THE INTERNATIONAL BIBLIOGRAPHY OF SOCIOLOGY

This bibliography, with its sister publications, Anthropology, Economics, and Political Science (known together as the *International Bibliography of the Social Sciences* is an essential tool for librarians, academics and researchers wishing to keep abreast of the published literature in the social sciences.

The *IBSS* offers a large scale database of journal articles and monographs from all over the world and in over 25 languages, all with English title translations where needed.

From 1991, users already familiar with the bibliography will notice major changes in contents and currency. There is greater coverage of monographs as well as journals, with continued emphasis on international publications, especially those from the developing world and Eastern Europe. Indexing techniques have been refined: it now offers more specific subject and place indexes together with a name index. A subject index in French continues to be provided.

Prepared until 1989 at the *Fondation nationale des sciences politiques* in Paris, the *IBSS* is now compiled and edited by the *British Library of Political and Economic Science* at the *London School of Economics*. The UNESCO *Internatioanl Committee for Social Science Information and Documentation* continues to support the publication. The new *International Bibliography* not only maintains its traditional extensive coverage of periodical literature, but considerably extends its coverage of monographic material by incorporating most of that which would previously have been included in the *London Bibliography of the Social Sciences*, publication of which has now been discontinued.

Also available from Routledge

Copies of the *International Bibliography of the Social Sciences* for previous years.

Thematic Lists of Descriptors. Four subject volumes published in 1989, following the clasification and index terms of the relevant volume of the *IBSS*.

The *International Current Awareness Services* complement the *IBSS* with the same geographical sweep, but offering full contents information on current journals. These four new monthly sevices — Anthropology, Ecomomics, Political Science and Sociology — provide coverage, with indexing by keyword, of items received during the previous month, including not only articles but also items such as book reviews, short articles, interviews, speeches, reports, editorials and letters.

Copies of the *London Bibliography of the Social Sciences* for previous years are available from Schmidt Periodicals, Dettendorf, D-8201 Bad Feilnbach 2, Germany.

INTERNATIONAL BIBLIOGRAPHY OF THE SOCIAL SCIENCES
BIBLIOGRAPHIE INTERNATIONALE DES SCIENCES SOCIALES

[published annually in four parts / paraissant chaque année en quatre parties: since 1961/ jusqu'en 1961: UNESCO, Paris]

International bibliography of sociology / Bibliographie internationale de sociologie [red cover / couverture rouge] Vol.1:1951 (publ. 1952)

International bibliography of political science/ Bibliographie internationale de science politique [grey cover / couverturegrise] Vol.1: 1952 (publ. 1954)

International bibliography of economics / Bibliographie internationale de science economique [yellow cover / couverture jaune] Vol.1: 1952 (publ. 1955)

International bibliography of social and cultural anthropology / Bibliographie internationale d'anthropologie sociale et culturelle [green cover/ couverture vert] Vol.1: 1955 (publ. 1958)

Prepared by

THE BRITISH LIBRARY OF POLITICAL AND ECONOMIC SCIENCE

with the support of the UNESCO International Committee for Social Science Information and Documentation

Editor

Christopher J. Hunt
Librarian, British Library of Political and Economic Science

Editorial Manager

Christopher C.P. Doutney

Assistant Manager

Caroline S. Shaw

Consultant/Technical Manager

N.S.M. Cox

Editorial Assistants

Julie Hickey
Michael Leiser
Lucy Rantzen
Richard Waterstone

INTERNATIONAL BIBLIOGRAPHY OF THE SOCIAL SCIENCES

1988

INTERNATIONAL BIBLIOGRAPHY OF SOCIOLOGY

VOLUME XXXVIII

BIBLIOGRAPHIE INTERNATIONALE DES SCIENCES SOCIALES

BIBLIOGRAPHIE INTERNATIONALE DE SOCIOLOGIE

London and New York

First published in 1992 by
Routledge
(on behalf of The British Library of Political and Economic Science)

11 New Fetter Lane
London EC4P 4EE
&
29 West 35th Street
New York, NY 10001

© 1992, British Library of Political and Economic Science

Processed and composed in Great Britain by
Cowlard Ventures Limited, Shipston-on-Stour, Warwickshire

Typeset in Great Britain by
W.E. Baxter Limited, Lewes, East Sussex

Printed in Great Britain by
Mackays of Chatham PLC, Chatham, Kent

All rights reserved. No part of this book may be reprinted or reproduced or utilized in any form or by any electronic, mechanical, or other means, now known or hereafter invented, including photocoping and recording, or in any information storage or retrieval system, without permission in writing from the publishers.

British Library Cataloguing in Publication Data

A CIP catalogue record for this book is available from the British Library.
ISBN 0–415–06474–0
ISSN 0085–2066

Editorial Correspondence should be sent to:

International Bibliography of the Social Sciences
British Library of Political and Economic Science
London School of Economics
10 Portugal Street
London WC2A 2HD
United Kingdom

Telephone: (U.K.) 071-955-7144

Fax: (U.K.) 071-242-0392

HM
15
.I61
v.38
1988

CONTENTS

International Committee for Social Science
    Information andDocumentation   vii

Preface   viii-xviii

Selection criteria   xix

Correspondents   xx

List of periodicals consulted   xxi

List of abbreviations   lxxv

Classification scheme   lxxxviii

Bibliography for 1988   1

Author index   206

Placename index   264

Subject index   270

Index des matières   297

Immediate access to the world's journals

International Current Awareness Services

●Anthropology ●Economics ●Political Science ●Sociology

A major new bibliographic service providing rapid international coverage of the world's significant social science literature

First issues available October 1990

Users of *IBSS* will be aware that the merger in 1990 of the *IBSS* and the *London Bibliography of the Social Sciences* databases, under the auspices of the British Library of Political and Economic Science at the London School of Economics, has brought a substantial improvement in the breadth of coverage of literature.

This merger has not only enriched *IBSS* contents but allowed the development of a new *International Current Awareness Service (ICAS)* in each of the four subjects covered by *IBSS*.

ICAS is published monthly as an immediate, comprehensive and easy-to-use tool for accessing the latest in the world's constantly expanding social science literature.

Special features of *ICAS* include:

- monthly publication for each subject, permitting users to scan the contents of journals often *before* they reach the library shelf
- unparalleled coverage of the world's journal literature through a service that scans at least 120,000 articles per year
- access to literature in 30 languages with each accompanied by English language title translation and identification of any summaries in English
- reports of book reviews, making rapidly available invaluable information on monographs
- indexing of important papers in monographic works of edited collections, a unique feature in a bibliographic service
- full contents listings of journal parts, enabling the user to scan contents of all current journals in a single source
- coverage of significant interviews, speeches, reports, editorials and letters
- in-depth subject keyword attribution, giving the user ease and precision of usage unprecedented in any other current awareness service

Printed in standardized formats with clear typeset listings of contents pages, *ICAS* is produced in a high quality, easy-to-read layout. Average extent 100pp per issue.

ICAS ISSNs   Anthropology 0960 1511   Economics 0960 152X
               Political Science 0960 1538   Sociology 0960 1546

For further details, sample copies and annual subscription rates please contact:
Promotions Department, Routledge, 11 New Fetter Lane, London EC4P 4EE, Telephone: 071 583 9855

INTERNATIONAL COMMITTEE FOR SOCIAL SCIENCE INFORMATION AND DOCUMENTATION
LE COMITÉ INTERNATIONAL POUR L'INFORMATION ET LA DOCUMENTATION EN SCIENCES SOCIALES

Kyllikki Ruokonen, Helsinki School of Economics Library (Chair)
Jean Meyriat, Fondation nationale des sciences politiques, Paris (Secretary General)

MEMBERS

S.P. Agrawal, National Social Science Documentation Centre, New Delhi
Dominique Babini, Consejo Latinoamericano de Ciencias Sociales, Buenos Aires
James A. Beckford, University of Warwick, Coventry
Russell Bernard, University of Florida, Gainesville
Azuka Dike, University of Nigeria, Nsukka
Heinz Heineberg, Westfalische Wilhems-Universität, Münster
Christopher Hunt, British Library of Political and Economic Science, London
Serge Hurtig, Fondation nationale des sciences politiques, Paris
Massimo Livi-Bacci, Università degli studi di Firenze
Yoshiro Matsuda, Hitotsubashi University, Tokyo
Lars-Goran Nilsson, University of Umea
Boris Polunin, USSR Academy of Sciences, Moscow
Mark Perlman, University of Pittsburgh
William A. Steiner, Squire Law Library, Cambridge

ASSOCIATES

Margarita Almada de Ascencio, Universidad Nacional Autónoma de México
Wilhelm Bartenbach, Foundation Center, New York
Paul Kaegbein, Lehrstuhl für Bibliothekswissenschaft der Universität zu Köln
J.M. Ng'ang'a, Kenyatta University, Nairobi
E. Seusing, Bibliothek des Instituts für Weltwirtschaft an der Universität Kiel
Libuše Švábová, Czechoslovakian Academy of Sciences, Prague

PREFACE

The volumes covering 1988 are the second editions of the *International Bibliographies of the Social Sciences* to be compiled and edited by the British Library of Political and Economic Science of the London School of Economics. Under the sponsorship of the International Committee for Social Science Information and Documentation, established by UNESCO in 1950, the four divisions of the *International Bibliography* (Anthropology: Economics: Political Science: Sociology) have been published from Paris since 1952. Together they form the most extensive bibliography of the social sciences in existence, with a world wide coverage achieved by no other bibliographical series.

The British Library of Political and Economic Science has published the *London Bibliography of the Social Sciences* since 1931. In 47 volumes it forms an unrivalled record of twentieth century monograph literature in social sciences. The volume covering 1989 was issued early in 1990 and it will be the last of the series. The bulk of the data which would previously have been published as the *London Bibliography* will, from 1990 onwards, appear within the structure of the *International Bibliographies of the Social Sciences*.

The *International Bibliography of Sociology* has been compiled from two sources: analysis of the published literature (particularly as contained in periodicals) accessible to the editors; and contributions from correspondents throughout the world, reporting publications, details of which are not easily obtainable outside their countries of origin. These dual sources of data will continue to be the basis of the *Bibliography*. The *international* emphasis will be maintained, without bias towards the publications of any one country. Some 120,000 journal articles per year are scanned for indexing in the four divisions, and a selection is made from over 20,000 monograph titles. Material in over 25 languages is included, but all titles, in addition to being cited in their original form, also appear in English. The work is produced from a computer maintained data base. The long established subject classifications continue to be the basis for indexing, governing an alphabetical arrangement by keywords.

The annual volumes of the *International Bibliographies* are complemented by the *International Current Awareness Services in the Social Sciences*, issued in the same four subject divisions as the annual volumes, but on a monthly basis. The *Current Awareness Services* include full contents listings (indexed by keyword) of all relevant periodicals received at the editorial office in London during the previous month. They index not only principal articles but also more ephemeral material such as short articles and book reviews, omitted in the annual volumes. Together, the two publication series provide immediate access to new publications and form a permanent record of printed material in the social sciences.

C.J. Hunt,
Editor,
London School of Economics

PRÉFACE

Les volumes qui couvrent 1988 sont les deuxièmes éditions des *Bibliographies Internationales des Sciences Sociales* recueillies et dirigées sous les auspices de la British Library of Political and Economic Science de la London School of Economics. Paris est depuis 1952 siège de la publication des quatre sections de la *Bibliographie Internationale* (Anthropologie: Sciences Economiques: Sciences Politiques: Sociologie.) sous le patronage du Comité International pour l'Information et la Documentation des Sciences Sociales établi par l'UNESCO en 1950. Dans l'ensemble, elles constituent la bibliographie la plus étendue des Sciences Sociales qui jouit d'une portée mondiale sans pareille en série de bibliographie.

La British Library of Political and Economic Science publie la *London Bibliography of the Social Sciences* depuis 1931. Ses 47 volumes présentent des archives incomparables de la littérature monographique du vingtième siècle en ce qui concerne les Sciences Sociales. Le volume de 1989, publié au début de 1990, sera le dernier de la série. La plupart des données qu'on aurait trouvées auparavant à la *London Bibliography* paraîtront dès 1990 dans le cadre des Bibliographies Internationales des Sciences Sociales.

La *Bibliographie Internationale de la Sociologie* ramasse les informations de deux sources; l'analyse de la littérature publiée (surtout en périodiques) à la portée des directeurs; et des contributions des correspondants partout dans le monde qui fournissent des comptes de publications dont on ne pourrait guère se renseigner hors de leur pays d'origine. Cette dualité de sources des données continuera comme base de la *Bibliographie*. On continuera à souligner sa qualité internationale sans aucune prévention en faveur des publications d'un seul pays. Chaque année on parcourt environ 120,000 articles de périodiques pour les indexer selon les quatre sections, et on choisit parmi 20,000 titres de monographie. La bibliographie comprend des contributions en 25 langues, mais tout les titres paraîtront en anglais, ainsi qu'en leur langue d'origine. L'ouvrage se produit des donnés recueillies sur ordinateur. La classification par sujets bien établie continuera comme base de l'indexation et déterminera un rangement alphabétique selon des mots-clefs.

Comme complément aux volumes annuels des *Bibliographies Internationales*, il y a les *International Current Awareness Services in the Social Sciences*, publications mensuelles qui s'occupent des mêmes quatre sujets que les volumes annuels. Les *Current Awareness Services* comprennent des listes complètes du contenu, (indexées par Mot-clef) de tous les périodiques pertinents arrivés chez la rédaction pendant le mois précédent. Ils indexent non seulement les articles principaux mais aussi les matériaux plus éphémères comme par exemple des articles courts et des critiques de livres dont les volumes annuels ne font pas mention. Les deux séries de publications ensemble permettent un accès immédiat aux nouvelles publications et servent d'archives permanentes des matériaux imprimés en sciences sociales.

C.J. Hunt,
Rédacteur,
London School of Economics

PREFACIO

Los tomos que abarcan el año 1988 constituyen las segundas ediciones de las *Bibliografías Internacionales de las Ciencias Sociales* redactadas y compiladas por la British Library of Political and Economic Science, de la London School of Economics. Las cuatro divisiones de la *Bibliografía Internacional* (Antropología: Ciencias Económicas: Ciencias Políticas y Sociología) se han venido publicando en París desde el año 1952, por gentileza patrocinal del Comité Internacional de Información y Documentación de las Ciencias Sociales, establecido por UNESCO en el año 1950. En su conjunto, constituyen la bibliografía más extensa en materia de Ciencias Sociales, con alcance mundial, e inigualable en otras series bibliográficas.

La British Library of Political and Economic Science ya publicaba la *London Bibliography of the Social Sciences* a partir del año 1931. En sus 47 tomos, constituye un registro de literatura monográfica sin rival sobre temas sociocientíficos del siglo XX. El tomo que abarca el año 1989 se publicó a principios del 1990, siendo éste el último de aquella serie. La mayoría de los datos se habrían publicado en épocas anteriores bajo el título *London Bibliography*. A partir del año 1990, aparecerán dentro de la estructura de las *International Bibliographies of the Social Sciences*.

La *International Bibliography de Sociología* ha sido compilada con base en dos fuentes: el análisis de la literatura publicada (en particular, tal como contenidos en los periódicos) accesible a redactores, y las contribuciones de corresponsales de todas partes del mundo, publicaciones de tipo informe, detalles de los cuales no resultan ser fácilmente obtenibles fuera de sus países de orígen. Dichas fuentes duales de información seguirán siendo la base de la Bibliografía. Se mantendrá el énfasis internacional, sin tendencias hacia las publicaciones de un sólo país dado. Se exploran al año unos 120,000 artículos para pasar a índices en las cuatro divisiones, y se efectúa una selección de más de 20,000 títulos monográficos. Se incluyen temas en más de 25 idiomas, pero todos los antedichos títulos, además de ser citados en su forma original, también aparecen traducidos al idioma inglés. Se lleva a cabo el trabajo a partir de una base de datos mantenida en ordenadores. Siguen siendo la base de la tarea de la puesta en índices, las clasificaciones por materias como se establecieron antiguamente, las cuales controlan una esquematización alfabética por palabra clave.

Los tomos anuales de las *Bibliografías Internacionales* se ven complementados mediante los *International Current Awareness Services in the Social Sciences*, con acuerdo a cada una de las mismas cuatro divisiones que se emplearon para los tomos anuales, pero sobre una base mensual. *Los Servicios de Actualización de Conocimientos* comprenden relaciones completas de materias, con puesta en índice por palabra clave, en relación con citas de todos los periódicos aplicaderos recibidos en la Casa Editorial de Londres durante el mes anterior. Abarcan índices no sólo de los artículos principales, sino también más materia efémera tal como sueltos cortos y críticas literarias que fueron omitidos de los tomos anuales. En conjunto, ambas series de publicaciones facilitan un acceso inmediato a las nuevas publicaciones, y constituyen un registro permanente de materias impresas comprendidas dentro del marco de las Ciencias Sociales.

C.J. Hunt,
Redactor,
London School of Economics

ПРЕДИСЛОВИЕ

Тома занимающиеся 1988-ым годом являются вторыми изданиями Международных Библиографий социологии, составлены и изданы Британской Библиотекой политических и Экономических Наук Лондонского Экономического Училища. Под покровительством Международного Комитета Социологической Информации и Документации, основанной ЮНЕСКО в 1950 г., четыре части Международной Библиографии/Антропология: Экономика: Политические Науки: Социология/издавались из Парижа с 1952 года. Вместе они составляют найболее обширную существующую библиографию социологии, с распространенным по всему свету обхватом не достигнутым никакой другой серийной библиографией.

Британская Библиотека Политических и Экономических Наук издаёт Лондонскую Библиографию Социологии с 1931-го года. В 47 томах это составляет непревзойдённую запись монографической литературы социологии двадцатого века. Том обхватывающий 1989-ый год был издан в начале 1990-ого года и это будет последнее издание этой серии. Большая часть данных, которая раньше должна издаваться как Лондонская Библиография с 1990-ого года будет появляться в структуре Международных Библиографий Социологии.

Международная Библиография Социология была составлена из двух источников, анализ изданной литературы/ особенно тот в периодических изданиях/ доступный для редакторов; и вклад корреспондентов со всего мира, репортажные публикации, деталь которых трудно получить, кроме в странах их происхождения. Эти двойственного характера источники данных будут являться основой Библиографии. Будет продолжаться международное значение библиографии без оказывания предпочтения изданиям каких-либо стран.

Ежегодно просматривается некоторые 120000 журнальных статей с целью составления указателей в четырёх частях, и тогда составляется сборник из больше чем 20000 монографических титулов. Включаются материалы на больше чем 25-и языках, но все титулы, вдобавок цитируются и в оригинальной версии и по английски. Произведение издаётся с помощью компьютерской базы данных. Долгосуществующая система классификации по предметам продолжается и употребляется в качестве основы для составления указателей, которые ведут алфавитный порядок ключевых слов.

Годовые тома Международных Библиографий дополняются Международными Текущими Осведомительными Услугами в Социологии, изданными в тех же самых четырёх частях по предметам что и годовые тома, но их издаются ежемесячно. Текущие Осведомительные Услуги включают указатели полных содержаний/ индексираны по ключевым словам/ всех уместных периодических журналов полученных в редакции в Лондоне в течение прошлого месяца. Они указывают не только главные статьи но тоже более эфемерные/ скоропроходящие/ материалы такие как короткие статьи и рецензии книг, пропущены в годовых томах. Вместе, эти две серии изданий предоставляют прямой доступ к новым изданиям и являются постоянной записью напечатанных материалов социологии.

C.J. Hunt,
Редактор,
Лондонское Экономическое Училище

ببليوغرافية علم الاجتماع الدولية

المقدمة

المجلدات اجزاء السلسلة التي تشمل سنة ١٩٨٧ هي اول طبعات الببليوغرافيات الدولية للعلوم الاجتماعية التي صنفتها واعدتها للنشر المكتبة البريطانية لعلم السياسة والاقتصاد التابعة الى معهد لندن لعلم الاقتصاد (والمشهور باسم مدرسة لندن لعلم الاقتصاد) وقد نشرت الاجزاء الاربعة من الببليوغرافية الدولية (وهي اولاً دراسة المجتمعات البشرية وثانياً علم الاقتصاد وثالثاً علم السياسة ورابعاً علم الاجتماع) من باريس منذ سنة ١٩٥٢ تحت رعاية اللجنة الدولية لمعلومات وللتدوين المستند لعلم الاجتماع والتي اسستها اليونسكو عام ١٩٥٠ وتشكل معاً هذه الاجزاء ببليوغرافية لها اوسع نطاق في الوجود ويشمل مداها انحاء العالم بكامله الى حد لم يبلغه اية سلسلة ببليوغرافية اخرى.

لقد نشرت المكتبة البريطانية لعلم السياسة والاقتصاد، نشرت الببليوغرافية اللندنية للعلوم الاجتماعية منذ سنة ١٩٣١ وهي تتألف من ٤٧ جزء وتكوّن سجلاً للمؤلفات التي تبحث العلوم الاجتماعية في القرن العشرين لا يضاهيه ايّ آخر وقد نشر المجلد الذي يشمل سنة ١٩٨٩ في اوائل ١٩٩٠ ويكوّن الجزء الاخير في السلسلة. ستنشر بعد سنة ١٩٩٠ في مضمون اطار الببليوغرافيات الدولية للعلوم الاجتماعية، ستنشر معظم تلك المعلومات التي كانت قد تكون تنشر سابقاً تحت اسم الببليوغرافيات اللندنية.

تم جمع وتدوين معلومات ببليوغرافية علم الاجتماع الدولية من مصدرين - الاول من تحليل المؤلفات وعلى وجه خاص ما احتوته المجلات الدورية التي هي في مدى تناول المحررين وثم ما قدّمه المراسلون في جميع انحاء العالم مع مطبوعات تقريرية يصعب الحصول على تفاصيلها خارج البلاد مصدر تلك الطبوعات. هذا وان مصدري المعلومات هذين سيبقيا اساس الببليوغرافية كما انه يتم الاستمرار في تولية الناحية الدولية اهمية خاصة، لكن دون اي ميول او انحياز نحو مطبوعات اي بلد. يتم تصفّح حوالي ١٢٠٠٠ من مقالات المجلات سنوياً للادراج في قوائم الاجزاء الاربعة، كما يتم الانتقاء من بين ما يزيد عن ٢٠٠٠ عنوان

لمؤلفات تبحث العلوم ، كل موضوع منفرداً . ثم ان ضمن المحتويات هناك مواد في ما يزيد عن ٢٥ لغة ، هذا كما ان العناوين مدرجة في لغتها الاصلية بالاضافة الى تدوينها بالانجليزية ، وهذا الشغل ينتج من خلال مستودع للمعلومات والحقائق العلمية يزقّه دماغ الكتروني . هذا وستبقى تبويبات الموضوعات الجارية من مدة طويلة ، تبقى هذه التبويبات الاساس للادراج في القائمة ، تضبط وترتّب هجائياً عن طريق كلمات مفتاح معيّنة .

المجلدات السنوية من الببليوغرافيات الدولية ستستكملها مطبوعات خدمات الالمام الجاري الدولية للعلوم الاجتماعية وتصدر هذه المطبوعات في اجزاء الموضوعات الاربعة ذاتها ، لكنها تصدر على ترتيب شهري وتشمل مطبوعات خدمات الالمام الجاري قوائم محتويات كاملة (مدرجة عن طريق كلمات مفتاح معيّنة) لجميع المجلات الدورية التي وصلت مكتب التحرير في لندن خلال الشهر السالف ، حيث يدرجون ليس الموضوعات الرئيسية فقط ، بل كذلك مواد سريعة الزوال - كالمقالات القصيرة وعرض ونقد الكتب مثلاً وهذه مواد ليست من ضمن المجلدات السنوية - وهكذا توفر سلسلتا المؤلفات هاتان اتصالاً فورياً بالمؤلفات الجديدة وتشكلا سجلاً دائماً للمواد المطبوعة في ميادين العلوم الاجتماعية .

سي . جي . هنت
محرر
معهد لندن لعلم الاقتصاد
(مدرسة لندن لعلم الاقتصاد)

国际社会学书志

序文

　　涉及 1987 年的各卷为伦敦经济学院 (London School of Economics) 属英国政治、经济学图书馆 (British Library of Political and Economic Science) 编辑和编集国际社会科学书志 (International Bibliographies of the Social Sciences) 的初版。国际书志 (International Bibliography) 的四部分 (人类学:经济学:政治学:社会学) 由联合国教育科学及文化组织 (UNESCO) 1950 年成立的社会科学情报与文书国际委员会 (International Committee for Social Science Information and Documentation) 发起，自从 1952 年由巴黎而初版。该四部分形成目前世界上最广泛的社会科学书志，具有其他书志系列未达到的世界性范围。

　　自 1931 年以来，英国政治、经济学图书馆发行了社会科学的伦敦书志 (London Bibliography of the Social Sciences)。他的四十七卷形成关于社会科学二十世纪专题文献的无比记录。涉及 1989 年的卷于 1990 年初发行了，是上述系列的最后一卷。由 1990 年开始，以前所发行为伦敦书志 (London Bibliography) 的大部分资料将于国际社会科学书志的结构之内出版。

　　国际社会学书志由两种来源而编辑，即受编者容易会见已出版文献(特别是杂志)的解析以及来自全世界通讯员系统的贡献。他们报道在产地外不容易得到出版的详细资料。书志将继续以该资料的两种来源为基础。书志也将维持国际性的观点，不重视任何一个国家的出版物。为于上述四部分内的排列，每年发表于杂志内的约十二万论文被审视，由二万以上专题的书名做出选择。虽然资料原文的语言数二十五以上，但所有书名，除引用原文以外，又附有英文翻译。书志是采用计算机化数据库产生的。长期确定的题目分类法继续作为资料排列的基础。关键词按照字母顺序而排列。

　　年度出版的国际书志为关于社会科学国际目前认识的服务 (International Current Awareness Services in the Social Sciences) 所补充，后者采用国际书志同样四个题目分类但是每月一次发行。不但主要的论文而且缩写论和书评等，以及

年度出版各卷所略去的较为朝生暮死的资料均编入索引。该两个出版系列共同提供与新出版的资料的直接接口，成为关于社会科学出版资料的永久记录。

C.J.Hunt
编著
伦敦经济学院

VORWORT

Mit den Bänden für 1988 liegt die zweite Ausgabe der *Internationalen Bibliographien der Sozialwissenschaften* vor, die von der British Library of Political and Economic Science der London School of Economics erstellt und redigiert wurde. Die vier Teilbände der *Internationalen Bibliographie* (Anthropologie: Politologie: Soziologie: Volkswirtschaft) wurden seit 1952 mit finanzieller Unterstützung des 1950 von der UNESCO eingesetzten Internationalen Komitees für Sozialwissenschaftliche Information und Dokumentation in Paris herausgegeben. Zusammen bilden sie die umfangreichste bestehende sozialwissenschaftliche Bibliographie mit einer weltweiten Reichweite in der Datenerfassung, wie sie keine andere bibliographische Reihe bietet.

Die British Library of Political and Economic Science veröffentlicht seit 1931 die *London Bibliography of the Social Sciences*. In 47 Bänden bildet sie ein unübertroffenes Verzeichnis der in Einzeldarstellungen erschienenen sozialwissenschaftlichen Literatur des 20. Jahrhunderts. Mit dem Band für 1989, der Anfang 1990 erschien, wurde diese Reihe eingestellt. Der Großteil der Daten, die vormals in der *London Bibliography* erschienen wären, wird von 1990 an im Rahmen der *Internationalen Bibliographien der Sozialwissenschaften* veröffentlicht werden.

Für die *Internationale Bibliographie der Soziologie* wurden zwei Arten von Quellen herangezogen: zum einen die (insbesondere in Fachzeitschriften) veröffentlichte Literatur, die der Redaktion im Original zugänglich war; zum andern Beiträge von Korrespondenten, die weltweit Publikationen erfassen, über die außerhalb ihrer Ursprungsländer nur schwer Einzelheiten in Erfahrung zu bringen sind. Diese beiden Datenquellen werden auch weiterhin die Grundlage für die *Bibliographie* bilden. Die *internationale* Ausrichtung wird erhalten bleiben, ohne Bevorzugung der Publikationen eines bestimmten Landes. Jährlich werden ca. 120.000 Zeitschriftenartikel auf eine Aufnahme in die vier Teilbände hin durchgesehen und eine Auswahl aus über 20.000 Monographien getroffen. Die *Internationalen Bibliographien* enthalten Material in mehr als 25 Sprachen; sämtliche Titel erscheinen außer in ihrer Originalsprache auch in englischer Übersetzung. Die vier Teilbände werden mit Hilfe einer computergestützten Datenbank erstellt. Die seit langem gebräuchliche Gliederung der Sachregister wurde beibehalten und liegt der alphabetischen Anordnung nach Schlagworten zugrunde.

Die jährlichen Bände der *Internationalen Bibliographien* werden ergänzt durch die *International Current Awareness Services in the Social Sciences*, die wie die Jahresbände in vier Teilen, jedoch monatlich erscheinen. Die *Current Awareness Services* enthalten vollständige Inhaltsverzeichnisse aller im vorausgegangenen Monat bei der Londoner Redaktion eingegangenen Zeitschriften, ergänzt um ein Schlagwortregister. Sie verzeichnen nicht nur Hauptartikel, sondern auch vergänglicheres Material wie Kurzbeiträge und Buchbesprechungen, die in den Jahresbänden unberücksichtigt bleiben. Beide Veröffentlichungen zusammen bieten direkten Zugriff auf neue Publikationen und ergeben ein dauerhaftes Verzeichnis von Druckschriften in den Sozialwissenschaften.

C.J. Hunt,
Herausgeber,
London School of Economics

国際社会学書誌

序文

　　　　１９８７年の各分野を網羅している各巻は、London School of Economics（ロンドン・スクール・オブ・エコノミックス）の英国政治・経済学図書館によって編纂され編集された国際社会科学書誌の各巻の第１版です。１９５０年にユネスコにより設立された社会科学情報・文書取扱国際委員会後援の下に国際書誌の４部（人類学：経済学：政治学：社会学）は、１９５２年からパリで発行されてきております。此の４部各書誌は、現存の最も広範囲に亙る社会科学の書誌を形成し、他の書誌シリーズによっては成就されなかった世界的取材を網羅するものであります。

　　　　英国政治・経済学図書館は１９３１年より、社会科学ロンドン書誌を発行して来ております。その４７巻は２０世紀に於ける比類のない社会科学の各専攻文献の記録を形成するものです。１９８９年を網羅する版は１９９０年初期に発行されましたが、これは此のシリーズの最後のものとなります。ロンドン書誌として前に発行されれる筈だった膨大な資料は、１９９０年以降、国際社会科学書誌の構築の中に包含されることになります。

　　　　国際社会学書誌は、２つの出典から編纂されたものです。即ち、編集者が利用できる文献（特に期間誌に含まれているもの）の解析と全世界の報道員の寄稿、それは、該当各国以外では入手困難な刊行物の詳細な資料とから編纂されてきているものです。これらの資料の複式出典は継続して書誌の基礎になるものです。「国際性」の意味は、どの国の刊行物に対しても偏見無しに維持されている事を強調しています。毎年凡そ１２万のジャーナル記事が図書目録のために鑑査走査され、４部門に分けられ、その上、２万以上の専攻書名から選択が行われます。２５以上の各国語からの資料が包含されておりますが、すべての書名は該当国語によるものが列挙されており、それに加えて、英語でも表記されています。此の仕事はコンピュータによる維持されたデータ・ベースから作成されます。図書目録の基礎として長期に亙り定着している首題の分類法は、今迄と同様に行われ、ａｂｃ順の見出語によるように統制されています。

　　　　国際書誌年刊の各巻は、社会科学学に於ける国際現代意識サービスによって補足され、これは、各巻の年刊と同じ4部門の首題で発行されていますが、月刊を基礎にしております。現代意識サービスは、ロンドン編集事務所で受け取った前月間のすべての該当期間誌の全内容目録（見出語による目録）を含みます。これらの目録は主要記事ばかりでなく、年刊には省略される短い記事や書評などのような、その時だけの記事も含まれています。2つの刊行シリーズは共に、新刊行物への即時利用を提供し、社会科学の印刷資料の永久記録となります。

C．J．ハント
編集者
London School of
Economics.

SELECTION CRITERIA

1. Subject

Documents relevent to sociology.

2. Nature and form

Publications of known authorship and lasting significance to sociology, whether in serial or monographic form, typically works with a theoretical component intending to communicate new knowledge, new ideas or making use of new materials.

Previously published materials in all formats are omitted, including most translations. Also excluded are textbooks, materials from newspapers or news magazines, popular or purely informative papers, presentations of predominantly primary data and legislative or judicial texts and items of parochial relevance only.

CORRESPONDENTS FOR SOCIOLOGY

This bibliography has been compiled by combining the work of the editorial office in London, which has established a large core of source publications, and the contributions of our foreign correspondents who provide first-hand knowledge of their countries' publications. We would like to to take this opportunity to thank our correspondents for their long-standing assistance and for adapting so helpfully to our new methods of working.

ARGENTINA — Fundación José María Aragón, Buenos Aires - Corina de Seoane

FRANCE — Bibliothèque de la Fondation nationale des sciences politiques, Paris - Professor Jean Meyriat

GERMANY — Akademie der Wissenschaften der DDR, Zentralinstitüt für Geschichte, Berlin - Dr. W. Wächter

INDIA — National Social Science Documentation Centre, Indian Council of Social Science Research, New Delhi - Dr. K.G. Tyagi and Dr. Savitri Devi

JAPAN — Japanese Sociological Association, Tokyo - Dr. Mamoru Yamada

POLAND — Polska Akademia Nauk, Ośrodek Informacji Naukowej, Warsaw - Dr. Janusz Sach

USSR — USSR Academy of Sciences
 — Institute for Scientific Information in the Social Sciences, Moscow - Boris Polunin
 — N.N. Miklukho-Maklay Institute of Ethnography, Leningrad - Alla V. Paneyakh and Tat'yana N. Sintsova

It should be noted that this list is not exhaustive, but consists only of those who contribute material in a systematic fashion on a regular basis.

LIST OF PERIODICALS CONSULTED
LISTE DES PERIODIQUES CONSULTÉS

Acadiensis.:*Journal of the history of the Atlantic Region [Acadiensis] ISSN: 0004-5851. University of New Brunswick, Department of History*: Fredericton, N.B. E3B 5A3, U.S.A.

Acta politica. *[Acta Pol.] ISSN: 0001-6810. Boom*: Postbus 1058, 7940 KB Meppel, The Netherlands

Acta sociologica. *[Acta Sociol.] ISSN: 0001- 6993. Scandinavian Sociological Association*; **Publisher**: *Universitetsforlaget*: Journals Department, P.O.Box 2959 Tøyen, 0608-Oslo 6, Norway

Acta Universitatis Łódziensis.:*Folia sociologica [Acta Univ. Łódz. Folia Soc.] ISSN: 0208-600X. Wydawnictwo Uniwersutetu Łódzkiego*: ul. Jaracza 34, Łódz, Poland

Acta Universtatis Łódziensis.:*Folia oeconomica [Acta Univ. Łódz.] ISSN: 0208-6018. Wydawnictwo Uniwersytetu Łódzkiego*: ul. Nowotki 143, Łódz, Poland

Administration and society. *[Admin. Soc.] ISSN: 0095-3997. Sage Publications*: 2455 Teller Road, Newbury Park, CA. 91320, U.S.A.

Administration for development. *[Admin. Devel.] ISSN: 0311-4511. Administrative College of Papua New Guinea*: P.O. Box 1216, Boroko, Papua New Guinea

Administrative science quarterly. *[Adm. Sci. Qua.] ISSN: 0001-8392. Cornell University, Johnson Graduate School of Management*: Caldwell Hall, Cornell University, Ithaca, N.Y. 14853, U.S.A.

Adoption and fostering. *[Adopt. Fost.] ISSN: 0308-5759. British Agencies for Adoption and Fostering*: 11 Southwark Street, London SE1 1RQ, U.K.

Advances in public interest accounting. *[Ad. Pub. Inter. Acc.]; JAI Press*: 55 Old Post Road, No 2., Greenwich, CN. 06836, U.S.A.

Affari sociali internazionali. *[Aff. Soc. Int.]; Franco Angeli Editore*: viale Monza 106, 20127 Milan, Italy

Africa. *[Africa] ISSN: 0001-9720. International African Institute*: Connaught House, Aldwych, London, WC2A 2AE, U.K.; **Publisher**: *Manchester University Press*: Oxford Road, Manchester M13 9PL, U.K.

Africa insight. *[Afr. Insight] ISSN: 0256-2804. Africa Institute of South Africa*: P.O. Box 630, Pretoria 0001, South Africa

Africa quarterly. *[Afr. Q.] ISSN: 0001-9828. Indian Council for Cultural Relations*: Azad Bhavan, Indraprastha Estate, New Delhi 110 002, India

Africa today. *[Afr. Tod.] ISSN: 0001-9887. Africa Today Associates*: c/o Graduate School of International Studies, University of Denver, Denver, CO. 80208, U.S.A.

African affairs. *[Afr. Affairs] ISSN: 0001-9909. Royal African Society*: 18 Northumberland Avenue, London WC2N 5BJ, U.K.; **Publisher**: *Oxford University Press*: Pinkhill House, Southfield Road, Eynsham, Oxford OX8 1JJ, U.K.

African communist. *[Afr. Comm.] ISSN: 0001-9976. Inkululeko Publications*: P.O. Box 902, London N19 2YY, U.K.; **Subscriptions**: *idem*: P.O. Box 1027, Johannesburg 2000, South Africa

African notes. *[Afr. Not.] ISSN: 0002-0087. University of Ibadan, Institute of African Studies*: Ibadan, Nigeria

INTERNATIONAL BIBLIOGRAPHY OF SOCIOLOGY — 1988

African review. *[Afr. R.] ISSN: 0856-0056. University of Dar es Salaam, Department of Political Science and Public Administration*: P.O. Box 35042, Dar es Salaam, Tanzania

African studies. *[Afr. Stud.] ISSN: 0002-0184. Witwatersrand University Press*: P.O. Wits, 2050 South Africa

African studies review. *[Afr. Stud. R.] ISSN: 0002-0206. African Studies Association*: Credit Union Building, Emory University, Atlanta, GA. 30322, U.S.A.

African urban quarterly. *[Afr. Urb. Q.]; African Urban Quarterly*: P.O. Box 74165, Nairobi, Kenya

Africana bulletin. *[Afr. Bul.] ISSN: 0002-029X. Uniwersytet Warszawski, Instytut Krajów Rozwijających Się*: Ul. Obozna 8, 00-032 Warsaw, Poland

Africana research bulletin. *[Afr. Res. Bul.]; University of Sierra Leone, Institute of African Studies*: Freetown, Sierra Leone

Afrika Spectrum. *[Af. Spec.] ISSN: 0002-0397. Institut für Afrika-Kunde*: Neuer Jungfernstieg 21, 2000 Hamburg 36, Germany

Afrique contemporaine. *[Afr. Cont.] ISSN: 0002-0478. Documentation Française*: 29-31 Quai Voltaire, 75340 Paris Cedex 07, France

Afro-Asian solidarity. *[Af-As. Solid.]; Afro-Asian Peoples Solidarity Organisation (AAPSO)*: 89 Abdel Aziz Al-Seoud Street, 11451-61 Manial El-Roda, Cairo, Egypt

Ageing and society. *[Age. Soc.] ISSN: 0144-686X. Centre for Policy on Ageing/ British Society of Gerontology*; **Publisher**: *Cambridge University Press*: The Edinburgh Building, Shaftesbury Road, Cambridge CB2 2RU, U.K.

Agenda. *[Agenda] ISSN: 1013-0950. Agenda Collective*: P.O. Box 37432, Overport, 4067 Durban, South Africa

Agricultura y sociedad. *[Agr. Soc.] ISSN: 0211-8394. Ministerio de Agricultura, Pesca y Alimentacion*: Centro de Publicaciones, Paseo de Infanta Isabel 1, 28071 Madrid, Spain

Ahfad journal. *[Ahfad J.]; Ahfad University for Women*: P.O. Box 167, Omdurman, Sudan

Akademika. *[Akademika] ISSN: 0126-5008. Penerbit Universiti Kebangsaan Malaysia, Faculty of Social Sciences and Humanities*: 43500 UKM Bangi, Selangor D.E., Malaysia

Albania today. *[Alb. Today] ISSN: 0044-7072. Drejtoria Qendrore e Librit*: Pruga Konferenca e Pezec, Tirana, Albania

Allgemeines statistisches Archiv. *[All. Stat. A.] ISSN: 0002-6018. Deutsche Statistische Gesellschaft*; **Publisher**: *Vandenhoeck & Ruprecht*: Theaterstraße 13, 3400 Göttingen, Germany

American anthropologist. *[Am. Anthrop.] ISSN: 0002-7294. American Anthropological Association*: 1703 New Hampshire Avenue, N.W. Washington, DC. 20009, U.S.A.

American behavioral scientist. *[Am. Behav. Sc.] ISSN: 0002- 7642. Sage Publications*: 2455 Teller Road, Newbury Park, CA 91320, U.S.A.

American economic review. *[Am. Econ. Rev.] ISSN: 0002-8282. American Economic Association*: 2014 Broadway, Suite 305, Nashville, TN. 37203, U.S.A.

American historical review. *[Am. Hist. Rev.] ISSN: 0002-8702. American Historical Association*: 400 A Street S.E., Washington DC. 20003, U.S.A.

American Jewish history. *[Am. Jew. Hist.] ISSN: 0164-0178. American Jewish Historical Society*: 2 Thornton Road, Waltham, MA. 02154, U.S.A.

American journal of economics and sociology. *[Am. J. Econ. S.] ISSN: 0002-9246. American Journal of Economics and Sociology*: 42 East 72 Street, New York, NY. 10021, U.S.A.

American journal of Islamic social sciences. *[Am. J. Islam. Soc. Sci.] ISSN: 0742-6763. Association of Muslim Social Scientists/ International Institute of Islamic Thought*: P.O. Box 669, Herndon, VA 22070, U.S.A.

INTERNATIONAL BIBLIOGRAPHY OF SOCIOLOGY — 1988

American journal of orthopsychiatry. [*Am. J. Orthopsy.*] *ISSN: 0002-9432. American Orthopsychiatric Association:* 19 W. 44th Street, New York, NY. 10036, U.S.A.; **Subscriptions**: *AOA Publications*: Sales Office, 49 Sheridan Avenue, Albany, NY. 12201-1413, U.S.A.

American journal of political science. [*Am. J. Pol. Sc.*] *ISSN: 0092-5853. Midwest Political Science Association*; **Publisher**: *Journals Department, University of Texas Press*: 2100 Comal, Austin TX. 78722, U.S.A.

American journal of sociology. [*A.J.S.*] *ISSN: 0024-9602. University of Chicago Press*: Journals Division, P.O. Box 37005, Chicago, IL. 60637, U.S.A.

American philosophical quarterly. [*Am. Phil. Q.*] *ISSN: 0003-0481. Philosophy Documentation Center*: Bowling Green State University, Bowling Green, OH. 43403-0189, U.S.A.

American political science review. [*Am. Poli. Sci.*] *ISSN: 0003-0554. American Political Science Association*: 1527 New Hampshire Avenue, N.W., Washington, DC. 20036, U.S.A.

American psychologist. [*Am. Psychol.*] *ISSN: 0003-066X. American Psychological Association*: 1400 North Uhle Street, Arlington, VA. 22201, U.S.A.

American review of Canadian studies. [*Am. R. Can. S.*] *ISSN: 0272-2011. Association for Canadian Studies in the United States*: One Dupont Circle, Suite 620, Washington DC. 20036, U.S.A.

American sociological review. [*Am. Sociol. R.*] *ISSN: 0003-1224. American Sociological Association*: 1722 N. Street, N.W. Washington, DC. 20036, U.S.A.

American sociologist. [*Am. Sociol.*] *ISSN: 0003-1232. Transaction Periodicals Consortium*: Rutgers University, New Brunswick, NJ. 08903, U.S.A.

Anales de estudios económicos y empresariales. [*Anal. Est. Econ. Empres.*] *ISSN: 0213-7569. Universidad de Valladolid, Facultad de Ciencias Económicas y Empresariales*: c/o Ramón y Cajal n° 7, 47005 Valladolid, Spain

Análise social. [*Anál. Soc.*] *ISSN: 0003-2573. Junta Nacional de Investigação Científica e Tecnológia/ Instituto Nacional de Investigação Científica*; **Publisher**: *Instituto de Ciências Sociais da Universidade de Lisboa*: Avenida das Forças Armadas, Edificio I.S.C.T.E., Ala Sul, 1° andar, 1600 Lisbon, Portugal

Analysis. [*Analysis*] *ISSN: 0003-2638. Basil Blackwell*: 108 Cowley Road, Oxford OX4 1JF, U.K.; **Subscriptions**: *Marston Book Services*: P.O. Box 87, Oxford OX2 0DT, U.K.

Annales.:*Economies, sociétés, civilisations* [**Annales**] *ISSN: 0395-2649. C.N.R.S./ École des Hautes Etudes en Sciences Sociales*; **Publisher**: *Armand Colin*: 103 boulevard Saint-Michel, 75240 Paris Cedex 05, France; **Subscriptions**: *Armand Colin*: B.P.22, 41353 Vineuil, France

Annales de géographie. [*Ann. Géogr.*] *ISSN: 0003-4010. Armand Colin Éditeur*: 103, boulevard Saint-Michel, 75240 Paris Cedex 05, France; **Subscriptions**: *Armand Colin*: B.P. 22, 41353 Vineuil, France

Annales de l'IFORD. [*Ann. IFORD*]; *L'institut de formation et de recherche demographiques*: Section des Publications, B.P. 1556 Yaounde, Cameroon

Annales internationales de criminologie; International annals of criminology; Anales internacionales de criminologia. [*Ann. Inter. Crimin.*] *ISSN: 0003-4452. Société Internationale de Criminologie = International Society for Criminology = Sociedad Internacional de Criminologia*: 4 rue Mondavi, 75001 Paris, France

Annali della fondazione Luigi Micheletti. [*Ann. Fond. "L. Mich."*]; *Fondazione Luigi Micheletti, Centro di ricerca sull'età contemporanea*: Via Cairoli 9, 15122 Brescia, Italy

Annali di ca'foscari. [*A. Ca'fos.*]; *Università degli Studi di Venezia*: San Polo 2035, 1- 30125 Venice, Italy

Annals of regional science. [*Ann. Reg. Sci.*] *ISSN: 0570-1864. Western Regional Science Association*; **Publisher**: *Springer- Verlag*: Heidelberger Platz 3, W-1000 Berlin 33, Germany

INTERNATIONAL BIBLIOGRAPHY OF SOCIOLOGY — 1988

Annals of the American Academy of Political and Social Science. *[Ann. Am. Poli.]* *ISSN: 0002-7162. American Academy of Political and Social Science*: 3937 Chestnut Street, Philadelphia, PA 19104, U.S.A.; **Publisher**: *Sage Publications*: 2455 Teller Road, Newbury Park, CA 91320, U.S.A.

Annals of the Association of American Geographers. *[Ann. As. Am. G.]* *ISBN: 0004-5608. Association of American Geographers*: 1710 Sixteenth Street, N.W., Washington, DC. 20009, U.S.A.

Annals of the Institute of Social Science. *[Ann. Inst. Soc. Sci.]* *ISSN: 0563-8054. University of Tokyo, Institute of Social Science*: 7-3-1 Hongo, Bunkyo-ku, Tokyo 113, Japan

Année africaine. *[Ann. Afri.]* *ISSN: 0570-1937. Centre d'Etude d'Afique Noire/ Centre de Recherche et d'Etude sur les Pays d'Afrique Orientale*: Institut d'Etudes Politiques de Bordeaux, Domaine University, BP 101, 33405 Talence Cedex, France; **Publisher**: *Editions A. Pedone*: Paris, France

Année sociologique. *[Ann. Sociol.]* *ISSN: 0066-2399. Presses Universitaires de France*: 108 boulevard Saint- Germain, 75006 Paris, France; **Subscriptions**: *Presses Universitaires de France*: 14 avenue du Bois-de-l'Epine, BP 90, 91003 Evry Cedex, France

Annuaire de l'afrique du nord. *[Ann. Afr. Nord]* *ISSN: 0242- 7540. Editions du Centre National de la Recherche Scientifique*: 15 quai Anatole France, 75700 Paris, France

Annuaire des pays de l'Ocean indien. *[Ann. Pays Oc. Ind.]* *ISSN: 0247-400X. Université d'Aix-Marseille III, Centre d'études et de recherches sur les sociétés d l'Ocean indien*: 3 avenue Robert Schuman, 13628 Aix en Provence Cedex 1, France; **Publisher**: *Editions du Centre Nationale de la Recherche Scientifique*: 15 quai Anatole France, 75700 Paris, France

Annual review of information science and technology. *[Ann. R. Info. Sci. Tech.]* *ISSN: 0066-4200. American Society for Information Science*: 8720 Georgia Avenue, Suite 501, Silver Spring, MD. 20910-3602, U.S.A.; **Publisher**: *Elsevier Science Publishers (North-Holland)*: Sara Burgerhartstraat 25, P.O. Box 211, 1000 AE Amsterdam, The Netherlands

Annual review of psychology. *[Ann. R. Psych.]* *ISSN: 0066-4308. Annual Reviews*: 4139 El Camino Way, P.O. Box 10139, Palo Alto, CA. 94303-0897, U.S.A.

Annual review of public health. *[Ann. R. Pub. H.]* *ISSN: 0163-7525. Annual Reviews*: P.O. Box 4139, Palo Alto, CA. 94303 0897, U.S.A.

Annual review of sociology. *[Ann. R. Soc.]* *ISSN: 0360-0572. Annual Reviews*: 4139 El Camino Way, P.O. Box 10139, Palo Alto, CA. 94303-0899, U.S.A.

Antipode. *[Antipode]* *ISSN: 0066-4812. Basil Blackwell*: 108 Cowley Road, Oxford OX4 1JF, U.K.

Anuario de estudios centroamericanos. *[An. Est. Cent.Am.]* *ISSN: 0377-7316. Universidad de Costa Rica, Instituto de Investigaciones Sociales*: Apartado 75, 2060 Ciudad Universitaria, Rodrigo Facio, 2050 San Pedro de Montes de Oca, San Jose, Costa Rica

Applied economics. *[Appl. Econ.]* *ISSN: 0003 6846. Chapman and Hall*: 2-6 Boundary Row, London SE1 8HN, U.K.; **Subscriptions**: *International Thomson Publishing Services*: North Way, Andover, Hampshire SP10 5BE, U.K.

Apuntes. *[Apuntes]* *ISSN: 0252-1865. Revista Apuntes*: Apartado Postal 4683, Lima 1, Peru

Arab journal for the humanities. *[Arab J. Hum.]*; *Kuwait University*: P.O. Box 26585, Safat, 13126 Kuwait

Arab studies quarterly. *[Arab St. Q.]* *ISSN: 0271-3519. Institute of Arab Studies/ Association of Arab-American University Graduates*: 556 Trapelo Road, Belmont, MA. 02178, U.S.A.

Archiv für Kommunalwissenschaften. *[Arc. Kommunal.]* *ISSN: 0003- 9209. Deutsches Institut für Urbanistik*: Straße des 17. Juni 112, Postfach 12 62 24, 1000 Berlin 12, Germany; **Publisher**: *Verlag W. Kohlhammer*: Heßbrühlstraße 69, Postfach 80 04 30, 7000 Stuttgart 80 (Vaihingen), Germany

INTERNATIONAL BIBLIOGRAPHY OF SOCIOLOGY — 1988

Archiv für Rechts- und Sozialphilosophie; Archives de philosophie du droit et de philosophie sociale; Archives for philosophy of law and social philosophy; Archivo de filosofía juridica y social. *[Arc. Recht. Soz.] ISSN: 0001-2343. Internationale Vereinigung für Rechts- und Sozialphilosophie*; **Publisher**: *Franz Steiner Verlag*: Birkenwaldstraße 44, Postfach 10 15 26, D-7000 Stuttgart 1, Germany

Archív orientální. *[Arch. Orient.] ISSN: 0044-8699. Czechoslovak Academy of Sciences, Oriental Institute*; **Publisher**: *Academia Publishing House*: Vodičkova 40, 112 29 Prague 1, Czechoslovakia; **Subscriptions**: *John Benjamins*: Postbus 52519, 1007 HA Amsterdam, The Netherlands

Archives européennes de sociologie; European journal of sociology; Europäisches Archiv für Soziologie. *[Eur. J. Soc.] ISSN: 0003-9756. Cambridge University Press*: The Edinburgh Building, Shaftesbury Road, Cambridge CB2 2RU, U.K.

Archivio di studi urbani e regionali. *[Arch. St. Urb. Region.]; Franco Angeli editore*: Viale Monza 106, 20127 Milan, Italy

Area. *[Area] ISSN: 0004-0894. Institute of British Geographers*: 1 Kensington Gore, London SW7 2AR, U.K.

Armed forces and society. *[Arm. Forces Soc.] ISSN: 0095-327X. Inter-University Seminar on Armed Forces and Society*: Box 46, 1126 East 59th Street, Chicago, IL. 60637, U.S.A.; **Publisher**: *Transaction Periodicals Consortium*: Rutgers University, New Brunswick, NJ. 08903, U.S.A.; **Subscriptions**: *Swets Publishing Service*: Heereweg 347, 2161 CA. Lisse, The Netherlands

Asia journal of theology. *[Asia J. Theol.] ISSN: 0218-0812. Asia Journal of Theology*: 324 Onan Road, Singapore 1542

Asian and African studies. *[Asian. Afr. Stud.] ISSN: 0066-8281. University of Haifa, Gustav Heinemann Institute of Middle Eastern Studies*: Haifa 31999, Israel

Asian profile. *[Asian Prof.] ISSN: 0304-8675. Asian Research Service*: Rm. 704, Federal Building, 369 Lockhart Road, Hong Kong; **Subscriptions**: *idem*: G.P.O. Box 2232, Hong Kong

Asian studies review. *[Asian Stud. R.] ISSN: 0314-7533. Asian Studies Association of Australia*: c/o Social and Policy Studies in Education, University of Sydney, N.S.W. 2006, Australia

Asian survey. *[Asian Sur.] ISSN: 0004-4687. University of California Press*: Berkeley, CA. 94720, U.S.A.

Asian thought and society. *[Asian Thoug. Soc.] ISSN: 0361-3968. State University of New York-Oneonta/Boston College, Center for East Europe, Russia, and Asia/University of Hong Kong*; **Publisher**: *East-West Publishing*: 1 Bugbee Road, Oneonta, NY. 13820, U.S.A.

Australian aboriginal studies. *[Aust. Abor. S.] ISSN: 0729-4352. Australian Institute of Aboriginal and Torres Strait Islander Studies*: G.P.O. Box 553, Canberra ACT 2601, Australia

Australian and New Zealand journal of sociology. *[Aust. N.Z. J. Soc.] ISSN: 0004-8690. Australian Sociological Association*: c/o Research School of Social Sciences, Australian National University, GPO Box 4, Canberra, ACT 2601, Australia; **Publisher**: *La Trobe University Press*: Bundoora, Victoria 3083, Australia

Australian cultural history. *[Aust. Cult. Hist.] ISSN: 0728- 8433. University of New South Wales, School of History*: P.O. Box 1, Kensington, N.S.W. 2033, Australia

Australian geographer. *[Aust. Geogr.] ISSN: 0004-9182. Geographical Society of New South Wales*: P.O. Box 602, Gladesville, NSW 2111, Australia

Australian geographical studies. *[Aust. Geogr. Stud.] ISSN: 0004-9190. Institute of Australian Geographers*: Department of Geography and Oceanography, University College, University of New South Wales, Australian Defence Force Academy, Campbell, ACT 2600, Australia

Australian historical studies. *[Aust. Hist. St.] ISSN: 1031-461X. University of Melbourne*: Department of History, University of Melbourne, Parkville, Victoria 3052, Australia

Australian journal of linguistics. *[Aust. J. Ling.] ISSN: 0726-8602. Australian Linguistic Society*: Department of Linguistics, La Trobe University, Bundoora 3083, Victoria, Australia; **Publisher**: *Cambridge University Press*: The Edinburgh Building, Shaftesbury Road, Cambridge CB2 2RU, U.K.

Australian journal of political science. *[Aust. J. Pol. Sci] ISSN: 0032-3268. Australasian Political Studies Association*; **Publisher**: *Australian Defence Force Academy, Department of Politics*: Canberra, ACT 2600, Australia

Australian journal of public administration. *[Aust. J. Publ.] ISSN: 0313-6647. Royal Australian Institute of Public Administration*: Box 904, GPO, Sydney, N.S.W. 2001, Australia

Australian journal of social issues. *[Aust. J. Soc. Iss.] ISSN: 0157-6321. Australian Council of Social Services*: Box 45, Railway Square, Sydney 2000, N.S.W., Australia

Australian journal of statistics. *[Aust. J. Statist.] ISSN: 0004-9581. Australian Statistical Publishing Association*: Treasurer, Statistical Society of Australia, G.P.O. Box 573, Canberra, ACT 2601, Australia

Australian quarterly. *[Aust. Q.] ISSN: 0005-0091. Australian Institute of Political Science*: P.O. Box 145, Balmain NSW 2041, Australia

Australian studies. *[Aust. Stud.] ISSN: 0954-0954. British Australian Studies Association*: Sir Robert Menzies Centre for Australian Studies, 27-28 Russell Square, London WC1B 5DS, U.K.; **Publisher**: *University of Stirling, Department of English Studies*: Stirling FK9 4LA, U.K.

AWR bulletin. *[AWR B.] ISSN: 0014-2492. Association for the Study of the World Refugee Problem*: FL- 9490 Vaduz, P.O.B. 75, Liechtenstein; **Publisher**: *Wilhelm Braumueller, Universitäts-Verlagsbuchhandlung*: Servitengasse 5, A-1092, Vienna, Austria

Azania. *[Azania] ISSN: 0067-270X. British Institute in Eastern Africa*: P.O. Box 30710, Nairobi, Kenya/ 1 Kensington Gore, London SW7 2AR, U.K.

Banaras law journal. *[Banaras Law J.]*; *Banaras Hindu University, Law School*: Varanasi 221005, India

Bangladesh development studies. *[Bang. Dev. Stud.] ISSN: 0304-095X. Bangladesh Unnayan Gobeshona Protishthan = Bangladesh Institute of Development Studies*: G.P.O. Box No.3854, E-17 Agargaon, Sher-e-Bangla Nagar, Dhaka, Bangladesh

Bangladesh journal of public administration. *[Bang. J. Pub. Admin.]*; *Bangladesh Public Administration Training Centre*: Savar, Dhaka 1343, Bangladesh

BC studies. *[BC. Stud.] ISSN: 0005-2949. University of British Columbia*: 2029 West Mall, University of British Columbia, Vancouver B.C. V6T 1W5, Canada

Behavior science research. *[Behav. Sc. Res.] ISSN: 0094-3673. Society for Cross-Cultural Research*; **Publisher**: *Human Relations Area Files*: Box 2015, Yale Sta., New Haven, CT. 06520, U.S.A.

Behavioral science. *[Behav. Sci.] ISSN: 0005-7940. International Society for Systems Sciences/ Institute of Management Sciences*: P.O. Box 64025, Baltimore, Maryland 21264, U.S.A.

Benelux. *[Benelux]*; *Secretariaat-Generaal van de Benelux Economische unie = Secrétariat général de l'Union économique Benelux = Generalsekretariat der Benelux-Wirtschaftsunion*: Regentschapsstraat, 39 rue de la Régence, Brussels 1000, Belgium

Berkeley journal of sociology. *[Berkeley J. Soc.] ISSN: 0067-5830. Berkeley Journal of Sociology*: 458A Barrows Hall, Department of Sociology, University of California Berkeley, Berkeley, CA 94720, U.S.A.

INTERNATIONAL BIBLIOGRAPHY OF SOCIOLOGY — 1988

Bioethics. *[Bioethics] ISSN: 0269- 9702. Basil Blackwell*: 108 Cowley Road, Oxford OX4 1JF, U.K.

Biography. *[Biography] ISSN: 0162-4962. Center for Biographical Research*: Varsity College, University of Hawaii, Honolulu, HI. 96822, U.S.A.; **Publisher**: *University of Hawaii Press*: 2840 Kolowalu Street, Honolulu, HI. 96822, U.S.A.

Boletim informativo e bibliográfico de ciências sociais. *[Bol. Inf. Bibl. Soc.]*; *Associação Nacional de Pós-Graduação e Pesquisa em Ciências Sociais*: Editoria do BIB, Rua da Matriz 82, Botafogo 22.260. Rio de Janeiro RJ., Brazil

Boletin de la Asociacion Española de Orientalistas. *[B. Asoc. Españ. Orient.]*; *Universidad Autónoma*: Edificio Rectorado, Ciudad Universitaria de Canto Blanco, 28049 Madrid, Spain

Botswana notes and records. *[Bots. Not. Rec.] ISSN: 0525-5059. Botswana Society*: P.O. Box 71, Gaborone, Botswana

British journal of addiction. *[Br. J. Addict.] ISSN: 0952-0481. Society for the Study of Addiction to Alcohol and Other Drugs*: Addiction Reseach Unit, National Addiction Centre, 101 Denmark Hill, London SE5 8AF, U.K.; **Publisher**: *Carfax Publishing*: P.O. Box 25, Abingdon, Oxfordshire, OX14 3UE, U.K.

British journal of Canadian studies. *[Br. J. Can. Stud.] ISSN: 0269-9222. British Association for Canadian Studies*: Centre of Canadian Studies, 21 George Square, Edinburgh EH8, U.K.

British journal of clinical psychology. *[Br. J. Clin. Psycho.] ISSN: 0144-6657. British Psychological Society*: St. Andrews House, 48 Princess Road East, Leicester LE1 7DR, U.K.; **Subscriptions**: *The Distribution Centre*: Blackhorse Road, Letchworth, Herts. SG6 1HN, U.K.

British journal of criminology. *[Br. J. Crimin.] ISSN: 0007-0955. Institute for the Study and Treatment of Delinquency*; **Publisher**: *Oxford University Press*: Pinkhill House, Southfield Road, Eynsham, Oxford OX8 1JJ, U.K.

British journal of educational studies. *[Br. J. Educ. S.] ISSN: 0007-1005. Basil Blackwell*: 108 Cowley Road, Oxford OX4 1JF, U.K.; **Subscriptions**: *Marston Book Services*: P.O. Box 87, Oxford OX2 0DT, U.K.

British journal of industrial relations. *[Br. J. Ind. R.] ISSN: 0007-1080. London School of Economics*: Houghton Street, London WC2A 2AE, U.K.; **Publisher**: *Basil Blackwell*: 108 Cowley Road, Oxford, OX4 1JF, U.K.; **Subscriptions**: *Journals Subscriptions, Industrial Relations Department, Marston Book Services*: P.O. Box 87, Oxford OX2 0DT, U.K.

British journal of management. *[Br. J. Manag.] ISSN: 1045-3172. British Academy of Management*; **Publisher**: *John Wiley & Sons*: Baffins Lane, Chichester, West Sussex PO19 1UD, U.K.

British journal of psychology. *[Br. J. Psy.] ISSN: 0007- 1269. British Psychological Society*: St. Andrews House, 48 Princess Road East, Leicester LE1 7DR, U.K.

British journal of social psychology. *[Br. J. Soc. P.] ISSN: 0144-6665. British Psychological Society*: St. Andrews House, 48 Princess Road East, Leicester LE1 7DR, U.K.; **Subscriptions**: *Distribution Centre*: Blackhorse Road, Letchworth, Herts SG6 1HN, U.K.

British journal of social work. *[Br. J. Soc. W.] ISSN: 0045-3102. British Association of Social Workers*; **Publisher**: *Oxford University Press*: Pinkhill House, Southfield Road, Eynsham, Oxford, OX8 1JJ, U.K.

British journal of sociology. *[Br. J. Soc.] ISSN: 0007-1315. London School of Economics and Political Science*: Houghton Street, Aldwych, London WC2A 2AE; **Publisher**: *Routledge*: 11 New Fetter Lane, London EC4P 4EE, U.K.

British review of New Zealand studies. *[Br. R. N.Z. Stud.] ISSN: 0951-6204. University of Edinburgh, New Zealand Studies Committee*: 21 George Square, Edinburgh EH8 9LD, U.K.

INTERNATIONAL BIBLIOGRAPHY OF SOCIOLOGY — 1988

Bulletin des études africaines de l'INALCO. *[B. Ét. Afr. INALCO]*; *Institut national des langues et civilisations orientales*: 2 rue de Lille, 75007 Paris, France

Bulletin of concerned Asian scholars. *[B. Concern. Asia. Schol.] ISSN: 0007-4810*. *Bulletin of Concerned Asian Scholars*: 3239 9th Street, Boulder, CO. 80304-2112, U.S.A.

Bulletin of Eastern Caribbean affairs. *[B. E.Carib. Aff.] ISSN: 0254-7406*. *Institute of Social and Economic Research (Eastern Caribbean)*: University of the West Indies, Cave Hill, Barbados

Bulletin of economic research. *[B. Econ. Res.] ISSN: 0307-3378*. *Basil Blackwell*: 108 Cowley Road, Oxford OX4 1JF, U.K.

Bulletin of Latin American research. *[B. Lat. Am. Res.] ISSN: 0261-3050*. *Society for Latin American Studies*; **Publisher**: *Pergamon Press*: Headington Hill Hall, Oxford OX3 OBW, U.K.

Bulletin of Tanzanian affairs. *[B. Tanzan. Aff.] ISSN: 0952-2948*. *British Tanzania Society*: 14B Westbourne Grove Terrace, London W2 5SD, U.K.

Business history review. *[Bus. Hist. Rev.] ISSN: 0007-6805*. *Harvard Business School*: Baker Library 5A, Harvard Business School, Boston, MA. 02163, U.S.A.

Cahiers de l'homme. *[Cah. Homme] ISSN: 0068-5046*. *Éditions de l'École des Hautes Études en Sciences Sociales*: 131 boulevard Saint-Michel, F-75005 Paris, France

Cahiers de linguistique asie orientale. *[Cah. Ling. Asie Orient.] ISSN: 0153-3320*. *École des Hautes Etudes en Sciences Sociales, Centre de Recherches Linguistiques sur l'Asie Orientale*: 54 boulevard Raspail, 75006 Paris, France

Cahiers de l'ISSP. *[Cah. ISSP]*; *Université de Neuchâtel, Institut de Sociologie et de Science Politique, Faculté de droit et des sciences économiques*; **Publisher**: *Editions EDES*: Neuchâtel, Switzerland

Cahiers de Tunisie. *[Cah. Tunis.] ISSN: 0008-0012*. *Faculté des Lettres et Sciences Humaines de Tunis*: boulevard du 9 Avril 1938, Tunis, Tunisia

Cahiers des Amériques latines. *[Cah. Amer. Lat.] ISSN: 0008-0020*. *Université de la Sorbonne Nouvelle (Paris III), Institut des Hautes Etudes de l'Amérique Latine*: 28 rue Saint-Guillaume, 75007 Paris, France

Cahiers des sciences humaines. *[Cah. Sci. Hum.] ISSN: 0768-9829*. *Editions de l'ORSTOM, Institut Français de Recherche Scientifique pour le developpement en Cooperation*: Commission des Sciences Sociales, 213 rue la Fayette, 75480 Paris, France; **Subscriptions**: *Editions de l'ORSTOM*: Librairie-Vente- Publicité, 70-74 Route d;Aulnay, 93143 Bondy Cedex, France

Cahiers d'études africaines. *[Cah. Et. Afr.] ISSN: 0008-0055*. *Editions de l'Ecole des Hautes Etudes en Sciences Sociales*: 131 boulevard Saint-Michel, 75005 Paris, France; **Subscriptions**: *Centrale des Revues*: 11 rue Gossin, 92543 Montrouge Cedex, France

Cahiers d'études sur la méditerranée orientale et le monde turco-iranien. *[Cah. Ét. Méd. Ori. Tur-Iran.] ISSN: 0764-9878*. *Association Française pour l'Etude de la Méditerranée Orientale et le Monde Turco-Iranien*: 4 rue de Chevreuse, 75006 Paris, France

Cahiers d'histoire de l'institut de recherches Marxistes. *[Cah. Inst. Rech. Marx.] ISSN: 0246-9731*. *Société d'Edition des Publications de l'Institut des Recherches Marxistes*: 15 rue Montmartre, 75001 Paris, France; **Subscriptions**: *Institut de Recherches Marxistes*: 64 boulevard Auguste-Blanqui, 75013 Paris, France

Cahiers d'outre-mer. *[Cah. Outre-mer] ISSN: 0373-5843*. *Université de Bordeaux III, Institut de Geographie*: Domaine Universitaire, 33405 Talence, France

Cahiers du CEDAF/ ASDOC-studies. *[Cah. CEDAF] ISSN: 0250-1619*. *Centre d'Étude et de Documentation Africaines = Afrika Studie-en Documentatiecentrum*: 7 Place Royale, B-1000 Brussels, Belgium

Cahiers internationaux de sociologie. *[Cah. Int. Soc.]* ISSN: 0008-0276. *Presses Universitaires de France*: 108 boulevard Saint-Germain, 75006 Paris, France

California management review. *[Calif. Manag. R.]* ISSN: 0008-1256. *University of California, Walter A. Haas School of Business*: 350 Barrows Hall. University of California, Berkeley, CA. 94720, U.S.A.

Cambridge law journal. *[Camb. Law J.]* ISSN: 0008-1973. *University of Cambridge, Faculty of Law*; **Publisher**: *Cambridge University Press*: The Edinburgh Building, Shaftesbury Road, Cambridge CB2 2RU, U.K.

Canadian Association of African Studies newsletter; Association canadienne des études africaines bulletin. *[Can. Ass. Afr. S. News]* ISSN: 0228-8397. *Canadian Association of African Studies = Association canadienne des études africaines*: 308, 294 Albert Street, Ottawa, Ontario, K1P 6E6 Canada

Canadian historical review. *[Can. Hist. R.]* ISSN: 0008-3755. *University of Toronto Press*: 5201 Dufferin Street, Downsview, Ontario M3H 5T8, Canada

Canadian journal of African studies; Revue canadienne des études africaines. *[Can. J. Afr, St.]* ISSN: 0008-3968. *Canadian Association of African Studies = Association Canadienne des Etudes Africaines*: Innis College, University of Toronto, 2 Sussex Avenue, Toronto, Ontario, Canada M5S IAI

Canadian journal of philosophy. *[Can. J. Phil.]* ISSN: 0045-5091. *University of Calgary Press*: Calgary, Alberta, Canada T2N 1N4

Canadian journal of political and social theory. *[Can. J. Pol. Soc. Theo.]* ISSN: 0380-9420. *A. and M. Kroker*: Concordia University, 1455 de Maisonneuve West, Montreal, Quebec H3G 1M8, Canada

Canadian journal of political science; Revue canadienne de science politique. *[Can. J. Poli.]* ISSN: 0008-4239. *Canadian Political Science Association = Association canadienne de science politique/ Société québécoise de science politique*: Suite 205, 1 Stewart Street, Ottawa, Ontario, Canada K1N 6H7/ Université du Québec à Montréal, Montréal, Québec, Canada H3C 3PN; **Publisher**: *Wilfrid Laurier University Press*: 75 University Avenue W., Waterloo, Ontario N2L 3C5, Canada

Canadian journal of sociology; Cahiers canadiens de sociologie. *[Can. J. Soc.]* ISSN: 0318-6431. *University of Alberta, Department of Sociology*: Edmonton, Alberta T6G 2H4, Canada

Canadian journal of statistics; Revue canadienne de statistiques. *[Can. R. Stat.]* ISSN: 0319-5724. *Statistical Society of Canada = Société Statistique du Canada*: 675 Denbury Avenue, Ottawa, Ontario, Canada K2A 2P2

Canadian public administration; Administration publique du Canada. *[Can. Publ. Ad.]* ISSN: 0008-4840. *Institute of Public Administration of Canada*: 897 Bay Street, Toronto, Ontario, Canada M5S 1Z7

Canadian review of sociology and anthropology; Revue canadienne de sociologie et d'anthropologie. *[Can. R. Soc. A.]* ISSN: 0008-4948. *Canadian Sociology and Anthropology Association*: Concordia University, 1455 boulevard de Maisonneuve W., Montreal, Quebec H3G 1M8, Canada

Canadian review of studies in nationalism; Revue canadienne des études sur le nationalisme. *[Can R. Stud. N.]* ISSN: 0317-7904. *CRSN/RCEN*: University of Prince Edward Island, Charlottetown, P.E.I. Canada C1A 4P3

Canadian yearbook of international law; Annuaire canadien de droit international. *[Can. Yb. Int. Law]* ISSN: 0069-0058. *International Law Association, Canadian Branch*; **Publisher**: *University of British Columbia Press*: 303-6344 Memorial Road, Vancouver, B.C., V16 1WS Canada

Capital and class. *[Cap. Class]* ISSN: 0309-8786. *Conference of Socialist Economists*: Editorial Committee, Conference of Socialist Economists, 25 Horsell Road, London N5 1XL, U.K.

Caribbean quarterly. [*Car. Quart.*] *ISSN: 0008-6495. University of the West Indies, Department of Extra-Mural Studies*: Mona, Kingston 7, Jamaica

Caribbean studies; Estudios del Caribe; Études des Caraïbes. [*Carib. Stud.*] *ISSN: 0008-6533. Universidad de Puerto Rico, Facultad de Ciencias Sociales, Instituto de Estudios del Caribe*: P.O. Box 23361 University Station, Pío Piedras, Puerto Rico 00931

Central Asiatic journal. [*Cent. Asia. J.*]; *Otto Harrassowitz*: Taunusstrasse 5, 6200 Wiesbaden, Germany

CEPAL review. [*CEPAL R.*] *ISSN: 0251-2920. United Nations Economic Commission for Latin America and the Caribbean*: Casilla 179-D, Santiago, Chile; **Subscriptions**: *United Nations Publications, Sales Section*: Palais des Nations, 1211 Geneva 10, Switzerland

Child development. [*Child. Devel.*] *ISSN: 0009-3920. Society for Research in Child Development*: 5720 South Woodlawn Avenue, Chicago, IL. 60637, U.S.A.; **Publisher**: *University of Chicago Press*: c/o 5720 South Woodlawn Avenue, Chicago, IL. 60637, U.S.A.; **Subscriptions**: *idem*: Journals Division, P.O. Box 37005, Chicago, IL. 60637, U.S.A.

Children and society. [*Child. Soc.*] *ISSN: 0951-0605. National Children's Bureau of the United Kingdom*; **Publisher**: *Whiting and Birch*: P.O. Box 872, Forest Hill, London SE23 3HZ, U.K.

China quarterly. [*China Quart.*] *ISSN: 0009 4439. University of London, School of Oriental and African Studies*: Thornhaugh Street, Russell Square, London WC1H 0XG, U.K.

Ching feng. [*Ch. Feng*]; *Christian Study Centre on Chinese Religion and Culture*: 6/F Kiu Kin Mansion, No.566 Nathan Road, Kowloon, Hong Kong

Ciências sociais hoje. [*Ciên. Soc. Hoje.*]; *Associção Nacional de Pós-Graduação e Pesquisa em Ciencias Sociais*; **Publisher**: *Edições Vértice*: Rua Conde do Pinhal 78, Caixa Postal 678, 01501 São Paulo, SP. Brazil

Cities. [*Cities*] *ISSN: 0264-2751. Butterworth-Heinemann*: 88 Kingsway, London WC2 6AB, U.K.; **Subscriptions**: *Turpin Transactions*: Distribution Centre, Blackhorse Road, Letchworth, Herts. SG6 1HN, U.K.

Civilisations. [*Civilisations*] *ISSN: 0009-8140. Université Libre de Bruxelles, Institut de Sociologie*: 44 avenue Jeanneaterloo, 1050 Brussels, Belgium

Cognition. [*Cognition*] *ISSN: 0010-0277. Elsevier Science Publishers*: P.O. Box 211, 1000 AE Amsterdam, The Netherlands

Cognitive linguistics. [*Cogn. Ling.*] *ISSN: 0936-5907. Walter de Gruyter*: Postfach 110240, D-Berlin 11, Germany

Cognitive science. [*Cogn. Sci.*] *ISSN: 0364-0213. Cognitive Science Society*: Learning Research and Development Center, University of Pittsburgh, 3939 O'Hara Street, Pittsburgh, PA. 15260, U.S.A.; **Publisher**: *Ablex Publishing*: 355 Chestnut Street, Norwood, NJ. 07648, U.S.A.

Columbia law review. [*Columb. Law.*] *ISSN: 0010-1958. Columbia Law Review Association*: 435 West 116th Street, New York, NY. 10027, U.S.A.

Commentary. [*Commentary*] *ISSN: 0010- 2601. American Jewish Committee*: 165 East 56th Street, New York, NY. 10022, U.S.A.

Communautés. [*Communautés*] *ISSN: 0010-3462. Université Coopérative Internationale*; **Publisher**: *Bureau d' Ecole Coopératives et Communautaires*: 1 rue du 11 Novembre, 92129 Montrouge, France

Communication theory. [*Commun. Theory*] *ISSN: 1050-3293. International Communication Association*: 8140 Burnet Road, P.O. Box 9589, Austin, TX. 78766-9589, U.S.A.; **Publisher**: *Guilford Publications*: 72 Spring Street, New York, NY. 10012, U.S.A.

Communisme. [*Communisme*] *ISSN: 2209-7007. Éditions L'Age d'Homme*: 5 rue Férou, 75006 Paris, France

INTERNATIONAL BIBLIOGRAPHY OF SOCIOLOGY — 1988

Community development journal. *[Comm. Dev. J.]* ISSN: 0010-3802. *Oxford University Press*: Walton Street, Oxford OX2 6DP, U.K.; **Subscriptions**: *idem:* Journals Subscription Dept., Pinkhill House, Southfield Road, Eynsham, Oxon OX8 1JJ, U.K.

Comparative and international law journal of Southern Africa. *[Comp. Int. Law J. S.Afr.]* ISSN: 0010-4051. *University of South Africa, Institute of Foreign and Comparative Law*: P.O. Box 392, Pretoria, South Africa

Comparative political studies. *[Comp. Poli. S.]* ISSN: 0010- 4140. *Sage Publications*: 2455 Teller Road, Newbury Park, CA 91320, U.S.A.; **Subscriptions**: *Sage Publications*: 6 Bonhill Street, London EC2A 4PU, U.K.

Comparative politics. *[Comp. Polit.]* ISSN: 0010-4159. *City University of New York*: 33 West 42nd Street, New York, NY. 10036, U.S.A.

Comparative social research. *[Comp. Soc. Res.]* ISSN: 0195-6310. *JAI Press*: 55 Old Post Road No. 2., Greenwich, CT. 06836, U.S.A.

Comparative studies in society and history. *[Comp. Stud. S.]* ISSN: 0010- 4175. *Society for the Comparative Study of Society and History*; **Publisher**: *Cambridge University Press*: 40 West 20th Street, New York, NY. 10011, U.S.A.

Computer science in economics and management. *[Comp. Sci. Ec. Manag.]* ISSN: 0921-2736. *Kluwer Academic Publishers*: P.O. Box 17, 3300 AA Dordrecht, The Netherlands; **Subscriptions**: *Kluwer Academic Publishers*: P.O. Box 322, 3300 AH Dordrecht, The Netherlands

Contemporary Pacific. *[Cont. Pac.]* ISSN: 1043-898X. *Center for Pacific Islands Studies*: University of Hawaii at Manoa, 1890 East-West Road, 215 Moore Hall, Honolulu, Hawaii 96822, U.S.A.; **Publisher**: *University of Hawaii Press*: 2840 Kolowalu Street, Honolulu, Hawaii 96822-1888, U.S.A.

Continuity and change. *[Contin. Change]* ISSN: 0268-4160. *Cambridge University Press*: The Edinburgh Building, Shaftesbury Road, Cambridge CB2 2RU, U.K.

Contributions to Indian sociology. *[Contr. I. Soc.]* ISSN: 0069-9667. *Institute of Economic Growth*: University of Delhi, Delhi 110007, India; **Publisher**: *Sage Publications India*: 32 M-Block Market, Greater Kailash 1, New Delhi 110 048, India

Corruption and reform. *[Corr. Reform]* ISSN: 0169-7528. *Martinus Nijhoff Publishers*: P.O. Box 322, 3300 AH Dordrecht, The Netherlands

Crime and delinquency. *[Crime Delin.]* ISSN: 0011-1287. *Sage Publications*: 2455 Teller Road, Newbury Park, CA. 91320, U.S.A.

Crime and justice. *[Crime Just.]* ISSN: 0192-3234. *University of Chicago Press*: 5720 S. Woodlawn, Chicago, IL. 60637, U.S.A.

Crime, law and social change. *[Cr. Law Soc. Chan.]* ISSN: 0925 4994. *Kluwer Academic Publishers*: Spuiboulevard 50, P.O. Box 17, 3300 AA Dordrecht, The Netherlands

Criminal law review. *[Crim. Law Rev.]* ISSN: 0011-135X. *Sweet & Maxwell*: South Quay Plaza, 183 Marsh Wall, London E14 9FT, U.K.; **Subscriptions**: *idem:* Freepost, Andover, Hants, SP10 5BR, U.K.

Critica marxista. *[Crit. Marx.]* ISSN: 0011-152X. *Editori Riuniti Riviste*: via Serchio 9, 00198 Rome, Italy

Critica sociologica. *[Crit. Sociol.]* ISSN: 0011 1546. *S.I.A.R.E.S.*: Corso Vittorio Emanuele 24, 00186 Rome, Italy

Critical review. *[Crit. Rev.]* ISSN: 0891-3811. *Center for Independent Thought*: 942 Howard Street, Room 109, San Francisco, CA 94103, U.S.A.; **Publisher**: *Critical Review*: P.O. Box 14528, Chicago IL. 60614, U.S.A.

INTERNATIONAL BIBLIOGRAPHY OF SOCIOLOGY — 1988

Critical sociology. *[Crit. Sociol.] ISSN: 0896- 9205. University of Oregon, Department of Sociology*: OR. 97403, U.S.A.

Cuadernos americanos. *[Cuad. Am.] ISSN: 0185-156X. Universidad Nacional Autónoma de México*: Ciudad Universitaria, 04510 México, D.F., Apartado Postal 965, México 1.

Cuadernos de nuestra América. *[Cuad. Nues. Am.]; Centro de Estudios Sobre America*: Ave. 3ra no. 1805e/ 18 y 20, Playa Zona Postal 13, Havana, Cuba

Cultural studies. *[Cult. St.] ISSN: 0950-2386. Routledge*: 11 New Fetter Lane, London, EC4P 4EE, U.K.; **Subscriptions**: *Routledge*: Cheriton House, North Way, Andover, Hants SP10 5BE, U.K.

Culture et société. *[Cult. Soc.]; Ministère de la Jeunesse des Sports et de la Culture, Centre de Civilisation Burundaise*: B.P. 1095, Bujumbura, Burundi

Culture, medicine and psychiatry. *[Cult. Medic. Psych.] ISSN: 0165-005X. Kluwer Academic Publishers*: P.O. Box 322, 3300 AH Dordrecht, The Netherlands

Current history. *[Curr. Hist.] ISSN: 0011-3530. Current History*: Publications Office, 4225 Main Street, Philadelphia, PA. 19127, U.S.A.

Current sociology. *[Curr. Sociol.] ISSN: 0011-3921. International Sociological Association*; **Publisher**: *Sage Publications*: 6 Bonhill Street, London EC2A 4PU, U.K.

Curriculum journal. *[Curric. J.] ISSN: 0958-5176. Routledge*: 11 New Fetter Lane, London, EC4P 4EE, U.K.; **Subscriptions**: *Routledge*: Cheriton House, North Way, Andover, Hants SP10 5BE, U.K.

Cyprus review. *[Cyprus Rev.] ISSN: 1015-2881. Intercollege/ University of Indianapolis*: P.O. Box 4005, 17 Heroes Avenue, Ayios Andreas, Nicosia, Cyprus/ 1400 Hanna Avenue, Indianapolis, IN. 46227-3687, U.S.A.

Dædalus. *[Dædalus] ISSN: 0011-5266. American Academy of Arts and Sciences*: 136 Irving Street, Cambridge, MA. 02138, U.S.A.; **Subscriptions**: *Dædalus Business Office*: P.O. Box 515, Canton, MA. 02021, U.S.A.

Demografie. *[Demografie] ISSN: 0011-8265. Federální Statistický Úřad*; **Publisher**: *Panorama*: Hálkova 1, 120 72 Prague 2, Czechoslovakia

Demography. *[Demography] ISSN: 0070-3370. Population Association of America*: 1722 N. Street, N.W., Washington, DC. 20036, U.S.A.

Derechos humanos. *[Der. Human.] ISSN: 0327-1846. Asamblea Permanente por los Derechos Humanos*: Avenida Callao 569, Piso 1°, oficina 15, 1022 Buenos Aires, Argentina

Deutschland Archiv.:*Zeitschrift für das vereinigte Deutschland [Deut. Arch.] ISSN: 0012-1428. Verlag Wissenschaft und Politik*: Salierring 14-16, 5000 Cologne, Germany

Development. *[Development] ISSN: 1011-6370. Society for International Development*: Palazzo della Civiltà del Lavoro, Rome 00144, Italy

Development & socio-economic progress. *[Devel. & Socio-eco. Pro.]; Afro-Asian Peoples' Solidarity Organisation (AAPSO)*: 89 Abdel Aziz Al-Saoud Street, 11451- 61 Manial El-Roda, Cairo, Egypt

Diachronica. *[Diachronica] ISSN: 0176-4225. John Benjamins Publishing*: Amsteldijk 44, P.O. Box 52519, NL-1007 HA Amsterdam, The Netherlands

Dirasat.:*Series A — the humanities [Dirasat Ser. A.] ISSN: 0255-8033. Deanship of Academic Research*: University of Jordan, Amman, Jordan

Disasters.:*Journal of disaster studies and management [Disasters] ISSN: 0361-3666. Basil Blackwell*: 108 Cowley Road, Oxford OX4 1JF, U.K.

Dissent. *[Dissent] ISSN: 0012-3846. Foundation for the Study of Independent Social Ideas*: 521 Fifth Avenue, New York, NY. 10017, U.S.A.

INTERNATIONAL BIBLIOGRAPHY OF SOCIOLOGY — 1988

Documents. *[Documents] ISSN: 0151- 0827. Documents*: 50 rue de Laborde, 75008 Paris, France; **Subscriptions**: *idem:* 21 rue du Faubourg-Saint-Antoine, 75011 Paris, France

Droit social. *[Droit Soc.] ISSN: 0012-6438. Éditions Techniques et Économiques*: 3, rue Soufflot, 75005 Paris, France

E & S.:*Économie et statistique [E & S] ISSN: 0336-1451. Institut National de la Statistique et des Etudes Economiques*: 18 boulevard A. Pinard, 75675 Paris Cedex 14, France

East European quarterly. *[E. Eur. Quart.] ISSN: 0012-8449. University of Colorado*: 1200 University Avenue, Boulder, CO. 80309, U.S.A.

Eastern Africa social science research review. *[E.Afr. Soc. Sci. Res. R.]; Organization for Social Science Research in Eastern Africa - OSSREA*: P.O. Box 31971, Addis Ababa, Ethiopia

Eastern Buddhist. *[East. Bud.]; Eastern Buddhist Society*: Otani University, Koyama, Kita-ku, Kyoto 603, Japan

Ecological economics. *[Ecol. Eco.] ISSN: 0921-8009. International Society for Ecological Economics*; **Publisher**: *Elsevier Science Publishers*: P.O. Box 211, 1000 AE Amsterdam, The Netherlands

Economia. *[Economia] ISSN: 0012-9704. Universidad Central del Ecuador, Instituto de Investigaciones Economicas*: Apartado 1088, Quito, Ecuador

Economia & lavoro. *[Ec. Lav.] ISSN: 0012-978X. Fondazione Giacomo Brodolini*: via Torino 122, 00184 Rome, Italy; **Publisher**: *Marsilio Editori*: Marittima — Fabbricato 205, 30135, Venice, Italy

Economia y desarrollo. *[Econ. Desar.] ISSN: 0252- 8584. Universidad de la Habana, Facultad de Economia*: Calle O No.262 e/ 25 y 27, Vedado, Havana 4, Cuba

Economic affairs [London]. *[Econ. Affr.] ISSN: 0265-0665. Institute of Economic Affairs*: 2 Lord North Street, London, SW1P 3LB, U.K.; **Publisher**: *City Publications*: 3-4 St. Andrew's Hill, London EC4V 5BY, U.K.; **Subscriptions**: *Economic Affairs*: Magazine Subscription Department, Freepost, Luton LU1 5BR, U.K.

Economic and industrial democracy. *[Econ. Ind. Dem.] ISSN: 0143-831X. Arbetslivscentrum (The Swedish Center for Working Life)*: Box 5606, S-114 86 Stockholm, Sweden; **Publisher**: *Sage Publications*: 6 Bonhill Street, London EC2A 4PU, U.K.

Economic and social history in the Netherlands. *[Econ. Soc. Hist. Nether.] ISSN: 0925-1669. Nederlandsch Economisch-Historisch Archief = Netherlands Economic History Archive*: Cruquiusweg 31, 1019 AT Amsterdam, The Netherlands

Economic and social review. *[Econ. Soc. R.] ISSN: 0012-9984. Economic and Social Studies*: 4 Burlington Road, Dublin 4, Ireland

Economic development and cultural change. *[Econ. Dev. Cult. Change] ISSN: 0013-0079. University of Chicago Press*: Journals Division, 5720 S. Woodlawn, Chicago, IL. 60637, U.S.A.

Economic geography. *[Econ. Geogr.] ISSN: 0013-0095. Clark University*: Worcester, MA. 01610, U.S.A.; **Publisher**: *Commonwealth Press*: 44 Portland Street, Worcester, MA., U.S.A.

Economic history review. *[Econ. Hist. R.] ISSN: 0013-0117. Economic History Society*: P.O. Box 190, 1 Greville Road, Cambridge CB1 3QG, U.K.; **Publisher**: *Basil Blackwell*: 108 Cowley Road, Oxford OX4 1JF, U.K.

Economic inquiry. *[Econ. Inq.] ISSN: 0095-2583. Western Economic Association International*: 7400 Center Avenue, Suite 109, Huntington Beach, CA 92647-3039, U.S.A.; **Subscriptions**: *idem:* Subscription Services, P.O. Box 368, Lawrence, KS. 66044-0368, U.S.A.

Economic papers [Warsaw]. *[Econ. Papers [Warsaw]] ISSN: 0324-864X. Central School of Planning and Statistics in Warsaw, Research Institute for Developing Countries*: Al. Niepodległości 167, 02-521 Warsaw, Poland

INTERNATIONAL BIBLIOGRAPHY OF SOCIOLOGY — 1988

Economic review. Bank of Israel. [*Econ. Rev. Bank Israel*] *ISSN: 0334-441X. Bank of Israel, Research Department*: Kiryat Ben-Gurion, P.O.B. 780, Jerusalem 91007, Israel

Economics and philosophy. [*Econ. Philos.*] *ISSN: 0266-2671. Cambridge University Press*: 40 West 20th Street, New York, NY 10011, U.S.A.

Economie appliquée. [*Econ. App.*] *ISSN: 0013-0494. Institut de Sciences Mathematiques et Economiques Appliquées*: 11 rue Pierre et Marie Curie, 75005 Paris, France; **Publisher**: *Presses Universitaries de Grenoble*: B.P. 47 X, 38 040 Grenoble Cedex, France

Economie du centre-est. [*Econ. Cen.E.*] *ISSN: 0153-4459. Institut d'Économie Régionale Bourgogne-Franche-Comte*: 4 boulevard Gabriel, 21000 Dijon, France; **Publisher**: *Dijon Presses de l'Université de Bourgogne*

Economies et sociétés. [*Ec. Sociét.*] *ISSN: 0013-0567. I.S.M.E.A.*: 11, rue Pierre-et-Marie Curie, 75005 Paris, France; **Publisher**: *Presses Universitaires de Grenoble (PUG)*: B.P. 47 X, 38040 Grenoble Cedex, France

Economisch en sociaal tijdschrift. [*Econ. Soc. Tidj.*] *ISSN: 0013-0575. Universtaire Faculteiten Sint-Ignatius te Antwerpen*: Kipdorp 19, 2000 Antwerp, Belgium

Economist [Leiden]. [*Economist [Leiden]*] *ISSN: 0013-063X. Royal Netherlands Economic Association*; **Publisher**: *Stenfert Kroese Uitgevers*: P.O. Box 33, 2300 AA Leiden, The Netherlands

Economy and society. [*Econ. Soc.*] *ISSN: 0308-5147. Routledge*: 11 New Fetter Lane, London EC4P 4EE, U.K.

Education and urban society. [*Educ. Urban. Soc.*] *ISSN: 0013- 1245. Sage Publications*: 2455 Teller Road, Newbury Park, CA. 91320, U.S.A.

Ekistics. [*Ekistics*] *ISSN: 0013-2942. Athens Technological Organization, Athens Center of Ekistics*: 24 Strat. Syndesmou St., 10673 Athens, Greece; **Subscriptions**: *idem:* P.O. Box 3471, 10210 Athens, Greece

Electoral studies. [*Elec. Stud.*] *ISSN: 0261- 3794. Butterworth-Heinemann*: Linacre House, Jordan Hill, Oxford OX2 8DP, U.K.

Employee relations. [*Employ. Relat.*] *ISSN: 0142-5455. MCB University Press*: 62 Toller Lane, Bradford, West Yorkshire, BD8 9BY, U.K.

English world-wide. [*Eng. Wor.-wide*] *ISSN: 0172-8865. John Benjamins Publishing*: P.O. Box 75577, Amstedldijk 44, 1007 AN Amsterdam, The Netherlands

Environment and behavior. [*Envir. Behav.*] *ISSN: 0013-9165. Environmental Design Research Association*; **Publisher**: *Sage Publications*: 2455 Teller Road, Newbury Park CA. 91320, U.S.A.

Environment and planning A.:*International journal of urban and regional research* [*Envir. Plan.A.*] *ISSN: 0308-518X. Pion*: 207 Brondesbury Park, London NW2 5JN, U.K.

Environment and planning B.:*Planning and design* [*Envir. Plan. B.*] *ISSN: 0265-8135. Pion*: 207 Brondesbury Park, London NW2 5JN, U.K.

Environment and planning C.:*Government and policy* [*Envir. Plan. C.*] *ISSN: 0263 774X. Pion*: 207 Brondesbury Park, London NW2 5JN, U.K.

Environment and planning D.:*Society and space* [*Envir. Plan. D*] *ISSN: 0263-7758. Pion*: 207 Brondesbury Park, London, NW2 5JN, U.K

Espace géographique. [*Espace Géogr.*] *ISSN: 0046- 2497. Doin Editeurs*: 8 place de l'Odéon, 75006 Paris, France

Espace populations sociétés. [*Espace Pop. Soc.*] *ISSN: 0755-7809. Université des Sciences et Techniques de Lille- Flandres- Artois*: 59655 Villeneuve d'Ascq Cedex, France

Esprit. *[Esprit] ISSN: 0014-0759. Esprit*: 212 rue Saint-Martin, 75003 Paris, France

Estudios de Asia y Africa. *[Est. Asia Afr.] ISSN: 0185-0164. El Colegio de México*: Camino al Ajusco 20, Pedregal de Santa Teresa, 10740 México D.F., México

Estudios demográficos y urbanos. *[Est. Demog. Urb.] ISSN: 0186-7210. Colégio de México, Centro de Estudios Demográficos y de Desarrollo Urbano*: Departamento de Publicaciones, Camino al Ajusco 20, 10740 México D.F., México

Estudios sociológicos. *[Est. Sociol.] ISSN: 0185-4186. Colegio de México*: Camino al Ajusco 20, Pedregal de Santa Teresa, 10740 Mexico, D.F., Mexico

Estudos jurídicos. *[Est. Juríd.] ISSN: 0100-2538. Universidade do Vale do Rio dos Sinos*: 93.000 São Leopoldo RS, Brazil

Estudos leopoldenses. *[Est. Leop.] ISSN: 0014-1607. Universidade do Vale do Rio dos Sinos*: 93.000 São Leopoldo RS, Brazil

Ethics. *[Ethics] ISSN: 0014-1704. University of Chicago Press*: Journals Division, 5720 S. Woodlawn Avenue, Chicago, IL. 60637, U.S.A.

Ethnic and racial studies. *[Ethn. Racial] ISSN: 0141-9870. Routledge*: 11 New Fetter Lane, London EC4P 4EE, U.K.; **Subscriptions**: *Routledge Journals*: Cheriton House, North Way, Andover, Hants. SP10 5BE, U.K.

Ethnologica Helvetica. *[Ethnol. Helvet.]; Schweizerische Ethnologische Gesellschaft = Société Suisse d'Ethnologie = Swiss Ethnological Society*: c/o Institut für Ethnologie, Schwanengasse 7, CH-3011 Bern, Switzerland; **Subscriptions**: *Dietrich Reimer Verlag*: Unter den Eichen 57, D-1000 Berlin 45, Germany

Ethology & sociobiology. *[Ethol. Socio.] ISSN: 0162-3095. Elsevier Science Publishing (New York)*: 655 Avenue of the Americas, New York, NY. 10010, U.S.A.; **Subscriptions**: *Journals Fulfillment Department, Elsevier Science Publishing*: 655 Avenue of the Americas, New York, NY. 10010, U.S.A.

Études canadiennes; Canadian studies. *[Étud. Can.] ISSN: 0153-1700. Association Française d'Etudes Canadiennes*: Maison des Sciences de l'Homme d'Aquitaine, Domaine Universitaire, 33405 Talence, France

Études rurales. *[Rural Stud.] ISSN: 0014-2182. Laboratoire d'Anthropologie Sociale*: Collège de France, 52 rue du Cardinal Lemoine, 75005 Paris, France; **Publisher**: *Editions de l'Ecole des Hautes Etudes en Sciences Sociales*: 131 boulevard Saint-Michel, 75005 Paris, France; **Subscriptions**: *idem*: Centrale des Revues; **Subscriptions**: *11 rue Gossin, 92543 Montrouge Cedex, France*

Études rwandaises.:*Série lettres et sciences humaines [Ét. Rwand.]; Éditions de l'Université Nationale du Rwanda*: B.P. 56 Butare, Rwanda

Études sociales. *[Étud. Soc.]; Société d'Écomonie et de Science Sociales*: 80 rue Vaneau, 75007 Paris, France

Eure.:*Revista latinoamericana de estudios urbanos regionales [Eure] ISSN: 0250-7161. Pontificia Universidad Catolica de Chile, Facultad de Arquitectura y Bellas Artes, Instituto de Estudios Urbanos*: Los Navegantes 1919, Casilla 16.002, Correo 9, Santiago, Chile

Europa ethnica. *[Eur. Ethn.] ISSN: 0014-2492. Wilhelm Braumüller*: A-1092 Vienna, Servitengasse 5, Austria

European journal of operational research. *[Eur. J. Oper. Res.] ISSN: 0377-2217. Association of European Operational Research Societies*; **Publisher**: *Elsevier Science Publishers (North-Holland)*: P.O. Box 1991, 1000 BZ Amsterdam, The Netherlands

European journal of political research. *[Eur. J. Pol. R.] ISSN: 0304-4130. European Consortium for Political Research*: University of Essex, Wivenhoe Park, Colchester CO4 3SQ, U.K.; **Publisher**: *Kluwer Academic Publishers*: Spuiboulevard 50, P.O. Box 17, 3300 AA Dordrecht, The Netherlands; **Subscriptions**: *idem*: P.O. Box 322, 3300 AH Dordrecht, The Netherlands

INTERNATIONAL BIBLIOGRAPHY OF SOCIOLOGY — 1988

European journal of population; Revue européenne de démographie. *[Eur. J. Pop.]* ISSN: 0168-6577. *Elsevier Science Publishers (North Holland)*: P.O. Box 1991, 1000 BZ Amsterdam, The Netherlands

European journal of social psychology. *[Eur. J. Soc. Psychol.]* ISSN: 0046-2772. *European Association of Experimental Social Psychology*; **Publisher**: *John Wiley & Sons*: Baffins Lane, Chichester, West Sussex PO19 1UD, U.K.

European sociological review. *[Eur. Sociol. R.]* ISSN: 0266-7215. *Oxford University Press*: Pinkhill House, Southfield Road, Eynsham, Oxford OX8 1JJ, U.K.

Evaluation review. *[Eval. Rev.]* ISSN: 0193-841X. *Sage Publications*: 2455 Teller Road, Newbury Park, CA. 91320, U.S.A.

Families in society. *[Fam. Soc.]* ISSN: 1044-3894. *Family Service America*: 11700 West Lake Park Drive, Milwaukee, WI. 53224, U.S.A.; **Subscriptions**: *Families in Society*: Subscription Department, P.O. Box 6649, Syracuse, NY. 13217, U.S.A.

Feminist review. *[Feminist R.]* ISSN: 0141-7789. *Feminist Review*: 11 Carleton Gardens, Brecknock Road, London N19 5AQ, U.K.; **Publisher**: *Routledge*: 11 New Fetter Lane, London EC4P 4EE, U.K.

Folia linguistica historia. *[Folia Ling. Hist.]*; *Societas Linguistica Europaea*; **Publisher**: *Mouton de Gruyter*: Postfach 110240, D-1000 Berlin 11, Germany

Formation emploi. *[Form. Emp.]* ISSN: 0759-6340. *Documentation Française*: 29-31 quai Voltaire, 75340 Paris Cedex 07, France; **Subscriptions**: *La Documentation Française*: 124 rue Henri Barbusse, 93308 Aubervilliers Cedex, France

Free associations. *[Free Assoc.]* ISSN: 0267-0887. *Free Association Books*: 26 Freegrove Road, London N7 9RQ, U.K.

Free China review. *[Free China R.]* ISSN: 0016- 030X. *Kwang Hwa Publishing*: 2 Tientsin Street, Taipei, Taiwan

Gender and history. *[Gend. Hist.]* ISSN: 9053-5233. *Basil Blackwell*: 108 Cowley Road, Oxford OX4 1JF, U.K.; **Subscriptions**: *Marston Book Services*: P.O. Box 87, Oxford OX2 0DT, U.K.

Gender and society. *[Gender Soc.]* ISSN: 0891-2432. *Sociologists for Women in Society*; **Publisher**: *Sage Publications*: 2455 Teller Road, Newbury Park, CA. 91320, U.S.A.

Genève-Afrique. *[Genève-Afrique]* ISSN: 0016-6774. *Institut Univeristaire d'Études du Développement (IUED)*: Case postale 136, CH-1211 Geneva 21, Switzerland

Genus. *[Genus]* ISSN: 0016-6987. *Comitato Italiano per lo Studio dei Problemi della Popolazione*: Via Nomentana 41, 00161 Rome, Italy; **Subscriptions**: *Edizioni Scientifiche Inglesi Americane*: Via Palestro 30, 00185 Rome, Italy

Geoforum. *[Geoforum]* ISSN: 0016-7185. *Pergamon Press*: Headington Hill Hall, Oxford OX3 0BW, U.K.

Geografiska annaler.:*Series B — Human geography [Geog.ann. B.]* ISSN: 0435-3676. *Svenska Sällskapet för Antropologi och Geografi = Swedish Society for Anthropology and Geography*: University of Uppsala, Department of Physical Geography, Box 554, S-751 22 Uppsala, Sweden; **Subscriptions**: *Universitetsforlaget*: P.O. Box 2959, Tøyen, N-0608 Oslo 6, Norway

Geographia polonica. *[Geogr. Pol.]* ISSN: 0016-7282. *Polish Academy of Sciences, Institute of Geography and Spatial Organization*; **Publisher**: *Polish Scientific Publishers*: Krakowskie Przedmieście 7, 00-068 Warsaw, Poland

Geographical analysis. *[Geogr. Anal.]* ISSN: 0016-7363. *Ohio State University Press*: 1070 Carmack Road, Columbus, OH 43210, U.S.A.

Geographical journal. *[Geogr. J.]* ISSN: 0016-7398. *Royal Geographical Society*: 1 Kensington Gore, London SW7 2AR, U.K.

Geographical review. *[Geogr. Rev.] ISSN: 0016-7428. American Geographical Society*: Suite 600, 156 Fifth Avenue, New York, N.Y. 10010, U.S.A.

Geographical review of India. *[Geogr. Rev. Ind.] ISSN: 0375-6386. Geographical Society of India*: Department of Geography, University of Calcutta, 35 Ballygunge Circular Road, Calcutta 700 019, India

Geographical review of Japan. *[Geogr. Rev. Jpn.] ISSN: 0016 7444. Association of Japanese Geographers*: Japan Academic Societies Center, 2-4-16 Yayoi, Bunkyo-ku, Tokyo 113, Japan

Geographische Rundschau. *[Geogr. Rund.] ISSN: 0016-7460. Westermann Schulbuchverlag*: Georg-Westermann-Allee 66, 3300 Braunschweig, Germany

Geography. *[Geography]; Geographical Association*: 343 Fulwood Road, Sheffield S10 3PB, U.K.

Geography research forum. *[Geogr. Res. For.] ISSN: 0333-5275. Ben-Gurion University of the Negev, Department of Geography*: Beer-Sheeva 84105, Israel

Geschichte und Gesellschaft. *[Gesch. Ges.] ISSN: 0340-613X. Vandenhoeck und Ruprecht*: Postfach 3753, D-3400 Göttingen, Germany

Gestion 2000.:*Management et prospective [Gestion] ISSN: 0773-0543. Université Catholique de Louvain, Institut d'Administration et de Gestion*: 16 avenue de l'Espinette, B-1348 Louvain-la-Neuve, Belgium

Gewerkschaftliche Monatshefte. *[Gewerk. Monat.] ISSN: 0016-9447. Bundesvorstand des DGB*: Hans-Böckler-Straße 39, 4000 Düsseldorf 30, Germany; **Publisher**: *Bund-Verlag*: Postfach 900840, 5000 Cologne 90, Germany

Годишник на Висшия Финансово- Стопански Институт „Д. А. Ценов" - Свищов; Godishnik na visshiia finansovo- stopanski institut "D. A. Tsenov" - Svishtov. *[God. Vis. F. S. Inst. Tsenov - Svi.] ISSN: 0323-9470. Knigoizdatelstvo Georgi Bakalov*: Bulgaria

Göteborg studies in educational sciences. *[Göt. Stud. Ed. Sci.] ISSN: 0436-1121. Acta Universitatis Gothoburgensis*: Box 5096, S-402 22 Göteborg, Sweden

Government and opposition. *[Govt. Oppos.] ISSN: 0017-257X. Government and Opposition*: Houghton Street, London WC2A 2AE, U.K.

Groupwork. *[Groupwork] ISSN: 0951-824X. Whiting & Birch*: P.O. Box 872, Forest Hill, London SE23 3HL, U.K.

Hacienda pública española. *[Hac. Públ. Esp.] ISSN: 0210-1173. Instituto de Estudios Fiscales*: Ministerio de Economía y Hacienda, Plaza de Canalejas 3, 28014 Madrid, Spain

Hamburger Jahrbuch für Wirtschafts- und Gesellschaftspolitik. *[Ham. Jahrb. Wirt- Ges.pol.]; HWWA- Institut für Wirtschaftsforschung*; **Publisher**: *J.C.B. Mohr (Paul Siebeck)*: Postfach 2040, D-7400 Tubingen, Germany

Harvard law review. *[Harv. Law. Rev.] ISSN: 0017-811X. Harvard Law Review Association*: Gannett House, 1511 Massachusetts Avenue, Cambridge, MA. 02138, U.S.A.

Health policy and planning. *[Health Pol. Plan.] ISSN: 0268-1080. London School of Hygiene and Tropical Medicine*: Keppel (Gower) Street, London WC1E 7HT, U.K.; **Publisher**: *Oxford University Press*: Pinkhill House, Southfield Road, Eynsham, Oxford, OX8 1JJ, U.K.

Hemispheres. *[Hemispheres] ISSN: 0239-8818. Polish Academy of Sciences, Centre for Studies on non-European Countries*: Rynek 9, 50-106 Wroclaw, Poland

Heritage of Zimbabwe. *[Herit. Zimb.] ISSN: 0556-9605. History Society of Zimbabwe*: P.O. Box 8268, Causeway, Harare, Zimbabwe

High technology law journal. *[High Tech. Law J.] ISSN: 0885-2715. University of California Press*: 2120 Berkeley Way, Berkeley, CA. 94720, U.S.A.

INTERNATIONAL BIBLIOGRAPHY OF SOCIOLOGY — 1988

Himal. *[Himal] ISSN: 1012-9804. Himal Associates*: P.O. Box 42, Lalitpur, Nepal

Hispanic American historical review.*[HAHR]*— *[Hisp. Am. Hist. Rev.] ISSN: 0018-2168. American Historical Association, Conference on Latin American History*; **Publisher**: *Duke University Press*: Box 6697 College Station, Durham, NC 27708, U.S.A.

Historical journal. *[Hist. J.] ISSN: 0018-246X. Cambridge University Press*: The Edinburgh Building, Shaftesbury Road, Cambridge CB2 2RU, U.K.

Historical social research; Historische Sozialforschung. *[Hist. Soc. R.] ISSN: 0172-6404. Arbeitsgemeinschaft für Quantifizierung und Methoden in der historisch sozialwissenschaftlichen Forschung/ International Commission for the Application of Quantitative Methods in History/ Association for History and Computing*: Bachemerstr. 40, D-5000 Cologne 41, Germany/ University of London, Westfield College, Department of History, Kidderpore Avenue, London NW3 7ST, U.K.; **Publisher**: *Zentrum für Historische Sozialforschung*: Zentralarchiv für Empirische Sozialforschung, Universität zu Köln, Bachemerstr. 40, D-5000 Cologne, Germany

Historical studies. *[Hist. S.] ISSN: 0018-2559. University of Melbourne*: Parkville, Victoria 3052, Australia

History and theory. *[Hist. Theory] ISSN: 0018-2656. Wesleyan University*: 287 High Street, Middletown, CT. 06457, U.S.A.

History of the human sciences. *[Hist. Human Sci.] ISSN: 0952-6951. Routledge*: 11 New Fetter Lane, London EC4P 4EE, U.K.

Hitotsubashi journal of commerce and management. *[Hito. J. Comm. Manag.] ISSN: 0018-2796. Hitotsubashi University, Hitotsubashi Academy*: Kunitachi, Tokyo 186, Japan; **Subscriptions**: *Japan Publications*: P.O. Box 5030 Tokyo International, Tokyo, Japan

Hitotsubashi journal of social studies. *[Hito. J. Soc. Stud.] ISSN: 0073- 280X. Hitotsubashi University, Hitotsubashi Academy*: 2-1 Naka, Kunitachi, Tokyo 186, Japan

Homines. *[Homines] ISSN: 0252-8908. Universidad Interamericana de Puerto Rico*: Recinto Metropolitano, División de Ciencias Sociales, Apartado 1293, Hato Rey 00919, Puerto Rico

Homme et la société. *[Hom. Soc.] ISSN: 0018-4306. Centre National des Lettres/ Centre National de la Recherche Scientifique*; **Publisher**: *Editions l'Harmattan*: 5-7 rue de l'Ecole- Polytechnique, 75005 Paris, France

Housing policy debate. *[Hous. Pol. Deb.] ISSN: 1051-1482. Office of Housing Policy, Fannie Mae*: 3900 Wisconsin Avenue, NW Washington, DC 20016-2899, U.S.A.

Howard journal of criminal justice. *[Howard J. Crim. Just.] ISSN: 0265-5527. Howard League*: 708 Holloway Road, London N19 3NL, U.K.; **Publisher**: *Basil Blackwell*: 108 Cowley Road, Oxford OX4 1JF, U.K.

Human ethology newsletter. *[Human Eth. New.] ISSN: 0739-2036. International Society for Human Ethology*: Paedological Institute of the City of Amsterdam, Ijsbaanpad 9, 1076 CV Amsterdam, The Netherlands

Human nature. *[Hum. Nature] ISSN: 1045-6767. Aldine de Gruyter*: 200 Saw Mill River Road, Hawthorne, N.Y. 10532, U.S.A.

Human relations. *[Human Relat.] ISSN: 0018-7267. Plenum Press*: 233 Spring Street, New York, N.Y. 10013, U.S.A.

Human rights quarterly. *[Hum. Rights Q.] ISSN: 0275-0392. Johns Hopkins University Press*: Journals Publishing Division, 701 W. 40th Street, Suite 275, Baltimore, MD. 21211, U.S.A.

Humor. *[Humor] ISSN: 0933-1719. Mouton de Gruyter*: Postfach 110240, D-1000 Berlin 11, Germany

ICSSR newsletter. *[ICSSR News.] ISSN: 0018-9049. Indian Council of Social Science Research*: 35 Ferozeshah Road, New Delhi-110 001, India

INTERNATIONAL BIBLIOGRAPHY OF SOCIOLOGY — 1988

IDS Bulletin. *[IDS Bull.] ISSN: 0265-5012. Institute of Development Studies*: University of Sussex, Brighton BN1 9RE, U.K.

Ilmu alam. *[Il. Alam] ISSN: 0126-7000. Universiti Kebangsaan Malaysia, Geography Department*: 43600 UKM Bangi, Selangor D.E., Malaysia; **Publisher**: *Universiti Kebangsaan Malaysia Press*: 43600 UKM Bang, Selangor D.E., Malaysia

Immigrants and minorities. *[Imm. Minor.] ISSN: 0261-9288. Frank Cass*: Gainsborough House, 11 Gainsborough Road, London E11 1RS, U.K.

Impact of science on society. *[Impact Sci.] ISSN: 0019-2872. UNESCO*: 7 place de Fontenoy, 75700 Paris, France; **Subscriptions**: *Taylor and Francis*: Rankine Road, Basingstoke, Hampshire RG24 0PR, U.K.

Index on censorship. *[Index Censor.] ISSN: 0306-4220. Writers and Scholars International*: 39c Highbury Place, London N5 1QP, U.K.

Indian economic and social history review. *[Indian Ec. Soc. His. R.] ISSN: 0019- 4646. Indian Economic and Social History Association*; **Publisher**: *Sage Publications*: 32 M- Block Market, Greater Kailash-I, New Delhi 110 048, India

Indian geographical journal. *[Ind. Geograph. J.] ISSN: 0019-4824. Indian Geographical Society*: c/o The editor, Indian Geographical Journal, Department of Geography, University of Madras, Madras 600 005, India

Indian journal of industrial relations. *[Ind. J. Ind. Rel.] ISSN: 0019-5286. Shri Ram Centre for Industrial Relations and Human Resources*: 4E/16 Jhandewalan Extension, New Delhi- 110015, India

Indian journal of labour economics. *[Ind. J. Lab. Econ.]; Indian Society of Labour Economics*; **Publisher**: *Dr. R.C. Singh*: Department of Labour and Social Welfare, Patna University, Patna 800005, India

Indian journal of public administration. *[Indian J. Publ. Admin.] ISSN: 0019-5561. Indian Institute of Public Administration*: Indraprastha Estate, Ring Road East, New Delhi 110002, India

Indian journal of regional science. *[Ind. J. Reg. Sci.] ISSN: 0046-9017. Indian Institute of Technology, Regional Science Association*: Department of Architecture and Regional Planning, Kharagpur, West Bengal, India

Indian journal of social science. *[Ind. J. Soc. Sci.]; Indian Council of Social Science Research*; **Publisher**: *Sage Publications India*: 32 M- Block Market, Greater Kailash I, New Delhi 110 048, India

Indian journal of social work. *[Indian J. Soc. W.] ISSN: 0019-5634. Tata Institute of Social Sciences*: Deonar, Bombay 400 088, India

Indian labour journal. *[Indian. Lab. J.] ISSN: 0019-5723. Labour Bureau*: Cleremont Shimla - 171004, Uttar Pradesh, India; **Subscriptions**: *Controller of Publications*: Civil Lines, Delhi-110 054, India

Indo Asia. *[In. Asia] ISSN: 0019-719X. Burg-Verlag*: Untere Au 41, 7123 Sachsenheim-Hohenhaslach, Germany

Indogermanische Forschungen. *[Indoger. Fors.] ISSN: 0019-7262. Walter de Gruyter*: Postfach 110240, D-1000 Berlin 30, Germany

Indonesia circle. *[Ind. Cir.] ISSN: 0306-2848. Indonesia Circle*: School of Oriental and African Studies, Thornhaugh Street, Russell Square, London WC1H 0XG, U.K.

Industrial and labor relations review. *[Ind. Lab. Rel.] ISSN: 0019-7939. Cornell University, New York State School of Industrial and Labor Relations*: 207 ILR Research Building, Cornell University, Ithaca, New York 14851-0952, U.S.A.

INTERNATIONAL BIBLIOGRAPHY OF SOCIOLOGY — 1988

Industrial archaeology review. *[Ind. Arch. Rev.]* ISSN: 0309- 0728. *Association for Industrial Archaeology*: The Wharfage, Ironbridge, Telford, Shropshire TF8 7AW, U.K.

Industrial crisis quarterly. *[Ind. Crisis Q.]* ISSN: 0921-8106. *Industrial Crisis Institute*: New York, U.S.A.; **Publisher**: *Elsevier Science Publishers (North-Holland)*: P.O. Box 1991, 1000 BZ Amsterdam, The Netherlands; **Subscriptions**: *idem*: Journal Department, Postbus 211, 1000 AE Amsterdam, The Netherlands

Industrial law journal. *[Ind. Law J.]* ISSN: 0395-9332. *Industrial Law Society*: 28 Boundary Road, Sidcup, Kent DA15 8ST, U.K.; **Publisher**: *Oxford University Press*: Pinkhill House, Southfield Road, Eynsham, Oxford OX8 1JJ, U.K.

Industrial relations. *[Ind. Relat.]* ISSN: 0019- 8676. *University of California, Berkeley, Institute of Industrial Relations*: Berkeley CA. 94720, U.S.A.; **Publisher**: *Basil Blackwell*: 108 Cowley Road, Oxford OX4 1JF, U.K.

Industrial relations journal. *[Ind. Relat. J.]* ISSN: 0019-8692. *Basil Blackwell*: 108 Cowley Road, Oxford OX4 1JF, U.K.

Industrial relations journal of South Africa. *[Ind. Rel. J. S.Afr.]* ISSN: 0258-7181. *University of Stellenbosch Business School*: P.O. Box 610, Bellville 7535, South Africa

Information sociales. *[Inf. Soc.]* ISSN: 0046-9459. *Caisse Nationale des Allocations Familiales*: 23 rue Daviel, 75634 Paris Cedex 13, France

Informationen zur Raumentwicklung. *[Inf. Raum.]* ISSN: 0303-2493. *Bundesforschungsanstalt für Landeskunde und Raumordnung*: Am Michaelshof 8, Postfach 20 01 30, 5300 Bonn 2, Germany

Inquiry. *[Inquiry]* ISSN: 0020-174X. *Universitetsforlaget (Norwegian University Press)*: P.O. Box 2959 Tøyen, N-0608 Oslo 6, Norway

Institut d'histoire du temps present bulletin. *[Inst. Hist. T. Pres.]* ISSN: 0247-0101. *Institut d'Histoire du Temps Present*: 44 rue de l'Amiral Mouchez, 75014 Paris, France

Interfaces. *[Interfaces]* ISSN: 0092-2102. *Institute of Management Sciences and the Operations Research Society of America*: 290 Westminster Street, Providence, RI. 02903, U.S.A.

International and comparative law quarterly. *[Int. Comp. L.]* ISSN: 0020-5893. *British Institute of International and Comparative Law*: 17 Russell Square, London WC1B 5DR, U.K.

International economic review. *[Int. Econ. R.]* ISSN: 0020-6598. *University of Pennsylvania, Department of Economics/Osaka University, Institute of Social and Economic Research Association*: 3718 Locust Walk, University of Pennsylvania, Philadelphia, PA. 19104-6297, U.S.A./ 6-1 Mihagaoka, Ibaraki, Osaka 567, Japan

International journal. *[Int. J.]* ISSN: 0020-7020. *Canadian Institute of International Affairs*: 15 Kings College Circle, Toronto, Ontario, Canada M5S 2V9

International journal of American linguistics. *[Int. J. Am. Ling.]* ISSN: 0020-7071. *University of Chicago Press*: 5720 S Woodlawn Avenue, Chicago, IL. 60637, U.S.A.

International journal of comparative sociology. *[Int. J. Comp. Soc]* ISSN: 0020-7152. *E.J. Brill*: P.O. Box 9000, 2300 PA Leiden, The Netherlands

International journal of conflict management. *[Int. J. Confl. Manag.]* ISSN: 1044-4068. *3-R Executive Systems*: 3109 Copperfield Court, Bowling Green, KY. 42104, U.S.A.

International journal of health services. *[Int. J. Health. Ser.]* ISSN: 0020-7314. *Baywood Publishing*: 26 Austin Avenue, P.O. Box 337, Amityville, NY. 11701, U.S.A.

International journal of human resource management. *[Int. J. Hum. Res. Man.]* ISSN: 0958-5192. *Routledge*: 11 New Fetter Lane, London EC4P 4EE, U.K.; **Subscriptions**: *idem*: Subscriptions Department, Cheriton House, North Way, Andover, Hants SP10 5BE, U.K.

International journal of industrial organization. *[Int. J. Ind. O.]* ISSN: 0167-7187. *Elsevier Science Publishers (North-Holland)*: P.O. Box 1991, 1000 BZ Amsterdam, The Netherlands; **Subscriptions**: *idem*: Journal Department, P.O. Box 211, 1000 AE Amsterdam, The Netherlands

International journal of law and the family. *[Int. J. Law Fam.] ISSN: 0950- 4109. Oxford University Press*: Pinkhill House, Southfield Road, Eynsham, Oxford OX8 1JJ, U.K.

International journal of moral and social studies. *[Int. J. Moral Soc. S.] ISSN: 0267-9655. Journals*: 1 Harewood Row, London NW1 6SE, U.K.

International journal of offender therapy and comparative criminology. *[Int. J. Offen.] ISSN: 0306-624X. Guilford Press*: 72 Spring Street, New York, NY. 10012, U.S.A.

International journal of politics, culture and society. *[Int. J. Pol. C. S.] ISSN: 0891-4486. Human Sciences Press*: 233 Spring Street, New York, NY. 10013-1578, U.S.A.

International journal of psycho-analysis. *[Int. J.Psy.] ISSN: 0020-7578. Institute of Psychoanalysis*: 63 New Cavendish Street, London W1M 7RD, U.K.; **Publisher**: *Routledge*: 11 New Fetter Lane, London, EC4P 4EE, U.K.; **Subscriptions**: *Routledge*: Cheriton House, North Way, Andover, Hants SP10 5BE, U.K.

International journal of social economics. *[Int. J. Soc. E.] ISSN: 0306-8293. MCB University Press*: 62 Toller Lane, Bradford, West Yorkshire, BD8 9BY, U.K.

International journal of social psychiatry. *[Int. J. Soc. Psyc.] ISSN: 0020-7640. Avenue Publishing*: 55 Woodstock Avenue, London NW11 9RG, U.K.

International journal of the sociology of language. *[Int. J. S. Lang.] ISSN: 0165-2516. Mouton de Gruyter*: Postfach 110240, D-1000 Berlin 11, Germany

International journal of the sociology of law. *[Int. J. S. Law] ISSN: 0194-6595. Academic Press*: 24-28 Oval Road, London NW1 7DX, U.K.

International journal of therapeutic communities. *[Inter. J. Therap. Comm.] ISSN: 0196-1365. Association of Therapeutic Communities*: 14 Charterhouse Square, London, EC1M 6AX, U.K.; **Subscriptions**: *idem:* P.O. Box 109, Dorking Surrey, RH5 4FA, U.K.

International journal of urban and regional research. *[Int. J. Urban] ISSN: 0309-1317. Edward Arnold*: Mill Road, Dunton Green, Sevenoaks, Kent TN13 2YA, U.K.; **Subscriptions**: *Edward Arnold*: Subscriptions Department, 42 Bedford Square, London WC1B 3SL, U.K.

International labour review. *[Int. Lab. Rev.] ISSN: 0020-7780. International Labour Office (ILO)*: CH-1211 Geneva 22, Switzerland

International migration; Migrations internationales; Migraciones internacionales. *[Int. Migr.] ISSN: 0020- 7985. International Organization for Migration*: P.O. Box 71, 1211 Geneva 19, Switzerland

International migration review. *[Int. Migr. Rev.] ISSN: 0197- 9183. Center for Migration Studies*: 209 Flagg Place, Staten Island, NY. 10304-1199, U.S.A.

International minds. *[Inter. Minds] ISSN: 0957-1299. International Minds*: 19 Hugh Street, London SW1V 1QJ, U.K.

International organization. *[Int. Organ.] ISSN: 0020-8183. World Peace Foundation*; **Publisher**: *MIT Press*: 55 Hayward Street, Cambridge, MA. 02142, U.S.A.

International public relations review. *[Int. Pub. Relat. R.] ISSN: 0269-0357. International Public Relations Association*: Case postale 126, CH-1211 Geneva 20, Switzerland; **Publisher**: *Whiting and Birch*: 90 Dartmouth Road, Forest Hill, London SE23 3HZ, U.K.

International regional science review. *[Int. Reg. Sci. R.] ISSN: 0160-0176. Regional Research Institute*: West Virginia University, Morgantown, WV. 26506, U.S.A.

International review of administrative sciences. *[Int. Rev. Admin. Sci.] ISSN: 0020-8523. International Institute of Administrative Sciences, European Group of Public Administration*: rue Defacqz 1, Box 11, B-1050 Brussels, Belgium; **Publisher**: *Sage Publications*: 6 Bonhill Street, London EC2A 4PU, U.K.

INTERNATIONAL BIBLIOGRAPHY OF SOCIOLOGY — 1988

International review of applied economics. *[Int. R. Applied Ec.]* ISSN: 0269-2171. *Edward Arnold*: Mill Road, Dunton Green, Sevenoaks, Kent TN13 2YA, U.K.; **Subscriptions**: *Edward Arnold, Subscription Department*: 42 Bedford Square, WC1I 3SL, U.K.

International review of mission. *[Inter. R. Miss.]* ISSN: 0020-8582. *World Council of Churches, Commission on World Mission and Evangelism*: 150 route de Ferney, 1211 Geneva 2, Switzerland

International review of psycho-analysis. *[Int. Rev. Psy.]* ISSN: 0306-2643. *Institute of Psychoanalysis*: 63 New Cavendish Street, London W1M 7RD, U.K.; **Publisher**: *Routledge*: 11 New Fetter Lane, London, EC4P 4EE, U.K.; **Subscriptions**: *idem:* Cheriton House, North Way, Andover, Hants SP10 5BE, U.K.

International review of retail, distribution and consumer research. *[Int. R. Ret. Dist. Res.]* ISSN: 0959-3969. *Routledge*: 11 New Fetter Lane, London EC4P 4EE, U.K.

International review of social history. *[Int. Rev. S. H.]* ISSN: 0020- 8590. *International Institute for Social History*: Cruquiusweg 31, 1019 AT Amsterdam, The Netherlands; **Publisher**: *Van Gorcum*: POB 43, 9400 AA Assen, The Netherlands

International social science journal. *[Int. Soc. Sci. J.]* ISSN: 0020-8701. *Basil Blackwell/ UNESCO*: 108 Cowley Road, Oxford OX4 1JF, U.K./ UNESCO Periodicals Division, 7 place de Fontenoy, 75700 Paris, France

International socialism. *[Int. Soc.]* ISSN: 0020-8736. *Socialist Workers Party*: PO Box 82, London E3, U.K.; **Subscriptions**: *Bookmarks*: 265 Seven Sisters Road, London N4 2DE, U.K.

International sociology. *[Int. Sociol.]* ISSN: 0268-5809. *International Sociological Association*: Consejo Superior de Investigaciones Cientificas. Pinar 25, 28006 Madrid, Spain; **Publisher**: *Sage Publications*: 6 Bonhill Street, London EC2A 4PU, U.K.

International studies in the philosophy of science. *[Inter. Phil. Sci.]* ISSN: 0269-8595. *Carfax Publishing*: P.O. Box 25, Abingdon, Oxfordshire, OX14 3UE, U.K.

International studies quarterly. *[Int. Stud. Q.]* ISSN: 0020-8833. *International Studies Association*: University of South Carolina, Columbia SC. 29208, U.S.A.; **Publisher**: *Butterworth-Heinemann*: 80 Montvale Avenue, Stoneham, MA. 02180, U.S.A.

IRAL. *[IRAL]* ISSN: 0019-042X. *Julius Groos Verlag*: P.O. Box 102423, Hertzstraße 6, D-6900 Heidelberg 1, Germany

Irish geography. *[Irish Geogr.]* ISSN: 0075-0778. *Geographical Society of Ireland*: University College Dublin, Department of Geography, Belfield, Dublin 4, Ireland

Islam et sociétés au sud du Sahara. *[Islam Soc. S.Sah.]* ISSN: 0984-7685. *Editions de la Maison des Sciences de l'Homme*: Secrétariat scientifique, 54 boulevard Raspail, 75270 Paris Cedex 06, France; **Subscriptions**: *C.I.D.*: 131 boulevard Saint- Michel, 75005 Paris, France

Islamic quarterly. *[Islam. Q.]* ISSN: 0021-1842. *Islamic Cultural Centre*: 146 Park Road, London NW8 7RG, U.K.

Israel law review. *[Isr. Law R.]* ISSN: 0021-2237. *Israel Law Review Association*: c/o Faculty of Law, Hebrew University, Mt. Scopus, P.O.B. 24100, Jerusalem 91240, Israel

Israel yearbook on human rights. *[Isr. Y.book. Hum. Rig.]* ISSN: 0333-5925. *Tel Aviv University, Faculty of Law*; **Publisher**: *Martinus Nijhoff Publishers*: Spuiboulevard 50, 3311 GR Dordrecht, The Netherlands; **Subscriptions**: *Kluwer Academic Publishers*: P.O. Box 322, 3300 AH Dordrecht, The Netherlands

Issue. *[Issue]* ISSN: 0047-1607. *African Studies Association*: Credit Union Building, Emory University, GA. 30322, U.S.A.

Issues in reproductive and genetic engineering. *[Iss. Repro. Gen. Engin.]* ISSN: 0958- 6415. *Pergamon Press*: Fairview Park, Elmsford, NY. 10523, U.S.A.

INTERNATIONAL BIBLIOGRAPHY OF SOCIOLOGY — 1988

Jahrbuch.:*Asien - Afrika - Lateinamerika* [*Jahr. As. Afr. Lat.am.*]; *VEB Deutscher Verlag der Wissenschaften*: Postfach 1216, 1080 Berlin, Germany

Jahrbuch für christliche Sozialwissenschaften. [*Jahr. Christ. Sozialwiss.*] *ISSN: 0075-2584. Universität Münster, Institut für Christliche Sozialwissenschaften*; **Publisher**: *Verlag Regensberg*: Daimlerweg 58, Postfach 6748-6749, 4400 Münster, Germany

Jahrbuch für Geschichte von Staat, Wirtschaft und Gesellschaft Lateinamerikas. [*Jahrb. Ges. St. Wirt. Ges. Lat.am.*] *ISSN: 0075-2673. Böhlaù Verlag*: Niehler Straße 272-274, 5000 Cologne 60, Germany

Jahrbuch für Ostrecht. [*Jahrb. Ost.*] *ISSN: 0075-2746. Institut für Ostrecht München*: Kessenicher Straße 116, Postfach 120380, 5300 Bonn 1, Germany; **Publisher**: *Deutscher Bundes-Verlag*: 8000 München 2, Theresienstraße 40, Germany

Jahrbuch für Wirtschaftsgeschichte. [*Jahrb. Wirt. Gesch.*] *ISSN: 0075-2800. Akademie-Verlag Berlin*: Postfach 1233, Leipziger Straße 3-4 1086 Berlin, Germany

Jahrbücher für Geschichte Osteuropas. [*Jahrb. Gesch. O.eur.*] *ISSN: 0021-4019. Osteuropa Institut*: Scheinerstraße 11, D-8000 Munich 80, Germany; **Publisher**: *Franz Steiner Verlag*: Birkenwaldstraße 44, Postfach 10 15 26, D-7000 Stuttgart, Germany

Jahrbücher für Nationalökonomie und Statistik. [*Jahrb. N. St.*] *ISSN: 0021-4027. Gustav Fischer Verlag*: Wollgrasweg 49, 7000 Stuttgart 70, Germany

Japan Christian quarterly. [*Jpn. Christ. Q.*] *ISSN: 0021-4361. Japan Christian Quarterly*: Kyo Bun Kwan, 4-5-1 Ginza, Chou-ku, Tokyo 104, Japan

Japan digest. [*Jpn. Dig.*] *ISSN: 0960-1473. Japan Library*: Knoll House, 35 The Crescent, Sandgate, Folkestone, Kent CT20 3EE, U.K.

Japan forum. [*Jpn. Forum*] *ISSN: 0955-5803. British Association for Japanese Studies*; **Publisher**: *Oxford University Press*: Pinkhill House, Southfield Road, Eynsham, Oxford OX8 1JJ, U.K.

Japanese journal of religious studies. [*Jap. J. Relig. St.*] *ISSN: 0304- 1042. Nanzan Institute for Religion and Culture*: 18 Yamazato-chō, Shōwa-ku, Nagoya 466, Japan

Jewish journal of sociology. [*Jew. J. Socio.*] *ISSN: 0021-6534. Maurice Freedman Research Trust*: 187 Gloucester Place, London NW1 6BU, U.K.

Jewish quarterly review. [*Jew. Q. Rev.*] *ISSN: 0021-6682. Annenberg Research Institute*: 420 Walnut Street, Philadelphia, PA. 19106, U.S.A.

Jewish social studies. [*Jew. Soc. Stud.*] *ISSN: 0021-6704. Conference on Jewish Social Studies*: 2112 Broadway, New York, NY. 10023, U.S.A.

Journal de la Société de Statistique de Paris. [*J. Soc. Stat. Paris*] *ISSN: 0037- 914X. Société de Statistique de France*: B-212, INSEE, 12 rue Boulitte, 75675 Paris Cedex 14, France; **Subscriptions**: *UAP International*: 9 Place Vendôme, 75001 Paris, France

Journal for the scientific study of religion. [*J. Sci. S. Relig.*] *ISSN: 0021- 8294. Society for the Scientific Study of Religion*: Pierce Hall, Room 193, Purdue University, West Lafayette, IN. 47907, U.S.A.

Journal for the study of Judaism in the Persian, Hellenistic and Roman periods. [*J. S. Jud. Per. Hellen. Rom.*] *ISSN: 0047- 2212. E.J. Brill*: P.O. Box 900, 2300 PA Leiden, The Netherlands

Journal for the theory of social behaviour. [*J. Theory Soc. Behav.*] *ISSN: 0021-8308. Basil Blackwell*: 108 Cowley Road, Oxford OX4 1JF, U.K.

Journal of African law. [*J. Afr. Law*] *ISSN: 0221-8553. University of London, School of Oriental and African Studies*: Thornhaugh Street, Russell Square, London WC1H 0XG, U.K.

Journal of African Marxists. [*J. Afr. Marx.*] *ISSN: 0263-2268. Journal of African Marxists*: 23 Bevenden Street, London N1 6BH, U.K.

Journal of American studies. *[J. Am. Stud.] ISSN: 0021-8758. Cambridge University Press*: The Edinburgh Building, Shaftesbury Road, Cambridge CB2 2RU, U.K.

Journal of analytical psychology. *[J. Analyt. Psychol.] ISSN: 0021-8774. Routledge*: 11 New Fetter Lane, London, EC4P 4EE, U.K.; **Subscriptions**: *Routledge*: Cheriton House, North Way, Andover, Hants SP10 5BE, U.K.

Journal of applied psychology. *[J. Appl. Psychol.] ISSN: 0021-9010. American Psychological Association*: 1400 North Uhle Street, Arlington VA. 22201, U.S.A.

Journal of applied social psychology. *[J. Appl. Soc. Psychol.] ISSN: 0021-9029. V.H. Winston & Son*: 7961 Eastern Avenue, Silver Spring, MD. 20910, U.S.A.

Journal of architectural and planning research. *[J. Arch. Plan. Res.]; Locke Science Publishing*: P.O. Box 146413, Chicago, IL. 60614, U.S.A.

Journal of Asian and African affairs. *[J. Asian Afr. Aff.] ISSN: 1044- 2979. Journal of Asian andd African Affairs*: P.O. Box 23099, Washington, DC. 20026, U.S.A.

Journal of Asian and African studies [Leiden]. *[J. As. Afr. S.] ISSN: 0021 9096. E.J. Brill*: P.O. Box 9000, 2300 PA Leiden, The Netherlands

Journal of Asian studies. *[J. Asian St.] ISSN: 0021-9118. Association for Asian Studies*: 1 Lane Hall, University of Michigan, Ann Arbor, MI. 48109, U.S.A.; **Publisher**: *University of Wisconsin-Milwaukee*: Milwaukee, WI. 53201, U.S.A.

Journal of Australian political economy. *[J. Aust. Pol. Econ.] ISSN: 0156-5826. Australian Political Economy Movement*: P.O. Box 76, Wentworth Building, University of Sydney, NSW 2006, Australia

Journal of Australian studies. *[J. Aust. Stud.]; La Trobe University Press*: La Trobe University, Bundoora, Victoria, 3083 Australia

Journal of biogeography. *[J. Biogeogr.] ISSN: 0305-0270. Blackwell Scientific Publications*: Osney Mead, Oxford OX2, U.K.; **Subscriptions**: *idem*: P.O. Box 88, Oxford OX2 0EL, U.K.

Journal of biosocial science. *[J. Biosoc. Sc.] ISSN: 0021-9320. Biosocial Society*: Journal of Biosocial Science, Department of Biological Anthropology, Downing Street, Cambridge CB2 3DZ, U.K.; **Subscriptions**: *Portland Press*: Journal of Biosocial Science, P.O. Box 32, Commerce Way, Colchester CO2 8HP, U.K.

Journal of business & economic statistics. *[J. Bus. Econ. Stat.] ISSN: 0735-0015. American Statistical Association*: 1429 Duke Street, Alexandria, VA. 22314, U.S.A.

Journal of business and society. *[J. Bus. Soc.] ISSN: 1012-2591. Cyprus College*: P.O. Box 2006, Corner Stasinos and Diogenes Streets, Nicosia, Cyprus

Journal of Canadian studies; Revue d'études canadiennes. *[J. Can. Stud.] ISSN: 0021-9495. Trent University*: Box 4800, Peterborough, Ontario, Canada K9J 7B8

Journal of Caribbean studies. *[J. Car. Stud.] ISSN: 0190-2008. Association of Caribbean Studies*: P.O. Box 22202, Lexington, KY. 40522, U.S.A.

Journal of common market studies. *[J. Com. Mkt. S.] ISSN: 0021-9886. University Association for Contemporary European Studies*; **Publisher**: *Basil Blackwell*: 108 Cowley Road, Oxford, OX4 1JF, U.K.

Journal of communication. *[J. Comm.] ISSN: 0021-9916. Oxford University Press*: 200 Madison Avenue, New York 10016, U.S.A.

Journal of communist studies. *[J. Commun. S.] ISSN: 0268-4535. Frank Cass*: Gainsborough House, 11 Gainsborough Road, London W11 1RS, U.K.

Journal of community and applied social psychology. *[J. Comm. App. Soc. Psychol.] ISSN: 1052-9284. John Wiley & Sons*: Baffins Lane, Chichester, West Sussex PO19 1UD, U.K.

INTERNATIONAL BIBLIOGRAPHY OF SOCIOLOGY — 1988

Journal of comparative family studies. *[J. Comp. Fam. Stud.]* ISSN: 0047-2328. *University of Calgary, Department of Sociology*: 2500 University Drive, N.W., Calgary, Alberta T2N 1N4, Canada

Journal of conflict resolution. *[Confl. Resolut.]* ISSN: 0022-0027. *Peace Science Society (International)*; **Publisher**: *Sage Publications*: 2455 Teller Road, Newbury Park, CA. 91320, U.S.A.

Journal of contemporary African studies. *[J. Contemp. Afr. St.]* ISSN: 0258-9001. *Africa Institute of South Africa*: P.O. Box 630, Pretoria 0001, South Africa

Journal of contemporary Asia. *[J. Cont. Asia]* ISSN: 0047-2336. *Journal of Contemporary Asia Publishers*: P.O. Box 592, Manila, 1099 Philippines

Journal of criminal law. *[J. Crim. Law]* ISSN: 0022- 0183. *Pageant Publishing*: 5 Turners Wood, London NW11 6TD, U.K.; **Subscriptions**: *Bailey Management Services*: Warner House, Bowles Well Gardens, Folkestone, Kent CT19 6PH, U.K.

Journal of criminal law and criminology. *[J. Crim. Law]* ISSN: 0091-4169. *Northwestern University School of Law*: 357 East Chicago Avenue, Chicago, IL. 60611, U.S.A.

Journal of developing areas. *[J. Dev. Areas]* ISSN: 0022-037X. *Western Illinois University*: 900 West Adams Street, Macomb, IL. 61455, U.S.A.

Journal of developing societies. *[J. Dev. Soc.]* ISSN: 0169-796X. *E.J. Brill*: P.O.B. 9000, 2300 PA Leiden, The Netherlands

Journal of development studies. *[J. Dev. Stud.]* ISSN: 0022-0388. *Frank Cass*: Gainsborough House, 11 Gainsborough Road, London E11 1RS, U.K.

Journal of Eastern African research & development. *[J. E.Afr. Res. Devel.]* ISSN: 0251-0405. *Gideon S. Were*: P.O. Box 10622, Nairobi, Kenya

Journal of economic and social measurement. *[J. Econ. Soc.]* ISSN: 0747-9662. *International Organisations Services*: Van Diemenstraat 94, 1013 CN Amsterdam, The Netherlands

Journal of economic history. *[J. Econ. Hist.]* ISSN: 0022-0507. *Economic History Association/ University of Kansas*: Department of History, George Washington University, Washington DC. 20052, U.S.A./ 211 Watkins Home, Hall Center for the Humanities, Lawrence, KS. 66045, U.S.A.; **Publisher**: *Cambridge University Press*: 40 West 20th Street, New York, N.Y. 10011, U.S.A.

Journal of economic issues. *[J. Econ. Iss.]* ISSN: 0021-3624. *Association for Evolutionary Economics*: Department of Economics, University of Nebraska-Lincoln, Lincoln, NE. 68588, U.S.A.

Journal of economic literature. *[J. Econ. Lit.]* ISSN: 0022-8515. *American Economic Association*: 2014 Broadway, Suite 305, Nashville, TN. 37203, U.S.A.

Journal of economic psychology. *[J. Econ. Psyc.]* ISSN: 0167-4870. *International Association for Research in Economic Psychology*: Egmontstraat 13, 1050 Brussels, Belgium; **Publisher**: *Elsevier Science Publishers (North-Holland)*: P.O. Box 1991, 1000 BZ Amsterdam, The Netherlands; **Subscriptions**: *idem:* Journals Division, P.O. Box 211, 1000 AE Amsterdam, The Netherlands

Journal of environmental management. *[J. Environ. Manag.]* ISSN: 0301-4797. *Academic Press*: 24-28 Oval Road, London NW1 7DX, U.K.; **Subscriptions**: *idem:* Foots Cray, Sidcup, Kent, DA14 5HP, U.K.

Journal of experimental child psychology. *[J. Exper. Child Psychol.]* ISSN: 0022-0965. *Academic Press*: 1 East First Street, Duluth, MN. 55802, U.S.A.

Journal of experimental social psychology. *[J. Exp. S. Psychol.]* ISSN: 0022-1031. *Academic Press*: 1 East First Street, Duluth, MN. 55802, U.S.A.

INTERNATIONAL BIBLIOGRAPHY OF SOCIOLOGY — 1988

Journal of family history. [*J. Fam. Hist.*] *ISSN: 0363-1990. National Council on Family Relations*; **Publisher**: *JAI Press*: 55 Old Post Road, No. 2, P.O. Box 1678, Greenwich, CT. 06836-1678, U.S.A.

Journal of family law. [*J. Fam. Law*] *ISSN: 0022- 1066. University of Louisville, School of Law*: 2301 South Third Street, Louisville, KY. 40292, U.S.A.

Journal of family therapy. [*J. Fam. Ther.*] *ISSN: 0163-4445. Association for Family Therapy*: 6 Ileol, Seddon, Danescourt, Llandaff, Cardiff CF5 2QX, U.K.; **Publisher**: *Basil Blackwell*: 108 Cowley Road, Oxford OX4 1JF, U.K.; **Subscriptions**: *Marston Book Services*: P.O. Box 87, Oxford OX2 0DT, U.K.

Journal of family violence. [*J. Fam. Viol.*] *ISSN: 0885-7482. Plenum Publishing Corporation*: 233 Spring Street, New York, NY. 10013, U.S.A.

Journal of forensic psychiatry. [*J. For. Psy.*] *ISSN: 0958-5184. Routledge*: 11 New Fetter Lane, London, EC4P 4EE, U.K.; **Subscriptions**: *Routledge*: Cheriton House, North Way, Andover, Hants SP10 5BE, U.K.

Journal of health economics. [*J. Health Econ.*] *ISSN: 0167-6296. Elsevier Science Publishers (North-Holland)*: P.O. Box 1991, 1000 BZ Amsterdam, The Netherlands; **Subscriptions**: *idem*: P.O. Box 211, 1000 AE Amsterdam, The Netherlands

Journal of historical sociology. [*J. Hist. Soc.*] *ISSN: 0952-1909. Basil Blackwell*: 108 Cowley Road, Oxford OX4 1JF, U.K.

Journal of housing research. [*J. Hous. Res.*] *ISSN: 1052-7001. Office of Housing Policy, Fannie Mae*: 3900 Wisconsin Avenue, N.W., Washington, DC. 20016-2899, U.S.A.

Journal of human resources. [*J. Hum. Res.*] *ISSN: 0022-166X. University of Wisconsin Press*: 4315 Social Science Building, University of Wisconsin, 1180 Observatory Drive, Madison, WI. 53706, U.S.A.; **Subscriptions**: *University of Wisconsin Press*: 114 North Murray Street, Madison, WI. 53715, U.S.A.

Journal of Indian philosophy. [*J. Ind. Phil.*] *ISSN: 0022-1791. Kluwer Academic Publishers*: Spuiboulevard 50, P.O. Box 17, 3300 AA Dordrecht, The Netherlands; **Subscriptions**: *idem*: P.O. Box 322, 3300 AH Dordrecht, The Netherlands

Journal of industrial relations. [*J. Ind. Relat.*] *ISSN: 0022-1856. Journal of Industrial Relations*: GPO Box 4479, Sydney, NSW 2001, Australia

Journal of interdisciplinary economics. [*J. Interd. Ec.*] *ISSN: 0260-1079. A.B. Academic Publishers*: P.O. Box 42, Bicester, Oxon OX6 7NW, U.K.

Journal of interdisciplinary history. [*J. Interd. Hist.*] *ISSN: 0022-1953. Tufts University/Lafayette College*: 26 Winthrop Street, Medford, MA. 02155, U.S.A.; **Publisher**: *MIT Press*: 55 Hayward Street, Cambridge, MA. 02142, U.S.A.

Journal of Jewish studies. [*J. Jew. Stud.*] *ISSN: 0022-2097. Oxford Centre for Postgraduate Hebrew Studies*: 45 St. Giles, Oxford OX1 2LP, U.K.

Journal of labor economics. [*J. Labor Ec.*] *ISSN: 0734-306X. Economics Research Center/NORC*; **Publisher**: *University of Chicago Press*: Journals Division, P.O. Box 37005, Chicago, IL 60637, U.S.A.

Journal of labor research. [*J. Labor Res.*] *ISSN: 0195-3613. George Mason University, Department of Economics*: Fairfax VA. 22030, U.S.A.

Journal of language and social psychology. [*J. Lang. Soc. Psychol.*] *ISSN: 0261-927X. Multilingual Matters*: Bank House, 8a Hill Road, Clevedon, Avon BS21 7HH, U.K.

Journal of Latin American studies. [*J. Lat. Am. St.*] *ISSN: 0022- 216X. Cambridge University Press*: The Edinburgh Building, Shaftesbury Road, Cambridge CB2 2RU, U.K.

INTERNATIONAL BIBLIOGRAPHY OF SOCIOLOGY — 1988

Journal of law and society. *[J. Law Soc.] ISSN: 0263-323X. Basil Blackwell*: 108 Cowley Road, Oxford OX4 1JF, U.K.

Journal of law, economics, & organization. *[J. Law Ec. Organ.] ISSN: 8756-6222. Oxford University Press*: 2001 Evans Road, Cary, NC. 27513, U.S.A.

Journal of legal studies. *[J. Leg. Stud.] ISSN: 0047-2530. University of Chicago Press*: 5720 S. Woodlawn Avenue, Chicago, IL. 60637, U.S.A.

Journal of leisure research. *[J. Leis. Res.] ISSN: 0022-2216. National Recreation and Park Association*: 3101 Park Center Drive, Alexandria VA. 22302, U.S.A.

Journal of libertarian studies. *[J. Libert. Stud.] ISSN: 0363-2873. Center for Libertarian Studies*: P.O. Box 4091, Burlingame, CA. 94011, U.S.A.

Journal of linguistics. *[J. Linguist.] ISSN: 0022-2267. Linguistics Association of Great Britain*: c/o Department of Linguistics, University College of North Wales, Bangor, Gwynedd LL57 2DG, U.K.; **Publisher**: *Cambridge University Press*: The Edinburgh Building, Shaftesbury Road, Cambridge CB2 2RU, U.K.

Journal of management studies. *[J. Manag. Stu.] ISSN: 0022-2380. Basil Blackwell*: 108 Cowley Road, Oxford OX4 1JF, U.K.; **Subscriptions**: *Marston Book Services*: P.O. Box 87, Oxford OX2 0DT, U.K.

Journal of marriage and the family. *[J. Marriage Fam.] ISSN: 0022-2445. National Council on Family Relations*: 3989 Central Avenue Northeast, Suite 550, Minneapolis, MN. 55421, U.S.A.

Journal of mathematical sociology. *[J. Math. Sociol.] ISSN: 0022-250X. Gordon & Breach Science Publishers*: P.O. Box 786, Cooper Station, New York, NY. 10276, U.S.A.

Journal of Mauritian studies. *[J. Maur. Stud.]; Mahatma Gandhi Institute*: Moka, Mauritius

Journal of modern African studies. *[J. Mod. Afr. S.] ISSN: 0022-278X. Cambridge University Press*: The Edinburgh Building, Shaftesbury Road, Cambridge CB2 2RU, U.K.

Journal of modern history. *[J. Mod. Hist.] ISSN: 0022-2801. American Historical Association, Modern European History Section*; **Publisher**: *University of Chicago Press*: 5720 S. Woodlawn, Chicago, IL. 60637, U.S.A.

Journal of modern Korean studies. *[J. Mod. Kor. S.]; Mary Washington College*: Monroe Hall, 209E, Fredericksburg, VI. 22401, U.S.A.

Journal of multilingual and multicultural development. *[J. Multiling.] ISSN: 0143- 4632. Multilingual Matters*: Bank House, 8a Hill Road, Clevedon, Avon BS21 7HH, U.K.

Journal of occupational psychology. *[J. Occup. Psychol.] ISSN: 0305-8107. British Psychological Society*: St. Andrews House, 48 Princess Road East, Leicester LE1 7DR, U.K.

Journal of Pacific studies. *[J. Pac. Stud.] ISSN: 1011-3029. University of the South Pacific, School of Social and Economic Development*: Editorial Secretariat, P.O. Box 1168, Suva, Fiji

Journal of Palestine studies. *[J. Pal. Stud.] ISSN: 0377-919X. Institute for Palestine Studies*: 3501 M Street, N.W. Washington, DC. 20007, U.S.A.; **Publisher**: *University of California Press*: 2120 Berkeley Way, Berkeley, CA. 94720, U.S.A.

Journal of peasant studies. *[J. Peasant Stud.] ISSN: 0306-6150. Frank Cass*: Gainsborough House, 11 Gainsborough Road, London E11 1RS, U.K.

Journal of personality. *[J. Personal.] ISSN: 0022-3506. Duke University Press*: Box 6697, College Station, Durham, NC. 27708, U.S.A.

Journal of personality and social psychology. *[J. Pers. Soc. Psychol.] ISSN: 0022-3514. American Psychological Association*: 1400 North Uhle Street, Arlington, VA. 22201, U.S.A.

Journal of philosophy. *[J. Phil.] ISSN: 0022-362X. Journal of Philosophy*: 709 Philosophy Hall, Columbia University, New York, NY. 10027, U.S.A.

INTERNATIONAL BIBLIOGRAPHY OF SOCIOLOGY — 1988

Journal of phonetics. *[J. Phon.] ISSN: 0095- 4470. Academic Press*: 24-28 Oval Road, London NW1 7DX, U.K.

Journal of pidgin and creole languages. *[J. Pid. Creo. Lang.] ISSN: 0920-9034. John Benjamins Publishing*: Amsteldijk 44, P.O. Box 52519, 1007 HA Amsterdam, The Netherlands

Journal of planning literature. *[J. Plan. Lit.] ISSN: 0885-4122. Ohio State University Press*: 1070 Carmack Road, Columbus, OH. 43210-1002, U.S.A.

Journal of policy analysis and management. *[J. Policy An.] ISSN: 0276-8739. Association for Public Policy Analysis and Management*; **Publisher**: *John Wiley and Sons*: 605 Third Avenue, New York, NY. 10155, U.S.A.

Journal of political economy. *[J. Polit. Ec.] ISSN: 0022-3808. University of Chicago Press*: 5720 S. Woodlawn Avenue, Chicago, IL. 60637, U.S.A.

Journal of popular culture. *[J. Pop. Cult.] ISSN: 0022-3840. Modern Language Association of America, Popular Literature Section/ Midwest Modern Language Association, Folklore Section*; **Publisher**: *Popular Press*: Bowling Green State University, Bowling Green OH 43402, U.S.A.

Journal of population economics. *[J. Pop. Ec.] ISSN: 0933-1433. Springer-Verlag*: Heidelberger Platz 3, D-1000 Berlin 33, Germany

Journal of pragmatics. *[J. Prag.] ISSN: 0378-2166. Elsevier Science Publishers (North-Holland)*: P.O. Box 1991, 1000 BZ Amsterdam, The Netherlands

Journal of psychology. *[J. Psychol.] ISSN: 0022-3980. Heldref Publications*: 4000 Albemarle Street, NW, Washington, DC. 20016, U.S.A.

Journal of refugee studies. *[J. Refug. S.] ISSN: 0951-6328. University of Oxford, Refugee Studies Programme*: Queen Elizabeth House, 21 St. Giles, Oxford OX1 3LA, U.K.; **Publisher**: *Oxford University Press*: Pinkhill House, Southfield Road, Eynsham, Oxford OX8 1JJ, U.K.

Journal of regional policy. *[J. Reg. Pol.]; Isveimer*: via S. Giacomo, 19 Naples, Italy

Journal of religion in Africa. *[J. Relig. Afr.] ISSN: 0022-4200. E.J. Brill*: Postbus 9000, 2300 PA Leiden, The Netherlands

Journal of research in crime and delinquency. *[J. Res. Crim. Delin.] ISSN: 0022- 4278. National Council on Crime and Delinquency*: 685 Market Street, Suite 620, San Francisco, CA. 94105, U.S.A.; **Publisher**: *Sage Publications*: 2455 Teller Road, Newbury Park, CA. 91320, U.S.A.

Journal of rural development and administration. *[J. Rural Devel. Admin.] ISSN: 0047-2751. Academy for Rural Development*: Academy Town, Peshawar, Pakistan

Journal of rural studies. *[J. Rural St.] ISSN: 0743-0167. Pergamon Press*: Headington Hill Hall, Oxford OX3 0BW, U.K.

Journal of semantics. *[J. Sem.] ISSN: 0167-5133. IBM Germany Scientific Center*: Postfach 800880, D-7000 Stuttgart 80, Germany; **Publisher**: *Oxford University Press*: Pinkhill House, Southfield Road, Eynsham, OX8 1JJ, Oxford, U.K.

Journal of social and biological structures. *[J. Soc. Biol. Struct.] ISSN: 0140 1750. JAI Press*: 55 Old Post Road No.2, P.O. Box 1678, Greenwich, CT. 06836-1678, U.S.A.

Journal of social and clinical psychology. *[J. Soc. Clin. Psychol.] ISSN: 0736-7236. Guilford Publications*: 72 Spring Street, New York, NY. 10012, U.S.A.

Journal of social development in Africa. *[J. Soc. Devel. Afr.] ISSN: 1012- 1080. School of Social Work*: P/ Bag 66022 Kopje, Harare, Zimbabwe

Journal of social history. *[J. Soc. Hist] ISSN: 0022-4529. Carnegie Mellon University*: Pittsburgh, PA. 15213, U.S.A.

Journal of social issues. *[J. Soc. Issues] ISSN: 0022-4537. Society for the Psychological Study of Social Issues*; **Publisher**: *Plenum Publishing*: 233 Spring Street, NY. 10013, U.S.A.

Journal of social policy. *[J. Soc. Pol.] ISSN: 0047-2794. Social Policy Association*; **Publisher**: *Cambridge University Press*: The Edinburgh Building, Shaftesbury Road, Cambridge CB2 2RU, U.K.

Journal of social psychology. *[J. Soc. Psychol.] ISSN: 0022-4545. Heldref Publications*: 4000 Albemarle St., N.W. Washington DC. 20016, U.S.A.

Journal of social science. *[J. Soc. Sci.]; University of Malawi, Faculty of Social Science*: Chancellor College, P.O. Box 280, Zomba, Malawi

Journal of social sciences and humanities. *[J. Soc. Sci. Human.] ISSN: 0023-4044. Korean Research Center*: 228 Pyong- dong, Chongno-ku, Seoul, Korea

Journal of social studies. *[J. Soc. Stud. Dhaka]; Centre for Social Studies*: Room no. 1107, Arts Building, University of Dhaka, Dhaka 1000, Bangladesh

Journal of social, political and economic studies. *[J. Soc. Pol. E.] ISSN: 0193-5941. Council for Social and Economic Studies*: Suite C-2, 1133 13th St. N.W., Washington, DC. 20005-4297, U.S.A.

Journal of South Asian literature. *[J. S.Asian Lit.]; Asian Studies Center*: Michigan State University, East Lansing, MI. 48824-1035, U.S.A.

Journal of Southeast Asian studies. *[J. SE. As. Stud.] ISSN: 0022-4634. National University of Singapore, Department of History*: 10 Kent Ridge Crescent, Singapore 0511; **Publisher**: *Singapore University Press*: Yusof Ishak House, 10 Kent Ridge Crescent, Singapore 0511

Journal of Southern African studies. *[J. S.Afr. Stud.] ISSN: 0305- 7070. Oxford University Press*: Pinkhill House, Southfield Road, Eynsham, Oxford OX8 1JJ, U.K.

Journal of the American Planning Association. *[J. Am. Plann.] ISSN: 0194-4363. American Planning Association*: 1313 East 60th Street, Chicago, IL 60637-2891, U.S.A.

Journal of the American Statistical Association. *[J. Am. Stat. Ass.] ISSN: 0162-1459. American Statistical Association*: 1429 Duke Street, Alexandria, VA. 22314, U.S.A.

Journal of the Australian Population Association. *[J. Aust. Pop. Ass.] ISSN: 0814-5725. Australian Population Association*: Division of Demography and Sociology, Research School of Social Sciences, The Australian National University, GPO Box 4, Canberra ACT 2601, Australia

Journal of the economic and social history of the orient. *[J. Ec. Soc. Hist. O.] ISSN: 0022-4995. E.J. Brill*: P.O. Box 9000, 2300 PA Leiden, The Netherlands

Journal of the history of ideas. *[J. Hist. Ideas.] ISSN: 0022-5037. Journal of the History of Ideas*: Temple University, Philadelphia, PA. 19122, U.S.A.

Journal of the history of philosophy. *[J. Hist. Philos.] ISSN: 0022-5053. Journal of the History of Philosophy*: Business Office, Department of Philosophy, Washington University, One Brookings Drive, St. Louis, MO. 63130- 4899, U.S.A.

Journal of the history of the behavioral sciences. *[J. Hist. Beh. Sci.] ISSN: 0022-5061. Clinical Psychology Publishing*: 4 Conant Square, Brandon, VT. 05733, U.S.A.

Journal of the International Phonetic Association. *[J. Inter. Phon. Ass.]; International Phonetic Association*: Phonetics Laboratory, Department of Linguistics, UCLA, Los Angeles, CA. 90024-1543, U.S.A.

Journal of the Japanese and international economies. *[J. Jap. Int. Ec.] ISSN: 0889-1583. Tokyo Center for Economic Research*; **Publisher**: *Academic Press*: 1 East First Street, Duluth, MN. 55802, U.S.A.

Journal of the Market Research Society. *[J. Market R.] ISSN: 0025-3618. Market Research Society*: 15 Northburgh Street, London EC1V 0AH, U.K.; **Subscriptions**: *NTC Publications*: P.O. Box 69, Henley-on-Thames, Oxon RG9 2BZ, U.K.

INTERNATIONAL BIBLIOGRAPHY OF SOCIOLOGY — 1988

Journal of the Mysore University.:*Section A-Arts* [*J. Mysore Univ. Arts*]; K.T. Veerappa, M.A.: Prasaranga, Manasagangotri, Mysore-6, India

Journal of the Oriental Institute. [*J. Orient. Inst.*] *ISSN: 0030-5324*. Baroda 390 002, Gujarat, India

Journal of the Royal Statistical Society.:*Series A (statistics in society)* [*J. Roy. Stat. Soc. A.*] *ISSN: 0035-9238*. *Royal Statistical Society*: 25 Enford Street, London W1H 2BH, U.K.

Journal of theoretical politics. [*J. Theor. Pol.*] *ISSN: 0951-6928*. *Sage Publications*: 6 Bonhill Street, London EC2A 4PU, U.K.

Journal of urban economics. [*J. Urban Ec.*] *ISSN: 0094-1190*. *Academic Press*: 1 First East Street, Duluth, MN 55802, U.S.A.

Journal of urban history. [*J. Urban Hist.*] *ISSN: 0096-1442*. *Sage Publications*: 2455 Teller Road, Newbury Park, CA 91320, U.S.A.

Journal of West African languages. [*J. W.Afr. Lang.*] *ISSN: 0022-5401*. *West African Linguistics Society*: Summer Institute of Linguistics, 7500 W.Camp Wisdom Road, Dallas, TX. 75236, U.S.A.

Journal of world history. [*J. World. Hist.*] *ISSN: 1045-6007*. *World History Association*: Department of History and Politics, Drexel University, Philadephia, PA. 19104, U.S.A.; **Publisher**: *University of Hawaii Press*: 2840 Kolowalu Street, Honolulu, HI. 96822, U.S.A.

Journal. Institute of Muslim Minority Affairs. [*J. Inst. Muslim Minor. Aff.*] *ISSN: 0266-6952*. *Institute of Muslim Minority Affairs*: 46 Goodge Street, London W1P 1FJ, U.K.

Jurnal antropologi dan sosiologi. [*J. Antro. Sosiol.*] *ISSN: 0126-9518*. *Universiti Kebangsaan Malaysia, Department of Anthropology and Sociology*: 43600 UKM Bangi, Selangor D.E., Malaysia

Jurnal Pendidikan. [*J.Pendid.*] *ISSN: 0126-6020*. *Universiti Kebangsaan Malaysia Press*: 43600 UKM Bangi, Selangor Darul Ehsan, Malaysia

Jurnal psikologi malaysia. [*J. Psik. Mal.*] *ISSN: 0127-8029*. *Universiti Kebangsaan Malaysia Press*: 43600 UKM Bangi, Selangor D.E., Malaysia

Kansaneläkelaitoksen julkaisuja. [*Kansan. Julk.*] *ISSN: 0355-4821*. *Kansaneläkelaitoksen*: P.O. Box 78, SF- 00381, Helsinki 38, Finland

Kiswahili. [*Kiswahili*] *ISSN: 0856-048X*. *University of Dar es Salaam, Institute of Kiswahili Research*: P.O. Box 35110, Dar es Salaam, Tanzania

Kölner Zeitschrift für Soziologie und Sozialpsychologie. [*Kölner Z. Soz. Soz. psy.*] *ISSN: 0340-0425*. *Westdeutscher Verlag*: Postfach 5829, D-6200 Wiesbaden 1, Germany

Коммунист; Kommunist. [*Kommunist*] *ISSN: 0131-1212*. *Kommunisticheskaya Partiia Sovetskogo Soiuza. Tsentral'nyi Komitet*; **Publisher**: *Izdatel'stvo Pravda*: Ul. Pravdy 24, 125047, Moscow, U.S.S.R.

Korea journal. [*Korea J.*] *ISSN: 0023-3900*. *Korean National Commission for Unesco*: C.P.O. Box 64, Seoul, 100-022 Korea

Korea observer. [*Korea Obs.*] *ISSN: 0023-3919*. *Institute of Korean Studies*: C.P.O. Box 3410, Seoul 100-643, Korea

Korean social science journal. [*Korean Soc. Sci. J.*]; *Korean Social Science Research Council/ Korean National Commission for UNESCO*: Box Central 64, Seoul, Korea

Kredit und Kapital. [*Kred. Kap.*] *ISSN: 0023-4591*. *Gesellschaft zur Förderung der wissenschaftlichen Forschung über das Spar- und Girowesen*: Sigrid Wehrmeister, Adenauerallee 110, 5300 Bonn 1, Germany; **Publisher**: *Duncker & Humblot*: Postfach 410329, Dietrich-Schäfer-Weg 9, 1000 Berlin 41, Germany

Kwartalnik historii kultury materialnej. *[Kwart. Hist. Kult. Mater.]* ISSN: 0023-5881. *Polska Akademia Nauk, Instytut Historii Kultury Materialnej*; **Publisher**: *Państwowe Wydawnictwo Naukowe*: ul. Swierczewskiego 105, 00-140 Warsaw, Poland

Kyklos. *[Kyklos]* ISSN: 0023- 5962. *Helbing & Lichtenhahn Verlag*: CH-4051 Basel, Switzerland

L.S.E. quarterly. *[L.S.E. Q.]* ISSN: 0269 9710. *London School of Economics and Political Science*: Houghton Street, London WC2A 2AE, U.K.; **Publisher**: *Basil Blackwell*: 108 Cowley Road, Oxford OX4 1JF, U.K.

Labor law journal. *[Lab. Law J.]* ISSN: 0023-6586. *Commerce Clearing House*: 4025 W. Peterson Avenue, Chicago, IL. 60646, U.S.A.

Labour; Travail. *[Labour]* ISSN: 0700-3862. *Committee on Canadian Labour History = Comité de l'histoire du travail du Canada*: Department of History, Memorial University of Newfoundland, St. John's, Newfoundland. A1C 5S7, Canada

Labour, capital and society; Travail, capital et société. *[Labour Cap. Soc.]* ISSN: 0706- 1706. *McGill University, Centre for Developing Area Studies*: 3715 rue Peel, Montréal, Québec H31 1X1, Canada

Language. *[Language]* ISSN: 0097-8507. *Linguistic Society of America*: 428 East Preston Street, Baltimore, MD 21202, U.S.A.

Language in society. *[Lang. Soc.]* ISSN: 0047-4045. *Cambridge University Press*: 40 West 20th Street, New York, NY. 10011, U.S.A.

Language problems and language planning. *[Lang. Prob. Lang. Plan.]* ISSN: 0270- 2690. *John Benjamins Publishing*: P.O. Box 75577, Amstedldijk 44, 1007 AN Amsterdam, The Netherlands

Latin American research review. *[Lat. Am. Res. R.]* ISSN: 0023-8791. *Latin American Studies Association*: Latin American Institute, 801 Yale NE, University of New Mexico, Albuquerque, NM. 87131-1016, U.S.A.

Law and contemporary problems. *[Law Cont. Pr.]* ISSN: 0023-9186. *Duke University, School of Law*: Room 006, Durham, NC 27706, U.S.A.

Law and policy. *[Law Policy]* ISSN: 0265-8240. *Basil Blackwell*: 108 Cowley Road, Oxford OX4 1JF, U.K.; **Subscriptions**: *Marston Book Services*: P.O. Box 87, Oxford OX2 0DT, U.K.

Law and society review. *[Law Soc. Rev.]* ISSN: 0023-9216. *Law and Society Association*: Hampshire House, University of Massachusetts at Amherst, Amherst MA. 01003, U.S.A.

Linguistics. *[Linguistics]* ISSN: 0024-3949. *Mouton de Gruyter*: Postfach 110240, D-1000 Berlin 11, Germany

Linguistics and philosophy. *[Ling. Philos.]* ISSN: 0165-0157. *Kluwer Academic Publishers*: Spuiboulevard 50, P.O. Box 17, 3300 AA Dordrecht, The Netherlands

Links. *[Links]* ISSN: 0024-404X. *Verlag 2000*: Bleichstraße 5/7, Postfach 10 20 62, 6050 Offenbach 1, Germany

Literary and linguistic computing. *[Lit. Ling. Comput.]*; *Association for Literary and Linguistic Computing*; **Publisher**: *Oxford University Press*: Pinkhill House, Southfield Road, Eynsham, Oxford OX8 1JJ, U.K.

Local economy. *[Local. Ec.]* ISSN: 0269-0942. *Local Economy Policy Unit*: Southbank Polytechnic, Borough Road, London SE1 0AA, U.K.; **Publisher**: *Longman Group*: 6th Floor, Westgate House, The High, Harlow, Essex CM20 1YR, U.K.

Local population studies. *[Local. Pop. S.]* ISSN: 0143-2974. *Local Population Studies Society*: Tawney House, Matlock, Derbyshire, DE4 3BT, U.K.; **Subscriptions**: *Subscriptions Secretary*: 27 St. Margarets Road, St. Marychurch, Torquay, Devon, TQ1 4NU, U.K.

Lokayan bulletin. *[Lokay. B.]* ISSN: 0970-5406. *Lokayan Bulletin*: 13 Alipur Road, New Delhi 110 054, India

Maandschrift economie. *[Maan. Econ.] ISSN: 0013-0486. Wolters-Noordhoff*: Postbus 58, 9700 MB Groningen, The Netherlands

Majalah demografi Indonesia; Indonesian journal of demography. *[Maj. Dem. Indonesia] ISSN: 0126-0251. Indonesian Demographers Association*: Demographic Institute, Faculty of Economics, University of Indonesia, Jln. Salemba 4, Jakarta 10430, Indonesia

Malaysian journal of tropical geography. *[Malay. J. Trop. Geogr.] ISSN: 0127-1474. University of Malaya, Department of Geography*: Kuala Lumpur 59100, Malaysia

Management science. *[Manag. Sci.] ISSN: 0025-1909. Institute of Management Sciences*: 290 Westminster Street, Providence, RI. 02903, U.S.A.

Manchester School of economic and social studies. *[Manch. Sch. E.] ISSN: 0025-2034. Basil Blackwell*: 108 Cowley Road, Oxford, OX4 1JF, U.K.

Mankind quarterly. *[Mankind Q.] ISSN: 0025-2344. Cliveden Press*: Suite C-2, 1133 13th Street N.W., Washington, DC. 20005-4298, U.S.A.

Marxistische Blätter. *[Marx. Blät] ISSN: 0542-7770. Neue Impulse Verlag*: Hoffnungstraße 18, 4300 Essen 1, Germany

Mathematical social sciences. *[Math. Soc. Sc.] ISSN: 0165 4896. Elsevier Science Publishers (North-Holland)*: P.O. Box 1991, 1000 BZ Amsterdam, The Netherlands

Media culture and society. *[Media Cult. Soc.] ISSN: 0163-4437. Sage Publications*: 6 Bonhill Street, London EC2A 4PU, U.K.

Medizin Mensch Gesellschaft. *[Medi. Mensch Gesell.] ISSN: 0340-8183. Ferdinand Enke Verlag*: Postfach 10 12 54. D-7000 Stuttgart 10, Germany

Medunarodni problemi. *[Med. Prob.] ISSN: 0025-8555. Institut za Medunarodnu Politiku i Privredu*: Makedonska 25, Belgrade, Yugoslavia

Megamot. *[Megamot] ISSN: 0025-8679. National Institute for Research in the Behavioural Sciences, Henrietta Szold Institute*: 9 Colombia Street, Kiryat Menachem, Jerusalem 96583, Israel

Melbourne historical journal. *[Mel. Hist. J.] ISSN: 0076-6232. University of Melbourne, Department of History*: Parkville, Victoria 3052, Australia

Mens en maatschappij. *[Mens Maat.] ISSN: 0025-9454. Bohn Stafleu Van Loghum*: Postbus 246, 3990 GA Houten, The Netherlands; **Subscriptions**: *Intermedia*: Postbus 4, 2400 MA Alphen aan den Rijn, The Netherlands

Merhavim. *[Merhavim]; Tel Aviv University, Department of Geography*: Tel Aviv, Israel

Michigan law review. *[MI. law. R.] ISSN: 0026-2234. Michigan Law Review*: Hutchins Hall, Ann Arbor, MI. 48109-1215, U.S.A.

Middle East journal. *[Middle E. J.] ISSN: 0026- 3141. Middle East Institute*: 1761 N. Street, N.W., Washington, DC. 20036, U.S.A.; **Publisher**: *Indiana University Press*: 10th and Morton, Bloomington, IN. 47405, U.S.A.

Middle Eastern studies. *[Middle E. Stud.] ISSN: 0026-3206. Frank Cass*: Gainsborough House, 11 Gainsborough Road, London E11 1RS, U.K.

Migracijske teme. *[Migrac. Teme] ISSN: 0352-5600. University of Zagreb, Institute for Migration and Nationalities Studies/ Yugoslav Sociological Association, Section for Migration*: 41001 Zagreb, Trnjanska bb, p.p. 88, Yugoslavia

Milbank quarterly. *[Milbank Q.] ISSN: 0887-378X. Milbank Memorial Fund*; **Publisher**: *Cambridge University Press*: 40 West 20th Street, New York, NY. 10011, U.S.A.

Millennium. *[Millennium] ISSN: 0305-8298. Millenium Publishing Group*: London School of Economics and Political Science, Houghton Street, London WC2A 2AE, U.K.

INTERNATIONAL BIBLIOGRAPHY OF SOCIOLOGY — 1988

Mind. *[Mind] ISSN: 0026-4423. Oxford University Press*: Pinkhill House, Southfield Road, Eynsham, OX8 1JJ, U.K.

Mind and language. *[Mind Lang.] ISSN: 0268 1064. Basil Blackwell*: 108 Cowley Road, Oxford OX4 1JF, U.K.

Minerva. *[Minerva] ISSN: 0026-4695. International Council on the Future of the University*: 11 Dupont Circle, Suite 300, Washington DC. 20036-1257, U.S.A.; **Publisher**: *Minerva*: 19 Nottingham Road, London SW17 7EA, U.K.

Modern Asian studies. *[Mod. Asian S.] ISSN: 0026- 749X. Cambridge University Press*: The Edinburgh Building, Shaftesbury Road, Cambridge CB2 2RU, U.K.

Mondes en développement. *[Mon. Dévelop.] ISSN: 0302-3052. CECOEDUC/I.S.M.E.A.*: Avenue des Naïades 11, B- 1170 Brussels, Belgium/ Rue Pierre et Marie Curie 11, Institut Henri Poincaré, F-75005 Paris, France

Monthly review. *[Mon. Rev.] ISSN: 0027- 0520. Monthly Review Foundation*: 122 West 27th Street, New York, NY. 10001, U.S.A.

Monumenta Nipponica. *[Monu. Nippon.] ISSN: 0027-0741. Sophia University*: 7-1 Kioi-chō, Chiyoda-ku, Tokyo 102, Japan

Mouvement social. *[Mouve. Soc.] ISSN:, 0027-2671. Association «Le Mouvement Social»*: 9 rue Malher, 75004 Paris, France; **Publisher**: *Editions Ouvrières*: 47 rue Servan, 75011 Paris, France

Multilingua. *[Multilingua] ISSN: 0167-8507. Mouton de Gruyter*: Postfach 110240, D-1000 Berlin 30, Germany

Národní hospodářství. *[Nár. Hosp.] ISSN: 0032-0749. Panorama*: Hálkova 1, 12072 Prague, Czechoslovakia

National Museum papers. *[Nat. Mus. Pap.]; National Museum of the Philippines/ Concerned Citizens for the National Museum*: Executive House, P.Burgos Street, 1000 Malate, Metro-Manila, Philippines

Nationalities papers. *[Nat. Pap.] ISSN: 0090-5992. Association for the Study of Nationalities (U.S.S.R. and East Europe)*: Andris Skreija, Department of Sociology, University of Nebraska, Omaha, NE. 68182, U.S.A.

Natural resources forum. *[Nat. Res. For.] ISSN: 0165-0203. United Nations Department of Technical Cooperation for Development*: New York, NY. 10017, U.S.A.; **Publisher**: *Butterworth-Heinemann*: P.O. Box 63, Westbury House, Bury Street, Guildford, Surrey GU2 5BH, U.K.

Natural resources journal. *[Natur. Res. J.] ISSN: 0028-0739. University of New Mexico, School of Law*: Albuquerque, NM. 87131, U.S.A.

Negotiation journal. *[Negot. J.] ISSN: 0748-4526. Plenum Press*: 233 Spring Street, New York, N.Y. 10013, U.S.A.

NEHA-bulletin. *[NEHA-B.] ISSN: 0920-9875. Nederlandsch Economisch-Historisch Archief = Netherlands Economic History Archive*: Cruquiusweg 31, 1019 AT Amsterdam, The Netherlands

Netherlands' journal of social sciences/Sociologia Neerlandica. *[Neth. J. Soc. Sci.] ISSN: 0038-0172. Netherlands' Sociological and Anthropological Society*; **Publisher**: *Van Gorcum*: P.O. Box 43, 4900 AA Assen, The Netherlands

Neue Gesellschaft/ Frankfurter Hefte. *[Neue Ges. Frank.] ISSN: 0177-6738. Friedrich-Ebert-Stiftung*; **Publisher**: *Verlag J.H.W. Dietz Nachf.*: In der Raste 2, 5300 Bonn 1, Germany

Neue politische literatur. *[Neue Pol. Liter.] ISSN: 0028-3320. Verlag Peter Lang*: Eschborner Landstraße 42-50, Postfach 940225, 6000 Frankfurt 90, Germany; **Subscriptions**: *idem*: Jupiterstrasse 15, CH-3000 Bern 15, Switzerland

New community. [*New Comm.*] *ISSN: 0047-9586. Commission for Racial Equality*: London, U.K.; **Publisher**: *University of Warwick, Centre for Research in Ethnic Relations*: Coventry CV4 7AL, U.K.

New formations. [*New Form.*] *ISSN: 0950-2378. Routledge*: 11 New Fetter Lane, London EC4P 4EE, U.K.; **Subscriptions**: *Subscriptions Department, Routledge Journals*: Cheriton House, North Way, Andover, Hants. SP10 5BE, U.K.

New ground. [*New Gro.*]; *Environmental and Development Agency (EDA)*: P.O. Box 322, Newtown, 2113 South Africa

New internationalist. [*N.I.*] *ISSN: 0305-9529. New Internationalist Publications*: 42 Hythe Bridge Street, Oxford OX1 2EP, U.K.; **Subscriptions**: *New Internationalist*: 120-126 Lavender Avenue, Mitcham, Surrey CR4 3HP, U.K.

New left review. [*New Left R.*] *ISSN: 0028- 6060. New Left Review*: 6 Meard Street, London W1V 3HR, U.K.

New perspectives on Turkey. [*New Persp. Turk.*] *ISSN: 0896-6346. Simon's Rock of Bard College*: Great Barrington, MA., U.S.A.

New politics. [*New Polit.*] *ISSN: 0028-6494. New Politics Associates*: P.O. Box 98, Brooklyn, NY. 11231, U.S.A.

New quest. [*New Que.*] *ISSN: 0258-0381. Indian Association for Cultural Freedom*: 850/8A Shivajinagar, Pune 411 004, India

New technology, work and employment. [*New Tech. Work. Empl.*] *ISSN: 0268-1072. Basil Blackwell*: 108 Cowley Road, Oxford OX4 1JF, U.K.

New Vico studies. [*New Vico S.*] *ISSN: 0733-9542. Institute for Vico Studies*: 69 Fifth Avenue, New York, NY. 10003, U.S.A.

New York University journal of international law and politics. [*N.Y.U. J. Int'l. L. & Pol.*] *ISSN: 0028-7873. New York University Law Publications*: 110 West Third Street, New York, NY. 10012, U.S.A.

New York University law review. [*NY. U. Law. Re.*] *ISSN: 0028-7881. New York University Law Review*: 110 W. Third Street, New York, NY. 10012, U.S.A.

New Zealand journal of history. [*N.Z. J. Hist.*] *ISSN: 0028-8322. University of Auckland, History Department*: Private Bag, Auckland, New Zealand

NIAS. [*NIAS*] *ISSN: 0904- 597X. Nordic Institute of Asian Studies*: 84 Njalsgade, DK-2300 Copenhagen S, Denmark

Nieuwe West-Indische gids; New West Indian guide. [*Nie. West-Ind. Gids*] *ISSN: 0028-9930. Stichting Nieuwe West- Indische Gids/ Johns Hopkins University, Program in Atlantic History, Culture and Society*: Utrecht, The Netherlands/ Baltimore, M.D., U.S.A.; **Publisher**: *Foris*: Box 509, 3300 AM Dordrecht, The Netherlands

Nigerian field. [*Niger. F.*] *ISSN: 0029-0076. Nigerian Field Society*; **Subscriptions**: *Mr. P.V. Hartley/ Mrs H. Fell*: PMB 5320, Ibadan, Oyo State, Nigeria/ Limestone House, Alma Road, Tideswell, Buxton, Derbyshire SK17 8ND, U.K.

Nigerian forum. [*Nig. For.*] *ISSN: 0189-0816. Nigerian Institute of International Affairs*: Kofo Aboyomi Road, Victoria Island, G.P.O. Box 1727, Lagos, Nigeria

Nigerian journal of economic and social studies. [*Nig. J. Econ. Soc. Stud.*] *ISSN: 0029-0092. Nigerian Economic Society*: University of Ibadan, Department of Economics, Ibadan, Nigeria

Nonprofit and voluntary sector quarterly. [*Nonprof. Volun. Sec. Q.*] *ISSN: 0899-7640. Association for Research on Nonprofit Organizations and Voluntary Action*: Route 2, Box 696, Pullman, Washington 99163, U.S.A.; **Publisher**: *Jossey-Bass*: 350 Sansome Street, San Francisco, CA. 94104, U.S.A.

Nordic journal of linguistics. *[Nordic J. Linguist.] ISSN: 0332-5865. Nordic Association of Linguists*; **Publisher**: *Universitetsforlaget = Norwegian University Press*: Journals Department, P.O. Box 2959 Tøyen, 0608 Oslo 6, Norway

Notes and records of the Royal Society of London. *[Not. & Rec. Roy. Soc.] ISSN: 0035-9149. Royal Society of London*: 6 Carlton House Terrace, London SW1Y 5AG, U.K.

Nueva sociedad. *[Nueva Soc.]; Nueva Sociedad*: Apartado 61.712, Caracas 1060-A, Venezuela

Numen. *[Numen] ISSN: 0029-5973. International Association for the History of Religions*; **Publisher**: *E.J. Brill*: P.O. Box 9000, 2300 PA Leiden, The Netherlands

Oceania. *[Oceania] ISSN: 0029-8077. Oceania Publications, University of Sydney*: 116 Darlington Road, N.S.W. 2006, Australia

Oceanic linguistics. *[Oceanic Ling.] ISSN: 0029-8115. University of Hawaii Press*: 2840 Kolowalu Street, Honolulu, HI. 96822, U.S.A.

Odu. *[Odu] ISSN: 0029-8522. University of Ife Press*: Periodicals Department, University of Ife, Ile-Ife, Nigeria

Oral history. *[Oral Hist.] ISSN: 0143-0955. Oral History Society*: University of Essex, Department of Sociology, Wivenhoe Park, Colchester, Essex CO4 3SQ, U.K.

Ordo. *[Ordo] ISSN: 0048- 2129. Gustav Fischer Verlag*: Wollgrasweg 49, D-7000 Stuttgart, Germany

Organization studies. *[Organ. Stud.] ISSN: 0170-8406. European Group for Organizational Studies*; **Publisher**: *Walter de Gruyter*: Genthiner Str. 13, D-1000 Berlin 30, Germany

Organizational behavior and human decision processes. *[Organ. Beh. Hum. Dec. Proces.] ISSN: 0749- 5978. Academic Press*: 1 East First Street, Duluth, MN. 55802, U.S.A.

Orient. *[Orient] ISSN: 0030-5227. Deutsches Orient- Institut*: Mittelweg 150, 2000 Hamburg 13, Germany; **Publisher**: *Leske + Budrich*: Postfach 300551, 5090 Leverkusen 3, Germany

Orientalia lovaniensia periodica. *[Orient. Lovan. Period.]; Universitaire Stichting Van België*: Departement Oriëntalistiek, Blijde Inkomststraat 21, B-3000 Leuven, Belgium

Orita. *[Orita] ISSN: 0030-5596. University of Ibadan*: Department of Religious Studies, Ibadan, Nigeria

Österreichische Zeitschrift für öffentliches Recht und Völkerrechte. *[Öster. Z. Öffent. Völk.] ISSN: 0378-3073. Springer-Verlag*: Mölkerbastei 5, P.O. Box 367, A-1011 Vienna, Austria

Österreichische Zeitschrift für Politikwissenschaft. *[Öster. Z. Polit.]; Österreichische Gesellschaft für Politikwissenschaft*; **Publisher**: *Verlag für Gesellschaftskritik*: Kaiserstraße 91, A-1070 Vienna, Austria

Osteuropa. *[Osteuropa] ISSN: 0030-6428. Deutsche Gesellschaft für Osteuropakunde*: Schaperstraße 30, 1000 Berlin 15, Germany; **Publisher**: *Deutsche Verlags-Anstalt*: Neckarstraße 121, Postfach 1060 12, 7000 Stuttgart 10, Germany

Our generation. *[Our Gener.] ISSN: 0030-686X. Our Generation*: Suite 444, 3981 boulevard St-Laurent, Montréal, Québec H2W 1Y5, Canada

Oxford agrarian studies. *[Ox. Agrar. Stud.] ISSN: 0264-5491. Carfax Publishing*: P.O. Box 25, Abingdon, Oxfordshire OX14 3UE, U.K.

Pacific affairs. *[Pac. Aff.] ISSN: 0030-851X. University of British Columbia*: Vancouver, BC., Canada, V6T 1W5

Pacific historical review. *[Pac. Hist. R.] ISSN: 0030-8684. American Historical Association, Pacific Coast Branch*: 6339 Bunche Hall, Los Angeles, CA. 90024, U.S.A.; **Publisher**: *University of California Press*: 2120 Berkeley Way, Berkeley, CA. 94720, U.S.A.

INTERNATIONAL BIBLIOGRAPHY OF SOCIOLOGY — 1988

Pacific review. *[Pac. Rev.]* *ISSN: 0951-2748. Oxford University Press*: Pinkhill House, Southfield Road, Eynsham OX8 1JJ, U.K.

Pacific studies. *[Pac. Stud.]* *ISSN: 0275-3596. Institute for Polynesian Studies*: Brigham Young University- Hawaii, Laie, HI. 96762, U.S.A.

Pacific viewpoint. *[Pac. View.]* *ISSN: 0030-8978. Victoria University of Wellington, Department of Geography*: Private Bag, Wellington, New Zealand; **Publisher**: *Victoria University Press*: P.O. Box 600, Wellington, New Zealand

Pakistan development review. *[Pak. Dev. R.]* *ISSN: 0030-9729. Pakistan Institute of Development Economics*: P.O. Box 1091, Islamabad, Pakistan

Pakistan journal of history and culture. *[Pak. J. Hist. Cult.]* *ISSN: 1012-7682. National Institute of Historical and Cultural Research*: Rauf Centre, 102 Blue Area, Islamabad, Pakistan

Państwo i prawo. *[Pań. Prawo]* *ISSN: 0031-0980. Polska Academia Nauk, Instytut Nauk Prawnych*: Ul. Wiejska 12, 00-490 Warsaw, Poland

Papers. *[Papers]* *ISSN: 0210-2862. Universitat autònoma de Barcelona, Departament de Sociologia*: Servei de Publicacions, Edifici A, 08193 Barcelona, Spain

Papers in regional science. *[Pap. Reg. Sci.]* *ISSN: 0486-2902. Regional Science Association International*: University of Illinois at Urbana-Champaign, 1-3 Observatory, 901 South Mathews Avenue, Urbana, IL. 61801-3682, U.S.A.

Past and present. *[Past Pres.]*; *Oxford University Press*: Pinkhill House, Southfield Road, Eynsham, Oxford OX8 1JJ, U.K.

Patterns of prejudice. *[Patt. Prej.]* *ISSN: 0031-322X. Institute of Jewish Affairs*: 11 Hertford Street, London W1Y 7DX, U.K.

Peasant studies. *[Peasant Stud.]*; *University of Utah*: Department of History, University of Utah, Salt Lake City, UT. 84112, U.S.A.

Peninsule. *[Peninsule]*; *Cercle de Culture et de Recherches Laotiennes*: 14 rue Dame Genette, 57070 Metz, France

Pensée. *[Pensée]* *ISSN: 0031-4773. Institut de recherches marxistes*: 64, Boulevard Auguste-Blanqui, 75013 Paris, France

Pensiero politico. *[Pens. Pol.]* *ISSN: 0031-4846. Casa Editrice Leo S.Olschki*: Cas. Postale 66, 50100 Florence, Italy

Perception & psychophysics. *[Perc. Psych.]* *ISSN: 0031-5117. Psychonomic Society*: 1710 Fortview Road, Austin, TX. 78704, U.S.A.

Peripherie. *[Peripherie]* *ISSN: 0173-184X. Wissenschaftliche Vereinigung für Entwicklungstheorie und Entwicklungspolitik*: Institut für Soziologie, Scharnhorststraße 121, D-4400 Münster, Germany; **Publisher**: *Verlag Peripherie*: LN-Vertrieb, Gneisenaustraße 2, D-1000 Berlin 61, Germany

Pesquisa e planejamento econômico. *[Pesq. Plan. Ec.]* *ISSN: 0100-0551. Instituto de Planejamento Econômico e Social (IPEA)*: Av. Presidente Antônio Carlos 51, CEP 20 020, Rio de Janeiro, Brazil

Peuples méditerranéens; Mediterranean peoples. *[Peup. Médit.]* *ISSN: 0399-1253. Institut d'Études Méditerranéenes*: B.P. 188-07, 75326 Paris Cedex 07, France

Philippine quarterly of culture and society. *[Phil. Q. Cult. Soc.]* *ISSN: 0115-0243. University of San Carlos*: Publications Section, Cebu City 6000, Philippines

Philippine studies. *[Phil. Stud.]* *ISSN: 0031-7837. Ateneo de Manila University Press*: P.O. Box 154, Manila 1099, Philippines

INTERNATIONAL BIBLIOGRAPHY OF SOCIOLOGY — 1988

Philosophy & public affairs. *[Philos. Pub.]* ISSN: 0048-3915. *Princeton University Press*: 41 William Street, Princeton, NJ. 08540, U.S.A.; **Subscriptions**: *Johns Hopkins University Press*: Journals Division, 701 West 40th Street, Suite 275, Baltimore, MD. 21211, U.S.A.

Philosophy east and west. *[Philos. E.W.]* ISSN: 0031-8221. *University of Hawaii Press*: 2840 Kolowalu Street, Honolulu, HI. 96822, U.S.A.

Philosophy of the social sciences. *[Philos. S. Sc.]* ISSN: 0048-3931. *Sage Publications*: 2455 Teller Road, Newbury Park, CA. 91320, U.S.A.

Planning and administration. *[Plan. Admin.]* ISSN: 0304-117X. *International Union of Local Authorities*: 41 Wassenaarseweg, 2596 CG The Hague, The Netherlands

Planning outlook. *[Plan. Out.]* ISSN: 0032-0714. *University of Newcastle-upon-Tyne, Department of Town and Country Planning*: Newcastle-upon-Tyne NE1 7RU, U.K.

Planning practice and research. *[Plan. Pract. Res.]* ISSN: 0269-7459. *Pion*: 207 Brondesbury Park, London NW2 5JN, U.K.

Policy and politics. *[Policy Pol.]* ISSN: 0305-5736. *University of Bristol, School for Advanced Urban Studies*: Rodney Lodge, Grange Road, Bristol BS8 4EA, U.K.

Polin. *[Polin]* ISSN: 0268-1056; ISBN: 0 631 17624 1. *Institute for Polish-Jewish Studies*: 45 St. Giles, Oxford OX1 3LP, U.K.; **Publisher**: *Basil Blackwell*: 108 Cowley Road, Oxford OX4 1JF, U.K.

Polish perspectives. *[Polish Persp.]* ISSN: 0032-2962. *Polska Instytut Spraw Miedzynasodowych*: ul. Warecka 1a, P.O. Box 159, 00-950 Warsaw, Poland; **Subscriptions**: *Ars Polona*: Krakowskie Przedmieście 7, 00-068 Warsaw, Poland

Political geography quarterly. *[Polit. Geogr. Q.]* ISSN: 0260-9827. *Butterworth-Heinemann*: Westbury House, Bury Street, P.O. Box 63, Guildford, Surrey GU2 5BH, U.K.

Political psychology. *[Polit. Psych.]* ISSN: 0162-895X. *International Society of Political Psychology*; **Publisher**: *Plenum Publishing*: 233 Spring Street, New York, NY. 10013, U.S.A.

Political science quarterly. *[Pol. Sci. Q.]* ISSN: 0032-3195. *Academy of Political Science*: 475 Riverside Drive, Suite 1274, New York, NY. 10115-0012, U.S.A.

Political studies. *[Politic. Stud.]* ISSN: 0032-3217. *Political Studies Association of the United Kingdom*: c/o Jack Hayward, Department of Politics, The University, Hull HU6 7RX, U.K.; **Publisher**: *Basil Blackwell*: 108 Cowley Road, Oxford, OX4 1JF, U.K.

Political theory. *[Polit. Theory]* ISSN: 0090-5917. *Sage Publications*: 2111 West Hillcrest Drive, Newbury Park, CA. 91320, U.S.A.

Politics and society. *[Polit. Soc.]* ISSN: 0032-3292. *Butterworth-Heinemann*: 80 Montvale Avenue, Stoneham, MA. 02180, U.S.A.

Politics and society in Germany, Austria and Switzerland. *[Pol. Soc. Ger. Aust. Swit.]* ISSN: 0954-6030. *University of Nottingham, Institute of German, Austrian and Swiss Affairs*: University Park, Nottingham NG7 2RD, U.K.

Politics and the life sciences. *[Polit. Life]* ISSN: 0730-9384. *Association for Politics and the Life Sciences*: Northern Illinois University, DeKalb, IL. 60115-2854, U.S.A.

Politique africaine. *[Pol. Afr.]* ISSN: 0244-7827. *Association des chercheurs de politique africaine*; **Publisher**: *Editions Karthala*: 22-24 boulevard Arago, 75013 Paris, France

Politique internationale. *[Polit. Int.]* ISSN: 0221-2781. *Politique Internationale*: 11 rue du Bois de Boulogne, 75116 Paris, France

Politiques et management public. *[Pol. Manag. Publ.]* ISSN: 0758-1726. *Institut de Management Public*: 14 rue Corvisart, 75013 Paris, France

Politische Vierteljahresschrift. *[Polit. Viertel.] ISSN: 0032-3470. Deutsche Vereinigung für Politische Wissenschaft*; **Publisher**: *Westdeutscher Verlag*: Postfach 5829 D-6200 Wiesbaden 1, Germany

Population. *[Population] ISSN: 0032-4663. Institut National d'Études Démographiques*: 27 rue du Commandeur, 75675 Paris Cedex 14, France; **Publisher**: *Editions de l'Institut National d'Etudes Démographiques*: 27 rue du Commandeur, 75675 Paris Cedex 14, France

Population and development review. *[Pop. Dev. Rev.] ISSN: 0098-7921. Population Council*: One Dag Hammarskjold Plaza, New York, N.Y. 10017, U.S.A.

Population and environment. *[Popul. Envir.] ISSN: 0199-0039. Human Sciences Press*: 233 Spring Street, New York, N.Y. 10013-1578, U.S.A.

Population research and policy review. *[Pop. Res. Pol. R.] ISSN: 0167-5923. Kluwer Academic Publishers*: P.O. Box 17, 3300 AH Dordrecht, The Netherlands; **Subscriptions**: *idem:* P.O. Box 322, 3300 AH Dordrecht, The Netherlands

Population review. *[Popul. R.] ISSN: 0032-471X. Indian Institute for Population Studies*: 8976 Cliffridge Avenue, La Jolla, CA. 92037, U.S.A.

Population studies. *[Pop. Stud.] ISSN: 0032-4728. London School of Economics, Population Investigation Committee*: Houghton Street, Aldwych, London WC2A 2AE, U.K.

Pouvoirs. *[Pouvoirs] ISSN: 0152-0768. Presses Universitaires de France*: 108 boulevard Saint-Germain, 75006 Paris, France; **Subscriptions**: *Presses Universitaires de France*: Département des Revues, 14 avenue du Bois-de-l'Epine, BP 90, 91003 Evry Cedex, France

Praca i zabezpieczenie społeczne. *[Pra. Zab. Społ.] ISSN: 0032-6186. Państwowe Wydawnictwo Ekonomiczne*: Ul. Niecała 4a, Warsaw, Poland

Practice. *[Practice] ISSN: 0950-3153. British Association of Social Workers*: 16 Kent Street, Birmingham B5 6RD, U.K.; **Subscriptions**: *BASW-Practice*: c/o Whiting & Birch, P.O. Box 872, London SE23 3HL, U.K.

Praxis international. *[Prax. Int.] ISSN: 0260-8448. Basil Blackwell*: 108 Cowley Road, Oxford OX4 1JF, U.K.

Présence africaine. *[Prés. Afr.] ISSN: 0032-7638. Société Africaine de Culture*: 25 bis, rue des Ecoles, 75005 Paris, France

Presidential studies quarterly. *[Pres. Stud. Q.] ISSN: 0360- 4918. Center for the Study of the Presidency*: 208 East 75th Street, New York, NY. 10021, U.S.A.

Problèmes politiques et sociaux. *[Prob. Pol. Soc.] ISSN: 0015-9743. Documentation Française*: 29 quai Voltaire, 75007 Paris, France

Problems of communism. *[Probl. Commu.] ISSN: 0032-941X. US Information Agency*: 301 4th Street SW Washington, DC. 20547, U.S.A.; **Subscriptions**: *Superintendent of Documents*: US Government Printing Office, Washington DC. 20402, U.S.A.

Proceedings. American Statistical Association. *[Proc. Am. Stat. Ass.]; American Statistical Association*: 1429 Duke Street, Alexandria, VA. 22314, U.S.A.

Professional geographer. *[Prof. Geogr.] ISSN: 0033-0124. Association of American Geographers*: 1710 Sixteenth Street, N.W., Washington, DC. 20009-3198, U.S.A.

Progress in human geography. *[Prog. H. Geog.] ISSN: 0309-1325. Edward Arnold*: Mill Road, Dunton Green, Sevenoaks, Kent TN13 2YA, U.K.; **Subscriptions**: *Subscription Department, Edward Arnold Journals*: 42 Bedford Square, London WC1B 3SL, U.K.

Progress in planning. *[Prog. Plan.] ISSN: 0305-9006. Pergamon Press*: Headington Hill Hall, Oxford OX3 0BW, U.K.

Prokla.:*Probleme des Klassenkampfs [Prokla]; Vereinigung zur Kritik der politischen Ökonomie*; **Publisher**: *Rotbuch Verlag*: Potsdamer Str. 98, 1000 Berlin 30, Germany

Przegląd polonijny. *[Prz. Pol.] ISSN: 0137-303X. Polska Akademia Nauk, Komitet Badania Polonii;* **Publisher**: *Ossolineum, Publishing House of the Polish Academy of Sciences*: Rynek 9, 50-106 Wroclaw, Poland

Przegląd socjologiczny. *[Prz. Soc.] ISSN: 0033-2356. Łódzkie towarzystwo naukowe:* ul Rewolucji 1905 roku 41/43, Łódź, Poland; **Publisher**: *Zakład Narodowy im. Ossolińskich, Wydawnictwo Polskiej Akademii Nauk:* Poland

Przegląd statystyczny. *[Prz. Staty.] ISSN: 0033- 2372. Polska Akademia nauk, Komitet Statystyki i Ekonometrii:* ul. Miodowa 10, Warsaw, Poland; **Subscriptions**: *ARS Polona:* Krakowskie Przedmieście 7, 00-068 Warsaw, Poland

Psychoanalytic review. *[Psychoanal. Rev.] ISSN: 0033-2836.* 72 Spring Street, New York, NY. 10012, U.S.A.

Psychological bulletin. *[Psychol .B.] ISSN: 0033- 2909. American Psychological Association:* 1400 North Uhle Street, Arlington, VA. 22201, U.S.A.

Psychological review. *[Psychol. Rev.] ISSN: 0033-295X. American Psychological Association:* 1400 North Uhle Street, Arlington, VA. 22201, U.S.A.

Psychology and developing societies. *[Psychol. Devel. Soc.]; Sage Publications India:* 32 M-Block Market, Greater Kailash I, New Delhi 110 048, India

Psychotherapy research. *[Psychoth. Res.] ISSN: 0894-7597. Society for Psychotherapy Research;* **Publisher**: *Guilford Publications:* 72 Spring Street, New York, NY. 10012, U.S.A.

Public administration. *[Publ. Admin.] ISSN: 0033- 3298. Royal Institute for Public Administration:* 3 Birdcage Walk, London SW1H 9JH, U.K.; **Publisher**: *Basil Blackwell:* 108 Cowley Road, Oxford OX4 1JF, U.K.

Public administration and development. *[Publ. Adm. D.] ISSN: 0271-2075. Royal Institute of Public Administration:* Regent's College, Inner Circle, Regent's Park, London NW1 4NS, U.K.; **Publisher**: *John Wiley & Sons:* Baffins Lane, Chichester, West Sussex PO19 1UD, U.K.

Public administration review. *[Publ. Adm. Re.] ISSN: 0033-3352. American Society for Public Administration:* 1120 G. Street, NW, Suite 500, Washington, DC. 20005, U.S.A.

Public affairs quarterly. *[Publ. Aff. Q.] ISSN: 0887-0373. Philosophy Documentation Center/ North American Philosophical Publications:* Bowling Green State University, Bowling Green, OH. 43403, U.S.A.

Public choice. *[Publ. Choice] ISSN: 0048-5829. Kluwer Academic Publishers:* Spuiboulevard 50, Postbus 17, 3300 AA Dordrecht, The Netherlands

Public culture. *[Publ. Cult.] ISSN: 0899-2363. Center for Transnational Cultural Studies:* University Museum, University of Pennsylvania, 33rd and Spruce Streets, Pennsylvania, PA. 19104-6324, U.S.A.; **Publisher**: *University of Pennsylvania, University Museum:* University of Pennsylvania, 33rd and Spruce Streets, Pennsylvania, PA. 19104-6324, U.S.A.

Public enterprise. *[Publ. Enter.] ISSN: 0351-3564. International Center for Public Enterprises in Developing Countries:* Titova 104, 61109 Ljubljana, P.O. Box 92, Yugoslavia

Public opinion quarterly. *[Publ. Opin. Q.] ISSN: 0033-362X. American Association for Public Opinion Research:* P.O. Box 17, Princeton, NJ. 08540, U.S.A.; **Publisher**: *University of Chicago Press:* Journals Division, 5720 S. Woodlawn Avenue, Chicago, IL. 60637, U.S.A.

Publizistik. *[Publizistik] ISSN: 0033-4006. Deutsche Gesellschaft für Publizistik- und Kommunikationswissenschaft/ Österreichische Gesellschaft für Publizistik- und Kommunikationswissenschaft/ Schweizerische Gesellschaft für Kommunikations- und Medienwissenschaft:* Martin-Legros-Straße 53, D-5300 Bonn 1, Germany; **Publisher**: *Universitätsverlag Konstanz:* Postfach 102051, D-7750 Konstanz, Germany

INTERNATIONAL BIBLIOGRAPHY OF SOCIOLOGY — 1988

Quaderni di sociologia. *[Quad. Sociol.]* ISSN: 0033- 4952. *Edizioni di Comunità*: 20090 Segrate, Milan, Italy

Quadrant. *[Quadrant]* ISSN: 0033-5002. *Quadrant Magazine*: 46 George Street, Fitzroy, Melbourne, Victoria 3065, Australia

Quarterly journal of administration. *[Q. J. Admin.]* ISSN: 0001-8333. *Obafemi Awolowo University, Faculty of Administration*: Ile-Ife, Nigeria

Quarterly journal of economics. *[Q. J. Econ.]* ISSN: 0033-5533. *Harvard University*: Cambridge MA 02138, U.S.A.; **Publisher**: *MIT Press*: 55 Hayward Street, Cambridge, MA. 02142, U.S.A.

Quarterly review of economics and business. *[Q. R. Econ. Bu.]* ISSN: 0033-5797. *University of Illinois at Urbana-Champaign, Bureau of Economic and Business Research*: 428 Commerce West, 1206 South Sixth Street, Champaign, IL. 61820, U.S.A.

R&D management. *[R&D Manag.]* ISSN: 0033-6807. *Basil Blackwell*: 108 Cowley Road, Oxford OX4 1JF, U.K.

Race and class. *[Race Class]* ISSN: 0306-3965. *Institute of Race Relations*: 2-6 Leeke Street, King's Cross Road, London WC1X 9HS, U.K.

Rassegna italiana di sociologia. *[Rass. It. Soc.]* ISSN: 0486 0349. *Societá Editrice il Mulino*: Strada Maggiore 37, 40125 Bologna, Italy

Raven. *[Raven]* ISSN: 0951- 4066. *Freedom Press*: 84b Whitechapel High Street, London E1 7QX, U.K.

Recherches sociographiques. *[Rech. Soc.graph]* ISSN: 0034-1282. *Université Laval, Département de Sociologie*: Québec G1K 7P4, Canada

Regional science and urban economics. *[Reg. Sci. Urb. Econ.]* ISSN: 0166- 0462. *Elsevier Science Publishers (North-Holland)*: P.O. Box 1991, 1000 BZ Amsterdam, The Netherlands; **Subscriptions**: *idem:* Journals Division, P.O. Box 211, 1000 AE Amsterdam, The Netherlands

Regional studies. *[Reg. Stud.]* ISSN: 0034-3404. *Regional Studies Association*; **Publisher**: *Cambridge University Press*: The Edinburgh Building, Shaftesbury Road, Cambridge CB2 2RU, U.K.

Religion. *[Religion]* ISSN: 0048-721X. *Academic Press*: 24-28 Oval Road, London NW1 7DX, U.K.

Religion in communist lands. *[Relig. Comm. Lands]* ISSN: 0307-5974. *Keston College*: Heathfield Road, Keston, Kent BR2 6BA, U.K.

Research in Melanesia. *[R. Melan.]* ISSN: 0254-0665. *University of Papua New Guinea, Department of Anthropology and Sociology*: Box 320 University, Port Moresby, Papua New Guinea

Research in social movements, conflicts and change. *[R. Soc. Move. Con. Cha.]* ISSN: 0163-786X. *JAI Press*: 55 Old Post Road No.2, Greenwich, CT. 066830, U.S.A.

Research in social stratification and mobility. *[R. Soc. Strat. Mob.]* ISSN: 0276-5624. *JAI Press*: 55 Old Post Road No.2, Greenwich, CT. 066830, U.S.A.

Resources policy. *[Res. Pol.]* ISSN: 0301-4207. *Butterworth-Heinemann*: Linacre House, Jordan Hill, Oxford, OX2 8DP, U.K.

Response to the victimization of women and children. *[Resp. Victim. Women Child.]* ISSN: 0894-7597. *Center for Women Policy Studies*: Washington, DC., U.S.A.; **Publisher**: *Guilford Publications*: 72 Spring Street, New York, NY. 10012, U.S.A.

Review of African political economy. *[Rev. Afr. Pol. Ec.]* ISSN: 0305- 6244. *ROAPE Publications*: Regency House, 75-77 St. Mary's Road, Sheffield S2 4AN, U.K.

Review of black political economy. [*Rev. Bl. Pol. Ec.*] *ISSN: 0034-6446. National Economic Association/ Clark Atlanta University, Southern Center for Studies in Public Policy*: 240 Brawley Drive, S.W. Atlanta, GA. 30314, U.S.A.; **Publisher**: *Transaction Publishers*: Rutgers University, New Brunswick, NJ. 08903, U.S.A.

Review of Indonesian and Malaysian affairs.*[RIMA]*— [*R. Ind. Malay. Aff.*] *ISSN: 0034- 6594. University of Sydney, Department of Indonesian and Malayan Studies*: Sydney, NSW 2001, Australia

Review of international co-operation. [*R. Int. Co-op.*] *ISSN: 0034-6608. International Co-operative Alliance*: Route des Morillons 15, CH-1218 Le Grand Saconnex, Geneva, Switzerland

Review of politics. [*Rev. Polit.*] *ISSN: 0034-6705. University of Notre Dame*: P.O. Box B, Notre Dame, IN. 46556, U.S.A.

Review of radical political economics. [*Rev. Rad. Pol. Ec.*] *ISSN: 0486-6134. Union for Radical Political Economics*: c/o Dept. of Economics, University of California, Riverside, CA. 92521, U.S.A.

Review of rural and urban planning in Southern and Eastern Africa. [*R. Rur. Urb. Plan. S.& E.Afr.*]; *University of Zimbabwe, Department of Rural and Urban Planning*: P.O. Box MP 167, Mount Pleasant, Harare, Zimbabwe

Review of social economy. [*R. Soc. Econ.*] *ISSN: 0034-6764. Association for Social Economics*: c/o Department of Economics, Northern Illinois University, DeKalb, IL. 60115, U.S.A.

Review of the economic situation of Mexico. [*Rev. Econ. Sit. Mex.*] *ISSN: 0187-3407. Banco Nacional de Mexico, Department of Economic Research*: Av. Madero 21, Mexico, D.F. 06000, Mexico

Review of urban and regional development studies. [*R. Urban. Region. Dev. S.*]; *Applied Regional Science Conference*; **Publisher**: *Tokyo International University, Urban Development Institute*: Nakanishi Building 6F, 8-4 Takadanobaba 4-chome, Shinjuku-Ku, Tokyo 169, Japan

Review. Fernand Braudel Center. [*Rev. F. Braudel. Ctr.*] *ISSN: 0147-9032. State University of New York, Fernand Braudel Center*: P.O. Box 6000, Binghamton, NY. 13902-6000, U.S.A.

Revista brasileira de ciências sociais. [*Rev. Bras. Ciên. Soc.*] *ISSN: 0102-6909. Associação Nacional de Pós-Graduação e Pesquisa em Ciências Sociais*: Largo de São Francisco, 01-4° andar, s/408 Centro, Rio de Janeiro RJ., Cep 20051, Brazil; **Publisher**: *Editora Revista dos Tribunais*: Rua Conde do Pinhal 78, 01501 São Paulo, SP. Brazil

Revista de administración pública. [*Rev. Admin. Públ.*] *ISSN: 0034-7639. Centro de Estudios Constitucionales*: Fuencarral 45, 28004 Madrid, Spain

Revista de ciência política. [*Rev. Ciê. Pol.*] *ISSN: 0034-8023. Fundação Getulio Vargas*: Praia de Botafogo, 188-CEP 22.253 Caixa Postal 9.052, 20.000 Rio de Janeiro, Brazil

Revista de ciências sociais. [*Rev. Ciê. Soc.*] *ISSN: 0041-8862. Universidade Federal do Ceará, Centro de Humanidades, Departamento de Ciências Sociais e Filosofia*: Caixa Postal 3025, CEP 6000 Fortaleza, Ceará, Brazil

Revista de ciencias sociales. [*Rev. Cien. Soc.*] *ISSN: 0034-7817. Universidad de Puerto Rico, Facultad de Ciencias Sociales, Centro de Investigaciones Sociales*: Rio Piedras, Puerto Rico 00931

Revista de fomento social. [*Rev. Fom. Soc.*] *ISSN: 0015-6043. INSA-ETEA*: Escritor Castilla Aguayo 4, Apartado 439, 14004 Cordoba, Spain; **Publisher**: *CESI-JESPRE*: Pablo Aranda 3, 28006 Madrid, Spain

Revista mexicana de sociología. [*Rev. Mexicana Soc.*] *ISSN: 0035-0087. Universidad Nacional Autónoma de México*: Torre II de Humanidades 7° piso, Ciudad Universitaria, 04510 México D.F., Mexico

INTERNATIONAL BIBLIOGRAPHY OF SOCIOLOGY — 1988

Revista occidental. *[Rev. Occid.]; Instituto de Investigaciones Culturales Latinoamericanas (IICLA)*: Apartado 38, Correo Central, 22000 Tijuana, Baja California, N., Mexico

Revista paraguaya de sociología. *[Rev. Parag. Sociol.]; Centro Paraguayo de Estudios Sociológicos*: Eligio Ayala 973, Casilla no.2.157, Asunción, Paraguay

Reyue canadienne d'études de développement; Canadian journal of development studies. *[Rev. Can. Etud. Dével.] ISSN: 0225-5189. Université d'Ottawa, Institut de développement international et de coopération/ University of Ottawa, Institute for International Development and Co-operation*: 25 University Street, Ottawa, Ontario K1N 6N5, Canada

Revue de Corée. *[Rev. Cor.]; UNESCO*; **Publisher**: *Commission Nationale Coréene*: BP 64 Poste Centrale, Seoul, Korea

Revue de l'histoire des religions. *[R. Hist. Relig.] ISSN: 0035-1423. Centre National de la Recherche Scientifique/ Centre National des Lettres*: 1 place Aristide Briand, 92195 Meuden Cedex, France; **Publisher**: *Presses Universitaires de France*: 108 boulevard Saint-Germain, 75006, Paris, France; **Subscriptions**: *idem*: Département des Revues, 14 avenue du Bois-de-l'Epine, B.P. 90, 91003 Evry Cedex, France

Revue de l'Institut de sociologie. *[R. Inst. Sociol.] ISSN: 0770-1055. Institut de Sociologie*: 44 avenue Jeanne, (CP 124) B-1050 Brussels, Belgium

Revue de science criminelle et de droit pénal comparé. *[Rev. Sci. Crim. D. P.] ISSN: 0035-1733. Université Panthéon-Assas (Paris 2), Institut de Droit Comparé, Section de Science Criminelle*; **Publisher**: *Editions Sirey*: 22 rue Soufflot, 75005 Paris Cedex 05, France; **Subscriptions**: *Dalloz*: 35 rue Tournefort, 75240 Paris Cedex 05, France

Revue d'économie régionale et urbaine. *[R. Ec. Reg. Urb.] ISSN: 0180-7307. ADICUEER (Association des Directeurs d'Instituts et des Centres Universitaires d'Etudes Economiques Régionales)*: 4 Rue Michelet, 75006 Paris, France

Revue des études coopératives mutualistes et associatives. *[R. Et. Coop. Mut. Ass.] ISSN: 0035-2020. Coopérative d'Information et d'Edition Mutualiste*: 255 rue de Vaugirard, 75719 Paris Cedex 15, France

Revue d'histoire moderne et contemporaine. *[R. Hist. Mod. Cont.] ISSN: 0048-8003. Société d'histoire moderne et contemporaine*: 47 boulevard Bessières, 75017 Paris, France

Revue du monde muselman et de la Méditerranée. *[R. Mon. Musel. Med.] ISSN: 0997-1327. Association pour l'Etude des Sciences Humaines en Afrique du Nord et au Proche-Orient*; **Publisher**: *Editions EDISUD*: La Calade, 13090 Aix-en-Provence, France

Revue du travail. *[Rev. Trav.] ISSN: 0035-2705. Ministère de l'Emploi et du Travail*: Revue du Travail, rue Belliard 53, Brussels 1040, Belgium

Revue économique et sociale. *[R. Econ. Soc.] ISSN: 0035-2772. Société d'Études Economiques et Sociales*: Bâtiment des Facultés des Sciences Humaines (BFSH1), 1015 Lausanne-Dorigny, Switzerland

Revue européenne des sciences sociales.:*Cahiers Vilfredo Pareto [Rev. Eur. Sci. Soc.] ISSN: 0008-0497. Librairie DROZ*: 11 rue Massot, CH-1211 Geneva, Switzerland

Revue française d'administration publique. *[R. Fr. Admin. Publ.] ISSN: 0152-7401. Institut International d'Administration Publique*: 2 avenue de l'Observatoire, 75006 Paris, France; **Subscriptions**: *La Documentation Française*: 29-31 quai Voltaire, 75340 Paris Cedex 07, France

Revue française de science politique. *[R. Fr. Sci. Pol.] ISSN: 0035-2950. Fondation nationale des sciences politiques/ Association française de science politique*: 27 rue Saint-Guillame, 75341 Paris, France

Revue française de sociologie. *[Rev. Fr. Soc.] ISSN: 0035-2969. Institut de recherche sur les sociétés contemporaines*: 59-61 rue Pouchet, 75017 Paris, France; **Publisher**: *Editions du Centre National de la Recherche Scientifique*: 20-22 rue Saint-Amand, 75015 Paris, France; **Subscriptions**: *Centrale des Revues/ CDR*: 11 rue Gossin, 92543 Montrouge Cedex, France

INTERNATIONAL BIBLIOGRAPHY OF SOCIOLOGY — 1988

Revue française des affaires sociales. [*R. Fr. Aff. Soc.*] *ISSN: 0035-2985*. *Ministère des Affaires Sociales et de la Solidarité Nationale*: 1 place de Fontenoy, 75700 Paris, France; **Publisher**: *Masson*: 120 boulevard St. Germain, 75005 Paris Cedex 06, France

Revue Roumaine des sciences sociales.:*Série des sciences juridiques* [*Rev. Roumaine Sci. Soc. Sér. Sci. Jurid.*] *ISSN: 0035-4023*. *Editura Academiei Române*: Calea Victoriei 125, 79717 Bucharest, Romania; **Subscriptions**: *Rompresfilatelia*: P.O. Box 12-201, Calea Grivitei 64-66, Bucharest, Romania

Revue syndicale suisse. [*R. Synd. Suisse*] *ISSN: 0035-421X*. *Revue Syndicale Suisse*: Case Postale 64, 3000 Berne 23 , Switzerland

Revue tiers-monde. [*R. T-Monde*] *ISSN: 0040-7356*. *Université de Paris, Institut d'Étude du Développement Economique et Social*: 58 boulevard Arago, 75013 Paris, France; **Publisher**: *Presses Universitaires de France*: 108 boulevard Saint- Germain, Paris, France

Revue tunisienne de sciences sociales. [*R. Tun. Sci. Soc.*] *ISSN: 0035-4333*. *Université de Tunis, Centre d'Etudes et de Recherches Economiques et Sociales*: 23 rue d'Espagne, 1000 Tunis, Tunisia

Rivista internazionale di scienze sociali. [*Riv. Int. Sci. Soc.*] *ISSN: 0035-676X*. *Università Cattolica del Sacro Cuore*: Vita e Pensiero, Largo A. Gemelli, 1-1 20123 Milan, Italy

Rivista italiana di scienza politica. [*Riv. It. Sci. Pol.*] *ISSN: 0048-8402*. *Dipartimento di scienza politica e sociologia politica*: via S. Caterina d'Alessandria 3, 50129 Florence, Italy; **Publisher**: *Società Editrice il Mulino*: Strada Maggiore 37, 40125 Bologna, Italy

Rivista trimestrale di diritto pubblico. [*Riv. Trim. Pubbl.*] *ISSN: 0557-1464*. *A. Giuffrè Editore*: via Busto Arsizio 40, 20151 Milan, Italy

Rural africana. [*Rur. Afr.*] *ISSN: 0085- 5839*. *Michigan State University African Studies Center*: 100 Center for International Programs, E.Lansing, MI. 48824-1035, U.S.A.

Rural history.:*Economy, society, culture* [*Rural Hist.*] *ISSN: 0956-7933*. *Cambridge University Press*: The Edinburgh Building, Shaftesbury Road, Cambridge CB2 2RU, U.K.

Rural sociology. [*Rural Sociol.*] *ISSN: 0036- 0112*. *Rural Sociological Society*: Texas A & M University, College Station, U.S.A.; **Publisher**: *idem:* Department of Sociology, Wilson Hall, Montana State University, Bozeman, MT. 59715, U.S.A.

Saeculum. [*Saeculum*] *ISSN: 0080-5319*. *Verlag Karl Alber*: Hermann-Herder-Straße 4, 7800 Freiburg im Breisgau, Germany

Santé mentale au Québec. [*San. Ment. Qué*] *ISSN: 0383-6320*. *Revue Santé mentale au Québec*: C.P. 548, Succ. Places d'Armes, Montréal, Québec H2Y 3H3, Canada

Sarawak gazette. [*Sara. Gaz.*]; *Sarawak Museum*: Kuching, Sarawak

Sarjana. [*Sarjana*]; *University of Malaya, Faculty of Arts and Social Sciences*: Lembah Pantai, Kuala Lumpur 22-11, Malaysia

Savanna. [*Savanna*] *ISSN: 0331-0523*. *Ahmadu Bello University Press*: PMB 1094, Zaria, Kaduna State, Nigeria

Scandinavian economic history review. [*Sc. Ec. Hist. R.*] *ISSN: 0358-5522*. *Scandinavian Society for Economic and Social History*: Department of Economic History, Box 7083, S- 220 07 Lund, Sweden

Scandinavian housing and planning research. [*Scand. Hous. Plan. R.*] *ISSN: 0281-5737*. *Building Research Institute (Denmark)/ Ministry of Environment (Finland)/ Institute for Urban and Regional Research (Norway)/ Institute for Building Research (Sweden)*; **Publisher**: *Almqvist & Wiksell International*: P.O. Box 638, S-101 28 Stockholm, Sweden

Scandinavian journal of development alternatives. [*Scand. J. Devel. Altern.*] *ISSN: 0280-2791*. *Bethany Books*: P.O. Box 7444, S-103 91 Stockholm, Sweden

Scandinavian journal of the Old Testament. *[Scan. J. Old. Test.] ISSN: 0901-8328. University of Aarhus, Department of Old Testament Studies*: DK-8000 Aarhus C., Denmark; **Publisher**: *Aarhus University Press*

Schweizerische Zeitschrift für Volkswirtschaft und Statistik; Revue suisse d'économie politique et de statistique. *[Schw. Z. Volk. Stat.]; Schweizerische Gesellschaft für Statistik und Volkswirtschaft/ Société suisse de statistique et d'économie politique*: Hallwylstraße 15, CH-3003 Berne, Switzerland; **Publisher**: *Staempfli*: Hallerstrasse 7, Postfach 8326, CH-3001 Berne, Switzerland

Science and society. *[Sci. Soc.] ISSN: 0036-8237. Guilford Publications*: 72 Spring Street, New York, NY. 10012, U.S.A.

Science as culture. *[Sci. Cult.] ISSN: 0959-5431. Free Association Books*: 26 Freegrove Road, London N7 9RQ, U.K.

Science, technology & development. *[Sc. Tech. Devel.] ISSN: 0950-0707. Frank Cass*: Gainsborough House, 11 Gainsborough Road, London E11 1RS, U.K.

Scientific American. *[Sci. Am.] ISSN: 0036-8733. Scientific American*: 415 Madison Avenue, New York, NY. 10017, U.S.A.

Semiotica. *[Semiotica]; International Association for Semiotic Studies*; **Publisher**: *Walter de Gruyter*: Postfach 110240, D-1000 Berlin 11, Germany

SIER Bulletin. *[SIER B.]; University of Swaziland, Faculty of Education*: P/Bag, Kwaluseni, Swaziland

Signs. *[Signs] ISSN: 0097-9740. University of Chicago Press*: 5720 S. Woodlawn, Chicago, IL. 60637, U.S.A.; **Subscriptions**: *idem*: Journals Division, P.O. Box 37005, Chicago, IL. 60637, U.S.A.

Simulation and gaming. *[Simulat. Gam.] ISSN: 0037-5500. Sage Publications*: 2455 Teller Road, Newbury Park, CA. 91320, U.S.A.

Singapore journal of tropical geography. *[Sing. J. Trop. Geogr.] ISSN: 0129-7619. National University of Singapore*: Department of Geography, Kent Ridge, Republic of Singapore 0511

Sistema. *[Sistema] ISSN: 0210-0223. Fundación Sistema*: Fuencarral 127, 1° 28010, Madrid, Spain

Slavic review. *[Slavic R.] ISSN: 0037-6779. American Association for the Advancement of Slavic Studies*: 128 Encina Commons, Stanford University, Stanford, CA. 94305, U.S.A.

Slavonic and East European review. *[Slav. E.Eur. Rev.] ISSN: 0037-6795. University of London, School of Slavonic and East European Studies*: Malet Street, London WC1E 7HU, U.K.; **Publisher**: *Modern Humanities Research Association*: King's College, Strand, London EC2R 2LS, U.K.

Slovo. *[Slovo] ISSN: 0954-6839. School of Slavonic and East European Studies*; **Publisher**: *University of London*: Malet Street, London WC1E 7HU, U.K.

Social action. *[Soc. Act.] ISSN: 0037-7627. Indian Social Institute, Social Action Trust*: Lodi Road, New Delhi 130003, India

Social analysis. *[Soc. Anal.] ISSN: 0155-977X. University of Adelaide, Department of Anthropology*: G.P.O. Box 498, Adelaide 5A 5001, Australia

Social and economic studies. *[Soc. Econ. S.] ISSN: 0037-7651. University of the West Indies, Institute of Social and Economic Research*: Mona, Kingston 7, Jamaica

Social behaviour. *[Soc. Behav.] ISSN: 0885-6249. John Wiley & Sons*: Baffins Lane, Chichester, West Sussex PO19 1UD, U.K.

Social biology. *[Soc. Biol.] ISSN: 0037-766X. Society for the Study of Social Biology*: c/o Population Council, One Dag Hammarskjold Place, New York, NY. 10017, U.S.A.

INTERNATIONAL BIBLIOGRAPHY OF SOCIOLOGY — 1988

Social choice and welfare. *[Soc. Choice]* ISSN: 0176-1714. *Springer International*: Heidelberger Platz 3, W-1000 Berlin 33, Germany

Social cognition. *[Soc. Cogn.]* ISSN: 0278-616X. *Guilford Publications*: 72 Spring Street, New York, NY. 10012, U.S.A.

Social compass. *[Soc. Compass]* ISSN: 0037-7686. *International Federation of Institutes for Social and Socio-Religious Research (FERES)/ Centre de Recherches Socio-Religieuses*: Université Catholique de Louvain, Belgium; **Publisher**: *Sage Publications*: 6 Bonhill Street, London EC2A 4PU, U.K.

Social dynamics. *[Soc. Dyn.]* ISSN: 0253-3952. *Centre for African Studies, University of Cape Town*: Rondebosch 7700, South Africa

Social forces. *[Soc. Forc.]* ISSN: 0037-7732. *University of North Carolina, Department of Sociology*: 168 Hamilton Hall, University of North Carolina, Chapel Hill, NC. 27599-3210, U.S.A.; **Publisher**: *University of North Carolina Press*: P.O. Box 2288, Chapel Hill, NC. 27515, U.S.A.

Social history. *[Soc. Hist.]* ISSN: 0307-1022. *Routledge*: 11 New Fetter Lane, London EC4P 4EE, U.K.; **Subscriptions**: *Routledge*: Cheriton House, North Way, Andover, Hants SP10 5BE, U. K.

Social indicators research. *[Soc. Ind.]* ISSN: 0303-8300. *Kluwer Academic Publishers*: Spuiboulevard 50, P.O. Box 17, 3300 AA Dordrecht, The Netherlands

Social justice. *[Soc. Just.]* ISSN: 0094-7571. *Global Options*: P.O. Box 40601, San Francisco, CA. 94140, U.S.A.

Social networks. *[Soc. Networks]* ISSN: 0378-8733. *International Network for Social Network Analysis (INSNA)*; **Publisher**: *Elsevier Science Publishers (North-Holland)*: P.O. Box 1991, 1000 BZ Amsterdam, The Netherlands; **Subscriptions**: *idem*: Journals Division, P.O. Box 211, 1000 BZ Amsterdam, The Netherlands

Social philosophy & policy. *[Soc. Philos. Pol.]* ISSN: 0265-0525. *Bowling Green State University, Social Philosophy and Policy Center*: Bowling Green, Ohio 43403, U.S.A.; **Publisher**: *Basil Blackwell*: 108 Cowley Road, Oxford OX4 1JF, U.K.

Social policy. *[Soc. Pol.]* ISSN: 0037-7783. *Social Policy Corporation*: 25 West 43rd Street, Room 620, New York, NY. 10036, U.S.A.

Social policy and administration. *[Soc. Pol. Admin.]* ISSN: 0144-5596. *Basil Blackwell*: 108 Cowley Road, Oxford OX4 1JF, U.K.

Social problems. *[Soc. Prob.]* ISSN: 0037-7791. *Society for the Study of Social Problems*: N631, University of San Francisco, CA. 94143-0612, U.S.A.; **Publisher**: *University of California Press*: 2120 Berkeley Way, Berkeley, CA. 94720, U.S.A.

Social research. *[Soc. Res.]* ISSN: 0037-783X. *New School for Social Research, Graduate Faculty of Political and Social Science*: 66 West 12th Street, New York, NY. 10011, U.S.A.

Social science & medicine. *[Soc. Sci. Med.]* ISSN: 0277-9536. *Pergamon Press*: Hennock Road, Marsh Barton, Exeter, Devon EX2 8NE, U.K.; **Subscriptions**: *idem*: Headington Hill Hall, Oxford OX3 0BW, U.K.

Social science history. *[Soc. Sci. Hist.]* ISSN: 0145-5532. *Social Science History Association*; **Publisher**: *Duke University Press*: Box 6697 College Station, Durham, NC. 27708, U.S.A.

Social science information. *[Soc. Sci. Info.]* ISSN: 0539-0184. *Maison des Sciences de l'Homme/ Ecole des Hautes Etudes en Science Sociales*; **Publisher**: *Sage Publications*: 6 Bonhill Street, London EC2A 4PU, U.K.

Social science quarterly. *[Soc. Sci. Q.]* ISSN: 0038-4941. *Southwestern Social Science Association*: W.C. Hogg Building, The University of Texas at Austin, Austin, TX. 78713, U.S.A.; **Publisher**: *University of Texas Press*: P.O. Box 7819, Austin, TX. 78713, U.S.A.

INTERNATIONAL BIBLIOGRAPHY OF SOCIOLOGY — 1988

Social science teacher. *[Soc. Sci. Teach.] ISSN: 0309- 7544. Association for the Teaching of the Social Sciences*: 6 Rosemont Road, Aigburth, Liverpool L17 6BZ, U.K.

Social sciences. *[Soc. Sci.] ISSN: 0134-5486. Nauka Moscow*: 33/12 Arbat, Moscow G-2. 121818, U.S.S.R.

Social sciences in China. *[Soc. Sci. China] ISSN: 0252-9203. Chinese Academy of Social Science*; **Publisher**: *China Social Sciences Publishing House*: Jia 158 Gulouxidajie, Beijing 100720, China

Social scientist. *[Soc. Scient.] ISSN: 0970-0293. Indian School of Social Sciences*: 424 Vithalbhai Patel House, Rafi Marg, New Delhi 110 001, India; **Subscriptions**: *idem:* 15/15 Sarvapriya Vihar, New Delhi 110 016, India

Social security journal. *[Soc. Sec. J.] ISSN: 0726-1195. Australian Government Publishing Service*: G.P.O. Box 84, Canberra, A.C.T. 2601, Australia

Social service review. *[Soc. Ser. R.] ISSN: 0037- 7961. University of Chicago Press*: 5720 S. Woodlawn, Chicago, IL. 60637, U.S.A.; **Subscriptions**: *University of Chicago Press*: P.O. Box 37005, Chicago IL. 60637, U.S.A.

Social work and social sciences review. *[Soc. Work Soc. Sci. R.] ISSN: 0953-5225. Whiting and Birch*: 90 Dartmouth Road, London SE23 3HZ, U.K.

Social work education. *[Soc. Work. Ed.] ISSN: 0261-5479. Whiting and Birch*: P.O. Box 872, Forest Hill, London SE23 3HZ, U.K.

Socialisme. *[Socialisme] ISSN: 0037-8127. Institut Emile Vandervelde*: 13 boulevard de l'Empereur, Brussels 1000 , Belgium

Socialismo y participación. *[Soc. Part.]; CEDEP (Centro de Estudios para el Desarrollo y la Participación)*: Ediciones Socialismo y Participación, Av. José Faustino Sánchez Carrión 790, Lima 17, Peru

Socialistische standpunten. *[Social. Stand.]; Emile Vandervelde Instituut*: Grasmarkt 105/51, 1000 Brussels, Belgium

Sociétés contemporaines. *[Soc. Contemp.] ISSN: 1150-1944. Institut de Recherche sur les Sociétés Contemporaines (IRESCO), CNRS*: 59/61 rue Pouchet, 75849 Paris Cedex 17, France; **Publisher**: *L'Harmattan*: 16 rue Des Ecoles, 75005 Paris, France

Society. *[Society] ISSN: 0147-2011. Transaction*: Rutgers — The State University, New Brunswick, NJ 08903, U.S.A.

Socio-economic planning sciences. *[Socio. Econ.] ISSN: 0038- 0121. Pergamon Press*: Journals Production Unit, Hennock Road, Marsh Barton, Exeter EX2 8NE, U.K.; **Subscriptions**: *Pergamon Press*: Headington Hill Hall, Oxford OX3 0BW, U.K.

Sociolinguistics. *[Sociolinguistics] ISSN: 0257-7135. International Sociological Association, Research Committee on Socioloinguistics*; **Publisher**: *Foris Publications*: P.O. Box 509, 3300 AM Dordrecht, The Netherlands

Sociologia [Bratislavia]; Sociology. *[Sociologia [Brat.]] ISSN: 0049-1225. Slovak Academy of Sciences, Institute of Sociology*; **Publisher**: *VEDA*: Klemensova 19, 814 30 Bratislava, Czechoslovakia

Sociologia del Lavoro. *[Sociol. Lav.]; Università di Bologna, Centro Internazionale di Documentazione e Studi Sociologico Sui Problemi del Lavoro*: Casella postale 413, 40100 Bologna, Italy; **Publisher**: *Franco Angeli Editore*: Viale Monza 106, 20127 Milan, Italy

Sociologia della comunicazione. *[Sociol. Comun.]; Franco Angeli editore*: Viale Monza 106, 20127 Milan, Italy

Sociologia internationalis. *[Social. Int.] ISSN: 0038-0164. Verlag Duncker & Humblot*: Dietrich-Schäfer- Weg 9, 1000 Berlin 41, Germany

Sociologia [Rome]. *[Sociologia [Rome]] ISSN: 0038-0156. Istituto Luigi Sturzo*: Via delle Coppelle 35, 00186 Rome, Italy

Sociologia ruralis. *[Sociol. Rur.] ISSN: 0038-0199. European Society for Rural Sociology/ Société Européenne de Sociologie Rurale/ Europäischen Gesellschaft für Land- und Agrarsoziologie*: c/o Pavel Uttitz (Secretary Treasurer), Forschungsgesellschaft für Agrarpolitik und Agrarsoziologie e.V., Meckenheimer Allee 125, 5300 Bonn 1, Germany; **Publisher**: *Van Gorcum*: P.O. Box 43, 9400 AA, Assen, The Netherlands

Sociologia urbana e rurale. *[Sociol. Urb. Rur.]; Università di Bologna, Dipartimento di Sociologia, Centro Studi sui problemi della Città e del Territorio (CE.P.CI.T.)*: via Strada Maggiore 45, 40125 Bologna, Italy; **Subscriptions**: *Franco Angeli*: Viale Monza, 126, Milan, Italy

Sociological analysis. *[Sociol. Anal.] ISSN: 0038-0210. Association for the Sociology of Religion*: Marist Hall Room 108, CUA, Washington, DC. 20064, U.S.A.

Sociological methods and research. *[Sociol. Meth.] ISSN: 0049 1241. Sage Publications*: 2455 Teller Road, Newbury Park, CA. 91320, U.S.A.

Sociological perspectives. *[Sociol. Pers.] ISSN: 0731-1214. Pacific Sociological Association*: Department of Sociology, University of Nevada, Las Vegas, Nevada 89154, U.S.A.; **Publisher**: *JAI Press*: 55 Old Post Road, No.2, P.O. Box 1678, Greenwich, CT 06836-1678, U.S.A.

Sociological quarterly. *[Sociol. Q.] ISSN: 0038-0253. J.A.I. Press*: Old Post Road, No.2, P.O. Box 1678, Greenwich, CT. 06836-1678, U.S.A.

Sociological review. *[Sociol. Rev.] ISSN: 0038-0261. University of Keele*: Keele, Staffordshire ST5 5BG, U.K.; **Publisher**: *Routledge*: 11 New Fetter Lane, London EC4P 4EE, U.K.

Sociological theory. *[Sociol. Theory] ISSN: 0735-2751. American Sociological Association*: 1722 N. Street, N.W., Washington DC. 20036, U.S.A.; **Publisher**: *Basil Blackwell*: 3 Cambridge Center, Cambridge, MA. 02142, U.S.A.; **Subscriptions**: *Marston Book Services*: Journals Department, P.O. Box 87, Oxford OX2 0DT, U.K.

Sociologie du travail. *[Sociol. Trav.] ISSN: 0038-0296. Dunod*: 15 rue Gossin, 92543 Montrouge Cedex, France; **Subscriptions**: *CDR — Centrale des revues*: 11 rue Gossin, 92543 Montrouge Cedex, France

Sociologische gids. *[Sociol. Gids] ISSN: 0038-0334. Boom*: Postbus 1058, 7940 KB Meppel, The Netherlands

Sociologus. *[Sociologus] ISSN: 0038-0377. Duncker & Humblot*: Postfach 41 03 29, Dietrich-Schäfer- Weg 9, Berlin 41, Germany

Sociology. *[Sociology] ISSN: 0038-0385. British Sociological Association*: 351 Station Road, Dorridge, Solihull, W. Midlands B93 8EY, U.K.

Sociology and social research. *[Social Soc. Res.] ISSN: 0038- 0393. University of Southern California*: Social Science Building, Rooms 168-169, University Park, Los Angeles, CA. 90089-0032, U.S.A.

Sociology of health and illness. *[Sociol. Health Ill.] ISBN: 0141-9889. Basil Blackwell*: 108 Cowley Road, Oxford OX4 1JF, U.K.; **Subscriptions**: *Marston Book Services*: P.O. Box 87, Oxford OX2 0DT, U.K.

Sociology of the sciences. *[Sociol. Sci.]; Kluwer Academic Publishers*: P.O. Box 17, 3300 AA Dordrecht, The Netherlands

Sojourn. *[Sojourn] ISSN: 0217-9520. Institute of Southeast Asian Studies*: Heng Mui Keng Terrace, Pasir Panjang, Singapore 0511

Социологические исследования (социс); Sotsiologicheskie issledovaniia (sotsis). *[Sot. Issle.] ISSN: 0132-1625. Akademii Nauk SSSR*; **Publisher**: *Izdatel'stvo Nauka*: Profsoiuznaja ul. 90, Moscow, U.S.S.R.

South African geographical journal; Suid-Afrikaanse geografiese tydskrif. *[S.Afr. Geogr. J.]* ISSN: 0373-6245. *South African Geographical Society = Suid-Afrikaanse Geografiese Vereniging*: Department of Geography and Environmental Studies, University of the Witwatersrand, P.O. Wits 2050, South Africa

South African historical journal; Suid-Afrikaanse historiese joernaal. *[S.Afr. Hist. J.]* ISSN: 0258-2473. *South African Historical Society*: Department of History, University of South Africa, P.O. Box 392, Pretoria 0001, South Africa

South African journal of economic history. *[S.Afr. J. Ec. Hist.]*; *Economic History Society of Southern Africa*: Department of History, Rand Afrikaans University, P.O. Box 524, Johannesburg 2000, South Africa

South African journal of economics; Suid-Afrikaanse tydskrif vir ekonomie. *[S. Afr. J. Econ.]* ISSN: 0038 2280. *Economic Society of South Africa*: P.O. Box 929, Pretoria, South Africa

South African journal of ethnology; Suid- Afrikaanse tydskrif vir etnologie. *[S.Afr. J. Ethnol.]*; *Association of Afrikaans Ethnologists = Vereniging van Afrikaanse Volkekundiges*; **Publisher**: *Bureau for Scientific Publications*: P.O. Box 1758, Pretoria 0001, South Africa

South African journal of labour relations. *[S. Afr. J. Labour Relat.]* ISSN: 0379-8410. *University of South Africa, School of Business Leadership*: P.O. Box 392, Pretoria 0001, South Africa

South African journal of sociology; Suid- Afrikaanse tydskrif vir sosiologie. *[S.Afr. J. Sociol.]*; *South African Sociological Association = Suid-Afrikaanse Sosiologievereniging*: School of Business Leadership, University of South Africa, P.O. Box 392, Pretoria 001, South Africa; **Publisher**: *Bureau for Scientific Publications*: P.O. Box 1758, Pretoria 0001, South Africa

South African journal on human rights. *[S. Afr. J. Human Rights]* ISSN: 0258-7203. *Centre for Applied Legal Studies*: University of the Witwatersrand, Wits 2050, South Africa; **Publisher**: *Juta*: P.O. Box 14373, Kenwyn 7790, South Africa

South African labour bulletin. *[S.Afr. Lab. B.]*; *Umanyano Publications*: 700 Medical Arts Building 220 Jeppe St. (cnr. Troye Street), Johannesburg, 2001 South Africa

South African sociological review. *[S.Afr. Sociol. R.]* ISSN: 1015-1370. *Association for Sociology in South Africa*: Department of Sociology, University of Cape Town, 7700 Rondebosch, South Africa

South Asia bulletin. *[S.Asia B.]* ISSN: 0732-3867. *South Asia Bulletin*: c/o Department of History, State University of New York, Albany, NY. 12222, U.S.A.

South Asia research. *[S.Asia R.]* ISSN: 0262-7280. *South Asia Research*: Room 472, School of Oriental and African Studies, Thornhaugh Street, Russell Square, London WC1H 0XG, U.K.

South Asian studies. *[S. Asian Stud.]* ISSN: 0266-6030. *Society for South Asian Studies*: c/o British Academy, 20- 21 Cornwall Terrace, London NW1 4QP, U.K.

Southeast Asian affairs. *[S.E.Asian Aff.]*; *Institute of Southeast Asian Studies*: Heng Mui Keng Terrace, Pasir Panjang, Singapore 0511

Southern economic journal. *[S. Econ. J.]* ISSN: 0038-4038. *Southern Economic Association/ University of North Carolina at Chapel Hill*: CB3540, UNC, Chapel Hill, NC 27599-3540, U.S.A.

Soviet Jewish affairs. *[Sov. Jew. Aff.]* ISSN: 0038-545X. *Institute of Jewish Affairs*: 11 Hertford Street, London W1Y 7DX, U.K.

Soviet studies. *[Sov. Stud.]* ISSN: 0038-5859. *Carfax Publishing*: P.O. Box 25, Abingdon, Oxfordshire OX14 3UE, U.K.

Soziale Welt. *[Soz. Welt.]* ISSN: 0038-6073. *Arbeitsgemeinschaft sozialwissenschaftlicher Institute*: Universität Bamberg, Feldkirchenstraße 21, 8600 Bamberg, Germany; **Publisher**: *Verlag Otto Schwartz*: Annastraße 7, 3400 Göttingen, Germany

INTERNATIONAL BIBLIOGRAPHY OF SOCIOLOGY — 1988

Soziologie. *[Soziologie]* ISSN: 0340- 918X. Deutsche Gesellschaft für Soziologie; **Publisher**: *Ferdinand Enke Verlag*: Postfach 10 12 54, D-7000 Stuttgart 10, Germany

Speaking of Japan. *[Speak. Jpn.]* ISSN: 0389-3510. Keizai Koho Center, Japan Institute for Social and Economic Affairs: 6-1 Otemachi 1-chome, Chiyoda-Ku, Tokyo 100, Japan

Sri Lanka journal of social sciences. *[Sri Lanka J. Soc. Sci.]* ISSN: 0258-9710. *Natural Resources, Energy & Science Authority of Sri Lanka*: 47/5 Maitland Place, Colombo 7, Sri Lanka

Sri Lanka journal of the humanities. *[Sri Lanka J. Human.]; University of Peradeniya*: Peradeniya, Sri Lanka

Staat und recht. *[Sta. Recht]* ISSN: 0038-8858. Märkische Verlag- und Druck-Gesellschaft: Friedrich-Engels- Straße 24, Postfach Postdam 1561, Germany

Statistician. *[Statistician]* ISSN: 0039-0526. Institute of Statisticians; **Publisher**: *Carfax Publishing Company*: P.O. Box 25, Abingdon, Oxfordshire OX14 3UE, U.K.

Stato e mercato. *[Sta. Mer.]; Società Editrice il Mulino*: Strada Maggiore 37, 40125 Bologna, Italy

Storia contemporanea. *[Stor. Contemp.]* ISSN: 0039-1875. *Società editrice il Mulino*: Strada Maggiore 37, Bologna, Italy

Studi storici. *[St. Stor.]* ISSN: 0039-3037. Istituto Gramsci; **Publisher**: *Editori Riuniti Riviste*: via Serchio 9, 00198 Rome, Italy

Studia demograficzne. *[Stud. Demogr.]* ISSN: 0039-3134. Polska Akademia Nauk, Komitet Nauk Demograficznych; **Publisher**: *Panstwowe Wydawnictwo Naukowe*: Miodowa 10, 00-251 Warsaw, Poland

Studies in comparative international development. *[Stud. Comp. ID.]* ISSN: 0039-3606. *Transaction Periodicals Consortium*: Dept. 4010, Rutgers University, New Brunswick, NJ. 08903, U.S.A.; **Subscriptions**: *Swets-Zeitlinger Publishing Services*: Heereweg 347, 2161 CA Lisse, The Netherlands

Studies in family planning. *[Stud. Fam. Pl.]* ISSN: 0039-3665. *Population Council*: One Dag Hammarskjold Plaza, New York, NY. 10017, U.S.A.

Studies in history. *[Stud. Hist.]* ISSN: 0257-6430. *Sage Publications India*: 32 M-Block Market, Greater Kailash I, New Delhi 110 048, India; **Subscriptions**: *idem*: 6, Bonhill Street, London EC2A 4PU, U.K.

Studies in history and philosophy of science. *[Stud. Hist. Phil. Sci.]* ISSN: 0039-3681. *Pergamon Press*: Headington Hill Hall, Oxford OX3 0BW, U.K.

Studies in law, politics, and society. *[Stud. Law. Pol. Soc.]; JAI Press*: 118 Pentonville Road, London N1 9JN, U.K.

Studies in political economy. *[Stud. Pol. Ec.]* ISSN: 0707-8552. *Studies in Political Economy*: P.O. Box 4729, Station E, Ottowa, Ontario, Canada K1S 5H9

Studies in Third World societies. *[St. Third Wor. Soc.]; College of William and Mary, Department of Anthropology*: Williamsburg, VA. 23185, U.S.A.

Survey of Jewish affairs. *[Sur. Jew. Aff.]* ISSN: 0741-6571. Institute of Jewish Affairs; **Publisher**: *Basil Blackwell*: 108 Cowley Road, Oxford OX4 1JF, U.K.

Tafsut. *[Tafsut]; Mouvement Culturel Berbère*; **Publisher**: *Université de Provence*: 13 621 Aix-en-Provence Cedex, France

Tareas. *[Tareas]* ISSN: 0494-7061. *Centro de Estudios Latineamericanos "Justo Arosemena"*: Apartado 6-3093, El Dorado Panamá, Panama City, Panama

Te reo. *[Te reo]* ISSN: 0494-8440. *Linguistic Society of New Zealand*: c/o University of Auckland, Private Bag, Auckland, New Zealand

INTERNATIONAL BIBLIOGRAPHY OF SOCIOLOGY — 1988

Technology and culture. *[Technol. Cul.] ISSN: 0040-165X. Society for the History of Technology*; **Publisher**: *University of Chicago Press*: 5720 South Woodlawn Avenue, Chicago, IL. 60637, U.S.A.

Technology and development. *[Tech. Devel.]; Institute for International Cooperation/ Japan International Cooperation Agency*: International Cooperation Center Building, 10-5 Ichigaya-Honmura-cho, Shinjuku-ku, Tokyo 162, Japan

Telos. *[Telos] ISSN: 0090-6514. Telos Press*: 431 E. 12th Street, New York, NY. 10009, U.S.A.

Temps modernes. *[Temps Mod.] ISSN: 0040-3075. Gallimard/ Les Temps Modernes*: 4, rue Férou, Paris 6e, France; **Subscriptions**: *B.S.I.*: 49, rue de la Vanne, 92120 Montrouge, France

Terrain. *[Terrain] ISSN: 0760-5668. Ministère de la Culture et de la Communication, Mission du Patrimoine ethnologique*: 65 rue de Richelieu, 75002 Paris, France

Terrorism. *[Terrorism] ISSN: 0149-0389. State University of New York, Institute for Studies in International Terrorism/ George Washington University, Elliot School of International Affairs*; **Publisher**: *Taylor & Francis*: 4 John Street, London WC1N 2ET, U.K.; **Subscriptions**: *idem*: Rankine Road, Basingstoke, Hampshire RG24 0PR, U.K.

Text. *[Text] ISSN: 0165-4888. Walter de Gruyter*: Postfach 110240, D-1000 Berlin 11, Germany

Theory and decision. *[Theory Decis.] ISSN: 0040-5833. Kluwer Academic Publishers*: P.O. Box 17, 3300 AA Dordrecht, The Netherlands; **Subscriptions**: *idem*: P.O. Box 322, 3300 AA Dordrecht, The Netherlands

Theory and society. *[Theory Soc.] ISSN: 0304-2421. Kluwer Academic Publishers*: Spuiboulevard 50, P.O. Box 17, 3300 AA Dordrecht, The Netherlands

Theory culture and society. *[Theory Cult. Soc.] ISSN: 0263-2764. Sage Publications*: 6 Bonhill Street, London EC2A 4PU, U.K.

Third World planning review. *[Third Wor. P.] ISSN: 0142-7849. Liverpool University Press*: P.O. Box 147, Liverpool L69 3BX, U.K.

Tidsskriftet antropologi. *[Tids. Antrop.] ISSN: 0109-1012. Stofskifte*: Frederiksholms Kanal 4, 1220 Copenhagen, Denmark

Tijdschrift voor economische en sociale geografie; Journal of economic and social geography. *[J. Econ. Soc. Geogr.] ISSN: 0040- 747X. Royal Dutch Geographical Society = Koninklijk Nederlands Aardrijkskundig Genootschap*: Weteringschans 12, 1017 SG Amsterdam, The Netherlands

Tijdschrift voor sociale geschiedenis. *[Tijd. Soc. Gesch.] ISSN: 0303-9935. Nederlandse Vereniging tot beoefening van de Sociale Geschiedenis*: c/o R. de Peuter, Instituut voor Geschiedenis, Lucas Bolwerk 5, 3512 EG Utrecht, The Netherlands

Town planning review. *[Town Plan. R.] ISSN: 0041-0020. University of Liverpool, Department of Civic Design (Town and Regional Planning)*; **Publisher**: *Liverpool University Press*: P.O. Box 147, Liverpool L69 3BX, U.K.

TRACE. *[TRACE] ISSN: 0185-6286. Centre d'Études Mexicaines et Centraméricaines*: Sierra Leona 330, 11000 Mexico D.F., Mexico

Transactions of the Institute of British Geographers.:*New series [Trans. Inst. Br. Geogr.]; Institute of British Geographers*: 1 Kensington Gore, London SW7 2AR, U.K.

Transactions of the Philological Society. *[Trans. Philolog. Soc.] ISSN: 0079-1636. Basil Blackwell*: 108 Cowley Road, Oxford OX4 1JF, U.K.

Transformation. *[Transformation] ISSN: 0258- 7696. Transformation*: Economic History Department, University of Natal, King George V Avenue, 4001 Durban, South Africa

Transition. *[Transition] ISSN: 1012-8263. University of Guyana, Faculty of Social Sciences and Institute of Development Studies*: P.O. Box 10110, Turkeyen, Georgetown, Guyana

INTERNATIONAL BIBLIOGRAPHY OF SOCIOLOGY — 1988

Travail et emploi. *[Trav. Emp.] ISSN: 0224-4365. Ministère du Travail, de l'Emploi et de la Formation Professionnelle, Service des études et de la statistique*: Bureau 3205A, 1 place de Fontenoy, 75700 Paris, France; **Publisher**: *Documentation Fraçaise*: 29-31 quai Voltiare, 75340 Paris Cedex 07, France

Tribus. *[Tribus] ISSN: 0082-6413. Linden- Museum Stuttgart*: Linden-Museum Stuttgart/ Staatliches Museum für Völkerkunde, Hegelplatz 1 D-7000 Stuttgart 1, Germany

Tricontinental. *[Tricontinental] ISSN: 0864-1595. Executive Secretariat of the Organization of Solidarity of the Peoples of Africa, Asia and Latin America (OSPAAAL)*: Apartado Postale 4224 y 6130, Calle C No. 668 e/27 y 29 Vedado, Havana, Cuba

Tuttogiovani notizie. *[Tutt. Not.]; Osservatorio della Gioventu*: Facoltà di Scienze dell'Educazione dell'Università, Pontificia Salesiano, Rome, Italy; **Publisher**: *Editrice LAS*: Piazza dell'Ateneo Salesiano 1, 00139 Rome, Italy

Ufahamu. *[Ufahamu] ISSN: 0041-5715. African Activist Association*: James S. Coleman African Studies Centre, University of California, Los Angeles, CA. 90024-1130, U.S.A.

Unasylva. *[Unasylva] ISSN: 0041-6436. United Nations, Food and Agriculture Organization*: FAO, Via delle Terme di Caracalla, 00100 Rome, Italy

Unisa Latin American report. *[Unisa Lat.Am. Rep.] ISSN: 0256-6060. Unisa Centre for Latin American Studies*; **Publisher**: *University of South Africa*: P.O. Box 392, 0001 Pretoria, South Africa

Uniswa research journal. *[Uniswa Res. J.]; University of Swaziland*: P/ Bag, Kwaluseni, Swaziland

Universitas. *[Universitas] ISSN: 0049-5530. University of Ghana*: Department of English, P.O. Box 25, Legon, Ghana

Uomo. *[Uomo]; Università di Roma «La Sapienza», Dipartimento di Studi Glottoantropologici*: P.le Aldo Moro 5, 00185 Roma, Italy

Urban affairs annual reviews. *[Urb. Aff. Ann. R.] ISSN: 0083-4688. Sage Publications*: 2455 Teller Road, Newbury Park, CA. 91320, U.S.A.

Urban affairs quarterly. *[Urban Aff. Q.] ISSN: 0042-0816. Sage Publications*: 2455 Teller Road, Newbury Park, CA. 91320, U.S.A.

Urban anthropology. *[Urban Anthro.] ISSN: 0894-6019. The Institute*: 56 Centennial Avenue, Brockport, NY. 14420, U.S.A.

Urban forum. *[Urban For.] ISSN: 1015-3802. Witwatersrand University Press*: P.O. Wits, Johannesburg 2050, South Africa

Urban geography. *[Urban Geogr.] ISSN: 0272-3638. V.H. Winston & Son*: 7961 Eastern Avenue, Silver Spring, MD. 20910, U.S.A.

Urban law and policy. *[Urban Law P.] ISSN: 0165-0068. Elsevier Science Publishers (North-Holland)*: Journals Division, P.O. Box 211, 1000 AE Amsterdam, The Netherlands

Urban studies. *[Urban Stud.] ISSN: 0042 0980. University of Glasgow, Centre for Urban and Regional Research*: Adam Smith Building, University of Glasgow, Glasgow G12 8RT, U.K.; **Publisher**: *Carfax Publishing Company*: P.O.Box 25, Abingdon, Oxfordshire OX14 3UE, U.K.

Utafiti. *[Utafiti] ISSN: 0856-096X. University of Dar es Salaam, Faculty of Arts and Social Sciences*: P.O. Box 35151, Dar es Salaam, Tanzania

Verfassung und Recht in Übersee; Law and politics in Africa, Asia and Latin America. *[Verf. Rec. Über.] ISSN: 0506-7286. Hamburger Gesellschaft für Völkerrecht und Auswärtige Politik*: Rothenbaumchaussee 21-23, D-2000 Hamburg 13, Germany; **Publisher**: *Nomos Verlagsgesellschaft*: Postfach 610, D-7570 Baden-Baden, Germany

Вестник ленинградского университета ; Vestnik Leningradskogo universiteta.:серия 6 история кпсс, научный коммунизм, философия право = seriia 6, istoriia KPSS nauchnyi kommunizm filosofiia pravo *[Vest. Lenin. Univ. 6] ISSN: 0132- 4624; ISSN: 0233-7541. Izdatel'stvo Leningradskogo Universiteta*: Universiteta Nab. 7/9, 199034 Leningrad, U.S.S.R.

INTERNATIONAL BIBLIOGRAPHY OF SOCIOLOGY — 1988

ВЕСЦІ Акадэміі Навук БССР; Vestsi akademii navuk BSSR.:Сурыя грамадскіх навук; Seryia gramadskikh navuk *[V. Aka. BSSR] ISSN: 0321-1649. Akademii Navuk, BSSR*; **Publisher**: *Navuka i Tekhnika*: Zhodzinskaia 18, 220600 Minsk, Belorussia, U.S.S.R.

Vierteljahrshefte zur Wirtschaftsforschung. *[Vier. Wirt.schung] ISSN: 0340-1707. Deutsches Institut für Wirtschaftsforschung*: Königin-Luise-Straße 5, D- 1000 Berlin 33, Germany; **Publisher**: *Duncker & Humblot*: Dietrich- Schäfer-Weg 9, D-1000 Berlin 41, Germany

Viitorul social. *[Viit. Soc.]; Editura Academiei Române*: Calea Victoriei 125, 79717 Bucharest, Romania; **Subscriptions**: *Rompresfilatelia*: P.O. Box 12-201, Calea Grivitei 64- 66, 78104 Bucharest, Romania

Volonta. *[Volonta] ISSN: 0392-5013. Editrice A*: via Rovetta 27, 20127 Milan, Italy

Вопросы философии; Voprosy filosofii. *[Vop. Filo.] ISSN: 0042-8744. Akademiia Nauk SSR, Institut filosofii*; **Publisher**: *Izdatel'stvo Pravda*: Ul. Pravdy 24, 125047 Moscow, U.S.S.R.

Вопросы истории; Voprosy istorii. *[Vop. Ist.] ISSN: 0042-8779. Izdatel'stvo Pravda*: Ul. Pravdy 24, 125865 Moscow, U.S.S.R.

Вопросы истории КПСС; Voprosy istorii KPSS. *[Vop. Ist. KPSS] ISSN: 0320-8907. Izdatel'stvo Pravda*: Ul. Pravdy 24, 125865 Moscow, U.S.S.R.

Вопросы научного атеизма; Voprosy nauchnogo ateizma. *[Vop. Nau. At.] ISSN: 0321-0847. Akademiia Obshchestvennych Nauk, Institut Nauchnogo Ateizma*; **Publisher**: *Izdatel'stvo Mysl*: Leninsky Prospekt 15, Moscow V-17, U.S.S.R.

Weltwirtschaftliches Archiv. *[Welt.liches Arc.] ISSN: 0043-2636. Institut für Weltwirtschaft*: Düsternbrooker Weg 120, D-2300 Kiel, Germany; **Publisher**: *J.C.B. Mohr (Paul Siebeck)*: Wilhelmstraße 18 Postfach 2040, D-7400 Tübingen, Germany

West European politics. *[W. Eur. Pol.] ISSN: 0140-2382. Frank Cass*: Gainsborough House, 11 Gainsborough Road, London E11 1RS, U.K.

Western political quarterly. *[West. Pol. Q.] ISSN: 0043-4078. Western Political Science Association/ Pacific Northwest Political Science Association/ Southern California Political Science Association/ Northern California Political Science Association*; **Publisher**: *University of Utah*: Salt Lake City, UT. 84112, U.S.A.

Wirtschaftswissenschaft. *[Wirt.wissensch.] ISSN: 0043-633X. Verlag die Wirtschaft*: Am Friedrichchain 22, Berlin 1055, Germany

Wisconsin law review. *[Wiscon. Law R.] ISSN: 0043-650X. University of Wisconsin, Law School*: 975 Bascom Mall, Madison, WI. 53706-1399, U.S.A.

Wissenschaftliche Zeitschrift der Humboldt-Universität zu Berlin.:*Reihe Gesellschaftswissenschaften* *[Wissensch. Z. Humboldt-Univ.] ISSN: 0863-0623. Humboldt-Universität*: Mittelstraße 7/8, 1086 Berlin, Germany

Without prejudice. *[With. Prej.] ISSN: 1035-4220. Australian Institute of Jewish Affairs*: GPO Box 5402CC, Melbourne, Victoria 3001, Australia

Women's studies international forum. *[Wom. St. Inter. For.] ISSN: 0277-5395. Pergamon Press*: Fairview Park, Elmsford, NY. 10523, U.S.A.

Work and occupations. *[Work Occup.] ISSN: 0730-8884. Sage Publications*: 2455 Teller Road, Newbury Park CA. 91320, U.S.A.; **Subscriptions**: *Sage Publications*: 6 Bonhill Street, London EC2A 4PU, U.K.

Work, employment and society. *[Work Emp. Soc.] ISSN: 0950-0170. British Sociological Association*: 10 Portugal Street, London WC2A 2HU, U.K.; **Subscriptions**: *Business Manager*: Work, Employment and Society, 351 Station Road, Dorridge, Solihull, West Midlands B93 8EY, U.K.

Working papers in linguistics. *[Work. Pap. Ling.]; Ohio State University*: 204 Cunz Hall, 1841 Millikin Road, Columbus, OH. 43210-1229, U.S.A.

World Bank economic review. *[W.B. Econ. R.] ISSN: 0258-6770. International Bank for Reconstruction and Development*: World Bank, Washington, DC. 20433, U.S.A.; **Subscriptions**: *World Bank Publications*: Box 7247-8619, Philadelphia, PA. 19170-8619, U.S.A.

World development. *[World Dev.] ISSN: 0305-750X. Pergamon Press*: Headington Hill Hall, Oxford OX3 0BW, U.K.

World politics. *[World Polit.] ISSN: 0043-8871. Princeton University, Center of International Studies*: Bendheim Hall, Princeton, NJ. 08544, U.S.A.; **Publisher**: *Johns Hopkins University Press*: Journals Publishing Division, 701 W 40th Street, Suite 275, Baltimore, MD. 21211-2190, U.S.A.

World review. *[World Rev.]; Australian Institute of International Affairs*: P.O. Box 279, Indooroopilly, Queensland, 4068 Australia

World today. *[World Today] ISSN: 0043-9134. Royal Institute of International Affairs*: 10 St. James's Square, London SW1Y 4LE, U.K.

Wuqûf. *[Wuqûf] ISSN: 0930-9306. Hanspeter Mattes Verlag/ edition Wuqûf*: Postfach 13 22 42, 2000 Hamburg 13, Germany

XXI Secolo. *[XXI Secolo]; Fondazione Giovanni Agnelli*: via Giacosa 38, 10125 Turin, Italy

Yagl-Ambu. *[Yagl-Ambu] ISSN: 0254-0681. University of Papua New Guinea*: Box 320, University Post Office, Papua New Guinea

York papers in linguistics. *[York Pap. Ling.] ISSN: 0307-3238. University of York, Department of Language and Linguistic Science*: Heslington, York YO1 5DD, U.K.

Zaïre-Afrique. *[Za-Afr.] ISSN: 0049-8513. Centre d'Études pour l'Action Sociale (CEPAS)*: B.P. 3375 Kinshasa/ Gombe, Avenue Père Boka no.9, Zaire

Zambezia. *[Zambezia] ISSN: 0379-0622. University of Zimbabwe*: Publications Office, P.O. Box MP 45, Mount Pleasant, Harare, Zimbabwe

Zambia journal of history. *[Zamb. J. Hist.]; University of Zambia, Department of History*: P.O. Box 32379, Lusaka, Zambia

Zeitschrift für ausländisches öffentliches Recht und Völkerrecht. *[Z. Aus. Recht. Völk] ISSN: 0044-2348. Verlag W. Kohlhammer*: P.B. 800430, D-7000 Stuttgart 80, Germany

Zeitschrift für Missionswissenschaft und Religionswissenschaft. *[Z. Mission. Religion.] ISSN: 0044-3123. Internationales Institut für missionswissenschaftliche Forschungen*: Albertus-Magnus-Staße 39, 5300 Bonn 2, Germany; **Publisher**: *Aschendorffsche Verlagsbuchhandlung*: Postfach 1124, 4400 Münster, Germany

Zeitschrift für Politik. *[Z. Polit.] ISSN: 0044- 3360. Hochschule für Politik München*: Ludwigstraße 8, 8000 Munchen, Germany; **Publisher**: *Carl Heymanns Verlag*: Luxemburger Straße 449, 5000 Cologne 41, Germany

Zeitschrift für Sexualforschung. *[Z. Sexual.] ISSN: 0932-8114. Ferdinand Enke Verlag*: Postfach 10 12 54, D-7000 Stuttgart 10, Germany

Zeitschrift für Soziologie. *[Z. Soziol.] ISSN: 0340-1804. Ferdinand Enke Verlag*: Postfach 10 12 54, D-7000 Stuttgart 10, Germany

Zeitschrift für Unternehmensgeschichte. *[Z. Unter.gesch.] ISSN: 0342-2852. Gesellschaft für Unternehmensgeschichte*: Bonner Straße 211, 9. Etage, D-5000 Cologne 51, Germany; **Publisher**: *Franz Steiner Verlag*: Birkenwaldstraße 44, Postfach 10 15 26, D-7000 Stuttgart 1, Germany

Zeitschrift für Verkehrswissenschaft. *[Z. Verkehr.] ISSN: 0044-3670. Verkehrs-Verlag J. Fischer*: Paulusstraße 1, 4000 Düsseldorf 1, Germany

INTERNATIONAL BIBLIOGRAPHY OF SOCIOLOGY — 1988

Zeitschrift für Wirtschafts- und Sozialwissenschaften. *[Z. Wirt. Soz.] ISSN: 0342-1783. Gesellschaft für Wirtschafts- und Sozialwissenschafen — Verein für Sozialpolitik;* **Publisher**: *Duncker and Humblot*: Dietrich-Schäfer-Weg 9, 1000 Berlin 41, Germany

Zeitschrift für Wirtschaftspolitik. *[Z. Wirt.pol.] ISSN: 0721-3808. Universität zu Köln, Institut für Wirtschaftspolitik*: Postfach 41 05 29, Lindenburger Allee 32, 5000 Cologne 41, Germany

LIST OF ABBREVIATIONS USED
LISTE DES ABBREVIATIONS UTILISÉS

A.J.S. — American journal of sociology. — Chicago, IL.: *University of Chicago Press*
Acta Pol. — Acta politica. — Meppel: *Boom*
Acta Sociol. — Acta sociologica. — Oslo: *Scandinavian Sociological Association*
Acta Univ. Łódz. — Acta Universtatis Łódziensis.: *Folia oeconomica* — Łódz: *Wydawnictwo Uniwersytetu Łódzkiego*
Admin. Soc. — Administration and society. — Newbury Park, CA.: *Sage Publications*
Aff. Soc. Int. — Affari sociali internazionali. — Milan: *Franco Angeli Editore*
Afr. Cont. — Afrique contemporaine. — Paris: *Documentation Française*
Afr. Q. — Africa quarterly. — New Delhi: *Indian Council for Cultural Relations*
Afr. Stud. R. — African studies review. — Atlanta, GA.: *African Studies Association*
Afr. Tod. — Africa today. — Denver, CO.: *Africa Today Associates*
Afr. Urb. Q. — African urban quarterly. — Nairobi: *African Urban Quarterly*
Africa — Africa. — Manchester: *International African Institute*
Age. Soc. — Ageing and society. — Cambridge: *Centre for Policy on Ageing/ British Society of Gerontology*
Am. Anthrop. — American anthropologist. — Washington, DC.: *American Anthropological Association*
Am. Econ. Rev. — American economic review. — Nashville, TN: *American Economic Association*
Am. J. Pol. Sc. — American journal of political science. — Austin, TX: *Midwest Political Science Association*
Am. Phil. Q. — American philosophical quarterly. — Bowling Green, OH.: *Philosophy Documentation Center*
Am. Poli. Sci. — American political science review. — Washington, DC.: *American Political Science Association*
Am. Psychol. — American psychologist. — Arlington, VA: *American Psychological Association*
Am. Sociol. R. — American sociological review. — Washington, D.C.: *American Sociological Association*
Anal. Est. Econ. Empres. — Anales de estudios económicos y empresariales. — Valladolid: *Universidad de Valladolid, Facultad de Ciencias Económicas y Empresariales*
Ann. Afr. Nord — Annuaire de l'afrique du nord. — Paris: *Editions du Centre National de la Recherche Scientifique*
Ann. Am. Poli. — Annals of the American Academy of Political and Social Science. — Newbury Park, CA.: *American Academy of Political and Social Science*
Ann. R. Psych. — Annual review of psychology. — Palo Alto, CA.: *Annual Reviews*
Ann. R. Soc. — Annual review of sociology. — Palo Alto, CA.: *Annual Reviews*
Ann. Reg. Sci. — Annals of regional science. — Berlin: *Western Regional Sciençe Association*
Annales — Annales.: *Economies, sociétés, civilisations* — Paris: *C.N.R.S./ Ecole des Hautes Etudes en Sciences Sociales*
Antipode — Antipode. — Oxford: *Basil Blackwell*

INTERNATIONAL BIBLIOGRAPHY OF SOCIOLOGY — 1988

Appl. Econ. — Applied economics. — London: *Chapman and Hall*
Arc. Kommunal. — Archiv für Kommunalwissenschaften. — Stuttgart: *Deutsches Institut für Urbanistik*
Area — Area. — London: *Institute of British Geographers*
Asian Sur. — Asian survey. — Berkeley, CA: *University of California Press*
Aust. Cult. Hist. — Australian cultural history. — Kensington, NSW: *University of New South Wales, School of History*
Aust. Geogr. — Australian geographer. — Gladesville, NSW: *Geographical Society of New South Wales*
Aust. J. Pol. Sci — Australian journal of political science. — Canberra: *Australasian Political Studies Association*
Aust. J. Soc. Iss. — Australian journal of social issues. — Sydney: *Australian Council of Social Services*
Aust. N.Z. J. Soc. — Australian and New Zealand journal of sociology. — Bundoora: *Australian Sociological Association*
Aust. Q. — Australian quarterly. — Balmain: *Australian Institute of Political Science*
Aust. Stud. — Australian studies. — Stirling: *British Australian Studies Association*
AWR B. — AWR bulletin. — Vienna: *Association for the Study of the World Refugee Problem*
B. Concern. Asia. Schol. — Bulletin of concerned Asian scholars. — Boulder, CO.: *Bulletin of Concerned Asian Scholars*
B. E.Carib. Aff. — Bulletin of Eastern Caribbean affairs. — Cave Hill: *Institute of Social and Economic Research (Eastern Caribbean)*
Bang. Dev. Stud. — Bangladesh development studies. — Dhaka: *Bangladesh Unnayan Gobeshona Protishthan = Bangladesh Institute of Development Studies*
Bang. J. Pub. Admin. — Bangladesh journal of public administration. — Dhaka: *Bangladesh Public Administration Training Centre*
Behav. Sci. — Behavioral science. — Baltimore, MD: *International Society for Systems Sciences/ Institute of Management Sciences*
Berkeley J. Soc. — Berkeley journal of sociology. — Berkeley, CA.: *Berkeley Journal of Sociology*
Bol. Inf. Bibl. Soc. — Boletim informativo e bibliográfico de ciências sociais. — Rio de Janeiro: *Associação Nacional de Pós-Graduação e Pesquisa em Ciências Sociais*
Br. J. Addict. — British journal of addiction. — Abingdon: *Society for the Study of Addiction to Alcohol and Other Drugs*
Br. J. Crimin. — British journal of criminology. — London: *Institute for the Study and Treatment of Delinquency*
Br. J. Ind. R. — British journal of industrial relations. — Oxford: *London School of Economics*
Br. J. Psy. — British journal of psychology. — Leicester: *British Psychological Society*
Br. J. Soc. — British journal of sociology. — London: *London School of Economics and Political Science*
Br. J. Soc. P. — British journal of social psychology. — Leicester: *British Psychological Society*
Br. J. Soc. W. — British journal of social work. — Oxford: *British Association of Social Workers*
Cah. Amer. Lat. — Cahiers des Amériques latines. — Paris: *Université de la Sorbonne Nouvelle (Paris III), Institut des Hautes Etudes de l'Amérique Latine*
Cah. Int. Soc. — Cahiers internationaux de sociologie. — Paris: *Presses Universitaires de France*
Calif. Manag. R. — California management review. — Berkeley, CA.: *University of California, Walter A. Haas School of Business*

INTERNATIONAL BIBLIOGRAPHY OF SOCIOLOGY — 1988

Can R. Stud. N. — Canadian review of studies in nationalism; Revue canadienne des études sur le nationalisme. — Charlottetown: *CRSN/RCEN*
Can. J. Afr. St. — Canadian journal of African studies; Revue canadienne des études africaines. — Ottawa: *Canadian Association of African Studies = Association Canadienne des Etudes Africaines*
Can. J. Phil. — Canadian journal of philosophy. — Calgary: *University of Calgary Press*
Can. J. Pol. Soc. Theo. — Canadian journal of political and social theory. — Montreal: *A. and M. Kroker*
Can. J. Poli. — Canadian journal of political science; Revue canadienne de science politique. — Ottawa: *Canadian Political Science Association = Association canadienne de science politique/ Société québécoise de science politique*
Can. J. Soc. — Canadian journal of sociology; Cahiers canadiens de sociologie. — Edmonton: *University of Alberta, Department of Sociology*
Can. R. Soc. A. — Canadian review of sociology and anthropology; Revue canadienne de sociologie et d'anthropologie. — Montreal: *Canadian Sociology and Anthropology Association*
Can. R. Stat. — Canadian journal of statistics; Revue canadienne de statistiques. — Ottawa: *Statistical Society of Canada = Société Statistique du Canada*
Carib. Stud. — Caribbean studies; Estudios del Caribe; Etudes des Caraïbes. — Puerto Rico: *Universidad de Puerto Rico, Facultad de Ciencias Sociales, Instituto de Estudios del Caribe*
Child. Devel. — Child development. — Chicago, IL.: *Society for Research in Child Development*
Ciên. Soc. Hoje. — Ciências sociais hoje. — São Paulo: *Associção Nacional de Pós-Graduação e Pesquisa em Cięncias Sociais*
Cities — Cities. — London: *Butterworth-Heinemann*
Civilisations — Civilisations. — Brussels: *Université Libre de Bruxelles, Institut de Sociologie*
Comp. Poli. S. — Comparative political studies. — Newbury Park, CA.: *Sage Publications*
Comp. Polit. — Comparative politics. — New York, NY.: *City University of New York*
Comp. Stud. S. — Comparative studies in society and history. — New York, NY.: *Society for the Comparative Study of Society and History*
Confl. Resolut. — Journal of conflict resolution. — Newbury Park, CA.: *Peace Science Society (International)*
Contin. Change — Continuity and change. — Cambridge: *Cambridge University Press*
Contr. I. Soc. — Contributions to Indian sociology. — New Delhi: *Institute of Economic Growth*
Corr. Reform — Corruption and reform. — Dordrecht: *Martinus Nijhoff Publishers*
Cr. Law Soc. Chan. — Crime, law and social change. — Dordrecht: *Kluwer Academic Publishers*
Crime Delin. — Crime and delinquency. — Newbury Park, CA.: *Sage Publications*
Crime Just. — Crime and justice. — Chicago, IL.: *University of Chicago Press*
Crit. Marx. — Critica marxista. — Rome: *Editori Riuniti Riviste*
Curr. Hist. — Current history. — Philadelphia, PA.: *Current History*
Curr. Sociol. — Current sociology. — London: *International Sociological Association*
Dædalus — Dædalus. — Cambridge, MA.: *American Academy of Arts and Sciences*
Demografie — Demografie. — Prague: *Federální Statistický Uřad*
Dirasat Ser. A. — Dirasat.: *Series A — the humanities* — Amman: *Deanship of Academic Research*
Dissent — Dissent. — New York, NY.: *Foundation for the Study of Independent Social Ideas*
Documents — Documents. — Paris: *Documents*
E & S — E & S.: *Economie et statistique* — Paris: *Institut National de la Statistique et des Études Economiques*

INTERNATIONAL BIBLIOGRAPHY OF SOCIOLOGY — 1988

E.Afr. Soc. Sci. Res. R. — Eastern Africa social science research review. — Addis Ababa: *Organization for Social Science Research in Eastern Africa - OSSREA*
Ec. Sociét. — Economies et sociétés. — Grenoble: *I.S.M.E.A.*
Econ. Affr. — Economic affairs [London]. — London: *Institute of Economic Affairs*
Econ. Cen.E. — Economie du centre-est. — Dijon: *Institut d'Economie Régionale Bourgogne-Franche-Comte*
Econ. Dev. Cult. Change — Economic development and cultural change. — Chicago, IL.: *University of Chicago Press*
Econ. Geogr. — Economic geography. — Worcester, MA.: *Clark University*
Econ. Ind. Dem. — Economic and industrial democracy. — London: *Arbetslivscentrum (The Swedish Center for Working Life)*
Econ. Inq. — Economic inquiry. — Huntington Beach, CA.: *Western Economic Association International*
Econ. Papers [Warsaw] — Economic papers [Warsaw]. — Warsaw: *Central School of Planning and Statistics in Warsaw, Research Institute for Developing Countries*
Econ. Rev. Bank Israel — Economic review. Bank of Israel. — Jerusalem: *Bank of Israel, Research Department*
Economia — Economia. — Quito: *Universidad Central del Ecuador, Instituto de Investigaciones Economicas*
Economist [Leiden] — Economist [Leiden]. — Leiden: *Royal Netherlands Economic Association*
Educ. Urban. Soc. — Education and urban society. — Newbury Park, CA.: *Sage Publications*
Envir. Behav. — Environment and behavior. — Newbury Park, CA.: *Environmental Design Research Association*
Envir. Plan. D — Environment and planning D.: *Society and space* — London: *Pion*
Envir. Plan.A. — Environment and planning A.: *International journal of urban and regional research* — London: *Pion*
Espace Géogr. — Espace géographique. — Paris: *Doin Editeurs*
Esprit — Esprit. — Paris: *Esprit*
Est. Sociol. — Estudios sociológicos. — Pedregal de Santa Teresa: *Colegio de México*
Ethics — Ethics. — Chicago, IL.: *University of Chicago Press*
Ethn. Racial — Ethnic and racial studies. — London: *Routledge*
Etud. Can. — Etudes canadiennes; Canadian studies. — Talence: *Association Française d'Etudes Canadiennes*
Eur. J. Pol. R. — European journal of political research. — Dordrecht: *European Consortium for Political Research*
Eur. J. Pop. — European journal of population; Revue européenne de démographie. — Amsterdam: *Elsevier Science Publishers (North Holland)*
Eur. J. Soc. — Archives européennes de sociologie; European journal of sociology; Europäisches Archiv für Soziologie. — Cambridge: *Cambridge University Press*
Eur. J. Soc. Psychol. — European journal of social psychology. — Chichester: *European Association of Experimental Social Psychology*
Eur. Sociol. R. — European sociological review. — Oxford: *Oxford University Press*
Eure — Eure.: *Revista latinoamericana de estudios urbanos regionales* — Santiago: *Pontificia Universidad Catolica de Chile, Facultad de Arquitectura y Bellas Artes, Instituto de Estudios Urbanos*
Eval. Rev. — Evaluation review. — Newbury Park, CA.: *Sage Publications*
Fam. Soc. — Families in society. — Milwaukee, WI.: *Family Service America*

Feminist R. — Feminist review. — London: *Feminist Review*
Form. Emp. — Formation emploi. — Paris: *Documentation Française*
Genus — Genus. — Rome: *Comitato Italiano per lo Studio dei Problemi della Popolazione*
Geoforum — Geoforum. — Oxford: *Pergamon Press*
Geog.ann. B. — Geografiska annaler.: *Series B* — *Human geography* — Uppsala: *Svenska Sällskapet för Antropologi och Geografi = Swedish Society for Anthropology and Geography*
Geogr. Anal. — Geographical analysis. — Columbus, OH.: *Ohio State University Press*
Geogr. J. — Geographical journal. — London: *Royal Geographical Society*
Geogr. Pol. — Geographia polonica. — Warsaw: *Polish Academy of Sciences, Institute of Geography and Spatial Organization*
Geogr. Rev. — Geographical review. — New York, N.Y.: *American Geographical Society*
God. Vis. F. S. Inst. Tsenov - Svi. — Годишник на Висшия Финансово- Стопански Институт „Д. А. Ценов" - Свищов; Godishnik na visshiia finansovo- stopanski institut "D. A. Tsenov" - Svishtov. — Varna: *Knigoizdatelstvo Georgi Bakalov*
Govt. Oppos. — Government and opposition. — London: *Government and Opposition*
Hac. Públ. Esp. — Hacienda pública española. — Madrid: *Instituto de Estudios Fiscales*
Hist. Soc. R. — Historical social research; Historische Sozialforschung. — Cologne: *Arbeitsgemeinschaft für Quantifizierung und Methoden in der historisch sozialwissenschaftlichen Forschung/ International Commission for the Application of Quantitative Methods in History/ Association for History and Computing*
Hist. Theory — History and theory. — Middletown, CT.: *Wesleyan University*
Hito. J. Comm. Manag. — Hitotsubashi journal of commerce and management. — Tokyo: *Hitotsubashi University, Hitotsubashi Academy*
Howard J. Crim. Just. — Howard journal of criminal justice. — Oxford: *Howard League*
Hum. Rights Q. — Human rights quarterly. — Baltimore, MD.: *Johns Hopkins University Press*
Human Relat. — Human relations. — New York, N.Y.: *Plenum Press*
Imm. Minor. — Immigrants and minorities. — London: *Frank Cass*
Impact Sci. — Impact of science on society. — Paris: *UNESCO*
Ind. Lab. Rel. — Industrial and labor relations review. — Ithaca, N.Y.: *Cornell University, New York State School of Industrial and Labor Relations*
Ind. Rel. J. S.Afr. — Industrial relations journal of South Africa. — Bellville: *University of Stellenbosch Business School*
Ind. Relat. J. — Industrial relations journal. — Oxford: *Basil Blackwell*
Indian J. Soc. W. — Indian journal of social work. — Bombay: *Tata Institute of Social Sciences*
Inf. Raum. — Informationen zur Raumentwicklung. — Bonn: *Bundesforschungsanstalt für Landeskunde und Raumordnung*
Int. J. Comp. Soc — International journal of comparative sociology. — Leiden: *E.J. Brill*
Int. J. Health. Ser. — International journal of health services. — Amityville, NY.: *Baywood Publishing*
Int. J. Law Fam. — International journal of law and the family. — Oxford: *Oxford University Press*
Int. J. Pol. C. S. — International journal of politics, culture and society. — New York, NY.: *Human Sciences Press*
Int. J. S. Lang. — International journal of the sociology of language. — Berlin: *Mouton de Gruyter*
Int. J. S. Law — International journal of the sociology of law. — London: *Academic Press*
Int. J. Soc. E. — International journal of social economics. — Bradford: *MCB University Press*

Int. J. Soc. Psyc. — International journal of social psychiatry. — London: *Avenue Publishing*
Int. J. Urban — International journal of urban and regional research. — Sevenoaks: *Edward Arnold*
Int. Migr. Rev. — International migration review. — New York, NY.: *Center for Migration Studies*
Int. Organ. — International organization. — Cambridge, MA.: *World Peace Foundation*
Int. Soc. Sci. J. — International social science journal. — Oxford: *Basil Blackwell/ UNESCO*
Int. Sociol. — International sociology. — London: *International Sociological Association*
Int. Stud. Q. — International studies quarterly. — Stoneham, MA.: *International Studies Association*
Inter. J. Therap. Comm. — International journal of therapeutic communities. — London: *Association of Therapeutic Communities*
Inter. Phil. Sci. — International studies in the philosophy of science. — Abingdon: *Carfax Publishing*
Irish Geogr. — Irish geography. — Dublin: *Geographical Society of Ireland*
Isr. Law R. — Israel law review. — Jerusalem: *Israel Law Review Association*
J. Afr. Law — Journal of African law. — London: *University of London, School of Oriental and African Studies*
J. Appl. Psychol. — Journal of applied psychology. — Arlington, VA.: *American Psychological Association*
J. Appl. Soc. Psychol. — Journal of applied social psychology. — Silver Spring, MD.: *V.H. Winston & Son*
J. As. Afr. S. — Journal of Asian and African studies [Leiden]. — Leiden: *E.J. Brill*
J. Asian St. — Journal of Asian studies. — Ann Arbor, MI.: *Association for Asian Studies*
J. Aust. Stud. — Journal of Australian studies. — Bundoora: *La Trobe University Press*
J. Biosoc. Sc. — Journal of biosocial science. — Cambridge: *Biosocial Society*
J. Car. Stud. — Journal of Caribbean studies. — Lexington, KY.: *Association of Caribbean Studies*
J. Com. Mkt. S. — Journal of common market studies. — Oxford: *University Association for Contemporary European Studies*
J. Comm. — Journal of communication. — New York, N.Y.: *Oxford University Press*
J. Commun. S. — Journal of communist studies. — London: *Frank Cass*
J. Comp. Fam. Stud. — Journal of comparative family studies. — Calgary: *University of Calgary, Department of Sociology*
J. Cont. Asia — Journal of contemporary Asia. — Manila: *Journal of Contemporary Asia Publishers*
J. Contemp. Afr. St. — Journal of contemporary African studies. — Pretoria: *Africa Institute of South Africa*
J. Crim. Law — Journal of criminal law and criminology. — Chicago, IL.: *Northwestern University School of Law*
J. Dev. Soc. — Journal of developing societies. — Leiden: *E.J. Brill*
J. Econ. Soc. Geogr. — Tijdschrift voor economische en sociale geografie; Journal of economic and social geography. — Amsterdam: *Royal Dutch Geographical Society = Koninklijk Nederlands Aardrijkskundig Genootschap*
J. Exp. S. Psychol. — Journal of experimental social psychology. — Duluth, MN.: *Academic Press*
J. Fam. Hist. — Journal of family history. — Greenwich, CT.: *National Council on Family Relations*

INTERNATIONAL BIBLIOGRAPHY OF SOCIOLOGY — 1988

J. Hist. Soc. — Journal of historical sociology. — Oxford: *Basil Blackwell*
J. Hum. Res. — Journal of human resources. — Madison, WI.: *University of Wisconsin Press*
J. Ind. Relat. — Journal of industrial relations. — Sydney: *Journal of Industrial Relations*
J. Interd. Hist. — Journal of interdisciplinary history. — Cambridge, MA.: *Tufts University/ Lafayette College*
J. Jap. Int. Ec. — Journal of the Japanese and international economies. — Duluth, MN.: *Tokyo Center for Economic Research*
J. Labor Ec. — Journal of labor economics. — Chicago, IL.: *Economics Research Center/NORC*
J. Labor Res. — Journal of labor research. — Fairfax, VA: *George Mason University, Department of Economics*
J. Law Soc. — Journal of law and society. — Oxford: *Basil Blackwell*
J. Linguist. — Journal of linguistics. — Cambridge: *Linguistics Association of Great Britain*
J. Manag. Stu. — Journal of management studies. — Oxford: *Basil Blackwell*
J. Market R. — Journal of the Market Research Society. — London: *Market Research Society*
J. Marriage Fam. — Journal of marriage and the family. — Minneapolis, MN.: *National Council on Family Relations*
J. Math. Sociol. — Journal of mathematical sociology. — New York: *Gordon & Breach Science Publishers*
J. Mod. Afr. S. — Journal of modern African studies. — Cambridge: *Cambridge University Press*
J. Occup. Psychol. — Journal of occupational psychology. — Leicester: *British Psychological Society*
J. Pac. Stud. — Journal of Pacific studies. — Suva: *University of the South Pacific, School of Social and Economic Development*
J. Peasant Stud. — Journal of peasant studies. — London: *Frank Cass*
J. Pers. Soc. Psychol. — Journal of personality and social psychology. — Arlington, VA: *American Psychological Association*
J. Personal. — Journal of personality. — Durham, NC.: *Duke University Press*
J. Policy An. — Journal of policy analysis and management. — New York, N.Y.: *Association for Public Policy Analysis and Management*
J. Polit. Ec. — Journal of political economy. — Chicago: *University of Chicago Press*
J. Pop. Ec. — Journal of population economics. — Berlin: *Springer-Verlag*
J. Psychol. — Journal of psychology. — Washington, DC: *Heldref Publications*
J. Res. Crim. Delin. — Journal of research in crime and delinquency. — Newbury Park, CA.: *National Council on Crime and Delinquency*
J. S.Afr. Stud. — Journal of Southern African studies. — Oxford: *Oxford University Press*
J. Sci. S. Relig. — Journal for the scientific study of religion. — West Lafayette, IN.: *Society for the Scientific Study of Religion*
J. Soc. Issues — Journal of social issues. — New York, NY.: *Society for the Psychological Study of Social Issues*
J. Soc. Pol. — Journal of social policy. — Cambridge: *Social Policy Association*
J. Soc. Psychol. — Journal of social psychology. — Washington, DC.: *Heldref Publications*
J. Soc. Stud. Dhaka — Journal of social studies. — Dhaka: *Centre for Social Studies*
J. Theory Soc. Behav. — Journal for the theory of social behaviour. — Oxford: *Basil Blackwell*
Jahr. Christ. Sozialwiss. — Jahrbuch für christliche Sozialwissenschaften. — Münster: *Universität Münster, Institut für Christliche Sozialwissenschaften*

Jahrb. N. St. — Jahrbücher für Nationalökonomie und Statistik. — Stuttgart: *Gustav Fischer Verlag*
Jew. J. Socio. — Jewish journal of sociology. — London: *Maurice Freedman Research Trust*
Kölner Z. Soz. Soz. psy. — Kölner Zeitschrift für Soziologie und Sozialpsychologie. — Wiesbaden: *Westdeutscher Verlag*
Korean Soc. Sci. J. — Korean social science journal. — Seoul: *Korean Social Science Research Council/ Korean National Commission for UNESCO*
Kyklos — Kyklos. — Basel: *Helbing & Lichtenhahn Verlag*
L.S.E. Q. — L.S.E. quarterly. — Oxford: *London School of Economics and Political Science*
Lab. Law J. — Labor law journal. — Chicago, IL.: *Commerce Clearing House*
Labour — Labour. — Rome: *Fondazione Giacomo Brodolini*
Labour Cap. Soc. — Labour, capital and society; Travail, capital et société. — Montreal: *McGill University, Centre for Developing Area Studies*
Lang. Soc. — Language in society. — New York, NY.: *Cambridge University Press*
Language — Language. — Baltimore, MD.: *Linguistic Society of America*
Lat. Am. Res. R. — Latin American research review. — Albuquerque, NM.: *Latin American Studies Association*
Law Cont. Pr. — Law and contemporary problems. — Durham, NC: *Duke University, School of Law*
Law Soc. Rev. — Law and society review. — Amherst, MA.: *Law and Society Association*
Maan. Econ. — Maandschrift economie. — Groningen: *Wolters-Noordhoff*
Manag. Sci. — Management science. — Providence, RI.: *Institute of Management Sciences*
Med. Prob. — Medunarodni problemi. — Belgrade: *Institut za Medunarodnu Politiku i Privredu*
Media Cult. Soc. — Media culture and society. — London: *Sage Publications*
Mens Maat. — Mens en maatschappij. — Houten: *Bohn Stafleu Van Loghum*
MI. law. R. — Michigan law review. — Ann Arbor, MI.: *Michigan Law Review*
Middle E. J. — Middle East journal. — Bloomington, IN.: *Middle East Institute*
Middle E. Stud. — Middle Eastern studies. — London: *Frank Cass*
Milbank Q. — Milbank quarterly. — New York, NY.: *Milbank Memorial Fund*
Millennium — Millennium. — London: *Millenium Publishing Group*
Mind — Mind. — Oxford: *Oxford University Press*
Minerva — Minerva. — London: *International Council on the Future of the University*
Mon. Rev. — Monthly review. — New York, NY.: *Monthly Review Foundation*
Monu. Nippon. — Monumenta Nipponica. — Tokyo: *Sophia University*
Mouve. Soc. — Mouvement social. — Paris: *Association «Le Mouvement Social»*
Nat. Pap. — Nationalities papers. — Omaha, NE: *Association for the Study of Nationalities (U.S.S.R. and East Europe)*
Neth. J. Soc. Sci. — Netherlands' journal of social sciences/Sociologia Neerlandica. — Assen: *Netherlands' Sociological and Anthropological Society*
Neue Pol. Liter. — Neue politische literatur. — Frankfurt-am-Main: *Verlag Peter Lang*
New Left R. — New left review. — London: *New Left Review*
New Polit. — New politics. — Brooklyn, NY.: *New Politics Associates*
Nie. West-Ind. Gids — Nieuwe West-Indische gids; New West Indian guide. — Dordrecht: *Stichting Nieuwe West- Indische Gids/ Johns Hopkins University, Program in Atlantic History, Culture and Society*
Nueva Soc. — Nueva sociedad. — Caracas: *Nueva Sociedad*

NY. U. Law. Re. — New York University law review. — New York, N.Y.: *New York University Law Review*

Oceania — Oceania. — Sydney: *Oceania Publications, University of Sydney*

Oral Hist. — Oral history. — Colchester: *Oral History Society*

Organ. Beh. Hum. Dec. Proces. — Organizational behavior and human decision processes. — Duluth, MN.: *Academic Press*

Orient — Orient. — Leverkusen: *Deutsches Orient-Institut*

Our Gener. — Our generation. — Quebec: *Our Generation*

Pac. Stud. — Pacific studies. — Laie, HI.: *Institute for Polynesian Studies*

Pac. View. — Pacific viewpoint. — Wellington: *Victoria University of Wellington, Department of Geography*

Pań. Prawo — Państwo i prawo. — Warsaw: *Polska Academia Nauk, Instytut Nauk Prawnych*

Patt. Prej. — Patterns of prejudice. — London: *Institute of Jewish Affairs*

Pens. Pol. — Pensiero politico. — Florence: *Casa Editrice Leo S.Olschki*

Pensée — Pensée. — Paris: *Institut de recherches marxistes*

Peup. Médit. — Peuples méditerranéens; Mediterranean peoples. — Paris: *Institut d'Études Méditerranéenes*

Philos. Pub. — Philosophy & public affairs. — Princeton, N.J.: *Princeton University Press*

Philos. S. Sc. — Philosophy of the social sciences. — Newbury Park, CA.: *Sage Publications*

Plan. Out. — Planning outlook. — Newcastle-upon-Tyne: *University of Newcastle-upon-Tyne, Department of Town and Country Planning*

Pol. Manag. Publ. — Politiques et management public. — Paris: *Institut de Management Public*

Polish Persp. — Polish perspectives. — Warsaw: *Polska Instytut Spraw Miedzynasodowych*

Polit. Geogr. Q. — Political geography quarterly. — Guildford: *Butterworth-Heinemann*

Polit. Theory — Political theory. — Newbury Park, CA.: *Sage Publications*

Polit. Viertel. — Politische Vierteljahresschrift. — Wiesbaden: *Deutsche Vereinigung für Politische Wissenschaft*

Politic. Stud. — Political studies. — Oxford: *Political Studies Association of the United Kingdom*

Pop. Dev. Rev. — Population and development review. — New York, N.Y.: *Population Council*

Pop. Res. Pol. R. — Population research and policy review. — Dordrecht: *Kluwer Academic Publishers*

Pop. Stud. — Population studies. — London: *London School of Economics, Population Investigation Committee*

Popul. Envir. — Population and environment. — New York, N.Y.: *Human Sciences Press*

Popul. R. — Population review. — La Jolla, CA.: *Indian Institute for Population Studies*

Population — Population. — Paris: *Institut National d'Etudes Démographiques*

Pouvoirs — Pouvoirs. — Paris: *Presses Universitaires de France*

Pra. Zab. Społ. — Praca i zabezpieczenie społeczne. — Warsaw: *Państwowe Wydawnictwo Ekonomiczne*

Prés. Afr. — Présence africaine. — Paris: *Société Africaine de Culture*

Pres. Stud. Q. — Presidential studies quarterly. — New York, NY.: *Center for the Study of the Presidency*

Proc. Am. Stat. Ass. — Proceedings. American Statistical Association. — Alexandria, VA.: *American Statistical Association*

Prof. Geogr. — Professional geographer. — Washington, D.C.: *Association of American Geographers*

Prog. H. Geog. — Progress in human geography. — Sevenoaks: *Edward Arnold*
Prz. Pol. — Przegląd polonijny. — Wrocław: *Polska Akademia Nauk, Komitet Badania Polonii*
Psychol .B. — Psychological bulletin. — Arlington, VA.: *American Psychological Association*
Publ. Adm. D. — Public administration and development. — Chichester: *Royal Institute of Public Administration*
Publ. Adm. Re. — Public administration review. — Washington, DC.: *American Society for Public Administration*
Publ. Choice — Public choice. — Dordrecht: *Kluwer Academic Publishers*
Publ. Enter. — Public enterprise. — Ljubljana: *International Center for Public Enterprises in Developing Countries*
Publizistik — Publizistik. — Kontanz: *Deutsche Gesellschaft für Publizistik- und Kommunikationswissenschaft/ Österreichische Gesellschaft für Publizistik- und Kommunikationswissenschaft/ Schweizerische Gesellschaft für Kommunikations- und Medienwissenschaft*
Q. J. Admin. — Quarterly journal of administration. — Ile-Ife: *Obafemi Awolowo University, Faculty of Administration*
Q. J. Econ. — Quarterly journal of economics. — Cambridge, MA.: *Harvard University*
Q. R. Econ. Bu. — Quarterly review of economics and business. — Champaign, IL.: *University of Illinois at Urbana-Champaign, Bureau of Economic and Business Research*
R. Ec. Reg. Urb. — Revue d'économie régionale et urbaine. — Paris: *ADICUEER (Association des Directeurs d'Instituts et des Centres Universitaires d'Etudes Economiques Régionales)*
R. Fr. Admin. Publ. — Revue française d'administration publique. — Paris: *Institut International d'Administration Publique*
R. Fr. Sci. Pol. — Revue française de science politique. — Paris: *Fondation nationale des sciences politiques/ Association française de science politique*
R. Roum. Sci. Soc. — Revue roumaine des sciences sociales.: *Série de sociologie* — Bucharest: *Editura Academiei Române*
R. Soc. Move. Con. Cha. — Research in social movements, conflicts and change. — Greenwich, CT.: *JAI Press*
R. Soc. Strat. Mob. — Research in social stratification and mobility. — Greenwich, CT.: *JAI Press*
R. T-Monde —, Revue tiers-monde. — Paris: *Université de Paris, Institut d'Étude du Développement Economique et Social*
R. Tun. Sci. Soc. — Revue tunisienne de sciences sociales. — Tunis: *Université de Tunis, Centre d'Etudes et de Recherches Economiques et Sociales*
Race Class — Race and class. — London: *Institute of Race Relations*
Rass. It. Soc. — Rassegna italiana di sociologia. — Bologna: *Societá Editrice il Mulino*
Religion — Religion. — London: *Academic Press*
Rev. Bras. Ciên. Soc. — Revista brasileira de ciências sociais. — São Paulo: *Associação Nacional de Pós-Graduação e Pesquisa em Ciências Sociais*
Rev. Ciê. Pol. — Revista de ciência política. — Rio de Janeiro: *Fundação Getulio Vargas*
Rev. Cien. Soc. — Revista de ciencias sociales. — Puerto Rico: *Universidad de Puerto Rico, Facultad de Ciencias Sociales, Centro de Investigaciones Sociales*
Rev. Eur. Sci. Soc. — Revue européenne des sciences sociales.: *Cahiers Vilfredo Pareto* — Geneva: *Librairie DROZ*
Rev. F. Braudel. Ctr. — Review. Fernand Braudel Center. — Binghamton, NY.: *State University of New York, Fernand Braudel Center*

Rev. Fom. Soc. — Revista de fomento social. — Madrid: *INSA-ETEA*
Rev. Fr. Soc. — Revue française de sociologie. — Paris: *Institut de recherche sur les sociétés contemporaines*
Rev. Mexicana Soc. — Revista mexicana de sociología. — Mexico City: *Universidad Nacional Autónoma de México*
Rev. Parag. Sociol. — Revista paraguaya de sociología. — Asunción: *Centro Paraguayo de Estudios Sociológicos*
Rev. Polit. — Review of politics. — Notre-Dame, IN: *University of Notre Dame*
Rev. Rad. Pol. Ec. — Review of radical political economics. — Riverside: *Union for Radical Political Economics*
Rev. Roumaine Sci. Soc. Sér. Sci. Jurid. — Revue Roumaine des sciences sociales.: *Série des sciences juridiques* — Bucharest: *Editura Academiei Române*
Rev. Roumaine Sci.Soc. Série Sci. Econ. — Revue roumaine des sciences sociales.: *Série des sciences économiques* — Bucharest: *Editura Academiei Române*
Riv. Int. Sci. Soc. — Rivista internazionale di scienze sociali. — Milan: *Università Cattolica del Sacro Cuore*
Rural Sociol. — Rural sociology. — College Station, TX.: *Rural Sociological Society*
S. Afr. J. Econ. — South African journal of economics; Suid-Afrikaanse tydskrif vir ekonomie. — Pretoria: *Economic Society of South Africa*
S.Asia B. — South Asia bulletin. — Albany, NY.: *South Asia Bulletin*
Savanna — Savanna. — Zaria: *Ahmadu Bello University Press*
Schw. Z. Volk. Stat. — Schweizerische Zeitschrift für Volkswirtschaft und Statistik; Revue suisse d'économie politique et de statistique. — Bern: *Schweizerische Gesellschaft für Statistik und Volkswirtschaft/ Société suisse de statistique et d'économie politique*
Sci. Am. — Scientific American. — New York, NY.: *Scientific American*
Sci. Soc. — Science and society. — New York, NY.: *Guilford Publications*
Signs — Signs. — Chicago, IL.: *University of Chicago Press*
Simulat. Gam. — Simulation and gaming. — Newbury Park, CA.: *Sage Publications*
Sistema — Sistema. — Madrid: *Fundación Sistema*
Slovo — Slovo. — London: *School of Slavonic and East European Studies*
Soc. Anal. — Social analysis. — Adelaide: *University of Adelaide, Department of Anthropology*
Soc. Behav. — Social behaviour. — Chichester: *John Wiley & Sons*
Soc. Compass — Social compass. — London: *International Federation of Institutes for Social and Socio-Religious Research (FERES)/ Centre de Recherches Socio-Religieuses*
Soc. Forc. — Social forces. — North Carolina: *University of North Carolina, Department of Sociology*
Soc. Ind. — Social indicators research. — Dordrecht: *Kluwer Academic Publishers*
Soc. Just. — Social justice. — San Francisco, CA.: *Global Options*
Soc. Part. — Socialismo y participación. — Lima: *CEDEP (Centro de Estudios para el Desarrollo y la Participación)*
Soc. Philos. Pol. — Social philosophy & policy. — Oxford: *Bowling Green State University, Social Philosophy and Policy Center*
Soc. Pol. Admin. — Social policy and administration. — Oxford: *Basil Blackwell*
Soc. Prob. — Social problems. — Berkeley, CA.: *Society for the Study of Social Problems*
Soc. Sci. — Social sciences. — Moscow: *Nauka Moscow*
Soc. Sci. Med. — Social science & medicine. — Exeter: *Pergamon Press*

Soc. Sci. Q. — Social science quarterly. — Austin, TX.: *Southwestern Social Science Association*
Soc. Ser. R. — Social service review. — Chicago, IL: *University of Chicago Press*
Social Soc. Res. — Sociology and social research. — Los Angeles, CA.: *University of Southern California*
Socio. Econ. — Socio-economic planning sciences. — Exeter: *Pergamon Press*
Sociol. Anal. — Sociological analysis. — Washington, DC: *Association for the Sociology of Religion*
Sociol. Gids — Sociologische gids. — Meppel: *Boom*
Sociol. Lav. — Sociologia del Lavoro. — Milan: *Università di Bologna, Centro Internazionale di Documentazione e Studi Sociologico Sui Problemi del Lavoro*
Sociol. Meth. — Sociological methods and research. — Newbury Park, CA.: *Sage Publications*
Sociol. Pers. — Sociological perspectives. — Greenwich, CT.: *Pacific Sociological Association*
Sociol. Q. — Sociological quarterly. — Greenwich, CT.: *J.A.I. Press*
Sociol. Rev. — Sociological review. — London: *University of Keele*
Sociol. Rur. — Sociologia ruralis. — Assen: *European Society for Rural Sociology/ Société Européenne de Sociologie Rurale/ Europäischen Gesellschaft für Land- und Agrarsoziologie*
Sociol. Sci. — Sociology of the sciences. — Dordrecht: *Kluwer Academic Publishers*
Sociol. Theory — Sociological theory. — Cambridge, MA.: *American Sociological Association*
Sociol. Trav. — Sociologie du travail. — Paris: *Dunod*
Sociologia [Brat.] — Sociologia [Bratislavia]; Sociology. — Bratislava: *Slovak Academy of Sciences, Institute of Sociology*
Sociologia [Rome] — Sociologia [Rome]. — Rome: *Istituto Luigi Sturzo*
Sociologus — Sociologus. — Berlin: *Duncker & Humblot*
Sociology — Sociology. — Solihull: *British Sociological Association*
Sot. Issle. — Социологические исследования (социс); Sotsiologicheskie issledovaniia (sotsis). — Moscow: *Akademii Nauk SSSR*
Sov. Jew. Aff. — Soviet Jewish affairs. — London: *Institute of Jewish Affairs*
Sov. Stud. — Soviet studies. — Abingdon: *Carfax Publishing*
Soz. Welt. — Soziale Welt. — Göttingen: *Arbeitsgemeinschaft sozialwissenschaftlicher Institute*
Stud. Comp. ID. — Studies in comparative international development. — New Brunswick, NJ: *Transaction Periodicals Consortium*
Stud. Demogr. — Studia demograficzne. — Warsaw: *Polska Akademia Nauk, Komitet Nauk Demograficznych*
Stud. Fam. Pl. — Studies in family planning. — New York, NY.: *Population Council*
Stud. Hist. Phil. Sci. — Studies in history and philosophy of science. — Oxford: *Pergamon Press*
Tareas — Tareas. — Panama City: *Centro de Estudios Latineamericanos "Justo Arosemena"*
Telos — Telos. — New York, NY.: *Telos Press*
Theory Decis. — Theory and decision. — Dordrecht: *Kluwer Academic Publishers*
Third Wor. P. — Third World planning review. — Liverpool: *Liverpool University Press*
Town Plan. R. — Town planning review. — Liverpool: *University of Liverpool, Department of Civic Design (Town and Regional Planning)*
Ufahamu — Ufahamu. — Los Angeles, CA.: *African Activist Association*
Uomo — Uomo. — Rome: *Università di Roma «La Sapienza», Dipartimento di Studi Glottoantropologici*
Urb. Aff. Ann. R. — Urban affairs annual reviews. — Newbury Park, CA.: *Sage Publications*

Urban Aff. Q. — Urban affairs quarterly. — Newbury Park, CA.: *Sage Publications*
Urban Law P. — Urban law and policy. — Amsterdam: *Elsevier Science Publishers (North-Holland)*
Urban Stud. — Urban studies. — Abingdon: *University of Glasgow, Centre for Urban and Regional Research*
Vest. Lenin. Univ. 6 — Вестник ленинградского университета ; Vestnik Leningradskogo universiteta.: серия 6 история кпсс, научный коммунизм, философия право = seriia 6, istoriia KPSS nauchnyi kommunizm filosofiia pravo — Leningrad: *Izdatel'stvo Leningradskogo Universiteta*
Viit. Soc. — Viitorul social. — Bucharest: *Editura Academiei Române*
Vop. Filo. — Вопросы философии; Voprosy filosofii. — Moscow: *Akademiia Nauk SSR, Institut filosofii*
Vop. Ist. KPSS — Вопросы истории КПСС; Voprosy istorii KPSS. — Moscow: *Izdatel'stvo Pravda*
Welt.liches Arc. — Weltwirtschaftliches Archiv. — Tübingen: *Institut für Weltwirtschaft*
West. Pol. Q. — Western political quarterly. — Salt Lake City, UT.: *Western Political Science Association/ Pacific Northwest Political Science Association/ Southern California Political Science Association/ Northern California Political Science Association*
Wirt.wissensch. — Wirtschaftswissenschaft. — Berlin: *Verlag die Wirtschaft*
Work Emp. Soc. — Work, employment and society. — London: *British Sociological Association*
Work Occup. — Work and occupations. — Newbury Park, CA.: *Sage Publications*
World Dev. — World development. — Oxford: *Pergamon Press*
World Polit. — World politics. — Baltimore, MD.: *Princeton University, Center of International Studies*
World Rev. — World review. — Indooroophilly: *Australian Institute of International Affairs*
Yagl-Ambu — Yagl-Ambu. — Papua New Guinea: *University of Papua New Guinea*
Z. Polit. — Zeitschrift für Politik. — Cologne: *Hochschule für Politik München*
Zambezia — Zambezia. — Harare: *University of Zimbabwe*

CLASSIFICATION SCHEME
PLAN DE CLASSIFICATION

A: *Social Sciences. Research. Documentation — Sciences sociales. Recherche. Documentation*

A.1: Social sciences. Sociology — *Sciences sociales. Sociologie*

A.2: Research workers. Sociologists — *Chercheurs. Sociologues*

A.3: Organization of research. Research policy — *Organisation de la recherche. Politique de recherche*

A.4: Congresses. Meetings — *Congrès. Réunions*

A.5: Documents. Information processing — *Documents. Traitement de l'information*

B: Methodology. Theory — *Méthodologie. Théorie*

B.1: Epistemology. Research methods. Theory — *Epistémologie. Méthodes de recherche. Théorie*

B.1.1: Philosophy. Theory — *Philosophie. Théorie*

  Marxism *[Marxisme]*

B.1.2: Epistemology. Explanation. Understanding — *Epistémologie. Explication. Compréhension*

B.1.3: Research techniques. Sociological analysis — *Techniques de recherche. Analyse sociologique*

B.2: Data collection. Experiments — *Rassemblement des données. Expériences*

B.3: Mathematical analysis. Statistical analysis — *Analyse mathématique. Analyse statistique*

C: Individuals. Groups. Organizations — *Individus. Groupes. Organisations*

C.1: Psychology. Social psychology. Sociometry — *Psychologie. Psychologie sociale. Sociométrie*

C.2: Individuals. Personality — *Individus. Personnalité*

    Emotions *[Émotions]*; Personality *[Personnalité]*

C.3: Interpersonal relations — *Relations interpersonnelles*

C.4: Groups — *Groupes*

C.5: Bureaucracy. Organization — *Bureaucratie. Organisation*

C.6: Leadership. Role — *Commandement. Rôle*

C.7: Attitudes. Opinion — *Attitudes. Opinion*

D: Culture. Socialization. Social life — *Culture. Socialisation. Vie sociale*

D.1: Culture. Social environment. Value — *Culture. Milieu social. Valeur*

D.1.1: **Culture and cultural relations** — *Culture et relations culturelles*

D.1.2: **Social norms. Social control. Value systems** — *Normes sociales. Régulation sociale. Systèmes de valeurs*

D.1.3: **Alienation. Socialization. Social conformity** — *Aliénation. Socialisation. Conformité sociale*

D.2: Customs. Traditions — *Coutumes. Traditions*

D.3: Ethics. Morals — *Éthique. Morale*

D.4: Law. Regulation — *Loi. Réglementation*

D.5: Magic. Mythology. Religion — *Magie. Mythologie. Religion*

    Christianity *[Christianisme]*; Islam *[Islam]*

D.6: Science. Sociology of knowledge — *Science. Sociologie de la connaissance*

D.7: Communication. Language — *Communication. Langage*

> Communication *[Communication]*; Linguistics *[Linguistique]*; Media *[Moyens de communication]*

D.8: Art — *Art*

D.9: Education — *Éducation*

D.9.1: Educational sociology — *Sociologie de l'éducation*

D.9.2: Educational systems. Educational policy — *Systèmes d'enseignement. Politique de l'éducation*

D.9.3: Primary education. Secondary education — *Enseignement primaire. Enseignement secondaire*

D.9.4: School environment — *Milieu scolaire*

D.9.5: Higher education — *Enseignement supérieur*

D.9.6: Adult education — *Éducation des adultes*

D.9.7: Civic education. Technical education — *Instruction civique. Enseignement technique*

D.9.8: Academic success. School failure — *Réussite dans les études. Échec scolaire*

D.9.9: Pedagogy. Teaching. Teachers — *Pédagogie. Enseignement. Enseignants*

E: Social structure — *Structure sociale*

E.1: Social system — *Système social*

E.2: Social stratification — *Stratification sociale*

E.3: Social change — *Changement social*

F: Population. Family. Ethnic group — *Population. Famille. Groupe ethnique*

F.1: Demography. Genetics — *Démographie. Génétique*

F.2: Age groups — *Groupes d'âges*

> Ageing *[Vieillissement]*; Childhood *[Enfance]*

F.3: Population evolution. Population policy — *Évolution de la population. Politique démographique*

> Family planning *[Planification de la famille]*; Fertility *[Fécondité]*; Morbidity *[Morbidité]*; Mortality *[Mortalité]*

F.4: Marriage. Family — *Mariage. Famille*

F.4.1: Marriage. Nuptiality — *Mariage. Nuptialité*

> Marital separation *[Separation maritale]*

F.4.2: Family — *Famille*

> Domestic violence *[Violence familiale]*; Family disintegration *[Désintégration familiale]*; Family relations *[Relations familiales]*; Method and theory *[Méthode et théorie]*

F.5: Gender — *Sexe*

> Feminism *[Féminisme]*; Gender differentiation *[Différenciation sexuelle]*; Gender roles *[Rôles de sexe]*; Men *[Hommes]*; Women *[Femmes]*

F.6: Sexual behaviour — *Comportement sexuelle*

F.7: Ethnic groups — *Groupes ethniques*

> Ethnicity *[Ethnicité]*; Race relations *[Relations raciales]*; Racial discrimination *[Discrimination raciale]*

F.8: Migration — *Migration*

> International migration *[Migration internationale]*

G: Environment. Community. Rural. Urban — *Environment. Communauté. Rural. Urbain*

G.1: Ecology. Geography. Human settlements — *Écologie. Géographie. Etablissements humains*

G.2: Community — *Communauté*

G.3: Rural. Urban — *Rural. Urbain*

G.3.1: Rural sociology — *Sociologie rurale*

> Peasant studies *[Études paysannes]*; Rural development *[Développement rurale]*

G.3.2: Urban sociology — *Sociologie urbaine*

> Urban housing *[Logement urbain]*; Urban planning and development *[Aménagement et développement urbain]*; Urban transport *[Transport urbain]*; Urbanization *[Urbanisation]*

H: Economic life — *Vie économique*

H.1: Economic sociology — *Sociologie économique*

H.2: Economic systems — *Systèmes économiques*

H.3: Economic situation. Standard of living — *Situation économique. Niveau de vie*

H.4: Enterprises. Production — *Entreprises. Production*

H.5: Consumption. Market. Prices — *Consommation. Marché. Prix*

H.6: Credit. Financing. Money — *Crédit. Financement. Monnaie*

H.7: Economic policy. Planning — *Politique économique. Planification*

I: Labour — *Travail*

I.1: Industrial sociology. Sociology of work — *Sociologie industrielle. Sociologie du travail*

I.2: Employment. Labour market — *Emploi. Marché du travail*

I.3: Personnel management. Working conditions — *Administration du personnel. Conditions de travail*

I.4: Occupations. Vocational training — *Professions. Formation professionnelle*

I.5: Employees. Technicians. Workers — *Employés. Techniciens. Travailleurs*

I.6: Labour relations — *Relations du travail*

I.7: Leisure — *Loisir*

J: Politics. State. International relations — *Politique. État. Relations internationales*

J.1: Political science. Political sociology — *Science politique. Sociologie politique*

J.2: Political doctrines. Political thought — *Doctrines politiques. Pensée politique*

J.3: Constitution. State — *Constitution. État*

J.4: Public administration — *Administration publique*

J.5: Political parties. Pressure groups — *Partis politiques. Groupes de pression*

J.6: Political behaviour. Elections. Politics — *Comportement politique. Élections. Politique*

J.7: Army. Military sociology — *Armée. Sociologie militaire*

J.8: International relations — *Relations internationales*

K: Social problems. Social services. Social work — *Problèmes sociaux. Services sociaux. Travail social*

K.1: Social problems — *Problèmes sociaux*

> Child neglect and abuse *[Enfants martyrs et abandon d'enfant]*; Crime *[Délits]*; Criminal justice *[Justice criminelle]*; Drugs *[Drogue]*; Poverty *[Pauvreté]*

K.2: Social policy — *Politique sociale*

K.3: Social work — *Travail social*

K.4: Social services — *Services sociaux*

BIBLIOGRAPHY FOR 1988
BIBLIOGRAPHIE POUR 1988

A: Social Sciences. Research. Documentation — *Sciences sociales. Recherche. Documentation*

A.1: Social sciences. Sociology — *Sciences sociales. Sociologie*

1 Acerca de la relación entre la sociología italiana y el fascismo (1920-1945) *[In Spanish]*; [On the relations between Italian sociology and fascism (1920-1945)]. Marta Losito; Sandro Segre. *Est. Sociol.* **VI:18** 9-12:1988 pp. 491 – 516

2 Alexander Zinoviev, les fondements scientifiques de la sociologie *[In French]*; [Alexander Zinoviev, the scientific foundations of sociology]. Fabrice Fassio. Paris: La Pensée universelle, 1988: 220 p. *ISBN: 2214076972*.

3 Another type of Third World dependency — the social sciences. Frederick H. Gareau. *Int. Sociol.* **3:2** 6:1988 pp. 171 – 178

4 Asking too much, expecting too little. Stanley Lieberson. *Sociol. Pers.* **31:4** 10:1988 pp. 379 – 397

5 Auflösung des Sozialen? Die Verflüssigung des soziologischen „Gegenstandes" im Fortgang der soziologischen Theorie *[In German]*; The dissolution of the „social" in sociology? *[Summary]*. Heinz Bude. *Soz. Welt.* **39:1** 1988 pp. 4 – 17

6 Christliche Sozialwissenschaft — eine normative Gesellschaftstheorie in ordnungsethischen und dynamisch-evolutiven Ansätzen *[In German]*; [Christian social science — ethical and evolutionary perspectives on a normative social theory]. Franz Furger. *Jahr. Christ. Sozialwiss.* **29** 1988 pp. 17 – 28

7 Cinquante ans de sciences sociales à l'Université Laval — l'histoire de la Faculté des sciences sociales, 1938-1988 *[In French]*; [Fifty years of the social sciences at Laval University — history of the faculty of social sciences]. Albert Faucher *[Ed.]*. Sainte-Foy, (Québec): Faculté des sciences sociales de l'Université Laval, 1988: 390 p. *ISBN: 2763767176*.

8 Contemporary British society — a new introduction to sociology. Nicholas Abercrombie; Alan Warde; Keith Soothill; John Urry; Sylvia Walb. Cambridge: Polity, 1988: 400 p. *Includes bibliography and index.*

9 The development of the sociology of law in the socialist Republic of Romania. Sofia Popescu. *Rev. Roumaine Sci. Soc. Sér. Sci. Jurid.* **32:1** 1-6:1988 pp. 7 – 16

10 L'Egypte dans le regard des sciences sociales *[In French]*; Egypt as seen by the social sciences — the avatars of a model *[Summary]*. Alain Roussillon. *Peup. Médit.* **41-42** 10:1987-3:1988 pp. 3 – 26

INTERNATIONAL BIBLIOGRAPHY OF SOCIOLOGY — 1988

A.1: Social sciences. Sociology *[Sciences sociales. Sociologie]*

11 Eizou Shakaigaku Josetsu *[In Japanese]*; [An introduction to visual sociology]. Akeshi Watari; Shintarou Tanabe. Hiroshima: General Research Center of Hiroshima Shudo University, 1988: 121 p.

12 Expériences roumaines de sociologie interdisciplinaire (1925-1988) *[In French]*; [Romanian experiences of interdisciplinary sociology (1925-1988)]. H.H. Stahl. *R. Roum. Sci. Soc.* **32:2** 7-12:1988 pp. 115 – 120

13 The future of sociology. Edgar F. Borgatta *[Ed.]*; Karen S. Cook *[Ed.]*. Newbury Park, CA: Sage, 1988: 422 p. *ISBN: 0803930240.*

14 Gendai Shakaigaku — riron to bunseki *[In Japanese]*; [Sociology today — theory and analysis]. Heizo Kanaya *[Ed.]*. Kyoto: Horitubunkasha, 1988: p.207

15 Historische Sozialforschung als Erweiterung der Soziologie. Die Konvergenz sozialwissenschaftlicher und historischer Erkenntniskonzepte *[In German]*; Historical social research as an extention of sociology — the convergence of sociological and historical concepts of cognition *[Summary]*. Heinrich Best. *Kölner Z. Soz. Soz. psy.* **40:1** 1988 pp. 1 – 14

16 History in the system of social sciences. Ivan Kovalchenko. *Soc. Sci.* **XIX:3** 1988 pp. 85 – 100

17 The human sciences — their contributions to society and future research needs. Brendan Gail Rule *[Ed.]*; Baha Abu-Laban *[Ed.]*. Edmonton: University of Alberta Press, 1988: xvii, 293 p. (ill.) *ISBN: 0888641346; LofC: cn88-91158. Proceedings of a conference held in Edmonton, Alberta, Oct. 9-12, 1985; Includes bibliographical references.*

18 In defence of indigenisation in sociological theories. A. Muyiwa Sanda. *Int. Sociol.* **3:2** 6:1988 pp. 189 – 199

19 Информационное обеспечение обновления общественных наук в СССР и братских странах социализма *[In Russian]*; (Information basis of the renovation process of social sciences in the USSR and fraternal socialist countries); (L'assurance de l'information du renouvellement des sciences humaines dans l'U.R.S.S. et dans les pays du socialisme: *Title only in French*); (Informationssicherstellung der Erneuerung der Gesellschaftswissenschaften in der UdSSR und sozialistischen Bruderländern: *Title only in German*); (El aseguramiento de información a la renovación de las ciencias sociales en la URSS y en los países hermanos del socialismo: *Title only in Spanish*); *[Title only in Chinese]*. B.A. Виноградов. *Vop. Ist. KPSS* **2** 1988 pp. 46 – 59

20 The long, uncertain road to social science maturity. Fred Gareau. *Int. J. Comp. Soc* **XXIX:3-4** 9-12:1988 pp. 175 – 186

21 Making sense of postmodern sociology. John W. Murphy. *Br. J. Soc.* **XXXIX:4** 12:1988 pp. 600 – 614

22 Max Weber et la sociologie française *[In French]*; [Max Weber and French sociology]. Monique Hirschhorn. Paris: L'Harmattan, 1988: 229 p. *ISBN: 2858028664. Bibliography — p..207-226.* [Logiques sociales.]

23 Перестройка и социологическая наука *[In Russian]*; (Perestroika and sociology). В.Н. Иванов. *Sot. Issle.* **1** 1-2:1988 pp. 7 – 15

24 Philosophy of social science. Alexander Rosenberg. Boulder: Westview Press, 1988: xiv, 218 p. *ISBN: 0813306167. Bibliography — p.207-211.* [Dimensions of philosophy series.]

INTERNATIONAL BIBLIOGRAPHY OF SOCIOLOGY — 1988

A.1: Social sciences. Sociology *[Sciences sociales. Sociologie]*

25 Pragmatism and the progressive movement in the United States — the origin of the new social sciences. John Lugton Safford. Lanham: University Press of America, 1988: 255 p. *ISBN: 0819164380. Includes bibliography and index.*

26 A quarter-century of sociology at the University of Toronto, 1963-1988. Richard C Helmes-Hayes *[Ed.]*. Toronto: Canadian Scholars' Press, 1988: vii, 63 p. *ISBN: 0921627076; LofC: cn 88095217.*

27 The scope of sociology. Milton M. Gordon. New York: Oxford University Press, 1988: viii, 252 p. *ISBN: 0195053036; LofC: 88-20384. Includes index.*

28 Seeds of bankruptcy — sociological bias against business and freedom. David Marsland. London: Claridge Press, 1988: xii, 238 p. *ISBN: 1870626400.*

29 Shakaigaku Kougi *[In Japanese]*; [Lecture of sociology]. Haruhiko Hamaguchi; Haruo Sagaza *[Ed.]*. Tokyo: Press of Waseda University, 1988: 281 p.

30 La sociologie en France *[In French]*; [Sociology in France]. Jacques Ardoino *[Ed.]*. Paris: Editions la Découverte, 1988: 128 p. *ISBN: 2707117625. Bibliography — p.102-126.* [Repères.]

31 Sociólogos y sociología en Venezuela *[In Spanish]*; [Sociologists and sociology in Venezuela]. Gregorio A. Castro. Caracas: Unesco, 1988: 455 p. *LofC: 88-146982. Bibliography — p.. 441-455.*

32 Sociology and the new social thinking. Gennady V. Osipov. *Int. Sociol.* **3:4** 12:1988 pp. 319 – 333

33 Sociology of development — reflections on the present crisis. Nicos P. Mouzelis. *Sociology* **22:1** 2:1988 pp. 23 – 44

34 Sociology's lost human relations area files. Jonathan H. Turner; Alexandra R. Maryanski. *Sociol. Pers.* **31:1** 1:1988 pp. 19 – 34

35 Социология в Эстонской ССР: социол. наука в АН ЭССР в XI пятилетке (1981-1985 гг.) *[In Russian]*; [Sociology in the Estonian SSR — sociological science in the Estonian Academy of Sciences in the 11th five year plan (1981-1985)]. Iu.Iu. Kakhk *[Ed.]*; Kh.A. Kallus *[Ed.]*. Tallin: , 1987: 60 p.

36 Soviet sociology and sociology in the Soviet Union. Liah Greenfeld. *Ann. R. Soc.* **14** 1988 pp. 99 – 123

37 Die Soziologen auf der Suche nach ihrer Disziplin — zur Genealogie eines Wissenschaftsbildes (1945-1961) *[In German]*; [Sociologists in search of their discipline — the formation of a social science genealogy (1945-1961)]. Alex Demirović. *Prokla* **70:1** 3:1988 pp. 33 – 57

38 Toward an emancipatory sociology — abandoning universalism for true indigenisation. Peter Park. *Int. Sociol.* **3:2** 6:1988 pp. 161 – 170

39 Universalism and indigenisation in sociological theory — introduction. Akinsola Akiwowo. *Int. Sociol.* **3:2** 6:1988 pp. 155 – 160

A.2: Research workers. Sociologists — *Chercheurs. Sociologues*

1 Donald R. Cressey, 1919-1987. Don C. Gibbons *[Contrib.]*; Lloyd Ohlin *[Contrib.]*; Paul Colomy *[Contrib.]*; Kenneth Polk *[Contrib.]*; Don C. Gibbons *[Contrib.]*; Ross L. Matsueda *[Contrib.]*; Craig Reinarman *[Contrib.]*; Jeffrey Fagan *[Contrib.]*; John Irwin *[Contrib.]*; Joseph L. Albini *[Contrib.] and others*. Collection of 8 articles. **Crime Delin.** , *34:3*, 7:1988 pp. 236 – 354

2 G.H. Mead, socialism and the progressive agenda. Dmitri N. Shalin. *A.J.S.* **93:4** 1:1988 pp. 913 – 951

3 Kindai nihon shakai chousa-shi kenkyū no kadai *[In Japanese]*; [The sociological study of the history of social research in modern Japan]. Takao Kawai. **Hosog. Kenk** *Vol.61; No.1 - 1988*. pp. 67 – 96

4 Max Weber's 'Science as a vocation'. Peter Lassman *[Ed.]*; Irving Velody *[Ed.]*; Herminio Martins *[Ed.]*. London: Unwin Hyman, 1988: xvii, 220 p. *ISBN: 0043012116. Bibliography — p209-213*.

5 The nature of sociological research and practice worldwide — a perspective from India. T. K. Oommen. *Int. Sociol.* **3:3** 9:1988 pp. 309 – 312

6 Wright Mills no chousa kenkyū ni okeru shakai ninshiki *[In Japanese]*; [Wright Mills' understanding of society in his investigation]. Izumi Hotta. **Kin. Daig. Ky. Gak. Ken. Ki.** *Vol.20; No.2 - 1988*. pp. 1 – 17

A.3: Organization of research. Research policy — *Organisation de la recherche. Politique de recherche*

1 Action research note (2). Koichiro Kobayashi. **Res. B. Tokyo Univ. Grad. Sch. Soc.** *Vol.24. 1988*. pp. 1 – 17

2 The articulation of project work — an organizational process. Anselm Strauss. *Sociol. Q.* **29:2** Summer:1988 pp. 163 – 178

3 Central and East European social research — parts 1 & 2. Arien Mack *[Ed.]*; Timothy Garton Ash *[Contrib.]*; Elemér Hankiss *[Contrib.]*; Laszlo Bruszt *[Contrib.]*; Robert Manchin *[Contrib.]*; Mira Marody *[Contrib.]*; Lena Kolarska-Bobinska *[Contrib.]*; Marek Ziołkowski *[Contrib.]*; Krzysztof Kowak *[Contrib.]*; H. Gordon Skilling *[Contrib.] and others*. Collection of 14 articles. **Soc. Res.** , *55:1-2*, Spring-Summer:1988 pp. 3 – 318

4 El estado actual de la investigación social en América Latina *[In Spanish]*; [The current state of social research in Latin America]. Aníbal Quijano. *Rev. Cien. Soc.* **XXVII: 3-4** 9-12: 1988 pp. 155 – 169

5 Ethical and professional dimensions of socially sensitive research. Joan E. Sieber; Barbara Stanley. *Am. Psychol.* **43:1** 1:1988 pp. 49 – 55

6 Fujibayashi Keizō no roudou chōsa kan — sono shakaishi-teki houhou wo chūshin ni *[In Japanese]*; [The logic of labour research in Keizō Fuji-bayashi]. Yukio Saka. **Rodo Ty.** *Vol.240. 1988*. pp. 48 – 59

7 Ideological orientation and political control of Vietnamese social science. Edmund Dahlström. *Acta Sociol.* **31:2** 1988 pp. 105 – 117

8 "Inochi no denwa" ni kansuru hikaku bunka-teki kenyū (2) — Niigata, Nara, Kansai "inochi no denwa" wo shu field to shite *[In Japanese]*; [Comparative

A.3: Organization of research. Research policy *[Organisation de la recherche. Politique de recherche]*

cultural researches "life-line" — centering on Niigata, Nara, Kansai "inochi no denwa"]. Takashi Katano; Seiji Yagasaki; Hiroshi Yamamoto. *Hikaku Bunka* Vol.2. 1988. pp. 65 – 96

9 Inventions from R & D — organizational designs for efficient research performance. Frank Hull. *Sociology* **22:3** 8:1988 pp. 393 – 416

10 An operational research programme for monitoring and evaluation. K. Balachandra Kurup. *Soc. Ind.* **20:1** 2:1988 pp. 91 – 102

11 La recherche en sciences sociales en milieu étranger *[In French]*; Social science research abroad *[Summary]*. Louis-Jean Duclos. *R. Fr. Sci. Pol.* **38:1** 2:1988 pp. 48 – 68

12 Sociologie française et francophone — annuaire 1988 *[In French]*; [French and French language sociology — 1988 directory]. Centre National de la Recherche Scientifique; Association internationale des sociologues de langue française; Société française de sociologie; Association professionnelle des sociologues. Paris: Centre National de la Recherche Scientifique, 1988: 314 p. *ISBN: 2222042348.*

A.4: Congresses. Meetings — *Congrès. Réunions*

A.5: Documents. Information processing — *Documents. Traitement de l'information*

1 Bibliography of the works of Jean Piaget in the social sciences. J. McLaughlin. Lanham: University Press of America, 1988: 148 p. *ISBN: 0819167304.*

2 Guide to the Archiv für Sozialwissenschaft und Sozialpolitik group, 1904-1933 — a history and comprehensive bibliography. Regis A. Factor. New York: Greenwood, 1988: 214 p. *ISBN: 031322837x; LofC: 88-17770.* [Bibliographies and indexes in law and political science.]

3 Publications perish — sociology endures. Bernard Farber. *Sociol. Pers.* **31:1** 1:1988 pp. 3 – 18

4 Shoki Mannheim no ikou — "shii no Kouzou" wo megutte *[In Japanese]*; [Karl Mannheim's posthumous manuscripts]. Atsushi Sawai. *Shak.she Kenk.* Vol.10. 1988. pp. 34 – 50

5 Social scientists' information needs in the 1980s. Margaret Slater. *J. Doc.* **44:3** 9:1988 pp. 226 – 237

6 The supply and demand of social science information in the Netherlands — an exploratory research into the supply of social science information and the needs of its users. J. Lempert-Lenderink. Amsterdam: SWIDOC, 1988: 102 p. *ISBN: 0444856943. Bibliography — p.88-94.*

7 Telescience — scientific communication in the information age. Murray Aborn *[Ed.]*; James R. Beniger *[Contrib.]*; Melvin Kranzberg *[Contrib.]*; Richard Jay Solomon *[Contrib.]*; Theodor D. Sterling *[Contrib.]*; Fred W. Weingarten *[Contrib.]*; D. Linda Garcia *[Contrib.]*; Zellig Harris *[Contrib.]*; Paul Mattick *[Contrib.]*; Jacques Tocatlian *[Contrib.] and others*. Collection of 12 articles. **Ann. Am. Poli.**, *495:*, 1:1988 pp. 10 – 143

B: Methodology. Theory — *Méthodologie. Théorie*

B.1: Epistemology. Research methods. Theory — *Epistémologie. Méthodes de recherche. Théorie*

B.1.1: Philosophy. Theory — *Philosophie. Théorie*
Sub-divisions: Marxism *[Marxisme]*

1 The animal within — biology and the social sciences. Philip Kitcher. *L.S.E. Q.* **2:4** Winter:1988 pp. 339 – 360
2 The antinomies of neofunctionalism — a critical essay on Jeffrey Alexander. Hans Joas. *Inquiry* **31:4** 12:1988 pp. 471 – 494
3 Are we doing theory ethnocentrically? A comparison of modernization theory and Kemalism. Craig C. Hansen. *J. Dev. Soc.* **V:2** 7-10:l989 pp. 175 – 187
4 A behavioral theory of social structure. Jonathan H. Turner. *J. Theory Soc. Behav.* **18:4** 12:1988 pp. 335 – 372
5 Conceptual frameworks in comparative inquiry — divergent or convergent? Piotr Sztompka. *Int. Sociol.* **3:3** 9:1988 pp. 207 – 218
6 Contemporary social philosophy. Gordon Graham. Oxford: Basil Blackwell, 1988: viii,184 p. *ISBN: 0631157050. Bibliography — p179-181.*
7 Desconstrucción o nueva síntesis. Aproximaciones críticas a la noción de postmodernidad *[In Spanish]*; [Deconstruction or new synthesis. Critical approximations to the notion of postmodernity]. Luis Eduardo Gómez Sánchez. *Est. Sociol.* **VI:18** 9-12:1988 pp. 603 – 626
8 Durkheim and individualism. W. Watts Miller. *Sociol. Rev.* **36:4** 11:1988 pp. 647 – 673
9 Durkheim wo yomu shiza *[In Japanese]*; [Perspective for reading Durkheim]. Michio Nakajima. *Ann. Rep. St. Hum. Soc. Sci. Vol.31. 1988.* pp. 11 – 28
10 The genesis of Max Weber's Verstehende Soziologie. Soma Herva. *Acta Sociol.* **31:2** 1988 pp. 143 – 156
11 Hermeneutics and economics — a criticism of hermeneutical thinking in the social sciences. Hans Albert. *Kyklos* **41: 4** 1988 pp. 573 – 602
12 The idea of rationality and its relationship to social science — comments on Popper's philosophy of the social sciences. Michael Schmid. *Inquiry* **31:4** 12:1988 pp. 451 – 469
13 Is "neofunctionalism" really functional? Jonathan H. Turner; A.R. Maryanski. *Sociol. Theory* **6:1** Spring:1988 pp. 110 – 121
14 Kindai Shakaishisou no Kenkyū *[In Japanese]*; [Studies on the modern social thought]. Shoji Saito. Tokyo: Enaho Book Publishing Co., 1988: 165 p.
15 Koiron toshiteno Descartes no hoho *[In Japanese]*; [Methods of Descartes as an action theory]. Jiro Kawakoshi. *Seit.-gak. Ky. Daig. Vol.16. 1988.* pp. 16 – 31
16 Law, democracy and social justice. Roger Cotterrell *[Contrib.]*; Brian Bercusson *[Contrib.]*; Laurence Lustgarten *[Contrib.]*; Tony Prosser *[Contrib.]*; Sol Picciotto *[Contrib.]*; Elizabeth Kingdom *[Contrib.]*; Doreen

INTERNATIONAL BIBLIOGRAPHY OF SOCIOLOGY — 1988

B.1.1: Philosophy. Theory *[Philosophie. Théorie]*

McBarnet *[Contrib.]*; Stuart A. Scheingold *[Contrib.]*; Paul Hirst *[Contrib.]*. Collection of 10 articles. **J. Law Soc.**, *15:1*, Spring:1988 pp. 1 – 150

17 Luhmann no henbou — shakaigaku-teki auronomy no genri no tameni *[In Japanese]*; [Transformation of Luhmann — to principle of sociological autonomy]. Yasuo Baba. *Shak. Hyor. Vol.39; No.1 - 1988.* pp. 17 – 31

18 Max Weber on "Jewish rationalism" and the Jewish question. Gary Abraham. *Int. J. Pol. C. S.* **1:3** Spring:1988 pp. 358 – 391

19 Max Weber — essays in reconstruction. Wilhelm Hennis; Keith Tribe *[Tr.]*. London: Allen & Unwin, 1988: xii, 254 p. *ISBN: 0043013015; LofC: 87-12584.* eng, ger; Includes index.

20 On Georg Simmel's sociology of the sexes. Heinz-Jürgen Dahme. *Int. J. Pol. C. S.* **1:3** Spring:1988 pp. 412 – 430

21 Postmodernism, post-Fordism, and critical social theory. N. Albertsen. *Envir. Plan. D* **6(3):** 9:1988 pp. 339 – 366

22 Pragmatic identity of meaning and metaphor. J. van Brakel; J.P.M. Geurts. *Inter. Phil. Sci.* **2:2** Spring:1988 pp. 205 – 226

23 Rationality, value and preference. Kurt Baier. *Soc. Philos. Pol.* **5:2** Spring:1988 pp. 17 – 45

24 Razionalizzare l'irrazionale —Karl Mannheim e il vizio inveterato degli intellettuali tedeschi *[In Italian]*; Rationalizing the irrational —Karl Mannheim and the besetting sin of German intellectuals *[Summary]*. David Kettler; Volker Meja; Nico Stehr. *Rass. It. Soc.* **29:4** 10-12:1988 pp. 487 – 512

25 Rickert's value theory and the foundation of Weber's methodology. Guy Oakes. *Sociol. Theory* **6:1** Spring:1988 pp. 38 – 51

26 Riron shakaigaku ni okeru kouzou riron no kanousei — network ron no ichi sokumen *[In Japanese]*; [The growing importance of structural theory in sociology — one aspect of the network approach]. Toshio Kumada. *Surug. Univ. St. Vol.1. 1988.* pp. 63 – 72

27 Social causality. Jerald Hage; Barbara Foley Meeker *[Ed.]*. Boston, [Mass.]: Allen & Unwin, 1988: 236 p. *ISBN: 0043120296.* Includes bibliography and index. [Contemporary social research series. : No. 16]

28 The social world as will and idea — Schopenhauer's influence upon Durkheim's thought. Stjepan G. Mestrovic. *Sociol. Rev.* **36:4** 11:1988 pp. 674 – 705

29 Sociological metatheory — a defense of a subfield by a delineation of its parameters. George Ritzer. *Sociol. Theory* **6:2** Fall:1988 pp. 187 – 200

30 Taming Leviathan — reflections on some recent work on Hobbes. Daniel M. Farrell. *Ethics* **98:4** 7:1988 pp. 793 – 805

31 A treatise on social theory. Volume 2 — substantive social theory. W. G. Runciman. Cambridge: Cambridge University Press, 1988: 493 p. *ISBN: 0521249597. Bibliography — p.451-479.*

32 Weber niokeru keiyaku gainen no yakuwari to juyosei nitsuite *[In Japanese]*; [A study of the key word Verbrüderung in the sociology of Max Weber]. Nobaru Yonakuni. *B. Univ. Ryuk. Coll. Law. Lett. Vol.30. 1988.* pp. 1 – 30

33 Weber no Shakaigaku — gendaishakai heno Shikaku *[In Japanese]*; [Sociology of Max Weber — a perspective on modern society]. Masahito Suzuki. Kyoto : , 1988: 250 p.

INTERNATIONAL BIBLIOGRAPHY OF SOCIOLOGY — 1988

B.1.1: Philosophy. Theory *[Philosophie. Théorie]* —

Marxism *[Marxisme]*

34 Is "analytical Marxism" Marxism? Michael A. Lebowitz. *Sci. Soc.* **52:2** Summer:1988 pp. 191 – 214

35 Marxismus und Entwicklungssoziologie — der Weg in die Sackgasse *[In German]*; [Marxism and the sociology of development — towards a dead-end]. David Booth. *Prokla* **71:2** 6:1988 pp. 13 – 49

36 Neoclassical Marxism. W.H. Locke Anderson; Frank W. Thompson. *Sci. Soc.* **52:2** Summer:1988 pp. 215 – 228

37 Strategii de „reconstrucţie a marxismului" in sociologia occidentală a deceniului al nouălea *[In Romanian]*; (Strategies of "Marxist reconstruction" in the Western sociology of the 1990s); (Stratégies de la "reconstrucion du marxisme" dans la sociologie occidentale de la neuvième décennie: *Title only in French)*; (Стратегии «восстановления марксизма» в западный социологии девтого десятилетия: *Title only in Russian).* Maria Larionescu. *Viit. Soc.* **LXXXI** 7-8:1988 pp. 335 – 342

B.1.2: Epistemology. Explanation. Understanding —
Epistémologie. Explication. Compréhension

1 Clifford Geertz no kaishaku-gaku-teki bunka bunseki — sono shiten houhou to riron ni tsuite *[In Japanese]*; [On the interpretive cultural analysis of Clifford Geertz — its viewpoint, method and theory]. Masao Kuchiba. *Shak. Ron.* Vol.8. *1988.* pp. 35 – 59

2 "Kansatsu" to tasha-sei *[In Japanese]*; [Observation and otherness]. Natsuko Yoshizawa. *Philosophy* Vol.86. *1988.* pp. 85 – 105

3 Marxism and social research — the reality of epistemology. Morton G. Wenger. *Sci. Soc.* **52:2** Summer:1988 pp. 133 – 161

4 Ontological investigations — an inquiry into the categories of nature, man and society. Ingvar Johansson. London: Routledge, 1988: 368 p. *ISBN: 0415025885. Includes bibliography and index.*

5 The relation of theory and method — causal relatedness, historical contingency and beyond. Derek Layder. *Sociol. Rev.* **36:3** 8:1988 pp. 441 – 463

6 Towards a heuristic theory of problem structuring. Gerald F. Smith. *Manag. Sci.* **34:12** 12:1988 pp. 1489 – 1506

B.1.3: Research techniques. Sociological analysis —
Techniques de recherche. Analyse sociologique

1 Actions and structure — research methods and social theory. Nigel Fielding *[Ed.]*. London: Sage, 1988: 202 p. (ill) *ISBN: 0803981473. Bibliographies.*
2 Approaches to social research. Royce Singleton *[Ed.]*; et al. New York: Oxford University Press, 1988: xviii, 541 p. (ill) *ISBN: 019504469x; LofC: 87-12187. Bibliography — p497-515. Includes index.*
3 Computer simulation as a research tool — the DISCUSS model of group decision making. Garold Stasser. *J. Exp. S. Psychol.* **24:5** 9:1988 pp. 393 – 422
4 The contribution of rational choice theory to macrosociological research. Debra Friedman; Michael Hechter. *Sociol. Theory* **6:2** Fall:1988 pp. 201 – 218
5 Controversial issues in social research methods. J. Greenberg; Robert Folger *[Ed.]*. : Springer Verlag, New York: 230 p. *ISBN: 0387965718; LofC: lc87-023237. Bibliography — p.195-224.*
6 Doing research in organisations. Alan Bryman *[Ed.]*. London: Routledge, 1988: xii, 180 p. *ISBN: 0415002575. Bibliography — p.162-173.*
7 Doing social research. Therese L. Baker. New York: McGraw-Hill, 1988: xxvi, 483 p. (ill) *ISBN: 0070034532; LofC: 87-17333. Bibliography — p.454-461. - Includes index.*
8 Estilos de investigación sobre la clase obrera *[In Spanish]*; [Styles of research into the working class]. Enrique de la Garza Toledo. *Rev. Mexicana Soc.* **L:4** 10-12:1988 pp. 3 – 29
9 Ethnomethodology — a critical review. Paul Atkinson. *Ann. R. Soc.* **14** 1988 pp. 441 – 465
10 Factor analysis and the construct indicator relationship. John Bynner. *Human Relat.* **41:5** 1988 pp. 389 – 405
11 A feminist ethic for social science research. Nebraska Sociological Feminist Collective. Lewiston,N. Y.: Edwin Mellen Press, 1988: 247 p. *ISBN: 0889461201. Bibliography — p.219-235.*
12 Handbook of research methods — a guide for practitioners in the social sciences. Natalie L. Sproull. Metuchen, N.J.: Scarecrow, 1988: xiv,404 p. (ill) *ISBN: 0810821168. 88-, 303; Bibliography — p.389-395.*
13 Human inquiry in action — developments in new paradigm research. Peter Reason *[Ed.]*. London: Sage, 1988: 242 p. (ill) *ISBN: 0803980892. Includes bibliography and index.*
14 Methodology and techniques of research. R.K. Verma; Gopal Verma. New Delhi: Anmol, 1988: iii, 135 p.
15 The micro contribution to macro sociology. Randall Collins. *Sociol. Theory* **6:2** Fall:1988 pp. 242 – 253
16 The micro-macro problem in social theory. Norbert Wiley. *Sociol. Theory* **6:2** Fall:1988 pp. 254 – 261
17 Naze "shitsu-teki" data ga hitsuyou nanoka — Mita/ Yasuda ronsou saikou *[In Japanese]*; [Why do we need "qualitative" data? — reconsideration of "Mita-Yasuda dispute"]. Keisuke Ikoshi. *Sophia Stud. Soc. Vol.12. 1988.* pp. 21 – 42
18 Network analysis and methodological individualism. Thomas Mathien. *Philos. S. Sc.* **18:1** 3:1988 pp. 1 – 20

B.1.3: Research techniques. Sociological analysis [Techniques de recherche. Analyse sociologique]

19 On Durkheim's rules of sociological method. Mike Gane. London: Routledge, 1988: xi, 193 p. *ISBN: 0415002516. Bibliography—p.184-188.*

20 The politics and aesthetics of footnoting. Joseph Bensman. *Int. J. Pol. C. S.* **1:3** Spring:1988 pp. 443 – 470

21 Principles of theoretical analysis. Guillermina Jasso. *Sociol. Theory* **6:1** Spring:1988 pp. 1 – 20

22 Quantity and quality in social research. Alan Bryman. London: Unwin Hyman, 1988: viii, 198 p. *ISBN: 0043120393. Includes bibliography and index.* [Contemporary social research series. : No. 18]

23 The rediscovery of chronos — the new role of time in sociological theory. Mark Elchardus. *Int. Sociol.* **3:1** 3:1988 pp. 35 – 59

24 Rekishi-shuigi no gakushi hohoron *[In Japanese]*; [Historicism as a methodology of the history of sociology]. Toshihide Yokoi. *Shak.she Kenk.* *Vol.10. 1988.* pp. 82 – 98

25 Research design explained. Mark L. Mitchell; Janina M. Jolley *[Ed.]*. New York: Holt,Rinehart and Winston, 1988: xv, 428 p. *ISBN: 0030040248. Bibliography—p.411-415.*

26 The sacralization of social scientific discourse. Fred D'Agostino. *Philos. S. Sc.* **18:1** 3:1988 pp. 21 – 40

27 Selected issues on research methods. K.L. Bhowmik *[Ed.]*. New Delhi: Inter-India, 1988: xiv, 131 p. *ISBN: 81 210 0201 X.*

28 Shakai chousa no Kiso *[In Japanese]*; [Foundation of social research]. Keigo Inō; Minoru Abe; Muneyuki Kawatei; Kouichi Hiraoka; Masakatsu Murakami; Souhei Mori. Tokyo: Jusonbo, 1988: 137 p.

29 Teoreticko-metodologické východiská uplatňovania sociologických poznatkov v spoločenskej praxi *[In Czech]*; Теоретическо-методологические исходные пункты использования социологических знаний в общественной практике *[Russian summary]*; Theoretical-methodological solutions of the usage of sociological knowledge in social practice *[Summary]*; Theoretisch-methodologische Lösungen des Ausnutzung soziologischer Kenntnisse in der sozialen Praxis *[German summary]*. Ján Pichňa. *Sociologia [Brat.]* **20:3** 1988 pp. 255 – 273

30 Transcending general linear reality. Andrew Abbott. *Sociol. Theory* **6:2** Fall:1988 pp. 169 – 186

31 The use of mathematics in social explanation. M.H.I. Dore. *Sci. Soc.* **52:4** Winter:1988 pp. 456 – 469

32 Women's status and mode of production — a cross-cultural test. Lewellyn Hendrix; Zakir Hossain. *Signs* **13:3** Spring:1988 pp. 437 – 447

B.2: Data collection. Experiments — *Rassemblement des données. Expériences*

1 Aanzetten tot een contextuele theorie van het interview *[In Dutch]*; A contextual theory of the survey interview *[Summary]*. Jan van Dijk. *Mens Maat.* **63:3** 8:1988 pp. 277 – 293
2 Assessing the quality of longitudinal surveys. Robert F. Boruch; Robert W. Pearson. *Eval. Rev.* **12:1** 2:1988 pp. 3 – 59
3 Evaluation as scientific research. John A. Crane. *Eval. Rev.* **12:5** 10:1988 pp. 467 – 482
4 L'intervistatore come attore. Ovvero, le infedeltà che non importa superare *[In Italian]*; The interviewer as actor, or the infidelity that is not worth getting over *[Summary]*. Andrea Sormano. *Rass. It. Soc.* **29:3** 7-9:1988 pp. 347 – 382
5 Linear structural relationships (LISREL) in family research. Yoav Lavee. *J. Marriage Fam.* **50:4** 11:1988 pp. 937 – 948
6 Response bias using two-stage data collection — a study of elderly participants in a program. Marianne Goodfellow; Nancy-Ellen Kiernan; Frank Ahern; Michael A. Smyer. *Eval. Rev.* **12:6** 12:1988 pp. 638 – 654
7 The study of sensitive subjects — a research note. Julia Brannen. *Sociol. Rev.* **36:3** 8:1988 pp. 552 – 563
8 Survey research and social policy. James D. Wright. *Eval. Rev.* **12:6** 12:1988 pp. 595 – 606
9 Systematic data collection. Susan C. Weller; A. Kimball Romney *[Ed.]*. Newbury Park; London: Sage, 1988: 96 p. *ISBN: 0803930739; LofC: 87-23475*.
10 Uitwerking en beoordeling van een contextuele theorie van het interview *[In Dutch]*; Elaboration and evaluation of a contextual theory of the interview *[Summary]*. van der J. Zouwen. *Mens Maat.* **63:3** 8:1988 pp. 294 – 308

B.3: Mathematical analysis. Statistical analysis — *Analyse mathématique. Analyse statistique*

1 Alternative și opțiuni ale analizei statistice în sociologia contemporană *[In Romanian]*; (Alternatives and options of the statistic analysis in the contemporary sociology); (Alternatives et options de l'analyse statistique dans la sociologie contemporaine: *Title only in French*); (Альтернативы и выборы статиетического анализа в современном социологии: *Title only in Russian*). Dumitru Sandu. *Viit. Soc.* **LXXXI** 5-6:1988 pp. 245 – 252
2 The competing risks model — a method for analysing processes with multiple types of events. David S. Hachen. *Sociol. Meth.* **17:1** 8:1988 pp. 21 – 54
3 De computer bij kwalitatief-interpreterend onderzoek — een onderzieks- notitie *[In Dutch]*; Computer use and qualitative interpretive analysis — a research note *[Summary]*. V.A.M. Peters; F.P.J. Wester. *Sociol. Gids* **XXXV:5** 9-10:1988 pp. 332 – 345
4 Developments in K-linkage clustering for sociology. Dumitru Sandu. *R. Roum. Sci. Soc.* **32:1** 1-6:1988 pp. 31 – 44

B.3: Mathematical analysis. Statistical analysis [Analyse mathématique. Analyse statistique]

5 Discovering heterogeneity — continuous versus discrete latent variables. Otis Dudley Duncan; Magnus Stenbeck; Charles J. Brody. *A.J.S.* **93:6** 5:1988 pp. 1305 – 1321

6 Doing secondary analysis. Angela Dale; Sara Arber *[Ed.]*; Michael Procter *[Ed.]*. London: Allen & Unwin, 1988: 358 p. *ISBN: 0043120415. Includes bibliography and index.* [Contemporary social research series. : Vol. 17]

7 Erkenntnisziele zeitreihenanalytischer Forschung *[In German]*; [Objectives of time series analysis research]. Rainer Metz. *Hist. Soc. R.* **13:3** 1988 pp. 6 – 22

8 Estimation of contamination parameters and identification of outliers in multivariate data. Maia Berkane; P.M. Bentler. *Sociol. Meth.* **17:1** 8:1988 pp. 55 – 64

9 Formalizing the social expert's knowledge. Kathleen Carley. *Sociol. Meth.* **17:2** 11:1988 pp. 165 – 232

10 Latent structure models with direct effects between indicators - local dependence models. Jacques A. Hagenaars. *Sociol. Meth.* **16:3** 2:1988 pp. 379 – 405

11 Mathematical modelling and game theory — a rational choice for the social sciences? B.T. Coram. *Aust. N.Z. J. Soc.* **24:3** 11:1988 pp. 459 – 472

12 Measurement scales and statistics — what can significance tests tell us about the world? A.W. MacRae. *Br. J. Psy.* **:1-2-3-4** 2-5-8-11:1988 pp. 161 – 172

13 Measures of dependence for cross-lagged panel models. Lawrence S. Mayer; Steven S. Carroll. *Sociol. Meth.* **17:1** 8:1988 pp. 93 – 120

14 Modelling strategies — exploratory findings; Modélisdation de la monogame successire — résultats d'une exploration *[French summary]*. Jan Bartlema. *Eur. J. Pop.* **4:3** 4:1988 pp. 197 – 221

15 A note on approximating correlations from odds ratios. Mark P. Becker; Clifford C. Clogg. *Sociol. Meth.* **16:3** 2:1988 pp. 407 – 424

16 On fuzzy cliques in fuzzy networks. Xiaoyan Yan. *J. Math. Sociol.* **13:4** 1988 pp. 359 – 389

17 A paradigmatic crisis in the multiplacative modeling of mobility tables — the problem of circulation mobility as a anomaly. Kazimierz M Slomczynski; Tadeusz K. Krauze. *Am. Sociol. R.* **53:5** 10:1988 pp. 742 – 748

18 Проблеми на социалната статистика. Интеграция и интеграция и интеграционен подход при изграждането й *[In Bulgarian]*; Проблемы социальной статистики интеграция и интеграционный подход при ее разработке *[Russian summary]*; Problems of the social statistics. Integration and integrative approach to its establishment *[Summary]*. Ст.Т. Станев. *God. Vis. F. S. Inst. Tsenov - Svi.* **LXXVIII** 1988 pp. 143 – 210

19 Quantitative analysis of historical material as the basis for a new cooperation between history and sociology. Erwin K. Scheuch. *Hist. Soc. R.* **13:2** 1988 pp. 5 – 30

20 Shakai network no sūri model — hen net model wo chūshin ni *[In Japanese]*; [Mathematical model on social networks — mainly on biased network models]. Hiroshi Hiramatsu. *Soc. Theo. Meth.* *Vol.3; No.1 - 1988.* pp. 97 – 110

B.3: Mathematical analysis. Statistical analysis [Analyse mathématique. Analyse statistique]

21 Some new sources of social conflict — transformations of mixed-motive games. Robert E. Goodin. *Br. J. Soc.* **XXXIX:3** 9:1988 pp. 441 – 451
22 Statistical games and human affairs — the view from within. Roger J. Bowden. Cambridge: Cambridge University Press, 1988: 281 p. *ISBN: 0521361788*. Includes index.
23 Sūri Shakaigaku no Tenkai *[In Japanese]*; [Mathematical sociology in progress]. Michio Umino *[Ed.]*; Junsuke Hara *[Ed.]*; Shūichi Wada *[Ed.]*. *Sendai Vol.1988*. p. 488
24 Theories of measurement in social science — a critical review. Kurt Walter Schwager. Rotterdam: Erasmus Universiteits Drukkerij, 1988: 343,14 p. *Summary in Dutch, p323-327; Bibliography — p.328-343.*
25 True score or factor models — a secondary analysis of the ALLBUS-test-retest data. Willem E. Saris; Bas Van Den Putte. *Sociol. Meth.* **17:2** 11:1988 pp. 123 – 157
26 Unified theory and strategies of survey sampling. Arijit Chaudhuri; J. W. E. Vos *[Ed.]*. Amsterdam: North-Holland, 1988: p. cm *BNB: 87029499; ISBN: 0444703578. A. Chaudhuri and J.W.E. Vos; Bibliography — p..* [North-Holland series in statistics and probability. : Vol. 4]
27 Violations of probability theory — what do they mean? Deborah E. Frisch. *J. Theory Soc. Behav.* **18:2** 6:1988 pp. 137 – 148

C: Individuals. Groups. Organizations — *Individus. Groupes. Organisations*

C.1: Psychology. Social psychology. Sociometry — *Psychologie. Psychologie sociale. Sociométrie*

1 The anatomy of madness — essays in the history of psychiatry. Roy Porter *[Ed.]*; W. F. Bynum *[Ed.]*; Michael Shepherd *[Ed.]*. London: Routledge, -: xi, 353 p. *ISBN: 041500859x. Includes bibliography and index.*
2 Aptitude-treatment interaction research in the clinical setting — a review of attempts to dispel the "patient uniformity" myth. Kathryn A. Dance; Richard W. J. Neufeld. *Psychol .B.* **104:2** 9:1988 pp. 192 – 213
3 "Associationism". Hiroshi Uga. *B. Gen. Ed.* Vol.24-25. 1988. pp.25-41, 1-20
4 The behavioral and social sciences — achievements and opportunities. Dean R. Gerstein *[Ed.]*. Washington: National Academy Press, 1988: 282 p. *ISBN: 0309037492; LofC: 88-001618.*
5 Computer models of mind — computational approaches in theoretical psychology. Margaret A. Boden. Cambridge: Cambridge University Press, 1988: 289 p. *ISBN: 052124868x; LofC: 87-25625. Includes bibliography and index.* [Problems in the behavioural sciences. : No. 5]
6 Darwin's psychological theorizing — triangulating on habit. Daniel Rochowiak. *Stud. Hist. Phil. Sci.* **:2** 6:1988 pp. 215 – 242
7 Defensive reactance of psychologists to a metaphysical foundation for integrating different psychologies. E. Rae Harcum. *J. Psychol.* **122:3** 5:1988 pp. 217 – 235

INTERNATIONAL BIBLIOGRAPHY OF SOCIOLOGY — 1988

C.1: Psychology. Social psychology. Sociometry *[Psychologie. Psychologie sociale. Sociométrie]*

8 Un delirio ben fondato — aspetti psicologici del pensiero di Durkheim (1) *[In Italian]*; [A well-founded delirium — psychological aspects of Durkheim's thought (1)] *[Summary]*. Ornella Mastrobuoni. *Uomo* **1:1-2** 1988 pp. 75 – 97

9 The dynamics of inaction — psychological factors inhibiting arms control activism. Richard Karman Gilbert. *Am. Psychol.* **43:10** 10:1988 pp. 755 – 764

10 Elimination, enlightenment and the normative content of folk psychology. Jane Braaten. *J. Theory Soc. Behav.* **18:3** 9:1988 pp. 251 – 268

11 Etiology and treatment of the psychological side effects associated with cancer chemotherapy — a critical review and discussion. Michael P. Carey; Thomas G. Burish. *Psychol .B.* **104:3** 11:1988 pp. 307 – 325

12 The family and psychopathology. Michael J. Goldstein. *Ann. R. Psych.* **39:** 1988 pp. 283 – 300

13 Field dependence research — a historical analysis of a psychological construct. Janice Haaken. *Signs* **13:2** Winter:1988 pp. 311 – 330

14 The follow-up project on psychotherapeutic communities — design and preliminary results. J.E.A. Wagenborg; G.W. Tremonti; A.J. Hesselink; R.F. Koning. *Inter. J. Therap. Comm.* **9:3** 1988 pp. 129 – 152

15 The follow-up project on therapeutic communities — a collection of measures for change. A.M. Koster; J.E.A. Wagenborg. *Inter. J. Therap. Comm.* **9:3** 1988 pp. 163 – 176

16 It was worthwhile, wasn't it? Retrospective reflections on the follow-up project on psychotherapeautic communities. R.F. Koning; J.E.A. Wagenborg. *Inter. J. Therap. Comm.* **9:3** 1988 pp. 205 – 222

17 Knocking at the door — admissions procedures to psychotherapeutic communities. R.F. Koning. *Inter. J. Therap. Comm.* **9:3** 1988 pp. 153 – 162

18 Lay theories — everyday understanding of problems in the social sciences. Adrian Furnham. Oxford: Pergamon, 1988: 280p. *ISBN: 0080326943*. [International series in experimental social psychology.]

19 A narrative history of experimental social psychology — the Lewin tradition. Shelley Patnoe. New York: Springer-Verlag, 1988: 279 p. *ISBN: 0387968504*. [Recent research in psychology.]

20 On the politics of psychological constructs — stop the bandwagon, I want to get off. Martha T. Mednick. *Am. Psychol.* **44:8** 8:1988 pp. 1118 – 1123

21 On the social psychology of therapy evaluation — control treatments and the natural negotiation hypothesis. John D. Greenwood. *J. Theory Soc. Behav.* **18:4** 12:1988 pp. 373 – 390

22 Перестройка и общественная психология *[In Russian]*; (Perestroika and social psychology). Г.Г. Дилигенский. *Rab. Klass Sov.* **6:108** 1988 pp. 3 – 16

23 Persons in context — developmental processes. Niall Bolger *[Ed.]*. Cambridge: Cambridge University Press, 1988: 259 p. *ISBN: 052135577x; LofC: 87-036765*. [Human development in cultural and historical contexts.]

24 Phenomenological analysis and experimental method in psychology — the problem of their compatibility. Carl F. Graumann. *J. Theory Soc. Behav.* **18:1** 3:1988 pp. 33 – 50

INTERNATIONAL BIBLIOGRAPHY OF SOCIOLOGY — 1988

C.1: Psychology. Social psychology. Sociometry *[Psychologie. Psychologie sociale. Sociométrie]*

25 Placebos and common factors in two decades of psychotherapy research. Peter Horvath. *Psychol .B.* **104:2** 9:1988 pp. 214 – 225

26 Psychobiography and life narratives. Dan P. McAdams *[Ed.]*; Richard L. Ochberg *[Ed.]*; Alan C. Elms *[Contrib.]*; Abigail J. Stewart *[Contrib.]*; Carol Franz *[Contrib.]*; Lynne Layton *[Contrib.]*; David G. Winter *[Contrib.]*; Leslie A. Carlson *[Contrib.]*; Rae Carlson *[Contrib.]*; James William Anderson *[Contrib.] and others. Collection of 11 articles.* **J. Personal.** , *56:1*, 3:1988 pp. 1 – 326

27 Psychology and AIDS. Thomas E. Backer *[Ed.]*; Walter F. Batchelor *[Ed.]*; James M. Jones *[Ed.]*; Vickie M. Mays *[Ed.]*; Stephen F. Morin *[Contrib.]*; Nancy Pelosi *[Contrib.]*; Charles R. Schuster *[Contrib.]*; James D. Watkins *[Contrib.]*; Thomas J. Coates *[Contrib.]*; Ron D. Stall *[Contrib.] and others. Collection of 13 articles.* **Am. Psychol.** , *43:11*, 11:1988 pp. 835 – 897

28 Psychology in Australia. Ronald Taft; Ross H. Day. *Ann. R. Psych.* **39:** 1988 pp. 375 – 400

29 Psychotherapeutic community outcome in a Grand Prix contest — in search of a comparison. G.W. Tremonti; R.F. Koning. *Inter. J. Therap. Comm.* **9:3** 1988 pp. 193 – 204

30 Race and culture in psychiatry. Suman Fernando. London: Croom Helm, 1988: xviii, 216 p. *ISBN: 070994912x. Bibliography — p.186-204.*

31 The radical spirit — essays on psychoanalysis and society. Joel Kovel. London: Free Association, 1988: 349 p. *ISBN: 0946960577. Bibliography — p.335-343.*

32 Recent advances in social psychology — an international perspective. Joseph P. Forgas *[Ed.]*; J. Michael Innes *[Ed.]*. Amsterdam: North-Holland, 1988: 543 p. *ISBN: 0444885196. International Congress of Psychology. 24th. 1988. Sydney.*

33 The relevance and irrelevance of psychological research — the example of prison crowding. R. Barry Ruback; Christopher A. Innes. *Am. Psychol.* **43:9** 9:1988 pp. 683 – 693

34 The role of the case study method in the foundations of psychoanalysis. Adolf Grünbaum. *Can. J. Phil.* **18:4** 12:1988 pp. 623 – 658

35 Russian psychology — a critical history. David Joravsky. Oxford: Blackwell, 1988: 583 p. *ISBN: 0631163379. Bibliography — p.537-568.*

36 Social fabrics of the mind. Donald R. Omark *[Ed.]*; Michael R. A. Chance *[Ed.]*. Hove: Lawrence Erlbaum Associates, 1988: 341 p. *ISBN: 0863770975.*

37 Social psychology, past and present — an integrative orientation. Jay M. Jackson. Hillsdale,N.J.: Lawrence Erlbaum, 1988: 173 p. *ISBN: 0898599164. Bibliography.*

38 Sociometric research. Willem E. Saris *[Ed.]*; Irmtraud N. Gallhofer *[Ed.]*. Basingstoke: Macmillan, 1988: x, 246 p. (ill) *ISBN: 0333437233. Conference papers; Includes bibliographies.*

39 Stress management during noxious medical procedures — an evaluative review of outcome studies. Robin Ludwick-Rosenthal; Richard W.J. Neufeld. *Psychol .B.* **104:3** 11:1988 pp. 326 – 342

C.1: Psychology. Social psychology. Sociometry *[Psychologie. Psychologie sociale. Sociométrie]*

40 Sublimierungskonzept und Komplementaritätsprinzip. Bewerkungen zum Verhältnis von Psychoanalyse und Soziologie *[In German]*; On sublimation and complementarity — reflections upon the relationship between sociology and psychoanalysis *[Summary]*. Günter Naegeler. *Kölner Z. Soz. Soz. psy.* **40:3** 1988 pp. 464 – 484

41 Toward a formative psychology. George C. Rosenwald. *J. Theory Soc. Behav.* **18:1** 3:1988 pp. 1 – 32

C.2: Individuals. Personality — *Individus. Personnalité*

Sub-divisions: Emotions *[Émotions]*; Personality *[Personnalité]*

1 Age and outstanding achievement — what do we know after a century of research? Dean Keith Simonton. *Psychol .B.* **104:2** 9:1988 pp. 251 – 267

2 An application of the prototype scale construction strategy to the assessment of student motivation. Peter F. de Jong. *J. Personal.* **56:3** 9:1988 pp. 487 – 508

3 Appraisal of the self-schema construct in cognitive models of depression. Zindel V. Segal. *Psychol .B.* **103:2** 3:1988 pp. 147 – 162

4 Are the poor less intelligent? Or much ado about nothing. Anup Kumar Singh. *Indian J. Soc. W.* **XLIX:4** 10:1988 pp. 377 – 386

5 Attachment in late adolescence — working models, affect regulation, and representations of self and others. R. Rogers Kobak; Amy Sceery. *Child. Devel.* **59:1** 2:1988 pp. 135 – 146

6 Belief, desire, and revision. J. Collins. *Mind* **XCVII:** :1988 pp. 333 – 342

7 Biases resulting from the use of indexes — an application to attributional style and depression. Jeffrey M. Perloff; Jacqueline B. Persons. *Psychol .B.* **103:1** 1:1988 pp. 95 – 104

8 Causal processing — origins and development. Peter A. White. *Psychol .B.* **104:1** 7:1988 pp. 36 – 52

9 Children's understanding of representational change and its relation to the understanding of false belief and the appearance-reality distinction. Alison Gopnik; Janet W. Astington. *Child. Devel.* **59:1** 2:1988 pp. 26 – 37

10 Cognitive domains of the mood system. John D. Mayer; Michelle H. Mamberg; Alton J. Volanth. *J. Personal.* **56:3** 9:1988 pp. 453 – 486

11 The cognitive perspective on strategic decision-making. Charles R. Schwenk. *J. Manag. Stu.* **25:1** 1:1988 pp. 41 – 56

12 Cognitive processes underlying context effects in attitude measurement. Roger Tourangeau; Kenneth A. Rasinski. *Psychol .B.* **103:3** 5:1988 pp. 299 – 314

13 Cognitive significance without cognitive content. H. Wettstein. *Mind* **XCVII:** :1988 pp. 1 – 28

14 Comprehension monitoring and the apprehension of literal meaning. Gary Bonitatibus. *Child. Devel.* **59:1** 2:1988 pp. 60 – 70

15 Containing anxiety in institutions — selected essays. Isabel Menzies Lyth. London: Free Association, 1988: 269 p. *ISBN: 1853430005. Bibliography —p.259-264.*

16 The cooperative/ competitive strategy scale — a measure of motivation to use

C.2: Individuals. Personality *[Individus. Personnalité]*

cooperative or competitive strategies for success. Carolyn H. Simmons; Elizabeth A. Wehner; Suzette Settle Tucker; Cheryl Simrell King. *J. Soc. Psychol.* **128:2** 4:1988 pp. 199 – 205

17 Creativity syndrome — integration, application, and innovation. Michael D. Mumford; Sigrid B. Gustafson. *Psychol .B.* **103:1** 1:1988 pp. 27 – 43

18 The current state of differential association theory. Ross L. Matsueda. *Crime Delin.* **34:3** 7:1988 pp. 277 – 306

19 Desire as belief. D. Lewis. *Mind* **XCVII:** :1988 pp. 323 – 332

20 The development of political understanding in children between 6-15 years old. Anna Emilia Berti. *Human Relat.* **41:6** 1988 pp. 437 – 446

21 The difference between feeling and thinking. S. Everson. *Mind* **XCVII:** :1988 pp. 401 – 413

22 Dysrhythmia, dysphoria, and depression — the interaction of learned helplessness and circadian dysrhythmia in the pathogenesis of depression. D. Healy; J.M.G. Williams. *Psychol .B.* **103:2** 3:1988 pp. 163 – 178

23 The effect of decision strategy and task complexity on decision performance. Laurence Paquette; Thomas Kida. *Organ. Beh. Hum. Dec. Proces.* **41:1** 2:1988 pp. 128 – 142

24 The effects of response mode and importance on decision-making strategies — judgment versus choice. Robert S. Billings; Lisa L. Scherer. *Organ. Beh. Hum. Dec. Proces.* **41:1** 2:1988 pp. 1 – 19

25 Evolving conceptions of memory storage, selective attention, and their mutual constraints within the human information-processing system. Nelson Cowan. *Psychol .B.* **104:2** 9:1988 pp. 163 – 191

26 Humour in society — resistance and control. Chris Powell *[Ed.]*; George E. C. Paton *[Ed.]*. Basingstoke: Macmillan, 1988: xxii, 279 p. *ISBN: 0333440706. Includes bibliographies and index.*

27 Identity in the loose and popular sense. D.L.M. Baxter. *Mind* **XCVII:** :1988 pp. 575 – 584

28 Illusion and well-being — a social psychological perspective on mental health. Shelley E. Taylor; Jonathon D. Brown. *Psychol .B.* **103:2** 3:1988 pp. 193 – 210

29 The IQ controversy. Mark Snyderman; Stanley Rothman *[Ed.]*. New Brunswick: Transaction Books, [1988]: xi, 310 p. *ISBN: 0887381510.*

30 Jiishiki no akujunkan katei wo megutte *[In Japanese]*; [On the vicious circle of self-consciousness]. Hiroaki Ishikawa. *Sociologos Vol.12. 1988.* pp. 100 – 115

31 The knowledge-structure and inductivist strategies in causal attribution — a direct comparison. D.J. Hilton; C.S. Knibbs. *Eur. J. Soc. Psychol.* **18:1** 1-3:1988 pp. 79 – 92

32 Limited mental capacities and perceived control in attribution of responsibility. Frank D. Fincham; Robert E. Emery. *Br. J. Soc. P.* **27:3** 9:1988 pp. 193 – 207

33 Lost in a book — the psychology of reading for pleasure. Victor Nell. New Haven, Connecticut: Yale University Press, 1988: 336 p. (ill) *ISBN: 0300041152; LofC: 87-14283. Includes bibliography and index.*

34 Moderator variable approaches in personality research — a discussion. Roy F.

C.2: Individuals. Personality *[Individus. Personnalité]*

Baumeister *[Contrib.]*; Dianne M. Tice *[Contrib.]*; Sampo V. Paunonen *[Contrib.]*; Auke Tellegen *[Contrib.]*. *Collection of 3 articles.* **J. Personal.** , *56:3,* 9:1988 pp. 571 – 663

35 Nuclear fear — a history of images. Spencer R. Weart. Cambridge, Mass.: Harvard University Press, 1988: 535 p. (1ill) *ISBN: 0674628357; LofC: 87-25995. Includes index.*

36 On humour — its nature and its place in modern society. Michael Mulkay. Cambridge: Polity, 1988: 232 p. (ill) *ISBN: 0745605435. Bibliography, p.224-229. Includes index.*

37 On the social nature of human cognition — an analysis of the shared intellectual roots of George Herbert Mead and Lev Vygotsky. Jaan Valsiner; René van der Veer. *J. Theory Soc. Behav.* **18:1** 3:1988 pp. 117 – 136

38 Pain — synaptic or syntactic. James Walkup. *J. Theory Soc. Behav.* **18:3** 9:1988 pp. 309 – 322

39 Patterns of visual-spatial performance and "spatial ability" — dissociation of ethnic and sex differences. Terence J. Mayes; Gustav Jahoda; Irene Neilson. *Br. J. Psy.* **:1-2-3-4** 2-5-8-11:1988 pp. 105 – 120

40 Perpetrators' freedom of choice as a determinant of responsibility attribution. Dariusz Dolinski; Wojciech Gromski; Andrzej Szmajke. *J. Soc. Psychol.* pp. 441 – 449

41 Personal and impersonal identity. T.L.S. Sprigge. *Mind* **XCVII:** :1988 pp. 29 – 49

42 Perspectives on self-deception. Brian P. McLaughlin *[Ed.]*; Amélie Oksenberg Rorty *[Ed.]*. Berkeley: University of California Press, [1988]: 558 p. *ISBN: 0520052080. Bibliography — p.[553]-558.*

43 The psychobiology of loss — lessons from humans and nonhuman primates. Mark L. Laudenslager. *J. Soc. Issues* **44:3** 1988 pp. 19 – 36

44 The psychology of human thought. Robert J. Sternberg *[Ed.]*; Edward E. Smith *[Ed.]*. Cambridge: Cambridge University Press, 1988: 480 p. *ISBN: 0521322294. Includes index.*

45 Psychosocial functioning and depression — distinguishing among antecedents, concomitants, and consequences. Peter A. Barnett; Ian H. Gotlib. *Psychol .B.* **104:1** 7:1988 pp. 97 – 125

46 Reconceptualizing arousal — psychobiological states in motor performance. Rob Neiss. *Psychol .B.* **103:3** 5:1988 pp. 345 – 366

47 Relapse after recovery from unipolar depression — a critical review. Gayle Belsher; Charles G. Costello. *Psychol .B.* **104:1** 7:1988 pp. 84 – 96

48 The relation between stable/ unstable attribution and learned helplessness. Mario Mikulincer. *Br. J. Soc. P.* **27:3** 9:1988 pp. 221 – 230

49 The relationship of self-esteem and attributional style to young peoples' worries. Glynis M. Breakwell; Chris Fife-Schaw; John B. Devereux. *J. Psychol.* **122:3** 5:1988 pp. 207 – 216

50 Remembering your parents — reflections on the retrospective method. Charles F. Halverson. *J. Personal.* **56:2** 6:1988 pp. 435 – 443

51 Self-defeating behavior patterns among normal individuals — review and analysis of common self-destructive tendencies. Roy F. Baumeister; Steven J. Scher. *Psychol .B.* **104:1** 7:1988 pp. 3 – 22

C.2: Individuals. Personality [Individus. Personnalité]

52 Self-extensions — a conceptualization. Sandra Lancaster; Margaret Foddy. *J. Theory Soc. Behav.* **18:1** 3:1988 pp. 77 – 94
53 Self-serving attributions for performance in naturalistic settings — a meta-analytic review. Brian Mullen; Catherine A. Riordan. *J. Appl. Soc. Psychol.* **18:1** 1:1988 pp. 3 – 22
54 The social form of feeling. Alan Radley. *Br. J. Soc. P.* **27:1** 3:1988 pp. 5 – 18
55 Stress and coping in relation to health and disease. A.J.J.M. Vingerhoets *[Contrib.]*; F.H.G. Marcelissen *[Contrib.]*; James P. Henry *[Contrib.]*; L.J.P. van Doornen *[Contrib.]*; E.J.C. de Geus *[Contrib.]*; J.F. Orlebeke *[Contrib.]*; Susan Folkman *[Contrib.]*; Richard S. Lazarus; Zahava Solomon *[Contrib.]*; Hanoch Flum *[Contrib.]* and others. Collection of 14 articles. *Soc. Sci. Med.*, 26:3, 1988 pp. 277 – 392
56 Sympathy, empathy, and the stream of consciousness. Thomas Natsoulas. *J. Theory Soc. Behav.* **18:2** 6:1988 pp. 169 – 196
57 Thought without language. L. Weiskrantz *[Ed.]*. Oxford: Clarendon Press, 1988: 450 p. *A Fyssen Foundation symposium; Includes bibliography and index.*
58 Towards a contingency model of self- management. Oded Manor. *Inter. J. Therap. Comm.* **9:1** 1988 pp. 17 – 30

Emotions [Émotions]

59 Behind the happiness barrier. J.P. Roos. *Soc. Ind.* **20:2** 4:1988 pp. 141 – 163
60 A causal theory of experiential fear. Wayne Davis. *Can. J. Phil.* **18:3** 9:1988 pp. 459 – 484
61 Constructing emotions — weaving meaning from memories. Susan Kippax; June Crawford; Pam Benton; Una Gault; Jenny Noesjirwan. *Br. J. Soc. P.* **27:1** 3:1988 pp. 19 – 33
62 A developmental analysis of elementary school-aged children's concepts of pride and embarrassment. Laura Beizer Seidner; Deborah J. Stipek; Norma Deitch Feshbach. *Child. Devel.* **59:2** 4:1988 pp. 367 – 377
63 Embarrassment — a window on the self. Mary K. Babcock. *J. Theory Soc. Behav.* **18:4** 12:1988 pp. 459 – 484
64 Emotion and social context — an American-German comparison. Shula Sommers; Corinne Kosmitzki. *Br. J. Soc. P.* **27:1** 3:1988 pp. 35 – 49
65 Emotionsarbeit. Zur Kommerzialisierung von Gefühlen *[In German]*; Emotion work. The commercialization of feelings *[Summary]*. Jürgen Gerhards. *Soz. Welt.* **39:1** 1988 pp. 47 – 65
66 Expression of emotion. Wayne A. Davis. *Am. Phil. Q.* **25:4** 10:1988 pp. 279 – 292
67 Gendai shakai to kanjo — josetsu *[In Japanese]*; [Modern society and emotions — an introduction]. Masayuki Okahara; Kuniharu Kida. *Nen. Shak. Ron.* Vol.1. 1988. pp. 35 – 46
68 Grief as an emotion and as a disease — a social-constructionist perspective. James R. Averill; Elma P. Nunley. *J. Soc. Issues* **44:3** 1988 pp. 79 – 95
69 Habit, emotion, and self-conscious action. John D. Baldwin. *Sociol. Pers.* **31:1** 1:1988 pp. 35 – 58
70 Imagining emotions and appreciating fiction. Susan L. Feagin. *Can. J. Phil.* **18:3** 9:1988 pp. 485 – 500

C.2: Individuals. Personality *[Individus. Personnalité]* — Emotions *[Émotions]*

71 Impression-management and self-deception components of appraised emotional experience. Gordon L. Flett; Kirk R. Blankstein; Patricia Pliner; Carl Bator. *Br. J. Soc. P.* **27:1** 3:1988 pp. 67 – 77

72 In and out of context — influences of facial expression and context information on emotion attributions. Harald G. Wallbott. *Br. J. Soc. P.* **27:4** 12:1988 pp. 357 – 369

73 Infant discrimination of naturalistic emotional expressions — the role of face and voice. Albert J. Caron; Rose F. Caron; Darla J. MacLean. *Child. Devel.* **59:3** 6:1988 pp. 604 – 616

74 A longitudinal study of negative emotional states and adjustment from early childhood through adolescence. Jacqueline V. Lerner; Christopher Hertzog; Karen A. Hooker; Mahin Hassibi; Alexander Thomas. *Child. Devel.* **59:2** 4:1988 pp. 356 – 366

75 On emotions as judgements. Robert C. Solomon. *Am. Phil. Q.* **25:2** 4:1988 pp. 183 – 193

76 Passionate women and passionate men — sex differences in accounting for angry and weepy episodes. Muriel Egerton. *Br. J. Soc. P.* **27:1** 3:1988 pp. 51 – 66

77 Passions within reason — the strategic role of the emotions. Robert H. Frank. New York: W.W.Norton, 1988: 304 p. *ISBN: 0393026043. Bibliography.*

78 The psychology of love. Robert J. Sternberg *[Ed.]*; Michael L. Barnes *[Ed.]*. New Haven [Conn.]: Yale University Press, 1988: 395 p. *ISBN: 0300039506; LofC: 87-10656. Includes index.*

79 Self-discrepancies as predictors of vulnerability to distinct syndromes of chronic emotional distress. Timothy J. Strauman; E. Tory Higgins. *J. Personal.* **56:4** 12:1988 pp. 685 – 707

80 Shame and conformity — the deference-emotion system. Thomas J. Scheff. *Am. Sociol. R.* **53:3** 6:1988 pp. 395 – 406

81 The utility of happiness. Ruut Veenhoven. *Soc. Ind.* **20:4** 8:1988 pp. 333 – 354

82 Wenn Gefühle zum Arbeitsgegenstand werden. Gefühlsarbeit im Rahmen personenbezogener Dienstleistungstätigkeiten *[In German]*; When emotions become objects of labor — emotional labor within personal service occupations *[Summary]*. Wolfgang Dunkel. *Soz. Welt.* **39:1** 1988 pp. 66 – 85

Personality *[Personnalité]*

83 The authoritarian personality — an inadequate explanation for intergroup conflict in South Africa. J. Louw-Potgieter. *J. Soc. Psychol.* **128:1** 2:1988 pp. 75 – 87

84 Centrality and individual differences in the meaning of daily hassles. Rand J. Gruen; Susan Folkman; Richard S. Lazarus. *J. Personal.* **56:4** 12:1988 pp. 743 – 762

85 The construct validity of assertion — contributions of four assessment procedures and Norman's personality factors. Marc-André Bouchard; Francine Lalonde; Martin Gagnon. *J. Personal.* **56:4** 12:1988 pp. 763 – 783

86 Constructing the inner citadel — recent work on the concept of autonomy. John Christman. *Ethics* **99:1** 10:1988 pp. 109 – 124

87 Culture, personality and psychotherapy. Vijoy K. Varma. *Int. J. Soc. Psyc.* **34:2** Summer:1988 pp. 142 – 149

C.2: Individuals. Personality *[Individus. Personnalité]* — Personality *[Personnalité]*

88 Desire for control and the use of attribution processes. Jerry M. Burger; Lawton T. Hemans. *J. Personal.* **56**:3 9:1988 pp. 531 – 546

89 The effects of success and failure on children's use of defense mechanisms. Phebe Cramer; Robin Gaul. *J. Personal.* **56**:4 12:1988 pp. 729 – 742

90 Experiential being and the inherent self — towards a constructivist theory of the self. David D.V. Fisher. *J. Theory Soc. Behav.* **18**:2 6:1988 pp. 149 – 168

91 From inferred personalities toward personality in action. Donald W. Fiske. *J. Personal.* **56**:4 12:1988 pp. 815 – 833

92 Global self-evaluation and changes in self-description as a function of information discrepancy and favorability. J. Sidney Shrauger; Robert J. Kelly. *J. Personal.* **56**:4 12:1988 pp. 709 – 728

93 Group differences in measurable personality factors associated with parental divorce and remarriage. Stanley E. Wigle; Thomas S. Parish. *J. Psychol.* **122**:2 3:1988 pp. 109 – 112

94 In search of self in India and Japan — toward a cross-cultural psychology. Alan Roland. Princeton: Princeton University Press, 1988: xxxii, 386 p. *ISBN: 0691086176. Includes bibliography.*

95 Narcissism and the use of personal pronouns. Robert Raskin; Robert Shaw. *J. Personal.* **56**:2 6:1988 pp. 393 – 404

96 Object relations and ego development — comparison and correlates in middle childhood. Rachel Robb Avery; Richard M. Ryan. *J. Personal.* **56**:3 9:1988 pp. 547 – 569

97 On the integration of nomothetic and idiographic research methods in the study of personal meaning. Hubert J. M. Hermans. *J. Personal.* **56**:4 12:1988 pp. 785 – 812

98 The personality of vegetables — botanical metaphors for human characteristics. Robert Sommer. *J. Personal.* **56**:4 12:1988 pp. 665 – 683

99 Recalled parent-child relations and adult personality. Robert R. McCrae; Paul T. Costa. *J. Personal.* **56**:2 6:1988 pp. 417 – 434

100 The role of contextual factors in the relationship between physical activity and self-awareness. Michael H. Kernis; Bruce D. Grannemann; Talman Richie; Judy Hart. *Br. J. Soc. P.* **27**:3 9:1988 pp. 265 – 273

101 Self-concept development of Ghanaian school children. Osman Alawiye; Catherine Zeimat Alawiye. *J. Psychol.* **122**:2 3:1988 pp. 139 – 146

102 Self-ratings of personality — a naturalistic comparison of normative, ipsative, and idiothetic standards. William F. Chaplin; Kathryn E. Buckner. *J. Personal.* **56**:3 9:1988 pp. 509 – 530

103 Use of categorical and individuating information in making inferences about personality. Joachim Krueger; Myron Rothbart. *J. Pers. Soc. Psychol.* **55**:2 8:1988 pp. 187 – 195

104 Zelfwaardering bij meisjes en jongens — een biosociale benadering *[In Dutch]*; Self-esteem among girls and boys — a biosocial approach *[Summary]*. H. Brutsaert. *Sociol. Gids* **XXXV**:4 7-8:1988 pp. 268 – 280

C.3: Interpersonal relations — *Relations interpersonnelles*

1 Attachment and emotional health — a life span approach. Tamara Kotler; Mary Omodei. *Human Relat.* **41:8** 1988 pp. 619 – 640
2 The "Chong" space — a zone of non-exchange in Korean human relationships. Soo-Won Lee. *Korean Soc. Sci. J.* **14** 1988 pp. 120 – 130
3 Communication, social cognition, and affect. Lewis Donohew *[Ed.]*; Howard E. Sypher *[Ed.]*; E. Tory Higgins *[Ed.]*. Hillsdale, New Jersey: Erlbaum, 1988: xiii, 259 p. *ISBN: 089859975x*. [Communication.]
4 Comunicare culturală și personalitate *[In Romanian]*; (Cultural communication and personality); (Communication culturelle et personnalité: *Title only in French*); (Культурное сообщение и личность: *Title only in Russian*). Florin Ciotea. *Viit. Soc.* **LXXXI** 1-2:1988 pp. 43 – 50
5 Conflict resolution as the alternative to terrorism. Stephen P. Cohen; Harriet C. Arnone. *J. Soc. Issues* **44:2** 1988 pp. 175 – 189
6 Consciousness raising among mentally handicapped people — a critique of the implications of normalization. Susan E. Szivos; Eileen Travers. *Human Relat.* **41:9** 1988 pp. 641 – 653
7 Couples' cognitive/affective reactions to communication behaviors. Frank J. Floyd. *J. Marriage Fam.* **50:2** 5:1988 pp. 523 – 532
8 The decision to leave an abusive relationship — empirical evidence and theoretical issues. Michael J. Strube. *Psychol .B.* **104:2** 9:1988 pp. 236 – 250
9 Depression and interpersonal attraction — the role of perceived similarity. Abram Rosenblatt; Jeff Greenberg. *J. Pers. Soc. Psychol.* **55:1** 7:1988 pp. 112 – 119
10 Diagaku-sei no musume to chichioya no joucho kankei *[In Japanese]*; [Emotional relationship between college student daughters and their fathers]. Miyoko Nagatsu. *Aobag. Kiyo Vol.13. 1988.* pp. 59 – 72
11 Discussione and friendship — socialization processes in the peer culture of Italian nursery school children. William A. Corsaro; Thomas A. Rizzo. *Am. Sociol. R.* **53:6** 12:1988 pp. 879 – 894
12 Dramaturgical analysis of social interaction. Paul A. Hare; Herbert H. Blumberg *[Ed.]*. New York: Praeger, 1988: 177 p. *ISBN: 0275927628; LofC: 87-30534. Bibliography — p.159-167*.
13 Early family experience, social problem solving patterns, and children's social competence. Gregory S. Pettit; Kenneth A. Dodge; Melissa M. Brown. *Child. Devel.* **59:1** 2:1988 pp. 107 – 120
14 Effects of devil's advocacy on escalating commitment. Charles R. Schwenk. *Human Relat.* **41:10** 1988 pp. 769 – 782
15 Estimating the prevalence of shyness in the "global village" — pluralistic ignorance or false consensus? Peter R. Harris; Philip Wilshire. *J. Personal.* **56:2** 6:1988 pp. 405 – 415
16 Excuses — their effective role in the negotiation of reality. C.R. Snyder; Raymond L. Higgins. *Psychol .B.* **104:1** 7:1988 pp. 23 – 35
17 Extending the metaphor "system". C.J. Atkinson; P.B. Checkland. *Human Relat.* **41:10** 1988 pp. 709 – 725
18 La fiducia — un concetto fragile, una non meno fragile realtà *[In Italian]*; Trust — a fragile concept, a no less fragile reality *[Summary]*. Luis Roniger. *Rass. It. Soc.* **29:3** 7-9:1988 pp. 383 – 402

C.3: Interpersonal relations [Relations interpersonnelles]

19 Functional flexibility — a new conception of interpersonal flexibility. Delroy L. Paulhus; Carol Lynn Martin. *J. Pers. Soc. Psychol.* **55:1** 7:1988 pp. 88 – 101

20 Funsouriron saikou josetsu *[In Japanese]*; [Reconsideration of conflict theories]. Kouichi Ogawa. *Keio U. Shinbun Kenkyuusho Nenpou Vol.30.* *1988.* pp. 61 – 78

21 Gender differences in verbal ability — a meta-analysis. Janet Shibley Hyde; Marcia C. Linn. *Psychol .B.* **104:1** 7:1988 pp. 53 – 69

22 A generic measure of relationship satisfaction. Susan S. Hendrick. *J. Marriage Fam.* **50:1** 2:1988 pp. 93 – 98

23 Gratitude and obligation. Claudia Card. *Am. Phil. Q.* **25:2** 4:1988 pp. 115 – 128

24 Individual and social identities in intergroup relations. Willem Doise. *Eur. J. Soc. Psychol.* **18:2** 4-6:1988 pp. 99 – 111

25 Intergroup competition for the provision of step-level public goods — effects of preplay communication. Gary Bornstein; Amnon Rapoport. *Eur. J. Soc. Psychol.* **18:2** 4-6:1988 pp. 125 – 142

26 Interpersonal moral conflicts. Terrance McConnell. *Am. Phil. Q.* **25:1** 1:1988 pp. 25 – 36

27 Interpersonal processes in close relationships. Margaret S. Clark; Harry T. Reis. *Ann. R. Psych.* **39:** 1988 pp. 609 – 672

28 Local friendship ties and community attachment in mass society — a multilevel systemic model. Robert J. Sampson. *Am. Sociol. R.* **53:5** 10:1988 pp. 766 – 779

29 Matching for attractiveness in romantic partners and same-sex friends — a meta-analysis and theoretical critique. Alan Feingold. *Psychol .B.* **104:2** 9:1988 pp. 226 – 235

30 The nature of power. Barry Barnes. Cambridge: Polity Press, 1988: 205 p. *ISBN: 0745600735. Includes bibliography — p199-202; and index.*

31 The other side of dialogue — on making the other strange and the experience of otherness. Z.D. Gurevitch. *A.J.S.* **93:5** 3:1988 pp. 1179 – 1199

32 Peer interaction and problem solving — when are two heads better than one? Margarita Azmitia. *Child. Devel.* **59:1** 2:1988 pp. 87 – 96

33 Perceived voluntariness of consent of warrantless police searches. Dorothy K. Kagehiro. *J. Appl. Soc. Psychol.* **18:1** 1:1988 pp. 38 – 49

34 Personal relationships. Philip Blumstein; Peter Kollock. *Ann. R. Soc.* **14** 1988 pp. 467 – 490

35 Pluralism, corporatism, and Confucianism — political associations and conflict regulation in the United States, Europe, and Taiwan. L. Harmon Zeigler. Philadelphia: Temple University Press, 1988: xviii, 249 p. (ill.) *ISBN: 087722529x. Bibliography — p.229-241.*

36 The predictability of informal conversation. Christine Cheepen. London: Pinter, 1988: 224 p. *ISBN: 0861877071.*

37 Psychologie des influences sociales; The psychology of social influence. Angela St. James-Emler *[Tr.]*; Nicolas Emler *[Tr.]*; Geneviéve Paicheler. Cambridge: Cambridge University Press, 1988: vi, 225 p. (ill) *ISBN: 0521309409; LofC: 87-21827. eng, fre; Bibliography — p.211-219. Includes index.*

C.3: Interpersonal relations *[Relations interpersonnelles]*

38 The relation of empathy to aggressive and externalizing-antisocial behavior. Paul A. Miller; Nancy Eisenberg. *Psychol .B.* **103:3** 5:1988 pp. 324 – 344

39 Resolving conflict — dispute settlement mechanisms for Aboriginal communities and neighbourhoods. Kayleen Hazlehurst. *Aust. J. Soc. Iss.* **23:4** 11:1988 pp. 309 – 321

40 The role of rewards and fairness in developing premarital relationships. M. Rodney Cate; Sally A. Lloyd; Edgar Long. *J. Marriage Fam.* **50:2** 5:1988 pp. 443 – 452

41 Secrecy and status — the social construction of forbidden relationships. Laurel Richardson. *Am. Sociol. R.* **53:2** 4:1988 pp. 209 – 219

42 Self-esteem and facilitative close relationships — a cross-lagged panel correlation analysis. Duncan Cramer. *Br. J. Soc. P.* **27:2** 6:1988 pp. 115 – 126

43 La sociabilité, une pratique culturelle *[In French]*; [Sociability — a cultural activity]. François Héran. *E & S* **216** 12:1988 pp. 3 – 22

44 Social closure — the theory of monopolization and exclusion. Raymond Murphy. Oxford: Clarendon Press, 1988: 276 p. *ISBN: 0198272685. Bibliography — p.259-270.*

45 Social identifications — a social psychology of intergroup relations and group processes. Michael A. Hogg; Dominic Abrams *[Ed.]*. London: Routledge, 1988: xv, 268 p. *ISBN: 0415006945. Bibliographical references — p.[219]-256.*

46 Social networks of children, adolescents and college students. Suzanne Salzinger *[Ed.]*; John S. Antrobus *[Ed.]*; Muriel Hammer *[Ed.]*. Hillsdale (N.J.); Hove: Lawrence Erlbaum, 1988: 322 p. *ISBN: 0898599792; LofC: 87-6739.*

47 The social psychology of intergroup conflict — theory, research and applications. Wolfgang Stroebe *[Ed.]*. Berlin: Springer-Verlag, 1988: x,198 p. *ISBN: 3540176950.* [Springer series in social psychology.]

48 Sociology's lost human relations area files. Jonathan H. Turner; Alexandra R. Maryanski. *Sociol. Pers.* **31:1** 1:1988 pp. 19 – 34

49 Sougo koui heno "miburi kaiwa" ron-teki approach *[In Japanese]*; [An approach to interaction as "a conversation of gestures"]. Chihaya Kusayaangi. *Philosophy Vol.87. 1988.* pp. 175 – 201

50 Stereotypes and social judgment — extremity, assimilation, and contrast. Melvin Manis; Thomas E. Nelson; Jonathan Shedler. *J. Pers. Soc. Psychol.* **55:1** 7:1988 pp. 28 – 36

51 Strangers — the social construction of university and particularity. Zygmunt Bauman. *Telos* **78** Winter:1988-1989 pp. 7 – 42

52 The structure of conflict. Clyde Hamilton Coombs; George S. Avrunin *[Ed.]*. Hillsdale, New Jersey: Lawrence Erlbaum Associates, 1988: xi, 244 p. *ISBN: 0805800115. Bibliography — p.225-236.*

53 Women, therapy and dependency. Erica L. Hallebone. *Aust. J. Soc. Iss.* **23:4** 11:1988 pp. 268 – 286

C.4: Groups — *Groupes*

1 Axioms of cooperative decision making. Hervé Moulin. Cambridge: Cambridge University Press, 1988: xiv, 332 p. *ISBN: 0521360552. Bibliography — p.317-326.* [Econometric Society monographs. : No. 15]
2 Behavioral-cognitive groups for adult psychiatric patients. Pat McAuley; Mary Louise Catherwood; Ethel Quayle. *Br. J. Soc. W.* **18:5** 10:1988 pp. 455 – 472
3 The "black sheep effect" — extremity of judgement towards ingroup members as a function of group identification. J.M. Marques; V.Y. Yzerbyt; J.-P. Leyens. *Eur. J. Soc. Psychol.* **18:1** 1-3:1988 pp. 1 – 16
4 Context effects on intergroup discrimination — in-group bias as a function of experimenter's provenance. José M. Marques; Vincent Y. Yzerbyt; John B. Rijsman. *Br. J. Soc. P.* **27:4** 12:1988 pp. 301 – 318
5 The Eric Burden community — madness and community. Heather Hull; G.P. Pullen. *Inter. J. Therap. Comm.* **9:2** 1988 pp. 109 – 114
6 Factional competition in complex society. Elizabeth M. Brumfiel. *J. Soc. Stud. Dhaka* **:40** 4:1988 pp. 120 – 130
7 Free riders and zealots — the role of social networks. James S. Coleman. *Sociol. Theory* **6:1** Spring:1988 pp. 52 – 57
8 The good, the bad and the ugly — outcomes of residential psychotherapy. J.E.A. Wagenborg. *Inter. J. Therap. Comm.* **9:3** 1988 pp. 177 – 192
9 Group processes — dynamics within and between groups. Rupert Brown. Oxford: Basil Blackwell, 1988: xii, 295 p. (ill) *ISBN: 0631144382. Includes index.*
10 Groups that work — structure and process. Paul H. Ephross; Thomas V. Vassil *[Ed.]*. New York: Columbia University Press, 1988: xiv, 230 p. *ISBN: 0231057385. Bibliography — p221-226.*
11 How does the large group change the individual? Peter van der Linden. *Inter. J. Therap. Comm.* **9:1** 1988 pp. 31 – 40
12 Individual unionization decisions. Steven L. Premack; John E. Hunter. *Psychol .B.* **103:2** 3:1988 pp. 223 – 234
13 Ingroup and outgroup minorities — differential impact upon public and private responses. R. Martin. *Eur. J. Soc. Psychol.* **18:1** 1-3:1988 pp. 39 – 52
14 Interacción entre las creencias y la observancia de las normas en los grupos sociales — una teoria formal *[In Spanish]*; [A formal theory on interaction of beliefs and the observance of norms in social groups]. José Miguel Sánchez Molinero. *Anal. Est. Econ. Empres.* **3** 1988 pp. 9 – 18
15 Intergroup differentiation in a political context. Caroline Kelly. *Br. J. Soc. P.* **27:4** 12:1988 pp. 319 – 332
16 Interpersonal dimensions in a therapeutic community. J.S.B. Lindsay. *Inter. J. Therap. Comm.* **9:2** 1988 pp. 89 – 100
17 Justice norms and group dynamics — the case of the family. Jean M. Kellerhals; Josette Coenen-Huther; Marianne Modak. *Int. Sociol.* **3:2** 6:1988 pp. 111 – 128
18 Learning to grow — the necessity for educational processing in therapeutic community practice. Paul Barber. *Inter. J. Therap. Comm.* **9:2** 1988 pp. 101 – 108

C.4: Groups [Groupes]

19 Matsuyama shimin no juminishiki to neywork *[In Japanese]*; [Studying personal networks in Matsuyama]. Shinsuke Otani *[Ed.]*. : The Institute of Social Research in Matsuyama University, -: 234 p. Social networks

20 Methodological issues in social support and social network research. Patrick O'Reilly. *Soc. Sci. Med.* **26:8** 1988 pp. 863 – 873

21 Nihon shakai no shakai-teki kettei system to kanjin-shugi *[In Japanese]*; [Japanese social decision making-system and contextualism]. Toshiki Sato. *Sociologos Vol.12. 1988.* pp. 68 – 81

22 Organizational maintenance and the retention decision in groups. Lawrence S. Rothenberg. *Am. Poli. Sci.* **82:4** 12:1988 pp. 1129 – 1152

23 The paradox of group size in collective action — a theory of the critical mass. II. Pamela E. Oliver; Gerald Marwell. *Am. Sociol. R.* **53:1** 2:1988 pp. 1 – 8

24 The relationship between participation rate and liking ratings in groups. Willem Koomen. *Br. J. Soc. P.* **27:2** 6:1988 pp. 127 – 132

25 Shakai network no sūri model — hen net model wo chūshin ni *[In Japanese]*; [Mathematical model on social networks — mainly on biased network models]. Hiroshi Hiramatsu. *Soc. Theo. Meth. Vol.3; No.1 - 1988.* pp. 97 – 110

26 Shakaiteki network to shakaiteki shiji *[In Japanese]*; [Social network and social support]. Shin Watanabe. *Sophia Stud. Soc. Vol.12. 1988.* pp. 1 – 20

27 Social network analysis. John Scott. *Network analysis. Sociology* **22:1** 2:1988 pp. 109 – 127

28 Social network analysis and intercorporate relations. John Scott. *Hito. J. Comm. Manag.* **23:1** 12:1988 pp. 53 – 68

29 Social networks and collective action — a theory of the critical mass. III. Gerald Marwell; Pamela E. Oliver; Ralph Prahl. *A.J.S.* **94:3** 11:1988 pp. 502 – 534

30 Social organization and pathways of commitment — types of communal groups, rational choice theory, and the Kanter thesis. John R. Hall. *Am. Sociol. R.* **53:5** 10:1988 pp. 679 – 692

31 Structures and processes of social support. J. C. House; D. Umberson; K. R. Landis. *Ann. R. Soc.* **14** 1988 pp. 239 – 318

32 The taxonomy of social support — an ethnographic analysis among adolescent mothers. W. Thomas Boyce; Margarita Kay; Chris Uitti. *Soc. Sci. Med.* **26:11** 1988 pp. 1079 – 1085

33 Text, talk and discourse in a therapeutic community. G.E. Chapman. *Inter. J. Therap. Comm.* **9:2** 1988 pp. 75 – 88

34 The transforming nature of metaphors in group development — a study in group theory. Suresh Srivastva; Frank J. Barrett. *Human Relat.* **41:1** 1988 pp. 31 – 64

C.5: Bureaucracy. Organization — *Bureaucratie. Organisation*

1 Analyzing organizational conflicts using a model based on structural role theory. Boris Kabanoff. *Human Relat.* **41:11** 1988 pp. 841 – 870
2 Appraising and exploring organisations. S. Tyson *[Ed.]*; et al. London: Croom Helm, 1988: 230 p. (ill) *ISBN: 0709943407. Includes bibliographies and index.*
3 Attributions and organizational conflict — the mediating role of apparent sincerity. Robert A. Baron. *Organ. Beh. Hum. Dec. Proces.* **41:1** 2:1988 pp. 111 – 127
4 Bridging the gap — international organizations as organizations. Gayl D. Ness; Steven R. Brechin. *Int. Organ.* **42:2** Spring:1988 pp. 245 – 274
5 Communication and power in organizations — discourse, ideology, and domination. Dennis K. Mumby. Norwood, N.J.: Ablex, 1988: xvi, 194 p. *ISBN: 0893914800. Bibliography — p.169-179.* [People, communication, organization.]
6 Ecological models of organizations. Carroll Glenn *[Ed.]*. Cambridge, Massachusetts: Ballinger, 1988: xvi, 280 p. *ISBN: 0887302084. Bibliography — p.241-258.*
7 Explaining participation in coproduction — a study of volunteers. Richard A. Sundeen. *Soc. Sci. Q.* **69:3** 9:1988 pp. 547 – 568
8 Imperfect decisions in organizations — toward a theory of internal structure. Ronald A. Heiner. *Korean Soc. Sci. J.* **9:1** 1:1988 pp. 25 – 44
9 Incentives in collective action organizations. David Knoke. *Am. Sociol. R.* **53:3** 6:1988 pp. 311 – 329
10 Information technology and organizational change — causal structure in theory and research. M. Lynne Markus; Daniel Robey. *Manag. Sci.* **34:5** 5:1988 pp. 583 – 598
11 Intelligent planning — meaningful methods for sensitive situations. Ray Wyatt. London: Unwin Hyman, 1988: 286 p. *ISBN: 0047110198. Bibliography — p262-276.*
12 Is population ecology a useful paradigm for the study of organizations? Ruth C. Young. *A.J.S.* **94:1** 7:1988 pp. 1 – 24
13 Légitimité et modes de domination dans les organisations *[In French]*; Legitimacy and forms of domination in organizations *[Summary]*. Pierre-Éric Tixier. *Sociol. Trav.* **:4** :1988 pp. 615 – 630
14 Manager subordinate dyads — relationships among task and social contact, manager friendliness, and subordinate performance in management groups. Andrew Crouch; Philip Yetton. *Organ. Beh. Hum. Dec. Proces.* **41:1** 2:1988 pp. 65 – 82
15 Managing ambiguity and change. Louis R. Pondy *[Ed.]*; Richard Boland *[Ed.]*; Howard Thomas *[Ed.]*. : Wiley, 1988: 250 p. *ISBN: 0471918431.*
16 Managing voluntary organizations. G. A. Poulton. Chichester: Wiley, 1988: ix, 177 p. (ill) *ISBN: 0471914940; LofC: 88-17385. Bibliography — p.168-172.Includes index.* [Management in the social services.]
17 A mathematical model showing the effects of organizational structure on the dynamics of institutional bias. Joel Gersten; Roslyn Wallach Bologh. *J. Math. Sociol.* **13:3** 1988 pp. 283 – 310

C.5: Bureaucracy. Organization [Bureaucratie. Organisation]

18 Meditating cutbacks in human services — a case study in the negotiated order. David L. Altheide. *Sociol. Q.* **29:3** Fall:1988 pp. 339 – 355

19 The mindlessness of organizational behaviors. Blake E. Ashforth; Yitzhak Fried. *Human Relat.* **41:4** 1988 pp. 305 – 329

20 Organisation as social relationship, formalisation and standardisation — a Weberian approach to concept formation. Gangolf Peters. *Int. Sociol.* **3:3** 9:1988 pp. 267 – 282

21 Organization transitions and innovation-design. Peter A. Clark; Ken Starkey *[Ed.]*. London: Printer, 1988: 211 p. (ill) *ISBN: 0861876466; LofC: 87-25729. Bibliography — p.197-207. Includes index.*

22 Organizational change in Japanese factories. Robert M. Marsh; Hiroshi Mannari. Greenwich, Connecticut: JAI Press Inc., 1988: 313 p.

23 Organizational control of deviant behavior — the case of employee theft. Peter F. Parilla; Richard C. Hollinger; John P. Clark. *Soc. Sci. Q.* **69:2** 6:1988 pp. 261 – 280

24 Organizational demography. Shelby Stewman. *Ann. R. Soc.* **14** 1988 pp. 173 – 202

25 Organizational identity — a psychoanalytic exploration of organizational meaning. Michael A. Diamond. *Admin. Soc.* **20:2** 8:1988 pp. 166 – 190

26 Organizational learning. Barbara Levitt; James G. March. *Ann. R. Soc.* **14** 1988 pp. 319 – 340

27 Organizational population dynamics and social change. Michael T. Hannan. *Eur. Sociol. R.* **4:2** 9:1988 pp. 95 – 110

28 Organizations as multiple cultures — a rules theory analysis. Randall A. Rose. *Human Relat.* **41:2** 1988 pp. 139 – 170

29 Political behavior and physical design. Andrew D. Seidel *[Contrib.]*; Walter B. Kleeman *[Contrib.]*; Robert Sommer *[Contrib.]*; Katherine Steiner *[Contrib.]*; Richard M. Merelman *[Contrib.]*; Jon Lang *[Contrib.]*; James M. Mayo *[Contrib.]*. Collection of 6 articles. **Envir. Behav.**, *20:5*, 9:1988 pp. 531 – 663

30 Professionalism, variation, and organizational survival. David L. Torres. *Am. Sociol. R.* **53:3** 6:1988 pp. 380 – 394

31 Progettazione organizzativa, caratteristiche sociali delle organizzazioni, piccoli gruppi e loro dinamiche *[In Italian]*; [Organizational planning, social characteristics of organizations, small groups and their dynamics]. Francesca Forlani; Francesco Garibaldo; Luisa Masina. *Sociol. Lav.* **35-36** 1988-89 pp. 287 – 300

32 Public, private and hybrid organizations — an empirical examination of the role of publicness. Mark A. Emmert; Michael M. Crow. *Admin. Soc.* **20:2** 8:1988 pp. 216 – 244

33 The quest for organizational meaning. Identifying and interpreting the symbolism in organizational stories. Julianne Mahler. *Admin. Soc.* **20:3** 11:1988 pp. 344 – 368

34 Regional cultures, managerial behavior and entrepreneurship. Joseph W. Weiss *[Ed.]*. New York: Quorum, 1988: x,207 p. *ISBN: 0899303277; LofC: 87-32278.*

35 Reputational status of organizations in technical systems. Wesley Shrum; Robert Wuthnow. *A.J.S.* **93:4** 1:1988 pp. 882 – 912

C.5: Bureaucracy. Organization [Bureaucratie. Organisation]

36 Ressourcenzusammensetzung und Oligarchisierung freiwilliger Vereinigungen [In German]; Resource structure and oligarchic tendencies in voluntary associations [Summary]. Heinz-Dieter Horch. *Kölner Z. Soz. Soz. psy.* **40:3** 1988 pp. 527 – 550

37 Secrecy, information and politics — an essay on organizational decision making. Steven P. Feldman. *Human Relat.* **41:1** 1988 pp. 73 – 90

38 Social organizations and matching theory. F. Masarani; S.S. Gokturk. *Theory Decis.* **24:1** 1:1988 pp. 77 – 95

39 Soshiki ni okeru jikososhikika katei to gorisei [In Japanese]; [Self-organizing process and rationality in organizations]. Michio Ogiso. *Sophia Stud. Soc.* Vol.12. 1988. pp. 61 – 78

40 Soshiki no gouri-sei to innovation [In Japanese]; [Organizational rationality and innovation]. Takenori Takase. *Organ. Sc.* Vol.22; No.3 - 1988. pp. 15 – 24

41 Sources of citizens' bureaucratic contacts — a multivariate analysis. Steven A. Peterson. *Admin. Soc.* **20:2** 8:1988 pp. 152 – 165

42 Sporadic fluid and constricted processes — three types of strategic decision-making in organizations. David Cray; Geoffrey R. Mallory; Richard J. Butler; David J. Hickson; David C. Wilson. *J. Manag. Stu.* **25:1** 1:1988 pp. 13 – 40

43 Survey research and membership in voluntary associations. Frank R. Baumgartner; Jack L. Walker. *Am. J. Pol. Sc.* **32:4** 11:1988 pp. 908 – 928

44 Taishutsu-Kokuhatsu paradigm ni yoru soshiki no suitai — kaifuka katei no bunseki — A. Hirshman, exit, voice and loyalty wo tegakari to shite [In Japanese]; [Decline-recovery process of organizations and "exit-voice paradigm" — an analysis refering to exit, voice and loyalty by A. Hirshman]. Youichi Yanagawa. *Toy. Daig. Kei. Ron* Vol.33; No.3 - 1988. pp. 281 – 313

45 The task-related competency and compliance aspects of goal setting — a clarification. James S. Phillips; Sara M. Freedman. *Organ. Beh. Hum. Dec. Proces.* **41:1** 2:1988 pp. 34 – 49

46 Theoretical pluralism in organizational analysis — the phenomena of work design and organization. Lawrence Nurse. *Admin. Soc.* **20:1** 5:1988 pp. 92 – 108

47 The vortical environment — the fifth in the Emery-Trist levels of organizational environments. Oğuz N. Babüroğlu. *Human Relat.* **41:3** 1988 pp. 181 – 210

48 Weber kanryoseiron eno ichi shiten [In Japanese]; [The concept of Sachlichkeit in the theory of bureaucracy by Max Weber]. Katsuhiro Matsui. *Shak. Kenk.* Vol.52. 1988. pp. 121 – 136

49 What people say and what they do — the differential effects of informational cues and task design. Martin Kilduff; Dennis T. Regan. *Organ. Beh. Hum. Dec. Proces.* **41:1** 2:1988 pp. 83 – 97

50 Women managers — changing organizational cultures. Gisèle Asplund. Chichester: Wiley, [1988]: xvi, 196 p. *ISBN: 0471912921*.

C.6: Leadership. Role — Commandement. Rôle

1 Adoption of the sick role — a latent structure analysis of deviant and normative adaptation. Robert J. Johnson; Howard B. Kaplan; Steven S. Martin. *Soc. Sci. Q.* **69:2** 6:1988 pp. 281 – 298

2 Age and active-passive leadership style. James N. Schubert. *Am. Poli. Sci.* **82:3** 9:1988 pp. 763 – 772

3 Aging and political leadership. Angus McIntyre *[Ed.]*. Melbourne: Oxford University Press, 1988: viii, 316 p. *ISBN: 0195547977; LofC: 88168946. Includes bibliographies and index.*

4 Charisma and objectivity. Aaron Rhodes. *Eur. J. Soc.* **XXIX:1** 1988 pp. 12 – 30

5 Charismatic leadership — the elusive factor in organizational effectiveness. Jay A. Conger; Warren Bennis *[Foreword]*; Rabindra Nath Kanungo *[Ed.]*. San Francisco: Jossey-Bass, 1988: xxii, 352 p. *ISBN: 1555421024; LofC: 88-42784.* [Jossey-Bass management series.]

6 Culture and power — the state of research. Néstor García Canclini. *Media Cult. Soc.* **10:4** 10:1988 pp. 467 – 497

7 Exploitation, cooperation, collusion — an enquiry into patronage. Michael Korovkin. *Eur. J. Soc.* **XXIX:1** 1988 pp. 105 – 126

8 Humbuggery and manipulation — the art of leadership. F.G. Bailey. Ithaca,N.Y.: Cornell University Press, 1988: xiv, 187 p. *ISBN: 0801421543. Bibliography — p.176-181.*

9 In the eye of the beholder — leader images in Canada. Steven D. Brown; Ronald D. Lambert; Barry J. Kay; James E. Curtis. *Can. J. Poli.* **21:4** 12:1988 pp. 729 – 755

10 Interaction preludes to role setting — exploratory local action. Eric M. Leifer. *Am. Sociol. R.* **53:6** 12:1988 pp. 865 – 878

11 Leadership no dilemma — game riron-teki kousatsu *[In Japanese]*; [Dilemma of leadership — a game theoretic analysis]. Kunihiro Kimura. *Soc. Theo. Meth. Vol.3; No.1 - 1988.* pp. 27 – 41

12 Leadership performance in crisis — the longevity-complexity link. Michael D. Wallace; Peter Suedfeld. *Int. Stud. Q.* **32:4** 12:1988 pp. 439 – 451

13 Leadership, organizations and culture — an event management model. Peter B. Smith; Mark F. Peterson *[Ed.]*. London: Sage, 1988: 195 p. *ISBN: 0803980833.*

14 Narcissistic rage in leaders — the intersection of individual dynamics and group process. Mardi J. Horowitz; Ransom J. Arthur. *Int. J. Soc. Psyc.* **34:2** Summer:1988 pp. 135 – 141

15 Personalführung und -entwicklung im veränderten gesellschaftlichen Umfeld *[In German]*; [Personal leadership and development in changing social conditions]. Jan S. Krulis-Randa. *Schw. Z. Volk. Stat.* **124:3** 9:1988 pp. 349 – 365

16 Prisoners of leadership. Manfred F.R. Kets de Vries. *Human Relat.* **41:3** 1988 pp. 261 – 280

17 Qualitative research and the study of leadership. Alan Bryman; Michael Bresnen; Alan Beardsworth; Teresa Keil. *Human Relat.* **41:1** 1988 pp. 13 – 30

C.6: Leadership. Role *[Commandement. Rôle]*

18 Reaction to authoritarian leadership — a projective study. Satish Kumar Kalra. *Indian J. Soc. W.* **XLIX:1** 1:1988 pp. 27 – 44

19 Le rôle du leader charismatique dans la révolution iranienne *[In French]*; [The role of the charismatic leader in the Iranian revolution] *[Summary]*. F. Nahavandi. *Civilisations* **XXXVIII:2** 1988 pp. 125 – 141

20 Role taking reconsidered — linking competence and performance to social structure. Michael L. Schwalbe. *J. Theory Soc. Behav.* **18:4** 12:1988 pp. 411 – 436

21 The socialization to partisan legislative behavior — an extension of Sinclair's task force socialization thesis. James C. Garand. *West. Pol. Q.* **41:2** 6:1988 pp. 391 – 400

C.7: Attitudes. Opinion — *Attitudes. Opinion*

1 Action individuelle et action collective — réflexion sur les modes et procédures de satisfaction des besoins *[In French]*; Individual and collective action — the forms and means of satisfying needs *[Summary]*. José Kobielski. *Pol. Manag. Publ.* **6:1** 3:1988 pp. 1 – 20

2 Aggressive behaviour of children aged 6-11 — gender differences and their magnitude. John Archer; Norma A. Pearson; Karin E. Westeman. *Br. J. Soc. P.* **27:4** 12:1988 pp. 371 – 384

3 Altruism within the family reconsidered — do nice guys finish last? B. Douglas Bernheim; Oded Stark. *Am. Econ. Rev.* **78:5** 12:1988 pp. 1034 – 1045

4 Are people who co-operate 'rational altruists'? Alphons J.C. van de Kragt; Robyn M. Dawes; John M. Orbell. *Publ. Choice* **56:3** 3:1988 pp. 233 – 247

5 An assessment of Skinner's theory of animal behavior. John A. Mills. *J. Theory Soc. Behav.* **18:2** 6:1988 pp. 197 – 218

6 Attitude importance and attitude change. Jon A. Krosnick. *J. Exp. S. Psychol.* **24:3** 5:1988 pp. 240 – 255

7 Attitudes toward homosexuality — a cross cultural analysis of predictors. Larry Jensen; David Gambles; Joe Olsen. *Int. J. Soc. Psyc.* **34:1** Spring:1988 pp. 47 – 57

8 Behavioral momentum and the partial reinforcement effect. John A. Nevin. *Psychol .B.* **103:1** 1:1988 pp. 44 – 56

9 Categorization, accentuation and social judgement. Craig McGarty; R.E.C. Penny. *Br. J. Soc. P.* **27:2** 6:1988 pp. 147 – 157

10 Choice and rationality in social theory. Barry Hindess. London: Unwin Hyman, 1988: 128 p. *ISBN: 0043013066. Includes index.* [Controversies in sociology. : No. 22]

11 A configurational approach to the study of traditional behavior. Simonetta Tabboni. *R. Soc. Move. Con. Cha.* **10** 1988 pp. 225 – 234

12 Cultural change and attitude change — an assessment of postrevolutionary marriage and family attitudes in Iran. Abbas Tashakkori; Vaida D. Thompson. *Pop. Res. Pol. R.* **7:1** 1988 pp. 3 – 27

13 Deceptive behavior in social relationships — a consequence of violated expectations. Karen U. Millar; Abraham Tesser. *J. Psychol.* **122:3** 5:1988 pp. 263 – 274

C.7: Attitudes. Opinion *[Attitudes. Opinion]*

14 Differential attitudes of Chinese students toward people with disabilities — a cross-cultural perspective. Fong Chan; John J. Hedl; Harry J. Parker; Chow S. Lam; Tai-Nai Chan; Brenda Yu. *Int. J. Soc. Psyc.* **34:4** Winter:1988 pp. 267 – 273

15 Eccentrics — the scientific investigation. David Joseph Weeks; Kate Ward *[Ed.]*. Stirling: Stirling University Press, 1988: x,259 p. *ISBN: 0948812001. Bibliographical references.*

16 Ego defenses and the legitimation of behavior. Guy E. Swanson. Cambridge: Cambridge University Press, 1988: viii, 232 p. *ISBN: 0521343615; LofC: 87-3006. Bibliography — p.217-228. - Includes index.* [The Arnold and Caroline Rose monograph series of the American Sociological Association.]

17 Estimating probabilistic choice models from sparse data — a method and an application to groups. Joel H. Steckel; Donald R. Lehmann; Kim P. Corfman. *Psychol .B.* **103:1** 1:1988 pp. 131 – 139

18 False consensus and false uniqueness in estimating the prevalence of health-protective behaviors. Jerry Suls; Choi K. Wan; Glenn S. Sanders. *J. Appl. Soc. Psychol.* **18:1** 1:1988 pp. 66 – 79

19 Fatalism and deliberation. Robin Small. *Can. J. Phil.* **18:1** 3:1988 pp. 13 – 30

20 Helping — the effects of sex differences and locus of causality. Susan L. Hope; Howard F. Jackson; Michael J. Avis. *Br. J. Soc. P.* **27:3** 9:1988 pp. 209 – 219

21 Ideological dilemmas — a social psychology of everyday thinking. Michael Billig *[Ed.]*; et al. London: Sage, 1988: vii, 180 p. *ISBN: 0803980957. Bibliography — p.164-173.*

22 Идеологические отношения в обществе *[In Russian]*; [Ideological relations in society]. V.M. Prokopenko. Moscow: Izd-vo Moskovskogo universiteta, 1987: 84 p.

23 Ideologiczne aspekty kultury *[In Polish]*; [Ideological aspects of culture]. Jerzy Ładyka. *Nowe Drogi* **5:468** 5:1988 pp. 147 – 154

24 Ideology and society in India — sociological essays. C.N. Venu Gopal. New Delhi: Criterion, 1988: v, 173 p.

25 Improving attitude-behavior prediction models with economic variables — farmer actions toward soil conservation. Gary D. Lynne; Leandro R. Rola. *J. Soc. Psychol.* **128:1** 2:1988 pp. 19 – 28

26 L'intolérance — une problématique générale *[In French]*; [Intolerance — a general problem]. Lise Noël. Montréal: Boréal express, 1988: 308 p. *ISBN: 2890522512. Bibliography — p.275-306.*

27 Local residents' attitudes to oil and nuclear developments. J.R. Eiser; R. Spears; P. Webley; J. van der Pligt. *Soc. Behav.* **3:3** 9:1988 pp. 237 – 254

28 Moods and compliance. Sandra Milberg; Margaret S. Clark. *Br. J. Soc. P.* **27:1** 3:1988 pp. 79 – 90

29 National politics and collective action — recent theory and research in Western Europe and the United States. Sidney Tarrow. *Ann. R. Soc.* **14** 1988 pp. 421 – 440

30 The public and private use of consensus-raising excuses. Stephanie H. Smith; George I. Whitehead. *J. Personal.* **56:2** 6:1988 pp. 355 – 371

31 Public self-consciousness and consumption behavior. Stephen J. Gould; Benny Barak. *J. Soc. Psychol.* **128:3** 6:1988 pp. 393 – 400

C.7: Attitudes. Opinion *[Attitudes. Opinion]*

32 Razionalizzare l'irrazionale —Karl Mannheim e il vizio inveterato degli intellettuali tedeschi *[In Italian]*; Rationalizing the irrational —Karl Mannheim and the besetting sin of German intellectuals *[Summary]*. David Kettler; Volker Meja; Nico Stehr. *Rass. It. Soc.* **29:4** 10-12:1988 pp. 487 – 512

33 Recent developments in attitudes and social structure. K. Jill Kiecolt. *Ann. R. Soc.* **14** 1988 pp. 381 – 403

34 Relationships among three concepts of authoritarianism in adolescent schoolchildren. Ken Rigby. *J. Soc. Psychol.* **128:6** 12:1988 pp. 825 – 832

35 Relative contribution of specific and nonspecific treatment effects — meta-analysis of placebo-controlled behavior therapy research. Thomas G. Bowers; George A. Clum. *Psychol .B.* **103:3** 5:1988 pp. 315 – 323

36 Social categorization and behaviour in mixed-motive games — a Northern Ireland study. John Kremer; Anthony Gallagher; Peter Somerville; Gilbert Traylen. *Soc. Behav.* **3:3** 9:1988 pp. 229 – 236

37 Social identity and minimal groups — the effects of interpersonal and intergroup attitudinal similarity on intergroup discrimination. Michael Diehl. *Br. J. Soc. P.* **27:4** 12:1988 pp. 289 – 300

38 The social organization of self-help — a study of defensive weapon ownership. Douglas A. Smith; Craig D. Uchida. *Am. Sociol. R.* **53:1** 2:1988 pp. 94 – 102

39 Social responsivity as elementary human action. Joachim Israel. *Acta Sociol.* **31** 1988 pp. 231 – 240

40 Stereotypes — notes on the effect of identificational and dialogic functions in the interaction between code and usage. Robert Nicolaï. *Int. J. S. Lang.* **74** 1988 pp. 91 – 106

41 The structure and antecedents of the normative and attitudinal components of Fishbein's theory of reasoned action. Robert E. Burnkrant; Thomas J. Page. *J. Exp. S. Psychol.* **24:1** 1:1988 pp. 66 – 87

42 The subjective well-being of young adults — trends and relationships. Willard L. Rodgers; Jerald G. Bachman *[Ed.]*. Ann Arbor, Mich.: Survey Research Center, Institute for Social Research, University of Michigan, 1988: xiv, 231 p. (ill.) *ISBN: 0879443235; LofC: 88-009455. Bibliography, p. 227-230.* [Research report series. : No. Institute for Social Research]

D: Culture. Socialization. Social life — *Culture. Socialisation. Vie sociale*

D.1: Culture. Social environment. Value — *Culture. Milieu social. Valeur*

D.1.1: Culture and cultural relations — *Culture et relations culturelles*

1 All consuming images — the politics of style in contemporary culture. Stuart Ewen. New York: Basic Book Publisher, 1988: xi, 306 p. *ISBN: 0465001009. Bibliography — p.287-296.*
2 Anthropology in the twenty-first century. José Matos Mar. *Int. Soc. Sci. J.* **116** 5:1988 pp. 203 – 210
3 Bunka-jinruigaku heno approach *[In Japanese]*; [Approaches to cultural anthropology]. Kanji Ito; Toshinao Yoneyama. Kyoto: Minerva Shobo, 1988: 301 p.
4 Changing identities of the Southeast Asian Chinese since World War II. Jennifer W. Cushman *[Ed.]*; Gungwu Wang *[Ed.]*. [Hong Kong]: Hong Kong University Press, 1988: 344 p. *ISBN: 9622092071. Contains papers and abstracts from a symposium held at Australian National Uuniversity, Canberra in June 1985; Contains bibliographies.*
5 Le complexe de Marianne [The Marianne complex] *[In French]*. Paul Trouillas. Paris: Seuil, 1988: 317 p. (ill) *ISBN: 2020101890. Contains bibliographical references.* [L'histoire immédiate.]
6 Cultural history of northern India. Sushi Kumar Singh. New Delhi: Ramanand Vidya Bhawan, 1986: 184 p.
7 Culture and agency — the place of culture in social theory. Margaret Scotford Archer. Cambridge: Cambridge University Press, 1988: - *ISBN: 0521346231. Includes index.*
8 Culture and consciousness in Southern Africa. Terence Ranger *[Contrib.]*; Wyatt MacGaffey *[Contrib.]*; Elizabeth Gunner *[Contrib.]*; T. Dunbar Moodie *[Contrib.]*; Vivien Ndatshe *[Contrib.]*; British Sibuye *[Contrib.]*; Jeff Guy; Motlatsi Thabane *[Contrib.]*; John McCracken *[Contrib.]*; Norma Kriger *[Contrib.] and others. Collection of 9 articles.* **J. S.Afr. Stud.** , *14:2*, 1:1988 pp. 181 – 329
9 Culture and national relations. Leokadia Drobizheva. *Soc. Sci.* **XIX:1** 1988 pp. 48 – 58
10 Domination and cultural resistance — authority and power among an Andean people. Roger Neil Rasnake. Durham,N. C.: Duke University Press, 1988: 321 p. *ISBN: 0822308096; LofC: 87-35834. Bibliography — p.293-312.*
11 Durkheimian sociology — cultural studies. Jeffrey C. Alexander *[Ed.]*. Cambridge: Cambridge University Press, 1988: xi, 227 p. *ISBN: 0521346223. Includes bibliographical references.*
12 Economic and social acculturation among the Old Order Amish in select communities — surviving in a high-tech society. Jerry Savells. *J. Comp. Fam. Stud.* **XIX:1** Spring:1988 pp. 123 – 136
13 The effects of truth — re-presentations of the past and the imaging of community. Ana Maria Alonso. *J. Hist. Soc.* **1:1** 3:1988 pp. 33 – 57

D.1.1: Culture and cultural relations *[Culture et relations culturelles]*

14 The element of irrationality — Max Weber's diagnosis of modern culture. Jukka Gronow. *Acta Sociol.* **31:4** 1988 pp. 319 – 331

15 Estetizzazione e stilizzazione — due strategie di gestione della stile di vita *[In Italian]*; Aestheticisation and stylisation — two strategies of life-style management *[Summary]*. Birgitta Nedelmann. *Rass. It. Soc.* **29:4** 10-12:1988 pp. 513 – 535

16 Êtes-vous un vrai Français? *[In French]*; [Are you truly French?]. Maurice Tarik Maschino. Paris: B. Grasset, 1988: 251 p. *ISBN: 2246406919*.

17 A foreign egg in our nest? — American popular culture in New Zealand. Geoff Lealand. Wellington: Victoria University Press, 1988: 126 p. *ISBN: 0864730780. Bibliography, p. 122-126*..

18 Fremde Kultur und soziales Handeln — Max Webers Analyse der indischen Zivilisation *[In German]*; Non-western culture and social action — Max Weber's study of Indian civilization *[Summary]*. Martin Fuchs. *Kölner Z. Soz. Soz. psy.* **39:4** 1988 pp. 669 – 692

19 Furusato Japan — the culture and politics of nostalgia. Jennifer Robertson. *Int. J. Pol. C. S.* **1:4** Summer:1988 pp. 494 – 518

20 Galtonian genius, Kroeberian configurations, and emulation — a generational time-series analysis of Chinese civilization. Dean Keith Simonton. *J. Pers. Soc. Psychol.* **55:2** 8:1988 pp. 230 – 238

21 Gendai nihon ni okeru soshikika no shokeitai *[In Japanese]*; [The dualistic structure of social life in contemporary Japan]. Tsutomu Shiobara. ***Organ. Sc.*** *Vol.21; No.4 - 1988.* pp. 21 – 29

22 Gendai nihon shakai ron *[In Japanese]*; [The study of contemporary Japan]. Hirosuke Kawanishi *[Ed.]*. : Chiba College of Arts and Sciences, Chiba U., 1988: 278 p.

23 Gendai seinen bunka no ruikei to nichijou koudou, shuudan katudou no eikyou *[In Japanese]*; [The type of modern youth culture and the influence of action and group]. Michio Ohno. ***Seishounen Mondai*** *Vol.35; No.2 - 1988.* pp. 20 – 27

24 Hinkon no bunka to seikatsu sekai no sai-seisan — seikatsu sekai/ bunka/ shakaikouzou ni kansuru ichi shiron *[In Japanese]*; ["The culture of poverty" as a reproduction of the lifeworld — an essay of lifeworld, culture and social structure]. Takashi Okumura. ***Sociologos*** *Vol.12. 1988.* pp. 20 – 35

25 Historical consciousness and post traditional identity — remarks on the Federal Republic's orientation to the West. Jürgen Habermas. *Acta Sociol.* **31:1** 1988 pp. 3 – 13

26 Individualism, capitalism and the dominant culture — a note on the debate. Bryan Turner. *Aust. N.Z. J. Soc.* **24:1** 3:1988 pp. 47 – 64

27 Intercultural understanding — Max Weber and Leo Strauss. Ahmad Sadri; Mahmoud Sadri. *Int. J. Pol. C. S.* **1:3** Spring:1988 pp. 392 – 411

28 "Kata" to shite no nihon bunka — kabuki wo chūshin to shite *[In Japanese]*; [Japanese culture seen in terms of "pattern" (kata)]. Michikuni Ono. *Soc. Rev. [Kobe] Vol.5. 1988.* pp. 1 – 24

29 Latin American perspectives. Philip Schlesinger *[Ed.]*; José Marques de Melo *[Contrib.]*; Javier Esteinou Madrid *[Contrib.]*; Jesús Martín-Barbero *[Contrib.]*; Néstor García Canclini *[Contrib.]*; Colin Hoskins *[Contrib.]*; Rolf Mirus *[Contrib.]*; Greg Philo *[Contrib.]*. Collection of 7 articles. **Media Cult. Soc.** , *10:4*, 10:1988 pp. 395 – 522

D.1.1: Culture and cultural relations [Culture et relations culturelles]

30 Literature, culture, and society in the new Latin America. William H. Katra. *Lat. Am. Res. R.* **XXIII:2** 1988 pp. 170 – 188

31 Man, society and nature. P. Banerjee; S.K. Gupta. Shimla, Indian Institute of Advanced Study and Delhi: Motilal, 1988: xi, 200 p. *ISBN: 81 208 0566 6.*

32 Metodologiczne aspekty badań nad zagadnieniem obecności polskiej w kulturze Francji *[In Polish]*; Methodological aspects of research on the Polish presence in the culture of France *[Summary]*. Wiesław Śladkowski; Małgorzata Willaume. *Prz. Pol.* **XIV:4** 1988 pp. 53 – 66

33 Mukeiki hiko; Viva Nippon!? — ruminations on Japan's cultural, educational and industrial institutions. Tadao Ichikawa; Murray McDonald *[Ed.]*; Sumiko McDonald *[Ed.]*. Singapore: World Scientific Publishing Co., 1988: 198 p. *ISBN: 9971505916. Murray and Sumiko McDonald.*

34 New directions in study of culture. Robert Wuthnow; Marsha Witten. *Ann. R. Soc.* **14** 1988 pp. 49 – 67

35 Pancasila and the search for identity and modernity in Indonesian society — a cultural and ethical analysis. Eka Darmaputera. Leiden: E.J. Brill, 1988: x, 254 p. *ISBN: 9004084223; LofC: 88004304. Includes index; Bibliography —p.. [230]-238.*

36 Politique provinciale et identité franco-ontarienne *[In French]*; [Local politics and Franco-Ontarian identity] *[Summary]*. Sylvie Guillaume. *Etud. Can.* **:25** 1988 pp. 67 – 44

37 La relativité des cultures et le problème du jugement *[In French]*; [The relativity of cultures and problem of judgement]. Jean-Pierre Siméon. *Rev. Eur. Sci. Soc.* **XXVI:81** 1988 pp. 121 – 131

38 The rhythms of society. Michael Young *[Ed.]*; Tom Schuller *[Ed.]*. London: Routledge, 1988: 233 p. *ISBN: 0415025338. Includes bibliographical references.* [Reports of the Institute of Community Studies.]

39 La routine — analyse d'une composante de la vie quotidienne à travers les pratiques d'habiter *[In French]*; [Routine — an analysis of everyday life in terms of living habits] *[Summary]*. Yves Chalas. *Cah. Int. Soc.* **35:LXXXV** 7-12:1988 pp. 243 – 56

40 Social action and human nature. Axel Honneth; Hans Joas *[Ed.]*. Cambridge: Cambridge University Press, 1988: xii, 191 p. *ISBN: 0521326834. Bibliography —p.180-186.*

41 Social reality — perspectives and understanding. Janak Pandey *[Ed.]*. New Delhi: Concept, 1988: 156 p. *ISBN: 81 7022 199 4.*

42 Society and culture. New Delhi: Inter-India, 1988: xvi, 210 p. [Current Anthropological and Archaeological Perspectives. : Vol. 2]

43 Tradition, core values and intercultural development in plural societies. J.J. Smolicz. *Ethn. Racial* **11:4** 11:1988 pp. 387 – 410

44 A typology of lifestyles. James Horley; Barbara Carroll; Brian R. Little. *Soc. Ind.* **20:4** 8:1988 pp. 383 – 398

45 Understanding Soviet society. Michael Paul Sacks *[Ed.]*; Jerry G. Pankhurst *[Ed.]*. Boston: Allen & Unwin, 1988: 320 p. *ISBN: 0044450362. Includes bibliography and index.*

46 A viewpoint on society. Mohan Patil. New Delhi: NIB Pub, 1988: 118 p.

47 Weber, Simmel and the sociology of culture. Lawrence A. Scaff. *Sociol. Rev.* **36:1** 2:1988 pp. 1 – 30

D.1.2: Social norms. Social control. Value systems — *Normes sociales. Régulation sociale. Systèmes de valeurs*

1 Belonging in America — reading between the lines. Constance Perin. Madison: University of Wisconsin Press, 1988: 287 p. *ISBN: 0299115801. Bibliography — p.243-273.* [New directions in anthropological writing.]
2 Les censures de la pensée stéréotypée *[In French]*; Censuring stereotyped thought — official values and popular ripostes *[Summary]*. Amr Helmy Ibrahim. *Peup. Médit.* **41-42** 10:1987-3:1988 pp. 257 – 282
3 Cultures nigériennes et éducation — domaine Zarma-Songhay et Hausa *[In French]*; [Nigerian cultures and education — the Zarma-Songhay and Hausa region]. Diawara I.. *Prés. Afr.* **148** 1988 pp. 9 – 19
4 Evolution, systems of interdependence, and social values. Charles G. McClintock. *Behav. Sci.* **33: 1** 1: 1988 pp. 59 – 76
5 Gendai ikigai ni kansuru shakaigaku-teki kousatsu *[In Japanese]*; [A sociological perspective on lifestyle]. Naoyuki Okada. *5250 Vol.5. 1988.* pp. 103 – 124
6 Hostages to fortune — youth, values and the public interest. John Janeway Conger. *Am. Psychol.* **43:4** 4:1988 pp. 291 – 300
7 Im Spiegel der Medien — Wertewandel in der Bundesrepublik Deutschland — eine empirische Analyse anhand von Stern, ZDF-Magazin und Monitor im Zeitraum 1965 bis 1983 *[In German]*; [Changing values in West Germany, as reflected in the media — an empirical analysis with examples from "Stern", "ZDF - Magazin" and "Monitor" from the period between 1965 and 1983]. Matthias Schuppe. Frankfurt a.M.: P. Lang, 1988: 475 p. *ISBN: 3820413782.*
8 Japanese Teinen Taishoku — how cultural values affect retirement. John McCallum. *Age. Soc.* **8:1** 3:1988 pp. 23 – 41
9 Regulation and repression — the study of social control. Anne R. Edwards. Sydney: Allen and Unwin, 1988: 281 p. *ISBN: 0043321364. Bibliography — p244-273.* [Studies in society.]
10 Représentation idéologique et contrôle sociale *[In French]*; [Ideological representation and social control]. Josiane Boulad Ayoub. *Can. J. Pol. Soc. Theo.* **12:1-2** :1988 pp. 230 – 239
11 Tautology and paradox in the self-descriptions of modern society. Niklas Luhmann; Stephan Fuchs *[Tr.]*. *Sociol. Theory* **6:1** Spring:1988 pp. 21 – 37
12 Value attributions and value transmission between parents and children. Les B. Whitbeck; Viktor Gecas. *J. Marriage Fam.* **50:3** 8:1988 pp. 829 – 840
13 Verdrängung des Todes — kulturkritisches Vorurteil oder Strukturmerkmal moderner Gesellschaften? Systemtheoretische und wissenssoziologische Überlegungen *[In German]*; Repression of death — a prejudice of cultural criticism or a structural characteristic of modern societies? *[Summary]*. Armin Nassehi; Georg Weber. *Soz. Welt.* **39:4** 1988 pp. 377 – 396

D.1.3: Alienation. Socialization. Social conformity —
Aliénation. Socialisation. Conformité sociale

1 Child development and socialisation. B. G. Banerjee. New Delihi: Deep & Deep, 1987: 156 p.

2 Children of different worlds — the formation of social behavior. Beatrice B. Whiting; Carolyn Pope Edwards *[Ed.]*; Carol R. Ember *[Ed.]*. Cambridge, Mass.: Harvard University Press, 1988: xii, 337 p. (ill) *ISBN: 067411616x; LofC: 87-19742. Bibliography — p.316-329. Includes index.*

3 A critique of expectation states theory — theoretical assumptions and models of social cognition. J. David Knottnerus. *Sociol. Pers.* **31:4** 10:1988 pp. 420 – 445

4 Cultural capital — allusions, gaps and glissandos in recent theoretical developments. Michèle Lamont; Annette Lareau. *Sociol. Theory* **6:2** Fall:1988 pp. 153 – 168

5 Discussione and friendship — socialization processes in the peer culture of Italian nursery school children. William A. Corsaro; Thomas A. Rizzo. *Am. Sociol. R.* **53:6** 12:1988 pp. 879 – 894

6 Erving Goffman — exploring the interaction order. Paul Drew *[Ed.]*; Anthony Wootton *[Ed.]*. Cambridge: Polity, 1988, c1987: iv, 298 p. (ill) *ISBN: 0745603920. Includes bibliography and index.*

7 Étrangers à nous-mêmes *[In French]*; [Strangers to ourselves]. Julia Kristeva. Paris: Fayard, 1988: 293 p. *ISBN: 2213021775.*

8 Generic and generative dimensions of interactionism — towards the unfolding of critical directions. Livy Visano. *Int. J. Comp. Soc* **XXIX:3-4** 9-12:1988 pp. 230 – 244

9 Geschlechtsspezifische Sozialisation — neuere Beiträge und Perspektiven zur Entstehung des „weiblichen Sozialcharakters" *[In German]*; Gender socialization *[Summary]*. Regine Gildemeister. *Soz. Welt.* **39:4** 1988 pp. 486 – 503

10 Invisible boundaries — grooming for adult roles — a descriptive study of socialization in poor rural and urban slum setting in Gujarat. T.S. Saraswathi; Ranjana Dutta. New Delhi: Northern Book Centre, 1988: xviii, 246 p. *ISBN: 81 85119 49 X.*

11 The modernization of tradition and the emergence of new cultural structures. Nicolae Radu; Carmen Furtună; Carmen Grămadă. *R. Roum. Sci. Soc.* **32:1** 1-6:1988 pp. 21 – 30

12 On queueing. Zbigniew Czawartosz. *Eur. J. Soc.* **XXIX:1** 1988 pp. 3 – 11

13 Pobladores e integración social *[In Spanish]*; [Settlers and social integration]. Eugenio Tironi. *Rev. Parag. Sociol.* **25:71** 1-4:1988 pp. 55 – 79

14 Problém motivácie v prognóze sociálneho rozvoja *[In Czech]*; Проблема мотивации в прогнозе социального развития *[Russian summary]*; The problem of motivation in the prognosis of social development *[Summary]*; Das Problem der Motivation in der Prognose der sozialen Entwicklung *[German summary]*. Ján Bunčák. *Sociologia [Brat.]* **20:6** 1988 pp. 649 – 662

15 Psycho-social integration of the handicapped — a challenge to the society. Anima Sen. Delhi: Mittal, 1988: xiv, 366 p. *ISBN: 81 7099 060 2.*

D.1.3: Alienation. Socialization. Social conformity *[Aliénation. Socialisation. Conformité sociale]*

16 Ritual and conformity in Soviet society. Thomas O. Cushman. *J. Commun. S.* **4:2** 6:1988 pp. 162 – 180
17 Shakaiteki sougo sayou to shakaiteki jiko — Goffman no shiten kara *[In Japanese]*; [Social interaction and social self — from the viewpoint of Erving Goffman]. Tadashi Miyauchi. *J. App. Soc.* Vol.29. 1988. pp. 83 – 102
18 Social structure and personality development — the individual as a productive processor of reality. Klaus Hurrelmann. Cambridge: Cambridge University Press, 1988: ix, 163 p. (ill) *ISBN: 0521354749; LofC: 87-37205. Bibliography — p.147-158. - Includes index.*
19 Sozialisation durch Massenmedien *[In German]*; [Socialisation by mass media]. Ulrich Saxer *[Contrib.]*; Dieter Baacke *[Contrib.]*; Uwe Sander *[Contrib.]*; Ralf Vollbrecht *[Contrib.]*; Jan- Uwe Rogge *[Contrib.]*; Marie-Luise Kiefer *[Contrib.]*; Peter Vitouch *[Contrib.]*; Michael Charlton *[Contrib.]*; Klaus Neumann *[Contrib.]*; Kurt Luger *[Contrib.] and others.* Collection of 25 articles. **Publizistik** , *33*:2-3, 4-9:1988 pp. 165 – 576
20 Technologies of the self — a seminar with Michel Foucault. Luther H. Martin *[Ed.]*; Huck Gutman *[Ed.]*. London: Tavistock, 1988: 166 p.
21 A theory of social interaction. Jonathan H. Turner. Stanford, Calif.: Stanford University Press, 1988: xiv, 225 p. (ill.) *ISBN: 0804714630. Bibliography, p. [215]-220; Includes indexes.*

D.2: Customs. Traditions — *Coutumes. Traditions*

1 Kouri to dentou *[In Japanese]*; [Utility and tradition]. Hitoshi Ochiai. *Ann. Leg. Phil.* Vol.1988. pp. 61 – 73
2 Paris fashion — a cultural history. Valerie Steele. New York: , 1988: 317p., 4p of plates (ill(some col.)) *ISBN: 0195044657; LofC: 87-11143. Bibliography — p303-309. Includes index.*
3 Street life — the politics of carnival. P. Jackson. *Envir. Plan. D* **6(2):** 6:1988 pp. 213 – 227

D.3: Ethics. Morals — *Éthique. Morale*

1 The decline of guilt. Herbert Morris. *Ethics* **99:1** 10:1988 pp. 62 – 76
2 Ethical issues in professional life. Joan C. Callahan *[Ed.]*. New York: OUP, 1988: 470 p. *ISBN: 0195053621.*
3 Ethics and aging — the right to live, the right to die. Earl R. Winkler *[Ed.]*; James E. Thornton *[Ed.]*. Vancouver: University of British Columbia Press, 1988 *ISBN: 0774803029.*
4 Evaluating moral theories. Lansing Pollock. *Am. Phil. Q.* **25:3** 7:1988 pp. 229 – 240
5 Global moral commitment. Alan H. Goldman. *Am. Phil. Q.* **25:1** 1:1988 pp. 69 – 78
6 Gramsci e la concezione della vita morale *[In Italian]*; (Gramsci and the concept of moral life). Aldo Zanardo. *Crit. Marx.* **26:5** 9-10:1988 pp. 37 – 74

D.3: Ethics. Morals [Éthique. Morale]

7 Hare on moral weakness and the definition of morality. William Frankena. *Ethics* **98:4** 7:1988 pp. 779 – 792

8 Honour — its fate in socialist society. Ivan Kuvacic. *Int. J. Pol. C. S.* **2:1** Fall:1988 pp. 36 – 44

9 Hume and morality as a matter of fact. M. Platts. *Mind* **XCVII:** :1988 pp. 189 – 204

10 Intelligence and academia. James V. Schall. *Int. J. Soc. E.* **15:10** 1988 pp. 63 – 71

11 Marshallian ethics and economics — deconstructing the authority of science. Rudi Visker. *Philos. S. Sc.* **18:2** 6:1988 pp. 179 – 200

12 Moral judgement and human values. N.T. Feather. *Br. J. Soc. P.* **27:3** 9:1988 pp. 239 – 246

13 Moral reasoning and statecraft — essays presented to Kenneth W. Thompson. Reed M. Davis *[Ed.]*; Kenneth W. Thompson *[Ed.]*. Lanham: University Press of America, 1988: 193 p. *ISBN: 0819170186.*

14 The moral status of pity. Eamonn Callan. *Can. J. Phil.* **18:1** 3:1988 pp. 1 – 12

15 Morality, potential persons and abortion. John Bigelow; Robert Pargetter. *Am. Phil. Q.* **25:2** 4:1988 pp. 173 – 182

16 Natura e morale *[In Italian]*; Nature and morality *[Summary]*. Fabio Bazzani. *Crit. Marx.* **26:1** 1-2:1988 pp. 181 – 191

17 A new "slave revolt in morals"? The meaning of the debate over a feminist ethics. John Torpey. *Berkeley J. Soc.* **XXXIII** 1988 pp. 73 – 93

18 Нравственные проблемы быта в социалистическом обществе *[In Russian]*; [Moral problems of living in a socialist society]. A.I. Titarenko *[Ed.]*; O.M. Guseinov. Rostov: Izd-vo Rostovskogo Universiteta, 1987: 154 p.

19 On the uses of psychological theory and research in the process of ethical inquiry. Alan S. Waterman. *Psychol .B.* **103:3** 5:1988 pp. 283 – 298

20 Organizations and ethical individualism. Konstantin Kolenda *[Ed.]*. New York: Praeger, 1988: 172 p. *ISBN: 0275927601; LofC: 87-32673. Bibliography — p.159-167.*

21 Papers on the ethics of administration. N. Dale Wright *[Ed.]*. Provo,Utah: Brigham Young University, 1988: 252 p. *ISBN: 0887069614; LofC: 88-016737.*

22 Politics, innocence, and the limits of goodness. Peter Johnson. London: Routledge, 1988: 283 p. *ISBN: 0415010462. Bibliography — p.272-279. Includes index.*

23 The power of the professional person. Robert P. Lawry *[Ed.]*. Lanham, MD: University Press of America, 1988: x, 240 p. *ISBN: 0819169560. Papers from a series of conferences held at Case Western Reserve University during the 1985-1986 academic year, sponsored by the University's Center for Professional Ethics; Includes bibliographies.*

24 The problem of the criterion and coherence methods in ethics. Michael R. DePaul. *Can. J. Phil.* **18:1** 3:1988 pp. 67 – 86

25 Проблемы нравственного воспитания в условиях перестройки *[In Russian]*; (Problems of moral education under perestroika); (Les problèmes de l'éducation morale dans les conditions de la restructuration: *Title only in French*); (Probleme der moralischen Erziehung under den Bedingungen der

D.3: Ethics. Morals [Éthique. Morale]

Umgestaltung: *Title only in German);* (Problemas de la educación moral en las condiciones de la perestroika: *Title only in Spanish); [Title only in Chinese].* М.П. Мчедлов. *Vop. Ist. KPSS* **3** 1988 pp. 3 – 18

26 The Protestant ethic and legitimation of bureaucratic elites. Anthony P. Johnson. *Int. J. Pol. C. S.* **1:4** Summer:1988 pp. 585 – 597

27 Rationality and affectivity — the metaphysics of the moral self. Laurence Thomas. *Soc. Philos. Pol.* **5:2** Spring:1988 pp. 154 – 172

28 The relation between self-interest and justice in contractarian ethics. Christopher W. Morris. *Soc. Philos. Pol.* **5:2** Spring:1988 pp. 119 – 153

29 Relation of formal education to moral judgement development. Djilali Bouhamama. *J. Psychol.* **122:2** 3:1988 pp. 155 – 154

30 Relativismo teoreticoe relativismo morale *[In Italian];* [Theoretical relativism and moral relativism] *[Summary].* Alessandra Ciattini. *Uomo* **1:1-2** 1988 pp. 51 – 73

31 Seductions of crime — moral and sensual attractions in doing evil. Jack Katz. New York: Basic Books, 1988: 367 p. *ISBN: 0465076157; LofC: 88-047691.*

32 Sex differences in adult moral orientations. Michael W. Pratt; Gail Golding; William Hunter; Rosemarie Sampson. *J. Personal.* **56:2** 6:1988 pp. 373 – 391

33 The status of the human embryo — perspectives from moral tradition. G. R. Gordon Reginald Dunstan; Mary J. Seller *[Ed.].* London: King Edward's Hospital Fund for London, 1988: 119 p. *ISBN: 0197246443.*

34 Sulla fondazione razionale dell'etica *[In Italian];* (About the rational foundation of ethics). Vittoria Franco. *Crit. Marx.* **26:5** 9-10:1988 pp. 145 – 158

35 Symposium on Weber's "The protestant ethic". Richard van Dülen *[Contrib.];* Guy Oakes *[Contrib.];* Paul Piccone *[Contrib.]. Collection of 3 articles.* **Telos**, *78,* Winter:1988-1989 pp. 71 – 108

36 Treat me right — essays in medical law and ethics. Ian Kennedy. Oxford: Clarendon, 1988: 320 p. *ISBN: 0198255594. Includes bibliography and index.*

37 Two studies of Piaget's theory of moral judgment. Klaus Helkama. *Eur. J. Soc. Psychol.* **18:1** 1-3:1988 pp. 17 – 37

38 Values and morality of scientists — some unresolved problems. Arthur Vidich. *Int. J. Pol. C. S.* **1:3** Spring:1988 pp. 471 – 486

39 What is a person? M. F. Goodman *[Ed.].* Clifton,N.J.: Wiley Humana Press, 1988: 325 p. *ISBN: 0896031179; LofC: 86- 021487.* [Contemporary issues in Biomedicine, Ethics and Society.]

D.4: Law. Regulation — Loi. Réglementation

1 And how are the children? The effects of ideology and mediation of child custody law and children's well-being in the United States. Carol S. Bruch. *Int. J. Law Fam.* **2:1** 4:1988 pp. 106 – 126
2 Bengoshi akuses ni kansuru shakaigakuteki kenkyuu *[In Japanese]*; [Sociological study of the relationship between citizens and lawyers]. Tomohiro Otani. **Hiroshima Hogaku, Hiroshima Daigaku Hogakkai** *Vol.11; No.2 - 1988.* pp. 97 – 122
3 Black people and the criminal law — rhetoric and reality. Paul Gordon. *Int. J. S. Law* **16:3** 8:1988 pp. 295 – 313
4 The court disposal of young males, by race, in London in 1983. Monica A. Walker. *Br. J. Crimin.* **28:4** Autumn:1988 pp. 441 – 460
5 The dimensions of rape reform legislation. Ronald J. Berger; Patricia Searles; W. Lawrence Neuman. *Law Soc. Rev.* **22:2** 1988 pp. 329 – 357
6 Family law reform in Tanzania — a socio-legal report. Barthazar A. Rwezaura; Ulrike Wanitzek. *Int. J. Law Fam.* **2:1** 4:1988 pp. 1 – 26
7 Hou shakaigaku — kadai wo ou *[In Japanese]*; [Sociology of law — exploring socio-cultural theory]. Masaji Chiba. Tokyo: Seibundo, 1988: 222 p.
8 Law in practice — applications of psychology to legal decision making and legal skills. Sally M. Lloyd-Bostock. London: British Psychological Society and Routledge, 1988: xiii,177 p. (ill) *ISBN: 0901715670. Includes bibliographies and index.* [Psychology in action.]
9 The life-without-parole sanction — its current status and a research agenda. Derral Cheatwood. *Crime Delin.* **34:1** 1:1988 pp. 43 – 59
10 Literacy, law, and social order. Edward Stevens. DeKalb, Ill.: Northern Illinois University Press, 1988: xi, 278 p. (ill.) *ISBN: 0875801315. Bibliography, p. [257]-268.*
11 О социологии права *[In Russian]*; On sociology of law *[Summary]*. S.L. Sergevnin. *Vest. Lenin. Univ.* 6 **1:6** 3:1988 pp. 69 – 75
12 Philosophy of punishment. Robert M. Baird *[Ed.]*; Stuart E. Rosenbaum *[Ed.]*. Buffalo, N.Y.: Prometheus, [1988]: 151 p. *ISBN: 0879754176.* [Contemporary issues in philosophy.]
13 Punishment and the individual in the United States and Japan. V. Lee Hamilton; Joseph Sanders. *Law Soc. Rev.* **22:2** 1988 pp. 301 – 328
14 Secularization of family law in Greece. Michael P. Stathopoulos. *Isr. Law R.* **22:3** Winter-Spring:1988 pp. 365 – 376
15 Sociedade contemporânea e direito natural — uma visão filosófica dos valores jurídicos *[In Spanish]*; [Contemporary society and natural law — a philosophical view of juridical values]. Oliveiros Litrento. *Rev. Ciê. Pol.* **31** 1-3:1988 pp. 55 – 61
16 A transsexual's nightmare — the determination of sexual identity in English law. Jerold Taitz. *Int. J. Law Fam.* **2:2** 1988 pp. 139 – 154

D.5: Magic. Mythology. Religion — *Magie. Mythologie. Religion*

Sub-divisions: Christianity *[Christianisme]*; Islam *[Islam]*

1 Afro-American religious syncretism in Brazil and the United States — a Weberian perspective. Evandro M. Camara. *Sociol. Anal.* **48:4** Winter:1988 pp. 299 – 318

2 American Jewish converts to new religious movements. Charles Selengant. *Jew. J. Socio.* **XXX:2** 12:1988 pp. 95 – 109

3 The brain-mind relation, religious evolution, and forms of consciousness — an exploratory statement. Doyle Paul Johnson. *Sociol. Anal.* **49:1** Spring:1988 pp. 52 – 65

4 El capital simbólico — estructura social, politica y religión en España *[In Spanish]*; [Symbolic capital — social structure, policy and religion in Spain]. Rafael Díaz-Salazar. Madrid: Ediciones HOAC, 1988: 248 p. *ISBN: 8485121449*.

5 Changes in religious culture in post World War II Poland. Barbara Strassberg. *Sociol. Anal.* **48:4** Winter:1988 pp. 342 – 354

6 Conceptualizing religion from below — the Central American experience; *[French summary]*. Michael Gismondi. *Soc. Compass* **XXXV:2-3** 1988 pp. 343 – 370

7 Contemporary moral cultures and "the return of the sacred". Vytautas Kavolis. *Sociol. Anal.* **49:3** Fall:1988 pp. 203 – 216

8 The contextual significance of the charismatic movements in independent Nigeria. Matthews A. Ojo. *Africa* **58:2** 1988 pp. 175 – 192

9 Le culte des divinités locales dans une région de l'Himachal Pradesh *[In French]*; [The cult of local gods in a region of Himachal Pradesh]. Denis Vidal. Paris: Orstom, 1988: 319 p. *ISBN: 2709909359. Bibliography — p.306-314.* [Collection études et thèses.]

10 Cults, converts and charisma — the sociology of new religious movements. Thomas Robbins. *Curr. Sociol.* **36:1** Spring:1988 pp. 1 – 256

11 De-axialization/re-axialization — the case of Brazilian millennialism. Bernardo Arévalo De León. *Int. J. Comp. Soc* **XXIX:1-2** 1-4:1988 pp. 44 – 61

12 Diversities of gifts — field studies in southern religion. Ruel W. Tyson *[Ed.]*; James Lowe Peacock *[Ed.]*; Daniel Watkins Patterson *[Ed.]*. Urbana: University of Illinois Press, 1988: xiv, 218 p. (ill.) *ISBN: 0252015177. Includes bibliographies and index.* [Folklore and society.]

13 Epistemología y sociología de la religión *[In Spanish]*; [The epistemology and sociology of religion]. José Miguel Rodríguez. *Rev. Cien. Soc.* **:39** 3:1988 pp. 83 – 98

14 Folk religion among the Koreans in Japan. Takafumi Iida. *Jap. J. Relig. St.* Vol.15; No.2-3 - 1988. pp. 155 – 182

15 Forme di secolarizzazione nella società contemporanea — il caso italiano *[In Italian]*; Forms of secularisation in contemporary society — the example of Italy *[Summary]*. Franco Garelli. *Rass. It. Soc.* **29:1** 1-3:1988 pp. 89 – 121

16 The functions of religion — a reappraisal. Bryan R. Wilson. *Religion* **18** 7:1988 pp. 199 – 216

D.5: Magic. Mythology. Religion *[Magie. Mythologie. Religion]*

17 Gendai nihon ni okeru kazokuhendou to shuukyou *[In Japanese]*; [The changing family and religion in contemporary Japan]. Mitsugi Koutmoto. *Suu. Jih. Vol.77. 1988.* pp. 1 – 10

18 Gendai nihon no shin-shukyo *[In Japanese]*; [New religion in modern Japan]. Kenya Numata. Osaka: Sogensha, 1988: 281 p.

19 Hasidism — the surprising utopia. Shlomo Fischer. *Int. J. Comp. Soc* **XXIX:1-2** 1-4:1988 pp. 76 – 92

20 Hayarigami no tanjo — "kubinashi jizou" wo jirei to shite *[In Japanese]*; [The birth of Hayarigami (a popular God)]. Iwayumi Suzuki. *Rev. Area St. Vol.4. 1988.* pp. 33 – 45

21 Ideology and atheism in the Soviet Union. William Peter van den Bercken. Berlin: Mouton de Gruyter, 1988: 191 p. *ISBN: 0899253849. Bibliography — p.177-186.* [Religion and society.]

22 Is there a religious factor in health care utilization? A review. Preston L. Schiller; Jeffery S. Levin. *Soc. Sci. Med.* **27:12** 1988 pp. 1369 – 1379

23 Islam in perspective — a guide to Islamic society, politics and law. Patrick Bannerman. London: Routledge for Royal Institute of International Affairs, 1988: 278 p. *ISBN: 0415010152.*

24 The Javanese conception of order and its relationship to millenarian motifs and imagery. Sarit Helman. *Int. J. Comp. Soc* **XXIX:1-2** 1-4:1988 pp. 126 – 138

25 Magic, communication and efficacy. M.F.C. Bourdillon. *Zambezia* **15:i** 1988 pp. 27 – 42

26 Musical chairs — patterns of denominational change. Andrew M. Greely; Michael Hout. *Social Soc. Res.* **72:2** 1:1988 pp. 75 – 86

27 Das New-Age-Syndrom — zur Kultursoziologie vagabundierender Religiosität *[In German]*; [The "New Age" syndrome — the sociology of a vagabond spirituality]. Gottfried Küenzlen. *Z. Polit.* **35:3** 9:1988 pp. 237 – 248

28 Obituary and ancestral worship — analysis of a contemporary cultural form in Nigeria. Olatunde Bayo Lawuyi. *Sociol. Anal.* **48:4** Winter:1988 pp. 372 – 379

29 The organizational dilemmas of ethnic churches — a case study of Japanese Buddhism in Canada. Mark R. Mullins. *Sociol. Anal.* **49:3** Fall:1988 pp. 217 – 233

30 Orthodoxy, religious discordance and alienation. Larry R. Petersen. *J. Sci. S. Relig.* **27:3** 9:1988 pp. 362 – 377

31 Patterns of religious tension in Malaysia. Raymond L.M. Lee. *Asian Sur.* **XXVIII:4** 4:1988 pp. 400 – 418

32 The politics of religion and social change. Jeffrey K. Hadden *[Ed.]*; Anson Shupe *[Ed.]*. New York: Paragon House, 1988: - [Religion and the political order. : No. 2]

33 The problem of nihilism — a sociological approach. Meerten B. Ter Borg. *Sociol. Anal.* **49:1** Spring:1988 pp. 1 – 16

34 Psychology of religion. Richard L. Gorsuch. *Ann. R. Psych.* **39:** 1988 pp. 201 – 222

35 The quest for purity — dynamics of puritan movements. Walter E. A. van Beek *[Ed.]*. Berlin: Mouton de Gruyter, 1988: 273 p. *ISBN: 0899253768.* [Religion and society. : No. 26]

36 The rationality of magic. Michal Buchowski. *Philos. S. Sc.* **18:4** 12:1988 pp. 509 – 518

D.5: Magic. Mythology. Religion [Magie. Mythologie. Religion]

37 Religion and the persistence of identity. Phillip E. Hammond. *J. Sci. S. Relig.* **27:1** 3:1988 pp. 1 – 11

38 Religion and the problem-solving process — three styles of coping. Kenneth I. Pargament; Joseph Kennell; William Hathaway; Nancy Grevengoed; Jon Newman; Wendy Jones. *J. Sci. S. Relig.* **27:1** 3:1988 pp. 90 – 104

39 Religion as a sociological category. I. C. Jarvie. *Oceania* **59:1** 9:1988 pp. 29 – 39

40 Religion et évolution démographique en Inde *[In French]*; Religión y evolución demográfica en India *[Spanish summary]*; Religion and demographic change in India *[Summary]*. Roland Breton. *Population* **43:6** 11-12:1988 pp. 1089 – 1122

41 Religion, economics, and society. James T. Richardson *[Ed.]*; David G. Bromley *[Ed.]*; Bruce C. Busching *[Contrib.]*; Barbara Hargrove *[Contrib.]*; Lynn D. Nelson *[Contrib.]*; John R. Hall *[Contrib.]*; Joseph B. Tamney; Ronald Burton *[Contrib.]*; Stephen Johnson *[Contrib.]*. Collection of 6 articles. **Sociol. Anal.**, *49:S,* 12:1988 pp. 1 – 96

42 Religion, ethnicity and the role of the state — explaining conflict in Assam. Alfred T. Darnell; Sunita Parikh. *Ethn. Racial* **11:3** 7:1988 pp. 263 – 281

43 Religion, solidarity and class struggle. Marx, Durkheim and Gramsci on the religion question; *[French summary]*. Anthony Mansueto. *Soc. Compass* **XXXV:2-3** 1988 pp. 261 – 277

44 Religiosity, life meaning and wellbeing — some relationships in a sample of women. Kerry Chamberlain; Sheryl Zika. *J. Sci. S. Relig.* **27:3** 9:1988 pp. 411 – 420

45 Religious change and secularization — the transmission of religious values in Australia. Ian McAllister. *Sociol. Anal.* **49:3** Fall:1988 pp. 249 – 263

46 Religious ideology and interpersonal relationships within the family; *[French summary]*; *[Spanish summary]*. Vanaja Dhruvarajan. *J. Comp. Fam. Stud.* **XIX:2** Summer:1988 pp. 273 – 285

47 The sati of Deorala — an attributional study of social reactions. Ajit K. Dalal; Atul K. Singh; Ambalika Sinha; Usha Sah. *Indian J. Soc. W.* **XLIX:4** 10:1988 pp. 349 – 358

48 A scientific approach to religious development — proposals and a case illustration. Susan Kwilecki. *J. Sci. S. Relig.* **27:3** 9:1988 pp. 307 – 325

49 La secolarizzazione — contributi per l'analisi empirica *[In Italian]*; [Secularization — contributions towards an empirical analysis]. Loredana Sciolla *[Contrib.]*; Luca Ricolfi *[Contrib.]*; Franco Garelli *[Contrib.]*; Giovanni Filoramo *[Contrib.]*. Collection of 4 articles. **Rass. It. Soc.**, *29:1,* 1-3:1988 pp. 3 – 145

50 Sex, ethnic and social class differences in parareligious beliefs among Israeli adolescents. Moshe Zeidner; Benjamin Beit-Hallahmi. *J. Soc. Psychol.* **128:3** 6:1988 pp. 333 – 343

51 Shinshuukyou ni okeru senzo rei sinkou no isou *[In Japanese]*; [The topological space of ancestor worship and spiritualism of the new religious movement in modern Japan society]. Mitsugi Koumoto. *Mei. Daig. Ky. Ron. Vol.212. 1988.* pp. 153 – 173

52 Situated fraternization — the eudaemonic sublimation of religion. Carl Kavadlo. *Int. J. Pol. C. S.* **2:2** Winter:1988 pp. 257 – 276

D.5: Magic. Mythology. Religion *[Magie. Mythologie. Religion]*

53 Sociology and religion — a bibliography selected from the ATLA database. Albert E. Hurd *[Ed.]*. Chicage: American Theological Library Association, 1988: 541 p.

54 Sociology of religion and American religious history — retrospect and prospect. David G. Hackett. *J. Sci. S. Relig.* **27:4** 12:1988 pp. 461 – 474

55 Spiritual politics — religion and America since World War II. Mark Silk. London: Simon and Schuster, 1988: 206 p. *ISBN: 0671439103.*

56 Teología y ciencias sociales *[In Spanish]*; [Theology and the social sciences]. Gustavo Gutiérrez. *Tareas* pp. 97 – 122

57 The transformative impact of the study of new religions on the sociology of religion. Thomas Robbins. *J. Sci. S. Relig.* **27:1** 3:1988 pp. 12 – 31

58 The transmission of religious beliefs and practices from parents to firstborn early adolescent sons. Cynthia A. Clark; Everett L. Worthington; Donald B. Danser. *J. Marriage Fam.* **50:2** 5:1988 pp. 463 – 472

59 Trends in Judaism in the Soviet Union. Avraham Greenbaum. *Nat. Pap.* **XVI:2** Fall:1988 pp. 191 – 200

60 The universal man — Tagore's vision of the religion of humanity. Santinath Chottopadhyay. Calcutta: Naya Prokash, 1987: xxii, 210 p. *ISBN: 81 85169 16 0.*

Christianity *[Christianisme]*

61 La acción social de la Iglesia en el marco de la sociedad actual *[In Spanish]*; [The social action of the church in the framework of today's society]. Fernando Fuente Alcantara. *Rev. Fom. Soc.* **43:171** 7-9:1988 pp. 259 – 270

62 American Catholicism and the international family planning movement. Peter J. Donaldson. *Pop. Stud.* **XLII:3** 11:1988 pp. 367 – 374

63 Approche démographique de l'implantation hors d'Europe des congrégations religieuses féminines d'origine française *[In French]*; A demographic approach to the spread of women's religious orders of French origin outside Europe *[Summary]*; *[Spanish summary]*. Elisabeth Dufourcq. *Population* **43:1** 1-2:1988 pp. 45 – 76

64 The Catholic Church and politics in Nicaragua and Costa Rica. Philip J. Williams. Basingstoke: Macmillan in association with St. Antony's College, Oxford, 1988: xvi, 228 p. *ISBN: 0333471288. Bibliography — p.207-221.*

65 Les catholiques et la question wallonne *[In French]*; [The Catholics and the Walloon question]. Jacques Leclercq; Pierre Sauvage *[Ed.]*. Mont-sur-Marchienne: Institut Jules Destrée, 1988: 239 p. [Écrits politiques wallons. : No. 1]

66 The changing role of the Roman Catholic Church in the Philippines. Tony Anderton. *World Rev.* **27:2** 6:1988 pp. 12 – 36

67 Demographic transitions in religious organizations — a comparative study of priest decline in Roman Catholic dioceses. Richard A. Schoenherr; Lawrence A. Young; José Pérez Vilarino. *J. Sci. S. Relig.* **27:4** 12:1988 pp. 461 – 474

68 The divorce referendum in the Republic of Ireland — resisting the tide. William Duncan. *Int. J. Law Fam.* **2:1** 4:1988 pp. 62 – 75

69 Economic and social acculturation among the Old Order Amish in select communities — surviving in a high-tech society. Jerry Savells. *J. Comp. Fam. Stud.* **XIX:1** Spring:1988 pp. 123 – 136

D.5: Magic. Mythology. Religion *[Magie. Mythologie. Religion]* — **Christianity** *[Christianisme]*

70 An exploration of the attribution styles of Christian fundamentalists and of authoritarians. Michael B. Lupfer; Patricia L. Hopkinson; Patricia Kelley. *J. Sci. S. Relig.* **27:3** 9:1988 pp. 389 – 398

71 Mass media religion — the social sources of the electronic church. Stewart M. Hoover. Newbury Park: Sage Publications, 1988: 250 p. *LofC: 87-036859; ISBN: 0-8039-2994-3.* [Communication and human values.]

72 I movimenti cristiani e la teologia della secolarizzazione nell'europa occidentale *[In Italian]*; [The Christian movement and secularization theology in Western Europe]. Giuseppe Alberigo. *Pens. Pol.* **XXI:2** 5-8:1988 pp. 149 – 185

73 Organizational homogeneity, growth, and conflict in Brazilian Protestantism. Reed E. Nelson. *Sociol. Anal.* **48:4** Winter:1988 pp. 319 – 327

74 Polônia, a pé — a mística de uma romaria católica *[In Portuguese]*; [Poland on foot — the mystique of a Catholic pilgrimage]. Rubem César Fernandes. *Ciên. Soc. Hoje.* pp. 185 – 195

75 Le protestantisme doit-il mourir? — la différence protestante dans une France pluriculturelle *[In French]*; [Must Protestantism die? — the Protestant difference in a multicultural France]. Jean Baubérot. Paris: Editions du Seuil, 1988: 274 p. *ISBN: 2020103656. Bibliography — p.. 267-[275].*

76 Religion and business — the Catholic Church and the American economy; *[French summary]*. Manuel Velasquez; Gerald Canavagh. *Calif. Manag. R.* **30:4** 1988 pp. 124 – 140

77 Religious values, practices and pregnancy outcomes — a comparison of the impact of sect and mainstream Christian affiliation. J.M. Najman; G.M. Williams; J.D. Keeping; J. Morrison; M.J. Andersen. *Soc. Sci. Med.* **26:4** 1988 pp. 401 – 408

78 Role commitment processes revisited — American Catholic priests 1970 and 1985. Mary Jeanne Verdieck; Joseph J. Shields; Dean R. Hoge. *J. Sci. S. Relig.* **27:4** 12:1988 pp. 524 – 535

79 Sociologie du catholicisme *[In French]*; [The sociology of Catholicism]. E. Poulat *[Contrib.]*; J. Maitre *[Contrib.]*; Y. Lambert *[Contrib.]*; J. Potel *[Contrib.]*; J. Palard *[Contrib.]*; R. Courcy *[Contrib.]*; L. Voyé *[Contrib.]*; G. Cholvy *[Contrib.]*; J.-F. Mayer *[Contrib.]*; D. Hervieu-Léger *[Contrib.]* and others. Collection of 10 articles. **Contin. Change**, *3:3*, 12:1988 pp. 23 – 231

80 Symposium on Weber's "The protestant ethic". Richard van Dülen *[Contrib.]*; Guy Oakes *[Contrib.]*; Paul Piccone *[Contrib.]*. *Collection of 3 articles.* **Telos**, *78*, Winter:1988-1989 pp. 71 – 108

81 Vatican II, ecumenism and a Parsonian analysis of change. Michael F. Aloisi. *Sociol. Anal.* **49:1** Spring:1988 pp. 17 – 28

Islam *[Islam]*

82 Charisma and brotherhood in African Islam. Donal B. Cruise O'Brien *[Ed.]*; Christian Coulon *[Ed.].* : Clarendon, 1988: vi, 223 p. *ISBN: 019822723x; LofC: 88-12437. Bibliography — p.205-213.*

83 Discovering Islam — making sense of Muslim history and society. Akbar S. Ahmed. London: Routledge & Kegan Paul, 1988: x, 251 p. *ISBN: 0710210493; LofC: 87-4967. Bibliography — p.238-239. Includes index.*

D.5: Magic. Mythology. Religion *[Magie. Mythologie. Religion]* — Islam *[Islam]*

84 Islam and women. Malladi Subbamma. New Delhi: Sterling, 1988: xviii, 140 p. *ISBN: 81 207 0742 7.*

85 Islamic fundamentalism. Dilip Hiro. London: Paladin, 1988: xv, 304 p. *ISBN: 0586086447. Bibliography — p.294-296.*

86 Islamic fundamentalism and modernity. W. Montgomery Watt. : Routledge, 1988: 158 p. *ISBN: 0415006236. Bibliography — p.153-155.*

87 Les Marabouts de l'arachide — la confrérie mouride et les paysans du Sénégal *[In French]*; [The Marabouts — the mouride brotherhood and the Senegal peasants]. Jean Copans. Paris: l'Harmattan, 1988: 279 p. *ISBN: 2738402771.*

88 Les Musulmans dans la société française *[In French]*; [Muslims in French society]. Gilles Kepel *[Ed.]*; Rémy Leveau *[Ed.]*. Paris: Presses de la Fondation Nationale des Sciences Politiques, 1988: 207 p. *ISBN: 2724605586.* [[Références].]

89 The new Islamic presence in Western Europe. Tomas Gerholm *[Ed.]*; Yngve Georg Lithman *[Ed.]*. London: Mansell, 1988: viii, 293 p. (ill) *ISBN: 0720118867; LofC: 87-31259. Includes bibliographies and index.*

90 Shi'i thought from the south of Lebanon. Chibli Mallat. Oxford: Centre for Lebanese Studies, 1988: 42 p. *ISBN: 1870552075.* [Papers on Lebanon. : No. 7]

D.6: Science. Sociology of knowledge — *Science. Sociologie de la connaissance*

1 Artificial intelligence. Seymour Papert *[Contrib.]*; Hubert L. Dreyfus *[Contrib.]*; Stuart E. Dreyfus *[Contrib.]*; Robert Sokolowski *[Contrib.]*; Pamela McCorduck *[Contrib.]*; Jack D. Cowan *[Contrib.]*; David H. Sharp *[Contrib.]*; Jacob T. Schwartz *[Contrib.]*; George N. Reeke *[Contrib.]*; Gerald M. Edelman *[Contrib.] and others. Collection of 14 articles.* **Dædalus**, *117:1,* Winter:1988 pp. 1 – 311

2 Asuwada principle — an analysis of Akiwowo's contributions to the sociology of knowledge from an African perspective. M. Akin. Makinde. *Int. Sociol.* **3:1** 3:1988 pp. 61 – 76

3 Australian science and its public. R.W. Home. *Aust. Cult. Hist.* **:7** :1988 pp. 86 – 103

4 Ciencia y razón *[In Spanish]*; [Science and reason]. Georg Henrik von Wright. *Sistema* **83** 3:1988 pp. 13 – 24

5 Common sense and the human sciences. Raymond Boudon. *Int. Sociol.* **3:1** 3:1988 pp. 1 – 22

6 Conoscenza e intervento — verso approcio interattivo *[In Italian]*; Knowledge and intervention — towards an interactive approach *[Summary]*. Giovanni B. Sgritta. *Rass. It. Soc.* **29:4** 10-12:1988 pp. 537 – 562

7 Explanation in science. James W. McAllister *[Contrib.]*; Josep Corbí *[Contrib.]*; Marin Marinov *[Contrib.]*; James Robert Brown *[Contrib.]*; Ulrich Röseberg *[Contrib.]*; Del Ratzsch *[Contrib.]*; Michael Detlefsen *[Contrib.]. Collection of 7 articles.* **Inter. Phil. Sci.**, *3:1,* Autumn:1988 pp. 2 – 116

D.6: Science. Sociology of knowledge *[Science. Sociologie de la connaissance]*

8 Fostering understanding between scientists and the public. Zhang Daoyi. *Impact Sci.* **38:4(152)** 1988 pp. 355 – 362

9 Il futuro ed i limiti della scienza *[In Italian]*; (Science future and science limits). Giuliano Toraldo di Francia. *Crit. Marx.* **26:2** 3-4:1988 pp. 111 – 120

10 „Herrschaft kraft Wissen" in der Risikogesellschaft *[In German]*; Domination via knowledge in the "risk society" *[Summary]*. Rainer Wolf. *Soz. Welt.* **39:2** 1988 pp. 164 – 187

11 Imputing beliefs — a controversy in the sociology of knowledge. Alan Scott. *Sociol. Rev.* **36:1** 2:1988 pp. 31 – 56

12 Issues in the popularization of science. Sergie P. Kapitza. *Impact Sci.* **38:4(152)** 1988 pp. 317 – 326

13 Karl Mannheim and the contemporary sociology of knowledge. Brian Longhurst. Basingstoke: Macmillan, 1988: xii, 202 p. *ISBN: 0333457064.* Bibliography — p.175-195. Includes index.

14 Knowledge and reflexivity — new frontiers in the sociology of knowledge. Steve Woolgar *[Ed.]*. London: Sage, 1988: 256 p. (ill) *ISBN: 0803981201.* Includes bibliography and index.

15 Knowledge and the role of theories. Paul K. Feyerabend. *Philos. S. Sc.* **18:2** 6:1988 pp. 157 – 178

16 Koki Schultz to chi no shakaigaku no kanousei *[In Japanese]*; [Schultz's late theory and the potentialities of his sociology of knowledge]. Kazuhisa Nishihara. *Gend. Shi. Seid. Tokyo* Vol.16; No.7 - 1988. pp. 40 – 60

17 Mannheim as a sociologist of knowledge. Hans Speier. *Int. J. Pol. C. S.* **2:1** Fall:1988 pp. 81 – 94

18 New materials, new machines. John V. Wood *[Contrib.]*; T. Fred Smith *[Contrib.]*; Jacqueline Juillard *[Contrib.]*; Jacqueline Jozefonvicz *[Contrib.]*; Marcel Jozefowicz *[Contrib.]*; S.C. Mehendale *[Contrib.]*; K.C. Rustagi *[Contrib.]*; John Woodhead Galloway *[Contrib.]*; Eric Labouze *[Contrib.]*; Guri Marchuk *[Contrib.]* and others. Collection of 8 articles. **Impact Sci.**, *38:1(149)*, 1988 pp. 3 – 95

19 Public dialogue on science in Sweden. Annagreta Dyring. *Impact Sci.* **38:4(152)** 1988 pp. 327 – 336

20 The public perception of science. Jean Dhombres *[Contrib.]*; Peter Pockley *[Contrib.]*; Robert G. Calvora *[Contrib.]*; Andrew O. Urevbu *[Contrib.]*; Günter Kröber *[Contrib.]*; Rahat Nabi Khan *[Contrib.]*. Collection of 6 articles. **Impact Sci.**, *38:2(151)*, 1988 pp. 209 – 271

21 The rhetoric of science — strategies for logical leaping. Charles Kurzman. *Berkeley J. Soc.* **XXXIII** 1988 pp. 131 – 158

22 Science as power — discourse and ideology in modern society. Stanley Aronowitz. : Macmillan, 1988: 384 p. *ISBN: 0333475461.*

23 Science in its confrontation with society. Robert G. Calvora. *Impact Sci.* **38:2(151)** 1988 pp. 231 – 238

24 Science popularization in a changing world. Yves Coppens *[Contrib.]*; Michael Shortland *[Contrib.]*; Sergei P. Kapitza *[Contrib.]*; Annagreta Dyring *[Contrib.]*; Diane Saunier *[Contrib.]*; Zhang Daoyi *[Contrib.]*; Saliou Touré *[Contrib.]*; Dorte Olesen *[Contrib.]*; Sidney Harris *[Contrib.]*; Michael Mosley *[Contrib.]* and others. Collection of 11 articles. **Impact Sci.**, *38:4(152)*, 1988 pp. 301 – 409

D.6: Science. Sociology of knowledge *[Science. Sociologie de la connaissance]*

25 Science, scientists and society — public attitudes towards science and technology. Rahat Nabi Khan. *Impact Sci.* **38:2(151)** 1988 pp. 257 – 271
26 Science, technology and African values. Andrew O. Urevbu. *Impact Sci.* **38:2(151)** 1988 pp. 239 – 248
27 Scienza e cultura scientifica *[In Italian]*; (Science and scientific culture). Antonio Di Meo. *Crit. Marx.* **26:2** 3-4:1988 pp. 33 – 42
28 Scienza e potere in Russia e in Unione Sovietica *[In Italian]*; Science and power in Russia and Soviet Union *[Summary]*. Silvano Tagliagambe. *Crit. Marx.* **26:6** 11-12:1988 pp. 23 – 49
29 La situazione delle scienze in Italia *[In Italian]*; (The situation of sciences in Italy). Antonio Di Meo *[Contrib.]*; Enrico Bellone *[Contrib.]*; Carlo Bernardini *[Contrib.]*; Paolo Budinich *[Contrib.]*; Maria Luisa Dalla Chiara *[Contrib.]*; Giorgio Di Maio *[Contrib.]*; Giorgio Levi *[Contrib.]*; Alberto Oliverio *[Contrib.]*; Giuliano Toraldo Di Francia *[Contrib.]*; Giuseppe Chiarante *[Contrib.] and others*. *Crit. Marx.* , *26:2*, 3-4:1988 pp. 33 – 130
30 Social epistemology. Steve Fuller. Bloomington [Ind.]: Indiana University Press, 1988: xv, 316 p. *ISBN: 0253352274. Bibliography — p295-311.* [Science, technology, and society.]
31 The social psychology of knowledge. Arie W. Kruglanski *[Ed.]*; Daniel Bar-Tal *[Ed.]*. Cambridge: Cambridge University Press, 1988: - *ISBN: 052132114x*.
32 The sociology of knowledge — towards redemption of a failed promise. William Buxton; David Rehorick. *Int. J. Pol. C. S.* **2:1** Fall:1988 pp. 66 – 80
33 The sociology of scientific knowledge — can we ever get it straight? Peter T. Manicas; Alan Rosenberg. *J. Theory Soc. Behav.* **18:1** 3:1988 pp. 51 – 76
34 Tra politica e scienza *[In Italian]*; (Between politics and science). Giuseppe Chiarante. *Crit. Marx.* **26:2** 3-4:1988 pp. 121 – 130
35 When intellectual paradigms shift — does the end of the old mark the beginning of the new? Jacob Neusner. *Hist. Theory* **27:3** 1988 pp. 241 – 260

D.7: Communication. Language — *Communication. Langage*

Sub-divisions: Communication *[Communication]*; Linguistics *[Linguistique]*; Media *[Moyens de communication]*

1 ABC — the alphabetization of the popular mind. Ivan Illich; Barry Sanders *[Ed.]*. London: Boyars, 1988: xi, 166 p. *ISBN: 0714528919. Bibliography — p.128-166.*
2 The context principle and some Indian controversies over meaning. B.K. Matilal; P.K. Sen. *Mind* **XCVII:** :1988 pp. 73 – 97
3 Feminism and censorship — the current debate. Gail Chester *[Ed.]*; Julienne Dickey *[Ed.]*. Bridport: Prism Press, 1988: 282 p. *ISBN: 1853270229. Bibliography — p.279.*
4 The future of ethnic languages in Australia. Anne Pauwels *[Ed.]*; Joshua A. Fishman *[Ed.]*; Anne Pauwels *[Contrib.]*; Camilla Bettoni *[Contrib.]*; John Gibbons *[Contrib.]*; Mark Garner *[Contrib.]*; Ludmila Kouzmin *[Contrib.]*; Michael G. Clyne *[Contrib.]*; Susanne Döpke *[Contrib.]*; Uldis Ozolins *[Contrib.] and others*. Collection of 9 articles. *Int. J. S. Lang.* , 72, 1988 pp. 5 – 134

D.7: Communication. Language [Communication. Langage]

5 The information society — an international perspective. Raul Luciano Katz. New York: Praeger, 1988: 216 p. (ill) *ISBN: 0275926591; LofC: 87-25884.* Includes bibliography and index.

6 Języki społeczności etnicznych. Wartości rdzenne a zachowywanie kultury — doświadczenia australijskie ze szczególnym uwzględnieniem grup — greckiej, łotewskiij i polskiej. Część I *[In Polish]*; Community languages, core values and cultural maintenance — the Australian experience with special references to Greek, Latvian and Polish groups. Part 1 *[Summary]*. Jerzy J. Smolicz; Margaret J. Secombe. *Prz. Pol.* **XIV:4** 1988 pp. 5 – 24

7 Language planning and attitudes. Florian Coulmas *[Ed.]*; Moha Ennaji *[Contrib.]*; John B. Pride *[Contrib.]*; Ru-Shan Liu *[Contrib.]*; Calvin Veltman *[Contrib.]*; Marie-Noële Denis *[Contrib.]*; Robert Nicolaï *[Contrib.]*; Roeland van Hout *[Contrib.]*; Henk Münstermann *[Contrib.]*; Joshua A. Fishman *[Contrib.] and others. Collection of 6 articles.* **Int. J. S. Lang.**, *74*, 1988 pp. 5 – 140

8 Language planning in Ireland. Pádraig Ó. Riagáin *[Ed.]*; Joshua A. Fishman *[Ed.]*; Pádraig Ó. Riagáin *[Contrib.]*; Patrick Commins *[Contrib.]*; Hilary Tovey *[Contrib.]*; John Harris *[Contrib.]*; Micheál Ó Gliasáin *[Contrib.]*; Dónall P.Ó. Baoill *[Contrib.]*; Jeffrey L. Kallen *[Contrib.]. Collection of 8 articles.* **Int. J. S. Lang.**, *70*, 1988 pp. 5 – 142

9 Language, interaction, and social problems. Douglas W. Maynard *[Contrib.]*; Jack Whalen *[Contrib.]*; Don H. Zimmermann *[Contrib.]*; Marilyn R. Whalen *[Contrib.]*; Hugh Mehan *[Contrib.]*; John Wills *[Contrib.]*; Carol Brooks Gardner *[Contrib.]*; Paul Drew *[Contrib.]*; Elizabeth Holt *[Contrib.]*; Gail Jefferson *[Contrib.] and others.* **Soc. Prob.**, *35:4*, 10:1988 pp. 311 – 492

10 Latin American perspectives. Philip Schlesinger *[Ed.]*; José Marques de Melo *[Contrib.]*; Javier Esteinou Madrid *[Contrib.]*; Jesús Martín-Barbero *[Contrib.]*; Néstor García Canclini *[Contrib.]*; Colin Hoskins *[Contrib.]*; Rolf Mirus *[Contrib.]*; Greg Philo *[Contrib.]. Collection of 7 articles.* **Media Cult. Soc.**, *10:4*, 10:1988 pp. 395 – 522

11 Las legislaciones sobre las lenguas minoritarias en Europa Occidental — ámbitos de valoración *[In Spanish]*; [Legislation on the minority languages of Western Europe — scope for improving status]. Santiago Petschen. *Sistema* **83** 3:1988 pp. 113 – 122

12 Semantic representation of meaning — a critique. Benny Shanon. *Psychol .B.* **104:1** 7:1988 pp. 70 – 83

13 Translation, interpretation and understanding. Richard C. Jennings. *Philos. S. Sc.* **18:3** 9:1988 pp. 343 – 354

14 The uses of history — language, ideology, and law in the United States and South Africa. Elizabeth Mertz. *Law Soc. Rev.* **22:4** 1988 pp. 661 – 685

15 Whose information society? A view from the periphery. Mark Hepworth; Kevin Robins. *Media Cult. Soc.* **10:3** 7:1988 pp. 323 – 343

Communication [Communication]

16 Are "powerless" communication strategies the Japanese norm? Patricia J. Wetzel. *Lang. Soc.* **17:4** 12:1988 pp. 555 – 564

17 Aufstieg und Fall des „Two-Step-Flow of Communication". Kritik einer

D.7: Communication. Language *[Communication. Langage]* — **Communication** *[Communication]*

sozialwissenschaftlichen Hypothese *[In German]*; The rise and fall of the "two-step-flow of communication" — critique of a social-science hypothesis *[Summary]*. Klaus Merten. *Polit. Viertel.* **29:4** 12:1988 pp. 610 – 635

18 Communication and cross-cultural adaptation — an integrative theory. Young Yun Kim. Clevedon: Multilingual Matters, 1988: 223 p. *ISBN: 090502883x. Bibliography — p.175-213*. [Intercommunication. : No. 2]

19 Communication as predictor of the perception of commonality among Caribbean Island groups. Humphrey A. Regis. *J. Car. Stud.* **6:3** Autumn:1988 pp. 259 – 273

20 Communication in a multilingual society — some missed opportunities. Rajendra Singh; Jayant Lele; Gita. Martohardjono. *Lang. Soc.* **17:1** 3:1988 pp. 43 – 59

21 Communication reconstructed. Robyn Penman. *J. Theory Soc. Behav.* **18:4** 12:1988 pp. 391 – 410

22 The concept of preference in conversation analysis. Jack. Bilmes. *Lang. Soc.* **17:2** 6:1988 pp. 161 – 181

23 Confrontation and politeness strategies in physician-patient interactions. Lynne S. Robins; Fredric M. Wolf. *Soc. Sci. Med.* **27:3** 1988 pp. 217 – 221

24 The context of oral and written language — a framework for mode and medium switching. Denise E. Murray. *Lang. Soc.* **17:3** 9:1988 pp. 351 – 373

25 Effectiveness of cigarette advertisements on women — an experimental study. Barbara Loken; Beth Howard-Pitney. *J. Appl. Psychol.* **73:3** 8:1988 pp. 378 – 382

26 Literacy and orality — studies in the technology of communication. Ruth Finnegan. Oxford: Basil Blackwell, 1988: 256 p. *Includes bibliography and index.*

27 Mass communication and modern culture — contribution to a critical theory of ideology. John B. Thompson. *Sociology* **22:3** 8:1988 pp. 359 – 383

28 Mass communications research methods — a step-by-step approach. H. J. Hsia. Hillsdale,N. J.: Lawrence Erlbaum, 1988: 629 p. *ISBN: 0898599148.*

29 The mass media and village life — an Indian study. Paul Hartmann; B.R. Patil; Anita Dighe. New Delhi and London: Sage Publications, 1988: 286 p. *Bibliography — p.270-272.*

30 Mass-communication kenkyū no shakaigaku-taki tenbou *[In Japanese]*; [Sociological approach to the research for mass communication]. Hakuchi Tanaka. ***Kenyunenshi*** *Vol.32. 1988.* pp. 63 – 78

31 A new look at informal communication — the role of the physical environment. David E. Campbell; Toni A. Campbell. *Envir. Behav.* **20:2** 3:1988 pp. 211 – 226

32 Nonverbal communication in advertising. S. Hecker; D. W. Stewart *[Ed.]*. Lexington, Mass: Lexington Books, 1988: - *ISBN: 0669141720; LofC: lc87-017143.*

33 Politeness in context — intergenerational issues. Nikolas Coupland; Karen Grainger; Justine Coupland. *Lang. Soc.* **17:2** 6:1988 pp. 253 – 262

34 The political economy of information. Vincent Mosco *[Ed.]*; Janet Wasko *[Ed.]*. Madison, Wisc.: University of Wisconsin Press, 1988: 334 p. cm *ISBN: 0299115704. Includes bibliographies and index.* [Studies in communication and society.]

D.7: Communication. Language *[Communication. Langage]* — **Communication** *[Communication]*

35 The politics of representation — writing practices in biography, photography, and policy analysis. Michael J. Shapiro. Madison: University of Wisconsin Press, 1988: 203 p. *ISBN: 0299116301.*

36 Putting on appearances — gender and advertising. Diane L. Barthel. Philadelphia: Temple University Press, 1988: ix, 219 p. *ISBN: 0877225281; LofC: 87-020010. Includes index.* [Women in the political economy.]

37 The quantitative study of communicative success — politeness and accidents in aviation discourse. Charlotte. Linde. *Lang. Soc.* **17:3** 9:1988 pp. 375 – 399

38 Rumor as communication — contextualist approach. Ralph L. Rosnow. *J. Comm. 38:1* pp. 12 – 28

39 Sign languages of aboriginal Australia — cultural, semiotic and communicative perspectives. Adam Kendon. Cambridge: Cambridge University Press, 1988: 542 p. *ISBN: 0521360080. Bibliography — p.513-528.*

40 Social conflict and alternative mass communications — public art and politics in the service of Spanish-Basque nationalism. Lyman Chaffee. *Eur. J. Pol. R.* **16:5** 1988 pp. 545 – 572

41 The social construction of written communication. Bennett A Rafoth *[Ed.]*; Donald L Rubin *[Ed.]*. Norwood, N.J.: Ablex, 1988: 330 p. *ISBN: 0893914363. Includes indexes.* [Writing research.]

42 Social semiotics. Robert Hodge; Gunther Kress *[Ed.]*. Cambridge: Polity, 1988: ix, 285 p. *ISBN: 0745602533. Bibliography — p.273-279. Includes index.*

43 Sougo koui heno "miburi kaiwa" ron-teki approach *[In Japanese]*; [An approach to interaction as "a conversation of gestures"]. Chihaya Kusayaangi. *Philosophy Vol.87. 1988.* pp. 175 – 201

44 Technologies of control — the new interactive media for the home. Kevin G. Wilson. Madison, Wis.: University of Wisconsin Press, 1988: xi, 180 p. *ISBN: 0299113701.* [Studies in communication and society.]

45 The telecom mosaic — assembling the new international structure. Robert R. Bruce; Jeffrey P. Cunard *[Ed.]*; Mark D. Director *[Ed.]*. London: Butterworths, 1988: 7, 447 p. *ISBN: 0408026707; LofC: 88- 14661.*

46 Terms of address — problems of patterns and usage in various languages and cultures. Friederike Braun. Berlin: Mouton de Gruyter, 1988: 372 p. *ISBN: 0899254322. Bibliography — p.313-365.* [Contributions to the sociology of language. : No. 50]

47 The theatre of consumption — on comparing American and Japanese advertising. Stephen Kline. *Can. J. Pol. Soc. Theo.* **12:3** :1988 pp. 101 – 120

48 Variation across speech and writing. Douglas Biber. Cambridge: Cambridge University Press, 1988: 299 p. *ISBN: 0521320712. Includes index; Bibliography — p.280-291.*

49 Women and politeness — the Javanese example. Nancy J. Smith-Hefner. *Lang. Soc.* **17:4** 12:1988 pp. 535 – 554

Linguistics *[Linguistique]*

50 Adolescent social structure and the spread of linguistic change. Penelope. Eckert. *Lang. Soc.* **17:2** 6:1988 pp. 183 – 207

51 Bilingualism in society and school. J. N. Jørgensen *[Ed.]*. Clevedon:

INTERNATIONAL BIBLIOGRAPHY OF SOCIOLOGY — 1988

D.7: Communication. Language *[Communication. Langage]* — **Linguistics** *[Linguistique]*

Multilingual Matters, 1988: xii, 340 p. *ISBN: 1853590169. Conference proceedings; Includes bibliographies and index.* [Copenhagen studies in bilingualism. : Vol. 5]

52 Codeswitching — anthropological and sociolinguistic perspectives. Monica Heller *[Ed.]*. Berlin: Mouton de Gruyter, 1988: 278 p. (ill.) *ISBN: 0899254128. Includes bibliographies and index.* [Contributions to the sociology of language. : No. 48]

53 Colour terms in Russian — reflections of typological constraints in a single language. Greville Corbett; Gerry Morgan. *J. Linguist.* **24:1** 3:1988 pp. 31 – 64

54 Complainable matters — the use of idiomatic expressions in making complaints. Paul Drew; Elizabeth Holt. *Soc. Prob.* **35:4** 10:1988 pp. 398 – 417

55 Culture and language development — language acquisition and language socialization in a Samoan village. Elinor Ochs. Cambridge: Cambridge University Press, 1988: - *ISBN: 0521344549. Includes index.* [Studies in the social and cultural foundations of language. : No. 6]

56 La dynamique des langues dans la fédération canadienne *[In French]*; [Language dynamics in the Canadian federation] *[Summary]*. Jacques Leclerc. *Étud. Can.* **:25** 1988 pp. 7 – 22

57 Forms of address in post-revolutionary Iranian Persian — a sociolinguistic analysis. Mohammad Hossein. Keshavarz. *Lang. Soc.* **17:4** 12:1988 pp. 565 – 575

58 The ideology of English — French perceptions of English as a world language. Jeffra Flaitz. Berlin: Mouton de Gruyter, 1988: xiii, 225 p. (ill.) *ISBN: 0899254330. Includes index.* [Contributions to the sociology of language. : No. 49]

59 Language and ethnic identity. William B. Gudykunst *[Ed.]*. Clevedon: Multilingual Matters, 1988: 172 p. *ISBN: 1853590215. Includes bibliography and index.*

60 Language and society — steps towards an integrated theory. Jayant Lele; R Singh *[Ed.]*. Leiden: E.J. Brill, 1988: xix, 146 p. *ISBN: 9004087893. Includes index.* [Monographs and theoretical studies in sociology and anthropology in honour of Nels Anderson.]

61 Language diversity — problem or resource? Sandra L. McKay *[Ed.]*; Sau-ling Cynthia Wong *[Ed.]*. Cambridge, Mass.: Newbury House, 1988: xiii, 386 p. (ill) *ISBN: 0066326087; LofC: 88-1450. Includes bibliographies.*

62 Language planning in Morocco and changes in Arabic. Moha Ennaji. *Int. J. S. Lang.* **74** 1988 pp. 9 – 40

63 Language shift and narrative performance — on the structure and function of Arvanítika narratives. Lukas D. Tsitsipis. *Lang. Soc.* **17:1** 3:1988 pp. 61 – 86

64 Language, interaction, and social problems. Douglas W. Maynard. *Soc. Prob.* **35:4** 10:1988 pp. 311 – 334

65 Langue et disparités de statut économique au Québec 1970 et 1980 *[In French]*; [Language and disparity in economic statues in Quebec 1970 and 1980]. François Vaillancourt. Quebec (Province): Conseil de la langue française, 1988: 232 p. [Dossiers du Conseil de la langue française. : No. 28]

D.7: Communication. Language *[Communication. Langage]* — Linguistics *[Linguistique]*

66 Linguistique et colonialisme — petit traité de glottophagie *[In French]*; [Linguistics and colonialism — a short treatise on glottophagy]. Louis-Jean Calvet. Paris: Payot, 1988, c1974: 248 p. *ISBN: 2228880280.* [Bibliothèque scientifique Payot.]

67 Le marché des langues en sciences — le français et l'identité nationale *[In French]*; [The growth of languages in science — French and national identity] *[Summary]*. Michel Leclerc. *Étud. Can.* :**25** 1988 pp. 23 – 40

68 Mental representations — the interface between language and reality. Ruth M. Kempson *[Ed.]*. Cambridge: Cambridge University Press, 1988: 227 p. *ISBN: 0521342511. Includes index.*

69 Mind and media — the epistemic functions of literacy. David R. Olson. *J. Comm.* **38:3** 1988 pp. 27 – 36

70 Modelling the language shift process of Hispanic immigrants. Calvin Veltman. *Int. Migr. Rev.* **XXII:4** Winter:1988 pp. 545 – 562

71 New perspectives on language maintenance and language shift II. James R. Dow *[Ed.]*; Joshua A. Fishman *[Ed.]*; Robert H. Buchheit *[Contrib.]*; James R. Dow *[Contrib.]*; Werner Enninger *[Contrib.]*; Vasilikie Demos *[Contrib.]*; Kamal K. Sridhar *[Contrib.]*; Melvyn C. Resnick *[Contrib.]*; April R. Komenaka *[Contrib.]*. Collection of 7 articles. **Int. J. S. Lang.**, *69*, 1988 pp. 5 – 116

72 On being literate — living with difference. Margaret Meek. London: Bodley Head, 1988: 266 p. *ISBN: 0370311906. Includes bibliography and index.*

73 The regional dynamics of language differentiation in Belgium — a study in cultural-political geography. Alexander B. Murphy. Chicago, Ill.: University of Chicago, Committee on Geographical Studies, 1988: 249 p. *ISBN: 0890651329. Includes index; Bibliography — p.205-244.* [Geography Research paper.]

74 Sociolinguística latinoamericana *[In Spanish]*; [Socio-linguistics in Latin America]. Rainer Enrique Hamel *[Ed.]*; Yolanda Lastra de Suarez *[Ed.]*; Héctor Muñoz Cruz *[Ed.]*. Mexico: Unam-Investigaciones Antropologicas, 1988: 240 p. *ISBN: 9683603467.* [Serie Antropológica. : No. 56]

75 Sociolinguistics and pidgin-creole studies. John R. Rickford *[Ed.]*; Joshua A. Fishman *[Ed.]*; John R. Rickford *[Contrib.]*; Dennis R. Craig *[Contrib.]*; Robert B. Le Page *[Contrib.]*; Peter Mühlhäusler *[Contrib.]*; Suzanne Romaine *[Contrib.]*; Albert Valdman *[Contrib.]*; Jeffrey P. Williams *[Contrib.]*; Donald Winford *[Contrib.]* <u>and others</u>. Collection of 11 articles. **Int. J. S. Lang.**, *71*, 1988 pp. 5 – 130

76 The sociolinguistics of Dutch. Judith Stalpers *[Ed.]*; Florian Coulmas *[Ed.]*; Joshua A. Fishman *[Ed.]*; Florian Coulmas *[Contrib.]*; Judith Stalpers *[Contrib.]*; Pieter H. van der Plank *[Contrib.]*; Anton M. Hagen *[Contrib.]*; Herman Giesbers *[Contrib.]*; Pete van de Craen *[Contrib.]*; Roland Willemyns *[Contrib.]* <u>and others</u>. Collection of 8 articles. **Int. J. S. Lang.**, *73*, 1988 pp. 5 – 136

77 Sociolinguistics of urban vernaculars — case studies and their evaluation. Norbert Dittmar *[Ed.]*; Peter Schlobinski *[Ed.]*. Berlin: W. de Gruyter, 1988: 275 p. *ISBN: 0899255124. Bibliography — p.259-275.* [Soziolinguistik und Sprachkontakt.]

78 Spanish language use and attitudes — a study of two New York City communities. Ofelia García; Isabel Evangelista; Mabel Martínez; Carmen Disla; Bonifacio Paulino. *Lang. Soc.* **17:4** 12:1988 pp. 475 – 511

D.7: Communication. Language *[Communication. Langage]* — Linguistics *[Linguistique]*

79 Standardizing written Japanese — a factor in modernization. Nanette Twine. *Monu. Nippon.* **43:4** Winter:1988 pp. 429 – 454

80 Terms of address — problems of patterns and usage in various languages and cultures. Friederike Braun. Berlin: Mouton de Gruyter, 1988: 372 p. *ISBN: 0899254322. Bibliography — p.313-365.* [Contributions to the sociology of language. : No. 50]

81 The use of Welsh — a contribution to sociolinguistics. Martin J. Ball *[Ed.]*. Clevedon: Multilingual Matters, 1988: 341 p. *ISBN: 0905028996. Bibliography — p.320-331.* [Multilingual Matters. : No. 36]

82 What are you cookin' on a hot? Movement constraints in the speech of a three-year-old blind child. Bob Wilson; Ann M. Peters. *Language* **64:4** 1988 pp. 249 – 273

Media *[Moyens de communication]*

83 The alternative public realm — the organization of the 1980s anti-nuclear press in West Germany and Britain. John D.H. Downing. *Media Cult. Soc.* **10:2** 4:1988 pp. 163 – 181

84 The apologetics of suppression — the regulation of pornography as act and idea. Steven G. Gey. *MI. law. R.* **86:7** 6:1988 pp. 1564 – 1634

85 Arab scientific journalism — achievements and aspirations. Radwan Mawlawi. *Impact Sci.* **38:4(152)** 1988 pp. 397 – 409

86 Bantu world and the origins of a captive African commercial press in South Africa. Les Switzer. *J. S.Afr. Stud.* **14:3** 4:1988 pp. 351 – 370

87 The British, Canadian, and U.S. pornography commissions and their use of social science research. Edna F. Einsiedel. *J. Comm.* **38:2** 1988 pp. 108 – 121

88 Cableviewing. Carrie Heeter; Bradley S. Greenberg *[Ed.]*. Norwood,N. J.: Ablex Publishing, 1988: 316 p. *ISBN: 0893914665; LofC: 88-010450. Bibliography.*

89 Camera politica — the politics and ideology of contemporary Hollywood film. Michael Ryan; Douglas Kellner *[Ed.]*. Bloomington, Ind.: Indiana University Press, 1988: 328 p. *ISBN: 0253313341. Includes index.*

90 Consumerism, the media, and malnutrition in the Pacific Islands. Randolph R. Thaman. *J. Pac. Stud.* **14:** 1988 pp. 68 – 96

91 Doctoring the media — the reporting of health and medicine. Anne Karpf. London: Routledge, 1988: x, 288 p. *ISBN: 0415002508.*

92 East of Dallas — the European challenge to American television. Alessandro Silj; Manuel Alvarado *[Ed.]*. London: BFI, 1988: x,224 p. (ill) *ISBN: 0851702252. Bibliography — p.220-224. Includes index.*

93 The end of conversation — the impact of mass media on modern society. Franco Ferrarotti. New York: Greenwood, 1988: 192 p. *ISBN: 0313260877; LofC: 87-24966. Includes bibliography and index.* [Contributions in sociology. : No. 71]

94 From a raised eyebrow to a turned back — the FCC and children's product-related programming. Dale Kunkel. *J. Comm.* **38:4** 1988 pp. 90 – 107

95 "Hitting paydirt" — capacity theory and sports announcers' use of clichés. Wayne Wanta; Dawn Leggett. *J. Comm.* **38:4** 1988 pp. 82 – 89

D.7: Communication. Language *[Communication. Langage]* — Media *[Moyens de communication]*

96 Housou kenkyū no kadai to tenbou *[In Japanese]*; [Tasks facing broadcasting studies]. Takeshi Sato. *Hosog. Kenk Vol.38. 1988.* pp. 7 – 31

97 How first-time viewers comprehend editing conventions. Renée Hobbs; Richard Frost; Arthur Davis; John Stauffer. *J. Comm.* **38:4** 1988 pp. 50 – 60

98 Images of the enemy — reporting the new Cold War. Brian McNair. London: Routledge, 1988: 216 p. (ill) *ISBN: 0415006457. Based on author's thesis (Ph.D.); Bibliography — p.210-212.*

99 Impact of cigarette advertising on aggregate demand for cigarettes in New Zealand. Jane Chetwynd; Pat Coope; Roderick J. Brodie; Elisabeth Wells. *Br. J. Addict.* **83:4** 4:1988 pp. 409 – 414

100 Information source reliance and knowledge acquisition — Canadian/ U.S. comparisons regarding acid rain. Mary Ann E. Steger; John C. Pierce; Nicholas P. Lovrich; Brent S. Steel. *West. Pol. Q.* **41:4** 9:1988 pp. 747 – 764

101 International handbook of broadcasting systems. Philip T. Rosen *[Ed.]*. New York: Greenwood, 1988: xvii, 308 p. *ISBN: 0313243484; LofC: 87-29986. Includes index.*

102 Is good, popular science television possible? Michael Mosley. *Impact Sci.* **38:4(152)** 1988 pp. 387 – 395

103 Is it easy to be truthful? Reflections in a movie theater. Nikolai Khramov. *New Polit.* **II:1 (New series)** Summer:1988 pp. 131 – 138

104 Die Kernenergie in der Presse. Eine Analyse zum Einfluß subjektiver Faktoren auf die Konstruktion von Realität *[In German]*; Nuclear energy and the press — an analysis of the influence of subjective factors on the construction of reality *[Summary]*. Hans Mathias Kepplinger. *Kölner Z. Soz. Soz. psy.* **40:4** 1988 pp. 659 – 683

105 Ku vzt'ahu marxistickej sociológie, žurnalistiky a masovej komunikácie *[In Czech]*; К соотношению марксистской социологии, журналистики и массовой коммуникации *[Russian summary]*; On the relationship of Marxist sociology, journalism and mass media *[Summary]*; Zur Beziehung der marxistischen Soziologie, der Journalistik und der Massenmedien *[German summary]*. Samuel Brečka. *Sociologia [Brat.]* **20:5** 1988 pp. 523 – 535

106 Laws of media — the new science. Marshall McLuhan. Toronto: Univiversity of Toronto Press, 1988: 252 p. *ISBN: 0802057829.*

107 The living room celebration of the Olympic Games. Eric W. Rothenbuhler. *J. Comm.* **38:4** 1988 pp. 61 – 81

108 Une maladie dans l'espace public — le sida dans six quotidiens français [An illness in the public arena —AIDS in six French dailies] *[In French]*. Claudine Herzlich; Janine Pierret. *Annales* **43:5** 9-10:1988 pp. 1109 – 1134

109 Mass media and the spiral of silence — the Philippines from Marcos to Aquino. Hernando González. *J. Comm.* **38:4** 1988 pp. 33 – 49

110 The mass media and village life — an Indian study. Paul Hartmann; B.R. Patil; Anita Dighe. New Delhi and London: Sage Publications, 1988: 286 p. *Bibliography — p.270-272.*

111 Media imperialism and the videocassette recorder — the case of Turkey. Christine Ogan. *J. Comm.* **38:2** 1988 pp. 93 – 106

D.7: Communication. Language *[Communication. Langage]* — Media *[Moyens de communication]*

112 Media, minds and men — a history of media in Sweden. Bo Peterson. [Uppsala]: Almqvist and Wiksell, 1988: 366 p. *ISBN: 9122012060.*

113 Narrative form and moral force — the realization of innocence and guilt through investigative journalism. James S. Ettema; Theodore L. Glasser. *J. Comm.* **38:3** 1988 pp. 8 – 26

114 News analysis — case studies of international and national news in the press. Teun A. van Dijk. Hillsdate, N.J.: Lawrence Erlbaum Associates, 1988: xvi, 325 p. *ISBN: 0805800646. Bibliographical references — p303-313.*

115 News as discourse. Teun A. van Dijk. Hillsdale, N.J.: Lawrence Erlbaum Associates, 1988: viii, 200 p. *ISBN: 0805800654.* [Communication.]

116 Orwellian language and the media. Paul Chilton. London: Pluto Press, 1988: 127 p. *ISBN: 0745301738.*

117 The popular press and political democracy. Colin Sparks. *Media Cult. Soc.* **10:2** 4:1988 pp. 209 – 223

118 Pornography, politics, and the press — the U.S. Attorney General's commission on pornography. David L. Paletz. *J. Comm.* **38:2** 1988 pp. 122 – 136

119 La presse en France *[In French]*; [The French press]. Yves Guillauma. Paris: Éditions La Découverte, 1988: 127 p. *ISBN: 2707117617.* [Repères.]

120 Print media coverage of new religious movements — a longitudinal study. Barend van Driel; James T. Richardson. *J. Comm.* **38:3** 1988 pp. 37 – 61

121 Le prospettive della comunicazione locale *[In Italian]*; Perspectives of local communication *[Summary]*. Vincenzo Vita. *Crit. Marx.* **26:6** 11-12:1988 pp. 93 – 110

122 Public interest and the business of broadcasting — the broadcast industry looks at itself. Jon T. Powell *[Ed.]*; Wally Gair *[Ed.]*. New York: Quorum Books, 1988: x,193 p. *ISBN: 0899301983; LofC: 88-3098. Bibliography — p.183-187. Includes index.*

123 Public perceptions of the new media — a survey of British attitudes. Ralph Negrine; André Goodfriend. *Media Cult. Soc.* **10:3** 7:1988 pp. 303 – 322

124 "Racial" referents — images of European/Aboriginal relations in Australian feature films 1955-1984. Kevin M. Brown. *Sociol. Rev.* **36:3** 8:1988 pp. 474 – 502

125 Radio vs. television — their cognitive impact on children of different socioeconomic and ethnic groups. Patricia Greenfield; Jessica Beagles-Roos. *J. Comm.* **38:2** 1988 pp. 71 – 92

126 The ravens of Odin — the press in the Nordic nations. Robert G Picard. Ames: Iowa State University Press, 1988: 153 p. *ISBN: 0813815185. Bibliography — p.141-148.*

127 Representing native Kenya on film — Lorang's Way and the Turkana people. N. Frank Ukadike. *Ufahamu* **XVII:1** :1988 pp. 3 – 14

128 Research methods and the new media. Frederick Williams; Ronald E. Rice *[Ed.]*; Everett M. Rogers *[Ed.]*. New York: Free Press, 1988: xii,212 p. *ISBN: 0029353327. Bibliography — p193-206.* [The Free Press series in communication technology and society.]

129 Sengo joseizasshi seisuiki *[In Japanese]*; [The history of women's magazines after World War II, Japan]. Teruko Inoue. *Bessatsu Rekishi Dokuhon Vol.9. 1988.* pp. 170 – 175

D.7: Communication. Language *[Communication. Langage]* — Media *[Moyens de communication]*

130 Sozialisation durch Massenmedien *[In German]*; [Socialisation by mass media]. Ulrich Saxer *[Contrib.]*; Dieter Baacke *[Contrib.]*; Uwe Sander *[Contrib.]*; Ralf Vollbrecht *[Contrib.]*; Jan- Uwe Rogge *[Contrib.]*; Marie-Luise Kiefer *[Contrib.]*; Peter Vitouch *[Contrib.]*; Michael Charlton *[Contrib.]*; Klaus Neumann *[Contrib.]*; Kurt Luger *[Contrib.] and others*. Collection of 25 articles. **Publizistik** , *33:2-3,* 4-9:1988 pp. 165 – 576

131 Split signals — television and politics in the Soviet Union. Ellen Propper Mickiewicz. New York: Oxford University Press, 1988: xi, 286 p. *ISBN: 0195054636. Includes index.* [Communication and society.]

132 Technologies of control — the new interactive media for the home. Kevin G. Wilson. Madison, Wis.: University of Wisconsin Press, 1988: xi, 180 p. *ISBN: 0299113701.* [Studies in communication and society.]

133 Television advertisements for alcoholic drinks do reinforce under-age drinking. P.P. Aitken; D.R. Eadie; D.S. Leathar; R.E.J. McNeill; A.C. Scott. *Br. J. Addict.* **83:12** 12:1988 pp. 1399 – 1419

134 Television and ethics — a bibliography. Thomas W. Cooper. Boston: G.K. Hall, 1988: 203 p. *ISBN: 0816189668; LofC: 88- 007206.*

135 Television and its audience. Patrick Barwise; Andrew Ehrenberg *[Ed.]*. London: Sage, 1988: xii, 206 p. *ISBN: 0803981546. Bibliography — p.179-188.* [Sage communication in society series.]

136 Television and its audience — international research perspectives. Phillip Drummond *[Ed.]*; Richard Paterson *[Ed.]*. London: British Film Institute, 1988: x, 334 p. *ISBN: 0851702244. Includes index.*

137 Television and the black audience — cultivating moderate perspectives on racial integration. Paula W. Matabane. *J. Comm.* **38:4** 1988 pp. 21 – 32

138 Television as a social issue. Stuart Oskamp *[Ed.]*. Newbury Park: Sage, 1988: 390 p. *ISBN: 0803930690. Bibliographies.* [Applied social psychology annual. : No. 8]

139 Television in Chile — a history of experiment and reform. Valerio Fuenzalida. *J. Comm.* **38:2** 1988 pp. 49 – 58

140 Trouble in the backyard — Soviet media reporting on the Afghanistan conflict. John D.H. Downing. *J. Comm.* **38:2** 1988 pp. 5 – 32

141 A turn-taking system for British news interviews. David Greatbatch. *Lang. Soc.* **17:3** 9:1988 pp. 401 – 430

142 TV broadcasting in Europe and the new technologies. Gareth Locksley. Luxembourg: Office for Official Publications of the European Communities, 1988: 384 p. (ill.) *ISBN: 9282587592.*

143 Ukete no kaishaku sagyou to mass media no eikyouryoku *[In Japanese]*; [Interpretative-practices of the audience and the influence of mass media]. Yumiko Ehara. *Jpn. Jour. Rev. Vol.37. 1988.* pp. 51 – 66

144 Uncovering Soviet disasters — exploring the limits of glasnost. James E. Oberg. New York: Random House, 1988: xviii, 317 p. 8 p.of plates (ill) *ISBN: 0394560957.*

145 The unseen voice — a cultural study of Australian radio. Lesley Johnson. London: Routledge, 1988: 243 p. *ISBN: 0415027632. Bibliography — p.226-233.*

146 Vingt ans de cinéma en Iran (1969-1989) *[In French]*; [Twenty years of Iranian cinema (1969-1989)] *[Summary]*. Farrokh Gaffary. *Civilisations* **XXXVIII:2** 1988 pp. 179 – 195

D.7: Communication. Language *[Communication. Langage]* — **Media** *[Moyens de communication]*

147 Violence and terror in the mass media. George Gerbner; Nancy Signorielli *[Ed.]*. Paris: Unesco, 1988: 45 p. *ISBN: 9231026038. Bibliography — p.. 29-45*. [Reports and papers on mass communication. : No. 102]
148 Violence and terror in the mass media — an annotated bibliography. Nancy Signorielli *[Comp.]*; George Gerbner *[Comp.]*. New York: Greenwood, 1988: xxi, 233 p. *ISBN: 0313261202; LofC: 87-29556. Includes index.* [Bibliographies and indexes in sociology.]
149 What's the meaning of this? Viewers' plural sense-making of TV news. Peter Dahlgren. *Media Cult. Soc.* **10:3** 7:1988 pp. 285 – 302
150 World families watch television. James Lull *[Ed.]*. Newbury Park: Sage, 1988: 264 p. *ISBN: 0803932545.* [Communication and human values.]

D.8: Art — *Art*

1 Black culture, white youth — the reggae tradition from JA to UK. Simon Jones. Basingstoke: Macmillan Education, 1988: xxviii, 251 p. *ISBN: 0333452542. Includes index.* [Communications and culture.]
2 Conservatism in the new Australian cinema. Brian McFarlane. *Aust. Cult. Hist.* **:7** :1988 pp. 37 – 48
3 "Coughing up fire" — soundsystems, music and cultural politics in S.E. London. Les Back. *J. Car. Stud.* **6:2** Spring:1988 pp. 203 – 218
4 Criticizing and evaluating the visual arts in India — a preliminary example. Joanna Williams. *J. Asian St.* **47:1** 2:1988 pp. 3 – 28
5 Disease and representation — images of illness from madness to AIDS. Sander L. Gilman. Ithaca,N.Y.: Cornell University Press, 1988: 320 p. *ISBN: 0801494761*.
6 Drifting blues — "taishū ongaku" ron no otoshiana; [Drifting blues — a pitfall of T. Nakamura's perspective on popular music]. Nobutoshi Nakagawa. *Critique Vol.11. 1988.* pp. 88 – 97
7 Economic and social aspects of the performing arts in Japan — symphony orchestras and opera. Yoshimasa Kurabayashi; Yoshiro Matsuda *[Ed.]*. Tokyo: Kinokuniya, 1988: 431 p. *ISBN: 431400486x. Bibliography — p.409-416.* [Economic Research Series.]
8 Economic importance of arts in Britain. John Myerscough. London: Policy Studies Institute, 1988: 221 p. *ISBN: 0853743541. Bibliography — p.220-221.* [PSI Research Report. : No. 672]
9 A fotografia e as ciências humanas *[In Portuguese]*; [Photography and the human sciences]. Miriam Lifchitz Moreira Leite. *Bol. Inf. Bibl. Soc.* **:25** :1988 pp. 83 – 90
10 Graffiti as career and ideology. Richard Lachmann. *A.J.S.* **94:2** 9:1988 pp. 229 – 250
11 Literature and everyday life. Brian Robinson. *Antipode* **20:3** 12:1988 pp. 180 – 206
12 Music for pleasure — essays in the sociology of pop. Simon Frith. Cambridge: Polity in association with Blackwell, 1988: viii, 232 p. (ill) *ISBN: 0745604927. Includes index.*

D.8: Art [Art]

13 Noudouteki uketezou no tankyu *[In Japanese]*; [Toward a conceptualization of active audience]. Kazuto Kojima. *Shin. Hy. Vol.37. 1988.* pp. 233 – 249
14 Picturing power — visual depiction and social relations. Gordon Fyfe *[Ed.]*; John Law *[Ed.]*. London: Routledge, 1988: 281 p. (ill) *ISBN: 0415031443. Includes bibliographies.* [Sociological review monographs.]
15 Political behavior and physical design. Andrew D. Seidel *[Contrib.]*; Walter B. Kleeman *[Contrib.]*; Robert Sommer *[Contrib.]*; Katherine Steiner *[Contrib.]*; Richard M. Merelman *[Contrib.]*; Jon Lang *[Contrib.]*; James M. Mayo *[Contrib.]*. *Collection of 6 articles.* **Envir. Behav.** , *20:5,* 9:1988 pp. 531 – 663
16 Sociology and literature — the voice of fact and the writing of fiction. A. McHoul. *Aust. N.Z. J. Soc.* **24:2** 7:1988 pp. 208 – 225
17 La structuration ethnolinguistique de la chanson caribéenne anglophone *[In French]*; [The ethnolinguistic structuring of anglophone Caribbean songs]. Jacques M. Aly. *Prés. Afr.* **148** 1988 pp. 54 – 67
18 Study of the arts — a reappraisal. Judith R. Blau. *Ann. R. Soc.* **14** 1988 pp. 269 – 292
19 Travelling circus — an interpretation. Yoram S. Carmeli. *Eur. J. Soc.* **XXIX:2** 1988 pp. 258 – 282

D.9: Education — *Éducation*

1 Academic freedom and responsibility. Malcolm Tight *[Ed.]*. Milton Keynes: Open University Press, 1988: 160 p. *ISBN: 0335095313. Includes index.*
2 Adapting to deprivation — an examination of inflated educational expectations. Robert Agnew; Diane H. Jones. *Sociol. Q.* **29:2** Summer:1988 pp. 315 – 337
3 Biotechnology — big money comes to the university. James B. Rule. *Dissent* **35:4** Fall:1988 pp. 430 – 436
4 Christianity and educational provision in international perspective. Witold Tulasciewicz *[Ed.]*; Colin Brock *[Ed.]*. London: Routledge, 1988: 378 p. *ISBN: 041500568x. Includes index.*
5 The curriculum as social studies. Alan Barcan. *Aust. Q.* **60:4** Summer:1988 pp. 448 – 460
6 The democratic basis of modern education. Ion Holban. *R. Roum. Sci. Soc.* **32:1** 1-6:1988 pp. 11 – 20
7 Educating poor minority children. James P. Comer. *Sci. Am.* **259:5** 11:1988 pp. 24 – 30
8 Education and balanced urban-rural development in South Africa — preliminary considerations. Mokubung Nkomo. *Afr. Q.* **XXVIII:3-4** 1988-1989 pp. 36 – 51
9 Education in the southern coastal plain. Robert J. Maxwell; Eleanor Krassen Maxwell. *Social Soc. Res.* **72:4** 7:1988 pp. 242 – 248
10 Educational selection, inequality and development in Barbados — which way now? Pedro L.V. Welch. *B. E.Carib. Aff.* **14:1-2** 3-6:1988 pp. 31 – 40
11 Educational theorizing in an emancipatory context — a case for a Caribbean curriculum. Clement London. *J. Car. Stud.* **6:2** Spring:1988 pp. 163 – 178

D.9: Education *[Éducation]*

12 Educational thought and ideology in modern Japan — state authority and intellectual freedom. Teruhisa Horio; Stephen Platzer *[Ed.]*. Tokyo: Tokyo University Press, 1988: 410 p. *ISBN: 0860083527.*
13 Equality of educational opportunity. M. T. Hallinan. *Ann. R. Soc.* **14** 1988 pp. 249 – 268
14 Formal education and initial employment — unravelling the relationship between schooling and skills over time. Alfred A. Hunter. *Am. Sociol. R.* **53:5** 10:1988 pp. 753 – 765
15 La France illettrée *[In French]*; [Illiterate France]. Jean-Pierre Vélis; Françoise Silvéréano *[Ed.]*. Paris: Éditions du Seuil, 1988: 272 p. *ISBN: 2020100886.* [L'épreuve des faits.]
16 "Gender to kyouiku" kenkyū no gendaiteki kadai — kakusareta "ryouiki" no jizoku *[In Japanese]*; [Contemporary research on "gender and education" — reviews and perspectives]. Masako Amano. **Shak. Hyor.** *Vol.39; No.3 - 1988.* pp. 266 – 283
17 International organizations in education. Michael D. Stephens *[Ed.]*. London: Routledge, 1988: xxi, 165 p. *ISBN: 0415021839. Includes index.*
18 The Islamic revival and Indonesian education. R. Murray Thomas. *Asian Sur.* **XXVIII:9** 9:1988 pp. 897 – 915
19 Kokusai-ka Shakai no Katei Kyouiku *[In Japanese]*; [Family and education in contemporary Japan]. Fumie Kumagai. Tokyo: Kobundo Shuppansha, 1988: 171 p.
20 Literacy in St. Lucia — theoretical and practical parameters of the language experience. Didacus Jules. *B. E.Carib. Aff.* **14:1-2** 3-6:1988 pp. 11 – 23
21 Minority education — from shame to struggle. Tove Skutnabb-Kangas *[Ed.]*; Jim Cummins *[Ed.]*. Clevedon: Multilingual Matters, 1988: 410 p. *ISBN: 1853590037. Bibliographies.* [Multilingual matters. : No. 40]
22 Nihon no Kyouiku to Nationalism *[In Japanese]*; [Education and nationalism in Japan]. Eiichiro Tamura. Tokyo: Akashi Shoten, 1988: 251 p.
23 The social history of American education. B. Edward McClellan *[Ed.]*; William J. Reese *[Ed.]*. Illinois: University of Illinois Press, 1988: 370 p. *ISBN: 0252014618. Contains bibliographical references.*
24 Soviet education — the gifted and the handicapped. James Riordan *[Ed.]*. London: Routledge, 1988: 194 p. *ISBN: 0415005744. Includes index.*
25 Waving the flag for old Chicago. Fred B. Lindstrom *[Ed.]*; Ronald A. Hardert *[Contrib.]*; Ralph H. Turner *[Contrib.]*; Jonathan H. Turner *[Contrib.]*; Bernard Farber *[Contrib.]*; Rose Marie Ohm *[Contrib.]*. Collection of 9 articles. **Sociol. Pers.** , *31:3*, 7:1988 pp. 267 – 376
26 Whom must we treat equally for educational opportunity to be equal? Christopher Jencks. *Ethics* **98:3** 4:1988 pp. 518 – 533

D.9.1: Educational sociology — *Sociologie de l'éducation*

1 Democratización escolar y conflictividad en la construcción de un "nueva orden". Un estudio antropólogico *[In Spanish]*; [Educational democratization and conflicts in the construction of a "new order". An anthropological study]. Elena Libia Achilli. *Rev. Parag. Sociol.* **25:72** 5-8:1988 pp. 69 – 85

2 Education and society — studies in the politics, sociology and geography of education. L. Bondi *[Ed.]*; M. H. Matthews *[Ed.]*. London: Routledge, 1988: 272 p. (ill) *ISBN: 0415004519. Contains bibliographical references.*

D.9.2: Educational systems. Educational policy — *Systèmes d'enseignement. Politique de l'éducation*

1 Bilingual education — evaluation politics and practices. Peter Behuniak; John A. Hubert; Hernan LaFontaine; Robert J. Nearine. *Eval. Rev.* **12:5** 10:1988 pp. 483 – 509

2 Education and integration in Israel — the first twenty years. Bernard Steinberg. *Jew. J. Socio.* **XXX:1** 6:1988 pp. 17 – 36

3 Excellence and equity in education — models for success. Leonard A. Valverde *[Ed.]*; Geneva Gay *[Contrib.]*; Henry T. Trueba *[Contrib.]*; Ricardo R. Fernandez *[Contrib.]*; Gangjian Shu *[Contrib.]*; Eugene E. Garcia *[Contrib.]*; A. Reynaldo Contreras *[Contrib.]*. **Educ. Urban. Soc.**, *20:4*, 8:1988 pp. 315 – 413

4 Governing education — a sociology of policy since 1945. Andrew McPherson; Charles D. Raab *[Ed.]*. Edinburgh: Edinburgh University Press, 1988: xxiii,555 p. *ISBN: 0852245157. Bibliography — p.508-537. Includes index.*

5 Understanding home schools — emerging research and reactions. J. Gary Knowles *[Ed.]*; Brian D. Ray *[Contrib.]*; Maralee Mayberry *[Contrib.]*; Jon Wartes *[Contrib.]*; Jane A. van Galen *[Contrib.]*; Adrienne Charvoz *[Contrib.]*; Cheryl Wright *[Contrib.]*. *Collection of 8 articles.* **Educ. Urban. Soc.**, *21:1*, 11:1988 pp. 3 – 113

D.9.3: Primary education. Secondary education — *Enseignement primaire. Enseignement secondaire*

1 Containing attrition in school-based research — an innovative approach. Phyllis L. Ellickson; Domenica Bianca; Diane C. Schoeff. *Eval. Rev.* **12:4** 8:1988 pp. 331 – 351

2 Denomination and type of school attended — the transmission of an error. Don Anderson. *J. Aust. Stud.* :22 5:1988 pp. 33 – 39

3 A gender agenda — a sociological study of teachers, parents and pupils in their primary schools. Terry D. Evans. Sydney: Allen and Unwin, 1988: ix,163 p. *ISBN: 0043030092. Bibliography — p154-159. Includes index.* [Studies in society.]

4 Gender in American public schools — thinking institutionally. Elisabeth Hansot; David Tyack. *Signs* **13:4** Summer:1988 pp. 741 – 760

5 Kousoku, hensachi, shiken *[In Japanese]*; [School code, selection system and examination]. Shouzan Shibano. *Sein.-Shin. Vol.67. 1988.* pp. 24 – 30

D.9.3: Primary education. Secondary education [Enseignement primaire. Enseignement secondaire]

6 Nigerian primary school's compliance with Nigeria national policy on education — an evaluation of continuous assessment practices. Anthony Ali; Augustine Akubue. *Eval. Rev.* **12:6** 12:1988 pp. 625 – 637

7 Parents' financial and cultural resources, grades, and transition to secondary school in the Federal Republic of Germany. Paul M. de Graaf. *Eur. Sociol. R.* **4:3** 12:1988 pp. 209 – 222

8 Псйхологические проьлемы профессионального самоопределения школьнихов *[In Russian]*; The psychological problems of the professional self- determination of secondary school students *[Summary]*. V.A. Yakunin; S.E. Reskina. *Vest. Lenin. Univ. 6* **20:3** 1988 pp. 44 – 48

9 Reactions to drug education — a comparison of two videos produced for schools. Christine Eiser; J. Richard Eiser; Mary Pritchard. *Br. J. Addict.* **83:8** 8:1988 pp. 955 – 963

10 Représentations du devenir et reproduction sociale — le cas des lycéens d'Elbeuf *[In French]*; Conceptions of the future and social reproduction — the case of Elbeuf secondary school students *[Summary]*. Olivier Galland. *Sociol. Trav.* **:3** Summer:1988 pp. 399 – 418

11 Violent schools — unsafe schools. The case of Hawaii. Michael Haas. *Confl. Resolut.* **32:4** 12:1988 pp. 727 – 758

D.9.4: School environment — *Milieu scolaire*

1 Rethinking school leadership. Robert O. Slater *[Ed.]*; Marshall Sashkin *[Contrib.]*; Kent D. Peterson *[Contrib.]*; Catherine Marshall *[Contrib.]*; Rick Ginsberg *[Contrib.]*; Jameson W. Doig *[Contrib.]*; Robert K. Wimpelberg *[Contrib.]*. Collection of 7 articles. **Educ. Urban. Soc.**, *20:3*, 5:1988 pp. 235 – 310

D.9.5: Higher education — *Enseignement supérieur*

1 America's state colleges. V.R. Cardozier. *Minerva* **XXVI:4** Winter:1988 pp. 549 – 574

2 Blacklisting social science departments with poor Ph.D. submission rates. Richard A. Colombo; Donald G. Morrison. *Manag. Sci.* **34:6** 6:1988 pp. 696 – 706

3 The concept of productivity in institutions of higher education. Université du Québec. Sillery, Québec: Presses de l'Université du Quebéc, 1988: 163, 186 p. *ISBN: 276050476x.*

4 The crisis in higher education — competence, delight and the common good. Marjorie Reeves. Milton Keynes: Society for Research into Higher Education & Open University Press, 1988: 98 p. *ISBN: 0335095305; LofC: 88-22467. Includes index and bibliography.*

5 Dezvoltarea învăţămintului superior şi problematica mobilităţii sociale *[In Romanian]*; (Development of higher education and the problematique of social mobility); (Développement de l'enseignement supérieur et problématique de la mobilité sociale: *Title only in French*); (Развитие высшего образования и проблематика социальной мобильности: *Title only in Russian*). Mitulescu Sorin; Iaona Petre. *Viit. Soc.* **LXXXI** 9-10:1988 pp. 413 – 421

D.9.5: Higher education *[Enseignement supérieur]*

6 Les disparités de carriéres individuelles à l'université — une dialectique de la sélection et de l'autosélection *[In French]*; [Disparities in individual university careers — a dialectic of selection and self-selection]. Marie Duru; Alain Mingat. *Contin. Change* **3:3** 12:1988 pp. 309 – 340

7 The economic value of higher education. Larry L. Leslie; Paul T. Brinkman *[Ed.]*. New York: American Council on Education/Macmillan, 1988: 276 p. *ISBN: 0029186013. Bibliography.*

8 Efficiency and equity in Greek higher education. George Psacharopoulos. *Minerva* **XXVI:2** Summer:1988 pp. 119 – 137

9 Engineering education and research in Montreal — social constraints and opportunities. Yves Gingras; Robert Gagnon. *Minerva* **XXVI:1** Spring:1988 pp. 53 – 65

10 The Free University of Berlin — a political history. James F. Tent. Bloomington, Ind.: Indiana University Press, 1988: xiv, 507 p. *ISBN: 0253326664; LofC: 87-046407. Bibliography.*

11 Gendai daigakusei no bengaku to yoka *[In Japanese]*; [Leisure and college life of current university students in Japan]. Kiyoshi Takeuchi. *Seish. Mon.* Vol.35; No.4 - 1988. pp. 4 – 12

12 Higher education in a learning society — meeting new demands for education and training. Jerold W. Apps. San Francisco: Jossey-Bass, 1988: 241 p. *ISBN: 1555421156. Bibliography — p.221-233.*

13 Higher education in partnership with industry — opportunities and strategies for training, research, and economic development. David R. Powers *[Ed.]*. San Francisco: Jossey-Bass, 1988: xxv, 367 p. (ill) *ISBN: 1555420710; LofC: 87-46348. Includes bibliographies and index.* [The Jossey-Bass higher education series.]

14 How colleges work — the cybernetics of academic organization and leadership. Robert Birnbaum. San Francisco: Jossey-Bass, 1988: xx, 253 p. (ill) *ISBN: 1555421261; LofC: 88-4277. Bibliography — p.231-244. Includes index.* [Jossey-Bass higher education series.]

15 Incentives in academics — why is there tenure? Lorne H. Carmichael. *J. Polit. Ec.* **96:3** 6:1988 453- 472

16 Интеграцıя высшей школы с наукой и производством *[In Russian]*; [Integration of the higher institutes with science and manufacturing]. I.P. Iakovlev. Leningrad: Leningradskii Universitet, 1987: 128 p.

17 Leadership and management in universities — Britain and Nigeria. Titus Oshagbemi. Berlin: de Gruyter, 1988: 249 p. *ISBN: 311011514x. Bibliography — p.235-241.* [de Gruyter studies in organization. : No. 14]

18 Muslim society, higher education and development in Southeast Asia. Sharom Ahmat *[Ed.]*; Sharon Siddique *[Ed.]*. : Singapore, 1988: 219 p. *ISBN: 9971988909.*

19 Neutrality and commitment in South African universities — a philosophical analysis. Paul Taylor. *J. Contemp. Afr. St.* **7:1/2** 4/10:1988 pp. 185 – 202

20 Policies implication of the rate of return criterion in higher educational investment planning — the case of Bangladesh. Mir Obaidur Rahman. *Bang. J. Pub. Admin.* **2:2** 7:1988 pp. 157 – 174

21 Presiones y resistencias al cambio en la educación superior de México *[In Spanish]*; [Pressures and resistance to change in higher education in Mexico]. N. Jorge Padua. *Est. Sociol.* **VI:16** 1-4:1988 pp. 129 – 178

D.9.5: Higher education *[Enseignement supérieur]*

22 Private challenges to public goods — transformations in Australian higher education. D. Stone. *Aust. Q.* **60:1** Autumn:1988 pp. 40 – 62
23 Some statistical and DEA evaluations of relative efficiencies of public and private institutions of higher learning. Taesik Ahn; Abraham Charnes; William W. Cooper. *Socio. Econ.* :**6** 1988 pp. 259 – 269
24 Universities and the myth of cultural decline. Jerry Herron. Detroit: Wayne State University Press, 1988: 144 p. *LofC: 88-010081; ISBN: 0-8143-2068-6.*
25 The university means business — universities, corporations and academic work. Janice Newson; Howard Buchbinder *[Ed.]*. Toronto: Garamond Press, 1988: 103 p. *ISBN: 0920059384. Bibliography — p.98-103.*
26 Women of academe — outsiders in the sacred grove. Nadya Aisenberg; Mona Harrington *[Ed.]*. Amherst, Mass.: University of Massachusetts Press, 1988: 280 p. *ISBN: 0870236067; LofC: 87-30067. Includes bibliography.*

D.9.6: Adult education — *Éducation des adultes*

1 Adult education for rural development — a university strategy. A. Musa; G. Tahir. *Savanna* **9:1** 6:1988 pp. 64 – 69
2 La lutte contre l'analphabétisme en Turquie *[In French]*; [The struggle against illiteracy in Turkey]. Ali Arayici. *R. Tun. Sci. Soc.* **25:94/95** 1988 pp. 43 – 74

D.9.7: Civic education. Technical education — *Instruction civique. Enseignement technique*

D.9.8: Academic success. School failure — *Réussite dans les études. Échec scolaire*

1 Determinants of postsecondary educational attainment for 1980 high school seniors. Eva E. Eagle; Carlyle E. Maw. *Proc. Am. Stat. Ass.* pp. 88 – 93
2 The education level of the Jewish population and labor force in Israel, 1950-80. Shmuel Amir. *Econ. Rev. Bank Israel* **61** 2:1988 pp. 63 – 99
3 Educational achievement in Japan — lessons for the West. Richard Lynn. Basingstoke: Macmillan in association with the Social Affairs Unit, 1988: xii, 157 p. *ISBN: 0333445317. Includes index.* [Studies in social revaluation.]
4 Educational attainment and cohort size. David C. Stapleton; Douglas J. Young. *J. Labor Ec.* **6:3** 7:1988 pp. 330 – 361
5 Kyouiku tassei ni oyobusu chiiki kouka no bunseki *[In Japanese]*; [An analysis of educational attainment and its regional variations]. Fumiaki Ojima. *Journal of Osaka University of Economics Vol.186. 1988.* pp. 77 – 97
6 Overeducation and the earnings of black, Hispanic, and white male workers. Richard R. Verdugo; Naomi Turner Verdugo. *Sociol. Pers.* **31:2** 4:1988 pp. 190 – 212
7 The perceived causal structure of examination failure. Peter K. Lunt. *Br. J. Soc. P.* **27:2** 6:1988 pp. 171 – 179

D.9.8: Academic success. School failure *[Réussite dans les études. Échec scolaire]*

8 The role of teacher logic and clarity in student achievement. Kyung-Chul Huh. *Korean Soc. Sci. J.* **14** 1988 pp. 131 – 157

9 School type and academic achievement — 1985. Josephine Jordan. *Zambezia* **15:i** 1988 pp. 43 – 52

10 The use of educational qualifications under Soviet-type socialism. J.L. Porket. *Sov. Stud.* **XL:4** 10:1988 pp. 585 – 601

D.9.9: Pedagogy. Teaching. Teachers — *Pédagogie. Enseignement. Enseignants*

1 The cost of quality — teacher testing and racial-ethnic representativeness in public education. Nelson C. Dometrius; Lee Sigelman. *Soc. Sci. Q.* **69:1** 3:1988 pp. 70 – 82

2 L'insegnamento della scienze *[In Italian]*; (The teachings of sciences). Carlo Bernardini. *Crit. Marx.* **26:2** 3-4:1988 pp. 49 – 56

3 Koto-kyoiku ni okeru kyoshi-kyoiku no ichi *[In Japanese]*; [Teacher education in Japan — current status and trends in Japanese higher education]. Takekazu Ehara. *J. Ed. Soc. Vol.43. 1988.* pp. 56 – 69

4 Kyoushi no genzai to kyoushi kenkyū no konnichi-teki kadai *[In Japanese]*; [Teachers today and future research on teaching profession]. Kojiro Imazu. *J. Ed. Soc. Vol.43. 1988.* pp. 5 – 17

5 Latent class models of teacher attitudes and perceptions. Mary R. Papageorgiou; Sharon A. Bobbitt. *Proc. Am. Stat. Ass.* pp. 17 – 24

6 Research on teachers in public and independent schools — how the organizational context shapes the job. Pearl R. Kane. *Proc. Am. Stat. Ass.* pp. 25 – 32

7 Teachers' collective bargaining outcomes and tradeoffs. John Thomas Delaney. *J. Labor Res.* **IX:4** Autumn:1988 pp. 363 – 377

8 Why teach? A comparative study of Caribbean and North American college students attraction to teaching. Arthur G. Richardson. *B. E.Carib. Aff.* **14:1-2** 3-6:1988 pp. 24 – 30

E: Social structure — *Structure sociale*

E.1: Social system — *Système social*

1 Continuity and change in German social structure. Erwin K. Scheuch. *Hist. Soc. R.* **13:2** 1988 pp. 31 – 121

2 Essays on social action and social structure. Bo Anderson. Uppsala: Uppsala University, 1988: 181 p. *ISBN: 9155422527. Bibliographies.* [Acta Universitatis Upsaliensis.]

3 Gendai shakai no kouzou *[In Japanese]*; [The structure of modern society]. Sadamitsu Nakagiri. Tokyo: Kōbundo Shuppansha, 200 p.

4 Network connections and the distribution of power in exchange networks. Toshio Yamagishi; Mary R. Gillmore; Karen S. Cook. *A.J.S.* **93:4** 1:1988 pp. 833 – 851

E.1: Social system [Système social]

5 Power relations in exchange networks. Barry Markovsky; David Willer; Travis Patton. *Am. Sociol. R.* **53:2** 4:1988 pp. 220 – 236

6 Shakai taiseiron *[In Japanese]*; [Reconsideration on the social system]. Yasuo Yokoyama. *Bung-bu. Rob. Riss. Daig. Vol.88. 1988.* pp. 63 – 87

7 Social structures — a network approach. Barry Wellman *[Ed.]*; S. D. Berkowitz *[Ed.]*. Cambridge: Cambridge University Press, 1988: xii, 513 p. (ill) *ISBN: 0521244412. Includes index.* [Structural analysis in the social sciences. : No. 2]

8 Stability and cyclicity in social systems. Wolfgang Weidlich. *Behav. Sci.* **33: 4** 10: 1988 pp. 241 – 256

9 Stellung und Entwicklung der sozialen Infrastruktur im gesellschaftlichen Reproduktionsprozeß des Territoriums *[In German]*; Status and development of social infrastructure in the social reproduction process at local level *[Summary]*; Значение и развитие социальной инфраструктуры в общественном процессе воспроизводства на данной территории *[Russian summary]*; (Position et développement de l'infrastructure sociale au sein du processus de reproduction social du territoire: *Title only in French).* Peter Grimmer; Karl-Heinz Sieber. *Wirt.wissensch.* **36:9** 1988 pp. 1400 – 1408

10 T.Parsons ni okeru shakaikozobunseki to kazokuriron *[In Japanese]*; [Some considerations on the analysis of social structure and the family theory in the work of Talcott Parsons]. Masafumi Kimura. *Osaka Shog. Daig. Ron. Vol.81. 1988.* pp. 97 – 115

E.2: Social stratification — Stratification sociale

1 Adolescent social structure and the spread of linguistic change. Penelope Eckert. *Lang. Soc.* **17:2** 6:1988 pp. 183 – 207

2 Behind the planter's back — lower class responses to marginality in Bequia Island, St Vincent. Neil Price. Basingstoke: Macmillan, 1988: 272 p. (ill) *ISBN: 0333474600. Includes bibliography and index.* [Warwick University Caribbean studies.]

3 Can we at least say goodbye to social class? An examination of the usefulness and stability of some alternative methods of measurement. Sarah O'Brien; Rosemary Ford. *J. Market R.* **30:3** 7:1988 pp. 289 – 332

4 Caste adaptation in modernizing Indian society. Harold A. Gould. Delhi: Chaukya, 1988: vii, 188 p. *ISBN: 81 7001 045 4.*

5 Caste origins as determinants of social class — the case of industrial workers. G.N. Ramu. *J. Dev. Soc.* **V:2** 7-10:1989 pp. 188 – 202

6 The challenge of class analysis. Wallace Clement. Ottawa: Carleton University Press, 1988: 203 p. *ISBN: 0886290759; LofC: cn88-90239. Includes bibliographical references.* [Carleton library series. : No. 149]

7 Class and social organisation in Finland, Sweden and Norway. Göran Ahrne *[Ed.]*; et al. Uppsala: Uppsala University, 1988: 154 p. *ISBN: 9155421962. Bibliography — p.149-154.* [Acta Universitatis Upsaliensis.]

8 Class formation and peasantry. Bishnu C. Barik. Jaipur: Rawat, 1988: xiii, 219 p.

9 Class identification and gender role norms among employed married women. Leonard Beeghley; John Cochran. *J. Marriage Fam.* **50:3** 8:1988 pp. 719 – 729

E.2: Social stratification *[Stratification sociale]*

10 Class identification in Norway — explanatory factors and life-cycle differences. Knud Knudsen. *Acta Sociol.* **31:1** 1988 pp. 69 – 79

11 Class identification of men and women in the 1970s and 1980s. Nancy Davis; Robert V. Robinson. *Am. Sociol. R.* **53:1** 2:1988 pp. 103 – 112

12 Class structure and patterns of social closure in Australia and New Zealand. F.L. Jones; Peter Davis. *Sociology* **22:2** 5:1988 pp. 271 – 297

13 Class, gender and the relations of distribution. Joan Acker. *Signs* **13:3** Spring:1988 pp. 473 – 497

14 Classes in Britain — Marxist and official. Gordon Marshall. *Eur. Sociol. R.* **4:2** 9:1988 pp. 141 – 154

15 Les classes sociales en France — un débat inachevé, 1789-1989 *[In French]*; [Social classes in France, the unfinished debate]. Larry Portis; Christiane Passevant *[Ed.]*. Paris: Éd. Ouvrières, 1988: 190 p. *ISBN: 2708225677. Bibliography — p.179-182.* [Collection Portes ouvertes.]

16 Closure and fluidity in the class structure. F.L. Jones; Peter Davis. *Aust. N.Z. J. Soc.* **24:2** 7:1988 pp. 226 – 247

17 Cross-class families. Håkon Leiulfsrud; Alison E. Woodward. *Acta Sociol.* **31:2** 1988 pp. 175 – 180

18 Daitoshi inner-area niokeru shakai ido to chiiki keisei *[In Japanese]*; [Social mobility and community structure in the inner metropolitan area]. Hideki Takenaka; Yuetsu Takahashi. *Comprehensive Urban Studies, Centre for Urban Studies of Tokyo Metropolitan U.* Vol.34. 1988. pp. 35 – 50

19 Defining and measuring the underclass. Erol R. Ricketts; Isabel V. Sawhill. *J. Policy An.* **7:2** Winter:1988 pp. 316 – 325

20 The demography of inequality in Brazil. Charles H. Wood; José Alberto Magno de Carvalho *[Ed.]*. Cambridge: Cambridge University Press, 1988: xii, 301 p. *ISBN: 052135174x. Includes bibliography and index.* [Cambridge Latin American studies.]

21 A divided working class — ethnic segmentation and industrial conflict in Australia. Constance Lever-Tracy; Michael Quinlan *[Ed.]*. London: Routledge & Kegan Paul, 1988: xviii, 338 p. (ill) *ISBN: 0710208146. Bibliography — p.321-329. Includes index.*

22 Dynamics of atrocities on scheduled castes in rural India. Rabindra K. Mohanty. *Indian J. Soc. W.* **XLIX:1** 1:1988 pp. 51 – 66

23 "Echte" en "onechte" Brahmanen — de effecten van het Britse kastebewustzijn *[In Dutch]*; "Real" and "spurious" Brahmans — the effect of the British caste consciousness *[Summary]*. Peter van der Veer. *Sociol. Gids* **XXXV:3** 5-6:1988 pp. 199 – 211

24 Egalitarianism and the separateness of persons. Dennis McKerlie. *Can. J. Phil.* **18:2** 6:1988 pp. 205 – 226

25 Estilos de investigación sobre la clase obrera *[In Spanish]*; [Styles of research into the working class]. Enrique de la Garza Toledo. *Rev. Mexicana Soc.* **L:4** 10-12:1988 pp. 3 – 29

26 The expanding middle — some Canadian evidence on the deskilling debate; *[French summary]*. John Myles. *Can. R. Soc. A.* **25:3** 8:1988 pp. 335 – 364

27 The formation of dominant classes in Zambia — critical notes. P. Mufune. *Afr. Tod.* **35:2** :1988 pp. 5 – 20

28 Gender and class analysis — the position of women in the class structure. Janeen Baxter. *Aust. N.Z. J. Soc.* **24:1** 3:1988 pp. 106 – 123

E.2: Social stratification [Stratification sociale]

29 Gender, class, and space. G. Pratt; S. Hanson. *Envir. Plan. D* **6(1):** 3:1988 pp. 15 – 36

30 Gender, household and social class. Norman Bonney. *Br. J. Soc.* **XXXIX:1** 3:1988 pp. 28 – 46

31 Les haitiens — politique de classe et de couleur *[In French]*; [Haitians — the politics of class and colour]. Lyonel Paquin. Port-au-Prince: Imprimerie Le Natal, 1988: 327 p. *fre, eng.*

32 Inequalities? Social class differentials in health in British youth. Patrick West. *Soc. Sci. Med.* **27:4** 1988 pp. 291 – 296

33 Inequality in Sweden — trends and current situation. Joachim Vogel *[Ed.]*. Stockholm: Statistics Sweden, 1988: 512 p. *ISBN: 9161801453.*

34 The influence of class and race on clinical assessments by MSW students. Robert Paviour. *Soc. Ser. R.* **62:4** 12:1988 pp. 684 – 693

35 Intellectuals and the CPC in the post-Mao period — a study in perceptual role conflict. Richard Franklin. *J. Dev. Soc.* **V:2** 7-10:1989 pp. 203 – 217

36 Is equality of opportunity a false ideal for society? S.J.D. Green. *Br. J. Soc.* **XXXIX:1** 3:1988 pp. 1 – 27

37 Kasoka chiiki no shakai idou — Kagoshima-ken Satamachi 3 chiku no chiiki idou to shokugyou sentaku *[In Japanese]*; [Social mobility in sparsely-populated areas]. Chihiro Ushijama. ***Kenkyusho Nenpo Vol.18.*** *1988.* pp. 159 – 176

38 Kinship and class in the West Indies — a genealogical study of Jamaica and Guyana. Raymond T. Smith. Cambridge: Cambridge University Press, 1988: x, 205 p. *ISBN: 0521345227; LofC: 87-11662. Bibliography — p.185-194. - Includes index.* [Cambridge studies in social anthropology.]

39 Klassenstruktur und Klassenbewußtsein in der Bundesrepublik Deutchland — Erste empirische Ergebnisse *[In German]*; Class structure and class consciousness in the Federal Republic of Germany — first empirical results *[Summary]*. Barbara Erbslöh; Thomas Hagelstange; Dieter Holtmann; Joachim Singelmann; Hermann Strasser. *Kölner Z. Soz. Soz. psy.* **40:2** 1988 pp. 245 – 261

40 Komplexitätssteigerung und dezentrale Kontextsteuerung. Zur system-theorischen Bewältigung des Klassenkampfes *[In German]*; [Intensification of complexity and decentralized context management. On the systems-theoretical conceptualization of the class struggle]. Michael Hartmann. *Eur. J. Soc.* **XXIX:1** 1988 pp. 51 – 77

41 Landlords and capitalists — the dominant class of Chile. Maurice Zeitlin; Richard Earl Ratcliff *[Ed.]*. Princeton, N.J.: Princeton University Press, 1988: xxiv, 288 p. *ISBN: 0691077576. Bibliography — p.259-284.*

42 The life style of the eunuchs. M. D. Vyas; Yogesh Shingals. New Delhi: Anmol, vii, 116 p. *ISBN: 81 7041 026 6.*

43 Measuring status inconsistency — more trouble than it's worth? Wayne Curtis Brown; Gary A. Crester; Thomas E. Lasswell. *Sociol. Pers.* **31:2** 4:1988 pp. 213 – 237

44 La mediación de las clases sociales *[In Spanish]*; [The mediation of the social classes]. Ferran Brunet. *Tareas* pp. 123 – 142

45 The missing link? The relationship between spatial mobility and social mobility. Mike Savage. *Br. J. Soc.* **XXXIX:4** 12:1988 pp. 554 – 576

E.2: Social stratification [Stratification sociale]

46 Mobilité sociale et équité *[In French]*; [Social mobility and fairness]. Mohamed Cherkaoui. *Rev. Fr. Soc.* **XXIX:2** 4-6:1988 pp. 227 – 245

47 The modern African elite of South Africa. Lynette Dreyer. Basingstoke: Macmillan, 1988: 240 p. *ISBN: 0333464109. Includes index.*

48 The new Indian middle class in Britain. Vaughan Robinson. *Ethn. Racial* **11:4** 11:1988 pp. 456 – 473

49 Nihon no kaiso 100nen *[In Japanese]*; [Japanese social stratification in 20th century]. Takatoshi Imada. *Quart. Soc. Ser. Res. Vol.1; No.2 - 1988.* pp. 30 – 35

50 Organizing collective interests — causes of cross- national differences in working-class formation. Tom Colbjørnsen. *R. Soc. Strat. Mob.* **7** 1988 pp. 247 – 272

51 Proletarianization in the British class structure? Gordon Marshall; David Rose. *Br. J. Soc.* **XXXIX:4** 12:1988 pp. 498 – 518

52 Race, class, and opportunity — changing realities and perceptions. Roy L. Austin; Steven Stack. *Sociol. Q.* **29:3** Fall:1988 pp. 357 – 369

53 Social class differences in infant mortality — the problem of competing hypothesis. Charlotte Humphrey; Jonathan Elford. *J. Biosoc. Sc.* **20:4** 10:1988 pp. 497 – 504

54 Social class in modern Britain. Gordon Marshall *[Ed.]*; et al. London: Hutchinson, 1988: xv, 314 p. *ISBN: 0091679400. Bibliography — p.276-287. Includes index.*

55 The social consciousness of the intelligentsia. Stanisław Widerszpil. *Polish Persp.* **XXXI:3** 1988 pp. 15 – 21

56 Social differentiation in Australian cities. James Forrest. *Geoforum* **19:3** 1988 pp. 277 – 294

57 Social inequality in Canada — patterns, problems, policies. James E. Curtis *[Ed.]*; et al. Scarborough, Ontario: Prentice-Hall, 1988: viii, 520 p. *ISBN: 0138156069.*

58 Social mobility in tribal Madhya Pradesh. Jayanta Sarkar. New Delhi: B.R. Pub, 1986: 80 p.

59 Social status — construct and external validity. Bo Ekehammar; Jim Sidanius; Ingrid Nilsson. *J. Soc. Psychol.* **128:4** 8:1988 pp. 473 – 481

60 Social stratification and economic change. David Rose *[Ed.]*. London: Hutchinson, 1988: 303 p. *ISBN: 009164691x. Includes bibliographies and index.*

61 Social stratification, work and personality. Kenneth I. Spenner. *Ann. R. Soc.* **14** 1988 pp. 69 – 97

62 Sociale stratificatie en maatschappelijke oriëntaties *[In Dutch]*; Social stratification and values *[Summary]*. Roel Bosker; Wim Meijnen; Rolf van der Velden. *Mens Maat.* **63:2** 5:1988 pp. 156 – 174

63 Socialist entrepreneurs — embourgeoisement in rural Hungary. Ivan Szelenyi; Robert Manchin; et al. Cambridge: Policy, 1988: 272 p. (ill) *ISBN: 0745604609. Includes bibliography and index.*

64 Sociología y clases sociales en Colombia - 2 vols *[In Spanish]*; [Sociology and social classes in Colombia — 2 vols]. Alvaro Villar Gaviria. Bogotá: Carlos Valencia, 1988: - *ISBN: 9589044360.*

65 Some social and political implications of the contemporary fragmentation of the "service class" in Britain. Mike Savage; Peter Dickens; Tony Fielding. *Int. J. Urban* **12:3** 9:1988 pp. 455 – 476

E.2: Social stratification [Stratification sociale]

66 Социальная дифференциация и интеграция в условиях перестройки *[In Russian]*; (Social differentiation and integration under perestroika). М.Н. Руткевич. *Sot. Issle.* **6** 11-12:1988 pp. 22 – 31
67 Status generalization — new theory and research. Martha Foschi *[Ed.]*; Murray Webster *[Ed.]*. Stanford, Calif.: Stanford University Press, 1988: xiv, 536 p. (ill.) *ISBN: 0804714215. Includes index.*
68 Status inconsistency and criss-cross in an adolescent society. Uwe Engel. *Int. Sociol.* **3:3** 9:1988 pp. 283 – 300
69 Strategische Gruppen, Klassenbildung und Staat in der Peripherie. Eine Kritik des Bielefelder Ansatzes *[In German]*; Strategic groups, class formation, and the state in peripheral societies — a critique of the Bielefeld approach *[Summary]*. John P. Neelsen. *Kölner Z. Soz. Soz. psy.* **40:2** 1988 pp. 284 – 315
70 Stratification approaches to class measurement. F.L. Jones. *Aust. N.Z. J. Soc.* **24:2** 7:1988 pp. 279 – 284
71 The structure of organizations and the structure of class. Peter M.E. Hedström; Eva Wallin. *R. Soc. Strat. Mob.* **7** 1988 pp. 225 – 246
72 Temporality and class analysis — a comparative study of the effects of class trajectory and class structure on class consciousness in Sweden and the United States. Erik Olin Wright; Kwang-Yeong Shin. *Sociol. Theory* **6:1** Spring:1988 pp. 58 – 84
73 Teoría de las élites y elitismo (apuntes para un análisis histórico y actual) *[In Spanish]*; [Theory of elites and elitism (notes for historical and contemporary analysis)]. Ettore A. Albertoni. *Sistema* **83** 3:1988 pp. 43 – 56
74 Thai ni okeru keizai-kouzou-henka *[In Japanese]*; [Economic growth and social structure change in Thailand]. Tsuneo Kito. *Win Vol.57-58. 1988.* pp.20-21, 20-21
75 The transformation of the southern racial state — class and race determinants of local-state structures. David R. James. *Am. Sociol. R.* **53:2** 4:1988 pp. 191 – 208

E.3: Social change — *Changement social*

1 Any complete theory of social change inevitably incorporates a normatively grounded theory of moral choice. Stephen Chilton. *J. Dev. Soc.* **IV:2** 7-10:1988 pp. 135 – 148
2 Commercialization and commoditization — a dialogue between perspectives. Peter Vandergeest. *Sociol. Rur.* **XXVIII:1** 1988 pp. 7 – 29
3 Components of social change in urban areas. Peter Congdon; John Shepherd. *Urban Stud.* **25:3** 6:1988 pp. 173 – 189
4 Condorcet kara Saint-Simon he — koten jisshou-shugi-teki shakai-hendou-ron no seisei *[In Japanese]*; [French positivism's contribution to social change theory — from Condorcet to Saint-Simon]. Hidetaka Tanaka. *Shisō Vol.771. 1988.* pp. 77 – 98
5 Contradictions in social change — reflections on the ideological transformation of present-day Europe. Carlo Mongardini. *R. Soc. Move. Con. Cha.* **10** 1988 pp. 213 – 224

E.3: Social change [Changement social]

6 Divergence and convergence in international development — a decomposition analysis of inequality in the world system. Walter Gillis Peacock; Greg A. Hoover; Charles D. Killian. *Am. Sociol. R.* **53:6** 12:1988 pp. 838 – 852

7 Les doctrines sociales en France et l'évolution de la société française du XVIIIe siècle à nos jours *[In French]*; [Social doctrines in France and the development of French society from the 18th century to the present day]. Marie-Madeleine Martin. Paris: Dervy-Livres, 1988: 365 p. *ISBN: 2850762865*.

8 Die dunkle Seite der Soziologie. Zum Problem gesellschaftlicher Fluktuationen *[In German]*; The darker side of sociology — on the problem of societal fluctuations *[Summary]*. Walter L. Bühl. *Soz. Welt.* **39:1** 1988 pp. 18 – 46

9 Economic and social change in the north-east. Habung Payeng. New Delhi: Criterion, 1988: vii, 157 p.

10 Essays in Jewish historiography. Ada Rapoport-Albert *[Ed.]*; Shaye J.D. Cohen *[Contrib.]*; Jacob Neusner *[Contrib.]*; Robert Chazan *[Contrib.]*; Bruno Chiesa *[Contrib.]*; Louis Jacobs *[Contrib.]*; Robert Bonfil *[Contrib.]*; Natalie Zemon Davis *[Contrib.]*; Michael A. Meyer *[Contrib.]*. Collection of 9 articles. **Hist. Theory**, *27:4*, 1988 pp. 1 – 175

11 Forces of change in the Middle East. Paul Jabber. *Middle E. J.* **42:1** Winter:1988 pp. 7 – 15

12 Is Spencer's theory an evolutionary theory? Valerie A.. *A.J.S.* **93:5** 3:1988 pp. 1200 – 1223

13 The Japanese trajectory — modernization and beyond. Gavan McCormack *[Ed.]*; Yoshio Sugimoto *[Ed.]*. Cambridge: Cambridge University Press, 1988: viii, 300 p. (ill) *ISBN: 0521345154; LofC: 88-1722*. Includes index.

14 Kiki no jidai ni okeru America shakai-shinka-shugi — higeki no yogensha Veblen to mirai wo kousou suru Dewey *[In Japanese]*; [American social evolutionalism in the crisis times — the tragic prophecy of Veblen and the future idea of Dewey]. Motohiro Matsuoka. *J. Soc. Vol.101. 1988.* pp. 23 – 39

15 Korea's Confucian heritage and social change. Quee-Young Kim. *J. Dev. Soc.* **IV:2** 7-10:1988 pp. 255 – 269

16 Marx, Weber and development sociology — beyond the impasse. Peter Vandergeest; Frederick H. Buttel. *World Dev.* **16:6** 6:1988 pp. 683 – 695

17 La modernisation des activités productives dans les pays socialistes européens *[In French]*; [The modernization of production in the socialist countries of Europe]. A. Gueullette *[Contrib.]*; M. Lavigne *[Contrib.]*; W. Andreff *[Contrib.]*; E. Brunal *[Contrib.]*; I. Samson *[Contrib.]*; J. Blaha *[Contrib.]*; I. Major *[Contrib.]*; T. Bauer *[Contrib.]*; M. Laki *[Contrib.]*; K.A. Soos *[Contrib.]* and others. Collection of 6 articles. **Ec. Sociét.**, *22:2*, 2:1988 pp. 3 – 201

18 Modernitätsbegriffe und Modernitätskritik in der Soziologie *[In German]*; Concepts and critique of modernity in sociological theory *[Summary]*. Johannes Berger. *Soz. Welt.* **39:2** 1988 pp. 224 – 235

19 Mokuteki shikou katei to shiteno kindaika *[In Japanese]*; [Modernization as a goal-orientated process — application and limitation of political system theory]. Teruya Oda. *Sociologos Vol.12. 1988.* pp. 54 – 67

20 Mouvements sociaux et action politique — existe-t-il une théorie de la

E.3: Social change [Changement social]

    mobilisation des ressources? *[In French]*; [Social movements and political action — is there a theory of resource mobilization?]. Didier Lapeyronnie. *Rev. Fr. Soc.* **XXIX:4** 10-12:1988 pp. 593 – 619

21 Neopatriarchy — a theory of distorted change in Arab society. Hisham Sharabi. New York: Oxford University Press, 1988: xi, 196 p. *ISBN: 0195051416; LofC: 87-34876. Bibliography — p177-185. Includes index.*

22 An operational analysis of the phenomenon of the other underdevelopment in the Arab world and in the Third World. Mahmoud Dhaouadi. *Int. Sociol.* **3:3** 9:1988 pp. 219 – 234

23 The principles of social evolution. C.R. Hallpike. Oxford: Clarendon Press, 1988: xi, 412 p.

24 I processi di modernizzazione nelle società tradizionali. Il caso dell'Indonesia esterna *[In Italian]*; Modernization processes in outer Indonesia *[Summary]*. Pietro Scarduelli. *Rass. It. Soc.* **29:2** 4-6:1988 pp. 209 – 230

25 Science, technology and social change. Steven Yearley. London: Unwin Hyman, 1988: vii, 199 p. *ISBN: 0043012582. Includes bibliography and index.*

26 Small urban centers and social change in south-eastern Zaire. Mukohya Vwakyanakazi. *Afr. Stud. R.* **31:3** 12:1988 pp. 85 – 94

27 Systems simulation. The simulation of social system evolution with spiral loops. Peter P. Merten. *Behav. Sci.* **33: 2** 4: 1988 pp. 131 – 157

28 Transcending the impasse — metatheory, theory and empirical research in the sociology of development and underdevelopment. Leslie Sklair. *World Dev.* **16:6** 6:1988 pp. 697 – 709

29 Trends in world social development — the social progress of nations, 1970-1987. Richard J. Estes. Westport, Conn.: Praeger, 1988: xx, 218 p. *ISBN: 0275926133; LofC: 87-36132. Bibliography — p.211-216.*

30 Trop archaïques ou trop modernes? Les citadines grecques face à l'occidentalisation *[In French]*; Too archaic or too modern? Greek women and the encounter with westernization during the years just after independence *[Summary]*. Eleni Varikas. *Peup. Médit.* **44:45** 7-12:1988 pp. 269 – 292

31 Understanding modernity — toward a new perspective going beyond Durkheim and Weber. Richard Münch. London: Routledge, 1988: 342 p. *ISBN: 041501283x. Bibliography — p.306-327.*

32 When the north winds blow — a note on small towns and social transformation in the Nilotic Sudan. John W. Burton. *Afr. Stud. R.* **31:3** 12:1988 pp. 49 – 60

F: Population. Family. Ethnic group — *Population. Famille. Groupe ethnique*

F.1: Demography. Genetics — *Démographie. Génétique*

1 The accuracy of U.N. population projections. Peter Pflaumer. *Proc. Am. Stat. Ass.* pp. 299 – 304

2 Análisis y predicción de la población española (1910-2000) *[In Spanish]*; [Analysis and forecasting of the Spanish population (1910-2000)]. Juan del Hoyo Bernat; Antonio García Ferrer *[Ed.]*. Madrid: Fundación de Estudios de Economía Aplicada, 1988: 308 p. [Coleccion Estudios.]

3 The component structure of elderly population growth in the Netherlands — 1950-1980; Les composantes structurelles de la croissance de la population âgée en Hollande — 1950-1980 *[French summary]*. David F. Sly; William J. Serow. *Eur. J. Pop.* **4:4** 7:1988 pp. 271 – 281

4 Consolidación y fluctuación de la población en "squatter settlements" *[In Spanish]*; [Population consolidation and fluctuation in squatter settlements] *[Summary]*. Ralf Engelhardt. *Rev. Cien. Soc.* **XXVII: 3-4** 9-12: 1988 pp. 119 – 143

5 Demografía historica en españa *[In Spanish]*; [Historical demography history in Spain]. Vicente Pérez Moreda *[Ed.]*; David Sven Reher *[Ed.]*. Madrid: Ediciones el Arquero, 1988: 607 p. *ISBN: 8486902037.*

6 Demografia între ştiinţa şi acţiune socială *[In Romanian]*; (Demography between science and social action); (La démographie entre science et action: *Title only in French*); (Демография как наука и социальное действие: *Title only in Russian*). Vladimir Trebici. *Viit. Soc.* **LXXXI** 1-2:1988 pp. 69 – 74

7 Démographie africaine — tendances et perspectives *[In French]*; African demography — trends and prospects *[Summary]*. Mpembele Sala-Diakanda. *Afr. Cont.* **145** 1:1988 pp. 3 – 27

8 Dynamique de population en économie de plantation — le plateau de Dayes au sud-ouest du Togo *[In French]*; [Population dynamics in a plantation economy — the Dayes plateau in south-west Togo]. A. Quesnel; P. Vimard *[Ed.]*. Paris: ORSTOM, 1988: 460 p. *ISBN: 2709909421. Bibliography — p.431-441.* [Collection études et thèses.]

9 Formation and dissolution of one-person households in the United States and West Germany. James Witte; Herbert Lahmann. *Social Soc. Res.* **73:1** 10:1988 pp. 31 – 42

10 Immigration et régulation de la structure par âge d'une population *[In French]*; Inmigracion y regulación de la estructura por edad de una población *[Spanish summary]*; Immigration and the control of the age structure of a population *[Summary]*. Didier Blanchet. *Population* **43:2** 3-4:1988 pp. 957 – 974

11 Merging populations, stochastic dominance and Lorenz curves. O. Stark; S. Yitzhaki. *J. Pop. Ec.* **1:2** 1988 pp. 157 – 161

12 Methods and models in demography. Colin Newell. London: Belhaven, 1988: 217 p. *ISBN: 1852930160. Includes index.*

F.1: Demography. Genetics [Démographie. Génétique]

13 Micro-approaches to demographic research. John C. Caldwell; Allan G. Hill *[Ed.]*; Valerie J. Hull *[Ed.]*. London: Kegan Paul International in association with Australian International Development Assistance Bureau Seminars for Development Program [and] International Union for the Scientific Study of the Population, 1988: xvi, 500 p. *ISBN: 0710302975. Bibliography — p.471-500.*

14 Mobilitatea populaţiei pe teritoriul judeţului Giurgiu *[In Romanian]*; (The mobility of population on the territory of Giurgiu country); (La mobilité de la population sur le territoire du district de Giurgiu: *Title only in French)*; (Мобильность населения на территории уезда Джуржу: *Title only in Russian).* Ilinca Nicolae. *Viit. Soc.* **LXXXI** 11-12:1988 pp. 533 – 540

15 Modeling multigroup populations. Robert Schoen. New York: Plenum, 1988: xii, 308 p. *ISBN: 0306426498. Bibliography — p.287-295.* [Plenum series on demographic methods and population analysis.]

16 Le monde caché de la mobilité des populations urbaines *[In French]*; The hidden world of urban population mobility *[Summary].* Azouz Begag. *Espace Géogr.* **XVII:4** 10-12:1988 pp. 245 – 255

17 On inequality before death and life table summary measures. Jacques Silber. *Genus* **XLIV:1-2** 1-6:1988 pp. 25 – 41

18 On tests for sex preferences. Siu Fai Leung. *J. Pop. Ec.* **1:2** 1988 pp. 95 – 114

19 Orthodoxy and revisionism in American demography. Dennis Hodgson. *Pop. Dev. Rev.* **14:4** 12:1988 pp. 541 – 569

20 Population and development. Budai Tapari *[Ed.]*; E. D'Sa *[Contrib.]*; John Burton *[Contrib.]*; Philip J. Hughes *[Contrib.]*; Marjorie Sullivan *[Contrib.]*; David King *[Contrib.]*. Collection of 5 articles. **Yagl-Ambu**, *15:2,* 6:1988 pp. 1 – 83

21 Population forecasting — an application of Box-Jenkins technique. Sanabel El-Attar. *Proc. Am. Stat. Ass.* pp. 305 – 310

22 Practical uses of multistate population models. Robert Schoen. *Ann. R. Soc.* **14** 1988 pp. 341 – 361

23 Predictability of demographic variables in the short run; Prévisibilité à court terme des variables démographiques *[French summary].* Joop de Beer. *Eur. J. Pop.* **4:4** 7:1988 pp. 283 – 296

24 Progrès génétiques et biologiques — effets sur la démographie et la population *[In French]*; [Progress in genetics and biology — effects on demography and population]. Alexandre Minkowski. Paris: La Documentation Française, 1988: 75 p. *ISBN: 2110020865.*

25 Projecting the older population of the United States — lessons from the past and prospects for the future. Jack M. Guralnik; Machiko Yanagishita; Edward L. Schneider. *Milbank Q.* **66:2** 1988 pp. 283 – 308

26 La qualité du suivi des échantillons dans les enquêtes démographiques — un bilan *[In French]*; The quality of follow-up studies of the sample in the demographic surveys. An appraisal *[Summary]*; *[Spanish summary].* Benoît Riandey. *Population* **43:4-5** 7-10:1988 pp. 829 – 854

27 Religion et évolution démographique en Inde *[In French]*; Religion and demographic change in India *[Summary]*; *[Spanish summary].* Roland Breton. *Population* **43:6** 11-12:1988 pp. 1089 – 1122

28 Simulating the aging of the Netherlands. Henk A. Becker. *Simulat. Gam.* **19:2** 6:1988 pp. 186 – 209

F.1: Demography. Genetics *[Démographie. Génétique]*

29 Socio-economic aspects of population structure — case study of Uttar Pradesh. M. Abuzar. Jaipur: Rawat, 1988: xvi, 179 p. *ISBN: 81 7033 049 1.*

30 Stochastic processes in demography and applications. Suddhendu Biswas; Vijay Kumar Sehgal *[Ed.]*. New Delhi: Wiley Eastern, 1988: xiii, 359 p. *ISBN: 0470210486.*

F.2: Age groups — *Groupes d'âges*

Sub-divisions: Ageing *[Vieillissement]*; Childhood *[Enfance]*

1 Adolescent development. Anne C. Petersen. *Ann. R. Psych.* **39:** 1988 pp. 583 – 608

2 Age, crime and the early life course. Yossi Shavit; Arye Rattner. *A.J.S.* **93:6** 5:1988 pp. 1457 – 1470

3 The diffuseness of age. J.W. Boyd; J.J. Dowd. *Soc. Behav.* **3:2** 6:1988 pp. 85 – 103

4 Immigration et régulation de la structure par âge d'une population *[In French]*; Regulating the age structure of a population through migration *[Summary]*; *[Spanish summary]*. Didier Blanchet. *Population* **43:2** 3-4:1988 pp. 293 – 310

5 Integrating process and structure in the concept of youth — a case for secondary analysis. Gill Jones. *Sociol. Rev.* **36:4** 11:1988 pp. 706 – 732

6 Jongerenprotest en tweede feministische golf — een sociologische verglijking *[In Dutch]*; Youth revolt and second wave feminism — a sociological comparison *[Summary]*. L.B. van Snippenburg. *Sociol. Gids* **XXXV:2** 3-4:1988 pp. 102 – 115

7 Jóvenes y viejos ante el empleo *[In Spanish]*; [Young and old in employment]. Luis Puchol. *Rev. Fom. Soc.* **43:170** 4-6:1988 pp. 149 – 164

8 Louts and legends — male youth culture in an inner city school. J. C. Walker; Christine Hunt *[Ed.]*. Sydney: Allen & Unwin, 1988: xiv, 192 p. *ISBN: 0043303927. Bibliography — p.183-187 Includes index.*

9 Measurement of intergenerational relations. David J. Mangen *[Ed.]*; Vern L. Bengtson *[Ed.]*; Pierre H. Landry *[Ed.]*. Newbury Park, California: Sage, 1988: 253 p. *ISBN: 0803929897. Bibliography — p.239-250.*

10 Omogenizare și diferențiere in circumstanțele de viață și de activitate ale tinerilor *[In Romanian]*; (Homogenization and differentiation in the life conditions of young people); (Homogéneisation et différentiation dans les circonstances de vie jeunes gens: *Title only in French*); (Гомогенизация и дифференциация в жиз ни и деятельности молодёжи: *Title only in Russian*). Dumitru Bazac. *Viit. Soc.* **LXXXI** 11-12:1988 pp. 499 – 506

11 Patterns of transition to adulthood — a comparative study of Israeli society. Tamar Rapoport; Edna Lomsky-Feder. *Int. Sociol.* **3:4** 12:1988 pp. 415 – 432

12 Recent social trends — changes in personal aspirations of American youth. Eileen M. Crimmins; Richard A. Easterlin. *Social Soc. Res.* **72:4** 7:1988 pp. 217 – 223

13 Rural youth. Dharam Raj Singh. Allahabad: Chugh, 1987: vii, 190 p. *ISBN: 81 85076 29 4.*

F.2: Age groups [Groupes d'âges]

14 De samenhang tussen leeftijd en postmaterialistische waardenpatronen — een inhoudelijke uiteenlegging in socialisatie-en levensloopeffecten [In Dutch]; The empirical relation between age and postmaterialist values — a theoretical decomposition of socialisation and life course effects [Summary]. Nan Dirk de Graad; Paul M. de Graaf. Sociol. Gids **XXXV:6** 11-12:1988 pp. 397 – 417

15 Sedai sa bijinesu ron [In Japanese]; [Marketing the generation gap]. Terue Ohashi. : Toyokeizaishinposha, 1988: 243 p.

16 Sociological aspects of the third age. Trăilă Cernescu; Marilena Gânju. R. Roum. Sci. Soc. **32:1** 1-6:1988 pp. 57 – 64

17 Soviet youth — pioneers of change. Jim Riordan. Sov. Stud. **XL:4** 10:1988 pp. 556 – 572

18 Turning points and transitions — perceptions of the life course. Tamara K. Hareven; Kanji Masaoka. J. Fam. Hist. **13:3** 1988 pp. 271 – 289

19 Youth and the developing international perspective. Kenneth Cushner [Ed.]; Gail Wiener-Hughes [Contrib.]; Kenneth Cushner [Contrib.]; Bettina Hansel [Contrib.]; Augene H. Wilson [Contrib.]; J.E. Rash [Contrib.]. Collection of 6 articles. **Educ. Urban. Soc.** , 20:2, 2:1988 pp. 131 – 225

20 Youth in India. S. Saraswathi. New Delhi: Indian Council of Social Science Research, 1988: ix, 507 p.

21 Youth participation and development. D. Paul Chowdhry. Delhi: Atma, 1988: xx, 407 p. ISBN: 81 7043 101 8.

Ageing [Vieillissement]

22 Abundance of life — human development policies for an aging society. Harry R. Moody. New York: Columbia University Press, 1988: ix, 307 p. ISBN: 0231065922. Bibliography, p. [267]-300. [Columbia studies of social gerontology and aging.]

23 Adulthood and old age under apartheid — a psychosocial consideration. Helen Q. Kivnick. Age. Soc. **8:4** 12:1988 p.425-440

24 Age discrimination and the mandatory retirement controversy. Martin Lyon Levine. Baltimore: John Hopkins U.P., 1988: 231 p. ISBN: 0801833574.

25 Aged females — the most deprived among the deprived. M. Deva Sahayam. Indian J. Soc. W. **XLIX:3** 7:1988 pp. 261 – 270

26 Ageing and the impact of new technology. Glynis M. Breakwell; Chris Fife-Schaw. Soc. Behav. **3:2** 6:1988 pp. 119 – 130

27 Ageing as a challenge for sociological theory. Martin Kohli. Age. Soc. **8:4** 12:1988 pp. 369 – 394

28 Ageing, technology and society. Howard Giles [Ed.]; Karen Henwood [Ed.]; Susan Condor [Ed.]; Dennis Basil Bromley [Contrib.]; J.W. Boyd [Contrib.]; J.J. Dowd [Contrib.]; E.B. Ryan [Contrib.]; R.K.B. Heaven [Contrib.]; Glynis M. Breakwell [Contrib.]; Chris Fife-Schaw [Contrib.] and others. Collection of 9 articles. **Soc. Behav.** , 3:2, 6:1988 pp. 59 – 196

29 Ageing, technology, and society — an introduction and future priorities. Howard Giles; Susan Condor. Soc. Behav. **3:2** 6:1988 pp. 59 – 69

30 Aging and society — a Canadian perspective. Mark W. Novak. Scarborough, Ont.: Nelson Canada, 1988: xviii, 461 p. (ill.) ISBN: 0176034153; LofC: cn88-93559. Includes indexes; Bibliography — p. 375-446.

F.2: Age groups *[Groupes d'âges]* — Ageing *[Vieillissement]*

31 Aging and the family. Stephen J. Bahr *[Ed.]*; Evan T. Peterson *[Ed.]*. Lexington, Mass.: Lexington Books, 1988: ix, 321 p. *ISBN: 0669177024*.

32 Aging in a rural place — the elusive source of well-being. V.R. Kivett. *J. Rural St.* **4:2** 1988 pp. 125 – 134

33 Aging in Canadian society — a survey. Maureen Baker. Toronto: McGraw-Hill Ryerson, 1988: x, 150 p. *ISBN: 0075491737. Bibliography — p.124-141.*

34 The aging in India — problems and potentialities. A.B. Bose *[Ed.]*; K.D. Gangrade *[Ed.]*. New Delhi: Abhinav, 1988: xvi, 132 p. *ISBN: 81 710 7230 6*.

35 Aging in rural America. J.A. Krout *[Ed.]*; P.J. Krout *[Contrib.]*; G.D. Rowles *[Contrib.]*; V.R. Kivett *[Contrib.]*; D. Shenk *[Contrib.]*; D. McTavish; A. Martin Matthews *[Contrib.]*; P.G. Windley *[Contrib.]*; R.J. Scheidt; R.T. Coward *[Contrib.]* *and others. Collection of 7 articles.* **J. Rural St.** , *4:2*, 1988 pp. 99 – 168

36 Alte Menschen — ihr "Standort" in unserer Gesellschaft *[In German]*; [Elderly people — their "location" in our society]. Wendelin Strubelt *[Ed.]*; Hansjörg Bucher *[Contrib.]*; Martina Kocks *[Contrib.]*; Hans- Joachim Schulze *[Contrib.]*; Jan Künzler *[Contrib.]*; Leopold Rosenmayr *[Contrib.]*; Erika Haindl *[Contrib.]*; Gerhard Haag *[Contrib.]*; Robert Wischer *[Contrib.]*; Christa Kliemke *[Contrib.]* *and others. Collection of 11 articles.* **Inf. Raum.** , *:1/2*, 1988 pp. 1 – 120

37 Black elderly in rural America — a comprehensive study. Arnold G. Parks. Bristol, Ind.: Wyndham Hall Press, 1988: 333 p. *ISBN: 1556050550*.

38 Daily life in later life — comparative perspectives. Karen Altergott *[Ed.]*. Newbury Park: Sage Publications, 1988: 252 p. *ISBN: 080392898x; LofC: 88-003245.* [Sage focus editions. : No. 99]

39 Dependency and old age — theoretical accounts and practical understandings. Tim Dant. *Age. Soc.* **8:2** 6:1988 pp. 171 – 188

40 Do job opportunities decline with age? Robert M. Hutchens. *Ind. Lab. Rel.* **42:1** 10:1988 pp. 89 – 99

41 The elderly in rural environments. J.A. Krout. *J. Rural St.* **4:2** 1988 pp. 103 – 114

42 Elderly migration — for sun and money. Gary M. Fournier; David W. Rasmussen; William J. Serow. *Pop. Res. Pol. R.* **7:2** 1988 pp. 189 – 199

43 The environment for aging — interpersonal, social and spatial contexts. Russell A. Ward; Susan R. Sherman *[Ed.]*; Mark La Gory *[Ed.]*. Tuscaloosa: University of Alabama Press, 1988: 272 p. (ill) *ISBN: 0817303421; LofC: 86- 24940*.

44 Ethics and aging — the right to live, the right to die. Earl R. Winkler *[Ed.]*; James E. Thornton *[Ed.]*. Vancouver: University of British Columbia Press, 1988 *ISBN: 0774803029*.

45 Gendai kazoku to kourei-shakai no sho-mondai *[In Japanese]*; [Modern family and problems of aged society]. Hiromitsu Matsuyama. **The Journal of Sociology** *Vol.103. 1988*. pp. 72 – 85

46 Health care, health status, and cohort mortality in the elderly. Larry J. Brant *[Contrib.]*; Megan E. Greene *[Contrib.]*; Dwight B. Brock *[Contrib.]*; Daniel J. Foley *[Contrib.]*; Rebecca B. Rosenstein *[Contrib.]*; Wlliam D. Spector *[Contrib.]*; Walter F. Freiberger *[Contrib.]*; Kyung S. Bay *[Contrib.]*; Janet Ross Kerr *[Contrib.]*; Bert Kestenbaum *[Contrib.]* *and others. Collection of 6 articles.* **Proc. Am. Stat. Ass.** , pp. 412 – 446

INTERNATIONAL BIBLIOGRAPHY OF SOCIOLOGY — 1988

F.2: Age groups *[Groupes d'âges]* — *Ageing [Vieillissement]*

47 Intersections of gender and aging. Judith A. Levy. *Sociol. Q.* **29:4** Winter:1988 pp. 479 – 486

48 Kinship, responsibility and care for elderly people. Graham Allan. *Age. Soc.* **8:3** 9:1988 pp. 249 – 268

49 Kourei-ka shakai to kazoku *[In Japanese]*; [Family problems in aging society]. Kōzō Iwao. ***University Extension journal of Kanazawa University Vol.8.*** *1988.* pp. 17 – 31

50 Koureisha no shakai kouzou no ichi ni tsuite *[In Japanese]*; [Aged people and social structure]. Atsuhiro Terada. ***Annual Report of the Researches, Nihon Daigaku Vol.9.*** *1988.* pp. 121 – 128

51 Koureisha no stress — roujin daigaku jukousei no baai *[In Japanese]*; [Social stress of the aged]. Akitoshi Nishishita. ***Journal for the Study of Gerontology Vol.8.*** *1988.* pp. 45 – 51

52 Die Lebenssituation alter Menschen im ländlichen Raum. Gesellschaftliche Integration und Lebensbedingungen *[In German]*; [Elderly people in rural areas. Social integration and living conditions]. Erika Haindl. *Inf. Raum.* **:1/2** 1988 pp. 37 – 47

53 Life transitions in the elderly. William E. Powell *[Ed.]*; Pat Conway *[Contrib.]*; Sheldon S. Tobin *[Contrib.]*; Barbara S. Cain *[Contrib.]*; Lenore A. Kola *[Contrib.]*; Ruth E. Dunkle *[Contrib.]*; Zev Harel *[Contrib.]*; Gari Lesnoff-Caravaglia *[Contrib.]*; Virginia S. Burlingame *[Contrib.]*. Collection of 9 articles. **Fam. Soc.** , *69:9*, 11:1988 pp. 539 – 592

54 Naissance du vieillard — essai sur l'histoire des rapports entre les vieillards et la société en France *[In French]*; [Birth of the elderly — study on the history of the relations between the elderly and society in France]. Jean-Pierre Gutton. Paris: Aubier, 1988: 281 p. *ISBN: 2700722205. Bibliography — p..277-279.*

55 Old and poor — a critical assessment of the low-income elderly. William F. Clark; Marleen L. Clark *[Ed.]*; Anabel O. Pelham *[Ed.]*. Lexington, Mass.: Lexington Books, 1988: x, 222p. *ISBN: 0669110787. Bibliography — p.209-218.*

56 On the survival of centenarians and the span of life. Väinö Kannisto. *Pop. Stud.* **XLII:3** 11:1988 pp. 389 – 406

57 The over-forty society — issues for Canada's ageing population. Blossom T. Wigdor; David K. Foot *[Ed.]*. Toronto: J. Lorimer, 1988: 135 p. *ISBN: 1550280872. Bibliography — p.131-135.*

58 La popolazione anziana del canton Ticino — un'indagine sui bisogni e sui modi di vita *[In Italian]*; [The elderly population of Ticino canton — an investigation into their needs and their way of life]. Emilio Gerosa. Milano: F. Angeli, 1988: 492 p. *ISBN: 8820428830.* [Collana di sociologia.]

59 A population profile of very old men and women in the United States. Charles F. Longino. *Sociol. Q.* **29:4** Winter:1988 pp. 559 – 564

60 Retired and aging people — a study of their problems. P.N. Sati. Delhi: Mittal, 1988: xii, 264 p. *ISBN: 81 709 9042 4.*

61 Retirement and the lifestyles of older women. Wolfgang Voges; Hannelore Pongratz. *Age. Soc.* **8:1** 3:1988 pp. 63 – 83

62 Simulating the aging of the Netherlands. Henk A. Becker. *Simulat. Gam.* **19:2** 6:1988 pp. 186 – 209

F.2: Age groups *[Groupes d'âges]* — *Ageing [Vieillissement]*

63 Structural characteristics of social networks and their relationship with social support in the elderly — who provides support? Teresa E. Seeman; Lisa F. Berkman. *Soc. Sci. Med.* **26:7** 1988 pp. 737 – 749

64 Themes in Soviet social gerontology. Anna L. Howe. *Age. Soc.* **8:2** 6:1988 pp. 147 – 169

65 Toshi koureisha to chiiki shūan *[In Japanese]*; [The aged in cities and the locality-based groups]. Isamu Kaneko. *The Toshi Mondai Vol.79; No.4 - 1988.* pp. 41 – 52

Childhood *[Enfance]*

66 Acquiring culture — cross cultural studies in child development. Gustav Jahoda *[Ed.]*; I.M. Lewis *[Ed.]*. London: Croom Helm, 1988: ix, 340, [16] p. of plates *Bibliography — p.307-333. Includes index.*

67 Agents of modernity — children's care for children in urban Norway. Marianne Gullestad. *Soc. Anal.* **23** 8:1988 pp. 38 – 52

68 Answering back — parental perspectives on the children's hearings system. Alison Petch. *Br. J. Soc. W.* **18:1** 1988 pp. 1 – 24

69 Children and prejudice. Frances Aboud. Oxford: Basil Blackwell, 1988: x, 149 p. (ill) *ISBN: 0631149392. Includes index.* [Social psychology and society.]

70 Children's household work — its nature and functions. Jacqueline J. Goodnow. *Psychol .B.* **103:1** 1:1988 pp. 5 – 26

71 Children's rights and children's lives. Onora O'Neill. *Ethics* **98:3** 4:1988 pp. 445 – 463

72 Economic activities of children — dimensions causes and consequences. B.M. Dinesh. Delhi: Daya, 1988: xi, 151 p. *ISBN: 81 7035 040 9.*

73 The effect of seasonal maternal employment on young Senegalese children's behavior. Marianne N. Bloch. *J. Comp. Fam. Stud.* **XIX:3** Autumn:1988 pp. 397 – 418

74 Family secrets — child sexual abuse. Mary McIntosh *[Contrib.]*; Mary MacLeod *[Contrib.]*; Esther Saraga *[Contrib.]*; Linda Gordon *[Contrib.]*; Liz Kelly *[Contrib.]*; Jenny Kitzinger *[Contrib.]*; Ann Scott *[Contrib.]*; Mica Nava *[Contrib.]*; Elizabeth Woodcraft *[Contrib.]*; Gina Betcher *[Contrib.]* and others. Collection of 15 articles. **Feminist R.** , *28*, Spring:1988 pp. 6 – 17

75 Free South Africa's children — a symposium on children in detention. Gay McDougall *[Contrib.]*; Edward M. Kennedy *[Contrib.]*; Barbara A. Mikulski *[Contrib.]*; Jerry Coovadia *[Contrib.]*; Patrick Makhoba *[Contrib.]*; Pule Nape *[Contrib.]*; Sylvia Jele *[Contrib.]*; Audrey Coleman *[Contrib.]*; Michael Rice *[Contrib.]*; Marumo Moerane *[Contrib.]* and others. Collection of 9 articles. **Hum. Rights Q.** , *10:1*, 2:1988 pp. 10 – 108

76 The history of childhood since the "invention of childhood" — some issues in the eighties. Bruce Bellingham. *J. Fam. Hist.* **13:3** 1988 pp. 347 – 358

77 Individual differences in children and adolescents — international perspectives. Donald H. Saklofske *[Ed.]*; Sybil B. G. Eysenck *[Ed.]*. London: Hodder and Stoughton, 1988: 341 p. *ISBN: 034041295x. Includes bibliographies and index.*

78 Infância e sociedade no Brasil — uma análise da literatua *[In Portuguese]*; [Childhood and society in Brazil — a study of the literature]. Maria Rosilene Barbosa Alvim; Licia do Prado Valladares. *Bol. Inf. Bibl. Soc.* **:26** :1988 pp. 3 – 37

F.2: Age groups [Groupes d'âges] — Childhood [Enfance]

79 Knowing children — participant observation with minors. Gary Alan Fine; Kent L. Sandstrom *[Ed.]*. Beverly Hills, Calif.: Sage Publications, 1988: 88 p. *ISBN: 0803933649. Bibliography — p.79-84.* [Qualitative research methods. : Vol. 15]

80 Nonverbal communication skills in Down's syndrome children. Peter Mundy; Marian Sigman; Connie Kasari; Nurit Yirmiya. *Child. Devel.* **59:1** 2:1988 pp. 235 – 249

81 Population infantile consultant pour des troubles psychologiques *[In French]*; Profiles of children undergoing treatment for psychological disorders *[Summary]*; *[Spanish summary]*. Philippe Chevallier. *Population* **43:3** 5-6:1988 pp. 611 – 638

82 The public world of childhood. John R. Morss. *J. Theory Soc. Behav.* **18:3** 9:1988 pp. 323 – 345

83 Rethinking childhood. Leena Alanen. *Acta Sociol.* **31:1** 1988 pp. 53 – 67

84 Self-in-relation theory and latency-age boys. Sylvia Ridlen Wenston; Kent D. Jarratt. *Fam. Soc.* **69:4** 4:1988 pp. 231 – 237

85 Social development in infant twins — peer and mother-child relationships. Deborah Lowe Vandell; Margaret Tresch Owen; Kathy Shores Wilson; V. Kay Henderson. *Child. Devel.* **59:1** 2:1988 pp. 168 – 177

86 Street children of Cali. Lewis Aptekar. Durham: Duke University Press, 1988: xxi, 235 p. *Bibliography — p.224-230. Includes index.*

87 Whose neglect? The role of poverty-related factors in child neglect cases and court decisions in the United States. Leroy H. Pelton; Marguerite G. Rosenthal. *Int. J. Law Fam.* **2:2** 1988 pp. 167 – 182

F.3: Population evolution. Population policy — Évolution de la population. Politique démographique

Sub-divisions: Family planning *[Planification de la famille]*; Fertility *[Fécondité]*; Morbidity *[Morbidité]*; Mortality *[Mortalité]*

1 Ausblick auf die Zukunft der schweizerischen Bevölkerung — Bevölkerungsperspektiven 1986- 2025 *[In German]*; [Outlook for the future of Swiss population — the prospects for the population 1986-2025]. Werner Haug. *Schw. Z. Volk. Stat.* **124:2** 6:1988 pp. 193 – 211

2 The causes of demographic change — experimental research in South India. John Charles Caldwell; P. H. Reddy *[Ed.]*; Pat Caldwell *[Ed.]*. Madison,Wisc.: University of Wisconsin Press, 1988: 285 p. *ISBN: 0299116107.* [Social demography.]

3 Demographic transitions and the life course — lessons from Japanese and American comparisons. Dennis P. Hogan; Takashi Mochizuki. *J. Fam. Hist.* **13:3** 1988 pp. 291 – 305

4 Evolution demographique, croissance economique et bien-être social *[In French]*; Demographic change, economic growth and social welfare *[Summary]*. Anatoly Vichnievski. *Eur. J. Pop.* **4:1** 9:1988 pp. 69 – 94

5 How economic development can overcome culture — demographic change in Punjab, India. Alaka Malwade Basu. *Pop. Res. Pol. R.* **7:1** 1988 pp. 29 – 48

6 The impact of migration on the population changes in Jordan. Mousa M. Samha. *Dirasat Ser. A.* **XV:2** 2:1988 pp. 41 – 55

F.3: Population evolution. Population policy [Évolution de la population. Politique démographique]

7 In time of plague. Adrien Mack *[Ed.]*; Charles E. Rosenberg *[Contrib.]*; William H. Foege *[Contrib.]*; Joshua Lederberg *[Contrib.]*; Dorothy Nelkin *[Contrib.]*; Sander L. Gilman *[Contrib.]*; Lewis Thomas *[Contrib.]*; Barbara Gutmann Rosenkrantz *[Contrib.]*; S. Baruch *[Contrib.]*; Allan M. Brandt *[Contrib.]* and others. Collection of 14 articles. *Soc. Res.* , **55**:3, Autumn:1988 pp. 323 – 529

8 India's population policy — critical issues for future. Sheo Kumar Lal *[Ed.]*; Ambika Chandani *[Ed.]*. Meerut: Twenty-first Century, 1987: xxiv, 180 p.

9 An interest-group theory of population growth. M.S. Kimenyi; W.F. Shughart; R.D. Tollison. *J. Pop. Ec.* **1:2** 1988 pp. 131 – 139

10 Modeling fertility with mortality as a competing risk — an application. Arvind Pandey; C.M. Suchindran. *Proc. Am. Stat. Ass.* pp. 127 – 132

11 Moving disability beyond "stigma". Adrienne Asch *[Ed.]*; Michelle Fine *[Ed.]*; Jessica Scheer *[Contrib.]*; Nora Groce *[Contrib.]*; Harlan Hahn *[Contrib.]*; Elaine Makas *[Contrib.]*; Joseph W. Schneider *[Contrib.]*; Stephen C. Ainlay *[Contrib.]*; Gelya Frank *[Contrib.]*; Grace M. Mest *[Contrib.]* and others. Collection of 14 articles. *J. Soc. Issues* , **44**:1, 1988 pp. 1 – 192

12 New demographics and old designs — the Chinese family amid induced population transition. H. Yuan Tien; Che-Fu Lee. *Soc. Sci. Q.* **69:3** 9:1988 pp. 605 – 628

13 Population growth and development in the Third World — the neoclassic context. John G. Patterson; Nanda R. Shrestha. *Stud. Comp. ID.* **XXIII:2** Summer:1988 pp. 3 – 32

14 Современные особенности динамики городского и сельского населения сша *[In Russian]*; [Current peculiarities of the dynamics of urban and rural populations of the USA]. I.M. Kuzina; V.M. Kharitonov. *Prob. Amerik. Vol.5. 1988.* pp. 238 – 360

15 Tendencias de la población en squatter-settlements — estudio de un caso en Salvador, Brasil *[In Spanish]*; [Population trends in squatter settlements — case study in Salvador, Brazil]. Ralf Engelhardt. *Rev. Mexicana Soc.* **L:4** 10-12:1988 pp. 187 – 208

Family planning *[Planification de la famille]*

16 Abortion politics as symbolic politics — an investigation into belief systems. Amy Fried. *Soc. Sci. Q.* **69:1** 3:1988 pp. 137 – 154

17 Abortion, doctors and the law — some aspects of the legal regulation of abortion in England from 1803 to 1982. John Keown. Cambridge: Cambridge University Press, 1988: x, 212 p. *ISBN: 052134574x. Includes index.* [Cambridge history of medicine.]

18 Abortivita' volontaria e progetti di vita femminile *[In Italian]*; [Abortion on demand and planning women's lives]. Carla Bielli; Filomena Racioppi. *Genus* **XLIV:3-4** 7-12:1988 pp. 185 – 205

19 American Catholicism and the international family planning movement. Peter J. Donaldson. *Pop. Stud.* **XLII:3** 11:1988 pp. 367 – 374

20 Attitudes of urban Sudanese men toward family planning. Mona A. Khalifa. *Stud. Fam. Pl.* **19:4** 7-8:1988 pp. 236 – 243

21 Beyond supply — the importance of female family planning workers in rural Bangladesh. Ruth Simmons; Laila Baqee; Michael A. Koenig; James F. Phillips. *Stud. Fam. Pl.* **19:1** 1-2:1988 pp. 29 – 38

F.3: Population evolution. Population policy *[Évolution de la population. Politique démographique]* — **Family planning** *[Planification de la famille]*

22 Community development and family planning — an Egyptian experiment. J. Mayone Stycos *[Ed.]*; et al. Boulder: Westview, 1988: 224 p. *ISBN: 0813375991; LofC: 88-12057. Bibliography.*

23 Compensatory payments and vasectomy acceptance in urban Sri Lanka. V. de Silva; S. Thapa; L.R. Wilkens; M.G. Farr; K. Jayasinghe; J.E. McMahan. *J. Biosoc. Sc.* **20:2** 4:1988 pp. 143 – 156

24 A consumer intercept study of oral contraceptive users in the Dominican Republic. Edward C. Green. *Stud. Fam. Pl.* **19:2** 3-4:1988 pp. 109 – 117

25 The contraceptive confidence idea — an empirical investigation. Máire Ní Bhrolcháin. *Pop. Stud.* **XLII:2** 7:1988 pp. 205 – 226

26 Contraceptive discontinuation among married women in the United States. William R. Grady; Mark D. Hayward; Francesca A. Florey. *Stud. Fam. Pl.* **19:4** 7-8:1988 pp. 227 – 235

27 Contraceptive social marketing and community-based distribution systems in Colombia. Ricardo Vernon; Gabriel Ojeda; Marcia C. Townsend. *Stud. Fam. Pl.* **19:6** 11-12:1988 pp. 354 – 360

28 The domestic servant as family planning innovator — an Indian case study. Alaka Malwade Basu; Ramamani Sundar. *Stud. Fam. Pl.* **19:5** 9-10:1988 pp. 292 – 298

29 The effect of economic factors on contraceptive choice in Jamaica and Thailand — a comparison of mixed multinomial logit results. John S. Akin; Brad J. Schwartz. *Econ. Dev. Cult. Change* **36:3** 4:1988 pp. 503 – 528

30 The effect of schooling and labor market expectations on teenage childbearing. Elaine McCrate. *Rev. Rad. Pol. Ec.* **20:2:3** 1988 pp. 203 – 207

31 Family planning accessibility and adoption — the Korean population policy and program evaluation study. James A. Palmore *[Ed.]*; et al. Honolulu, Hawaii: East-West Population Institute, East-West Center, 1988: 125 p. *ISBN: 0866381066. Bibliography.* [Papers of the East-West Population Institute.]

32 Family planning and child survival — 100 developing countries. John A. Ross *[Ed.]*. New York: Center for Population and Family Health, Columbia University, 1988: 247 p. *ISBN: 0962095206.*

33 Family planning programme in India — its impact in rural and urban areas, 1970-1980. Kohli Chandra Shanta. Delhi: Mittal, 1987: xiv, 265 p. *ISBN: 81 7099 023 8.*

34 Fertility and contraception in the Marshall Islands. Susan J. Levy; Richard Taylor; Ilona L. Higgins; Deborah A. Grafton-Wasserman. *Stud. Fam. Pl.* **19:3** 5-6:1988 pp. 179 – 185

35 Husband's approval of contraceptive use in metropolitan Indonesia — program implications. Mohamad R. Joesoef; Andrew L. Baughman; Budi Utomo. *Stud. Fam. Pl.* **19:3** 5-6:1988 pp. 162 – 168

36 The Hutterites and fertility control. Bron B. Ingoldsby; Max E. Stanton. *J. Comp. Fam. Stud.* **XIX:1** Spring:1988 pp. 137 – 142

37 The masculine side of planned parenthood — an explanatory analysis; *[French summary]*; *[Spanish summary]*. Akin Adebayo. *J. Comp. Fam. Stud.* **XIX:1** Spring:1988 pp. 55 – 67

38 Les médecins face à l'avortement *[In French]*; [Doctors confronted by abortion] *[Summary]*. Michèle Ferrand. *Documents* **:2** :1988 pp. 367 – 380

F.3: Population evolution. Population policy *[Évolution de la population. Politique démographique]* — Family planning *[Planification de la famille]*

39 Physicians views of periodic abstinence methods — a study in four countries. Robert Snowden; Kathy I. Kennedy; Federico Leon; Viginia C. Orense; Harin W. Perera; Rodney Phillips; Ian Askew; Anna Flynn; Lawrence J. Severy. *Stud. Fam. Pl.* **19:4** 7-8:1988 pp. 215 – 226

40 Population control and family planning in India. Mamta Lakshmanna. Delhi: Discovery, 1988: vii, 201 p. *ISBN: 81 7141 026 X.*

41 Population policy and individual choice. M. Nerlove. *J. Pop. Ec.* **1:1** 1988 pp. 17 – 31

42 Predicting Mexican-American family planning intentions — an application and test of a social psychological model. Stephen R. Jorgensen; Russell P. Adams. *J. Marriage Fam.* **50:1** 2:1988 pp. 107 – 119

43 Preference for son, desire for additional children and contraceptive use in Bangladesh. M.A. Mannan. *Bang. Dev. Stud.* **XVI:3** 9:1988 pp. 31 – 58

44 Prevalence of contraceptive use — trends and issues. W. Parker Mauldin; Sheldon J. Segal. *Stud. Fam. Pl.* **19:6** 11-12:1988 pp. 335 – 353

45 A proposito dell'effetto Cernobyl sul comportamento riproduttivo della popolazione Italiana — il caso della Lombardia *[In Italian]*; [The effect of Chernobyl on the reproductive behaviour of the Italian population — the case of Lombardy]. Gian Carlo Blangiardo. *Genus* **XLIV:1-2** 1-6:1988 pp. 99 – 121

46 Social marketing of oral rehydration therapy and contraceptives in Egypt. Karen F.A. Fox. *Stud. Fam. Pl.* **19:2** 3-4:1988 pp. 95 – 108

47 The timing of the second birth. Howard Wineberg. *Social Soc. Res.* **72:2** 1:1988 pp. 96 – 101

48 Tubal sterilization — questioning the decision. Charles W. Warren; Richard S. Monteith; J. Timothy Johnson; Mark W. Oberle. *Pop. Stud.* **XLII:3** 11:1988 pp. 407 – 418

49 The war against population — the economics and ideology of world population control. Jacqueline Kasun. San Francisco: Ignatius Press, 1988: 225 p. *ISBN: 0898701910.*

Fertility *[Fécondité]*

50 Age at first birth in Canada — a hazards model analysis. K. Vaninadha Rao; T.R. Balakrishnan. *Genus* **XLIV:1-2** 1-6:1988 pp. 53 – 73

51 Application of Granger-Sims causality tests to monthly fertility data, 1958-1984. D.J. Macunovich; R.A. Easterlin. *J. Pop. Ec.* **1:1** 1988 pp. 71 – 88

52 La baisse de la fécondité arabe *[In French]*; Descenso de la fecundidad árabe *[Spanish summary]*; The decline in Arab birth rates *[Summary]*. Philippe Fargues. *Population* **43:6** 11-12:1988 pp. 975 – 1004

53 Comportements démographiques — une fécondité maîtrisée *[In French]*; [Demographic behaviour — controlled fertility] *[Summary]*. Guy Desplanques. *Documents* **:2** :1988 pp. 353 – 366

54 Contraceptive use and fertility in Paraguay, 1987. Richard S. Monteith; Juan Maria Carron; Charles W. Warren; Mercedes Maria Melian; Dario Castagnino; Leo Morris. *Stud. Fam. Pl.* **19:5** 9-10:1988 pp. 284 – 291

55 Cultural dynamics and economic theories of fertility change. Ron Lesthaeghe; Johan Surkyn. *Pop. Dev. Rev.* **14:1** 3:1988 pp. 1 – 45

F.3: Population evolution. Population policy [Évolution de la population. Politique démographique] — Fertility [Fécondité]

56 Determinants of reproductive change in a traditional society — evidence from Matlab, Bangladesh. James F. Phillips; Ruth Simmons; Michael A. Koenig; Chakraborty J.. *Stud. Fam. Pl.* **19:6** 11-12:1988 pp. 313 – 334

57 The dynamics of Labrador Inuit fertility — an example of cultural and demographic change. David Z. Scheffel. *Popul. Envir.* **10:1** Fall:1988 pp. 32 – 47

58 The effects of family planning effort and development on fertility — an intervening variables framework. Stewart E. Tolnay; Daniel G. Rodeheaver. *Neue Pol. Liter.* **XXIII:3** Fall:1988 pp. 28 – 49

59 The effects of improved child survival on family planning practice and fertility. Cynthia B. Lloyd; Serguey Ivanov. *Stud. Fam. Pl.* **19:3** 5-6:1988 pp. 141 – 161

60 La fecondité de certaines générations feminines en Roumanie *[In French]*; [The fertility of certain generations of women in Romania]. Vasile Ghetău. *R. Roum. Sci. Soc.* **32:1** 1-6:1988 pp. 45 – 56

61 La fécondité des Inuit du nouveau-Québec depuis 1931 — passage d'une fécondité naturelle à une fécondite contrôlée *[In French]*; La fecundidad de la poblacion inuit de nuevo Quebec a partir de 1931 — el paso de una fecundidad natural a una fecundidad controlada *[Spanish summary]*; Birth rates among the Inuit of New Quebec since 1931 — the transition from natural to controlled fertility *[Summary]*. Robert Choinière; Norbert Robitaille. *Population* **43:2** 3-4:1988 pp. 427 – 450

62 Fertility and indices of women's status — a study of relationships in Nigeria. Bamikale J. Feyisetan; Oladimeji Togunde. *Genus* **XLIV:1-2** 1-6:1988 pp. 229 – 249

63 Fertility as mobility — Sinic transitions. Susan Greenhalgh. *Pop. Dev. Rev.* **14:4** 12:1988 pp. 629 – 674

64 Fertility decline in a developing country — the case of Papua New Guinea. Harsha N. Mookherjee. *Popul. R.* **32:1-2** 1-12:1988 pp. 49 – 56

65 Fertility of women married once or more than once. Howard Wineberg. *Social Soc. Res.* **72:4** 7:1988 pp. 260 – 266

66 Fertility patterns — their relationship to child physical abuse and child neglect. Susan J. Zuravin. *J. Marriage Fam.* **50:4** 11:1988 pp. 983 – 993

67 Fruchtbarkeitstafeln *[In German]*; Fertility life tables *[Summary]*. Werner Grünewald. *Jahrb. N. St.* **204:3** 3:1988 pp. 241 – 254

68 The impact of income redistribution on fertility in Canada. Robert E. Wright. *Genus* **XLIV:1-2** 1-6:1988 pp. 139 – 157

69 Infertility — his and hers. Arthur L. Greil; Thomas A. Leitko; Karen L. Porter. *Gender Soc.* **2:2** 6:1988 pp. 172 – 199

70 A model of age-specific fecundability. James A. Wood; Maxime Weinstein. *Pop. Stud.* **XLII:1** 3:1988 pp. 85 – 114

71 Mouvement saisonnier des naissances — influence du rang et de la légitimité dans quelques pays d'Europe occidentale *[In French]*; Seasonal peaks in birth rate — influence of rank and legitimacy in few Western European countries *[Summary]*; *[Spanish summary]*. France Prioux. *Population* **43:3** 5-6:1988 pp. 587 – 610

72 Natural human fertility — social and biological determinants. Peter Diggory *[Ed.]*; Malcolm Potts *[Ed.]*; Sue Teper *[Ed.]*. London: Macmillan in

F.3: Population evolution. Population policy [Évolution de la population. Politique démographique] — Fertility [Fécondité]

association with the Eugenics Society, 1988: xix, 201 p. (ill) ISBN: 0333457242. Includes bibliographies and index. [Studies in biology, economy and society.]

73 O dwóch modelach demometrycznych płodności kobiet *[In Polish]*; (О двух демометрических моделях рождаемости женщин: *Title only in Russian)*; (On two demometric models of female fertility). Elżbieta Golata; Mieczyslaw Kędelski. *Stud. Demogr.* **3(93)** 1988 pp. 21 – 36

74 Occupational status, earnings, and fertility expectations — development and estimation of a causal model. Vijaya Krishnan. *Economist [Leiden]* **136:3** 1988 pp. 358 – 382

75 On forecasting mortality. S. Jay Olshansky. *Milbank Q.* **66:3** 1988 pp. 482 – 530

76 On the altered appetites of pregnancy — conceptions of food, body and person. Anne Murcott. *Sociol. Rev.* **36:4** 11:1988 pp. 733 – 764

77 The pace of births over the life course — implications for the minority-group status hypothesis. Nan E. Johnson. *Soc. Sci. Q.* **69:1** 3:1988 p. 95

78 Population growth and socioeconomic progress in less developed countries — determinants of fertility transition. Peter N. Hess. New York: Praeger, 1988: 166 p. *ISBN: 0275929795; LofC: 87-038472. Bibliography — p.157-162.*

79 A reformulation of the economic theory of fertility. Gary S. Becker; Robert J. Barro. *Q. J. Econ.* **CIII:1** 2:1988 pp. 1 – 26

80 Reverse survival methods of estimating birth rates under non-stable conditions. Kilambi Venkatacharya; Tesfay Teklu. *Genus* **XLIV:1-2** 1-6:1988 pp. 73 – 99

81 Révolution démographique et fécondité en URSS du XIXe siècle à la période contemporaine *[In French]*; The demographic revolution and fertility in the USSR from the nineteenth century to the present day *[Summary]*; *[Spanish summary]*. Anatole Vichnevskij. *Population* **43:4-5** 7-10:1988 pp. 799 – 814

82 The roles of individuals' socioeconomic characteristics and the government family planning program in China's fertility decline. Feng Wang. *Pop. Res. Pol. R.* **7:3** 1988 pp. 255 – 276

83 Shakai hendou no ichi sokumen to shiteno shussei-ryoku teika — kakushin kasetsu to junnou kasetsu *[In Japanese]*; [Fertility decline as an aspect of social change — innovation or adjustment]. Noriko Tsuya. *The Journal of Sociology* Vol.105. 1988. pp. 54 – 71

84 A simple model for birth interval survival. John C. Barrett. *Genus* **XLIV:1-2** 1-6:1988 pp. 41 – 53

85 Static versus dynamic analysis of the interaction between female labour-force participation and fertility; L'analyse statique opposée à l'analyse dynamique de l'interaction entre la participation au marché du travail féminin et la fécondité *[French summary]*. Erik Klijzing; Jacques Siegers; Nico Keilman; Loek Groot. *Eur. J. Pop.* **4:2** 4:1988 pp. 97 – 116

86 Teenage fertility in developing countries. Vijayan Pillai. *Stud. Comp. ID.* **XXIII:4** Winter:1988 pp. 3 – 14

F.3: Population evolution. Population policy [Évolution de la population. Politique démographique] —

Morbidity [Morbidité]

87 Les accidents de l'enfant et de l'adolescent — la place de la recherche *[In French]*; [Accidents in childhood and adolescence — the role of research]. Michel Manciaux; C. J. Romer *[Ed.]*. Paris: La Documentation française, 1988: 275 p. *ISBN: 2110020482.*

88 Africa and AIDS — dependent development, sexism, and racism. Charles W. Hunt. *Mon. Rev.* **39:9** 2:1988 pp. 10 – 22

89 AIDS and human rights — an international perspective. Martin Breum *[Ed.]*; Aart Hendriks *[Ed.]*. Copenhagen: Danish Center of Human Rights, 1988: 174 p. *ISBN: 8750027492.*

90 AIDS and the human community. Erich H. Loewy. *Soc. Sci. Med.* **27:4** 1988 pp. 297 – 303

91 AIDS and the pursuit of happiness — some problems associated with psychosocial discrimination. Michael W. Ross. *Aust. J. Soc. Iss.* **23:2** 5:1988 pp. 103 – 112

92 The AIDS crisis — a United States health care perspective. Lawrence C. Shulman; Joanne E. Mantell. *Soc. Sci. Med.* **26:10** 1988 pp. 979 – 988

93 AIDS education in a therapeutic community — implementation and results among high-risk clients and staff. Robert P. Galea; Benjamin F. Lewis; Lori A. Baker. *Inter. J. Therap. Comm.* **9:1** 1988 pp. 9 – 16

94 AIDS funding — competing needs and the politics of priorities. Nancy Krieger. *Int. J. Health. Ser.* **18:4** 1988 pp. 521 – 542

95 AIDS in Africa — the social and policy impact. Norman Miller *[Ed.]*; Richard C. Rockwell *[Ed.]*. Lewiston: Edwin Mellin, 1988: xxxi, 326 p. *ISBN: 0889461872.* [Studies in African health and medicine. : No. 10]

96 AIDS north and south — diffusion patterns of a global epidemic and a research agenda for geographers. William B. Wood. *Prof. Geogr.* **40:3** 8:1988 pp. 266 – 279

97 AIDS — bridging the gap between information and practice. Stephen L. Buckingham *[Ed.]*. **Fam. Soc.**, *69:6*, 6:1988 pp. 324 – 399

98 AIDS — cultural analysis, cultural activism. Douglas Crimp *[Ed.]*; et al. Cambridge, Mass.: MIT, 1988: 272 p. (ill) *ISBN: 026203140x.*

99 AIDS — lessons from the gay comunity. Cindy Patton. *Feminist R.* **30** Autumn:1988 pp. 104 – 111

100 AIDS — principles, practices & politics. Inge B. Corless *[Ed.]*; Mary Pittman-Lindeman *[Ed.]*. Cambridge: Hemisphere Pub. Corp., 1988: xvii, 252 p. *ISBN: 0891167951. Includes bibliographies and index.*

101 AIDS — social representations, social practices. Peter Aggleton *[Ed.]*; Graham Hart *[Ed.]*; Peter Davies *[Ed.]*. Basingstoke: Falmer, 1988: 276 p. *ISBN: 1850004307. Conference proceedings; Includes index.*

102 AIDS — the burdens of history. Elizabeth Fee *[Ed.]*; Daniel M. Fox *[Ed.]*. Berkeley: California University Press, 1988: 362 p. *LofC: 88-040242; ISBN: 0-520-06395-3.*

103 Blaming others — prejudice, race and worldwide AIDS. Jon Tinler *[Ed.]*; Renée Sabatier; Tade Aina; Martin Foreman; Marty Radlett. London: Panos, 1988: 120 p.

F.3: Population evolution. Population policy [Évolution de la population. Politique démographique] — Morbidity [Morbidité]

104 The child's world of illness — the development of health and illness behaviour. Simon R. Wilkinson. Cambridge: Cambridge University Press, 1988: x, 288 p. (ill) *ISBN: 052132873x; LofC: 87-26825. Bibliography — p.270-284. Includes index.*

105 The developing geography of AIDS — a case study of the West Midlands. Sandra Winn. *Area* **20:1** 3:1988 pp. 61 – 67

106 Disability beyond stigma — social interaction, discrimination, and activism. Michelle Fine; Adrienne Asch. *J. Soc. Issues* **44:1** 1988 pp. 3 – 21

107 Disease as natural hazard. Nancy D. Lewis; Jonathan D. Mayer. *Prog. H. Geog.* **12:1** 3:1988 pp. 15 – 33

108 Family responsibility and caregiving in the qualitative analysis of the Alzheimer's disease experience. Jaber F. Gubrium. *J. Marriage Fam.* **50:1** 2:1988 pp. 197 – 207

109 For a sociology/anthropology of illness — towards a delineation of its disciplinary specificities. Dipankar Gupta. *Int. Sociol.* **3:4** 12:1988 pp. 403 – 413

110 Health inequalities in European countries. John Fox *[Ed.]*. Aldershot: Gower, 1988: 414 p. *ISBN: 0566054973. Includes bibliographies and index.*

111 Heterogeneity, intrafamily distribution and child health. Mark R. Rosenzweig; Kenneth I. Wolpin. *J. Hum. Res.* **XXIII:4** Fall:1988 pp. 437 – 461

112 HIV-AIDS — a social work perspective. M. Bamford *[Ed.]*; Roger Gaitley *[Ed.]*; Riva Miller *[Ed.]*. Birmingham: British Association of Social Workers, 1988: v,125 p. *ISBN: 0900102659. Bibliography — p.119-120.*

113 Les homosexuels et le sida — sociologie d'une épidémie *[In French]*; [Homosexuals and AIDS — sociology of an epidemic]. Michael Pollak. Paris: A.M. Métailié, 1988: 212 p. *ISBN: 286424053x. Notes bibliographiques.*

114 Image, myth and metaphor in the AIDS epidemic. V. Gallego. *Aust. Q.* **60:1** Autumn:1988 pp. 85 – 93

115 Implicaţii sociale ale sindromului de imunodeficieţă dobindită *[In Romanian]*; (Social implication of the acquired immune deficiency syndrome); (Implications sociales du syndrome d'immunodéficience acquise: *Title only in French*); (Социальные последствия синдрома приобретенного иммунодефицита: *Title only in Russian*). Lucian Huiban. *Viit. Soc.* **LXXXI** 7-8:1988 pp. 320 – 334

116 Jakarta kampung morbidity variations — some policy implications. Ralph Lenz. *Soc. Sci. Med.* **26:6** 1988 pp. 641 – 649

117 Living arrangements and women's health. Ofra Anson. *Soc. Sci. Med.* **26:2** 1988 pp. 201 – 208

118 Living with chronic illness — the experience of patients and their families. Robert Anderson *[Ed.]*; Michael Bury *[Ed.]*. London: Unwin Hyman, 1988: 319 p. *ISBN: 0043620663. Includes bibliography and index.*

119 Man and viruses. Hugues de Thé *[Contrib.]*; Oyewale Tomori *[Contrib.]*; Pierre Sonigo *[Contrib.]*; Ji-ming Zhu *[Contrib.]*; Frank Fenner *[Contrib.]*; Jonathan Mann *[Contrib.]*; A. Latif Ibrahim *[Contrib.]*; Aini Ideris *[Contrib.]*; Adama Diallo *[Contrib.]*; David Robinson *[Contrib.]* and others. Collection of 10 articles. **Impact Sci.**, *38:2*, 1988 pp. 105 – 201

F.3: Population evolution. Population policy *[Évolution de la population. Politique démographique] — Morbidity [Morbidité]*

120 Mental handicap in the community. Alan Leighton *[Ed.]*. New York: Woodland-Faulkner, 1988: xxi, 233 p. *ISBN: 0859414477*.

121 Moving the mentally ill into the community — the problems of acceptance and the effect of contact. Penelope Cousens; June Crawford. *Aust. J. Soc. Iss.* **23:3** 8:1988 pp. 196 – 207

122 The mystery of RSI. Sara Kiesler; Tom Finholt. *Am. Psychol.* **43:12** 12:1988 pp. 1004 – 1015

123 A national study of HIV infection, AIDS and community nursing staff in England. Senga Bond *[Ed.]*. Newcastle upon Tyne: University of Newcastle upon Tyne, School of Health Care Sciences, Health Care Research Unit, 1988: various pagings *ISBN: 1870399234. Bibliography — 3 leaves.* [Report.]

124 Psychology and AIDS. Thomas E. Backer *[Ed.]*; Walter F. Batchelor *[Ed.]*; James M. Jones *[Ed.]*; Vickie M. Mays *[Ed.]*; Stephen F. Morin *[Contrib.]*; Nancy Pelosi *[Contrib.]*; Charles R. Schuster *[Contrib.]*; James D. Watkins *[Contrib.]*; Thomas J. Coates *[Contrib.]*; Ron D. Stall *[Contrib.] and others. Collection of 13 articles.* **Am. Psychol.** , *43:11,* 11:1988 pp. 835 – 897

125 Psycho-social integration of the handicapped — a challenge to the society. Anima Sen. Delhi: Mittal, 1988: xiv, 366 p. *ISBN: 81 7099 060 2.*

126 El SIDA en méxico — los efectos sociales *[In Spanish]*; [AIDS in Mexico — the social effects]. Francisco Galván Díaz *[Ed.]*. México: U. Aut. Metropolitana, 1988: 399 p. *ISBN: 9684070179.*

127 Social aspects of AIDS. Peter Aggleton *[Ed.]*; Hilary Homans *[Ed.]*. London: Falmer, 1988: vii, 194 p. *ISBN: 1850003637. Includes bibliographies and index.*

128 Social policy for pollution-related diseases. Michael R. Reich *[Contrib.]*; Leslie I. Boden *[Contrib.]*; J. Raymond Miyares *[Contrib.]*; David Ozonoff *[Contrib.]*; Edward J. Burger *[Contrib.]*; Bruce Aronson *[Contrib.]*; Takehisa Awaji *[Contrib.]*; Tsuneo Tsukatani *[Contrib.]*; Stephen M. Soble *[Contrib.]*; Janis H. Brennan *[Contrib.] and others. Collection of 11 articles.* **Soc. Sci. Med.** , *27:10,* 1988 pp. 1011 – 1123

129 Sorting out the cuckoo's nest — a factorial survey approach to the study of popular conceptions of mental illness. Quint C. Thurman; Julie A. Lam; Peter H. Rossi. *Sociol. Q.* **29:4** Winter:1988 pp. 565 – 588

130 Spouses of discharged psychiatric patients — factors associated with their experience of burden. Samual Noh; William R. Avison. *J. Marriage Fam.* **50:2** 5:1988 pp. 377 – 389

131 Stress and coping in relation to health and disease. A.J.J.M. Vingerhoets *[Contrib.]*; F.H.G. Marcelissen *[Contrib.]*; James P. Henry *[Contrib.]*; L.J.P. van Doornen *[Contrib.]*; E.J.C. de Geus *[Contrib.]*; J.F. Orlebeke *[Contrib.]*; Susan Folkman *[Contrib.]*; Richard S. Lazarus; Zahava Solomon *[Contrib.]*; Hanoch Flum *[Contrib.] and others. Collection of 14 articles.* **Soc. Sci. Med.** , *26:3,* 1988 pp. 277 – 392

132 The travel needs and habits of non-elderly physically handicapped people. M. Doyle. Loughborough: Loughborough University of Technology, 1988: 2 vols. *ISBN: 0904947122.*

133 Vulnerability factors in the transition to university — self-reported mobility history and sex differences as factors in psychological disturbance. Shirley Fisher; Bruce Hood. *Br. J. Psy.* **:1-2-3-4** 2-5-8-11:1988 pp. 309 – 320

F.3: Population evolution. Population policy *[Évolution de la population. Politique démographique]* —

Mortality *[Mortalité]*

134 Child mortality in the Nigerian city — its levels and socioconomic differentials. Gbolahan A. Oni. *Soc. Sci. Med.* **27:6** 1988 pp. 607 – 614

135 Child survival in India. Thomas R. Leinbach. *Third Wor. P.* **10:3** 8:1988 pp. 255 – 270

136 Diet, mortality and life expectancy. A cross national analysis. Vijayendra Rao. *J. Pop. Ec.* **1:3** 1988 pp. 225 – 233

137 Differences in infant mortality among Texas Anglos, Hispanics, and Blacks. Eve Powell-Griner. *Soc. Sci. Q.* **69:2** 6:1988 pp. 452 – 467

138 The effect of legalization and public funding of abortion on neonatal mortality — an intervention analysis. Michael K. Miller; C. Shannon Stokes; Rex H. Warland. *Pop. Res. Pol. R.* **7:1** 1988 pp. 79 – 92

139 Évolution comparée de la mortalité en République tchèque et en France depuis 1950 *[In French]*; Mortality movements in the Czech Republic and France since 1950 *[Summary]*; *[Spanish summary]*. Jitka Rychtaříková; Jacques Vallin; France Meslé. *Population* **43:3** 5-6:1988 pp. 555 – 586

140 Increasing trends in some cancers in older Americans — fact or artifact? Devra Lee Davis; Abraham M. Lilienfeld; Alan M. Gittelsohn; Mary Ellen Scheckenbach. *Int. J. Health. Ser.* **18:1** 1988 pp. 35 – 68

141 Infant mortality and social work — legacy of success. Terri Combs-Orme. *Soc. Ser. R.* **62:1** 3:1988 pp. 83 – 102

142 Infant mortality in India — differentials and determinants. Aurudh K. Jain *[Ed.]*; Pravin Visaria *[Ed.]*. New Delhi: Sage, 1988: - *ISBN: 0803995458.*

143 Marginalidad y mortalidad infantil *[In Spanish]*; [Marginality and infant mortality]. René Jiménez Ornelas. *Rev. Mexicana Soc.* **L:4** 10-12:1988 pp. 171 – 185

144 Mesure et analyse de la mortalité, nouvelles approches *[In French]*; [Measuring and analysing mortality, new approaches]. Jacques Vallin *[Ed.]*; Stanislaus D'Souza *[Ed.]*; Alberto Palloni *[Ed.]*. [Paris]: Institut national d'études démographiques, 1988: vii, 458 p. (ill.) *ISBN: 2733201190. actes d'un séminaire international tenu à Sienne du 7 au 12 juillet 1987; Includes bibliographical references and indexes.* [Travaux et documents.]

145 Models of mystery — physician and patient perceptions of sudden infant death syndrome. Anne L. Wright. *Soc. Sci. Med.* **26:6** 1988 pp. 587 – 595

146 La mortalidad en México — niveles, tendencias y determinantes *[In Spanish]*; [Mortality in Mexico — levels, trends and determinants]. Mario Bronfman *[Ed.]*; José Gómez de León C. *[Ed.]*. Pedregal de Sta.Teresa [Mexico]: El Colegio de México, 1988: 468 p. *ISBN: 968120395x. Bibliography — p.462-464.*

147 Mortality and living conditions — relative mortality levels and their relation to the physical quality of life in urban populations. Jon Anson. *Soc. Sci. Med.* **27:9** 1988 pp. 901 – 910

148 On forecasting mortality. S. Jay Olshansky. *Milbank Q.* **66:3** 1988 pp. 482 – 530

149 Racial and residential differences in U.S. infant death rates — a temporal analysis. Nan E. Johnson; Khalida P. Zaki. *Rural Sociol.* **53:2** Summer:1988 pp. 207 – 219

F.3: Population evolution. Population policy *[Évolution de la population. Politique démographique]* — **Mortality** *[Mortalité]*

150 Shi no rinsho shakaigaku josetsu *[In Japanese]*; [An introduction to clinical sociology of death]. Hiroaki Taguchi. *Kumamoto Journal of Culture and Humanities, Kumamoto U. Japan* Vol.24. *1988.* pp. 15 – 31

151 Social class differences in infant mortality — the problem of competing hypothesis. Charlotte Humphrey; Jonathan Elford. *J. Biosoc. Sc.* **20:4** 10:1988 pp. 497 – 504

152 Społeczno-ekonomiczne czynniki zróznicowania umieralnosci w wielkich miastach w polsc *[In Polish]*; (Социально-экономические факторы дифференциации смертности в больших городах в Польше: *Title only in Russian*); (Socioeconomic factors of differentiation of mortality in large cities). Alicja Mazur. *Stud. Demogr.* **3(93)** 1988 pp. 57 – 76

153 Violent deaths among Mexican-, Puerto Rican- and Cuban-born migrants in the United States. Donna Shai; Ira Rosenwaike. *Soc. Sci. Med.* **26:2** 1988 pp. 269 – 276

F.4: Marriage. Family — *Mariage. Famille*

F.4.1: Marriage. Nuptiality — *Mariage. Nuptialité*
Sub-divisions: Marital separation *[Separation maritale]*

1 Behavioral antecedents of relationship stability and adjustment — a five-year longitudinal study. Erik E. Filsinger; Stephen J. Thoma. *J. Marriage Fam.* **50:3** 8:1988 pp. 785 – 795

2 Bereavement and widowhood. Robert O. Hansson *[Ed.]*; Margaret S. Stroebe *[Ed.]*; Wolfgang Stroebe *[Ed.]*; Mark L. Laudenslager *[Contrib.]*; Robert S. Weiss *[Contrib.]*; Colin Murray Parkes *[Contrib.]*; Paul C. Rosenblatt *[Contrib.]*; James R. Averill *[Contrib.]*; Elma P. Nunley *[Contrib.]*; Catherine M. Sanders *[Contrib.]* and others. Collection of 14 articles. *J. Soc. Issues*, *44:3*, 1988 pp.1-216.

3 Between two worlds — modern wives in a traditional setting. Stella R Quah. Singapore: Institute of Southeast Asian Studies, 1988: 66 p. *ISBN: 9971988852; LofC: 88942133.* Includes bibliographical references. [Field report series.]

4 Changing emotion norms in marriage — love and anger in U.S. women's magazines. Francesca M. Cancian; Steven L. Gordon. *Gender Soc.* **2:3** 9:1988 pp. 308 – 342

5 The changing relationship of marital status to reported happiness. Norval D. Glenn; Charles N. Weaver. *J. Marriage Fam.* **50:2** 5:1988 pp. 317 – 324

6 Class, kinship density, and conjugal role segregation. Malcolm D. Hill. *J. Marriage Fam.* **50:3** 8:1988 pp. 731 – 741

7 Commitment and the modern union — assessing the link between premarital cohabitation and subsequent marital stability. Neil G. Bennett; Ann Kilmas Blanc; David E. Bloom. *Am. Sociol. R.* **53:1** 2:1988 pp. 127 – 138

8 Courtship behavior of the remarried. Kathleen M. O'Flaherty; Laura Workman Eells. *J. Marriage Fam.* **50:2** 5:1988 pp. 499 – 506

9 Cultural change and attitude change — an assessment of postrevolutionary marriage and family attitudes in Iran. Abbas Tashakkori; Vaida D. Thompson. *Pop. Res. Pol. R.* **7:1** 1988 pp. 3 – 27

F.4.1: Marriage. Nuptiality *[Mariage. Nuptialité]*

10 La découverte du conjoint. II. Les scènes de rencontre dans l'espace social *[In French]*; Finding a spouse. II. The meeting place in social space *[Summary]*; *[Spanish summary]*. Michel Bozon; François Héran. *Population* **43:1** 1-2:1988 pp. 121 – 150

11 The demographic effect of mixed marriages; L'effet démographique des mariages mixtes *[French summary]*. Fjalar Finnäs. *Eur. J. Pop.* **4:2** 4:1988 pp. 145 – 156

12 Determinants and consequences of marital instability in northwest Ethiopia. Asmerom Kidane; Azbaha Haile. *E.Afr. Soc. Sci. Res. R.* **IV:1** January:1988 pp. 57 – 68

13 The determinants of depression in two-income marriages. Patricia M. Ulbrich. *J. Marriage Fam.* **50:1** 2:1988 pp. 121 – 131

14 Determinants of marital instability — a Cox-regression model. Evelyn L. Lehrer. *Appl. Econ.* **20:2** 2:1988 pp. 195 – 210

15 Domestic violence and control. Jan E. Stets. New York: Springer-Verlag, 1988: xii, 166 p. *ISBN: 0387966285. Bibliography — p.159-162.*

16 Effects of prior marriage children on adjustment in remarriage — a Canadian study; *[French summary]*; *[Spanish summary]*. Charles Hobart; David Brown. *J. Comp. Fam. Stud.* **XIX:3** Autumn:1988 pp. 381 – 396

17 L'exigence et le plaisir. Mariage et changement social en Grèce; Demand and pleasure. Marriage and social change in Greece *[Summary]*. Roberta Shapiro. *Peup. Médit.* **44:45** 7-12:1988 pp. 117 – 135

18 Family in India and North America — change and continuity among the Lingayat families; *[French summary]*; *[Spanish summary]*. Dan A. Chekki. *J. Comp. Fam. Stud.* **XIX:2** Summer:1988 pp. 329 – 343

19 Feminist perspectives on wife abuse. Kersti Yllö *[Ed.]*; Michele Bograd *[Ed.]*. Beverly Hills: Sage, 1988: 318 p. *ISBN: 0803930526.*

20 Gakusei no sei-yakuwari-kan to kekkon-kan *[In Japanese]*; [Students' conception of gender roles and alternative patterns of mate selection]. Hideki Watanabe. ***Bulletin of the University of Electro-Communications** Vol.1; No.1 - 1988.* pp. 215 – 241

21 Gay and lesbian domestic partnerships — expanding the definition of family. Linda M. Poverny; Wilbur A. Finch. *Fam. Soc.* **69:2** 2:1988 pp. 116 – 121

22 Gendai no joshi tandai-sei no kekkon-kan ni tsuite (josetsu) *[In Japanese]*; [Junior college girl student's view on marriage — an introduction]. Yoshibumi Ono. ***Bulletin of Shukugawa Gakuin Junior College** Vol.13. 1988.* pp. 47 – 59

23 Grounds for divorce. Gwynn Davis *[Ed.]*; Mervyn Murch *[Ed.]*. Oxford: Clarendon, 1988: x, 177 p. *ISBN: 019825220x. Bibliography — p.169-171.*

24 Inequality and intermarriage — a paradox of motive and constraint. Steven Rytina; Peter M. Blau; Terry Blum; Joseph Schwartz. *Soc. Forc.* **66:3** 3:1988 pp. 645 – 675

25 The influence of economic development on patterns of conjugal power and extended family residence in India; *[French summary]*; *[Spanish summary]*. George H. Conklin. *J. Comp. Fam. Stud.* **XIX:2** Summer:1988 pp. 187 – 205

26 Intermarriage and ethnic relations in Singapore. Sharon Mengchee Lee. *J. Marriage Fam.* **50:1** 2:1988 pp. 255 – 265

F.4.1: Marriage. Nuptiality *[Mariage. Nuptialité]*

27 Interspousal violence. Merlin B. Brinkerhoff; Eugen Lupri. *Can. J. Soc.* **13:4** Fall:1988 pp. 407 – 434
28 Intraethnic, interethnic, and interracial marriages among Asian Americans in California, 1980. Larry Hajime Shinagawa; Gin Yong Pang. *Berkeley J. Soc.* **XXXIII** 1988 pp. 95 – 114
29 Jane Austen — the matrix of matrimony. T. Vasudeva Reddy. Jaipur: Bohra, 1987: ii, 182 p.
30 Les jeunes immigrées et le mariage mixte *[In French]*; Young women immigrants and mixed marriage — salvation or perdition? *[Summary]*. Jocelyne Streiff-Fenart. *Peup. Médit.* **44:45** 7-12:1988 pp. 137 – 154
31 Knowledge of and attitude towards the legislation on age at marriage and their influence on ideal age at marriage. N. Audinarayana. *Indian J. Soc. W.* **XLIX:3** 7:1988 pp. 253 – 260
32 Leisure-activity patterns and marital satisfaction — a further test. Thomas B. Holman; Mary Jacquart. *J. Marriage Fam.* **50:1** 2:1988 pp. 69 – 77
33 Linguistic intermarriage in the United States. Gillian Stevens; Robert Schoen. *J. Marriage Fam.* **50:1** 2:1988 pp. 267 – 279
34 A macrosociological analysis of change in the marriage rate — Canadian women, 1921-25 to 1981-85. Frank Trovato. *J. Marriage Fam.* **50:2** 5:1988 pp. 507 – 521
35 Marital adjustment to adult diabetes — interpersonal congruence and spouse satisfaction. Mark Peyrot; James F. McMurry; Richard Hedges. *J. Marriage Fam.* **50:2** 5:1988 pp. 363 – 376
36 Marital happiness among mixed and homogeneous marriages in Israel. Leonard Weller; Yacov Rofé. *J. Marriage Fam.* **50:1** 2:1988 pp. 245 – 254
37 Marital roles and power — perceptions and reality in an urban setting. G.N. Ramu. *J. Comp. Fam. Stud.* **XIX:2** Summer:1988 pp. 207 – 228
38 Marital roles and power — perceptions and reality in the urban setting; *[French summary]*; *[Spanish summary]*. G.N. Ramu. *J. Comp. Fam. Stud.* **XIX:2** Summer:1988 pp. 207 – 227
39 Marital satisfaction and communication practices — comparisons among India and American couples; *[Spanish summary]*; *[French summary]*. Paul Yelsma; Kuriakose Athappily. *J. Comp. Fam. Stud.* **XIX:1** Spring:1988 pp. 37 – 54
40 Marital satisfaction in later life — the effects of nonmarital roles. Gary R. Lee. *J. Marriage Fam.* **50:3** 8:1988 pp. 775 – 783
41 Marital satisfaction in pregnancy — stability and change. Lonnie R. Snowden; Tracy L. Schott; Suzanne J. Awalt; Jo Gillis-Knox. *J. Marriage Fam.* **50:2** 5:1988 pp. 325 – 333
42 Marital strain, coping, and depression among Mexican-American women. William A. Vega; Bohdan Kolody; Ramon Valle. *J. Marriage Fam.* **50:2** 5:1988 pp. 391 – 403
43 Marriage among Muslims — preference and choice in Northern Pakistan. Hastings Donnan. Delhi: Hindustan Pub, 1988: xiv, 231 p.
44 Marriage in two cultures. Mary Stopes-Roe; Raymond Cochrane. *Br. J. Soc. P.* **27:2** 6:1988 pp. 159 – 169
45 Marriage, divorce and inheritance — the Uganda Council of Women's movement for legislative reform. Winifred Brown. Cambridge: African Studies Centre, 1988: vii,91 p. *ISBN: 0902993232.* [Cambridge African monographs.]

F.4.1: Marriage. Nuptiality [Mariage. Nuptialité]

46 Mate selection values — a comparison of Malaysian and United States students; [French summary]; [Spanish summary]. Antoinette Liston; Connie J. Salts. *J. Comp. Fam. Stud.* **XIX:3** Autumn:1988 pp. 361 – 370

47 Measurement issues in marital research — a review and critique of contemporary survey instruments. Ronald M. Sabatelli. *J. Marriage Fam.* **50:4** 11:1988 pp. 891 – 915

48 Modernity and the quality of marriage in Israel — the impact of socio-cultural factors on marital satisfaction; [French summary]; [Spanish summary]. Ruth Katz; Rosana Briger. *J. Comp. Fam. Stud.* **XIX:3** Autumn:1988 pp. 371 – 380

49 Nichteheliche Lebensgemeinschaften — eine Möglichkeit zur Veränderung des Geschlechterverhältnisses? [In German]; Cohabitation — an alternative to traditional gender relations? [Summary]. Sibylle Meyer; Eva Schulze. *Kölner Z. Soz. Soz. psy.* **40:2** 1988 pp. 337 – 356

50 Les nouveaux couples — nombre, caractéristiques et attitudes [In French]; Las nuevas uniones — número, características y actitudes [Spanish summary]; New couples — number, characteristics and attitudes [Summary]. Henri Leridon; Catherine Villeneuve-Gokalp. *Population* **43:2** 3-4:1988 pp. 331 – 374

51 Parental divorce and attitudes toward marriage and family life. Paul R. Amato. *J. Marriage Fam.* **50:2** 5:1988 pp. 453 – 461

52 Polyandry in India — demographic, economic, social, religious and psychological concomitants of plural marriages in women. Manis Kumar Raha. Delhi: Gian, 1987: xv, 440 p. *ISBN: 81 212 0105 5.*

53 Predictors of spousal support for the work commitments of husbands. Joe F. Pittman; Dennis K. Orthner. *J. Marriage Fam.* **50:2** 5:1988 pp. 335 – 348

54 Problèmes liés à l'étude de la nuptialité des migrants [In French]; Problems related to migrants' marriage rates [Summary]; [Spanish summary]. Michèle Tribalat. *Population* **43:2** 3-4:1988 pp. 375 – 390

55 Rates of courtship and first marriage in Thailand. Mark R. Montgomery; Paul P.L. Cheung; Donna B. Sulak. *Pop. Stud.* **XLII:3** 11:1988 pp. 375 – 388

56 The "real" marriage squeeze — mate selection, mortality, and the mating gradient. Jean E. Veevers. *Sociol. Pers.* **31:2** 4:1988 pp. 169 – 189

57 Sapporo Sendai Fukuoka sanshi ni okeru shokonnenrei to mikonritu no youinbunseki [In Japanese]; [Causal analysis of age at marriage and the unmarried in Sapporo, Sendai and Fukuoka]. Tohru Suzuki. *Kazoku Kenkyuu Nenpou* Vol.13. 1988. pp. 23 – 34

58 Serial marriage — a heuristic analysis of an emerging family form. Gene H. Brody; Eileen Neubaum; Rex Forehand. *Psychol .B.* **103:2** 3:1988 pp. 211 – 222

59 Spouses of discharged psychiatric patients — factors associated with their experience of burden. Samual Noh; William R. Avison. *J. Marriage Fam.* **50:2** 5:1988 pp. 377 – 389

60 A theory of marriage timing. Valerie Kincaide Oppenheimer. *A.J.S.* **94:3** 11:1988 pp. 563 – 591

61 Towards an organizational model of marital instability. Francis G. Castles; Elizabeth Seddon. *Aust. J. Soc. Iss.* **23:2** 5:1988 pp. 113 – 128

62 The widening gap in black and white marriage rates — the impact of population composition and differential marriage propensities. Robert Schoen; James R. Kluegel. *Am. Sociol. R.* **53:6** 12:1988 pp. 895 – 907

F.4.1: Marriage. Nuptiality *[Mariage. Nuptialité]*

63 With this ring — first marriage patterns, trends and prospects in Australia. Gordon A. Carmichael. Canberra: Dept. of Demography, Australian National University and Institute of Family Studies, 1988: xviii, 233 p. (ill) *ISBN: 0731503988. Includes bibliographical references (p.[221]-233).* [Australian family formation project.]

64 Work, love and marriage. Janet Mattinson. London: Duckworth, 1988: 232 p. *ISBN: 071562220x. Includes index.*

65 Young adults and parental divorce — exploring important issues. Teresa M. Cooney. *Human Relat.* **41:11** 1988 pp. 805 – 822

Marital separation *[Separation maritale]*

66 Après la séparation — diversité et stabilité des comportements *[In French]*; After separation — variety and stability in behaviour *[Summary]*; *[Spanish summary]*. Patrick Festy. *Population* **43:3** 5-6:1988 pp. 517 – 536

67 Divorce and kin ties — the importance of gender. Naomi Gerstel. *J. Marriage Fam.* **50:1** 2:1988 pp. 209 – 219

68 The divorce referendum in the Republic of Ireland — resisting the tide. William Duncan. *Int. J. Law Fam.* **2:1** 4:1988 pp. 62 – 75

69 Family "divorce heritage" and its intergenerational transmission — towards a system-level perspective. William R. Catton. *Sociol. Pers.* **31:4** 10:1988 pp. 398 – 419

70 The impact of first-birth timing on divorce — new evidence from a longitudinal analysis based on the central population register of Norway; L'effet de la première naissance sur le divorce — nouveaux résultats d'une analyse longitudinale basée sur le registre central de population de Norvège *[French summary]*. Øystein Kravdal. *Eur. J. Pop.* **4:3** 4:1988 pp. 247 – 269

71 The impact of parental divorce on children's educational attainment, marital timing, and likelihood of divorce. Verna M. Keith; Barbara Finlay. *J. Marriage Fam.* **50:3** 8:1988 pp. 797 – 809

72 Impasses of divorce — the dynamics and resolution of family conflict. Janet R. Johnston; Linda E. G. Campbell *[Ed.]*. New York: Free Press, 1988: 270 p. *ISBN: 0029166217. Bibliography.*

73 Outcomes of marital separation — a longitudinal test of predictors. Leslie A. Morgan. *J. Marriage Fam.* **50:2** 5:1988 pp. 493 – 498

74 Rikon no Ningen-gaku — case study *[In Japanese]*; [The study of humans in divorce — case study]. Kenji Tamura; Makie Tamura. Tokyo: System 5, 1988: 374 p.

75 Sons, daughters and the risk of marital disruption. S. Philip Morgan; Diane N. Lye; Gretchen A. Condran. *A.J.S.* **94:1** 7:1988 pp. 110 – 129

F.4.2: Family — *Famille*

Sub-divisions: Domestic violence *[Violence familiale]*; Family disintegration *[Désintégration familiale]*; Family relations *[Relations familiales]*; Method and theory *[Méthode et théorie]*

1 The abolitionists — the family and marriage under attack. Ronald Fletcher. London: Routledge, 1988: 220 p. *ISBN: 0415008557. Includes bibliography and index.*

2 Advantages of breastfeeding according to Turkish mothers living in Istanbul and Stockholm. Tahire Koctürk. *Soc. Sci. Med.* **27:4** 1988 pp. 405 – 410

3 Children, parents and the state. Andrew Bainham. London: Sweet & Maxwell, 1988: xix, 237 p. *ISBN: 0421363207. Includes index.* [Modern legal studies.]

4 Le corps paradoxal — regards de femmes sur la maternité *[In French]*; [The paradoxical body — women's views on motherhood]. Anne Quéniart. Montréal: Éditions Saint-Martin, 1988: 249 p. *ISBN: 2890351432. Bibliography — p..213-223.*

5 Cross-class families. Håkon Leiulfsrud; Alison E. Woodward. *Acta Sociol.* **31:2** 1988 pp. 175 – 180

6 Cultural change and attitude change — an assessment of postrevolutionary marriage and family attitudes in Iran. Abbas Tashakkori; Vaida D. Thompson. *Pop. Res. Pol. R.* **7:1** 1988 pp. 3 – 27

7 Discourses in Dutch child welfare inquiries. C.H.C.J. van Nijnatten. *Br. J. Crimin.* **28:4** Autumn:1988 pp. 494 – 512

8 Does wanting to become pregnant with a first child affect subsequent maternal behaviors and infant birth weight? William Marsiglio; Frank L. Mott. *J. Marriage Fam.* **50:4** 11:1988 pp. 1023 – 1036

9 Employment and economic problems. Catherine S. Chilman *[Ed.]*; Fred M. Cox *[Ed.]*; Elam W. Nunnally *[Ed.]*. Newbury Park: Sage, 1988: 269 p. *ISBN: 080392707x; LofC: 88-6539. Bibliography — p.237-254. Includes index.* [Families in trouble series. : Vol. 1]

10 The evolution of modern family law in Japan. Fujiko Isono. *Int. J. Law Fam.* **2:2** 1988 pp. 183 – 202

11 Exploitation in the domestic division of labour — an Australian case study. Ken Dempsey. *Aust. N.Z. J. Soc.* **24:3** 11:1988 pp. 420 – 436

12 Exploring adoptive family life — the collected adoption papers of H. David Kirk. B. Tansey *[Ed.]*. Port Angeles, WA: Ben-Simon, 1988: xiii,247 p. *ISBN: 0914539035.*

13 Las familias monoparentales — seminario hispano frances celebrado en Madrid diciembre 1987 *[In Spanish]*; [Single parents — Spanish-French seminar held in Madrid in December 1987]. Julio Iglesias de Ussel *[Ed.]*. Madrid: Instituto de la Mujer, 1988: 220 p. [[Serie debate].]

14 Families with a difference — varieties of surrogate parenthood. Michael Humphrey; Heather Humphrey *[Ed.]*. London: Routledge, 1988: p. cm *ISBN: 0415006899. Includes index; Bibliography.*

15 The family and hierarchy. Steven L. Nock. *J. Marriage Fam.* **50:4** 11:1988 pp. 957 – 966

16 Family background, postmaterialism and life style. Nan Dirk De Graaf; Paul M. De Graaf. *Neth. J. Soc. Sci.* **24: 1** 4: 1988 pp. 50 – 64

F.4.2: Family *[Famille]*

17 Family in India and North America. Dan A. Chekki *[Ed.]*; George H. Conklin *[Contrib.]*; G.N. Ramu *[Contrib.]*; Edwin D. Driver *[Contrib.]*; Aloo E. Driver *[Contrib.]*; Gura Bhargava *[Contrib.]*; A.A. Khatri *[Contrib.]*; Vanaja Dhruvarajan *[Contrib.]*; Bruce La Brack *[Contrib.]*; Josephine C. Naidoo *[Contrib.] and others.* Special issue — collection of 9 articles. **J. Comp. Fam. Stud.** , *XIX:2*, Summer:1988 pp. 171 – 343

18 Family law reform in Tanzania — a socio-legal report. Barthazar A. Rwezaura; Ulrike Wanitzek. *Int. J. Law Fam.* **2:1** 4:1988 pp. 1 – 26

19 Family sense of coherence and family adaptation. Aaron Antonovsky; Talma Sourani. *J. Marriage Fam.* **50:1** 2:1988 pp. 79 – 92

20 Family stories — events (temporarily) remembered. Peter Martin; Gunhild O. Hagestad; Patricia Diedrick. *J. Marriage Fam.* **50:2** 5:1988 pp. 533 – 541

21 The family system in remarriage — an exploratory study. Charles Hobart. *J. Marriage Fam.* **50:3** 8:1988 pp. 649 – 661

22 Городская и сельская семья *[In Russian]*; [The urban and the rural family]. D.I. Valentei *[Ed.]*. Moscow: Mysl', 1987: 278 p.

23 Household headship among unmarried mothers in six Latin American countries. de Susan Vos; Kerry Richter. *Int. J. Comp. Soc* **XXIX:3-4** 9-12:1988 pp. 214 – 229

24 Household, family, and social stratification — inheritance and labor strategies in a Catalan village (nineteenth and twentieth centuries). Dolors Comas d'Argemir. *J. Fam. Hist.* **13:1** 1988 pp. 143 – 163

25 Husbands' and wives' satisfaction with the division of labor. Mary Holland Benin; Joan Agostinelli. *J. Marriage Fam.* **50:2** 5:1988 pp. 349 – 361

26 Inter- und intragenerativer Wandel in Mirgrantenfamilien *[In German]*; Inter- and intragenerative change in migrant families *[Summary]*. Bernhard Nauck. *Soz. Welt.* **39:4** 1988 pp. 504 – 521

27 Kazoku-kouzou no henka to hoken - iryou *[In Japanese]*; [Changes in family structure and medical care]. Michitoshi Kumon. **Studies in Humanities and Social Sciences** *Vol.35. 1988.* pp. 73 – 86

28 "Kindaikazoku" gainen to nihonkindai no kazokuzou *[In Japanese]*; [The family in modern Japan through the study of family history]. Kazue Muta. ***Saga U. Kyouyou-Bu Kenkyuu Kiyou*** *Vol.20. 1988.* pp. 165 – 178

29 Kokusai-ka Shakai no Katei Kyouiku *[In Japanese]*; [Family and education in contemporary Japan]. Fumie Kumagai. Tokyo: Kobundo Shuppansha, 1988: 171 p.

30 Last chance children — growing up with older parents. Monica B. Morris. New York: Columbia University Press, 1988: xii, 170 p. *ISBN: 0231066945.* Bibliography — p167-170.

31 The law and practice relating to the adoption of children in Tanzania. Barthazar A. Rwezaura; Ulrike Wanitzek. *J. Afr. Law* **32:2** Autumn:1988 pp. 124 – 163

32 Lessons from the Rockefeller Foundation's experiments on the minority female single parent program. Robert F. Boruch; Michael Dennis; Kim Carter-Greer. *Eval. Rev.* **12:4** 8:1988 pp. 396 – 426

33 The long-term effects of family structure on gender-role attitudes. K. Jill Kiecolt; Alan C. Acock. *J. Marriage Fam.* **50:3** 8:1988 pp. 709 – 717

34 Managing childcare and work responsibilities. Julia Evetts. *Sociol. Rev.* **36:3** 8:1988 pp. 503 – 531

F.4.2: Family [Famille]

35 The masculine side of planned parenthood — an exploratory analysis. Akin Adebayo. *J. Comp. Fam. Stud.* **XIX:1** Spring:1988 pp. 55 – 68

36 Mother, madonna, whore — the idealization and denigration of motherhood. Estela V. Welldon. London: Free Association Books, 1988: 216 p. *ISBN: 1853430390. Includes bibliography and index.*

37 Mothers of misery — child abandonment in Russia. David L. Ransel. Princeton: Princeton University Press, 1988: 330 p. *ISBN: 069105522x; LofC: 88-009726. Bibliography — p.309-324.*

38 Mothers without custody. Geoffrey L. Greif; Mary S. Pabst *[Ed.].* Lexington: Lexington Books, 1988: 292 p. *ISBN: 0669130249; LofC: 86-045006. Bibliography.*

39 New mothers at work — employment and childcare. Julia Brannen; Peter Moss *[Ed.].* London: Unwin, 1988: vi, 200 p. *ISBN: 0046120483. Bibliography — p195-196. Includes index.*

40 "Off school sick" — mothers' accounts of school sickness absence. Alan Prout. *Sociol. Rev.* **36:4** 11:1988 pp. 765 – 789

41 Parenting styles and substance use during childhood and adolescence. Robert H. Coombs; John Landsverk. *J. Marriage Fam.* **50:2** 5:1988 pp. 473 – 482

42 Pets, families, and the life course. Alexa Albert; Kris Bulcroft. *J. Marriage Fam.* **50:2** 5:1988 pp. 543 – 552

43 The politics of breastfeeding. Gabrielle Palmer. : Pandora, 1988: xii, 309 p. *ISBN: 0863582206.*

44 Predicting first marriage and first birth patterns in Canada — an application of Coale-McNeil model. K. Vaninadha Rao; K.S. Murty. *Proc. Am. Stat. Ass.* pp. 121 – 126

45 Quality of family life, social support, and stress. Joe F. Pittman; Sally A. Lloyd. *J. Marriage Fam.* **50:1** 2:1988 pp. 53 – 67

46 Relationship between family structure and reactions to frustration of school-going adolescents. Pares Chandra Biswas. *Indian J. Soc. W.* **XLIX:4** 10:1988 pp. 359 – 366

47 Religious ideology and interpersonal relationships within the family; *[French summary]; [Spanish summary].* Vanaja Dhruvarajan. *J. Comp. Fam. Stud.* **XIX:2** Summer:1988 pp. 273 – 285

48 Research on step-families. Marilyn Ihinger-Tallman. *Ann. R. Soc.* **14** 1988 pp. 25 – 48

49 "Secrecy" — what can artificial reproduction learn from adoption? Erica Haimes. *Int. J. Law Fam.* **2:1** 4:1988 pp. 46 – 61

50 The shaking of the foundations — family and society. Ronald Fletcher. London: Routledge, 1988: xiv, 287 p. *ISBN: 0710215169. Bibliography — p.276-282. Includes index.*

51 Shift work and child care among young dual-earner American parents. Harriet B. Presser. *J. Marriage Fam.* **50:1** 2:1988 pp. 133 – 148

52 Single parent families — consequences for single parents. Shalini Bharat. *Indian J. Soc. W.* **XLIX:3** 7:1988 pp. 227 – 237

53 The single parent family and the child's mental health. Irma Moilanen; Paula Rantakallio. *Soc. Sci. Med.* **27:2** 1988 pp. 181 – 186

54 Social support, locus of control, and parenting in three low-income groups of mothers — black teenagers, black adults, and white adults. Joseph H. Stevens. *Child. Devel.* **59:3** 6:1988 pp. 635 – 642

F.4.2: Family *[Famille]*

55 Soren ni okeru kazoku hendou *[In Japanese]*; [Family change in the USSR]. Kenji Murai. **Annals of the Japanese Association for Soviet and East European Studies** Vol.X VI. *1988.* pp. 77 – 83

56 State and family in Singapore — restructuring a developing society. Janet W. Salaff. Ithaca, N.Y.: Cornell University Press, 1988: xv, 301 p. (ill) *ISBN: 0801421403; LofC: 87-47962. Includes index.* [Anthropology of contemporary issues.]

57 Surrogate motherhood. Martha A. Field. Cambridge, Mass.: Harvard University Press, 1988: 215 p. *ISBN: 0674857488; LofC: 88-017459. Bibliography.*

58 Teenage fathers. Bryan E. Robinson. Lexington, Mass.: D. C. Heath, 1988: xvi, 173 p. *ISBN: 0669145866; LofC: lc86-045896. Bibliography — p.160-166.*

59 The transmission of religious beliefs and practices from parents to firstborn early adolescent sons. Cynthia A. Clark; Everett L. Worthington; Donald B. Danser. **J. Marriage Fam. 50:2** 5:1988 pp. 463 – 472

60 Trois modes d'organisation domestique selon deux normes familiales font six types de famille *[In French]*; De tres modos de organización doméstica y dos formas de organización familiar resultan seis tipos de familia *[Spanish summary]*; Three modes of domestic organisation multiplied by two family norms equals six family types *[Summary]*. Georges Menahem. **Population 43:6** 11-12:1988 pp. 1005 – 1034

61 Unemployment, income and the family — an action research approach. Janice McGhee; David Fryer. **Publ. Adm. D. 4:4** 12:1988 pp. 237 – 252

62 Variant family forms. Catherine S. Chilman *[Ed.]*; Elam W. Nunnally *[Ed.]*; Fred M. Cox *[Ed.]*. Newbury Park: Sage, 1988: 336 p. *ISBN: 0803927096; LofC: 88-6539. Bibliography — p.290-319. Includes index.* [Families in trouble series. : Vol. 5]

63 Die Verteilung von Aufgaben und Pflichten im ehelichen Haushalt *[In German]*; The division of labour in a family household *[Summary]*. Victor Thiessen; Harald Rohlinger. **Kölner Z. Soz. Soz. psy. 40:4** 1988 pp. 640 – 658

64 Women as single parents — confronting institutional barriers in the courts, the workplace and the housing market. Elizabeth A. Mulroy *[Ed.]*. Dover, Mass.: Auburn House, 1988: 311 p. *BNB: 88011920.*

65 Work role characteristics, family structure demands, and work/family conflict. Patricia Voydanoff. **J. Marriage Fam. 50:3** 8:1988 pp. 749 – 761

66 Work/ family policies, the changing role of fathers and the presumption of shared responsibility for parenting. Graeme Russell; Deidre James; Jodie Watson. **Aust. J. Soc. Iss. 23:4** 11:1988 pp. 249 – 267

Domestic violence *[Violence familiale]*

67 Confronting child abuse — research for effective program design. Deborah Daro. New York: Free Press, 1988: 356 p. *ISBN: 0029069319; LofC: 87-027169. Bibliography.*

68 Coping with family violence — research and policy perspectives. Gerald T. Hotaling *[Ed.]*; et al. Newbury Park, Calif.: Sage, 1988: 323 p. *ISBN: 0803927223; LofC: 88-001874. Conference papers; Bibliography.*

69 Family abuse and its consequences — new directions in research. Gerald T. Hotaling *[Ed.]*. Newbury Park, CA: Sage Publications, 1988: 318 p. *ISBN: 0803927207.*

F.4.2: Family *[Famille]* — *Domestic violence [Violence familiale]*

70 Family secrets — child sexual abuse. Mary McIntosh *[Contrib.]*; Mary MacLeod *[Contrib.]*; Esther Saraga *[Contrib.]*; Linda Gordon *[Contrib.]*; Liz Kelly *[Contrib.]*; Jenny Kitzinger *[Contrib.]*; Ann Scott *[Contrib.]*; Mica Nava *[Contrib.]*; Elizabeth Woodcraft *[Contrib.]*; Gina Betcher *[Contrib.] and others*. Collection of 15 articles. **Feminist R.** , *28*, Spring:1988 pp. 6 – 17

71 Family violence. Lloyd E. Ohlin *[Ed.]*; Michael H Tonry *[Ed.]*. Chicago: University of Chicago Press, 1988: 595 p. *ISBN: 0226808068*. [Crime and justice. : Vol. .11]

72 Handbook of family violence. Vincent B. Van Hasselt *[Ed.]*. New York: Plenum, 1988: xviii, 500 p. *ISBN: 030642648x; LofC: 87-7204*. Includes bibliographies and index.

73 Physical punishment of children — Sweden and the U.S.A. Warren W. DeLey. *J. Comp. Fam. Stud.* **XIX:3** Autumn:1988 pp. 419 – 432

74 Violence and pregnancy — are pregnant women at greater risk of abuse? Richard J. Gelles. *J. Marriage Fam.* **50:3** 8:1988 pp. 841 – 847

75 The violent family — victimization of women, children and elders. Nancy Hutchings *[Ed.]*. New York: Human Sciences Press, 1988: 201 p. *ISBN: 0898853834*.

Family disintegration *[Désintégration familiale]*

76 Continuous parenting and the clean break — the aftermath of marriage breakdown. Margaret Harrison. *Aust. J. Soc. Iss.* **23:3** 8:1988 pp. 208 – 218

77 Divorce mediation and the legal process. Robert Dingwall *[Ed.]*; John Eekelaar *[Ed.]*. Oxford: Clarendon, 1988: 224 p. *ISBN: 0198255764; LofC: 87-28142*. Includes bibliography and index. [Oxford socio-legal studies.]

78 Effects of parental separation and reentry into union on the emotional well-being of children. Nazli Baydar. *J. Marriage Fam.* **50:4** 11:1988 pp. 967 – 981

79 The impact of divorce on children. David H. Demo; Alan C. Acock. *J. Marriage Fam.* **50:3** 8:1988 pp. 619 – 648

80 The interests of children after parental divorce — a long-term perspective. Mavis Maclean; M.E.J. Wadsworth. *Int. J. Law Fam.* **2:2** 1988 pp. 155 – 166

81 Intergenerational consequences of family disruption. Sara McLanahan; Larry Bumpass. *A.J.S.* **94:1** 7:1988 pp. 130 – 152

82 Kazoku-kino to rikon *[In Japanese]*; [Functions of the family and divorce]. Yasuhiko Yuzawa. Tokyo: Yasuda Life Welfare Foundation, 1988: 150 p.

83 The "problem of duty" — family desertion in the progressive era. Martha May. *Soc. Ser. R.* **62:1** 3:1988 pp. 40 – 60

84 Putting asunder — a history of divorce in western society. Roderick Phillips. Cambridge: Cambridge University Press, 1988: 672 p. *ISBN: 0521324343*. Bibliography — p.641-663.

Family relations *[Relations familiales]*

85 Activité féminine et structures familiales. Quelle dépendance? *[In French]*; Women's employment and family structure. What are the relationships? *[Summary]*; *[Spanish summary]*. Jacques Véron. *Population* **43:1** 1-2:1988 pp. 103 – 120

F.4.2: Family [Famille] — Family relations [Relations familiales]

86 Adolescents' and parents' conceptions of parental authority. Judith G. Smetana. *Child. Devel.* **59:2** 4:1988 pp. 321 – 335

87 L'affaiblissement de l'autorité paternelle *[In French]*; The weakening of paternel authority *[Summary]*. Françoise Hurstel. *Pensée* **261** 1-2: 1988 pp. 35 – 49

88 Attitudes toward women's familial roles — changes in the United States 1977-1985. Karen Oppenheim Mason. *Gender Soc.* **2:1** 3:1988 pp. 39 – 57

89 Child-mother attachment and the self in six-year-olds. Jude Cassidy. *Child. Devel.* **59:1** 2:1988 pp. 121 – 134

90 Children in de facto relationships. Siew-Ean Khoo. *Aust. J. Soc. Iss.* **23:1** 2:1988 pp. 38 – 49

91 Children's contact with absent parents. Judith A. Seltzer; Suzanne M. Bianchi. *J. Marriage Fam.* **50:3** 8:1988 pp. 663 – 677

92 Daughters who care — daughters caring for mothers at home. Jane Lewis; Barbara Meredith *[Ed.]*. London: Routledge, 1988: vi, 194 p. *ISBN: 0422619302. Bibliography — p.160-171.Includes index.*

93 Diagaku-sei no musume to chichioya no joucho kankei *[In Japanese]*; [Emotional relationship between college student daughters and their fathers]. Miyoko Nagatsu. *Aobag. Kiyo Vol.13. 1988.* pp. 59 – 72

94 Do mutual children cement bonds in stepfamilies? Lawrence H. Ganong; Marilyn Coleman. *J. Marriage Fam.* **50:3** 8:1988 pp. 687 – 698

95 Explaining intergenerational conflict when adult children and elderly parents live together. J. Jill Suitor; Karl Pillemer. *J. Marriage Fam.* **50:4** 11:1988 pp. 1037 – 1047

96 Family configuration, family interaction, and intellectual attainment. Prudence A. Widlak; Carolyn C. Perrucci. *J. Marriage Fam.* **50:1** 2:1988 pp. 33 – 44

97 Family divisions and inequality in the family. Paul Close *[Ed.]*. Basingstoke: Macmillan, 1988: 260 p. *ISBN: 0333436571.*

98 Family member adjustment and family dynamics in established single-parent and two-parent families. Robert G. Green; Patricia D. Crooks. *Soc. Ser. R.* **62:4** 12:1988 pp. 600 – 613

99 Family ties and aging. Ingrid Arnet Connidis. Scaborough,Ont.: Butterworths, 1988: 130 p. *ISBN: 0409811831. Bibliography.* [Perspectives on individual and population aging.]

100 Father-child relationships and the status of women — a cross-cultural study. Scott Coltrane. *A.J.S.* **93:5** 3:1988 pp. 1060 – 1095

101 Fatherhood today — men's changing role in the family. Phyllis Bronstein *[Ed.]*; Carolyn Pape Cowan *[Ed.]*. New York: Wiley, 1988: xix, 364 p. *ISBN: 0471836273.*

102 Homosexuality and the family. Frederick W. Bozett *[Ed.]*. New York: Harrington Park Press, 1988: 204 p. *ISBN: 0918393574.*

103 Just the two of us — parent-child relationships in single-parent homes. Barbara J. Risman; Kyung Park. *J. Marriage Fam.* **50:4** 11:1988 pp. 1049 – 1062

104 Kakudai kazoku ni okeru sedaikan kankei *[In Japanese]*; [Intergenerational relationship in extended-families in rural Japan]. Hiroko Sato. *Tokohagakuin U. Research Review Faculty of Education Vol.9. 1988.* pp. 1 – 16

F.4.2: Family *[Famille]* — *Family relations [Relations familiales]*

105 Kinship patterns and household composition — older unmarried Hungarian women, 1984; Relations de parenté et structure des ménages —les femmes hongroises très âgées et sans conjoint, en 1984 *[French summary]*. Douglas A. Wolf. *Eur. J. Pop.* **4:4** 7:1988 pp. 315 – 337

106 Maternal social networks and mother-infant interactions in full-term and very low birthweight, preterm infants. Cynthia L. Zarling; Barton J. Hirsch; Susan Landry. *Child. Devel.* **59:1** 2:1988 pp. 178 – 185

107 Nonmaternal care in the first year of life and the security of infant-parent attachment. Jay Belsky; Michael J. Rovine. *Child. Devel.* **59:1** 2:1988 pp. 157 – 167

108 Parental self-esteem and its relationship to child rearing practices, parent-adolescent interaction, and adolescent behavior. Stephen A. Small. *J. Marriage Fam.* **50:4** 11:1988 pp. 1063 – 1072

109 Patterns of adult-child associations in 18 cultures — an index of the "nuclear family"; *[French summary]*; *[Spanish summary]*. Wade C. Mackey. *J. Comp. Fam. Stud.* **XIX:1** Spring:1988 pp. 69 – 84

110 Patterns of functioning in families of remarried and first-married couples. Charles W. Peek; Nancy J. Bell; Terry Waldren; Gwendolyn T. Sorell. *J. Marriage Fam.* **50:3** 8:1988 pp. 699 – 708

111 Postdivorce reorganization of relationships between divorcing children and their parents. Colleen Leahy Johnson. *J. Marriage Fam.* **50:1** 2:1988 pp. 221 – 231

112 Relationships in remarried families. Charles Hobart. *Can. J. Soc.* **13:3** Summer:1988 pp. 261 – 282

113 Relationships with former in-laws after divorce — a research note. Anne-Marie Ambert. *J. Marriage Fam.* **50:3** 8:1988 pp. 679 – 686

114 Religious ideology and interpersonal relationships within the family. Vanaja Dhruvarajan. *J. Comp. Fam. Stud.* **XIX:2** Summer:1988 pp. 273 – 286

115 A right to know one's parentage? Katherine O'Donovan. *Int. J. Law Fam.* **2:1** 4:1988 pp. 27 – 45

116 Shared filial responsibility — the family as the primary caregiver. Sarah H. Matthews; Tena Tarler Rosner. *J. Marriage Fam.* **50:1** 2:1988 pp. 185 – 195

117 Sibling support and older widows' well-being. Shirley L. O'Bryant. *J. Marriage Fam.* **50:1** 2:1988 pp. 173 – 183

118 Social- emotional adaptation and infant-mother attachment in siblings — role of the mother in cross-sibling consistency. Mary J. Ward; Brian E. Vaughn; Martha D. Robb. *Child. Devel.* **59:3** 6:1988 pp. 643 – 651

119 Strangers in the house — the world of stepsiblings and half-siblings. William R. Beer. New Brunswick, N.J.: Transaction Books, 1988: 146 p. *ISBN: 0887382622. Includes index; Bibliography.*

120 Tanshin funin kazoku no kiki tekiou katie — "funin kikan" to "tsuma no kachikan" ni chakumoku shite *[In Japanese]*; [Understanding family stress and coping under job-induced separation (tanshin-funin)]. Takao Minami; Mitsuhiro Ura; Akihide Inaba. ***Philosophy*** *Vol.86. 1988.* pp. 199 – 227

121 The timing of parenthood and intergenerational relations. Audrey Vanden Heuvel. *J. Marriage Fam.* **50:2** 5:1988 pp. 483 – 491

122 Women's employment and family relations — a review. Glenna Spitze. *J. Marriage Fam.* **50:3** 8:1988 pp. 595 – 618

F.4.2: Family [Famille] —

Method and theory [Méthode et théorie]

123 An analytic simulation model of the family. Barry Edmonston; Ashok Mada Limra. *Proc. Am. Stat. Ass.* pp. 145 – 150

124 Causal modeling in family research. Deborah D. Godwin. *J. Marriage Fam.* **50**:4 11:1988 pp. 917 – 927

125 The changing sociological construct of the family. Patricia Wilson; Ray Pahl. *Sociol. Rev.* **36**:2 5:1988 pp. 233 – 266

126 Commitment to social fatherhood — predicting adolescent males' intentions to live with their child and partner. William Marsiglio. *J. Marriage Fam.* **50**:2 5:1988 pp. 427 – 441

127 Conceptualising the family. Jan Trost. *Int. Sociol.* **3**:3 9:1988 pp. 301 – 308

128 Current theorizing on the family — an appraisal. Jetse Sprey. *J. Marriage Fam.* **50**:4 11:1988 pp. 875 – 890

129 L'évolution des modèles familiaux dans les pays de l'Est européen et en URSS *[In French]*; [The development of family models in Eastern Europe and U.S.S.R.]. Basile Kerblay *[Ed.]*. Paris: Institut d'études slaves, 1988: 226 p. *ISBN: 2720402346.* [Cultures et sociétés de l'Est. : No. 9]

130 The family as project. Jaber F. Gubrium. *Sociol. Rev.* **36**:2 5:1988 pp. 273 – 296

131 Family assessment — a guide to methods and measures. Harold D. Grotevant; Cindy I. Carlson *[Ed.]*. New York: Guilford Press, 1988, c1989: 500 p. *ISBN: 0898627338. Includes indexes.*

132 Family matters — sociology and contemporary Canadian families. Karen L. Anderson. Toronto: Methuen, 1988: 266 p. *ISBN: 0458814601. Bibliography — p.257-260.*

133 The family photo assessment process (FPAP) — a method for validating cross-cultural comparisons of family social indentities; *[French summary]*; *[Spanish summary]*. Lynn Blinn. *J. Comp. Fam. Stud.* **XIX**:1 Spring:1988 pp. 17 – 35

134 Feminism, children, and the new families. Myra H. Strober *[Ed.]*; Saford M. Dornbuch *[Ed.]*. New York: The Guildford Press, 1988: 366 p. *ISBN: 0898620783.*

135 Gendai kazokuron ni okeru jakkan no kihon mondai *[In Japanese]*; [Some fundamental problems of modern family studies]. Hiromu Maeno. **Shakaigaku Ronsou, Nihon Daigaku** *Vol.102. 1988.* pp. 34 – 47

136 Justice norms and group dynamics — the case of the family. Jean M. Kellerhals; Josette Coenen-Huther; Marianne Modak. *Int. Sociol.* **3**:2 6:1988 pp. 111 – 128

137 Kazoku riron ni okeru gender to power *[In Japanese]*; [Gender and power in family theories]. Yoriko Meguru. **Shakaigaku Hyouron** *Vol.39; No.3 - 1988.* pp. 10 – 21

138 Kazoku system-ron no shakaigaku-teki kentou *[In Japanese]*; [Sociological study of family system]. Hideo Yagi. **Jinbun Ronshū** *Vol.24; No.1 - 1988.* pp. 1 – 19

139 Linear structural relationships (LISREL) in family research. Yoav Lavee. *J. Marriage Fam.* **50**:4 11:1988 pp. 937 – 948

140 Oyako doukyo no kazoku-hattatsu-ron-teki kousatsu *[In Japanese]*; [A family development approach to the Japanese three-generation family]. Kikuko Kato. *Japanese Sociological Review* *Vol.39; No.3 - 1988.* pp. 56 – 70

F.4.2: Family [Famille] — Method and theory [Méthode et théorie]

141 Panel analysis in family studies. David R. Johnson. *J. Marriage Fam.* **50:4** 11:1988 pp. 949 – 955
142 Recent directions in family research — India and North America. Dan A. Chekki. *J. Comp. Fam. Stud.* **XIX:2** Summer:1988 pp. 171 – 186
143 Reuben Hill and the state of family sociology; *[French summary]*; *[Spanish summary]*. Bert N. Adams. *J. Comp. Fam. Stud.* **XIX:3** Autumn:1988 pp. 345 – 359
144 Social learning and systems approaches to marriage and the family. Robert J McMahon *[Ed.]*; Ray DeV. Peters *[Ed.]*. New York: Brunner/Mazel, 1988: xiv, 325 p. *ISBN: 0876304773. Banff International Conferences on Behavior Modification. 17th. 1985; Includes bibliographies and index.*
145 The transition to parenthood — current theory and research. Gerald Y. Michaels *[Ed.]*; Wendy A. Goldberg *[Ed.]*. Cambridge: Cambridge University Press, 1988: 381 p. *ISBN: 0521354188. Includes index.* [Cambridge studies in social and emotional development.]
146 Two models for microsimulation of family life cycle and family structure. Salvatore Bertino; Antonella Pinnelli; Maurizio Vichi. *Genus* **XLIV:1-2** 1-6:1988 pp. 1 – 25
147 Value attributions and value transmission between parents and children. Les B. Whitbeck; Viktor Gecas. *J. Marriage Fam.* **50:3** 8:1988 pp. 829 – 840
148 Wie normal ist die Normalfamilie? — empirische Untersuchungen *[In German]*; [How normal is the normal family? — empirical studies]. M. Cierpka *[Ed.]*; E. Nordmann *[Ed.]*. Berlin: Springer-Verlag, 1988: 186 p. *ISBN: 3540193413.*

F.5: Gender — *Sexe*

Sub-divisions: Feminism *[Féminisme]*; Gender differentiation *[Différenciation sexuelle]*; Gender roles *[Rôles de sexe]*; Men *[Hommes]*; Women *[Femmes]*

Feminism *[Féminisme]*

1 Anarchism, existentialism, feminism, and ambiguity. L. Susan Brown. *Our Gener.* **19:2** Spring-Summer:1988 pp. 1 – 18
2 Becoming feminine — the politics of popular culture. Leslie G. Roman *[Ed.]*; Elizabeth Ellsworth *[Ed.]*; Linda K. Christian-Smith *[Ed.]*. London: Falmer Press, 1988: 213 p. *ISBN: 1850003289.*
3 Crossing boundaries — feminisms and the critique of knowledge. Barbara Caine *[Ed.]*; E. A. Grosz *[Ed.]*; Marie de Lepervanche *[Ed.]*. Sydney: Unwin Hyman, 1988: 211 p. *ISBN: 0043050042.*
4 Cultural feminism versus post-structuralism — the identity crisis in feminist theory. Linda Alcoff. *Signs* **13:3** Spring:1988 pp. 405 – 436
5 Defining feminism — a comparative historical approach. Karen Offen. *Signs* **14:1** Autumn:1988 pp. 119 – 157
6 Domestic labour and the feminist movement in Italy since the 1970s. Mariarosa Dalla Costa. *Int. Sociol.* **3:1** 3:1988 pp. 23 – 34
7 The failure of feminism. Nicholas Davidson. New York: Prometheus, 1988: 392 p. *BNB: 87007190; ISBN: 0879754084.*

F.5: Gender [Sexe] — Feminism [Féminisme]

8 Feminism and criminology in Britain. Loraine Gelsthorpe; Allison Morris. *Br. J. Crimin.* **28:2** Spring:1988 pp. 93 – 110

9 Feminism to kenryoku kouzou *[In Japanese]*; [Feminism and power effects]. Yumiko Ehara. Tokyo: Keisou-Shoubou, 1988: 224 p.

10 Feminist consciousness — European/American theory, Jamaican stories. Evelyn O'Callaghan. *J. Car. Stud.* **6:2** Spring:1988 pp. 143 – 162

11 Feminist organizing for change — the contemporary women's movement in Canada. Nancy Adamson; Margaret McPhail *[Ed.]*; Linda Briskin *[Ed.]*. Toronto: Oxford University Press, 1988: iv, 332 p. *ISBN: 0195406583. Includes bibliography — p.307-328 ; and index.*

12 Feminist political organisation in Iceland — some reflections on the experience of Kwenna Frambothid. Lena Dominelli; Gudrun Jonsdottir. *Feminist R.* **30** Autumn:1988 pp. 36 – 60

13 Feminist politics in Japan. Vera Mackie. *New Left R.* **:167** 1/2:1988 pp. 53 – 76

14 Feminist research — in search of a new paradigm? Aino Saarinen. *Acta Sociol.* **31:1** 1988 pp. 35 – 51

15 Feminist rhetoric — discources on the male monopoly of thought. Mary E. Hawkesworth. *Polit. Theory* **16:3** 8:1988 pp. 444 – 467

16 Feminist scholarship, relational and instrumental control, and a power-control theory of gender and delinquency. John Hagan; John Simpson; A.R. Gillis. *Br. J. Soc.* **XXXIX:3** 9:1988 pp. 301 – 336

17 Home economics and feminism — the Hestian synthesis. Patricia J. Thompson. Charlottetown, P.E.I.: Home Economic Publishing Collective, 1988: 111 p. *ISBN: 0919013104. Based on the proceedings of a workshop held prior to the Canadian Home Economics Association conference, 1986, Charlotteville, P.E.I.; Bibliography — p.103-104.*

18 Jongerenprotest en tweede feministische golf — een sociologische verglijking *[In Dutch]*; Youth revolt and second wave feminism — a sociological comparison *[Summary]*. L.B. van Snippenburg. *Sociol. Gids* **XXXV:2** 3-4:1988 pp. 102 – 115

19 Multiple jeopardy, multiple consciousness — the context of a black feminist ideology. Deborah K. King. *Signs* **14:1** Autumn:1988 pp. 42 – 72

20 The new feminist scholarship — some precursors and polemics. Mirra Komarovsky. *J. Marriage Fam.* **50:3** 8:1988 pp. 585 – 593

21 La paysanne égyptienne et le «féminisme traditionnel» *[In French]*; Feminist debate and "traditional feminism" — the changing role and status of peasant women in Egypt *[Summary]*. Mona Abaza. *Peup. Médit.* **41-42** 10:1987-3:1988 pp. 135 – 151

22 The political context of feminist attitudes in Israel. Dafna N. Izraeli; Ephraim Tabory. *Gender Soc.* **2:4** 12:1988 pp. 463 – 481

23 Transcending bureaucracy — feminist politics at a shelter for battered women. Noelie Maria Rodriguez. *Gender Soc.* **2:2** 6:1988 pp. 214 – 227

24 Two types of feminism. Gordon Graham. *Am. Phil. Q.* **25:4** 10:1988 pp. 303 – 312

25 Under western eyes — feminist scholarship and colonial discourses. Chandra Mohanty. *Feminist R.* **30** Autumn:1988 pp. 61 – 88

26 Women and the illness role — rethinking feminist theory; *[French summary]*. Marion Pirie. *Can. R. Soc. A.* **25:4** 11:1988 pp. 628 – 648

F.5: Gender *[Sexe]* —

Gender differentiation *[Différenciation sexuelle]*

27 Accommodating inequality — gender and housing. Sophie Watson. Sydney: Allen & Unwin, 1988: x, 157 p. *ISBN: 0043202292. Bibliography.*

28 Biyou no shakaigaku josetsu — biyou-koui no seisa *[In Japanese]*; [Sociology of cosmetics (1) — sex difference]. Nobuko Iijima. *St.And. Soc. Rev.* Vol.21; No.2 - 1988. pp. 151 – 174

29 Bringing the men back in — sex differentiation and the devaluation of women's work. Barbara F. Reskin. *Gender Soc.* **2:1** 3:1988 pp. 58 – 81

30 Class, gender and the relations of distribution. Joan Acker. *Signs* **13:3** Spring:1988 pp. 473 – 497

31 Disaggregating the sexual division of labour — a transatlantic case study. Joy Parr. *Comp. Stud. S.* **30:3** 1988 pp. 511 – 533

32 Discriminación de la mujer en el mercado de trabajo español — una aproximación empírica a la discriminación salarial *[In Spanish]*; [Sex discrimination against women in the Spanish labour market — an empirical outline of wage discrimination]. María Amalia Peinado López. Madrid: Centro de Publicaciones, Ministerio de Trabajo y Seguridad Social, 1988: 198 p. (ill.) *ISBN: 8474344816. "RET. 88-1.293."; Bibliography — p.. [195]-198.* [Colección Informes.]

33 Equality and sex discrimination law. Katherine O'Donovan; Erika Szyszczak *[Ed.]*. Oxford: Basil Blackwell, 1988: 254 p. *ISBN: 0631147713. Includes index.*

34 Gender in Caribbean development — papers presented at the inaugural seminar of the University of the West Indies, Women and Development Studies Project. Patricia Mohammed *[Ed.]*; Catherine Shepherd *[Ed.]*; Lucille Mathurin Mair *[Ed.]*. Mona, Jamaica: The University of the West Indies Women and Development Studies Project, 1988: xvii,372 p. (ill.) *ISBN: 9768057009.*

35 Gender politics and social theory. Sylvia Walby. *Sociology* **22:2** 5:1988 pp. 215 – 232

36 Indicators of gender equality for American states and regions. David B. Sugarman; Murray A. Straus. *Soc. Ind.* **20:3** 6:1988 pp. 229 – 270

37 Male bias in the development process. Diane Elson (ed). Manchester: Univ. of Manchester Press, 1988 *Includes index.*

38 The politics of gender in exile. Diana Kay. *Sociology* **22:1** 2:1988 pp. 1 – 21

39 The politics of the gender gap — the social construction of political influence. Carol M. Mueller *[Ed.]*. Newbury Park: Sage, 1988: 316 p. *ISBN: 0803927320.* [Sage yearbooks in women's policy studies. : Vol. 12]

40 Sex-related wage differentials and women's interrupted labor careers — the chicken or the egg. Reuben Gronau. *J. Labor Ec.* **6:3** 7:1988 pp. 277 – 301

41 The social-institutional bases of gender stratification — Japan as an illustrative case. Mary C. Brinton. *A.J.S.* **94:2** 9:1988 pp. 300 – 334

42 A study of how female and male managers in some public service organizations in Nigeria perceive work-related variables — some implications; *[Arabic summary]*; Comment les dirigeants femmes et dirigeants hommes dans certains organes gouvernementaux du Nigeria perçoivent les variables relatives au travail — quelques implications *[French summary]*; Un estudio de como la mujer y el hombre gerentes en algunas organizaciones de

F.5: Gender *[Sexe]* — *Gender differentiation [Différenciation sexuelle]*

servicios publicos de Nigeria registran variables relativas al trabajo — algunas implicaciones *[Spanish summary]*. G.U. Imanyi. *Publ. Enter.* **8:4** 12:1988 pp. 355 – 363

43 Ursachen der Unterrepräsentanz von Frauen in universitären Spitzenpositionen *[In German]*; Underrepresentation of women in higher university positions *[Summary]*. Mechthild Brothun. *Kölner Z. Soz. Soz. psy.* **40:2** 1988 pp. 316 – 336

Gender roles *[Rôles de sexe]*

44 The etiology of intolerance of homosexual politics. James L. Gibson; Kent L. Tedin. *Soc. Sci. Q.* **69:3** 9:1988 pp. 587 – 604

45 Gender identity and sex role conflict among working women and men. Leonard H. Chusmir; Christine S. Koberg. *J. Psychol.* **122:6** 11: 1988 pp. 567 – 575

46 Husband-wife role variation as a factor in the social space definition of farmers. John Everitt. *Soc. Sci. Q.* **69:1** 3:1988 pp. 155 – 176

47 The impact of occupation, performance and sex on sex role stereotyping. Sandra J. Hartman; Rodger W. Griffeth; Lynn Miller; Angelo Kinicki. *J. Soc. Psychol.* pp. 451 – 463

48 Sex ratios and women's roles — a cross-national analysis. Scott J. South; Katherine Trent. *A.J.S.* **93:5** 3:1988 pp. 1096 – 1115

49 Sex ratios, economic power, and women's roles — a theoretical extension and empirical test. Scott J. South. *J. Marriage Fam.* **50:1** 2:1988 pp. 19 – 31

50 Sex-role attitude change and reporting of rape victimization, 1973-1985. James D. Orcutt; Rebecca Faison. *Sociol. Q.* **29:4** Winter:1988 pp. 589 – 604

51 Social location and gender-role attitudes — a comparison of black and white woman. Karen Dugger. *Gender Soc.* **2:4** 12:1988 pp. 425 – 448

52 Socialisation, education and women — explorations in gender identity. Karuna Chanana *[Ed.]*. London: Sangam, 1988: 320 p. *ISBN: 0861318293. Conference proceedings; Includes bibliographies and index.* [Perspectives in Indian development.]

53 Wandering in the wilderness — the search for women role models. Berenice Fisher. *Signs* **13:2** Winter:1988 pp. 211 – 233

54 Working parents — transformations in gender roles and public policies in Sweden. Phyllis Moen. London: Adamantine, 1988: 181 p. (ill) *ISBN: 0744900123. Bibliography — p.159-175.* [Adamantine studies on the individual in society.]

Men *[Hommes]*

55 The men from the boys — rites of passage in male America. Ray Raphael. Lincoln: Nebraska U.P., 1988: xvii, 228 p. *ISBN: 0803238886.*

56 Men only — an investigation into men's organisations. Barbara Rogers. London: Pandora, 1988: 283 p. *ISBN: 0863580831.*

Women *[Femmes]*

57 Becoming feminine — the politics of popular culture. Leslie G. Roman *[Ed.]*; Elizabeth Ellsworth *[Ed.]*; Linda K. Christian-Smith *[Ed.]*. London: Falmer Press, 1988: 213 p. *ISBN: 1850003289.*

F.5: Gender *[Sexe]* — *Women [Femmes]*

58 Canadian women — a history. Alison Prentice *[Ed.]*. Toronto: Harcourt Brace Jovanovich, 1988: 496 p. *ISBN: 0774731125. Bibliography.*

59 Catholic women and the creation of a new social reality. Ruth A. Wallace. *Gender Soc.* **2:1** 3:1988 pp. 24 – 38

60 The changing lives of American women. Steven D. McLaughlin *[Ed.]*. Chapel Hill: North Carolina University Press, 1988: 250 p. *LofC: 88-009699; ISBN: 0-8078-1813-5. Bibliography.*

61 Changing patterns — women in Canada. Sandra Burt *[Ed.]*; Lorraine Code *[Ed.]*; Lindsay Dorney *[Ed.]*. Toronto: McClelland and Stewart, 1988: 354 p. *ISBN: 0771028539.*

62 Conceptualisations of women within Australian egalitarian thought. Susan Baggett Barham. *Comp. Stud. S.* **30:3** 1988 pp. 483 – 510

63 Enterprising women — home, work, and minority cultures in Britain. Sallie Westwood *[Ed.]*; Parminder Bhachu *[Ed.]*. London: Routledge, 1988: x, 210 p. *ISBN: 0415006864. Includes index; Bibliographies.*

64 Equality and sex discrimination law. Katherine O'Donovan; Erika Szyszczak *[Ed.]*. Oxford: Basil Blackwell, 1988: 254 p. *ISBN: 0631147713. Includes index.*

65 European Community action on behalf of women — the limits of legislation. Sonia Mazey. *J. Com. Mkt. S.* **XXVII: 1** 9: 1988 pp. 63 – 84

66 The female body and the law. Zillah R. Eisenstein. Berkeley: University of California Press, 1988: 235 p. *ISBN: 0520063090. Includes bibliographical references and index.*

67 Female circumcision — a critical appraisal. Alison T. Slack. *Hum. Rights Q.* **10:4** 1988 pp. 437 – 486

68 Female population, literacy and employment — some observations. Jyoti Rani; B. Rajaiah. *Indian J. Soc. W.* **XLIX:3** 7:1988 pp. 245 – 252

69 Feminist politics in Japan. Vera Mackie. *New Left R.* **:167** 1/2:1988 pp. 53 – 76

70 Les femmes et la modernité *[In French]*; [Women and modern life]. Monique Gadant *[Contrib.]*; Pima Madami *[Contrib.]*; Dorrah Mahfoudh *[Contrib.]*; Dahbia Abrous *[Contrib.]*; Naget Khadda *[Contrib.]*; Ghjermana Zerbi de *[Contrib.]*; Mona Abaza *[Contrib.]*; Roberta Shapiro *[Contrib.]*; Jocelyne Streiff-Fenart *[Contrib.]*; Najib El Bernoussi *[Contrib.]* and others. Collection of 16 articles. **Peup. Médit.**, 44:45, 7-12:1988 pp. 5 – 349

71 The fish don't talk about the water — gender transformation, power, and resistance among women in Sri Lanka. Carla Risseeuw. Leiden: E.J. Brill, 1988: xiv, 399 p. (ill.) *ISBN: 9004090118. Bibliography, p. [376]-396; Includes index.*

72 Health and the social power of women. Carol P. MacCormack. *Soc. Sci. Med.* **26:7** 1988 pp. 677 – 683

73 Josei no life course no sedai-kan oyobi sedai-nai kattou *[In Japanese]*; [Life course of women in terms of inter- and intra-generational conflicts]. Kiyomi Morioka. *Shakaigaku Hyoron Vol.39; No.3 - 1988.* pp. 2 – 9

74 Kou-gakureki Josei no life course — Tsudajuku daigaku shussin-sha no sedai-kan Hikaku *[In Japanese]*; [Life course patterns of women of the high academic career — the case of graduates of Tsuda college]. Kazuo Aoi *[Ed.]*. Tokyo: Keisō Shobō, 358 p.

75 Legal and scholarly activism — recent women's studies on India — a review article. Gail Minault. *J. Asian St.* **47:4** 11:1988 pp. 814 – 820

F.5: Gender [Sexe] — Women [Femmes]

76 Life spaces — gender, household, employment. Beth Moore Milroy *[Ed.]*; Caroline Andrew *[Ed.]*. Vancouver: University of British Columbia Press, 1988: vi, 214 p. *ISBN: 0774802952. Bibliography.*

77 Mujer y salud mental *[In Spanish]*; [Women and mental health]. Carmen Sáez Buanaventura *[Ed.]*; Lourdes del Río García *[Ed.]*; Pastora Sánchez Carrero *[Ed.]*. Madrid: Instituto de la Mujer, 1988: 222 p. *ISBN: 8450529263.* [Serie documentos.]

78 Nationalité et citoyenneté. Les femmes algériennes et leurs droits *[In French]*; Nationalism and mores — Algerian women and their rights *[Summary]*. Monique Gadant. *Peup. Médit.* **44:45** 7-12:1988 pp. 293 – 337

79 Palestinian women — triple burden, single struggle; Femmes palestiniennes — triple fardeau, combat singulier *[French summary]*. Rosemary Sayigh. *Peup. Médit.* **44:45** 7-12:1988 pp. 247 – 268

80 Passage through midlife — women's changing family roles and economic well-being. Ken R. Smith; Phyllis Moen. *Sociol. Q.* **29:4** Winter:1988 pp. 503 – 524

81 Patriarchy and class — African women in the home and the workforce. Sharon Stichter *[Ed.]*; Jane L. Parpart *[Ed.]*. Boulder,Col.: Westview, 1988: vi, 233 p. *ISBN: 0813374162; LofC: 88- 219.*

82 Personal voices — Chinese women in the 1980s. Emily Honig; Gail Hershatter *[Ed.]*. Stanford: Stanford University Press, 1988: vi, 387 p. *ISBN: 0804714169. Bibliography — p.363-380.*

83 The politics of women's rights. April Carter. London: Longman, 1988: viii,240 p. *ISBN: 058229519x. Includes bibliography and index.* [Politics today.]

84 Pozycja społeczno-zawodowa kobiet z wyzsym wykształceniem (ze szczególnym uwzglednieniem warunków Polskich) *[In Polish]*; (Socio-professional position of women with academic background (with special reference to the Polish conditions)). Halina Mortimer-Szymcak. *Acta Univ. Łódz.* **76** 1988 pp. 63 – 81

85 La prostitución de las mujeres *[In Spanish]*; [Prostitution and women]. Spain. Instituto de la Mujer. Madrid: Instituto de la Mujer, 1988: 254 p. *ISBN: 8477990077. Bibliography — p.247-254.* [Serie estudios.]

86 Race and class bias in qualitative research on women. Lynn Weber Cannon; Elizabeth Higginbotham; Marianne L. A. Leung. *Gender Soc.* **2:4** 12:1988 pp. 449 – 462

87 Rural women and technological advancement. Malkit Kaur. Delhi: Discovery, 1988: xiv, 213 p.

88 Rural women in education — a study in underachievement. Prem Lata Sharma. New Delhi: Sterling, 1988: vi, 95 p. *ISBN: 81 2070 785 0.*

89 Ser mujer en América Latina *[In Spanish]*; [The woman in Latin America]. Patricia Bifani *[Contrib.]*; Maria Noemi Castilhos Brito *[Contrib.]*; Laura Beatriz Gingold *[Contrib.]*; Inés Vásquez *[Contrib.]*; Tosca Hernández *[Contrib.]*; Ana Victoria Jiménez Alvarez *[Contrib.]*; María Eugenia Santillán *[Contrib.]*; Ana Luisa González Arévalo *[Contrib.]*; Graciela Esquivel Vilchis *[Contrib.]*; Migdaleder Mazuera *[Contrib.] and others. Collection of 10 articles.* **Nueva Soc.** ,1-2:1988 pp. 94 – 186

90 Short-changed — women and economic policies. Rhonda Sharp; Ray Broomhill *[Ed.]*. Sydney: Allen & Unwin, 1988: xv, 198 p. (ill) *ISBN: 0043202195; LofC: 88071847. Includes indexes; Bibliography — p. 178-188.*

F.5: Gender *[Sexe]* — Women *[Femmes]*

91 Socialisation, education and women — explorations in gender identity. Karuna Chanana *[Ed.]*. London: Sangam, 1988: 320 p. *ISBN: 0861318293. Conference proceedings; Includes bibliographies and index.* [Perspectives in Indian development.]

92 Status of women in Islam. Ashghar Ali Engineer *[Ed.]*. Delhi: Ajanta, 1987: viii, 128 p. *ISBN: 81 202 0190 6.*

93 The strongest part of the family — a study of Lao refugee women in Columbus, Ohio. Karen L. S. Muir. New York: AMS Press, 1988: 191 p. *ISBN: 0404194273; LofC: 87-045782. Bibliography.* [Immigrant communities & ethnic minorities in the United States & Canada. : No. 17]

94 The struggle for the liberation of women in Third World. Udobata Onunwa. *Ufahamu* **XVII:1** :1988 pp. 44 – 56

95 Suborinación y liberación de la mujer *[In Spanish]*; [The subordination and liberation of women]. Sonia Abarca *[Contrib.]*; Mirta González *[Contrib.]*; Zinnia Méndez *[Contrib.]*; Mayra Achío *[Contrib.]*; Patricia Mora *[Contrib.]*; Bernardo Bolaños *[Contrib.]*; Hannia Rodríguez *[Contrib.]*. Collection of 5 articles. **Rev. Cien. Soc.** , *:39*, 3:1988 pp. 7 – 68

96 Towards a typology of female entrepreneurs. Stanley Cromie; John Hayes. *Sociol. Rev.* **36:1** 2:1988 pp. 87 – 113

97 Ursachen der Unterrepräsentanz von Frauen in universitären Spitzenpositionen *[In German]*; Underrepresentation of women in higher university positions *[Summary]*. Mechthild Brothun. *Kölner Z. Soz. Soz. psy.* **40:2** 1988 pp. 316 – 336

98 Woman herself — a transdisciplinary perspective on women's identity. Robyn Rowland. Melbourne: Oxford University Press, 1988: viii, 232 p. *ISBN: 0195544757; LofC: 89212295. Includes index; Includes bibliographical references (p.[213]-219).*

99 Women and capitalist development in Sri Lanka, 1977-1987. Asoka Bandarage. *B. Concern. Asia. Schol.* **20:2** 1988 pp. 57 – 81

100 Women and child development — some contemporary issues. Reddy G. M. Narayan; Reddy Suma Narayan. Allahabad: Chugh, 1987: xiv, 156 p. *ISBN: 81 85076 28 6.*

101 Women and international relations. Fred Halliday *[Contrib.]*; J. Ann Tickner *[Contrib.]*; Jean Bethke Elshtain *[Contrib.]*; Philip Windsor *[Contrib.]*; Sarah Brown *[Contrib.]*; Anne Marie Goetz *[Contrib.]*; Georgina Ashworth *[Contrib.]*; Kathleen Newland *[Contrib.]*. *Collection of 8 articles.* **Millennium** , *17:3*, Winter:1988 pp. 419 – 538

102 Women and mental illness — the social context of female neurosis. Agnes Miles. Brighton: Wheatsheaf, 1988: viii, 168 p. *ISBN: 0745001432. Bibliography — p155-163. - Includes index.*

103 Women and the illness role — rethinking feminist theory; *[French summary]*. Marion Pirie. *Can. R. Soc. A.* **25:4** 11:1988 pp. 628 – 648

104 Women and the politics of empowerment. Ann Bookman *[Ed.]*; Sandra Morgen *[Ed.]*. Philadelphia: Temple University Press, 1988: xi, 324 p. *ISBN: 0877225044.* [Women in the political economy.]

105 Women in Ireland — an annotated bibliography. Anna Brady. New York: Greenwood, 1988: 520 p. *ISBN: 0313244863; LofC: 87-25043. Includes index.* [Bibliographies and indexes in women's studies.]

F.5: Gender *[Sexe]* — *Women [Femmes]*

106 Women in political theory — from ancient misogyny to contemporary feminism. Diana H. Coole. Brighton: Wheatsheaf, 1988: vii, 324 p. *ISBN: 0745001440. Bibliography — p304-316. - Includes index.*

107 Women with disabilities — essays in psychology, culture and politics. Michelle Fine *[Ed.]*; Adrienne Asch *[Ed.]*. Philadelphia: Temple University Press, 1988: 347 p. *ISBN: 0877224749; LofC: 87-10099.* [Health,society and policy.]

108 Women's quest for economic equality. Victor R. Fuchs. Cambridge,Mass.: Harvard University Press, 1988: 171 p. *ISBN: 0674955455; LofC: 88-007209. Bibliography.*

109 Women's rights and Catholicism in Ireland. Evelyn Mahon. *New Left R.* **166** 1988 pp. 13 – 78

110 Women's status and mode of production — a cross-cultural test. Lewellyn Hendrix; Zakir Hossain. *Signs* **13:3** Spring:1988 pp. 437 – 447

F.6: Sexual behaviour — *Comportement sexuelle*

1 Acquired immune deficiency syndrome and sexual behavior changes in a college student sample. Masako Ishii-Kuntz. *Social Soc. Res.* **73:1** 10:1988 pp. 13 – 18

2 Age, gender and adultery. Annette Lawson; Colin Samson. *Br. J. Soc.* **XXXIX:3** 9:1988 pp. 409 – 440

3 The Americanization of sex. Edwin M. Schur. Philadelphia: Temple University Press, 1988: xiv, 229 p. *ISBN: 0877225214; LofC: 87-017993. Includes index.*

4 Attitudes toward homosexuality — a cross cultural analysis of predictors. Larry Jensen; David Gambles; Joe Olsen. *Int. J. Soc. Psyc.* **34:1** Spring:1988 pp. 47 – 57

5 Behavioural research in sexuality. H.C. Ganguli. New Delhi: Vikas, 1988: ix, 222 p.

6 Biological predispositions and social control in adolescent sexual behaviour. J. Richard Udry. *Am. Sociol. R.* **53:5** 10:1988 pp. 709 – 722

7 Coercion and consent — classic liberal concepts in texts on sexual violence. Judith Vega. *Int. J. S. Law* **16:1** 2:1988 pp. 75 – 89

8 Concern with AIDS and the sexual behavior of college students. Leo Carroll. *J. Marriage Fam.* **50:2** 5:1988 pp. 405 – 411

9 Crisis — heterosexual behaviour in the age of AIDS. William H. Masters; Virginia E. Johnson *[Ed.]*; Robert C. Kolodny *[Ed.]*. London: Weidenfeld & Nicolson, 1988: 243 p. *ISBN: 0297793926.*

10 Daigakusei no sei ishki to sei kodo *[In Japanese]*; [Sexual attitudes and behavior among university students]. Kyoko Yoshizumi. *Fac. Lett. R. Ot. Gak. Vol.22. 1988.* pp. 111 – 134

11 Eroticism and love. Paul Gregory. *Am. Phil. Q.* **25:4** 10:1988 pp. 339 – 346

12 Family secrets — child sexual abuse. Mary McIntosh *[Contrib.]*; Mary MacLeod *[Contrib.]*; Esther Saraga *[Contrib.]*; Linda Gordon *[Contrib.]*; Liz Kelly *[Contrib.]*; Jenny Kitzinger *[Contrib.]*; Ann Scott *[Contrib.]*; Mica Nava *[Contrib.]*; Elizabeth Woodcraft *[Contrib.]*; Gina Betcher *[Contrib.]* and others. Collection of 15 articles. **Feminist R.** , 28, Spring:1988 pp. 6 – 17

F.6: Sexual behaviour *[Comportement sexuelle]*

13 Female circumcision — a critical appraisal. Alison T. Slack. *Hum. Rights Q.* **10**:4 11:1988 pp. 437 – 486

14 Gays/justice — a study of ethics, society, and law. Richard D. Mohr. New York: Columbia U.P., 1988: 357 p. *ISBN: 0231067348.*

15 The history of prostitution — its extent, causes and effects through out the world. William W. Sanger. New Delhi: Inter-India, 1986: xiv, 708 p.

16 Homosexualités et tolérance sociale *[In French]*; [Homosexuality and social tolerance]. Louis Richard *[Ed.]*; Marie-Thérèse Seguin *[Ed.]*. Moncton, N.-B.: Éditions d'Acadie, 1988: 194 p. *ISBN: 2760001512; LofC: cn88-6067.*

17 Human mating patterns. A. J. Boyce *[Ed.]*; C. G. N. Mascie-Taylor *[Ed.]*. Cambridge: Cambridge University Press, 1988: vii, 237 p. (ill) *ISBN: 0521334322. Includes bibliographies and index.* [Society for the Study of Human Biology symposium series. : No. 28]

18 Ideology and public policy — the case against pornography. Dany Lacombe. Toronto: Garmond, 1988: 128 p. *ISBN: 0920059449. Bibliography — p.117-128.* [Network basics series.]

19 In search of Eve — transsexual rites of passage. Anne Bolin. South Hadley (Mass.): Bergin and Garvey, 1988: xii,210 p. *ISBN: 0897890825. Bibliography — p.195-206.*

20 Influence of attitudes, significant others, and aspirations on how adolescents intend to resolve a premarital pregnancy. Jan F. Brazzell; Alan C. Acock. *J. Marriage Fam.* **50**:2 5:1988 pp. 413 – 425

21 Lesbianism — an annotated bibliography and guide to the literature, 1976-1986. Dolores J. Maggiore. Metuchen, N.J.: Scarecrow, 1988: vi, 150 p. *ISBN: 081082048x; LofC: 87-20613. Includes index.*

22 Male and female homosexuality — psychological approaches. Louis Diamant *[Ed.]*. Cambridge: Hemisphere Publishing Corporation, 1988: 292 p. *ISBN: 0891164499; LofC: 86-25816. Bibliographies.*

23 Our kind of polygamy. David G. Maillu. Nairobi: Heinemann Kenya, 1988: 187 p. *ISBN: 996646381x.*

24 Prostitution in Bangladesh — a study. Zarina Rahman Khan; H.K. Arefeen. *J. Soc. Stud. Dhaka* :**41** 7:1988 pp. 1 – 28

25 Radical records — thirty years of lesbian and gay history, 1957-1987. Bob Cant *[Ed.]*; Susan Hemmings *[Ed.]*. London: Routledge, 1988: xi, 266 p. *ISBN: 0710210574.*

26 A revision of the Reiss premarital sexual permissiveness scale. Susan Sprecher; Kathleen McKinney; Robert Walsh; Carrie Anderson. *J. Marriage Fam.* **50**:3 8:1988 pp. 821 – 828

27 Seishōnen no sei-kihan to sei-kyouiku *[In Japanese]*; [Sex norms and education adolescents]. Kazuo Katase. *Bess. Kyo. Gij. Vol.10.* pp. 77 – 116

28 The sexual trafficking in children — an investigation of the child sex trade. Daniel S. Campagna; Donald L. Poffenberger *[Ed.]*. Dover, Mass.: Auburn House, 1988: xiv, 250 p. *ISBN: 0865691541. Bibliography — p.234-241.*

29 Sociological research on male and female homosexuality. Barbara Risman; Pepper Schwartz. *Ann. R. Soc.* **14** 1988 pp. 125 – 147

30 A structural approach to sexual attitudes — interracial patterns in adolescents' judgments about sexual intimacy. Judith A. Howard. *Sociol. Pers.* **31**:1 1:1988 pp. 88 – 121

F.6: Sexual behaviour *[Comportement sexuelle]*

31 The treatment of sexual aggression — legal and ethical issues. Richard J. Freeman *[Ed.]*; Simon N. Verdun-Jones *[Ed.]*. Burnaby, B.C.: Criminology Research Centre,Simon Fraser University, 1988: 129 p. *ISBN: 0864910606*.
32 Virtue, order, health, and money — towards a comprehensive perspective on female prostitution in Asia. Truong Thanh-Dam. *Econ. Papers [Warsaw]* **22** 1988 pp. 166 – 216
33 Who remains celibate? Kathleen E. Kiernan. *J. Biosoc. Sc.* **20:3** 7:1988 pp. 253 – 263

F.7: Ethnic groups — *Groupes ethniques*

Sub-divisions: Ethnicity *[Ethnicité]*; Race relations *[Relations raciales]*; Racial discrimination *[Discrimination raciale]*

1 Aborigines and the state in Australia. Jeremy Beckett *[Ed.]*; Jan Larbalestier *[Contrib.]*; Gaynor M. MacDonald *[Contrib.]*; Tim Rowse *[Contrib.]*; Lee Sackett *[Contrib.]*. Collection of 6 articles. **Soc. Anal.** , *24*, 12:1988 pp. 3 – 84
2 Acculturation and assimilation among Mexican Americans — scales and population-based data. Helen P. Hazuda; Michael P. Stern; Steven M. Haffner. *Soc. Sci. Q.* **69:3** 9:1988 pp. 687 – 706
3 Analyzing the characteristics of blacks — a comparison of data from SIPP and CPS. Reynolds Farley; Lisa J. Neidert. *Proc. Am. Stat. Ass.* pp. 103 – 108
4 The Anglo-Indian community — survival of India. Evelyn Abel. Delhi: Chanakya, 1988: ix, 205 p. *ISBN: 81 7001 036 5*.
5 Anti-Shiism in Iraq under the monarchy. Elie Kedourie. *Middle E. Stud.* **24:2** 4:1988 pp. 249 – 254
6 The Arab internal refugees in Israel — the emergence of a minority within the minority. Majid Al-Haj. *Imm. Minor.* **7:2** 7:1988 pp. 149 – 166
7 Asian America — Chinese and Japanese in the United States since 1850. Roger Daniels. Seattle: University of Washington Press, 1988: 384 p. *ISBN: 0295966696. Bibliography — p.345-372*.
8 Aspetti e problemi della collettività italiana in Canada *[In Italian]*; [Aspects and problems of the Italian community in Canada]. Stefano Baldi. *Aff. Soc. Int.* **XVI:1** 1988 pp. 71 – 90
9 Assimilationist views of an ethnic region — the Cajun French experience in southwest Louisiana. Clifford J. Clarke. *Soc. Sci. Q.* **69:2** 6:1988 pp. 433 – 451
10 Bi-ethnic labor markets, mono-ethnic labor markets, and socioeconomic inequality. Moshe Semyonov. *Am. Sociol. R.* **53:2** 4:1988 pp. 256 – 266
11 Black people and the criminal law — rhetoric and reality. Paul Gordon. *Int. J. S. Law* **16:3** 8:1988 pp. 295 – 313
12 Blacks in administrative Natal — case studies in marginality. R. J. Evans. Pietermaritzburg: Natal Town and Regional Planning Commission, 1988: 660 p. *ISBN: 0869671669. Bibliography — p.58-9*. [Natal town and regional planning supplementary report. : Vol. 30]
13 Bridging the gap — reserve and off-reserve Indian interaction on the northwest coast; (Die Überwindung der Spaltung — Interaktion zwischen Indianern inner- und außerhalb der Reservate an der Nordwestküste: *Title only in German*). Erich Kasten. *Sociologus* **38:2** 1988 pp. 115 – 136

F.7: Ethnic groups [Groupes ethniques]

14 The burden of double roles — Korean wives in the USA. Kwang Chung Kim; Won Moo Hurh. *Ethn. Racial* **11:2** 4:1988 pp. 151 – 167

15 Canadian south Asian women in transition — a dualistic view of life; *[French summary]*; *[Spanish summary]*. Josephine C. Naidoo; J. Campbell Davis. *J. Comp. Fam. Stud.* **XIX:2** Summer:1988 pp. 311 – 327

16 Changing patterns of suburban racial composition, 1970-1980. John M. Stahura. *Urban Aff. Q.* **23:3** 3:1988 pp. 448 – 460

17 Les communautés cambodgienne et laotienne de Québec *[In French]*; [The Cambodian and Laotian communities of Quebec]. Louis-Jacques Dorais; Lise Pilon-Lê *[Ed.]*. Québec: Laboratoire de recherches anthropologiques, Université Laval, 1988: 242 p. [Documents de recherche.]

18 Community-level analyses of racial socioeconomic inequality — a cautionary note. Mark A. Fossett. *Sociol. Meth.* **16:4** 5:1988 pp. 454 – 491

19 The court disposal of young males, by race, in London in 1983. Monica A. Walker. *Br. J. Crimin.* **28:4** Autumn:1988 pp. 441 – 460

20 Deterioration of black economic conditions in the 1980s. Victor Perlo. *Rev. Rad. Pol. Ec.* **20:2:3** 1988 pp. 55 – 60

21 Dissent and tolerance in Chinese society. Stanley Rosen. *Curr. Hist.* *9:1988* pp.261-264, 278-281

22 Enterprising women — home, work, and minority cultures in Britain. Sallie Westwood *[Ed.]*; Parminder Bhachu *[Ed.]*. London: Routledge, 1988: x, 210 p. *ISBN: 0415006864. Includes index; Bibliographies.*

23 Essais sur la condition juive contemporaine *[In French]*; [Essays on the contemporary Jewish condition]. Raymond Aron; Perrine Simon-Nahum *[Ed.]*. Paris: Editions de Fallois, 1988: 318 p. *ISBN: 2877060217. Recueil de textes et de conférences, 1941-1983; Bibliogr. pp 315-318.*

24 The ethnic factor in security and development — perceptions of United Nations human-rights bodies. Russel Lawrence Barsh. *Acta Sociol.* **31:4** 1988 pp. 333 – 341

25 The ethnic success ethic — ubiquitous phenomenon in English-speaking societies? Brian M. Bullivant. *Ethn. Racial* **11:1** 1:1988 pp. 63 – 84

26 The ethos of the Hong Kong Chinese. Chao-chia Liu; Hsin-chi Kuan *[Ed.]*. Hong Kong: Chinese University Press, 1988: 217 p. *ISBN: 9622014313.*

27 From undesirable immigrant to model minority — the success story of Chinese in New Zealand. Rita Chi-Ying Chung; Frank H. Walker. *Imm. Minor.* **7:3** 11:1988 pp. 308 – 314

28 The future of American Jewry. Israel Finestein. *Jew. J. Socio.* **XXX:2** 12:1988 pp. 121 – 126

29 The future of ethnic languages in Australia. Anne Pauwels *[Ed.]*; Joshua A. Fishman *[Ed.]*; Anne Pauwels *[Contrib.]*; Camilla Bettoni *[Contrib.]*; John Gibbons *[Contrib.]*; Mark Garner *[Contrib.]*; Ludmila Kouzmin *[Contrib.]*; Michael G. Clyne *[Contrib.]*; Susanne Döpke *[Contrib.]*; Uldis Ozolins *[Contrib.] and others. Collection of 9 articles.* **Int. J. S. Lang.** , 72, 1988 pp. 5 – 134

30 The German presence in Queensland over the last 150 years — proceedings of an international symposium, August 24, 25, and 26, 1987, University of Queensland, Brisbane, Australia. Manfred Jurgensen *[Ed.]*; Alan Corkhill *[Ed.]*. St Lucia: Dept. of German, University of Queensland, 1988: xvi, 414 p. (ill. (some col.)) *ISBN: 0867762527; LofC: 89140861. Includes bibliographical references.*

F.7: Ethnic groups [Groupes ethniques]

31 The Hispanic experience in the United States — contemporary issues and perspectives. Barbara R. Sjostrom *[Ed.]*; Edna Acosta-Belén *[Ed.]*. New York: Praeger, 1988: xi, 261 p. (ill) *ISBN: 0275927407; LofC: 87-37690. Bibliography — p.243-254. Includes index.*

32 Hispanic U.S.A. — breaking the melting pot. Thomas Weyr. New York: Harper and Row, 1988: xiii, 241 p. *ISBN: 0060390662.*

33 "I'm proper number one fighter, me" — Aborigines, gender, and bureaucracy in central Australia. Jeff Collmann. *Gender Soc.* **2:1** 3:1988 pp. 9 – 23

34 The impact of stratification — assimilation or ethnic solidarity. Hanna Ayalon; Eliezer Ben-Rafael; Stephen Sharot. *R. Soc. Strat. Mob.* **7** 1988 pp. 305 – 326

35 La integración de los gitanos españoles *[In Spanish]*; [The integration of Spanish gypsies]. Angel de Miguel. *Rev. Fom. Soc.* **43:171** 7-9:1988 pp. 271 – 280

36 Irish migrants in the Canadas — a new approach. Bruce S Elliot. Montreal: McGill-Queens University Press/The Institute of Irish Studies, 1988: xvii, 371 p. *ISBN: 0773506071.* [McGill-Queen's studies in ethnic history. : No. 1]

37 The Kazaks of China — essays on an ethnic minority. Linda Benson *[Ed.]*; Ingvar Svanberg *[Ed.]*. Uppsala: Ubsaliensis S. Academiae, 1988: xii, 250 p. (ill) *ISBN: 9155422551. Includes bibliographical references.* [Acta Universitatis Upsaliensis.]

38 Lost illusions — Caribbean minorities in Britain and the Netherlands. Malcolm Cross *[Ed.]*; Han Entzinger *[Ed.]*. London: Routledge, 1988: x, 316 p. *ISBN: 0415006287. Bibliography — p.[285]-301.*

39 Minorities and criminality. Ronald B. Flowers. New York: Greenwood, 1988: 224 p. *ISBN: 0313253668; LofC: 88-5707. Includes bibliography and index.* [Contributions in criminology and penology.]

40 Minority peoples in the age of nation states. Gérard Chaliand *[Ed.]*; Michael Barrett *[Ed.]*; Ben Whitaker *[Intro.]*. London: Pluto, 1988: 160 p. *ISBN: 0745302769. eng, fre.*

41 The Mvskoke national question in Oklahoma. John H. Moore. *Sci. Soc.* **52:2** Summer:1988 pp. 163 – 190

42 Nigerian unity — integrative processes and problems. Lewis Walker; Dick Andzenge. *J. Dev. Soc.* **V:2** 7-10:1989 pp. 218 – 233

43 Overeducation and the earnings of black, Hispanic, and white male workers. Richard R. Verdugo; Naomi Turner Verdugo. *Sociol. Pers.* **31:2** 4:1988 pp. 190 – 212

44 Overseas Indians in Malaysia and the Caribbean — comparative notes. Ravindra K. Jain. *Imm. Minor.* **7:1** 3:1988 pp. 123 – 143

45 A Pakistani community in Britain. Alison Shaw. Oxford: Basil Blackwell, 1988: xiv,187 p. (ill) *ISBN: 0631152288. Includes index.*

46 Patronage, brokerage, entrepreneurship, and the Chinese community of New York. Bernard P. Wong. New York: AMS Press, 1988: ix, 348 p. (ill.) *ISBN: 0404194168. Bibliography — p.322-341.* [Immigrant communities and ethnic minorities in the United States & Canada.]

47 De Québécois à Ontarois — la communauté franco-ontarienne *[In French]*; [From Quebecois to Ontarois — the French community of Ontario]. Roger Bernard. Hearst: Le Nordir, 1988: 189 p. *ISBN: 0921272014. Bibliography — p..174-185.*

F.7: Ethnic groups [Groupes ethniques]

48 Race and alienation — observations on the impact of joblessness. Richard C. Hofstetter; Terry F. Buss. *Ethn. Racial* **11**:3 7:1988 pp. 305 – 318

49 Race and gender as psychological variables. Sandra Scarr. *Am. Psychol.* **43**:1 1:1988 pp. 56 – 59

50 The rise and decline of Australian multiculturalism — 1973-1988. Lois Foster; David Stockley. *Aust. J. Pol. Sci* **23**:2 11:1988 pp. 1 – 10

51 Sociology after the Holocaust. Zygmunt Bauman. *Br. J. Soc.* **XXXIX**:4 12:1988 pp. 469 – 497

52 Toward a Chicano social science. Irene I. Blea. New York: Praeger, 1988: 159 p. *ISBN: 0275924084; LofC: 88-6593. Includes bibliography and index.*

53 The transformation of the southern racial state — class and race determinants of local-state structures. David R. James. *Am. Sociol. R.* **53**:2 4:1988 pp. 191 – 208

54 U.S. Hispanics — a demographic and issue profile. Jaime Raigoza. *Popul. Envir.* **10**:2 Winter:1988 pp. 95 – 106

55 Les Vietnamiens au Canada — appartenance ethnique et identité nationale *[In French]*; [Vietnamese in Canada — ethnic roots and national identity] *[Summary]*. Tran Quang Ba. *Etud. Can.* :**25** 1988 pp. 75 – 84

56 Who are the "refuseniks"? A statistical and demographic analysis. Mordechai Altshuler. *Sov. Jew. Aff.* **18**:1 Spring:1988 pp. 3 – 15

Ethnicity [Ethnicité]

57 Afrikaner dissidents — a social psychological study of identity and dissent. Joha Louw-Potgieter. Clevedon: Multilingual Matters, 1988: 157 p. *ISBN: 1853590126. Bibliography — p.141-151.*

58 Barrio gangs — street life and identity in southern California. James Diego Vigil. Austin: Texas University Press, 1988: 202 p. *ISBN: 0292711190; LofC: 88-023386. Bibliography — p.181-196.* [Mexican American monograph. : No. 12]

59 Beyond Aztlan — ethnic autonomy in comparative perspective. Mario Barrera. New York: Praeger, 1988: xii, 209 p. (ill) *ISBN: 027592923x; LofC: 88-5432. Bibliography — p.177-198. Includes index.*

60 Ethnicity and assimilation. Robert M. Jiobu. Albany: State University of New York Press, 1988: xiv, 269 p. (ill.) *ISBN: 088706647x. Bibliography — p.255-265.*

61 Ethnicity and school performance — a comparative study of south Asian pupils in Britain and America. Margaret A. Gibson; Parminder K. Bhachu. *Ethn. Racial* **11**:3 7:1988 pp. 239 – 262

62 Ethnicity to Shakai Hendou *[In Japanese]*; [Ethnicity and social change]. Takamichi Kajita. Tokyo: Yūshindo, 1988: 320 p.

63 Ethnicity, race and nationalism in Australia — some critical perspectives. Gill Bottomley. *Aust. J. Soc. Iss.* **23**:3 8:1988 pp. 169 – 183

64 From communality to ethnicity — some theoretical considerations on the Maori ethnic revival. David Pearson. *Ethn. Racial* **11**:2 4:1988 pp. 168 – 191

65 Negritude — an annotated bibliography. Colette V. Michael. West Cornwall: Locust Hill Press, 1988: 315 p. *ISBN: 0933951159; LofC: 88-008848.*

66 Racial consciousness. Michael Banton. London: Longman, 1988: ix,153 p. (ill) *ISBN: 0582023858. GN269 B21; Bibliography — p147-150. Includes index.*

F.7: Ethnic groups *[Groupes ethniques]* — *Ethnicity [Ethnicité]*

67 Residential segregation and ethnic identification among Hispanics in Texas. Sean-Shong Hwang; Steve H. Murdock. *Urban Aff. Q.* **23**:3   3:1988 pp. 329 – 345

68 The sociopolitical process of identity formation in an ethnic community — the Chinese in New Zealand. Kwen Fee Lian. *Ethn. Racial* **11**:4   11:1988 pp. 506 – 532

69 Twenty girls — growing up, ethnicity and excitement in a south London microculture. Helena Wulff. Stockholm: Stockholm University,Department of Social Anthropology, 1988: 193 p. *ISBN: 9171467106*. [Stockholm studies in social anthropology. : Vol. 21]

Race relations *[Relations raciales]*

70 Anti-racism — a mania exposed. Russell Lewis. London: Quartet, 1988: 224 p. *ISBN: 0704300702*.

71 Ausländerintegration, Schule und Staat *[In German]*; Ethnic integration, the education system and the state in West Germany *[Summary]*. David Baker; Gero Lenbardt. *Kölner Z. Soz. Soz. psy.* **40**:1   1988 pp. 40 – 61

72 Black Africans and native Americans — color, race and caste in the evolution of red-black peoples. Jack D. Forbes. Oxford: Basil Blackwell, 1988: 352 p. *ISBN: 0631156658. Includes bibliography and index.*

73 Black American perceptions of black Africans. Michael C. Thornton; Robert J. Taylor. *Ethn. Racial* **11**:2   4:1988 pp. 139 – 150

74 The Chinese in Canada. Peter S. Li. Toronto: Oxford University Press, 1988: xi, 164 p. *ISBN: 0195406524. Bibliography, p. [143]-155.; Includes indexes.* [Studies in Canadian sociology.]

75 Chinos y antichinos en México — documentos para su estudio *[In Spanish]*; [The Chinese and anti-chinese in Mexico, documents for their study]. Humberto Monteón González *[Ed.]*; José Luis Trueba Lara *[Ed.]*. Guadalajara: Gobierno de Jalisco, 1988: 135 p. *ISBN: 9688323268*. [Colección Historia Serie — Documentos e Investigaciones. : No. 34]

76 Engagement und Distanzierung in der Westdeutschen Ausländerforschung — eine Untersuchung ihrer soziologischen Beiträge *[In German]*; [Commitment and distancing in West German research on foreigners — a study of their sociological contributions]. Annette Treibel. Stuttgart: Enke, 1988: 377 p. *ISBN: 3432975910*.

77 Ethnic hegemony and the Japanese of California. Robert M. Jiobu. *Am. Sociol. R.* **53**:3   6:1988 pp. 353 – 367

78 Fijian chiefs and Fiji Indians — ethnic reality surfaces in the south Pacific. Deryck Scarr. *World Rev.* **27**:4   11:1988 pp. 48 – 69

79 Les haitiens — politique de classe et de couleur *[In French]*; [Haitians — the politics of class and colour]. Lyonel Paquin. Port-au-Prince: Imprimerie Le Natal, 1988: 327 p. *fre, eng*.

80 Intergroup attitudes — black American perceptions of Asian Americans. Michael C. Thornton; Robert J. Taylor. *Ethn. Racial* **11**:4   11:1988 pp. 474 – 488

81 Jews in contemporary East Germany — the children of Moses in the land of Marx. Robin Ostow. Basingstoke: Macmillan, 1988: 169 p. *ISBN: 0333462998. Includes index.*

F.7: Ethnic groups [Groupes ethniques] — Race relations [Relations raciales]

82 The Jews of South Africa — what future? Tzippi Hoffman; Alan Fischer *[Ed.]*. Johannesburg: Southern Book Publishers, 1988: 393 p. *ISBN: 1868121577*.

83 Die Juden in Wien *[In German]*; [Jews in Vienna]. Hellmut Andics. München: Bucher, 1988: 416 p. (ill.) *ISBN: 3765805807; LofC: 89- 17838. Includes bibliographical references.*

84 Legends of people, myths of state — violence, intolerance and political culture in Sri Lanka and Australia. Bruce Kapferer. Washington, D.C.: Smithsonian Institution Press, 1988: 264 p. (ill) *ISBN: 0874745667; LofC: 87-42558.* [Smithsonian series in ethnographic inquiry.]

85 Optimism and pessimism about racial relations. Michael Banton. *Patt. Prej.* **22:1** Spring:1988 pp. 3 – 13

86 Portugais de France — essai sur une dynamique de double appartenance *[In French]*; [Portuguese in France — a study of the dynamics of double membership]. Maria do Céu Cunha. Paris: L'Harmattan, 1988: 158 p. *ISBN: 2738400426. Bibliography — p..153-158.*

87 Quiet riots — race and poverty in the United States. Roger W. Wilkins *[Ed.]*; Fred R. Harris *[Ed.]*. New York: Pantheon Books, 1988: 223 p. *ISBN: 0394574737.*

88 Race, class and conservatism. Thomas D. Boston. London: Unwin Hyman, 1988: xix, 172 p. *ISBN: 0043303684. Bibliography — p161-167.*

89 Racial conflict and resolution in New Zealand — the haka party incident and its aftermath 1979-1980. Kayleen M. Hazlehurst. Canberra: Australian National University, 1988: 65 p. (ill) *ISBN: 0731503910.*

90 "Racial" referents — images of European/Aboriginal relations in Australian feature films 1955-1984. Kevin M. Brown. *Sociol. Rev.* **36:3** 8:1988 pp. 474 – 502

91 Relative deprivation and the ethnic attitudes of blacks and Afrikaans-speaking whites in South Africa. Ans E.M. Appelgryn; Johan M. Nieuwoudt. *J. Soc. Psychol.* **128:3** 6:1988 pp. 311 – 323

92 Survey-based experiments on white racial attitudes toward residential integration. Howard Schuman; Lawrence Bobo. *A.J.S.* **94:2** 9:1988 pp. 273 – 299

Racial discrimination [Discrimination raciale]

93 Anti-racism — a mania exposed. Russell Lewis. London: Quartet, 1988: 224 p. *ISBN: 0704300702.*

94 Anti-semitism — banality or the darker side of genius? Albert S. Lindemann. *Religion* **18** 4:1988 pp. 183 – 195

95 L'anti-sémitisme — le Juif comme bouc émissaire *[In French]*; [Anti-semitism — the Jew as a scapegoat]. Yves Chevalier. Paris: Editions du Cerf, 1988: 464 p. *ISBN: 2204029122. Bibliography — p.407-451.* [Sciences humaines et religions.]

96 Les barbares — les immigrés et le racisme dans la politique belge *[In French]*; [Barbarians — immigrants and racism in Belgian politics]. Hugo Gijsels *[Ed.]*. Berchem: EPO, 1988: 184p.

97 Beyond the mother country — West Indians and the Notting Hill white riots. Edward Pilkington. London: Tauris, 1988: 182 p. *ISBN: 1850431132. Includes bibliography and index.*

F.7: Ethnic groups *[Groupes ethniques]* — Racial discrimination *[Discrimination raciale]*

98 Black youth, racism and the state — the politics of ideology and policy. John Solomos. Cambridge: Cambridge University Press, 1988: 285 p. *ISBN: 0521360196. Includes bibliography and index.* [Comparative ethnic and race relations.]

99 Blaming others — prejudice, race and worldwide AIDS. Renée Sabatier. London: Panos Institute, 1988: 167 p. *ISBN: 1870670035. Includes bibliographical references.*

100 Children and prejudice. Frances Aboud. Oxford: Basil Blackwell, 1988: x, 149 p. (ill) *ISBN: 0631149392. Includes index.* [Social psychology and society.]

101 Chinos y antichinos en México — documentos para su estudio *[In Spanish]*; [The Chinese and anti-chinese in Mexico, documents for their study]. Humberto Monteón González *[Ed.]*; José Luis Trueba Lara *[Ed.]*. Guadalajara: Gobierno de Jalisco, 1988: 135 p. *ISBN: 9688323268.* [Colección Historia Serie — Documentos e Investigaciones. : No. 34]

102 The economics of race and discrimination. John Majewski. *Econ. Affr.* **8:3** 2-3:1988 pp. 23 – 29

103 Ethnic inequality in a class society. Peter S. Li. Toronto: Wall & Thompson, 1988: xii, 165 p. *ISBN: 0921332033. Bibliography.*

104 Explaining and blaming — racism and sociology. Steven Fenton. *Patt. Prej.* **22:1** Spring:1988 pp. 21 – 30

105 Genocide — a critical bibliographic review. Israel W. Charny *[Ed.]*. London: Mansell, 1988: 300 p. *ISBN: 072011876x. Includes bibliographies and index.*

106 The ideology of racism. Samuel Kennedy Yeboah. London: Hansib Publishing, 1988: 311 p. *ISBN: 1870518071.*

107 Integration or disintegration? — towards a non-racist society. Ray Honeyford. London: Claridge, 1988: 309 p. *ISBN: 187062680x.*

108 Modern racial prejudice in America — social psychological dimensions and political modelling. Thomas F. Pettigrew. *Patt. Prej.* **22:4** Winter:1988 pp. 3 – 12

109 Moderner Antisemitismus in Deutschland *[In German]*; [Modern antisemitism in Germany]. Helmut Berding. Frankfurt: Suhrkamp, 1988: - *ISBN: 3518112570.* [Neue historische Bibliothek.]

110 The outsiders — Jews and corporate America. Abraham K. Korman. Lexington, Mass.: Lexington Books, 1988: xix, 203 p. *ISBN: 0669099872. Bibliography — p.189-195.*

111 Perceptions of injustice in a black community — dimensions and variation. James P. Adams; William W. Dressler. *Human Relat.* **41:10** 1988 pp. 753 – 767

112 Race prejudice and economic beliefs. Patrick C.L. Heaven; Adrian Furnham. *J. Soc. Psychol.* **128:4** 8:1988 pp. 483 – 489

113 Race, residence, discrimination and economic opportunity — modeling the nexus of urban racial phenomena. George C. Galster; W. Mark Keeney. *Urban Aff. Q.* **24:1** 9:1988 pp. 87 – 117

114 The racism of Jung. Farhad Dalal. *Race Class* **XXIX:3** Winter:1988 pp:1-22

115 Racism, peremptory challenges, and the democratic jury — the jurisprudence of a delicate balance. Brian J. Serr; Mark Maney. *J. Crim. Law* **79:1** Spring:1988 pp. 1 – 65

F.7: Ethnic groups [Groupes ethniques] — Racial discrimination [Discrimination raciale]

116 Trends in antiblack prejudice, 1972-1984 — region and cohort effects. Glenn Firebaugh; Kenneth E. Davis. *A.J.S.* **94:2** 9:1988 pp. 251 – 272

F.8: Migration — *Migration*

Sub-divisions: International migration *[Migration internationale]*

1 African migration decision-making process. Wilfred Mlay. *E.Afr. Soc. Sci. Res. R.* **IV:1** January:1988 pp. 69 – 81

2 Age patterns and model migration schedules in Poland. A. Potrykowska. *Geogr. Pol.* **54:** :1988 pp. 63 – 80

3 Les anglophones de Montreal — émigration et évolution des attitudes 1978-1983 *[In French]*; [English speakers in Montreal — emigration and attitude development 1978-1983]. Uli Locher. Quebec: Conseil de la langue française, 1988: 220 p. [Dossiers du Conseil de la langue française. : No. 29]

4 Application of two types of migration data to multiregional demographic projections. M. Kupiszewski. *Geogr. Pol.* **54:** :1988 pp. 43 – 62

5 Aspects of migration in an advanced industrial society. Franklin D. Wilson. *Am. Sociol. R.* **53:1** 2:1988 pp. 113 – 126

6 Children of circumstances — Israeli emigrants in New York. Moshe Shokeid. Ithaca; London: Cornell University Press, 1988: 226 p. *ISBN: 0801420784; LofC: 87-23934. Bibliography — p..215-221.*

7 The city connection — migration and family interdependence in the Philippines. Lillian Trager. Ann Arbor: Michigan University Press, 1988: 218 p. *ISBN: 0472063901; LofC: 88-022342. Bibliography.*

8 Economic returns to migration — marital status and gender differences. Nan L. Maxwell. *Soc. Sci. Q.* **69:1** 3:1988 pp. 108 – 121

9 Elderly migration as a response to economic incentives. Gary M. Fournier; David W. Rasmussen; William J. Serow. *Soc. Sci. Q.* **69:2** 6:1988 pp. 245 – 260

10 Elderly migration — for sun and money. Gary M. Fournier; David W. Rasmussen; William J. Serow. *Pop. Res. Pol. R.* **7:2** 1988 pp. 189 – 199

11 Family migration and female employment — the problem of underemployment among migrant married women. Donna Ruane Morrison; Daniel T. Lichter. *J. Marriage Fam.* **50:1** 2:1988 pp. 161 – 172

12 Family migration in an uncertain environment. Peter V. Schaeffer. *Socio. Econ.* **:5** 1988 pp. 221 – 227

13 Hokkaido chihou no dekasegi *[In Japanese]*; [Seasonal migratory labour in Hokkaido district]. Sakae Watababe; Shin Hada; Kunio Aida; Masanori Ishikawa. *Kenkyusho Nenpoh Vol.18. 1988.* pp. 95 – 118

14 Indonesia — the transmigration program in perspective. World Bank. Washington, D. C.: The World Bank, 1988: xlii, 227 p. *ISBN: 0821310925.* [A World Bank country study.]

15 Inter- und intragenerativer Wandel in Mirgrantenfamilien *[In German]*; Inter- and intragenerative change in migrant families *[Summary]*. Bernhard Nauck. *Soz. Welt.* **39:4** 1988 pp. 504 – 521

16 Labor standards enforcement and the realities of labor migration — protecting undocumented workers after Sure-tan, the IRCA, and Patel. Richard E. Burm. *NY. U. Law. Re.* **63:6** 12:1988 pp. 1342 – 1374

F.8: Migration [Migration]

17 The mechanism for migration in Poland. Z. Rykiel. *Geogr. Pol.* **54:** :1988 pp. 19 – 32

18 Méthodes de mesure de la mobilité spatiale — migrations internes, mobilité temporaire, navettes *[In French]*; [Methods of measuring spatial mobility — internal migration, temporary mobility, commuting]. Daniel Courgeau. Paris: Institut national d'études démographiques, 1988: ix, 301 p. (ill.) *ISBN: 2733220098. Bibliography p. 289-297.*

19 Metropolitan area population change due to economy-induced migration — measures. G.F. Sutton; J.K. Kindahl; R.A. Nakosteen. *Proc. Am. Stat. Ass.* pp. 151 – 155

20 Migracion en el occidente de Mexico *[In Spanish]*; [Migration in western Mexico]. Gustavo Lopez Castro *[Ed.]*; Sergio Pardo Galvan *[Ed.]*. [Mexico]: El Colegio de Michoacán, 1988: 280 p. *ISBN: 9687230444.*

21 Migrant careers and well-being of women. Judith Freidenberg; Graciela Imperiale; Mary Louise Skovron. *Int. Migr. Rev.* **XXII:2** Summer:1988 pp. 208 – 225

22 Los migrantes, las clases sociales y la acumulacion capitalista en Quito *[In Spanish]*; [Migrants, social class and capitalist accumulation in Quito]. Nelson Rodríguez A. *Economia* **85** 1:1988 pp. 73 – 99

23 Migrants' linkages with their place of origin — the case of a new town in northern Israel. Baruch A. Kipnis. *Oral Hist.* **19:4** 1988 pp. 447 – 455

24 Migration and caste formation in Europe — the Belgian case. Eugeen Roosens. *Ethn. Racial* **11:2** 4:1988 pp. 207 – 217

25 Migration as a factor differentiating demographic structure of Polish towns. E. Pytel-Tafel. *Geogr. Pol.* **54:** :1988 pp. 109 – 120

26 Migration in Botswana. H. Max Miller; James D. Tarver. *Afr. Urb. Q.* **3:3&4** 8&11:1988 pp. 278 – 285

27 Migration patterns and the effects of migration on household structure and production in an East Anatolian village. Ernst Struck. *J. Econ. Soc. Geogr.* **79:3** 1988 pp. 210 – 219

28 Migration transition in small northern and eastern Caribbean states. Jerome L. McElroy; Klaus de Albuquerque. *Int. Migr. Rev.* **XXII:3** Fall:1988 pp. 30 – 58

29 Migration trends and regional labour market change in Poland. P. Korcelli. *Geogr. Pol.* **54:** :1988 pp. 5 – 18

30 Migration — causes, correlates, consequences, trends and policies. Francis Cherunilam. Bombay: Himalaya, 1987: x, 158 p.

31 Migration, remittances and the Himalaya. William Whittaker. *Pac. View.* **29:1** 5:1988 pp. 1 – 24

32 Migration, remittances, and the family. Oded Stark; Robert E.B. Lucas. *Econ. Dev. Cult. Change* **36:3** 4:1988 pp. 465 – 482

33 Migrations among Polish urban agglomerations. Z. Rykiel. *Geogr. Pol.* **54:** :1988 pp. 101 – 108

34 Le migrazioni nel bacino de Mediterraneo *[In Italian]*; [Migration in the Mediterranean basin]. Alessandra Palmieri. *Aff. Soc. Int.* **XVI:3** 1988 pp.83-103. Migration

35 Migrazioni, migranti e migrazioni multiple *[In Italian]*; [Migration, migrants and multiple migration]. W. Maffenini. *Riv. Int. Sci. Soc.* **XCVI:3** 7-9:1988 pp. 494 – 519

F.8: Migration [Migration]

36 On marriage and migration; Mariage et migration [French summary]. Oded Stark. *Eur. J. Pop.* **4:1** 9:1988 pp. 23 – 37

37 Perspectives on migrant labouring and the village economy in developing countries — the Asian experience in a world context. Jonathan Rigg. *Prog. H. Geog.* **12:1** 3:1988 pp. 66 – 86

38 Policy aspects of development and individual mobility — migration and circulation from Ecuador's rural Sierra. Lawrence A. Brown; Jorge A. Brea; Andrew R. Goetz. *Econ. Geogr.* **64** 1988 pp. 147 – 170

39 Rural-urban migration and identity change — case studies from the Sudan. Fouad N. Ibrahim [Ed.]; Helmut S. Ruppert [Ed.]. Bayreuth: Druckhaus Bayreuth Verlagsgesellschaft, 1988: 176 p. (ill., maps) *ISBN: 3922808190; LofC: 89218579.* Includes bibliographical references. [Bayreuther geowissenschaftliche Arbeiten. : No. 11]

40 Rural-urban migration in Pakistan — the case of Karachi. Frits Selier. Lahore, Pakistan: Vanguard, 1988: 166 p. (ill) *ISBN: 9694020131; LofC: 89930092.* Includes bibliographical references.

41 Seeking immigration through matrimonial alliance — a study of advertisements in an ethnic weekly; [French summary]; [Spanish summary]. Gura Bhargava. *J. Comp. Fam. Stud.* **XIX:2** Summer:1988 pp. 245 – 259

42 Sociological implications of rural to rural migration — a case study of rural immigrants in Punjab. A.K. Gupta. Allahabad: Vohra, 1988: xiii, 148 p. *ISBN: 81 85072 19 1.*

43 The sociology of involuntary migration. Barbara E. Harrell-Bond; Laila Monahan. *Curr. Sociol.* **36:2** Summer:1988 pp. 1 – 153

44 Spatial barriers — concepts, use and an application to intra-regional migration. Z. Rykiel. *Geogr. Pol.* **54** :1988 pp. 33 – 42

45 A structural perspective on labour migration in underdeveloped countries. Nanda R. Shrestha. *Prog. H. Geog.* **12:2** 6:1988 pp. 179 – 207

46 Temporary townsfolk? Siwai migrants in urban Papua New Guinea. John Connell. *Pac. Stud.* **11:3** 7:1988 pp. 77 – 100

International migration [Migration internationale]

47 Africa's refugees — causes, solutions, and consequences. John R. Rogge. *E.Afr. Soc. Sci. Res. R.* **IV:1** January:1988 pp. 83 – 108

48 L'aménagement à contre-temps — nouveaux territoires immigrés à Marseille et Tunis [In French]; [Planning against the flow — new immigrant areas at Marseille and Tunis]. Alain Tarrius; Michel Peraldi [Ed.]; Geneviève Marotel [Ed.]. Paris: L'Harmattan, 1988: 152 p. *ISBN: 2858029210.* Bibliography — p.146-150. [Villes et entreprises.]

49 Caribbean skilled international migration and the transnational household. Elizabeth M. Thomas-Hope. *Oral Hist.* **19:4** 1988 pp. 423 – 432

50 Considerazioni socio-demografiche sulla emigrazione italiana 1950-1985 [In Italian]; [Socio- democratic considerations on Italian emigration]. Francesco Piccione. *Aff. Soc. Int.* **XVI:4** 1988 pp. 15 – 44

51 Contemporary American immigrants — patterns of Filipino, Korean and Chinese settlement in the United States. Luciano Mangiafico. New York: Praeger, 1988: 211 p. *ISBN: 0275927261; LofC: 87-17752.* Includes bibliography and index.

F.8: Migration *[Migration]* — International migration *[Migration internationale]*

52 Differential social integration among first generation Greeks in New York — participation in religious institutions. Anna Veglery. *Int. Migr. Rev.* **XXII:4** Winter:1988 pp. 627 – 657

53 Egyptian international labor migration and social processes — toward regional integration. Ralph R. Sell. *Int. Migr. Rev.* **XXII:3** Fall:1988 pp. 87 – 108

54 Emigration and immigration in Italy — recent trends. Francesco. Calvanese; Enrico. Pugliese. *Labour* **2:3** Winter:1988 pp. 181 – 199

55 L'emigrazione italiana in Brasile *[In Italian]*; [Italian migration to Brazil]. Diego Brasioli. *Aff. Soc. Int.* **XVI:3** 1988 pp. 29 – 36

56 En torno a la migración dominicana en P.R. *[In Spanish]*; [Dominican migration in Puerto Rico]. Laura L. Ortiz Negrón. *Rev. Cien. Soc.* **XXVII: 3-4** 9-12: 1988 pp. 147 – 153

57 Entering the working world — following the descendants of Europe's immigrant labour force. Czarina Wilpert *[Ed.]*. Aldershot: Gower, 1988: viii, 181 p. *ISBN: 0566056453.* [Studies in European migration.]

58 Ethnic associations and the welfare state — services to immigrants in five countries. Shirley Jenkins *[Ed.]*. New York: Columbia University Press, 1988: 299 p. *ISBN: 0231056907. Includes bibliographical references.* [Social Work and Social Issues.]

59 Les Français devant l'immigration *[In French]*; [The French faced with immigration]. Olivier Milza. Bruxelles: Editions Complexe, 1988: 217 p. *ISBN: 2870272510.* [Questions au XXe siècle.]

60 From India to Mauritius — a brief history of immigration and the Indo-Mauritian community. S. Chandrasekhar *[Ed.]*. La Jolla, Calif.: Population Review, 1988: 114 p. *ISBN: 096090803x.*

61 From settlers to skilled transients — the changing structure of British international migration. A.M. Findlay. *Oral Hist.* **19:4** 1988 pp. 401 – 410

62 Government policies and international migration of skilled workers in Sub-Saharan Africa. William T.S. Gould. *Oral Hist.* **19:4** 1988 pp. 433 – 445

63 Harvest of confusion — migrant workers in US agriculture. Philip L. Martin. Boulder: Westview Press, 1988: xvi, 238 p. *ISBN: 0813376122.* [Westview special studies in agriculture science and policy.]

64 Heirs of the Greek catastrophe — the social life of Asia Minor refugees in Piraeus. Renée Hirschon. Oxford: Clarendon Press, 1988: xvii, 280 p. *Bibliography — p.265-271. Includes index.*

65 Hispanic immigration and labor market segmentation. Gregory DeFreitas. *Ind. Relat.* **27:2** Spring:1988 pp. 195 – 214

66 Ideology and immigration — Australia, 1976 to 1987. Katharine Betts. Carlton, Vic: Melbourne University Press, 1988: ix, 234 p. (ill) *ISBN: 0522843514. Includes index; Bibliography — p.215-226.*

67 Illegal aliens — their employment and employers. Barry R. Chiswick. Kalamazoo: W.E.Upjohn Institute for Employment Research, 1988: 160 p. *ISBN: 0880990597; LofC: 88-010062. Bibliography.*

68 Immigrant and native ethnic enterprises in Mexican American neighborhoods — differing perceptions of Mexican immigrant workers. Niles Hansen; Gilberto Cardenas. *Int. Migr. Rev.* **XXII:2** Summer:1988 pp. 226 – 242

69 L'immigration *[In French]*; [Immigration]. Alain Limousin *[Contrib.]*; Agnès Hochet *[Contrib.]*; Joseph Krulic *[Contrib.]*; Patrick Weil *[Contrib.]*; Rémy Leveau *[Contrib.]*; Catherine Wihtol de Wenden *[Contrib.]*;

F.8: Migration *[Migration]* — International migration *[Migration internationale]*

Claude-Valentin Marie *[Contrib.]*; Diana Pinto *[Contrib.]*; Pierre Milza *[Contrib.]*; Bruno Etienne *[Contrib.] and others. Collection of 11 articles.* **Pouvoirs**, 47, 1988 pp. 1 – 144

70 L'immigration *[In French]*; [Immigration]. Jean Massot *[Contrib.]*; André Lebon *[Contrib.]*; Giampiero Rellini *[Contrib.]*; Maura Rolandi Ricci *[Contrib.]*; Carlos Castro-Almeida *[Contrib.]*; Guy Le Moigne *[Contrib.]*; Paul Simard *[Contrib.]*; Mark J. Miller *[Contrib.]*; Michel Cansot *[Contrib.]*; Arlette Vialle *[Contrib.] and others. Collection of 14 articles.* **R. Fr. Admin. Publ.**, 47, 7-9:1988 pp. 5 – 120

71 Immigration and the earnings of youth in the U.S. Benjamin N. Matta; Anthony V. Popp. *Int. Migr. Rev.* **XXII:1** Spring:1988 pp. 104 – 116

72 Immigration et intégration sociale des Haïtiens au Québec *[In French]*; [Immigration and social integration of Haitians in Quebec]. Wilfrid Dubuisson. Sherbrooke: Naaman; Port-au-Prince — Imprimerie Henri Deschamps, 1988: 148 p.

73 The institutional structure of immigration as a determinant of inter-racial competition — a comparison of Britain and Canada. Jeffrey G. Reitz. *Int. Migr. Rev.* **XXII:1** Spring:1988 pp. 117 – 146

74 International migration today. Reginald T. Appleyard *[Ed.]*; Charles Stahl *[Ed.]*. Paris: Unesco, 1988: 2 v. (ill.) *ISBN: 9231025279; LofC: 88- 212399.*

75 Iranian immigrants and refugees in Norway. Zahra Kamalkhani. Bergen: University of Bergen Department of Social Anthropology, 1988: 214 p. *Bibliography — p.203-214.* [Bergen Studies in Social Anthropology; Migration Project studies; Skriftserie. : No. 43]

76 Jewish immigration from Israel. Asher Friedberg; Aharon Kfir. *Jew. J. Socio.* **XXX:1** 6:1988 pp. 5 – 15

77 Kreativität und Leistung — Ursachen und Formen des Wandels der westdeutschen Kulturlandschaft unter dem Einfluß der Vertriebenen *[In German]*; [Creativity and achievement — changes in West German culture due to the influence of displaced persons]. Marion Frantzioch. *AWR B.* **26:1** 1988 pp. 4 – 17

78 Mexico y Estados Unidos — frente a la migración de los indocumentados *[In Spanish]*; [Mexico and the U.S.A. — facing illegal immigration]. Manuel García y Griego; Mónica Verea Campos *[Ed.]*. Mexico: Grupo Editorial Miguel Angel Porrú, 1988: 175 p. *ISBN: 9688421421. Bibliography — p.153-174.* [Las Ciencias Sociales.]

79 Migrant hands in a distant land — Australia's post-war immigration. Jock Collins. Sydney: Pluto, 1988: 302 p. *ISBN: 0949138193. Bibliography — p.286-298.*

80 Migrations et relations internationales — le cas haïtiano-dominicain *[In French]*; [Migration and international relations — the Haitian-Dominican case]. Suzy Castor. Port-au-Prince: Imprimerie le Natal, 1988: 134 p.

81 The mobility of labor and capital — a study in international investment and labor flow. Saskia Sassen. Cambridge: Cambridge University Press, 1988: xi, 224 p. *ISBN: 0521322278; LofC: 87-14586. Bibliography — p.202-220 Includes index.*

82 La mosaïque France — histoire des étrangers et de l'immigration *[In French]*; [The French mosaic — a history of foreigners and immigration]. Yves Lequin *[Ed.]*. Paris: Larousse, 1988: 480 p. (ill) *ISBN: 2035231140.*

F.8: Migration *[Migration]* — International migration *[Migration internationale]*

83 Palestinians in Lebanon — status ambiguity, insecurity and flux. Rosemary Sayigh. *Race Class* **XXX:1** 7-8:1988 pp. 13 – 32

84 Passage from India — Asian Indian immigrants in North America. Joan M. Jensen. New Haven: Yale University Press, 1988: x, 350 p. *ISBN: 0300038461. Bibliography — p.329-338.*

85 Peripherization of immigrant professionals — Korean physicians in the United States. Eui Hang Shin; Kyung-Sup Chang. *Int. Migr. Rev.* **XXII:4** Winter:1988 pp. 609 – 626

86 Les problèmes socio-éducatifs des immigrés en France *[In French]*; [Socio-educational problems of immigrants in France]. Ali Arayici. *R. Tun. Sci. Soc.* **25:92/93** 1988 pp. 155 – 180

87 Quality of life as an emigration factor in the eastern Caribbean. Graham M.S. Dann. *B. E.Carib. Aff.* **14:4** 9-10:1988 pp. 1 – 8

88 La question immigrée dans la France d'aujourd'hui *[In French]*; [The question of immigration in France today]. Jacques Voisard; Christiane Ducastelle *[Ed.]*. Paris: Calmann-Lévy, 1988: 151 p. *ISBN: 2702116337.*

89 Refugees and small business — the case of Soviet Jews and Vietnamese. Steven J. Gold. *Ethn. Racial* **11:4** 11:1988 pp. 411 – 438

90 Religions of immigrants from India and Pakistan — new threads in the American tapestry. Raymond Brady Williams. Cambridge: Cambridge University Press, 1988: - *ISBN: 0521351561. Includes bibliography.*

91 Remittances in temporary migration — a theoretical model and its testing with the Greek-German experience. Nicholas P. Glytsos. *Welt.liches Arc.* **124:3** 1988 pp. 524 – 549

92 I rifugiati in Italia *[In Italian]*; [Refugees in Italy]. Serenella Bellucci. *Aff. Soc. Int.* **XVI:3** 1988 pp. 37 – 44

93 Seeking immigration through matrimonial alliance — a study of advertisements in an ethnic weekly. Gura Bhargava. *J. Comp. Fam. Stud.* **XIX:2** Summer:1988 pp. 245 – 260

94 Skilled international labour migration. W.T.S. Gould *[Ed.]*; J. Salt *[Contrib.]*; A.M. Findlay *[Contrib.]*; P. White *[Contrib.]*; E.M. Thomas-Hope *[Contrib.]*. **Oral Hist.** , *19:4,* 1988 pp. 381 – 445

95 Skilled international migrants and urban structure in Western Europe. Paul White. *Oral Hist.* **19:4** 1988 pp. 411 – 422

96 South Asians as economic migrants in Britain. Badr Dahya. *Ethn. Racial* **11:4** 11:1988 pp. 439 – 455

97 Soviet Jewish emigration — a statistical test of two theories. Robert J. Brym. *Sov. Jew. Aff.* **18:3** Winter:1988 pp. 3 – 14

98 State incorporation of migrants and the reproduction of a middleman minority among Indochinese refugees. Jeremy Hein. *Sociol. Q.* **29:3** Fall:1988 pp. 463 – 478

99 Südostasien — Minderheiten, Migration, Flüchtlinge *[In German]*; [Southeast Asia — minorities, migration, refugees]. Werner Pfennig *[Ed.]*. Berlin: Quorum-Verl., 1988: 399 p. *ISBN: 3887262069. Werner Pfennig (Hrsg.).* [Berliner Studien zur internationalen Politik. : No. 12]

100 Swedish emigration to the United States reconsidered. Thor Norström. *Eur. Sociol. R.* **4:3** 12:1988 pp. 223 – 232

101 Towards a population policy — myths and misconceptions concerning the demographic effects of immigration. Christabel Young. *Aust. Q.* **60:2** Winter:1988 pp. 220 – 229

F.8: Migration *[Migration]* — **International migration** *[Migration internationale]*

102 Trade unions, Islam and immigration. Catherine Wihtol de Wenden. *Econ. Ind. Dem.* **9** 1988 pp. 65 – 82

103 Les Tunisiens de France — une forte concentration parisienne *[In French]*; [French Tunisian — strongly concentrated in Paris]. Salah Rimani; Michelle Guillon. Paris: CIEMI, [1988]: 153 p. (ill.) *ISBN: 2738401236; LofC: 89-127399. Bibliography — p.139- 142.* [Migrations et changements. : No. 19]

104 Wanderarbeiter aus der Türkei in der Europäischen Gemeinschaft — zur Zukunft der Gastarbeiterfrage in Europa *[In German]*; [Turkish migrant workers in the EEC — on the future of the European migrant labour question]. Kostas Dimakopoulos. Pfaffenweiler: Centaurus-Verlagsgesellschaft, 1988: 97 p. *ISBN: 3890852726. Includes bibliographical references.* [Rechtshistorische Reihe. : No. 70]

105 When borders don't divide — labor migration and refugee movements in the Americas. Patricia R. Pessar *[Ed.]*. New York: Center for Migration Studies, 1988: 220 p. *ISBN: 0934733260.*

G: Environment. Community. Rural. Urban —
Environment. Communauté. Rural. Urbain

G.1: Ecology. Geography. Human settlements — *Écologie. Géographie. Établissements humains*

1 Admission to citizenship. Herman R. van Gunsteren. *Ethics* **98:4** 7:1988 pp. 731 – 741

2 Bringing social theory to hazards research — conditions and consequences of the migration of environmental hazards. William C. Bogard. *Sociol. Pers.* **31:2** 4:1988 pp. 147 – 168

3 Contaminated communities — the social and pychological impacts of residential toxic exposure. Michael R. Edelstein. Boulder, Colo.: Westview, 1988: xviii, 217 p. (ill) *ISBN: 0813374472; LofC: 87-31653. Bibliography — p.199-210. Includes index.*

4 Desarrollo socioeconómico y el ambiente natural de Costa Rica — situación actual y perpectivas *[In Spanish]*; [Socio-economic development and the natural environment in Costa-Rica — the current situation and outlook]. Alonso Ramírez Solero *[Ed.]*; Tirso Maldonado Ulloa *[Ed.]*. San José: Heliconia, 1988: 159 p. *ISBN: 9977969000.*

5 Disease ecology — an introduction. Andrew Learmonth. Oxford: Basil Blackwell, 1988: x, 456 p. (ill) *ISBN: 0631148558; LofC: 87-11768. Bibliography — p364-424. Includes index.*

6 Ecology and human development. New Delhi: Inter-India, 1988: xviii, 155 p. *ISBN: 81 210 0195 1.* [Current anthropological and archaeological perspectives. : Vol. 5]

7 Evaluaciones de impacto ambiental — los aspectos sociales y la participacion publica *[In Spanish]*; [Environmental impact assessment — social aspects and public participation] *[Summary]*. Vincente Sánchez. *Eure* **XV:44** 12:1988 pp. 41 – 54

G.1: Ecology. Geography. Human settlements [Écologie. Géographie. Établissements humains]

8 France — géographie d'une societé [In French]; [France — geography of a society]. Armand Frémont. Paris: Flammarion, 1988: 290 p. ISBN: 2082128024. Bibliography — p.288-290.

9 The functioning and the development of Polish human geography. Zbigniew Rykiel. Prog. H. Geog. **12:3** 9:1988 pp. 391 – 408

10 Habitat, état et société au maghreb [In French]; [Habitat, state and society in Maghreb]. Pierre-Robert Baduel [Ed.]; Lahsen Abdelmaki [Contrib.]; Abdelghani Abouhani [Contrib.]; Samia Adjali [Contrib.]; Mohammed Ameur [Contrib.]; M. Ameur [Contrib.]; Abdelmajid Benabdellah [Contrib.]; Jean Bisson [Contrib.]; Sid Boubekeur [Contrib.]; Mohammed Bouhaba [Contrib.] and others. **Ann. Afr. Nord**, XXV, 1988 pp. 1 – 396

11 An historical geography of modern Australia — the restive fringe. J. M. Powell. Cambridge: Cambridge University Press, 1988: 430 p. (ill) ISBN: 0521256194. Includes bibliography and index. [Cambridge studies in historical geography.]

12 The historicity of human geography. Felix Driver. Prog. H. Geog. **12:4** 12:1988 pp. 497 – 506

13 Medical geography — selected papers from the 1986 Rutgers symposium. Robert Earickson [Contrib.]; Michael Greenberg [Contrib.]; Marian Craig [Contrib.]; Surinder M. Bhardwaj [Contrib.]; Madhusudana N. Rao [Contrib.]; Maggie Pearson [Contrib.]; D.R. Phillips [Contrib.]; J. Vincent [Contrib.]; Graham Betham [Contrib.]; G. Brent Hall [Contrib.] and others. Collection of 21 articles. **Soc. Sci. Med.**, 26:1, 1988 pp. 1 – 199

14 Organised groups, land use decisions, and ecological theory. James R. Hudson. Sociol. Pers. **31:1** 1:1988 pp. 122 – 141

15 Social policy for pollution-related diseases. Michael R. Reich [Contrib.]; Leslie I. Boden [Contrib.]; J. Raymond Miyares [Contrib.]; David Ozonoff [Contrib.]; Edward J. Burger [Contrib.]; Bruce Aronson [Contrib.]; Takehisa Awaji [Contrib.]; Tsuneo Tsukatani [Contrib.]; Stephen M. Soble [Contrib.]; Janis H. Brennan [Contrib.] and others. Collection of 11 articles. **Soc. Sci. Med.**, 27:10, 1988 pp. 1011 – 1123

16 Soil and vegetation changes under shifting cultivation in the miombo of East Africa. P. Stromgaard. Geog.ann. B. **70B:3** 1988 pp. 363 – 374

17 Space and living conditions in Poland — variations in the allocation of time according to size of settlement and macroregion. Maria Ciechocinska. Soc. Ind. **20:1** 2:1988 pp. 59 – 77

G.2: Community — *Communauté*

1 Community consultation in socially sensitive research — lessons from clinical trials of treatments for AIDS. Gary B. Melton; Robert J. Levine; Gerald P. Koocher; Robert Rosenthal; William C. Thompson. *Am. Psychol.* **43:7** 7:1988 pp. 573 – 581

2 Community development in a Mexican squatter settlement — a program evaluation. Scott Cummings; Leonora Finn Paradis; Cheryl Neal Alatriste; James Cornehls. *Pop. Res. Pol. R.* **7:2** 1988 pp. 159 – 188

3 Community organizations and crime. Wesley G. Skogan. *Crime Just.* **10** 1988 pp. 39 – 78

4 Components of neighborhood satisfaction — responses from urban and suburban single-parent women. Christine C. Cook. *Envir. Behav.* **20:2** 3:1988 pp. 115 – 149

5 The effect of changing household composition on neighbourhood satisfaction. Daphne Spain. *Urban Aff. Q.* **23:4** 6:1988 pp. 581 – 600

6 Gender, social control and community services. Lois Bryson; Anne Edwards. *Aust. N.Z. J. Soc.* **24:3** 11:1988 pp. 398 – 419

7 Hikou to Chiikishakai *[In Japanese]*; [Juvenile delinquency and community]. Kanehiro Hoshino. *Kokoro no Kagaku* Vol.22. *1988*. pp. 40 – 46

8 In service to America. Marvin Schwartz. London: University of Arkansas Press, 1988: 491 p. *ISBN: 1557280053*.

9 Kyoto-shi no community shisaku *[In Japanese]*; [Community policy of Kyoto]. Takahiro Shinohara. *Social Analysis* Vol.17. *1988*. pp. 33 – 39

10 The moral order of a suburb. M.P. Baumgartner. New York: Oxford University Press, 1988: 172 p. *ISBN: 019505413x. Includes index; Bibliography.*

11 Nagoya-shi no commmunity shisaku *[In Japanese]*; [Community policy of Nagoya]. Keiko Yasukochi. *Shakai Bunseki* Vol.17. *1988*. pp. 247 – 265

12 Neighborhood differences in attitudes toward policing — evidence for a mixed-strategy model of policing in a multi-ethnic setting. Roger G. Dunham; Geoffrey P. Alpert. *J. Crim. Law* **79:2** Summer:1988 pp. 504 – 523

13 People or place — variations in community leaders' subjective definitions of neighbourhood. Steven H. Haeberle. *Urban Aff. Q.* **23:4** 6:1988 pp. 616 – 634

14 Rhetoric, division and constraint — elements in local social mobilisation. Ed Young. *Sociol. Rev.* **36:2** 5:1988 pp. 297 – 319

15 The role of organizations in community participation — prevention of accidental injuries in a rural Swedish municipality. Lothar Schelp. *Soc. Sci. Med.* **26:11** 1988 pp. 1087 – 1093

16 The social history of a Bengal town. Indrani Ganguly. Bombay: Himalaya, 1987: xiii, 200 p.

17 Theme and variation in community policing. Jerome H. Skolnick; David H. Bayley. *Crime Just.* **10** 1988 pp. 1 – 37

G.3: Rural. Urban — Rural. Urbain

1 City versus countryside? The social consequences of development choices in China. Mark Selden. *Rev. F. Braudel. Ctr.* **XI:4** Autumn:1988 pp. 533 – 568
2 Explanations for the intensification of counterurbanization in the Federal Republic of Germany. Thomas Kontuly; Roland Vogelsang. *Prof. Geogr.* **40:1** 2:1988 pp. 42 – 54
3 The geography of urban-rural interaction in developing countries — essays for Alan B. Mountjoy. Robert B. Potter *[Ed.]*; P. T. H. Unwin *[Ed.]*; Alan B. Mountjoy *[Ed.]*. London: Routledge, 1988: 342 p. *ISBN: 0415004446. Includes index and bibliographies.*
4 Redistribution of the elderly population in Poland — regional and rural-urban dimensions. P. Korcelli; A. Potrykowska. *Geogr. Pol.* **54:** :1988 pp. 121 – 138
5 Rural-urban linkages in the Malawian context. D.P. Shaw. *Afr. Urb. Q.* **3:1:2** 2:5 pp. 95 – 99
6 Urban-rural linkages — research themes and directions. D. C. Funnell. *Geog.ann. B.* **70B:2** 1988 pp. 267 – 274

G.3.1: Rural sociology — *Sociologie rurale*
Sub-divisions: Peasant studies [*Études paysannes]*; Rural development [*Développement rurale]*

1 Aging in rural America. J.A. Krout *[Ed.]*; P.J. Krout *[Contrib.]*; G.D. Rowles *[Contrib.]*; V.R. Kivett *[Contrib.]*; D. Shenk *[Contrib.]*; D. McTavish; A. Martin Matthews *[Contrib.]*; P.G. Windley *[Contrib.]*; R.J. Scheidt; R.T. Coward *[Contrib.] and others. Collection of 7 articles.* **J. Rural St.** , *4:2*, 1988 pp. 99 – 168
2 Agrarian change in communist Laos. Grant Evans. Singapore: Institute of Southeast Asian Studies, 1988: 88 p. (ill) *ISBN: 9813035161; LofC: 89941218. Includes bibliographical references.* [ISEAS occasional paper.]
3 Agrarian relations and rural exploitation. B.C. Menta; A. Prasad. New Delhi: Ashish, 1988: xii, 268 p. *ISBN: 8170241634.*
4 La agricultura pampeana — tranformaciones productivas y sociales *[In Spanish]*; [Pampas agriculture — transformation in production and society]. Osvaldo Barsky *[Ed.]*. Buenos Aires: Fondo de Cultura Económica, 1988: 422 p. *ISBN: 950557035x.* [Sección de obras de economía.]
5 And here the world ends — the life of an Argentine village. Kristin Hoffman Ruggiero. Stanford, California: Stanford University Press, 1988: viii, 226 p. *Bibliography — p.213-227.*
6 Changing agrarian social structure in rural Rajasthan. H.S. Saxena. Jaipur: Classic, 1988: x, 184 p.
7 Comunidad y produccion en la agricultura andina *[In Spanish]*; [Community and production in Andian agriculture]. César Fonseca; Enrique Mayer *[Ed.]*. Lima: Asociación peruana para el fomento de las ciencias sociales, 1988: 212 p. *Bibliography — p.197-209.*

G.3.1: Rural sociology *[Sociologie rurale]*

8 Deforestation — social dynamics in watersheds and mountain ecosystems. Jack D. Ives *[Ed.]*; Douglas Pitt *[Ed.]*. London: Routledge, 1988: xiii, 247 p. *ISBN: 041500456x. edited by J. Ives and D. C. Pitt.* [European Year of the Environment.]

9 Ecology of rural India. Singh Pramod *[Ed.]*. New Delhi: Ashish, 1987: 2V. xvii, 310 p., xi, 217 p. *ISBN: 81 7024 089 1.*

10 The ecology of survival — case studies from Northeast African history. Douglas H. Johnson *[Ed.]*; David M. Anderson *[Ed.]*. London: Lester Crook, 1988: 340 p. (ill) *ISBN: 1870915003. Includes bibliography and index.*

11 The elderly in rural environments. J.A. Krout. *J. Rural St.* **4:2** 1988 pp. 103 – 114

12 Espaces ruraux et dynamiques sociales en Europe du sud *[In French]*; [Rural areas and social dynamics in southern Europe]. Fernando Medeiros. *Annales* **43:5** 9-10:1988 pp. 1081 – 1107

13 A failed graft — rural sociology in New Zealand. I. Carter. *J. Rural St.* **4:3** 1988 pp. 215 – 222

14 The green revolution and social inequalities in rural India. D.N. Dhanagare. *B. Concern. Asia. Schol.* **20:2** 1988 pp. 2 – 13

15 Indian village society in transition. P. Shankar. Delhi: Commonwealth, 1988: xv, 290 p. *ISBN: 81 9000 26 1.*

16 An investigation of villages in the Republic of Ireland. Desmond A. Gillmor. *Irish Geogr.* **21:2** 1988 pp. 57 – 68

17 Land and labor in South Asia. Inderjit Singh; World Bank. Washington, D. C.: The World Bank, 1988: viii, 236 p. *ISBN: 0821311298. Bibliography — p.184-236.* [World Bank discussion papers. : No. 33]

18 Land, power and people — rural elite in transition, 1801-1970. Singh Rajendra. New Delhi: Sage, 1988: 264 p. *ISBN: 81 7036 085 4.*

19 The mass media and village life — an Indian study. Paul Hartmann; B. R. Patil *[Ed.]*; Anita Dighe *[Ed.]*. New Delhi: Sage Publications, 1988: 286 p. (ill) *ISBN: b8956993; LofC: 88-18458. Bibliography — p.270-272.* [Communication and human values.]

20 Noson ni okeru sogofujososhiki no hensen *[In Japanese]*; [The changing process of the mutual-aid system in rural society]. Keiko Endo. **The Tohoku Gakuin University Review** Vol.92. 1988. pp. 65 – 91

21 La oligarquía agraria de Tlaxcala en los años setenta *[In Spanish]*; [The agrarian oligarchy of Tlaxcala in the 70s]. Mario Ramírez Rancaño. *Rev. Mexicana Soc.* **L:1** 1-3:1988 pp. 213 – 241

22 Participation in social research in rural Ethiopia. Siegfried Pausewang. *J. Mod. Afr. S.* **26:2** 6:1988 pp. 253 – 276

23 Reforma agraria y proceso de paz en Colombia *[In Spanish]*; [Agrarian reform and peace processes in Colombia]. Christian Gros. *Rev. Mexicana Soc.* **L:1** 1-3:1988 pp. 287 – 302

24 Representing reciprocity, reproducing domination — ideology and the labour process in Latin American contract farming. Roger A.J. Clapp. *J. Peasant Stud.* **16:1** 10:1988 pp. 5 – 39

25 Residential land tenure and housing development in the major villages of Botswana. John W. Bruce. *Afr. Urb. Q.* **3:1:2** 2:5 pp. 100 – 112

G.3.1: Rural sociology *[Sociologie rurale]*

26 Rich man's farming — the crisis in agriculture. Michael Franklin. London: Routledge, 1988: viii, 103 p. *ISBN: 0415010616. Includes index.* [Chatham House papers.]

27 Rural depopulation areas in Poland. A. Gawryszewski; A. Potrykowska. *Geogr. Pol.* **54:** :1988 pp. 81 – 100

28 Rural economy of Rajasthan. R.L. Godara. Delhi: Daya, 1988: vi, 165 p. *ISBN: 81 7035 038 7.*

29 Rural enterprise — case studies from developing countries. Malcolm Harper; Shailendra Vyakarnam *[Ed.].* London: Intermediate Technology, 1988: vi, 105 p. *ISBN: 1853390011.*

30 Rural families in Soviet Georgia — a case study in Ratcha province. Tamara Dragadze. London: Routledge, 1988: 250 p. *Includes bibliography and index.*

31 Rural Fiji. John Overton *[Ed.]*; Barbara Banks *[Ed.]*; Imam Ali *[Ed.].* Suva: University of the South Pacific, 1988: xii, 230 p. *ISBN: 9820200458. Bibliography — p.209-225.*

32 Rural Iraqi women and extension centers — policies and practices. S.K. Araji. *J. Rural St.* **4:3** 1988 pp. 263 – 273

33 Rural land-use planning in developed nations. Paul J. Cloke *[Ed.].* London: Unwin Hyman, 1988: 289 p. (ill) *ISBN: 0047110252; LofC: 88-016973. Includes bibliography and index.*

34 Rural small towns — an environmental context for aging. P.G. Windley; R.J. Scheidt. *J. Rural St.* **4:2** 1988 pp. 151 – 158

35 Rural suburbanisation and village expansion in the Rhine Rift valley — a cross-frontier comparison. M. T. Wild; P. N. Jones. *Geog.ann. B.* **70B:2** 1988 pp. 275 – 290

36 Rural women — management in farm and home. A. Laxmi Devi. New Delhi: Northern Book Centre, 1988: 180 p. *ISBN: 81 8511 920 1.*

37 Sado Higashi-hama no ichi gyoson ni okeru sonraku no tenkai to kouzou *[In Japanese]*; [The change and structure of a fishing village in Higashihama district, Sado island]. Yasuyuki Sato. ***Annual Bulletin of Rural Studies** Vol.24. 1988.* pp. 191 – 230

38 Sasanishiki no mura ni ikite — Miyagi-ken beisaku chitai no hitobito *[In Japanese]*; [Living in a rural village]. Yoshiko Sugaya. ***The Community** Vol.82. 1988.* pp. 1 – 108

39 Should we save the family farm? David Moberg. *Dissent* **35:2** Spring:1988 pp. 201 – 211

40 The social framework of rural exchange in Bangladesh. Geoffrey D. Wood. *J. Soc. Stud. Dhaka* **:40** 4:1988 pp. 1 – 30

41 Social risk and rural sociology. James A. Christenson. *Rural Sociol.* **53:1** 1988 pp. 1 – 24

42 Sonraku no shakai kozo to sono katsudo no tenkai katei *[In Japanese]*; [The social structure of the hamlet and its change over the past half century]. Yoshihiko Aikawa. ***Nogyokeizai Kenkyu** Vol.59; No.4 - 1988.* pp. 199 – 207

43 A study on the power structure of rural communities in Cheju Island. Haeng-Chull Shin. *Korean Soc. Sci. J.* **14** 1988 pp. 83 – 102

44 Success in small farmer development — paper making at Pang and Nanlibang, Nepal. Donald A. Messerschmidt. *World Dev.* **16:6** 6:1988 pp. 733 – 750

G.3.1: Rural sociology *[Sociologie rurale]*

45 Technological change and its impact on the rural structure of Pakistan. Karamat Ali. *S.Asia B.* **8:1&2** 1988 pp. 20 – 26

46 Thai nouson ni okeru shūgyou kouzou no chiiki-sa *[In Japanese]*; [A note on regional differences in occupational structure in rural Thailand]. Atsushi Kitahara. ***Southeast Asian Studies*** *Vol.26; No.3 - 1988.* pp. 27 – 52

47 Thai touhokubu sonraku ni okeru sonraku soshiki to shūkyou seikatsu — yobi chousa houkoku *[In Japanese]*; [Village organization and religious life in northeast Thailand]. Izuru Sahai; Boonyong Chunsuvimol. ***Bulletin of the Graduate School, Toyo University Graduate Program of Sociology*** *Vol.24. 1988.* pp. 67 – 82

48 Трудовые ресурсы села: (пробл сезон занятости) *[In Russian]*; [Working resources of the village]. I.V. Belokon'. Kiev: Science Dumka, 1987: 174 p. [AN USSR Council for Study of Production Powers of USSR.]

49 Uneven development and racial composition in the Deep South — 1970-1980. Glenna Colclough. *Rural Sociol.* **53:1** 1988 pp. 73 – 86

50 Urbanization, immigration, and rural change — a study of West Bengal. Biplab Dasgupta *[Ed.]*. Calcutta: A.Mukherjee, 1988: 523 p.

51 Village life in India — past and present. Bidyadhar Misra. Delhi: Ajanta, 1988: vi, 168 p. *ISBN: 81 2020 194 9.*

52 What's rural about rural aging? An Appalachian perspective. G.D. Rowles. *J. Rural St.* **4:2** 1988 pp. 115 – 124

53 Women participation in rural environment. G.P. Swarnkar. Allahabad: Chugh, 1988: xi, 136 p. *ISBN: 81 850 7637 5.*

Peasant studies *[Études paysannes]*

54 La agricultura campesina de la sierra — ¿es posible desarrollarla? *[In Spanish]*; [The mountain peasant farmer — is it possible to develop them?]. Daniel Cotlear. *Soc. Part.* **41** 3:1988 pp. 61 – 75

55 Los campesinos en el umbral de un nuevo milenio *[In Spanish]*; [Peasants on the verge of a new millenium]. Arturo Warman. *Rev. Mexicana Soc.* **L:1** 1-3:1988 pp. 3 – 12

56 Capital, state and peasantry — Japan. B.K. Jahangir. *J. Soc. Stud. Dhaka* **:42** 10:1988 pp. 95 – 108

57 Una discusión teórica del concepto de campesino — de los individuos a las relaciones *[In Spanish]*; [A theoretical look at the peasant concept — from individuals to relationships]. Fernando Cortés; Oscar Cuéllar. *Rev. Parag. Sociol.* **25:71** 1-4:1988 pp. 97 – 118

58 Entre faucilles et marteaux — pluractivités et stratégies paysannes *[In French]*; [Between the hammer and the sickle — peasant activities and strategies]. Gilbert Garrier *[Ed.]*; Ronald Hubscher *[Ed.]*. Lyon: Presses universitaires de Lyon; Paris — Éditions de la Maison des sciences de l'homme, 1988: 242 p. *ISBN: 2729703411.*

59 The "new peasant movement" in India. Gail Omvedt. *B. Concern. Asia. Schol.* **20:2** 1988 pp. 14 – 23

60 Our daily bread — the peasant question and family farming in the Colombian Andes. Nola Reinhardt. Berkeley: California U.P., 1988: 308 p. *ISBN: 0520062256.*

61 A parasztság társadalmi-termelési viszonyainak átalakulása 1930-1985 *[In*

G.3.1: Rural sociology *[Sociologie rurale]* — **Peasant studies** *[Études paysannes]*

Hungarian]; [A history of peasantry in 20th century Hungary]. Imre Tar. [Budapest]: Kossuth, 1988: 229 p. *ISBN: 9630932105.* Includes bibliographical references.

62 Les paysanneries du Michoacan au Mexique *[In French]*; [The peasantry of Michoacan, Mexico]. Thierry Linck *[Ed.]*; Roberto Santana *[Ed.]*. Paris: Éditions du CNRS, 1988: 193 p. *ISBN: 2222042690.*

63 Peasant economics — farm households and agrarian development. Frank Ellis. Cambridge: Cambridge University Press, 1988: xiv, 257 p. (ill) *ISBN: 0521324467; LofC: 87-14815. Bibliography — p.242-249. Includes index.* [Wye studies in agricultural and rural development.]

64 Peasants under peripheral capitalism. Hashim Wan. Bangi,Malaysia: Penerbit Universiti Kebangsaan Malaysia, 1988: 205 p. *ISBN: 9679421244. Bibliography — p.199-205.*

65 Theories of the exploited peasantry — a critical review. Antonio Yúnez N.. *J. Peasant Stud.* **15:2** 1:1988 pp. 190 – 217

Rural development *[Développement rurale]*

66 Coordination between government and voluntary organizations (NGOs) in Thailand's rural development. Maniemai Tongsawate; Walter E. J. Tips. *Publ. Adm. D.* **8:4** 10-12:1988 pp. 401 – 420

67 Development or dependence — the pattern of change in a Fijian village. Asesela Ravuvu. Suva: Institute of Pacific Studies, University of the South Pacific, 1988: xviii, 204 p. (ill. (some col.)) *ISBN: 9820200407. Includes index; Errata inserted; Bibliography — p.. 197-200.*

68 Dimensiuni ale dezvoltării socio-economice a ruralului și modul de locuire *[In Romanian]*; (Dwelling and the dimensions of the socio-economic development of the rural area); (Dimensions du développement socio-économique de l'environnement rural et l'habitat: *Title only in French*); (Размеры социально-экономического развития сельской среды и образ общежития: *Title only in Russian*). Alexandru R. Florian. *Viit. Soc.* **LXXXI** 1-2:1988 pp. 51 – 63

69 Integrated rural development in Tanzania. L. Kleemeier. *Publ. Adm. D.* **8:1** 1-3:1988 pp. 61 – 73

70 Off-farm employment and rural development — Pakistan — non-agricultural occupations in marginal farm households. Klaus Klennert. Aachen: Alano-Verlag, 1988: 497 p. *ISBN: 392400773x. Bibliography — p.479-493.* [Socioeconomic studies on rural development. : Vol. 81]

71 La politique de la Banque mondiale et le développement de stratégies alternatives pour le secteur rural au Mexique *[In French]*; [World Bank policy and the development of alternative strategies for the rural sector in Mexico]. Gonzalo Pineda Bravo. Louvain-la-Neuve: CIACO, 1988: 381 p.

72 Predictors of success in a participatory village development project in Thailand. Michael Useem; Lou Setti; Kanung Kanchanabucha. *Publ. Adm. D.* **8:3** 7-9:1988 pp. 289 – 303

73 The role of women in rural development. S. Giriappa. Delhi: Daya, 1988: 123 p. *ISBN: 81 703 5041 7.*

74 Rural development. New Delhi: Inter-India, 1988: xix, 294 p. [Current anthropological and archaeological perspectives. : Vol. 7]

G.3.1: Rural sociology [Sociologie rurale] — Rural development [Développement rurale]

75 Rural development and planning. Surendra Singh. New Delhi: Shree Pub, 1988: viii, 160 p.
76 Rural development in India — a study of industry, business and service sector. R.T. Tewari. New Delhi: Ashish, 1988: viii, 88 p. *ISBN: 8170241731.*
77 Rural development in India — poverty and development. K. Venkata Reddy. Bombay: Himalaya, 1988: xvi, 474 p.
78 Rural development issues. D. Vasudeva Rao. New Delhi: ESS ESS Pub, 1988: 84 p.
79 Rural transformation in tropical Africa. Douglas Rimmer *[Ed.]*. London: Belhaven, 1988: 177 p. (ill) *ISBN: 1852930128. Includes index.*
80 Small urban centers in rural development — what else is development other than helping your own home town? Aidan Southall. *Afr. Stud. R.* **31:3** 12:1988 pp. 1 – 15
81 Sociology of rural development. B.N. Thakur. New Delhi: Classical, 1988: vi, 202 p. *ISBN: 81 705 4080 1.*
82 Sociology of rural development in India. Raghvendra Pratap Singh. Delhi: Discovery, 1987: vi, 184 p.
83 Village republics — economic conditions for collective action in South India. Robert Wade. Cambridge: Cambridge University Press, 1988: xii, 238 p. (1ill) *ISBN: 0521301467; LofC: 86-33389. Bibliography — p.223-234. Includes index.* [Cambridge South Asian studies.]
84 Who shares? — co-operatives and rural development. D.W. Attwood *[Ed.]*; B.S. Baviskar *[Ed.]*. Delhi: Oxford University Press, 1988: x, 432 p. *ISBN: 0195621050. Bibliographies.*
85 Women, television and rural development. Binod C. Agrawal; Kumkum Rai. New Delhi: National, 1988: x, 99 p. *ISBN: 81 214 0107 0.*

G.3.2: Urban sociology — *Sociologie urbaine*

Sub-divisions: Urban housing *[Logement urbain]*; Urban planning and development *[Aménagement et développement urbain]*; Urban transport *[Transport urbain]*; Urbanization *[Urbanisation]*

1 Argentina's urban system and the economic crisis. Mabel Manzanal. *Cities* **5:3** 8:1988 pp. 260 – 267
2 Australian cities — the challenge of the 1980s. M.T. Daly. *Aust. Geogr.* **19:1** 5:1988 pp. 149 – 161
3 Cambios recientes en el sistema urbano Chileno — un analisis de la dinamica historica y particular de las organizaciones espaciales *[In Spanish]*; [Recent changes in the Chilean urban system — an analysis of the dynamics historical and in particular of spatial organizations] *[Summary]*. Fernando Soler Rioseco; Sergio León Balza. *Eure* **XIV:43** 10:1988 pp. 153 – 167
4 La Casbah d'Alger entre réhabilitation et réanimation *[In French]*; The Algiers Kasbah — between rehabilitation and recovery *[Summary]*. Djaffar Lesbet. *Peup. Médit.* 4-6:1988 pp. 59 – 78
5 Città e qualità ambientale *[In Italian]*; [The town and environmental quality]. Emma Finocchiaro. *Sociologia [Rome]* **XXII:1** 1988 pp. 15 – 81

G.3.2: Urban sociology [Sociologie urbaine]

6 City and urban fringe — a case study of Bareilly. H. Lal. New Delhi: Concept, 1987: xvi, 165 p. *ISBN: 81 7022 190 0.*

7 The city as a moral universe. Yi-Fu Tuan. *Geogr. Rev.* **78:3** 7:1988 pp. 316 – 324

8 Clichés of urban doom and other essays. Ruth Glass. Oxford: Basil Blackwell, 1988: 266 p. (ill) *ISBN: 0631128069. Includes index.*

9 Composition de la forme urbaine du Caire *[In French]*; Decomposing/ recomposing urban Cairo *[Summary]*. Mercedes Volait. *Peup. Médit.* **41-42** 10:1987-3:1988 pp. 105 – 118

10 Crafting urban partnerships. Implementing neighborhood assistance programs. Marshall R. Goodman. *Admin. Soc.* **20:3** 11:1988 pp. 251 – 274

11 Crisis in the built environment — the case of the Muslim city. Jamel Akbar. Singapore: Concept Media, 1988: 260 p. *ISBN: 9004087575. Bibliography.*

12 Une définition institutionnelle du lien social — la question du domicile de secours *[In French]*; An institutional definition of the social bond — residence *[Summary]*. Didier Renard. *R. Fr. Sci. Pol.* **38:3** 6:1988 pp. 370 – 386

13 Democracia urbana *[In Spanish]*; [Urban democracy]. Eduardo Neira Alva. *Soc. Part.* **44** 12:1988 pp. 7 – 32

14 Disposable people — forced evictions in South Korea. London: Catholic Institute for International Relations, 1988: 56 p. *ISBN: 1852870281.*

15 Dynamiques regionales et urbaines en Mediterranée *[In French]*; [Regional and urban change in the Mediterranean]. H. Regnault *[Contrib.]*; J.P. Carriere *[Contrib.]*; A. Trachen *[Contrib.]*; F. Charfi *[Contrib.]*; A. El Habaieb *[Contrib.]*; B. Semmoud *[Contrib.]*; J. Villaverde Castro *[Contrib.]*; B. Roux *[Contrib.]*; J.M. Miossec *[Contrib.]*; B. Morel *[Contrib.] and others. Collection of 5 articles.* **R. Ec. Reg. Urb.** , *4,* 1988 pp. 541 – 725

16 Elderly people in the socio-spatial structure of some Polish towns. G. Weclawowicz. *Geogr. Pol.* **54:** :1988 pp. 139 – 149

17 Espaces marchands et concentrations urbaines minoritaires — la petite Asie de Paris *[In French]*; [Retail areas and concentrations of urban minorities — the "little Asia" of Paris] *[Summary]*. Anne Raulin. *Cah. Int. Soc.* **35:LXXXV** 7-12:1988 pp. 225 – 42

18 L'État, «le bas», les cours — exclusion sociale et petite production immobilière à Abidjan *[In French]*; (The state, the poor — social exclusion and small-scale real estate in Abidjan); (Der Staat, «le bas», die Hinterhöfe — der soziale Ausschluß und die kleine Immobilienproduktion in Abidjan: *Title only in German)*; (El Estado, los probres los conventillos — exclusión social y pequeña producción inmobiliaria en Abidjan); (Gosudarstvo , «nizy», dvory — social'nye isključenija i melkoe žilioščnoe proizvodstvo v Abidžane: *Title only in Russian).* Alain Dubresson; Alphonse Yapi-Diahou. *R. T-Monde* **XXIX:116** 10-12:1988 pp. 1083 – 1100

19 Evaluating cities, multidimensionality, and diminishing returns. Stuart S. Nagel. *Eval. Rev.* **12:1** 2:1988 pp. 60 – 75

20 La formation des nouveaux territoires urbains et leur «crise» — les quartiers nord de Marseille *[In French]*; Forming new urban spaces and their «crisis» — the northern quarters of Marseilles *[Summary]*. Michel Anselme. *Peup. Médit. 4-6:1988* pp. 121 – 129

G.3.2: Urban sociology [Sociologie urbaine]

21 Future cities and information technology. Eskil Block; Tibor Hottovy [Ed.]. Gävle: National Swedish Institute for Building Research, 1988: 420 p. ISBN: 9154093074.

22 Gendai toshi no shakai-sou to shakai-shūdan — seikatsu to dentou no shiten kara [In Japanese]; [The life and tradition of modern Japanese cities]. Makoto Matsudaira. *Mun. Prob. Vol.79; No.4 - 1988*. pp. 17 – 28

23 Gentrification and distressed cities — an assessment of trends in intrametropolitan migration. Kathryn P. Nelson. Madison, Wis.: University of Wisconsin Press, 1988: xiii, 187 p. (ill.) ISBN: 0299111601. Bibliography — p.163-180. [Social demography.]

24 Gérer la complexité urbaine. Le cas de Naples [In French]; Managing urban complexity — the case of Naples [Summary]. Fabrizzio Mangoni. *Peup. Médit.* 4-6:1988 pp. 137 – 145

25 Growth of urban informal sector in a developing economy. Vishwa Mittar. New Delhi: Deep and Deep, 1988: 256 p.

26 Harajuku chiiki jūmin no seikatsu to fukushi — jyūmin ishiki chousa no bunseki wo toushite [In Japanese]; [The attitude of residents towards life and welfare in Harajuku, an urban community]. Youko Shouji; Kiyoshi Adachi; Miki Murai; Masayuki Sanbonmatsu. *Annual Report of the Social Work Research Institute* Vol.24. 1988. pp. 241 – 285

27 L'informel structuré. Les zabbâlîn du Caire [In French]; The Cairo garbage collectors [Summary]. Ragui Assaad. *Peup. Médit.* **41-42** 10:1987-3:1988 pp. 181 – 192

28 Intra metropolitan demographic structure — a Seattle example. Richard L. Morrill. *Ann. Reg. Sci.* **XXII:1** 3:1988 pp. 1 – 16

29 L'invasion, principale filière populaire de production foncière et immobilière à Lima [In French]; ("Invasion", a major popular means of providing real estate and property in Lima); (Die Invasion, das wichtigste Mittel der Immobilienproduktion durch die Armen in Lima: Title only in German); (La Invasión, principal vía popular de producción de bienes raíces e inmobiliarios en Lima: Title only in Spanish); (Vtorženie kak glavnaja otrasl' zemel'nogo i žiliščnogo proizvodstva v Lime: Title only in Russian). Anna Wagner. *R. T-Monde* **XXIX:116** 10-12:1988 pp. 1055 – 1066

30 Irrégularité urbaine et invention de la ville africaine au Cap-Vert [In French]; (Urban irregularity and inventing the African city in Cape Verde); (Städtische Unregelmäßigkeiten und Erfindung der afrikanischen Stadt in Kap Verde: Title only in German); (Irregularidad urbana e invento de la ciudad africana en Cabo Verde: Title only in Spanish); (Urbanističeskaja nereguljarnost' i izobretenie afrikanskogo goroda (Selenyj mys): Title only in Russian). Roger Navarro. *R. T-Monde* **XXIX:116** 10-12:1988 pp. 1101 – 1120

31 Land use planning and the mediation of urban change — the British planning system in practice. Patsy Healey [Ed.]; et al. Cambridge: Cambridge University Press, 1988: 295 p. 0521301440. [Cambridge human geography.]

32 Law and the urban poor in India. V.R. Krishna Iyer. Delhi: B.R.Publishing Corporation, 1988: xxiii, 119 p. ISBN: 81 701 8465 7.

33 The location of marginalised groups in the inner city. H.P.M. Winchester; P.E. White. *Envir. Plan. D* **6(1):** 3:1988 pp. 37 – 54

G.3.2: Urban sociology *[Sociologie urbaine]*

34 Managing Ontario's urban landscape. Allan R. Ruff. *Plan. Out.* **31:1** 1988 pp. 53 – 60

35 Metropolizacion en America Latina y el Caribe — calidad de vida y pobreza urbana *[In Spanish]*; [Metropolitan growth in Latin America and the Caribbean — quality of life and urban poverty] *[Summary]*. Patricio Gross Fuentes; Sergio Galilea Ocon; Ricardo Jordán Fuchs. *Eure* **XIV:43** 10:1988 pp. 7 – 51

36 Mortality and living conditions — relative mortality levels and their relation to the physical quality of life in urban populations. Jon Anson. *Soc. Sci. Med.* **27:9** 1988 pp. 901 – 910

37 Les morts de Villatina et le problème du sol urbain en Colombie *[In French]*; (The deaths at Villatina and the problem of land in urban areas in Colombia); (Die Toten von Villatina und das Problem des städtischen Grundbesitzes in Kolumbien: *Title only in German*); (Los muertos de Villatina y el problema del suelo urbano en Colombia: *Title only in Spanish*); (Mertvecy Villatina i problema gorodskof počvy v Kolumbii: *Title only in Russian*). Hugo Lopez Castaño. *R. T-Monde* **XXX:118** 4-6:1988 pp. 333 – 355

38 Naples á la fin des années quatre-vingt *[In French]*; Knowledge and action — Naples in the late '80s *[Summary]*. Giovanni Laino. *Peup. Médit. 4-6:1988* pp. 23 – 39

39 Les noms du social dans l'urbain en crise *[In French]*; What is to be called social in the urban crisis? *[Summary]*. Michel Peraldi. *Peup. Médit. 4-6:1988* pp. 5 – 21

40 Una nuova cultura per la città *[In Italian]*; A new culture for the city *[Summary]*. Corrado Morgia. *Crit. Marx.* **26:6** 11-12:1988 pp. 111 – 122

41 The paradigm shift in urban sociology. M. Gottdiener; Joe R. Feagin. *Urban Aff. Q.* **24:2** 12:1988 pp. 163 – 187

42 The politics of the urban crisis. Andrew Sills; Gillian Taylor *[Ed.]*; Peter Golding *[Ed.]*. London: Hutchinson, 1988: 180 p. *ISBN: 0091731291. Bibliography — p.172-177.*

43 Popular settlements in the city of Allahabad — findings from three case studies. Harikesh N. Misra. *Cities* **5:2** 5:1988 pp. 163 – 183

44 Poverty and the urban environment — an examination of the role of income levels in Sapele, Nigeria. Gideon E.D. Omuta. *Cities* **5:1** 2:1988 pp. 72 – 86

45 Power, community and the city — comparative urban and community research. Michael Peter Smith *[Ed.]*. New Brunswick: Transaction, 1988: 189 p. *ISBN: 0887387349.*

46 Le public et le privé dans les grandes actions de transformation urbaine *[In French]*; Public and private in major programs of urban transformation *[Summary]*. Liliana Padovani. *Peup. Médit. 4-6:1988* pp. 105 – 113

47 Reconceptualizing the links between home and work in urban geography. Susan Hanson; Geraldine Pratt. *Econ. Geogr.* **64** 1988 pp. 299 – 321

48 The red-light district in the West European city — a neglected aspect of the urban landscape. G.J. Ashworth; P.E. White; H.P.M. Winchester. *Geoforum* **19:2** 1988 pp. 201 – 212

49 Residential segregation and ethnic identification among Hispanics in Texas. Sean-Shong Hwang; Steve H. Murdock. *Urban Aff. Q.* **23:3** 3:1988 pp. 329 – 345

G.3.2: Urban sociology *[Sociologie urbaine]*

50 Residential segregation in American cities — a contrary review. George Galster. *Pop. Res. Pol. R.* **7:2** 1988 pp. 93 – 112

51 Residential segregation of blacks, Hispanics, and Asians by socioeconomic status and generation. Nancy A. Denton; Douglas S. Massey. *Soc. Sci. Q.* **69:4** 12:1988 pp. 797 – 817

52 Residential segregation of ethnic groups in West German cities. Johannes Michael Nebe. *Cities* **5:3** 8:1988 pp. 235 – 244

53 The rise and development of urban political machines — an alternative to Merton's functional analysis. Alan DiGaetano. *Urban Aff. Q.* **24:2** 12:1988 pp. 242 – 267

54 The role of information technology in managing cities. Kenneth L. Kraemer; John Leslie King. *Envir. Plan.A.* **14:2** 3-4:1988 pp. 23 – 47

55 The role of medium-sized towns in the spatial integration of Nigeria. Francis C. Okafor. *Afr. Urb. Q.* **3:3&4** 8&11:1988 pp. 253 – 264

56 The role of tourism in urban conservation — the case of Singapore. Russell A. Smith. *Cities* **5:3** 8:1988 pp. 245 – 259

57 Rural-urban linkages — the role of small urban centers in Nigeria. Lillian Trager. *Afr. Stud. R.* **31:3** 12:1988 pp. 29 – 38

58 El sector informal en Quito — 1985 *[In Spanish]*; [The informal sector in Quito — 1985]. Carlos Larrea Maldonado; Rafael Urriola. *Economia* **85** 1:1988 pp. 41 – 72

59 El sector informal urbano en el Ecuador *[In Spanish]*; [The urban informal sector in Ecuador]. María Mercedes Placencia. *Economia* **85** 1:1988 pp. 9 – 29

60 Sekatsu yoshiki henkaku toshiteno toshi-shugi *[In Japanese]*; [Urbanism as a reform of lifestyle]. Kenji Yamamoto. *The Kagoshima keizai Daigaku Shakaigakubu Ronshu Vol.7; No.1 - 1988.* pp. 1 – 16

61 Sharing the cities — residential desegregation in Harare, Windhoek and Mafeking. Claire Pickard-Cambridge. Johannesburg: South African Insitute of Race Relations, 1988: 53 p.

62 The social meaning of civic space — studying political authority through architecture. Charles T Goodsell. Lawrence, Kan.: University Press of Kansas, 1988: xviii, 229 p. *ISBN: 0700603476. Bibliography — p.[219]-223.* [Studies in government and public policy.]

63 Socio-spatial change in the Belfast urban area, 1971-1981. Paul Doherty. *Irish Geogr.* **21:1** 1988 pp. 11 – 19

64 South Africa's urban policy — a new form of influx control. Richard Tomlinson. *Urban Aff. Q.* **23:4** 6:1988 pp. 487 – 510

65 South Asian urban experience. R. C. Sharma. New Delhi: Criterion, 1988: xvi, 344 p.

66 Soziologische Stadtforschung *[In German]*; [Urban sociology]. Jürgen Friedrichs *[Ed.]*. Opladen: Westdeutscher Verlag, 1988: 440 p. (ill.) *ISBN: 3531120220; LofC: 89-101133. Includes summaries in English; Includes bibliographies.* [Kölner Zeitschrift für Soziologie und Sozialpsychologie.]

67 Subnational urban hierarchies in West Africa. Frank W. Young. *Afr. Urb. Q.* **3:3&4** 8&11:1988 pp. 212 – 218

68 Suburbanization and segregation in U.S. metropolitan areas. Douglas S. Massey; Nancy A. Denton. *A.J.S.* **94:3** 11:1988 pp. 592 – 626

G.3.2: Urban sociology *[Sociologie urbaine]*

69 Tecnologia y ambiente urbano — participacion y control social en las politicas publicas *[In Spanish]*; [Technology and urban environment — participation and social control in public policy] *[Summary]*. Susana Finquelievich. *Eure* **XV:44** 12:1988 pp. 17 – 30

70 Tokyo no inner area ni okeru kinrin kankei — Sumida-ku K-chiku chousa yori *[In Japanese]*; [Social relationships among neighbors in Tokyo's inner-city]. Shinji Nozawa; Yūetsu Takajashi. *Comprehensive Urban Studies Vol.34. 1988.* pp. 51 – 64

71 "Tokyo" no toshika to seikatsu henyou — sono han'iki kakutei no mondai wo chūshin to shite; [Tokyo as a natural city — a study of regional sociology]. Noriaki Gotō. *Shak. Ron. Vol.103. 1988.* pp. 33 – 53

72 Toshin no anomie ishiki — Fukuoka-shi to Naha-shi to no yobiteki hikaku bunseki *[In Japanese]*; [Anomie consciousness in the urban centre of the metropolis — preliminary comparative analysis between Fukuaka and Naha]. Tsutomu Yamamoto. *Social Analaysis Vol.17. 1988.* pp. 317 – 334

73 The transnationalization of urbanization in Japan. Mike Douglass. *Int. J. Urban* **12:3** 9:1988 pp. 425 – 454

74 Understanding residential segregation in American cities — interpreting the evidence. W.A.V. Clark. *Pop. Res. Pol. R.* **7:2** 1988 pp. 113 – 121

75 Urban basic services scheme — a strategy for improving the living conditions of the urban poor — an evaluation. N. Ashok Kumar; V. Gnaneshwar. *Indian J. Soc. W.* **XLIX:3** 7:1988 pp. 215 – 226

76 The urban black community as network — toward a social network perspective. Melvin L. Oliver. *Sociol. Q.* **29:4** Winter:1988 pp. 623 – 645

77 Urban environment in India — problems and prospects. Kamala Kant Dubey *[Ed.]*; Alok Kumar Singh *[Ed.]*. New Delhi: Inter-India, 1988: 1988 p.

78 Urban living — the individual in the city. D. J. Walmsley. Harlow: Longman Scientific & Technical, 1988: xiv,204 p. (ill) *ISBN: 058230167x; LofC: 87-2944. Bibliography — p159-190. Includes index.*

79 Urban reform and its consequences — a study in representation. Susan Welch; Timothy Bledsoe *[Ed.]*. Chicago: University of Chicago Press, 1988: xx, 154 p. *ISBN: 0226892999. Bibliography, p. 137-147.*

80 Urban social movements in the Third World. Frans J. Schuurman *[Ed.]*; Ton van Naerssen *[Ed.]*. London: Routledge, 1988: 240 p. *ISBN: 0415009197. Includes bibliographical references.*

81 Urban system of a developing economy — a study of Allahabad city region. H.N. Misra. New Delhi: Heritage, 1988: xiii, 251 p. *ISBN: 81 7026 138 4.*

82 Les urbanistes dans le doute *[In French]*; [Urbanism in doubt]. Michel Peraldi *[Contrib.]*; Giovanni Laino *[Contrib.]*; Alfons Segura *[Contrib.]*; Jean-Christophe Baudouin *[Contrib.]*; Djaffar Lesbet *[Contrib.]*; Abdelatif Baltagi *[Contrib.]*; Alain Tarrius *[Contrib.]*; Liliana Padovani *[Contrib.]*; Antida Gazzola *[Contrib.]*; Michel Anselme *[Contrib.] and others. Collection of 12 articles.* **Peup. Médit.** ,4-6:1988 pp. 5 – 145

83 Washington, D. C. — inner-city revitalization and minority suburbanization. Dennis E. Gale. Philadelphia: Temple University Press, 1988: 238 p. *ISBN: 087722496x; LofC: 87-010001.* [Comparative American cities.]

84 "Yuppies" — marketingretoriek of nieuwe sociale groepering? *[In Dutch]*; "Yuppies" — marketing rhetoric or new social group? *[Summary]*. Paul Dekker; Peter Ester. *Sociol. Gids* **XXXV:2** 3-4:1988 pp. 82 – 101

G.3.2: Urban sociology *[Sociologie urbaine]* —

Urban housing *[Logement urbain]*

85 Cities, housing and profits — flat break-up and the decline of private renting. Chris Hamnett; Bill Randolph *[Ed.]*. London: Hutchinson, 1988: 297 p. (ill) *ISBN: 0091732352. Bibliography — p.279-284. - Includes index.*

86 Hope for the homeless in the US — lessons from the Third World. Leland S. Burns. *Cities* **5:1** 2:1988 pp. 33 – 40

87 Housing allocation, tenure and mobility in Eastern Europe. John P. Huttman. *Urban Law P*. **9:4** 1988 pp. 277 – 294

88 Housing and the working class in an Indian metropolis. Ian Blore. *Publ. Adm. D*. **4:4** 12:1988 pp. 557 – 568

89 The housing construction process in Nigeria — implications for urban growth and development. Tunde Agbola. *Cities* **5:2** 5:1988 pp. 184 – 192

90 The invisible homeless — a new urban ecology. Richard H. Ropers. New York: Insight Books/Human Sciences Pr., 1988: 242 p. *ISBN: 0898854067. Bibliography — p.217-234.*

91 Joint housing studies — housebuilders, planners and the availability of land. Yvonne Rydin. *Envir. Plan.A*. **14:2** 3-4:1988 pp. 69 – 80

92 Le logement des pauvres dans les grandes villes du Tiers Monde *[In French]*; (Housing for the poor in large Third World cities). Michel Rochefort *[Ed.]*; Anna Wagner *[Contrib.]*; Monique Roussel *[Contrib.]*; Alain Dubresson *[Contrib.]*; Alphonse Yapi-Diahou *[Contrib.]*; Roger Navarro *[Contrib.]*; Patrick Canel *[Contrib.]*; Christian Girard *[Contrib.]*; Jean-François Tribillon *[Contrib.]*; Alain Marie *[Contrib.] and others. Collection of 9 articles.* **R. T-Monde** , *XXIX:116*, 10-12:1988 pp. 1045 – 1214

93 Luta pela moradia popular em São Paulo — movimentos de moradia — 1975-85 *[In Portuguese]*; [The struggle for popular housing in São Paulo — housing movements — 1975-85]. Maria da Glória M. Gohn. *Ciên. Soc. Hoje.* pp. 311 – 333

94 Un paradigme à l'épreuve des faits, l'autoconstruction en ville africaine *[In French]*; (A paradigm borne out by fact — self-construction in African cities); (Ein Paradigma unter Beweisprobe — Wohnungsbau in Eigenregie in einer afrikanischen Stadt: *Title only in German)*; (Un paradigma a la prueba de los hechos — la autoconstrucción en ciudad africana: *Title only in Spanish)*; (Paradigma pri ispytanii faktami — samovol'noe stroitel'stvo v afrikanskih gorodah: *Title only in Russian)*. Patrick Canel; Christian Girard. *R. T-Monde* **XXIX:116** 10-12:1988 pp. 1121 – 1134

95 The practical application of modern theoretical concepts in housing — a case study of Hal El-Salam, Ismail, Egypt. Hany B. Serag El-Din; Dina K. Shehayeb. *Afr. Urb. Q*. **3:1:2** 2:5 pp. 16 – 33

96 La problemática habitacional y los cambios en el uso del suelo *[In Spanish]*; [The problem of housing and changes in land use]. Martín Lovera Sánchez. *Rev. Mexicana Soc*. **L:4** 10-12:1988 pp. 209 – 225

97 Promoting the single-family house in Belgium — the social construction of model housing. Catherine Mougenot. *Int. J. Urban* **12:4** 12:1988 pp. 531 – 549

98 Slum and squatter settlements in sub-Saharan Africa — toward a planning strategy. Robert A. Obudho *[Ed.]*; Constance C. Mhlanga *[Ed.]*. New York: Praeger, 1988: xvi, 415 p. *ISBN: 0275923096; LofC: 87-11705. Bibliography — p.355-400. Includes index.*

G.3.2: Urban sociology [Sociologie urbaine] — Urban housing [Logement urbain]

99 Squatter settlements in Liberia — towards the integration of housing and population policies. Linda Lacey. *Afr. Urb. Q.* **3:3&4** 8&11:1988 pp. 219 – 230

100 Système d'habitat et ségrégation sociale dans l'agglomération de Tunis *[In French]*; Housing and social segregation in the Tunis urban area *[Summary]*. Abdelatif Baltagi. *Peup. Médit. 4-6:1988* pp. 79 – 86

101 Urban squatter housing in Third World. Ashok Ranjan Basu. Delhi: Mittal, 1988: xx, 316 p. *ISBN: 81 7099 047 5.*

102 Where we live — a social history of American housing. Irving Welfeld. New York: Simon and Schuster, 1988: 319 p. *ISBN: 0671638696; LofC: 88-013106. Bibliography.*

Urban planning and development [Aménagement et développement urbain]

103 Britain's first town planning act — a review of the 1909 achievement. Anthony Sutcliffe. *Town Plan. R.* **59:3** 7:1988 pp. 289 – 304

104 Building an urban future — race and planning in London. Thomas L. Blair. *Cities* **5:1** 2:1988 pp. 41 – 56

105 Business elites and urban development — case studies and critical perspectives. Scott Cummings *[Ed.]*. New York: State University of New York, 1988: 395 p. *ISBN: 0887065775.* [SUNY series on urban public policy.]

106 The changing Canadian inner city. Trudi E. Bunting *[Ed.]*; Pierre Filion *[Ed.]*. Waterloo,Ont.: University of Waterloo,Department of Geography, 1988: 175 p. *ISBN: 0921083289. Bibliography.* [University of Waterloo Department of Geography Publication Series. : No. 31]

107 The changing urban landscape: the case of London's high-class residential fringe. J.W.R. Whitehand. *Geogr. J.* **154:3** 11:1988 pp. 351 – 366

108 Cities of tomorrow — an intellectual history of urban planning and design in the twentieth century. Peter Hall. Oxford: Basil Blackwell, 1988: 473 p. (ill) *ISBN: 0631134441. Includes index; Bibliography — p401-452.*

109 The city that refused to die — Glasgow — the politics of urban regeneration. Michael Keating. Aberdeen: Aberdeen University Press, 1988: 211 p. *ISBN: 0080364128. Includes index; Bibliography — p201-206.*

110 Crise urbaine et aménagement du centre-ville. L'exemple du quartier Belsunce á Marseille *[In French]*; The urban crisis and downtown development — Belsunce quarter of Marseilles *[Summary]*. Jean-Christophe Baudouin. *Peup. Médit. 4-6:1988* pp. 49 – 57

111 Development of urban planning in Zimbabwe — an overview. K.H. Wekwete. *Cities* **5:1** 2:1988 pp. 57 – 71

112 Four metropoles in Western Europe — development and urban planning of London, Paris, Randstad Holland and the Ruhr region. Hans van der Cammen. Netherlands: Van Gorcum, 1988: 242 p. *ISBN: 9023224086.*

113 Further perspectives on Japanese urban planning. Ian Masser *[Contrib.]*; Takahiro Yorisaki *[Contrib.]*; M. Hirohara *[Contrib.]*; J.D. Alden *[Contrib.]*; M. Cassim *[Contrib.]*; Michael Hebbert *[Contrib.]*; Norihiro Nakai *[Contrib.]*. Collection of 3 articles. **Town Plan. R.** , *59:4*, 10:1988 pp. 351 – 395

114 Herat, the Islamic city — a study in urban conservation. Abdul Wasay Najimi. London: Curzon, 1988: 175 p. (ill) *ISBN: 0700701885. Bibliography — p.173-175.* [Scandinavian Institute of Asian Studies occasional papers.]

G.3.2: Urban sociology *[Sociologie urbaine]* — **Urban planning and development** *[Aménagement et développement urbain]*

115 Kokusai Chitsujo no Henka Katei ni okeru Hatten-tojoukoku no Toshika to Kindaika — tounan asia no jirei *[In Japanese]*; [Modernization of Southeast Asian cities]. Takeo Yazaki. Tokyo: Keio Tsushin, 1988: 174 p.

116 "Life on the upslope" — the postmodern landscape of gentrification. C.A. Mills. *Envir. Plan. D* **6(2):** 6:1988 pp. 169 – 190

117 Oubei no toshi kouzou saihen to koureisha no kyojūchi idou *[In Japanese]*; [Urban restructuring and elderly migration in post-industrial societies]. Yaeko Nishiyama. *Kinjo Gakuin Daigaku Ronso Vol.30. 1988.* pp. 21 – 37

118 Perspectives in urban geography. Vol. 15. City planning — administration and participation. C. S. Yadav *[Ed.]*. New Delhi: Concept, 1986: 339 p. [Concept's international series in geography. : No. 3]

119 Post-industrial cities — politics and planning in New York, Paris and London. H.V. Savitch. Princeton, N.J.: Princeton University Press, 1988: 368 p. *ISBN: 0691077738.*

120 Process and response in contemporary urban development — Melbourne in the 1980s. Chris Maher. *Aust. Geogr.* **19:1** 5:1988 pp. 162 – 181

121 Public infrastructure planning and management. Jay M. Stein *[Contrib.]*; Marshall Kaplan *[Contrib.]*; Douglass B. Lee *[Contrib.]*; Kenneth Newton *[Contrib.]*; Anthony James Catanese *[Contrib.]*; John E. Petersen *[Contrib.]*; Arthur C. Nelson *[Contrib.]*; Leon S. Eplan *[Contrib.]*; Catherine Ross *[Contrib.]*; Jon J. Lines *[Contrib.]* *and others. Collection of 13 articles.* **Urb. Aff. Ann. R.** , *33*, 1988 pp. 7 – 240

122 Revitalising the waterfront — international dimensions of dockland redevelopment. B. S. Hoyle *[Ed.]*; D. A. Pinder *[Ed.]*; M. S. Husain *[Ed.]*. London: Belhaven, 1988: 265 p. (ill) *ISBN: 1852930470. Includes bibliography and index.*

123 Self-help training for planning urban development — an innovation in on-the-job learning in Nigeria. Michael Mattingly. *Publ. Adm. D.* **8:2** 4-6:1988 pp. 203 – 217

124 Stadt und Stadtteilzentren — Gefährdungen und Entwicklungschancen *[In German]*; [The city and the inner-city — the dangers and the prospects for development]. Hannes Tank. *Arc. Kommunal.* **27:2** 1988 pp. 237 – 249

125 Three ways to build — the development process in the United States, Japan and Italy. Harvey Molotch; Serena Vicari. *Urban Aff. Q.* **24:2** 12:1988 pp. 188 – 214

126 Urban design as uneven development. James M. Mayo. *Envir. Behav.* **20:5** 9:1988 pp. 633 – 663

127 Urban design in capitalist society. R.J. King. *Envir. Plan. D* **6(4):** 12:1988 pp. 445 – 474

128 Urban development corporations and their alternatives. Paul Lawless. *Cities* **5:3** 8:1988 pp. 277 – 289

129 Urban development — theory, fact, and illusion. J. Vernon Henderson. New York: Oxford University Press, 1988: xi, 242 p. (ill.) *ISBN: 0195051572. Includes index; Bibliography, p. 235-238.*

130 Urban planning and the law in Kenya. A. Okoth Owiro. *Afr. Urb. Q.* **3:1:2** 2:5 pp. 69 – 79

131 Zoneamento — análise política de um instrumento urbanistico *[In Portuguese]*; Zoning — political analysis of an urbanistic instrument *[Summary]*;

G.3.2: Urban sociology *[Sociologie urbaine]* — **Urban planning and development** *[Aménagement et développement urbain]*

Constitution de zones — analyse politique d'un instrument urbanistique *[French summary]*. Antonio Octávio Cintra. *Rev. Bras. Ciên. Soc.* **3:6** 2:1988 pp. 39 – 52

Urban transport *[Transport urbain]*

132 City transport in developed and developing countries. Tom Rallis. Basingstoke: Macmillan, 1988: xiv,202p. (ill) *ISBN: 0333433270. Includes index.*

133 Transporte urbano, medio ambiente y planificacion *[In Spanish]*; [Urban transport, planning and environment]. Oscar Figueroa *[Contrib.]*; Etienne Henry *[Contrib.]*; Sergio Moreales *[Contrib.]*; Sergio Galilea *[Contrib.]*; Julio Hurtado *[Contrib.]*; Ovidio González *[Contrib.]*; Denise B. Pinheiro Machado *[Contrib.]*; Nora Clichevsky *[Contrib.]. Collection of 8 articles.* **Eure**, *XIV: 42*, 3: 1988 pp. 3 – 144

134 Urban land-use and transport interaction — policies and models. F. V. Webster *[Ed.]*; P. H. Bly *[Ed.]*; N. J. Paulley *[Ed.]*; John F. Brotchie *[Ed.]*. Aldershot: Avebury, 1988: xiv, 520 p. (ill) *ISBN: 0566057263; LofC: 88-14056. report of the International Study Group on Land-use / Transport Interaction (ISGLUTI); Includes bibliography.*

135 Urban passenger transport problems in Dar-es-Salaam, Tanzania. W.F. Banyikwa. *Afr. Urb. Q.* **3:1:2** 2:5 pp. 80 – 94

136 Urban transport in West Africa. Richard Barrett. Washington, D.C.: The World Bank, 1988: xiv, 125 p. *ISBN: 0821310429. Includes bibliographical references.* [World Bank technical paper; Urban transport series. : No. 81]

Urbanization *[Urbanisation]*

137 The components of urban population growth in Ghana and Sierra Leone. Toma J. Makannah. *Afr. Urb. Q.* **3:3&4** 8&11:1988 pp. 231 – 237

138 Croissance urbaine en Amazonie équatorienne — le cas de Coca, province de Napo *[In French]*; Crecimiento urbano en Amazonía ecuatoriana — el caso de coca, provincia del Napo *[Spanish summary]*; Urban growth in Equatorian Amazonia — the case of Coca, province of Napo *[Summary]*; Crescimento urbano na Amazõnia equatoriana. O caso de Coca, na provincia de Napo *[Portuguese summary]*. Blandine Gravelin. *Cah. Amer. Lat.* **7** 1988 pp. 81 – 87

139 Dinamica naturale e dinamica migratoria in provincia di Roma — analisi di un trentacinquennio di sviluppo (1951-1986) *[In Italian]*; (Natural and migratory dynamics in the province of Rome — thirty-five years of growth). Augusto Ascolani. *Genus* **XLIV:3-4** 7-12:1988 pp. 83 – 119

140 Directionally biased metropolitan growth — a model and a case study. Shaul Krakover; Emilio Casetti. *Econ. Geogr.* **64** 1988 pp. 17 – 28

141 Industrial capital, labour force formation and the urbanization process in Malaysia. T.G. McGee. *Int. J. Urban* **12:3** 9:1988 pp. 356 – 374

142 Komponen-komponen bagi pertumbuhan bandar di Semenanjung Malaysia, 1970-1980 *[In Malay]*; The components of urban growth in Peninsular Malaysia, 1970-1980. Malaysia. Jabatan Perangkaan. Kuala Lumpur: Jabatan Perangkaan Malaysia, [1988]: viii, 61 p. *ISBN: 9679999556; LofC: 88-949364. English and Malay.* [Kajian mengenai subjek demografi dan penduduk. : No. 4]

G.3.2: Urban sociology *[Sociologie urbaine]* — *Urbanization [Urbanisation]*

143 Major Arab cities — their growth and problems. M.A. Al Hammad. *Cities* **5:4** 11:1988 pp. 365 – 372

144 Market mechanisms and spontaneous urbanization in Egypt — the Cairo case. Galila El Kadi. *Int. J. Urban* **12:1** 3:1988 pp. 22 – 37

145 Metropolitan growth and migration in Peru. Gunnar Malmberg. Umea: Department of Geography,University of Umea, 1988: 267 p. *ISBN: 9171743294. Bibliography — p.253-266.* [Geographical reports.]

146 Migración y formas urbanas en el crecimiento de Tijuana — 1900-1984 *[In Spanish]*; [Migration and urban patterns in the growth of Tijuana — 1900-1984]. Arturo Ranfla González; Guillermo B. Alvarez de la Torre. *Rev. Mexicana Soc.* **L:4** 10-12:1988 pp. 245 – 275

147 Naissance d'une ville au Sénégal — évolution d'un groupe de six villages de Casamance vers une agglomération urbaine *[In French]*; [Birth of a Senegalese town — development of a group of six villages in Casamance into an urban agglomeration]. Pierre Nicolas; Malick Gaye *[Ed.]*. Paris: Karthala, 1988: 202 p. (ill) *ISBN: 2865371956.*

148 On urbanization in South Africa. H.S. Geyer. *S. Afr. J. Econ.* **56:2-3** 6-9:1988 pp. 154 – 172

149 Proceso de urbanización en el trapecio andino — propuestas de planificación para el desarrollo regional *[In Spanish]*; [Urbanization in the Andes — prospects for planning and regional development]. Ricardo Vergara. : Fundacion Friedrich Ebert, 1988: 128 p.

150 Processus d'urbanisation en Afrique *[In French]*; [Urbanization in Africa]. Catherine Coquery-Vidrovitch *[Ed.]*. Paris: L'Harmattan, 1988: - *ISBN: 2738400817.* [Villes et entreprises.]

151 Regional and metropolitan growth and decline in the United States. William H. Frey; Alden Speare *[Ed.]*. New York: Russell Sage Foundation, 1988: xxix, 586 p. *ISBN: 0871542935. Bibliography — p.559-564.* [Population of the United States in the 1980s.]

152 Small town urbanization in South Africa — a case study. Cecil Manona. *Afr. Stud. R.* **31:3** 12:1988 pp. 95 – 110

153 L'urbanisation de la Mauritanie — enquête dans trois villes secondaires *[In French]*; [The urbanization of Mauritania — inquiry in three secondary towns]. Jean-Paul Laborie; Jean-François Langumier *[Ed.]*. [Paris]: La Documentation française, [1988]: 92 p. *ISBN: 2110020601.*

154 Urbanization and development — the rural-urban transition in Taiwan. Alden Speare; Ching-lung Tsay *[Ed.]*. Boulder: Westview Press, 1988: xxii, 217 p. (ill.) *ISBN: 081337328x. Bibliography, p. 203-217.* [Brown University studies in population and development.]

155 Urbanization in India — spatial dimensions. Rao V. L. S. Prakasa. New Delhi: Concept, 1987: ix, 327 p.

156 The urbanization of the Third World. Josef Gugler *[Ed.]*. Oxford: Oxford University Press, 1988: 420 p. (ill) *ISBN: 0198232608. Includes bibliographies and index.*

157 The urbanization process with moving boundary. Wei-Bin Zhang. *Geogr. Anal.* **20:4** 10:1988 pp. 328 – 339

158 Women and urbanization. Susanne Thorbek. *Acta Sociol.* **31:4** 1988 pp. 283 – 301

H: Economic life — *Vie économique*

H.1: Economic sociology — *Sociologie économique*

1 Economic problems and socioeconomic beliefs and attitudes. James R. Kluegel. *R. Soc. Strat. Mob.* **7** 1988 pp. 273 – 304
2 Economies across cultures — towards a comparative science of the economy. Rhoda H. Halperin. Basingstoke: Macmillan, 1988: iv, 226 p. *ISBN: 0333452364. Includes index.*
3 Keizai shakaigaku josetsu — econo-sociology no teishou *[In Japanese]*; [An introduction to economic sociology]. Morio Onda. ***The Annual Review of Sociology*** *Vol.1. 1988.* pp. 55 – 66
4 Psychological economics — development, tensions, prospects. Peter E. Earl *[Ed.].* Boston [Mass.]: Kluwer, 1988: xi,274 p. (ill) *ISBN: 0898382343; LofC: 87-3050. Bibliography — p.243-266. Includes index.* [Recent economic thought series.]
5 Psychological foundations of economic behaviour. Paul J. Albanese *[Ed.].* Westport, Conn.: Praeger, 1988: 175 p. *ISBN: 0275927423; LofC: 87-38476. Includes index and bibliography.*
6 Social and psychological foundations of economic analysis. J. L. Baxter. Brighton: Wheatsheaf, 1988: 288 p. *ISBN: 0745004172. Includes bibliography and index.*
7 Sociological explanations of economic growth. Robert M. Marsh. *Stud. Comp. ID.* **XXIII:4** Winter:1988 pp. 41 – 76

H.2: Economic systems — *Systèmes économiques*

1 British rule and African civilization in Tanganyika. C.S.L. Chachage. *J. Hist. Soc.* **1:2** 6:1988 pp. 199 – 223
2 Crisis and critique — on the "logic" of late capitalism. Friedrich W Sixel. Leiden: E.J. Brill, 1988: vi, 158 p. *ISBN: 9004082840. Bibliography — p.143-154.* [Monographs and theoretical studies in sociology and anthropology in honour of Nels Anderson.]
3 Max Weber's conceptual portrait of feudalism. Gianfranco Poggi. *Br. J. Soc.* **XXXIX:2** 6:1988 pp. 211 – 227
4 Women in Jamaica's urban informal economy — insights from a Kingston slum. Faye V. Harrison. *Nie. West-Ind. Gids* **62:3-4** 1988 pp. 103 – 128

H.3: Economic situation. Standard of living — *Situation économique. Niveau de vie*

1 Change in marital status and short-term income dynamics. Martin H. David; Thomas S. Flory. *Proc. Am. Stat. Ass.* pp. 97 – 102

2 Childbearing and wives' foregone earnings. Charles A. Calhoun; Thomas J. Espenshade. *Pop. Stud.* **XLII:1** 3:1988 pp. 5 – 38

3 Democracy, economic development and income inequality. Edward N. Muller. *Am. Sociol. R.* **53:1** 2:1988 pp. 50 – 68

4 Development policies — sociological perspectives. Anthony Hall *[Ed.]*; James Midgley *[Ed.]*. Manchester: Manchester University Press, 1988: 154 p. *ISBN: 0719022746. Bibliography — p.134-148.*

5 Dual earning couples — trends of change in Great Britain. Norman Bonney. *Work Emp. Soc.* **2:1** 3:1988 pp. 89 – 102

6 The economic progress of European and East Asian Americans. Suzanne Model. *Ann. R. Soc.* **14** 1988 pp. 363 – 380

7 Economic segmentation and worker earnings in a US-Mexico border enclave. Scarlett G. Hardesty; Malcolm D. Holmes; James D. Williams. *Sociol. Pers.* **31:4** 10:1988 pp. 466 – 489

8 Education and earnings — empirical findings from alternative operationalizations. Robert Kominski. *Proc. Am. Stat. Ass.* pp. 82 – 87

9 Explaining relative incomes of low-income families in U.S. cities. Paul R. Blackley. *Soc. Sci. Q.* **69:4** 12:1988 pp. 835 – 859

10 Gender and poverty in Central Appalachia. Ann R. Tickamyer; Cecil H. Tickamyer. *Soc. Sci. Q.* **69:4** 12:1988 pp. 874 – 891

11 Growth, development and welfare — an essay on levels of living. Ajit K. Dasgupta. Oxford: Basil Blackwell, 1988: xi, 211 p. *ISBN: 0631143998; LofC: 87-36564. Includes index.*

12 A home divided — women and income in the Third World. Daisy Dwyer *[Ed.]*; Judith Bruce *[Ed.]*. Stanford: Stanford University Press, 1988: 289 p. *ISBN: 0804714851; LofC: 88-004938. Bibliography.*

13 Immigration and the earnings of youth in the U.S. Benjamin N. Matta; Anthony V. Popp. *Int. Migr. Rev.* **XXII:1** Spring:1988 pp. 104 – 116

14 Inequality observed — a study of attitudes towards income inequality. A. Szirman. Aldershot: Avebury, 1988: - *ISBN: 056605549x.*

15 A measure for the spatial dispersion of poverty areas and its relevance to the underclass debate. Richard Greene. *Proc. Am. Stat. Ass.* pp. 350 – 355

16 Методологические и метолические проблемы социологического изучения уровня жизни *[In Russian]*; [Methodological and methodical problems in the sociological study of the standard of living]. M.V. Pokrovskaya. Moscow: , 1987 pp. 28 – 53

17 On analysing earnings inequality in segmented labour markets. Lawrence E. Raffalovice. *Sociol. Meth.* **16:3** 2:1988 pp. 339 – 378

18 Recent widowhood, remarriage, and changes in economic well-being. Cathleen D. Zick; Ken R. Smith. *J. Marriage Fam.* **50:1** 2:1988 pp. 233 – 244

19 Seikatsu suijun shihyo — sono tokucho to pattern bunrui *[In Japanese]*; [Indicators of standard of living — its character and pattern analysis]. Hideki Yoshino. *NIRA Vol.1; No.2 - 1988.* pp. 12 – 15

H.3: Economic situation. Standard of living *[Situation économique. Niveau de vie]*

20 Sex-related wage differentials and women's interrupted labor careers — the chicken or the egg. Reuben Gronau. *J. Labor Ec.* **6:3** 7:1988 pp. 277 – 301
21 Spillover, standardization and stratification — earnings determination in the United States and Norway. Tom Colbjørnsen; Arne L. Kalleberg. *Eur. Sociol. R.* **4:1** 5:1988 pp. 20 – 31
22 Structure and processes of a phenomenon — the context of quality of life in India. Ramkrishna Mukherjee. *Soc. Ind.* **20:6** 12:1988 pp. 555 – 579
23 Toward a comprehensive "quality-of-life" index. Denis F. Johnston. *Soc. Ind.* **20:5** 10:1988 pp. 473 – 496
24 Trends in wage differentials between Jewish males of different ethnic origin during the 1970s. Shmuel Amir. *Econ. Rev. Bank Israel* **63** 12:1988 pp. 52 – 75
25 Wage determination, income distribution, and the design of change. Khalid Saeed. *Behav. Sci.* **33: 3** 7: 1988 pp. 161 – 186
26 Wage differentials due to gender. N. Smith; N. Westergård-Nielsen. *J. Pop. Ec.* **1:2** 1988 pp. 115 – 130
27 Wage growth and the black-white wage differential. John E. Garen. *Q. R. Econ. Bu.* **28:3** Autumn:1988 pp. 28 – 42
28 Wealth and well being. John Hart. London: Oxon, 1988: 256 p. *ISBN: 187067703x*.

H.4: Enterprises. Production — *Entreprises. Production*

1 An analytical investigation of policy effects on transit system performance measurement. M. Liotine; K.D. Lawrence. *Socio. Econ.* **:5** 1988 pp. 185 – 193
2 Automation, skill and the future of capitalism. Paul S. Adler. *Berkeley J. Soc.* **XXXIII** 1988 pp. 1 – 36
3 Automatisation et travail — le cas de la machine-outil *[In French]*; Automatisierung und Arbeit — der Fall der Werkzeugmaschinen *[German summary]*; Automation and work — machine tools *[Summary]*. Paul S. Adler; Bryan Borys. *Form. Emp.* **21** 1-3:1988 pp. 5 – 25
4 Beyond computopia — information, automation and democracy in Japan. Tessa Morris-Suzuki. London: Kegan Paul, 1988: ix, 221 p. (ill) *ISBN: 0710302932. Includes index.*
5 Computer als Schmetterling und Fledermaus. Über Technikbilder von Techniksoziologen *[In German]*; Computer as butterfly and bat. Images of technology in sociology *[Summary]*. Bernward Joerges. *Soz. Welt.* **39:2** 1988 pp. 188 – 204
6 Cooperative business ventures in the Soviet Union — the impact of social forces on private enterprise. Elisabeth Schillinger; Joel Jenswold. *Social Soc. Res.* **73:1** 10:1988 pp. 22 – 30
7 Corporate economic power and the state — a longitudinal assessment of two explanations. David Jacobs. *A.J.S.* **93:4** 1:1988 pp. 852 – 881
8 Corporate form — a unitary theory of technology, property and social class. John McDermott. *Rev. Rad. Pol. Ec.* **20:1** Spring:1988 pp. 21 – 45
9 Crisis agraria y diferenciación social en México *[In Spanish]*; [Agrarian crisis and social differentiation in Mexico]. Roger Bartra; Gerardo Otero. *Rev. Mexicana Soc.* **L:1** 1-3:1988 pp. 13 – 49

H.4: Enterprises. Production [Entreprises. Production]

10 Culture and management in Japan. Shuji Hayashi. : Tokyo, 1988: 194 p.
11 El empresario en el pensamiento societario contemporaneo *[In Spanish]*; [The enterprenuer in contemporary social thought]. Alfredo Hernández Sánchez. *Anal. Est. Econ. Empres.* **3** 1988 pp. 19 – 61
12 A family business? — the making of an international business elite. J. F. Marceau. Cambridge: Cambridge University Press, 1988: xii, 247 p. *ISBN: 0521267315. Bibliography — p.226-240.*
13 From research policy to social intelligence — essays for Stevan Dedijer. Jan Annerstedt *[Ed.]*; Andrew Jamison *[Ed.]*. Basingstoke: Macmillan, 1988: 180 p. (ill) *ISBN: 0333452755.*
14 From Taylorism to Fordism — a rational madness. Bernard Doray. London: Free Association, 1988: 7,230 p. *ISBN: 1853430102. Bibliography — p.210-221. Includes index.*
15 The green revolution, employment, and economic change in rural Java — a reassessment of trends under the New Order. Chris Manning. Singapore: Institute of Southeast Asian Studies, 1988: 95 p. *ISBN: 9813035021.* [ISEAS occasional paper. : No. 84]
16 A history of social psychological reactions to new technology. Jim Carlopio. *J. Occup. Psychol.* **61:1** 3:1988 pp. 67 – 77
17 Im Schatten der Schattenökonomie — die Hausarbeit *[In German]*; In the shadow of the shadow economy — housework *[Summary]*. Walburga von Zameck. *Jahrb. N. St.* **205:4** 10:1988 pp. 289 – 299
18 Industrial productivity — a psychological perspective. Ashok Pratap Singh. New Delhi: Sage, 1988: 158 p. (ill) *ISBN: 0803995679. Bibliography — p.132-150. Includes index.*
19 The information society. William J. Martin. London: Aslib, 1988: 200 p. *ISBN: 0851422195. Includes bibliography and index.*
20 The information society — issues and illusions. David Lyon. Cambridge: Polity, 1988: x, 196 p. (ill) *ISBN: 0745602606. Bibliography — p179-186. - Includes index.*
21 Information technologies and organizations — lessons from the 1980s and issues for the 1990s. Frank Blacker. *J. Occup. Psychol.* **61:2** 6:1988 pp. 113 – 127
22 Interlocking directorates and communities of interest among American railroad companies. William G. Roy; Philip Bonacich. *Am. Sociol. R.* **53:3** 6:1988 pp. 368 – 379
23 Making time — ethnographies of high-technology organizations. Frank A. Dubinskas *[Ed.]*. Philadelphia: Temple University Press, 1988: 232 p. (ill.) *ISBN: 0877225354. Includes bibliographies.*
24 Managerial leadership in the post-industrial society. Philip Sadler. Aldershot: Gower, 1988: 169 p. (ill) *ISBN: 0566026112. Includes bibliography and index.*
25 Managerial promotion — the effects of socialization, specialization, and gender. Kathy Cannings. *Ind. Lab. Rel.* **42:1** 10:1988 pp. 77 – 88
26 Методологические и социальные проблемы компьютеризации *[In Russian]*; (Methodological and social problems of computerization); (Les problèmes méthodologiques et sociaux de la computerisation: *Title only in French*); (Methodologische und gesellschaftliche Probleme der

INTERNATIONAL BIBLIOGRAPHY OF SOCIOLOGY — 1988

H.4: Enterprises. Production *[Entreprises. Production]*

Computerisierung: *Title only in German);* (Problemas metodológicos y sociales de la computerización: *Title only in Spanish).* К.А. Зуев. *Vop. Filo.* **5** 1988 pp. 43 – 55

27 Nuove tecnologie, nuovi modelli di organizzazione sociale e cambiamento sociale *[In Italian];* [New technology, new models of social organization and social change]. Gert Schmidt. *Sociol. Lav.* **35-36** 1988-89 pp. 104 – 114

28 Organizational growth of small firms — an outcome of markets and hierarchies. Mark H. Lazerson. *Am. Sociol. R.* **53:3** 6:1988 pp. 330 – 342

29 Problem statements in managerial problem solving. Roger J. Volkema. *Socio. Econ.* **:5** 1988 pp. 213 – 220

30 The process of technological change — new technology and social choice in the workplace. Jon Clark *[Ed.].* Cambridge: Cambridge University Press, 1988: xiv, 250 p. (ill) *ISBN: 0521323037; LofC: 87-6641. Bibliography — p.239-244. Includes index.* [Management and industrial relations series.]

31 Productivity in organizations. John P. Campbell *[Ed.];* Richard J. Campbell *[Ed.].* San Francisco: Jossey-Bass, 1988: xxvi, 451 p. *ISBN: 1555421008; LofC: 88-42780.*

32 La produzione post-fordista — un ruolo nuovo per la forza lavoro *[In Italian];* [Post-Fordist production — a new role for the labour force]. Bryn Jones. *Sociol. Lav.* **35-36** 1988-89 pp. 203 – 216

33 Programmed capitalism — a computer-mediated global society. Maurice Estabrooks. Armonk, N.Y.: M. E. Sharpe, 1988: 205 p. *ISBN: 0873324803; LofC: 88-004476. Bibliography.*

34 Proto-industry, women's work and the household economy in the transition to industrial capitalism. Sonya O. Rose. *J. Fam. Hist.* **13:2** 1988 pp. 181 – 193

35 Questioning technology — a critical anthology. John Zerzan *[Ed.];* Alice Carnes *[Ed.].* London: Freedom Press, 1988: 222 p. *ISBN: 0900384441.*

36 The revenge of Athena — science, exploitation and the Third World. Ziauddin Sardar *[Ed.].* London: Mansell, 1988: 270 p. *ISBN: 0720118913. Includes bibliographical references.*

37 Service-ka shakai no shinten to katei-seikatsu *[In Japanese];* [Progress of service society and its impact on home life]. Takahiko Furuta. **Kat. Kag.** *Vol.55; No.2 - 1988.* pp. 2 – 14

38 The social basis of the microelectronics revolution. Alfonso Hernan Molina. Edinburgh: Edinburgh University Press, 1988: 260 p. (ill) *ISBN: 0852245947. Includes bibliography and index.*

39 The social consequences of the differentiation of agriculture and forestry. A case study of two villages in Finnish forest periphery. Jukka Oksa; Pertti Rannikko. *Acta Sociol.* **31** 1988 pp. 217 – 229

40 The social effects of computer technology — proceedings of two conferences June 15-16, 1984 and June 21-22, 1985. Dean Harper. New York: Program in Sociology, University of Rochester, 1988: 177 p. *Includes bibliographies.*

41 Sozialpolitik im Betrieb — soziale Erfordernisse des wissenschaftlich-technischen Fortschritts *[In German];* [Social policy in enterprises — social requirements of scientific-technical progress]. Gerhard Tietze *[Ed.];* Gunnar Winkler *[Ed.].* Berlin: Dietz, 1988: 207 p. (ill.) *ISBN: 3320011146.*

INTERNATIONAL BIBLIOGRAPHY OF SOCIOLOGY — 1988

H.4: Enterprises. Production *[Entreprises. Production]*

42 Spatial differentiation in the social impact of technology — the case of the Irish Republic. Dirk-Jan F. Kamann. Aldershot: Avebury, 1988: 314 p. (ill) *ISBN: 0566057670. Includes bibliography and index.*

43 Technological change and the future of work. Belinda Probert; Judy Wajcman. *J. Ind. Relat.* **30:3** 9:1988 pp. 432 – 448

44 Technology and gender — women's work in Asia. Cecilia Ng *[Ed.]*. Selangor: Universiti Pertanian Malaysia,Women's Studies Unit, 1988: 150 p.

45 Technology in everyday life — conceptual queries. Bernward Joerges. *J. Theory Soc. Behav.* **18:2** 6:1988 pp. 219 – 238

46 Tecnologia e «azienda sistema» *[In Italian]*; [Technology and "business systems"]. Giorgio Gosetti. *Sociol. Lav.* **35-36** 1988-89 pp. 115 – 131

47 Threats and opportunities for middle management — new technology and competitive banking. M.L. Bowles; M. Lewis. *J. Ind. Relat.* **30:1** 3:1988 pp. 54 – 67

48 Towards a typology of female entrepreneurs. Stanley Cromie; John Hayes. *Sociol. Rev.* **36:1** 2:1988 pp. 87 – 113

49 El trabajador frente a la automatización — efectos sociales y percepción de los trabajadores *[In Spanish]*; [The worker faceed with automation — social effects and worker perception]. Lais Wendel Abramo. *Rev. Mexicana Soc.* **L:4** 10-12:1988 pp. 61 – 99

50 Transmission héréditaire et systèmes de production — le cas de la Soule (Pyrénées-Atlantiques) *[In French]*; Inheritance and production systems — la Soule (Pyrénées-Atlantiques) *[Summary]*. Ramon Barcelo. *Sociol. Trav.* **:3** Summer:1988 pp. 443 – 460

51 Work and flexible automation in Britain — a review of developments and possibilities. Bryn Jones. *Work Emp. Soc.* **2:4** 12:1988 pp. 451 – 486

H.5: Consumption. Market. Prices — *Consommation. Marché. Prix*

1 A ascensão do fetichismo consumista *[In Portuguese]*; The rise of consumer fetishism *[Summary]*; L'ascension du fétichisme consommateur *[French summary]*. Jeffrey Needell. *Rev. Bras. Ciên. Soc.* **3:8** 10:1988 pp. 39 – 58

2 L'évolution du budget des ménages — le poids des dépenses d'habitation et de transport *[In French]*; [The development of the household budget — the size of living and transport expenditure]. Mireille Moutardier. *E & S* **207** 2:1988 pp. 41 – 51

3 The food "surplus" — a staple illusion of economics — a cruel illusion for populations. David F. Durham; Jim C. Fandrem. *Popul. Envir.* **10:2** Winter:1988 pp. 115 – 121

4 Perspectives on trade, mobility and gender in a rural market system — Borno, north-east Nigeria. R.E. Porter. *J. Econ. Soc. Geogr.* **79:2** 1988 pp. 82 – 92

5 Saggio sui mercati illegali *[In Italian]*; [Comments on the black market]. Pino Arlacchi. *Rass. It. Soc.* **29:3** 7-9:1988 pp. 403 – 437

6 Scrapping a durable consumption good. Gerrit Antonides. Alblasserdam: Offsetdrukkerij Kanters B.V., 1988: 224 p. *Bibliography — p.184-198.*

7 The sociology of consumption — an anthology. Per Otnes *[Ed.]*. Oslo/ New Jersey: Solum Forlag/ Humanities Press, 1988: 192 p.

H.5: Consumption. Market. Prices *[Consommation. Marché. Prix]*

8 Der Wandel der Kochkunst als genußorientierte Speisengestaltung — Webers Theorie der Ausdifferenzierung und Rationalisierung als Grundlage einer Ernährungssoziologie *[In German]*; The change in the art of cooking to enjoyment oriented meal creation — Weber's theory of rationalization and differentiation as the basis of nutritional sociology *[Summary]*. Eva Barlösius; Wolfgang Manz. *Kölner Z. Soz. Soz. psy.* **40**:4 1988 pp. 728 – 746

H.6: Credit. Financing. Money — *Crédit. Financement. Monnaie*

1 From capital in production to capital in exchange. Ben Fine. *Sci. Soc.* **52**:3 Fall:1988 pp. 326 – 336
2 The gender gap on Wall Street — an empirical analysis of confidence in investment decision making. Ralph Estes; Jinoos Hosseini. *J. Psychol.* **122**:6 11: 1988 pp. 577 – 590
3 "Inflation" no image no ichi kenkyū *[In Japanese]*; [A study of inflation images]. Fumimasa Ishigami. ***Bulletin of Tokai Industrial College*** *Vol.2. 1988.* pp. 25 – 41

H.7: Economic policy. Planning — *Politique économique. Planification*

1 California development agreements and British planning agreements — the struggle of the public land use planner. Betty Smith. *Town Plan. R.* **59**:3 7:1988 pp. 277 – 288
2 California's housing element — a backdoor approach to metropolitan governance and regional planning. William C. Baer. *Town Plan. R.* **59**:3 7:1988 pp. 263 – 276
3 Development control in Western Europe. H.W.E. Davies *[Contrib.]*; D. Edwards *[Contrib.]*; John V. Punter *[Contrib.]*; A.J. Hooper *[Contrib.]*. Collection of 5 articles. **Town Plan. R.** , *59:2*, 4:1988 pp. 127 – 226
4 The impact of informationization on regional development. Yutaka Oishi. ***Keio Communication Review*** *Vol.9. 1988.* pp. 22 – 32
5 Marketing the city — concepts, processes and Dutch applications. G.J. Ashworth; H. Voogd. *Town Plan. R.* **59**:1 1:1988 pp. 65 – 80
6 Public policy in an ethnically plural society — approaches of London boroughs towards black business development. P.A. Memon. *Town Plan. R.* **59**:1 1:1988 pp. 45 – 64

I: Labour — *Travail*

I.1: Industrial sociology. Sociology of work — *Sociologie industrielle. Sociologie du travail*

1 L'analyse du travail — pratiques, concepts, enjeux *[In French]*; Die Arbeitanalyse — Praktiken, Konzepte und Bedeutung *[German summary]*; The analysis of work — practices, concepts and challenges *[Summary]*. Jacques Merchiers; Jean-Francois Troussier. *Form. Emp.* **23** 7-9:1988 pp. 57 – 70

2 Dalla sociologia industriale alla sociologia del lavoro — una panoramica sulla ricerca inglese a partire dagli anni '60 *[In Italian]*; [From industrial sociology to a sociology of work — the survey of English research from the 1960s onwards]. Duncan Gallie. *Sociol. Lav.* **35-36** 1988-89 pp. 15 – 47

3 Die doppelte Wirklichkeit der Unternehmen und ihre Konsequenzen für die Industriesoziologie *[In German]*; The double reality of enterprise and its consquences for industrial sociology *[Summary]*. Friedrich Weltz. *Soz. Welt.* **39:1** 1988 pp. 97 – 103

4 The employment relation as a social relation. James N. Baron. *J. Jap. Int. Ec.* **:3-4** 9-12:1988 pp. 492 – 525

5 Industriesoziologie als Katharsis *[In German]*; Industrial sociology as catharsis *[Summary]*. Bärbel Kern; Horst Kern; Michael Schumann. *Soz. Welt.* **39:1** 1988 pp. 86 – 96

6 On work — historical, comparative and theoretical approaches. R. E. Pahl *[Ed.]*. Oxford: Basil Blackwell, 1988: 752 p. (ill) *ISBN: 0631157611*. Bibliographies.

7 Sangyou shakaigaku *[In Japanese]*; [Industrial sociology]. Akihiro Ishikawa *[Ed.]*. Tokyo: Science-sha, 1988: 211 p.

I.2: Employment. Labour market — *Emploi. Marché du travail*

1 Accounting for changes in the labor supply of recently divorced women. William R. Johnson; Jonathan Skinner. *J. Hum. Res.* **XXIII:4** Fall:1988 pp. 417 – 436

2 Acteurs et institutions. La dynamique des marchés du travail *[In French]*; Actors and institutions — labor market dynamics *[Summary]*. Catherine Paradeise. *Sociol. Trav.* **:1** :1988 pp. 79 – 106

3 Action and information in the job mobility process — the search decision. Charles N. Halaby. *Am. Sociol. R.* **53:1** 2:1988 pp. 9 – 25

4 Activité féminine et structures familiales. Quelle dépendance? *[In French]*; Women's employment and family structure. What are the relationships? *[Summary]*; *[Spanish summary]*. Jacques Véron. *Population* **43:1** 1-2:1988 pp. 103 – 120

5 After redundancy — the experience of economic insecurity. John Westergaard; Iain Noble *[Ed.]*; Alan Walker *[Ed.]*. Cambridge: Polity, 1988: xii, 205 p. *ISBN: 0745601510*. Bibliography — p195-202.

INTERNATIONAL BIBLIOGRAPHY OF SOCIOLOGY — 1988

I.2: Employment. Labour market *[Emploi. Marché du travail]*

6 AIDS and employment law. Christopher Southam; Gillian Howard *[Ed.]*. London: Financial Training, 1988: xvii, 290 p. *ISBN: 1851850937.*

7 Arbeitsmarkt und soziale Netzwerke. Die Bedeutung sozialer Kontakte beim Zugang zu Arbeitsplätzen *[In German]*; Labor markets and social networks — the role of ties for getting a job *[Summary]*. Peter Preisendörfer; Thomas Voss. *Soz. Welt.* **39:1** 1988 pp. 104 – 119

8 Arbeitsmarktsegmentation in der Bundesrepublik Deutschland — eine empirische Überprüfung von Segmentationstheorien aus der Perspektive des Lebenslaufs *[In German]*; Labour market segmentation in the Federal Republic of Germany — an empirical examination of segmentation theories from a life course perspective *[Summary]*. Hans-Peter Blossfeld; Karl Ulrich Mayer. *Kölner Z. Soz. Soz. psy.* **40:2** 1988 pp. 262 – 283

9 Child labour in India — extent and associated factors. Ramesh Kanbargi. *Indian J. Soc. W.* **XLIX:3** 7:1988 pp. 239 – 244

10 The choice of part-time work among Swedish one-child mothers; En Suède, les mères d'enfant unique préfèrent le travail à temps partiel *[French summary]*. Eva M. Bernhardt. *Eur. J. Pop.* **4:2** 4:1988 pp. 117 – 144

11 Combating child labour. A. Bekele *[Ed.]*; Jo Boyden *[Ed.]*. Geneva: International Labour Office, 1988: xiii, 226 p. (ill.) *ISBN: 9221063887. Includes bibliographical references.*

12 Depression in unemployed Swedish women. Ellen M. Hall; Jeffrey V. Johnson. *Soc. Sci. Med.* **27:12** 1988 pp. 1349 – 1356

13 Determinants of maternal employment for white preschool children — 1960-1980. David J. Eggebeen. *J. Marriage Fam.* **50:1** 2:1988 pp. 149 – 159

14 Education and employment in the informal sector — a review of some recent African research. Eva M. Rathgeber. *Can. J. Afr. St.* **22:2** :1988 pp. 270 – 287

15 El empleo a domicilio en el medio rural — la nueva manufactura *[In Spanish]*; [Home employment in the rural environment — the new factory]. Patricia Arias. *Est. Sociol.* **VI:18** 9-12:1988 pp. 535 – 552

16 Employers, labour markets, and redistribution under state socialism — an interpretation of housing policy in Hungary 1960-1983. C.G. Pickvance. *Sociology* **22:2** 5:1988 pp. 193 – 214

17 Equal employment opportunity in Japan — a view from the west. Linda N. Edwards. *Ind. Lab. Rel.* **41:2** 1:1988 pp. 240 – 250

18 Female workers in Addis Ababa. Jose Van Kesteren. *E.Afr. Soc. Sci. Res. R.* **IV:1** January:1988 pp. 17 – 31

19 Feminization of the labour force — paradoxes and promises. Jane Jenson *[Ed.]*; Elisabeth Hagen *[Ed.]*; Ceallaigh Reddy *[Ed.]*. Cambridge: Polity, 1988: 290 p. *ISBN: 0745605486. Includes index.* [Europe and the international order.]

20 Gender and recruitment — people and places in the labour market. Margaret M. Curran. *Work Emp. Soc.* **2:3** 9:1988 pp. 335 – 351

21 Getting equal — labour market regulation and women's work. Carol O'Donnell; Philippa Hall *[Ed.]*. Sydney: Allen & Unwin, 1988: xii, 173 p. *ISBN: 0043020054; LofC: 87-22302. Includes index.*

22 Graduates at work — degree courses and the labour market. John Brennan;

INTERNATIONAL BIBLIOGRAPHY OF SOCIOLOGY — 1988

I.2: Employment. Labour market *[Emploi. Marché du travail]*

Philip McGeevor *[Ed.]*. London: Kingsley, 1988: vi, 151 p. (ill) *ISBN: 1853025003. Bibliography — p.151.* [Higher education policy. : No. 1]

23 The impact of redundancy on subsequent labour market experience. Mark Wooden. *J. Ind. Relat.* **30:1** 3:1988 pp. 3 – 31

24 Industrial labor markets and job mobility rates. David S. Hachen. *R. Soc. Strat. Mob.* **7** 1988 pp. 35 – 69

25 Information theory and employer recruitment practices. Margaret J. Nowak. *J. Ind. Relat.* **30:2** 6:1988 pp. 277 – 293

26 An investigation of sex discrimination in recruiters' evaluations of actual applicants. Laura M. Graves; Gary N. Powell. *J. Appl. Psychol.* **73:1** 2:1988 pp. 20 – 29

27 Labor market segmentation in the Federal Republic of Germany — an empirical study of segmentation theories from a life course perspective. Hans-Peter Blossfield; Karl Ulrich Mayer. *Eur. Sociol. R.* **4:2** 9:1988 pp. 123 – 140

28 Labour market segmentation and income determination in Poland. Henryk Domanski. *Sociol. Q.* **29:1** Spring:1988 pp. 47 – 62

29 Il lavoro femminile in Italia — linee di tendenza dell'analisi sociologica *[In Italian]*; [Female labour in Italy — trends in sociological analysis]. Bianca Beccalli. *Sociol. Lav.* **35-36** 1988-89 pp. 187 – 199

30 Mercato del lavoro e occupazione *[In Italian]*; [Labour market and occupations]. Richard K. Brown. *Sociol. Lav.* **35-36** 1988-89 pp. 303 – 317

31 Mercato del lavoro e occupazione — il caso italiano negli anni 80 *[In Italian]*; [Labour market and occupations — the Italian case of the 80s]. Paolo Calza Bini. *Sociol. Lav.* **35-36** 1988-89 pp. 318 – 336

32 A model for analyzing youth labor market policies. Alan L. Gustman; Thomas L. Steinmeier. *J. Labor Ec.* **6:3** 7:1988 pp. 376 – 396

33 Обшественное разделение труа и его производительность *[In Russian]*; [Social division of labour and its productivity]. S.A. Kuz'min. *Isvest. SSSR. Ser. Ekon. Vol.3. 1988.* pp. 3 – 12

34 Occupational health risks for Mexican women — the case of the maquiladora along the Mexican-United States border. Melbourne F. Hovell; Carol Sipan; Richard C Hofstetter; Barbara C. DuBois; Andrew Krefft; John Conway; Monica Jasis; Hope L. Isaacs. *Int. J. Health. Ser.* **18:4** 1988 pp. 617 – 628

35 The older worker. Monroe Berkowitz *[Ed.]*. Madison, Wis.: Industrial Relations Research Association, 1988: v, 228 p. *ISBN: 0913447412].* [Industrial Relations Research Association series.]

36 Older workers and the peripheral workforce — the erosion of gender differences. Angela Dale; Claire Bamford. *Age. Soc.* **8:1** 3:1988 pp. 43 – 62

37 One firm, two labour markets — the case of McDonald's in the fast-food industry. Toby L. Parcel; Marie B. Sickmeier. *Sociol. Q.* **29:1** Spring:1988 pp. 29 – 46

38 Opportunity models — adapting vacancy models to national occupational structures. Roderick J. Harrison. *R. Soc. Strat. Mob.* **7** 1988 pp. 3 – 33

39 Play the white man — the social construction of fairness and competition in equal opportunity policies. Janette Webb; Sonia Liff. *Sociol. Rev.* **36:3** 8:1988 pp. 532 – 551

I.2: Employment. Labour market [Emploi. Marché du travail]

40 Psychological effects of unemployment on workers and their families. Ramsay Liem; Joan Huser Liem. *J. Soc. Issues* **44:4** 1988 pp. 87 – 105

41 Racial differences in underemployment in American cities. Daniel T. Lichter. *A.J.S.* **93:4** 1:1988 pp. 771 – 792

42 Reflexiones sobre el trabajo a domicilio en la zona noreste de Guanajuato *[In Spanish]*; [Reflexions on work at home in the northeastern zone of Guanajuato]. Sandra Treviño Siller. *Est. Sociol.* **VI:18** 9-12:1988 pp. 583 – 601

43 Scientists in organizations — discrimination processes in an internal labour market. Yehouda A. Shenhav; Yitchak Haberfeld. *Sociol. Q.* **29:3** Fall:1988 pp. 451 – 462

44 Sex segregation in the paid workforce — the New Zealand case. Patricia Gwartney-Gibbs. *Aust. N.Z. J. Soc.* **24:2** 7:1988 pp. 264 – 278

45 Social resources, situational constraints, and re-employment. Maarten Sprengers; Fritz Tazelaar; Hendrik D. Flap. *Neth. J. Soc. Sci.* **24: 2** 10: 1988 pp. 98 – 116

46 Some remarks on informal work, social polarization and the social structure. R.E. Pahl. *Int. J. Urban* **12:2** 6:1988 pp. 247 – 267

47 Sources of variation in labour market segmentation — a comparison of youth labour markets in Canada and Britain. David N. Ashton. *Work Emp. Soc.* **2:1** 3:1988 pp. 1 – 24

48 Spatial labour markets. L. van der Laan *[Ed.]*; T. van der Meulen *[Ed.]*; G.H.M. Evers *[Contrib.]*; G.A. van der Knaap *[Contrib.]*; J.B.R. Gaspersz *[Contrib.]*; W. van Voorden *[Contrib.]*; W.C.G.M. van Paridon *[Contrib.]*; D. Massey *[Contrib.]*; B. Kruijt *[Contrib.]*; R. van Geuns *[Contrib.] and others. Collection of 10 articles.* **J. Econ. Soc. Geogr.** , *78:5*, 1988 pp. 325 – 398

49 Strukturelle Einflußfaktoren der gewerblichen Beschäftigung von Frauen im Wandel der Zeit *[In German]*; Organizational modernization and women's labour force participation *[Summary]*. Reinhard Stockmann. *Soz. Welt.* **39:3** 1988 pp. 330 – 360

50 Technology and local labour markets — what will happen to women's work? Lise Drewes-Nielsen. *Acta Sociol.* **31** 1988 pp. 249 – 263

51 Technology and the labour process — Australasian case studies. Evan Willis *[Ed.]*. Sydney: Allen & Unwin, 1988: 201 p. *ISBN: 004337008x.* [Studies in society.]

52 Third World workers — comparative international labour studies. Peter C.W. Gutkind *[Ed.]*; Dipesh Chakrabarty *[Contrib.]*; Carolyn A. Brown *[Contrib.]*; Hing Ai Yun *[Contrib.]*; Martin J. Murray *[Contrib.]*; Patricia Todd *[Contrib.]*; Jomo Kwame Sundaram *[Contrib.]*; Carolyne Dennis *[Contrib.]*; Ken Post *[Contrib.]*; Christopher Pycroft *[Contrib.] and others. Collection of 11 articles.* **J. As. Afr. S.** , *XXIII:1-2*, 1-4:1988 pp. 1 – 198

53 Unemployment and mental health — some British studies. Peter Warr; Paul Jackson; Michael Banks. *J. Soc. Issues* **44:4** 1988 pp. 47 – 68

54 Unemployment and psychiatric distress — social resources and coping. Margaret E. Ensminger; David D. Celentano. *Soc. Sci. Med.* **27:3** 1988 pp. 239 – 247

55 What is a good job? A new measure of labor-market success. Christopher Jencks; Lauri Perman; Lee Rainwater. *A.J.S.* **93:6** 5:1988 pp. 1322 – 1357

I.2: Employment. Labour market *[Emploi. Marché du travail]*

56 What mediates sex discrimination in hiring decisions? Peter Glick; Cari Zion; Cynthia Nelson. *J. Pers. Soc. Psychol.* **55:2** 8:1988 pp. 178 – 186

57 White, black and Hispanic female youths in central city labour markets. George Farkus; Margaret Barton; Kathy Kushner. *Sociol. Q.* **29:4** Winter:1988 pp. 605 – 621

58 Why does unemployment come in couples? — an analysis of (un)employment and (non)employment homogamy tables for Canada, the Netherlands and the United States in the 1980s. Wout Ultee; Jos Dessens; Wim Jansen. *Eur. Sociol. R.* **4:2** 9:1988 pp. 111 – 122

59 Womanpower — the Arab debate on women at work. Nadia Hijab. Cambridge: Cambridge University Press, 1988: - *ISBN: 052126443x. Includes bibliography and index.* [Cambridge Middle East library.]

60 Women and home-based work — the unspoken contract. Kathleen Christensen. New York: Henry Holt, 1988: 201 p. *ISBN: 080500386x; LofC: 87-8527.*

61 Women and paid work — issues of equality. Audrey Hunt *[Ed.]*; R. Lindley *[Foreword]*. Basingstoke: Macmillan, 1988: xviii, 237 p. (ill) *ISBN: 0333454200. Bibliography — p.222-230. Includes index.* [Warwick studies in employment.]

62 Women and work in Shenzhen. Phyllis Andors. *B. Concern. Asia. Schol.* **20:3** 1988 pp. 22 – 41

63 Women at work. Rosalind M. Schwartz *[Ed.]*. Los Angeles: University of California at Los Angeles, Institute of Industrial Relations and Center for the Study of Women, 1988: 210 p. *ISBN: 0892151455; LofC: 88-013247. Bibliography.* [Monograph and research series.]

64 Women's employment and multinationals in Europe. Diane Elson *[Ed.]*; Ruth Pearson *[Ed.]*. Basingstoke: Macmillan, 1988: 227 p. *ISBN: 0333438779. Includes index.*

65 Women's participation in the labour force — a methods test in India for improving its measurement. Richard Anker; M.E. Khan; R.B. Gupta. Geneva: International Labour Office, 1988: xiv, 204 p. [Women, work and development. : Vol. 16]

66 Women's participation in the medical profession — the Indian case. Nigar Fatima Abidi. *Int. Sociol.* **3:3** 9:1988 pp. 235 – 249

67 Worker power, firm power, and the structure of labour markets. Neil Fligstein; Roberto M. Fernandez. *Sociol. Q.* **29:1** Spring:1988 pp. 5 – 28

68 The worth of women's work — a qualitative synthesis. Anne Statham *[Ed.]*; Eleanor M. Miller *[Ed.]*; Hans O. Mauksch *[Ed.]*. Albany: State University of New York Pr, 1988: 331 p. *ISBN: 0887065910; LofC: 87-6472.*

69 Young adults and long-term unemployment. Susan McRae; Michael White *[Ed.]*. London: Policy Studies Institute, 1988: 160 p. *ISBN: 085374372x.*

70 Youth unemployment and ill health — results from a 2-year follow-up study. Anne Hammarström; Janlert Urban; Töres Theorell. *Soc. Sci. Med.* **26:10** 1988 pp. 1025 – 1033

71 Youth unemployment in China. Langrui Feng. *Int. Soc. Sci. J.* **116** 5:1988 pp. 285 – 296

72 Youth unemployment in Great Britain. P. E. Hart. Cambridge: Cambridge University Press, 1988: x, 142 p. (ill) *ISBN: 0521353483; LofC: 87-25597. Bibliography — p.133-140. - Includes index.* [Occasional papers.]

I.3: Personnel management. Working conditions — Administration du personnel. Conditions de travail

1 Absenteeism and accidents in a dangerous environment — empirical analysis of underground coal mines. Paul S. Goodman; Steven Garber. *J. Appl. Psychol.* **73:1** 2:1988 pp. 81 – 86
2 An adaptation of models of prosocial behavior to supervisor interventions with troubled employees. Gregory A. Bayer; Lawrence H. Gerstein. *J. Appl. Soc. Psychol.* **18:1** 1:1988 pp. 23 – 37
3 AIDS — human rights versus the duty to provide a safe workplace. Marco Leo Colosi. *Lab. Law J.* *10:1988* pp. 677 – 687
4 Alcohol drinking patterns and work areas — epidemiological study of factory and rural workers in Florence, Italy. Allaman Allamani; Francesco Cipriani; Stefano Innocenti; Canio Lomuto; Marco Marchi; Antonio Morettini. *Br. J. Addict.* **83:10** 10:1988 pp. 1169 – 1178
5 Aspects of the correlation between labour productivity and remuneration. G.H. Zaman; Zizi Beli. *Rev. Roumaine Sci.Soc. Série Sci. Econ.* **32:2** 7-12:1988 pp. 127 – 136
6 Behind the silicon curtain — the seductions of work in a lonely era. Dennis Hayes. London: Free Association, 1988: 215 p. *ISBN: 1853430706. Includes bibliography and index.*
7 Can sex be considered in promotion determinations? Dawn D. Bennett-Alexander. *Lab. Law J.* *4:1988* pp. 232 – 241
8 Causes of health and safety hazards in Canadian agriculture. Wilfred B. Denis. *Int. J. Health. Ser.* **18:3** 1988 pp. 419 – 436
9 Comparative perspectives on work structures and inequality. Arne L. Kalleberg. *Ann. R. Soc.* **14** 1988 pp. 203 – 225
10 The concept of work feeling. Lloyd E. Sandelands. *J. Theory Soc. Behav.* **18:4** 12:1988 pp. 437 – 458
11 Democratizing occupational health — the Scandinavian experience of work reform. Björn Gustavsen. *Int. J. Health. Ser.* **18:4** 1988 pp. 675 – 690
12 Early retirement. Ann McGoldrick; Cary L. Cooper *[Ed.].* Aldershot: Gower, 1988: x,330 p. (ill) *ISBN: 056605244x. Bibliography — p.304-320. Includes index.*
13 The effect of applicant age, job level, and accountability on the evaluation of job applicants. Randall A. Gordon; Richard M. Rozelle; James C. Baxter. *Organ. Beh. Hum. Dec. Proces.* **41:1** 2:1988 pp. 20 – 33
14 Estimating alcohol-related absenteeism in New Zealand. Sally Casswell; Lynnette Gilmore; Toni Ashton. *Br. J. Addict.* **83:6** 6:1988 pp. 677 – 682
15 Examining the nature of domestic labour. Colin C. Williams. Aldershot: Avebury, 1988: 196 p. (ill) *ISBN: 0566056836. Includes bibliography.*
16 Gender risk and access to tax-favored fringe benefits — a split labor market approach. Guy C. Dalto. *Pop. Res. Pol. R.* **7:3** 1988 pp. 239 – 253
17 Gender-cohort succession and retirement among older men and women, 1951 to 1984. Stanley DeViney; Angela M. O'Rand. *Sociol. Q.* **29:4** Winter:1988 pp. 525 – 540
18 The health and safety of workers — case studies in the politics of professional responsibility. Ronald Bayer *[Ed.].* Oxford: Oxford University Press, 1988: 308 p. *ISBN: 0195053656; LofC: 87-28111. Includes index.*

I.3: Personnel management. Working conditions *[Administration du personnel. Conditions de travail]*

19 Human resource training and development. Gary P. Latham. *Ann. R. Psych.* **39:** 1988 pp. 545 – 582

20 In the business of child care — employer initiatives and working women. Judith D. Auerbach. New York: Praeger, 1988: 171 p. (ill) *ISBN: 0275928586; LofC: 87-27393. Includes bibliography and index.*

21 Inequality in the automated office — the impact of computers on the division of labour. Angelika Volst; Ina Wagner. *Int. Sociol.* **3:2** 6:1988 pp. 129 – 154

22 Japanese Teinen Taishoku — how cultural values affect retirement. John McCallum. *Age. Soc.* **8:1** 3:1988 pp. 23 – 41

23 Job quits in theoretical and empirical perspective. Ross M. Stolzenberg. *R. Soc. Strat. Mob.* **7** 1988 pp. 99 – 133

24 Job requirements and religious practices — conflict and accommodation. Douglas Massengill; Donald J. Petersen. *Lab. Law J. 7:1988* pp. 402 – 410

25 Leaner and possibly fitter — the management of redundancy in Britain; Amaigri et peut-être plus apte — la gestion de la réduction du personnel en Grande-Bretagne *[French summary]*. Peter Turnbull. *West. Pol. Q.* **19:3** Autumn:1988 pp. 201 – 213

26 Learned helplessness at work. Lennart Lennerlöf. *Int. J. Health. Ser.* **18:2** 1988 pp. 207 – 222

27 Manpower planning and development in an organization. John Fyfe. *Publ. Adm. D.* **8:3** 7-9:1988 pp. 305 – 315

28 Maternity leave in Australia — employee and employer experiences — report of a survey. Helen Glezer. Melbourne: Australian Institute of Family Studies, 1988: xv, 164 p. [Australian Institute of Family Studies monograph. : No. 7]

29 Motivation in personnel management — the case of Bendel State Civil Service Commission. Andrew O. Igbineweka; Anthony Ehidiamen Ehizulen. *Q. J. Admin.* **XXII:3-4** 4-7:1988 pp. 169 – 190

30 Oligopoly capitalism, labour organization, and wages of workers in American manufacturing industries. E.M. Beck; Lee Watson. *Sociol. Q.* **29:1** Spring:1988 pp. 83 – 95

31 Organizational change in Japanese factories. Robert M. Marsh; Hiroshi Mannari *[Ed.].* Greenwich, Conn.: Jai Press, 1988: 313 p. *ISBN: 0892327774. Bibliography.* [Monographs in organizational behavior and industrial relations. : No. 9]

32 Otto no teinen zen/ go ni okeru tsuma no shūgyou jyoutai no henka *[In Japanese]*; [Impact of husband's retirement on labor-force participation]. Kiyoko Okamura. *Shakai Rounengaku Vol.28. 1988.* pp. 19 – 29

33 Outside ownership and workers' earnings and tenure. Randy Hodson; Patricia Seitz. *Sociol. Q.* **29:1** Spring:1988 pp. 63 – 81

34 Politique paternaliste et division sexuelle du travail — le cas de l'industrie japonaise *[In French]*; A case of paternalistic policy and sexual division of labour — the Japanese industry *[Summary]*. Helena Hirata; Kurumi Sugita. *Mouve. Soc.* **144** 7-9:1988 pp. 71 – 91

35 Public support for mandatory drug-alcohol testing in the workplace. Edward J. Latessa; Lawrence F. Travis; Francis T. Cullen. *Crime Delin.* **34:4** 10:1988 pp. 379 – 392

I.3: Personnel management. Working conditions *[Administration du personnel. Conditions de travail]*

36 Relation of job stressors to affective, health, and performance outcomes — a comparison of multiple data sources. Paul E. Spector; Daniel J. Dwyer; Steve M. Jex. *J. Appl. Psychol.* **73:1** 2:1988 pp. 11 – 19

37 Religious discrimination in the workplace — who's accommodating who? Thomas D. Brierton. *Lab. Law J.* *5:1988* pp. 299 – 306

38 Rethinking occupational health and safety legislation. Adrian Brooks. *J. Ind. Relat.* **30:3** 9:1988 pp. 347 – 362

39 The right to refuse in Québec — five-year evolution of a new mode of expressing risk. Marc Renaud; Chantal St-Jacques. *Int. J. Health. Ser.* **18:3** 1988 pp. 401 – 418

40 Roudou no ningen-ka to shou-shūdan katsudou *[In Japanese]*; [Quality of working life and small group activity]. Toshio Ueda. Tokyo: Senbundo, 1988: 254 p.

41 Scaling an Islamic work ethic. Abbas Ali. *J. Soc. Psychol.* **128:5** 10:1988 pp. 575 – 583

42 Self-esteem at work — research, theory, and practice. Joel Brockner. Lexington, Mass.: Lexington Books, 1988: xii, 258 p. (ill.) *ISBN: 0669097551. Bibliography, p. [233]-248.*

43 Social class and cardiovascular disease — the contribution of work. Michael Marmot; Tores Theorell. *Int. J. Health. Ser.* **18:4** 1988 pp. 659 – 674

44 Social epidemiology and the work environment. S. Leonard Syme. *Int. J. Health. Ser.* **18:4** 1988 pp. 635 – 646

45 Soziologie und menschengerechte Arbeitsgestaltung Arbeitsschutz, ein Berufsfeld für Soziologen? *[In German]*; Sociology and the humanization of working conditions *[Summary]*. Wolfgang Slesina; Alfons Schröer; Christian von Ferber. *Soz. Welt.* **39:2** 1988 pp. 205 – 223

46 Structural discrimination against foreigners and work-related health risks. Maria Oppen. *Econ. Ind. Dem.* **9** 1988 pp. 43 – 64

47 The structure of job satisfaction among New England fishermen and its application to fisheries management policy. Richard B. Pollnac; John J. Poggie. *Am. Anthrop.* **90:4** 12:1988 pp. 888 – 901

48 Le syndrome des 3 P — pression horaire, pression hiérarchique, pas de perspective professionelle *[In French]*; The "3 P" syndrome — time pressure, hierarchical pressure, no career prospects *[Summary]*. Jacques Broda. *Sociol. Trav.* **:1** :1988 pp. 19 – 36

49 Les temps sociaux *[In French]*; [Social time]. Daniel Mercure *[Ed.]*; Anne Wallemacq *[Ed.]*. Bruxelles: De Boeck-Wesmael, 1988: 271 p. *ISBN: 2804111261.*

50 Turnover and employment stability in a large West German company. Andreas Diekmann; Peter Preisendörfer. *Eur. Sociol. R.* **4:3** 12:1988 pp. 233 – 248

51 Les usages professionnels de la micro-informatique *[In French]*; Occupational utilizations of personal computers *[Summary]*. Josiane Jouët. *Sociol. Trav.* **:1** :1988 pp. 107 – 124

52 The vagaries of sex bias — conditions regulating the undervaluation, equivaluation, and overvaluation of female job applicants. Madeline E. Heilman; Richard F. Martell; Michael C. Simon. *Organ. Beh. Hum. Dec. Proces.* **41:1** 2:1988 pp. 98 – 110

I.3: Personnel management. Working conditions *[Administration du personnel. Conditions de travail]*

53 Women's attitudes towards work. Shirley Dex. Basingstoke: Macmillan, 1988: 187 p. (ill) *ISBN: 0333458095. Bibliography — p.177-182.*

54 Work hazards and safety organization in the Third World. Arne Wangel. *Acta Sociol.* **31:4** 1988 pp. 343 – 349

55 Work organisation and industrial relations in data processing departments — a comparative study of the United Kingdom, Denmark and the Netherlands. Andrew L. Friedman *[Ed.]*. Luxembourg: Office for Official Publications of the European Communities, 1988: xvi, 259 p. *ISBN: 9282587606. Bibliography — p.. 257-259.*

56 Work organisation in a regional newspaper — the impact of market and of trade unionism; L'organisation du travail dans un journal régional — l'impact du marché et du syndicalisme *[French summary]*. Paul Smith. *West. Pol. Q.* **19:3** Autumn:1988 pp. 214 – 221

57 Work without end — abandoning shorter hours for the right to work. Benjamin Kline Hunnicutt. Philadelphia: Temple University Press, 1988: x, 404 p. (ill.) *ISBN: 0877225206. Includes index.* [Labor and social change.]

58 Work, locality and social control. Michael Maguire. *Work Emp. Soc.* **2:1** 3:1988 pp. 71 – 87

59 Workers' perceptions, knowledge and responses regarding occupational health and safety — a report on a Canadian study. Vivienne Walters; Ted Haines. *Soc. Sci. Med.* **27:11** 1988 pp. 1189 – 1196

60 Workplace democracy and worker health — strategies for implementation. Steven Deutsch. *Int. J. Health. Ser.* **18:4** 1988 pp. 647 – 658

61 Worksite health promotion. Peter Conrad *[Contrib.]*; Roberta B. Hollander *[Contrib.]*; Joseph J. Lengermann *[Contrib.]*; Paul M. Roman *[Contrib.]*; Terry C. Blum *[Contrib.]*; Jennie J. Kronenfeld *[Contrib.]*; Kirby L. Jackson *[Contrib.]*; Keith E. Davis *[Contrib.]*; Steven N. Blair *[Contrib.]*; M.A. Spilman *[Contrib.]* <u>and others</u>. Collection of 10 articles. *Soc. Sci. Med.*, *26:5*, 1988 pp. 485 – 575

I.4: Occupations. Vocational training — *Professions. Formation professionnelle*

1 Comparisons of male and female student aspirants to a scientific career — perceptions of promising science talents. Gabriel Bar-Haïm; John M. Wilkes. *Int. J. Comp. Soc* **XXIX:3-4** 9-12:1988 pp. 187 – 201

2 Continuities and change in skilled work — a comparison of five paper manufacturing plants in the UK, Australia and the USA. Roger Penn; Hilda Scattergood. *Br. J. Soc.* **XXXIX:1** 3:1988 pp. 69 – 85

3 Cross-national variation in occupational distributions, relative mobility chances, and intergenerational shifts in occupational distributions. Robert M. Hauser; David B. Grusky. *Am. Sociol. R.* **53:5** 10:1988 pp. 723 – 741

4 Degrees of success — career aspirations and destinations of college, university and polytechnic graduates. C. J. Boys; J. Kirkland *[Ed.]*. London: Kingsley, 1988: 133 p. *ISBN: 185302502x. Includes index.* [Higher education policy series. : No. 2]

5 Desired occupational change among working women. Dennis A. Ahlburg. *J. Ind. Relat.* **30:1** 3:1988 pp. 68 – 82

I.4: Occupations. Vocational training [Professions. Formation professionnelle]

6 Do odds ratios really control for the availability of occupational positions in status contingency tables? Roderick Harrison. *Eur. Sociol. R.* **4:1** 5:1988 pp. 65 – 79

7 Ethics and professionalism. John H. Kultgen. Philadelphia: University of Pennsylvania Press, 1988: xii, 394 p. *ISBN: 0812280946. Includes indexes; Bibliography, p. [375]- 383.*

8 Formation professionelle ouvrière — trois modèles européens *[In French]*; Die Berufsausbildung der Arbeiter — drei europäische Muster *[German summary]*; Vocational training — three European models *[Summary]*. Myriam Campinos-Dubernet; Jean-Marc Grando. *Form. Emp.* **21** 1-3:1988 pp. 5 – 29

9 Gender and promotion in segmented job ladder systems. Thomas A. DiPrete; Whitman T. Soule. *Am. Sociol. R.* **53:1** 2:1988 pp. 26 – 40

10 Job mobility and earnings — an internal labour market analysis. John Creedy; Keith Whitfield. *J. Ind. Relat.* **30:1** 3:1988 pp. 100 – 117

11 Job mobility in Australia — theories, evidence and implications. Thorsten Stromback. *J. Ind. Relat.* **30:2** 6:1988 pp. 258 – 276

12 Joining forces — police training, socialization, and occupational competence. Nigel G. Fielding. London: Routledge, 1988: x, 228 p. *ISBN: 041500683x. Bibliography — p[216]-222.*

13 Kaigai haken shain no shakai-shinrigaku *[In Japanese]*; [The social psychology of corporate sojourners]. Takeo Ogawa. *J. Yamag. Univ. Lit. Soc. Vol.39. 1988.* pp. 177 – 198

14 Male-female differences in occupational choice and the demand for general and occupation-specific human capital. Nadja Zalokar. *Econ. Inq.* **XXVI:1** 1:1988 pp. 59 – 74

15 Measuring the efficiency of public programs — costs and benefits in vocational rehabilitation. Monroe Berkowitz *[Ed.]*. Philadelphia: Temple University Press, 1988: ix, 267 p. (ill.) *ISBN: 0877225273; LofC: 87-018080. Includes bibliographies and index.*

16 La mobilità occupazionale in Emilia-Romagna. Lo studio della mobilità relativa *[In Italian]*; Occupational mobility in Emilia Romagna *[Summary]*. Antonio Cobalti. *Rass. It. Soc.* **29:3** 7-9:1988 pp. 313 – 346

17 Modele de analiză a mobilității socioprofesionale *[In Romanian]*; (Models for analysing socio-professional mobility); (Modèles d'analyse de la mobilité socio-professionnelle: *Title only in French)*; (Аналитические модели социопрофессиональноай ориентации: *Title only in Russian)*. Doina Dragomirescu. *Viit. Soc.* **LXXXI** 11-12:1988 pp. 521 – 528

18 More universalism, less structural mobility — the American occupational structure in the 1980s. Michael Hout. *A.J.S.* **93:6** 5:1988 pp. 1358 – 1400

19 Nogyo setaiin no shugyo keireki *[In Japanese]*; [Occupational careers of farm family members]. Toyomi Ishihara. *Nogyo Sogo Kenkyu Vol.42; No.2 - 1988.* pp. 89 – 120

20 Occupational gender mix and men's experience of the work role. Pamela K. Adelmann. *Publ. Adm. D.* **4:4** 12:1988 pp. 225 – 236

21 Occupational stress amongst general practice dentists. Cary L. Cooper; Jane Watts; A.J. Baglioni; Mike Kelly. *J. Occup. Psychol.* **61:2** 6:1988 pp. 163 – 174

I.4: Occupations. Vocational training [Professions. Formation professionnelle]

22 Occupazione femminile e struttura occupazionale in Gran Bretagna [In Italian]; [Female occupations and occupational structure in Great Britain]. Rosemary Crompton. *Sociol. Lav.* **35-36** 1988-89 pp. 173 – 186
23 Organizational dynamics and career patterns. Peter Preisendörfer; Yvonne Burgess. *Eur. Sociol. R.* **4:1** 5:1988 pp. 32 – 45
24 Parental influence and teenagers' motivations to train for technological jobs. Glynis M. Breakwell; Chris Fife-Schaw; John Devereux. *J. Occup. Psychol.* **61:1** 3:1988 pp. 79 – 88
25 Psychological and sociological approaches to the study of occupational illness — a critical review. Michael Quinlan. *Aust. N.Z. J. Soc.* **24:2** 7:1988 pp. 189 – 207
26 The psychological effects of traditional and of economically peripheral job settings in Japan. Carmi Schooler; Atsushi Naoi. *A.J.S.* **94:2** 9:1988 pp. 335 – 355
27 The selection and training of primary health care workers in Ecuador — issues and alternatives for public policy. Karen R. Mangelsdorf. *Int. J. Health. Ser.* **18:3** 1988 pp. 471 – 494
28 The sociology of the professions. Dead or alive? Keith Macdonald; George Ritzer. *Work Occup.* **15:3** 8:1988 pp. 251 – 272
29 Work experience and psychological development through the life span. Kathryn M. Borman [Ed.]; Jeylan T. Mortimer [Ed.]. Boulder, Colo.: Westview Press, 1988: viii, 306 p. (ill.) *ISBN: 0813374677; LofC: 87-028190. Includes bibliographies and indexes.* [AAAS selected symposium. : No. 107]

I.5: Employees. Technicians. Workers — *Employés. Techniciens. Travailleurs*

1 The ambiguous future of professional and technical workers in manufacturing — some hypotheses. Erica Schoenberger. *Acta Sociol.* **31** 1988 pp. 241 – 247
2 Blue, white and pink collar workers in Australia — technicians, bank employees and flight attendants. Claire Williams. Sydney: Allen & Unwin, 1988: vii, 202 p. *ISBN: 0043100236. Includes bibliographical references (p. 190-195).* [Studies in society.]
3 Educational credentials and hiring decisions — what employers look for in new employees. David B. Bills. *R. Soc. Strat. Mob.* **7** 1988 pp. 71 – 97
4 Falling through the net — employment change and worker participation; Passer à travers les mailles du filet — les changements dans l'emploi et la participation des travilleurs [French summary]. Linda Dickens. *Ind. Relat. J.* **19:2** Summer:1988 pp. 139 – 153
5 Haben Industriefacharbeiter besondere Probleme mit dem Umweltthema? [In German]; Do skilled industrial workers have particular difficulties with the environmental debate [Summary]. Hartwig Heine; Rüdiger Mautz. *Soz. Welt.* **39:2** 1988 pp. 123 – 143
6 Industrial labour in Africa — continuity and change among Nigerian factory workers. Hans Dieter Seibel; Ukandi Godwin Damachi [Ed.]; Detlev Holloh

I.5: Employees. Technicians. Workers *[Employés. Techniciens. Travailleurs]*

[Ed.]; Sabine Herwegen *[Ed.]*. Saarbrücken: Breitenbach, 1988: x, 185 p. ISBN: 3881564128. *Includes bibliographical references (p. 163-166).* [Kölner Beiträge zur Entwicklungsländerforschung. : No. 11]

7 Japanese management progress — mobility into middle management. Mitsuru Wakabayashi; George Graen; Michael Graen; Martin Graen. *J. Appl. Psychol.* **73:2** 5:1988 pp. 217 – 227

8 Kanri-shoku to Shokuba no Jinji. Roumu *[In Japanese]*; [Manager's roles in enterprise]. Tadashi Umezawa. Tokyo: Gyousei, 1988: 322 p.

9 Management techniques in the public sector. Jamal Khan. *B. E.Carib. Aff.* **14:4** 9-10:1988 pp. 22 – 35

10 Manager zwischen Marx und Markt — Generaldirektoren in der DDR *[In German]*; [Managers between Marx and markets — general managers in East Germany]. Hans Herbert Götz. Freiburg im Breisgau: Herder Taschenbuch Verlag, 1988: 128 p. *ISBN: 3451085925.* []

11 Managerial lives in transition — advancing age and changing times. Ann Howard; Douglas W. Bray *[Ed.]*. New York: The Guilford Press, 1988: xvi,462 p. *ISBN: 0898621267. Bibliography — p.449-454.* [Adult development and aging.]

12 The moral manager. Clarence C. Walton. : Ballinger, 1988: 278 p. *ISBN: 0887303099.*

13 Patrons, entrepreneurs et dirigeants *[In French]*; [Bosses, entrepreneurs and leaders]. Bernd Marin *[Contrib.]*; Henri Weber *[Contrib.]*; Michel Bauer *[Contrib.]*; Elie Cohen *[Contrib.]*; Pierre-Éric Tixier *[Contrib.]*. Collection of 6 articles. *Sociol. Trav.* , :4, :1988 pp. 515 – 646

14 The position of the Soviet physician — the bureaucratic professional. Mark G. Field. *Milbank Q.* **66:2 Suppl.** 1988 pp. 182 – 201

15 The professional status of physicians in the Nordic countries. Elianne Riska. *Milbank Q.* **66:2 Suppl.** 1988 pp. 133 – 147

16 Professionals in distress — issues, syndromes, and solutions in psychology. Richard R. Kilburg *[Ed.]*; Peter E. Nathan *[Ed.]*; Richard W. Thoreson *[Ed.]*. Washington: American Psychological Association, 1988: 299 p. *ISBN: 0912704438; LofC: 85-18487. Bibliographies.*

17 The property rights of jobs — job entitlement versus managerial prerogative in manufacturing firms. Kevin T. Leicht; Michael Wallace. *R. Soc. Strat. Mob.* **7** 1988 pp. 189 – 223

18 Qu'est-ce que le patronat? Enjeux théoriques et résultats empiriques *[In French]*; What is the "patronat"? Theoretical issues and empirical results *[Summary]*. Bernd Marin. *Sociol. Trav.* **:4** :1988 pp. 515 – 544

19 The reproduction of social control — a study of prison workers at San Quentin. Barbara A. Owen. New York: Praeger, 1988: viii, 160 p. *ISBN: 0275928187; LofC: 87-36113. Bibliography — p.141-155. Includes index.*

20 Senmonshoku, senmonshoku-ka gainen ni kansuru ichi kosatsu *[In Japanese]*; [A consideration of concepts of profession and professionalization]. Satoshi Tokii. *Review of Miyazakisangyo-Keiei University Vol.1; No.1 - 1988.* pp. 19 – 31

21 Sociological approaches to the professions. Thomas Brante. *Acta Sociol.* **31:2** 1988 pp. 119 – 142

I.5: Employees. Technicians. Workers *[Employés. Techniciens. Travailleurs]*

22 Sociology and the qualifications of managerial staff in Czechoslovakia. Jaroslav Kohout. *Int. Sociol.* **3:4** 12:1988 pp. 335 – 342

23 A study of how female and male managers in some public service organizations in Nigeria perceive work-related variables — some implications; *[Arabic summary]*; Comment les dirigeants femmes et dirigeants hommes dans certains organes gouvernementaux du Nigeria perçoivent les variables relatives au travail — quelques implications *[French summary]*; Un estudio de como la mujer y el hombre gerentes en algunas organizaciones de servicios publicos de Nigeria registran variables relativas al trabajo — algunas implicaciones *[Spanish summary]*. G.U. Imanyi. *Publ. Enter.* **8:4** 12:1988 pp. 355 – 363

24 Third World workers — comparative international labour studies. Peter C.W. Gutkind *[Ed.]*. Leiden: Brill, 1988: 200 p. *ISBN: 9004087885*. Bibliography. [International studies in sociology and social anthropology. : No. 49]

25 Value differences among leaders and the workforce in Australia. Brian Graetz; Ian McAllister. *Aust. N.Z. J. Soc.* **24:1** 3:1988 pp. 83 – 105

26 Women managers — changing organizational cultures. Gisèle Asplund. Chichester: Wiley, [1988]: xvi, 196 p. *ISBN: 0471912921*.

27 Workers in Latin America — Latin American labour as an object of sociological analysis; Travailleurs d'Amérique latine — le travail en Amérique latine, élément d'analyse sociologique *[French summary]*. Francisco Zapata. *Labour Cap. Soc.* **21:1** 4:1988 pp. 110 – 125

28 Working lives in catering. Yiannis Gabriel. London: Routledge & Kegan Paul, 1988: viii, 190 p. *ISBN: 0710209231*. Bibliography — *p.184-187. Includes index*.

I.6: Labour relations — *Relations du travail*

1 Cambiamento tecnologico e organizzazione del lavoro nell'Inghilterra contemporanea *[In Italian]*; [Technological change and labour organizations in present day England]. Roger Penn. *Sociol. Lav.* **35-36** 1988-89 pp. 51 – 93

2 Commitment and the company — manager-worker relations in the absence of internal labor markets. William Finlay. *R. Soc. Strat. Mob.* **7** 1988 pp. 163 – 188

3 Communication and labour relations in South Africa — a strategic approach. Lorna A. Hill; Arminius A. Archer. *Ind. Rel. J. S.Afr.* **8:2** 1988 pp. 43 – 58

4 The composition of public sector compensation — the effects of unionization and bureaucratic size. William J. Hunter; Carol H. Rankin. *J. Labor Res.* **XI:1** Winter:1988 pp. 29 – 42

5 Control of work and worker control — a conflict theory of the governance of transaction costs in work relations. Terry Boswell. *R. Soc. Strat. Mob.* **7** 1988 pp. 135 – 161

6 Corporate characteristics and union organizing. Cheryl L. Maranto. *Ind. Relat.* **27:3** Fall:1988 pp. 352 – 370

7 A cross-section analysis of the postwar decline in American trade union membership. William J. Moore; Robert J. Newman. *J. Labor Res.* **IX:2** Spring:1988 pp. 111 – 125

I.6: Labour relations *[Relations du travail]*

8 Democracy, new technology and old fashioned unions. Eric Hammond. Nottingham: Trent Polytechnic, [1988]: 51 p. *ISBN: 1870864301*. [Trent Business School open lectures in industrial relations.]

9 Do female representatives make a difference? Women full-time officials and trade union work. Edmund Heery; John Kelly. *Work Emp. Soc.* **2:4** 12:1988 pp. 487 – 505

10 The ecology of organizational mortality — American labor unions, 1836-1985. Michael T. Hannan; John Freeman. *A.J.S.* **94:1** 7:1988 pp. 25 – 52

11 Education and union membership. Greg Hundley. *Br. J. Ind. R.* **XXVI:2** 7:1988 pp. 195 – 201

12 Employer associations and bargaining structures — an Australian perspective. David Plowman. *Br. J. Ind. R.* **XXVI:3** 11:1988 pp. 371 – 396

13 Employment flexibility, unions and companies in France; Flexibilité de l'emploi, syndicats et entreprise en France *[French summary]*. Jean-François Amadieu. *Ind. Relat. J.* **19:2** Summer:1988 pp. 117 – 123

14 Etre militante de soi-même. Le féminisme dans le syndicat italien *[In French]*; To be a militant of one's self. Feminism in Italian trade unions *[Summary]*. Monique Gadant; Pima Madami. *Peup. Médit.* **44:45** 7-12:1988 pp. 7 – 28

15 Gender differences in union attitudes, participation and priorities. John Benson; Gerry Griffin. *J. Ind. Relat.* **30:2** 6:1988 pp. 203 – 214

16 The importance of strike size in strike research. Jack W. Skeels; Paul McGrath; Gangadha Arshanapalli. *Ind. Lab. Rel.* **41:4** 7:1988 pp. 582 – 591

17 Individual morality and industrialized work — some theoretical considerations. Wolfgang Lempert. *Econ. Ind. Dem.* **9:4** 11:1988 pp. 475 – 496

18 Industrial relations and the German model. Karen Williams. Aldershot: Avebury, 1988: vii,148 p. (ill) *ISBN: 0566056038. Includes bibliography.*

19 Labour arbitrator's performance views from union and management perspectives. Donald P. Crane; John B. Miner. *J. Labor Res.* **XI:1** Winter:1988 pp. 43 – 54

20 Male and female arbitrator perceptions of the arbitration process. Donald J. Petersen; Marsha Katz. *Lab. Law J.* 2:1988 pp. 110 – 119

21 Moving the status quo — the growth of trade union political funds; *[French summary]*. John W. Leopold. *Ind. Relat. J.* **19:4** Winter:1988 pp. 286 – 295

22 La négociation des nouvelles technologies — une transformation des règles du jeu? *[In French]*; Bargaining on new technologies — new rules of the game? *[Summary]*. Jean-Daniel Reynaud. *R. Fr. Sci. Pol.* **38:1** 2:1988 pp. 5 – 22

23 New technology and industrial relations in Scandinavia. Gert Graversen *[Ed.]*; Russell D. Lansbury *[Ed.]*. Aldershot: Avebury, 1988: 153 p. (ill) *ISBN: 0566056550.*

24 On the explanation of industrial relations diversity — labour movements, employers and the state in Britain and Sweden. James Fulcher. *Br. J. Ind. R.* **XXVI:2** 7:1988 pp. 246 – 274

25 La participation — un clair-obscur *[In French]*; Participation/chiaroscuro *[Summary]*. Anni Borzeix; Danièle Linhart. *Sociol. Trav.* **:1** :1988 pp. 37 – 54

26 Participation, worker's control and self-management. György Széll. *Curr. Sociol.* **36:3** Winter:1988 pp. 1 – 259

I.6: Labour relations [Relations du travail]

27 The political economy of industrial relations — theory and practice in a cold climate. Richard Hyman. Basingstoke: Macmillan, 1988: xvi, 259 p. *ISBN: 0333464303. Includes bibliographies and index.*

28 Le relazione industriali in Gran Bretagna e in Italia oggi — convergenze e divergenze *[In Italian]*; [Industrial relations in Great Britain and Italy today — similarities and differences]. Colin Crouch. *Sociol. Lav.* **35-36** 1988-89 pp. 357 – 376

29 Le relazioni industriali oggi in Italia *[In Italian]*; [Industrial relations today in Italy]. Guido Baglioni. *Sociol. Lav.* **35-36** 1988-89 pp. 377 – 385

30 Representing employee interests — works councils and the rank and file — representation strategies and avoidance rituals. Ad Teulings. *Econ. Ind. Dem.* **9:2** 5:1988 pp. 179 – 195

31 The role of the trade unions in conscientizing the workers. R.E.D. Taylor. *Ind. Rel. J. S.Afr.* **8:1** 1988 pp. 43 – 48

32 Satisfaction with union representation. Jack Fiorito; Daniel G. Gallagher; Cynthia V Fukami. *Ind. Lab. Rel.* **41:2** 1:1988 pp. 294 – 307

33 Social workers and labor unions. Howard Jacob Karger. New York: Greenwood, 1988: 195 p. *ISBN: 0313258678; LofC: 88-3127. Bibliography — p.183-188.* [Contributions in labor studies.]

34 Sociologie des cadres syndicaux, cas de Gabes *[In French]*; [Sociology of trade unions, the Gabes case]. Salah Hamzaoui. *R. Tun. Sci. Soc.* **25:92/93** 1988 pp. 113 – 154

35 Strikes in Scotland; Les grèves en Ecosse *[French summary]*. Michael Jackson. *Ind. Relat. J.* **19:2** Summer:1988 pp. 106 – 116

36 Sub-systems of industrial relations — the spatial dimension in Britain. P.B. Beaumont; R.I. Harris. *Br. J. Ind. R.* **XXVI:3** 11:1988 pp. 397 – 408

37 A symposium — behavioral research in industrial relations. David Lewin *[Ed.]*; George Strauss *[Contrib.]*; James B. Dworkin *[Contrib.]*; Sidney P. Feldman *[Contrib.]*; James M. Brown *[Contrib.]*; Charles J. Hobson *[Contrib.]*; John Thomas Delaney *[Contrib.]*; Donna Sockell *[Contrib.]*; Joel Brockner *[Contrib.]*; Susan Schwochau *[Contrib.] and others*. Collection of 8 articles. **Ind. Relat.** , *27:1,* Winter:1988 pp. 1 – 129

38 La syndicalisation des femmes en Tunisie *[In French]*; The unionization of women in Tunisia *[Summary]*. Dorrah Mahfoudh. *Peup. Médit.* **44:45** 7-12:1988 pp. 29 – 47

39 Teachers' collective bargaining outcomes and tradeoffs. John Thomas Delaney. *J. Labor Res.* **IX:4** Autumn:1988 pp. 363 – 377

40 Union action and the free-rider dilemma. Bert Klandermans. *R. Soc. Move. Con. Cha.* **10** 1988 pp. 77 – 92

41 Unionism and voter turnout. John Thomas Delaney; Marick F. Masters; Susan Schwochau. *J. Labor Res.* **IX:3** Summer:1988 pp. 221 – 236

42 Vacation time and unionism in the U.S. and Europe. Francis Green; Michael J. Potepan. *Ind. Relat.* **27:2** Spring:1988 180-194

43 Who joins unions in the public sector? The effects of individual characteristics and the law. Greg Hundley. *J. Labor Res.* **IX:4** Autumn:1988 pp. 301 – 323

44 Why are trade unions becoming more popular? Unions and public opinion in Britain. Edwards P.K.; George Sayers Bain. *Br. J. Ind. R.* **XXVI:3** 11:1988 pp. 311 – 326

I.6: Labour relations [Relations du travail]

45 Why do workers belong to trade unions? A social psychological study in the UK electronics industry. David Guest; Philip Dewe. *Br. J. Ind. R.* **XXVI:2** 7:1988 pp. 178 – 194

46 Workers' participation. Curt Tausky *[Ed.]*; Anthony F. Chelte *[Ed.]*; Raymond Russell *[Contrib.]*; Robert N. Stern *[Contrib.]*; Frank Hull *[Contrib.]*; Koya Azumi *[Contrib.]*; Vladimir Shlapentokh *[Contrib.]*; Rick Fantasia *[Contrib.]*; Dan Clawson *[Contrib.]*; Gregory Graham *[Contrib.] and others.* Collection of 6 articles. **Work Occup.**, *15:4*, 11:1988 pp. 363 – 488

47 Workplace democracy in Bulgaria — from subordination to partnership in industrial relations; *[French summary]*. Isidor Wallimann; Christo Stojanov. *Ind. Relat. J.* **19:4** Winter:1988 pp. 310 – 321

48 Workplace hazards and workers' desires for union representation. James C. Robinson. *J. Labor Res.* **IX:3** Summer:1988 pp. 237 – 249

I.7: Leisure — *Loisir*

1 Chance and skill in gambling — a search for distinctive features. Gideon Keren; Willem A. Wagenaar. *Soc. Behav.* **3:3** 9:1988 pp. 199 – 217

2 Commitment and leisure. Boas Shamir. *Sociol. Pers.* **31:2** 4:1988 pp. 238 – 258

3 The effect of socio-economic development on household travel behavior in Saudi Arabia. Parviz Amir Koushki. *Socio. Econ.* :3 1988 pp. 131 – 136

4 The evolution of leisure — historical and philosophical perspectives. Thomas L. Goodale; Geoffrey Godbey *[Ed.]*. State College, Pa.: Venture Publishing, 1988: 291 p. *ISBN: 091025124x; LofC: 88-050288.*

5 Freedom and constraint — the paradoxes of leisure. Fred Coalter *[Ed.]*. London: Routledge, 1988: 240 p. *ISBN: 041500649x.*

6 Fútbol — pasión de multitudes y de elites — un estudio institucional de la Asiciación de Fútbol Argentino (1934-1986) *[In Spanish]*; [Football — the passion of the masses and of the élite — an institutional study of the Football Association of Argentina (1934-1986)]. Ariel Scher; Héctor Palomino *[Ed.]*. Buenos Aires: Centro de Investigaciones Sociales sobre el Estado y la Administración, 1988: 245 p. *ISBN: 9509305138.* Bibliography — *p.241-245*. [Documentos del CISEA. : No. 92]

7 The future of leisure services. John Benington; Judy White *[Ed.]*. Harlow: Longman, 1988: xi,272 p. *ISBN: 0582026377.*

8 Gambling without guilt — the legitimation of an American pastime. John Rosecrance. Pacific Grove, Calif.: Brooks/Cole Publishing Company, 1988: 174 p. *ISBN: 0534089542; LofC: 87-24419.*

9 Is there discrimination in the "black man's game"? James V. Koch; C. Warren Vander Hill. *Soc. Sci. Q.* **69:1** 3:1988 p. 83

10 Lazer e consumo cultural das elites *[In Portuguese]*; Leisure and cultural consumption among the elites *[Summary]*; Loisir et consommation culturelle des elites *[French summary]*. Maria Cecilia Spina Forjaz. *Rev. Bras. Ciên. Soc.* **3:6** 2:1988 pp. 99 – 113

11 Leisure, sport and working-class cultures — theory and history. Bob Hollands *[Ed.]*; Hart Cantelon *[Ed.]*. Toronto: Garamond Press, 1988: 106 p. *ISBN: 0920059589.*

I.7: Leisure [Loisir]

12 Not just a game — essays in Canadian sport sociology. Jean Harvey *[Ed.]*; Hart Cantelon *[Ed.]*. Ottawa: University of Ottawa Press, 1988: xv, 323 p. *ISBN: 077660189x. Bibliography — p.[309]-323.*

13 El ocio en las sociedades avanzadas *[In Spanish]*; [Leisure in advanced societies]. Angel Zaragoza. *Sistema* **84** 5:1988 pp. 71 – 90

14 The place of "place" in cultural studies of sports. John Bale. *Prog. H. Geog.* **12:4** 12:1988 pp. 507 – 524

15 Politics and leisure. John Wilson. Boston [Mass.]: Allen & Unwin, 1988: 216 p. *ISBN: 0043012655. Includes index.* [Leisure and recreation studies. : No. 5]

16 The professionalization of public sector sport and leisure management. Barrie Houlihan. *Envir. Plan.A.* **14:3** 5-6:1988 pp. 69 – 82

17 The social meanings of leisure. Gilles Pronovost. *Int. Sociol.* **3:1** 3:1988 pp. 89 – 103

18 Sociology of sport — an annotated bibliography. Paul Redekop. New York: Garland Pub., 1988 *BNB: 87031176; ISBN: 0824084640. Includes index.* [Garland library of sociology.]

19 Sport and society in Latin America — diffusion, dependency, and the rise of mass culture. Joseph L. Arbena *[Ed.]*. New York: Greenwood, 1988: 162 p. *ISBN: 0313247749; LofC: 87-32271. Includes bibliography and index.* [Contributions to the study of popular culture.]

20 Sport et délinquance *[In French]*; [Sport and delinquency]. Jean-Yves Lassalle. Paris: Économica; Aix-en-Provence — Presses universitaires d'Aix-Marseille, 1988: 249 p. *ISBN: 2717816119. Bibliography — p..221-236.* [Le Point sur.]

21 Sports for sale — television, money, and the fans. David A. Klatell; Norman Marcus *[Ed.]*. New York: Oxford University Press, 1988: xi, 253 p. *ISBN: 0195038363; LofC: 88-18789. Bibliography — p.251-253. Includes index.*

22 Television and national sport — the United States and Britain. Joan M. Chandler. Urbana: University of Illinois Press, 1988: xvi, 240 p. *ISBN: 0252015169. Bibliography, p. 193-232.* [Sport and society.]

23 Tourism — candyfloss industry or job generator? Allan M. Williams; Gareth Shaw. *Town Plan. R.* **59:1** 1:1988 pp. 81 – 104

24 Tourist worlds — tourist advertising, ritual, and American culture. David M. Hummon. *Sociol. Q.* **29:2** Summer:1988 pp. 179 – 202

25 The Ulysses factor — evaluating visitors in tourist settings. Philip L. Pearce. New York: Springer-Verlag, 1988: 257 p. *ISBN: 0387968342. Bibliography — p.229-257.* [Recent research in psychology.]

26 Work and leisure — exploring a relationship. David T. Herbert. *Area* **20:3** 9:1988 pp. 241 – 252

J: Politics. State. International relations — *Politique. État. Relations internationales*

J.1: Political science. Political sociology — *Science politique. Sociologie politique*

1 La asunción neo-conservadora de Weber. El espíritu del capitalismo y la ética neo-conservadora *[In Spanish]*; [Weber's neo-conservative assumption. The spirit of capitalism and neo-conservative ethics]. José María Mardones. *Sistema* **83** 3:1988 pp. 25 – 42

2 Interpreting Indian politics — Rajni Kothari and his critics. Thomas Pantham. *Contr. I. Soc.* **22:2** 7-12:1988 pp. 229 – 246

3 State and society in Soviet thought. Ernest Gellner. Oxford: Basil Blackwell, 1988: ix, 193 p. *ISBN: 0631157875. Bibliography — p[182]-184.* [Explorations in social structures.]

4 States, war and capitalism — studies in political sociology. Michael Mann. Oxford: Basil Blackwell, 1988: 240 p. *ISBN: 0631159738. Bibliographies.*

J.2: Political doctrines. Political thought — *Doctrines politiques. Pensée politique*

1 A critique of recent trends in the analysis of ethnonationalism. William A. Douglas. *Ethn. Racial* **11:2** 4:1988 pp. 192 – 206

2 Del poder y sus fisonomías *[In Spanish]*; [Of power and its features]. Felip Lorda Alaiz. *Sistema* **84** 5:1988 pp. 91 – 122

3 A duty to kill — John of Salisbury's theory of tyrannicide. Cary J. Nederman. *Rev. Polit.* **50:3** Summer:1988 pp. 365 – 389

4 Elites, nationalism, and regime legitimacy in Czechoslovakia and Yugoslavia. Leslie Spencer. *Slovo* **1:1** 5:1988 pp. 25 – 39

5 From ethnic to civic nationalism — English Canada and Quebec. Raymond Breton. *Ethn. Racial* **11:1** 1:1988 pp. 85 – 102

6 Gorbachev and Gorbachevism. Walter Joyce *[Ed.]*; Hillel Ticktin *[Ed.]*; Stephen White *[Ed.]*; Ronald J. Hill *[Contrib.]*; Ellen Mickiewicz *[Contrib.]*; Nick Lampert *[Contrib.]*; Julian Cooper *[Contrib.]*; Walter Joyce *[Contrib.]*; Hillel Ticktin *[Contrib.]*; Alex Pravda *[Contrib.]* and others. collection of 14 articles. **J. Commun. S.** , *4:4*, 12:1988 pp. 1 – 173

7 Marxism and social revolution in India and other essays. P. C. Joshi. New Delhi: Patriot, 1986: xiv, 227 p.

8 Nationalism between modernization and demodernization. Gerhard Sonnert. *Can R. Stud. N.* **XV:1-2** 1988 pp. 43 – 51

9 Nationalism in Scotland and Wales — a post-industrial phenomenon? Donley T. Studlar; Ian McAllister. *Ethn. Racial* **11:1** 1:1988 pp. 48 – 62

10 O desenvolvimento econômico acelerado no discurso populista *[In Portuguese]*; The accelerated economic development in the populist speech *[Summary]*; Le développment economique accéléré dans le discours populiste *[French summary]*. Guita Grin Debert. *Rev. Bras. Ciên. Soc.* **3:8** 10:1988 pp. 59 – 70

J.2: Political doctrines. Political thought *[Doctrines politiques. Pensée politique]*

11 Perceptoral politics, yeomen democracy and the enabling state. David Marquand. *Govt. Oppos.* **23:3** Summer:1988 pp. 261 – 275

12 The theory of the cheating of the masses in modern times — the institutional roots of social immorality under capitalism and socialism. Anghel N. Rugina. *Int. J. Soc. E.* **15:8** 1988 pp. 3 – 44

13 Us and them — the psychology of ethnonationalism. Group for the Advancement of Psychiatry. New York: Brunner/Mazel, 1988: 147 p. *ISBN: 0876304811. Bibliography — p.129-136.*

J.3: Constitution. State — *Constitution. État*

1 The accomodation between communities in Lebanon — parliament and paraparliaments in plural societies; *[French summary]*. Antoine Nasri Messara. *Soc. Compass* **XXXV:4** 1988 pp. 625 – 636

2 Censorship — the knot that binds power and knowledge. Sue Curry Jansen. New York: Oxford University Press, 1988: 282 p. *ISBN: 0195053257. Bibliography — p.253-269.*

3 Communalism and constitution. Anirban Kashyap. New Delhi: Lancers, 1988: xii, 372 p. *ISBN: 81 7095 007 4.*

4 Community policing — rhetoric or reality. Jack R. Greene *[Ed.]*; Stephen D. Mastrofski *[Ed.]*. : Praeger, 1988: xiv, 279 p. *ISBN: 0275929523; LofC: 88-15559.*

5 Community problems, problem communities, and community policing in Toronto. Christopher Murphy. *J. Res. Crim. Delin.* **25:4** 11:1988 pp. 392 – 410

6 Economic and political explanations of human rights violations. Neil J. Mitchell; James M. McCormick. *World Polit.* **XL:4** 7:1988 pp. 476 – 498

7 Evaluating police work — an action research project. David J. Smith; Christine Horton *[Ed.]*. London: Policy Studies Institute, 1988: 243 p. *ISBN: 0853743533.* [PSI Research Report. : No. 687]

8 Free South Africa's children — a symposium on children in detention. Gay McDougall *[Contrib.]*; Edward M. Kennedy *[Contrib.]*; Barbara A. Mikulski *[Contrib.]*; Jerry Coovadia *[Contrib.]*; Patrick Makhoba *[Contrib.]*; Pule Nape *[Contrib.]*; Sylvia Jele *[Contrib.]*; Audrey Coleman *[Contrib.]*; Michael Rice *[Contrib.]*; Marumo Moerane *[Contrib.] and others. Collection of 9 articles.* **Hum. Rights Q.**, *10:1,* 2:1988 pp. 10 – 108

9 Haïti — sortir du cauchemar, sur les décombres d'une dictature, l'éloge de l'humain *[In French]*; [Haiti — emerging from the nightmare, on the ruins of a dictatorship, praising humanities]. Yves Saint-Gérard. Paris: L'Harmattan, 1988: 136 p. (ill.) *ISBN: 2738400361.*

10 Jinken wo kurashi no nakani *[In Japanese]*; [Human rights and humanity]. Toshihiko Konno. Tokyo: Kisousha, 1988: 244 p.

11 The London Metropolitan Police and their clients — victim and suspect attitudes. Michael G. Maxfield. *J. Res. Crim. Delin.* **25:2** 5:1988 pp. 188 – 206

12 Les mécanismes de régulation sociale — la justice, l'administration, la police *[In French]*; [The mechanisms of social regulation — justice, administration, police]. Jean-Jacques Gleizal *[Ed.]*; Gérard Boismenu *[Ed.]*. Montréal: Boréal; Lyon, Presses universitaires de Lyon: 1988: 257 p. *ISBN: 2890522385. Bibliography — p..233-253.*

J.3: Constitution. State [Constitution. État]

13 Neighborhood differences in attitudes toward policing — evidence for a mixed-strategy model of policing in a multi-ethnic setting. Roger G. Dunham; Geoffrey P. Alpert. *J. Crim. Law* **79:2** Summer:1988 pp. 504 – 523

14 Notes on the difficulty of studying the state (1977). Philip Abrams. *J. Hist. Soc.* **1:1** 3:1988 pp. 58 – 89

15 La police des polices *[In French]*; [Policing the police]. Jean-Marc Ancian. Paris: Balland, 1988: 250 p. *ISBN: 2253051284*. [Le Livre de poche.]

16 Police powers and public prosecutions — winning by appearing to lose? Katherine De Gama. *Int. J. S. Law* **16:3** 8:1988 pp. 339 – 357

17 Policing and social change. Christopher Corns. *Aust. N.Z. J. Soc.* **24:1** 3:1988 pp. 32 – 46

18 Policing for profit — the private security sector. Nigel South. London: Sage, 1988: 180 p. *ISBN: 0803981740*. *Includes bibliography and index.* [Sage contemporary criminology.]

19 Policing liberal society. Steve Uglow. Oxford: Oxford University Press, 1988: viii,165p. *ISBN: 0192192221*. *Includes bibliography and index.* [OPUS.]

20 Policing — the critical issues. Mike Stephens. Hemel Hempstead: Harvester. Wheatsheaf, 1988: 213 p. *ISBN: 0745004091*. *Includes bibliography and index.*

21 Politik und Repräsentation — Beiträge zur Theorie und zum Wandel politischer und sozialer Institutionen *[In German]*; [Politics and representation — contributions to the theory of political and social institutions and political and institutional change]. Bernhard Claussen *[Ed.]*; Wolfgang Luthardt *[Ed.]*; Arno Waschkuhn *[Ed.]*. [Marburg: SP-Verlag, 1988]: 334 p. *ISBN: 3924800634*. [Schriftenreihe der Hochschulinitiative Demokratischer Sozialismus.]

22 Problems of police-social work interaction — some American lessons. Mike Stephens. *Howard J. Crim. Just.* **27:2** 5:1988 pp. 81 – 91

23 The role of courts in society. Shimon Shetreet *[Ed.]*. Dordrecht: M. Nijhoff Publishers, 1988: 491 p. *ISBN: 9024736706; LofC: 87-036017*. *Includes index.*

24 Scandinavian citizenship. Helga M. Hernes. *Acta Sociol.* **31** 1988 pp. 199 – 215

25 State and society. J. Gledhill *[Ed.]*; B. Bender *[Ed.]*; M. T. Larsen *[Ed.]*. London: Unwin Hyman, 1988: 352 p. (ill) *ISBN: 0044450230; LofC: 88-016915*. *Includes index.* [One world archaeology.]

26 Theme and variation in community policing. Jerome H. Skolnick; David H. Bayley. *Crime Just.* **10** 1988 pp. 1 – 37

27 The transformation of the southern racial state — class and race determinants of local-state structures. David R. James. *Am. Sociol. R.* **53:2** 4:1988 pp. 191 – 208

J.4: Public administration — *Administration publique*

1 Civil service policies in Indonesia — an obstacle to decentralization? Dwight Y. King. *Publ. Adm. D.* **8:3** 7-9:1988 pp. 249 – 260
2 Credit and the rural poor — the changing policy environment in Bangladesh. J. Allister McGregor. *Publ. Adm. D.* **8:4** 10-12:1988 pp. 467 – 482
3 The ethics of public service — resolving moral dilemmas in public organizations. Kathryn G. Denhardt. New York: Greenwood, 1988: x, 197 p. *ISBN: 0313255172; LofC: 87-15060. Bibliography — p.187-193. Includes index.* [Contributions in political science. : No. 195]
4 The Hong Kong civil service and its future. Ian Scott *[Ed.]*; John P. Burns *[Ed.]*. Hong Kong: Oxford University Press, 1988: 264 p. *ISBN: 0195841735. Includes bibliography and index.*
5 Implicaciones de la adhesion de España a las comunidades Europeas en la reestructuración y saneamiento del sector público español en los años 1982-1988 *[In Spanish]*; [Implications for Spain's support towards the European communities in the restructuring and reorganization of the Spanish public sector in the period 1982-1988]. Jesús Rodrigo. *Hac. Públ. Esp.* **110/111** 1988 pp. 259 – 277
6 Koukyū kanryou no ishiki kouzou kara mita gendai nihon no seisaku kettei katei *[In Japanese]*; [Higher civil servants and policy making process in contemporary Japan]. Takashi Harada. ***Konan Women's University Researches*** Vol.24. 1988. pp. 47 – 73
7 Local government and development in a regional city — the case of Iloilo City, Philippines. Juergen Rüland; Tomas A. Sajo. *Publ. Adm. D.* **8:3** 7-9:1988 pp. 261 – 287
8 Local government and urban protest in Colombia. Charles David Collins. *Publ. Adm. D.* **8:4** 10-12:1988 pp. 421 – 436
9 Local politics — the law of the fishes. Marguerite S. Robinson. Delhi: Oxford University Press, 1988: xv, 345 p. *ISBN: 0195619927. Bibliography — p.303-337.Includes index.*
10 The local state and urban local government in Zambia. Carole Rakodi. *Publ. Adm. D.* **8:1** 1-3:1988 pp. 27 – 46
11 Segregation versus integration of public service communities in Jerusalem. Yael Azmon. *Publ. Adm. D.* **8:3** 7-9:1988 pp. 345 – 360
12 Ubiquitous anomie — public service in an era of ideological dissensus. Aaron Wildavsky. *Publ. Adm. Re.* **48:4** 7-8:1988 pp. 753 – 755

J.5: Political parties. Pressure groups — *Partis politiques. Groupes de pression*

1 After the working-class movement? An essay on what's "new" and what's "social" in the new social movements. Gunnar Olofsson. *Acta Sociol.* **31:1** 1988 pp. 15 – 34
2 Les CCC — l'État et le terrorisme *[In French]*; [The CCC — the state and terrorism]. Jos vander Velpen. Anvers: EPO, 1988: 220 p.
3 Corporate political groupings — does ideology unify business political behaviour? Alan Neustadtl; Dan Clawson. *Am. Sociol. R.* **53:2** 4:1988 pp. 172 – 190
4 The crisis of Fordism, transformations of the "Keynesian" security state, and new social movements. Joachim Hirsch. *R. Soc. Move. Con. Cha.* **10** 1988 pp. 43 – 56
5 Democratization processes as an objective of new social movements. Barbara A. Misztal; Bronislaw Misztal. *R. Soc. Move. Con. Cha.* **10** 1988 pp. 93 – 166
6 Ecologie et action publique — pour une démarche-qualité de type «système-acteur» *[In French]*; [Ecology and public action — a positional approach of the système-acteur type]. Gilles Barouch. *Pol. Manag. Publ.* **6:4** 12:1988 pp. 117 – 132
7 Élaboration des politiques publiques et mobilisation sociale — le cas de l'environnement, de la consommation et des femmes *[In French]*; [The elaboration of public policy and social mobilisation — the case of the environment, consumption and women]. Calliope Spanou. *R. Fr. Admin. Publ.* **48** 10-12:1988 pp. 641 – 651
8 The environmental dialogue in the GDR — literature, church, party and interest groups in their socio-political context. Anita M. Mallinckrodt. Lanham: University Press of America, 1988: ix, 198 p. *ISBN: 0819164348. Includes index.* [Studies in GDR culture and society.]
9 Fiji Indians and political discourse in Fiji — from the Pacific romance to the coups. John Dunham Kelly. *J. Hist. Soc.* **1:4** 12:1988 pp. 399 – 422
10 Front national — l'écho politique de l'anomie urbaine *[In French]*; [The National Front — a political echo of urban alienation]. Pascal Perrineau. *Esprit* **136-137** 3-4:1988 pp. 22 – 38
11 Grievances and participation in social movements. Karl-Dieter Opp. *Am. Sociol. R.* **53:6** 12:1988 pp. 853 – 864
12 How do movements survive failures or prophecy? Anthony B. von Fossen. *R. Soc. Move. Con. Cha.* **10** 1988 pp. 193 – 212
13 Identity, negation and violence. Edward W. Said. *New Left R.* **:171** 9/10:1988 pp. 46 – 62
14 Inside terrorist organizations. David C. Rapoport *[Ed.]*. London: Cass, 1988: 259 p. *ISBN: 0714633321; LofC: 87- 27734.*
15 Leadership and membership in the nuclear freeze movement — a specification of resource mobilization theory. Sam Marullo. *Sociol. Q.* **29:3** Fall:1988 pp. 407 – 427
16 El movimiento de mujeres y la politización de la vida cotidiana — algunas reflexiones en torno al problema del poder *[In Spanish]*; [The women's

J.5: Political parties. Pressure groups [Partis politiques. Groupes de pression]

movement and the politicization of daily life — some thoughts on the problem of power] *[Summary]*. Madeline Román. *Rev. Cien. Soc.* **XXVII: 3-4** 9-12: 1988 pp. 67 – 78

17 Nomads of the present — social movements and individual needs in contemporary society. Alberto Melucci; John Keane *[Ed.]*; Paul Mier *[Ed.]*. London: Hutchinson, 1988: 288 p. *ISBN: 0091729165. Bibliography — p262-280.*

18 Ökologische Probleme und Kritik an der Industriegesellschaft in der DDR heute *[In German]*; [Ecological problems and critique of industrial society in the GDR today]. Peter Wensierski. Köln: Wissenschaft und Politik, 1988: 129 p. *ISBN: 3804687210.*

19 Party politics and the North Indian peasantry — the rise of the Bharatiya Kranti Dal in Uttar Pradesh. Ian Duncan. *J. Peasant Stud.* **16:1** 10:1988 pp. 40 – 76

20 The peace movement — some questions concerning its social nature and structure. Artur Meier. *Int. Sociol.* **3:1** 3:1988 pp. 77 – 87

21 Peace movements and government peace efforts. Louis Kriesberg. *R. Soc. Move. Con. Cha.* **10** 1988 pp. 57 – 76

22 Peasant movements in Poland, 1980-1981 — state socialist economy and the mobilization of individual farmers. Maria Halamska. *R. Soc. Move. Con. Cha.* **10** 1988 pp. 147 – 160

23 The social functions of defeat. Piotr Sztompka. *R. Soc. Move. Con. Cha.* **10** 1988 pp. 183 – 192

24 Social movements and contemporary rights in Japan — relative success factors. Setsou Miyazawa. *Kobe University Law Review Vol.21. 1988.* pp. 63 – 77

25 Social movements in comparative perspective. Jan Pakulski. *R. Soc. Move. Con. Cha.* **10** 1988 pp. 247 – 267

26 Social movements of the core and the periphery. Bronislaw Misztal. *Aust. N.Z. J. Soc.* **24:1** 3:1988 pp. 65 – 82

27 Social movements, old and new. Charles Tilly. *R. Soc. Move. Con. Cha.* **10** 1988 pp. 1 – 18

28 The Solidarity movement in relation to society and the state — communication as an issue of social movement. Pawel Kuczynski; Krzysztof Nowak. *R. Soc. Move. Con. Cha.* **10** 1988 pp. 127 – 146

29 Status politics and the political agenda of the Christian right. Matthew C. Moen. *Sociol. Q.* **29:3** Fall:1988 pp. 429 – 437

30 The struggle for survival — peasant movements and societal change. Krzysztof Gorlach. *R. Soc. Move. Con. Cha.* **10** 1988 pp. 161 – 172

31 The student movement in Poland, 1980-1981. Barbara Wejnert. *R. Soc. Move. Con. Cha.* **10** 1988 pp. 173 – 182

32 "Teikei" no kenkyū josetsu *[In Japanese]*; ["Teikei" as social movement]. Yoshimitsu Taniguchi. *Sophia Stud. Soc. Vol.12. 1988.* pp. 79 – 98

33 The terrorist. Maxwell Taylor. London: Brasseys, 1988: ix, 205 p. *ISBN: 0080336035.*

34 The trajectory of social movement in America. Mayer N. Zald. *R. Soc. Move. Con. Cha.* **10** 1988 pp. 19 – 42

35 Undoukeisei no kouzouteki youin to shinriteki youin *[In Japanese]*; [Structure and interaction in social movements]. Kouzou Ukai. *Shak. Hyor. Vol.39; No.1 - 1988.* pp. 2 – 16

J.5: Political parties. Pressure groups [Partis politiques. Groupes de pression]

36 Women's movements of the world — an international directory and reference guide. Sally Shreir *[Ed.]*. Harlow: Longman, 1988: ix,384 p. *ISBN: 058200988x; LofC: 87-35031. Bibliography — p.383-384. Includes index.* [A Keesing's reference publication.]

37 Zur Frage der Bewegungen *[In German]*; [On the question of social movements]. Rocco Buttiglione. *Z. Polit.* **35:3** 9:1988 pp. 219 – 236

J.6: Political behaviour. Elections. Politics — *Comportement politique. Élections. Politique*

1 Coffee and democracy in modern Costa Rica. Anthony Winson. Basingstoke: Macmillan, 1988: 195 p. *ISBN: 0333472691. Includes bibliography and index.*

2 Cognitieve repsonsiviteit van de politieke elite in Nederland *[In Dutch]*; Cognitive responsiveness of the Dutch political elite *[Summary]*. Paul Dekker; Peter Ester. *Acta Pol.* **4** 1988 pp. 401 – 436

3 Community and upward mobility — dynamics of socialization and stateization. Slawomir Magala. *R. Soc. Move. Con. Cha.* **10** 1988 pp. 235 – 246

4 Community cohesion and working-class politics — workplace — residence separation and Labour support, 1966-1983. Munroe Eagles; Stephen Erfle. *Polit. Geogr. Q.* **7:3** 7:1988 pp. 229 – 250

5 Conflictividad social y legislación electoral en el Distrito Federal, 1976-1987 *[In Spanish]*; [Social tension and electoral legislation in Mexico City 1976-1987]. Luis Reygadas; Mónica Toussaint. *Est. Sociol.* **VI:16** 1-4:1988 pp. 39 – 66

6 Conflictos y contradicciones en el sistema electoral mexicano *[In Spanish]*; [Conflicts and contradictions in the Mexican electoral system]. Silvia Gómez Tagle. *Est. Sociol.* **VI:16** 1-4:1988 pp. 3 – 38

7 Les elecciones en el Distrito Federal entre 1964 y 1985 *[In Spanish]*; [Elections in Mexico City between 1964 and 1985]. Jacqueline Peschard. *Est. Sociol.* **VI:16** 1-4:1988 pp. 67 – 102

8 Elecciones en México; [Elections in Mexico]. Silvia Gómez Tagle *[Contrib.]*; Luis Reygadas *[Contrib.]*; Mónica Toussaint *[Contrib.]*; Jacqueline Peschard *[Contrib.]*; Tonatiuh Guillén López *[Contrib.]*. *Collection of 4 articles*. **Est. Sociol.** , *VI:16*, 1-4:1988 pp. 31 – 127

9 Estimating the extent of racially polarized voting in multicandidate contests. Bernard Grofman; Michael Migalski. *Sociol. Meth.* **16:4** 5:1988 pp. 427 – 453

10 Génération Gorbatchev *[In French]*; [The Gorbachev generation]. Virginie Coulloudon. [Paris]: J.C. Lattès, 1988: 324 p. *Bibliography — p..303-319.*

11 Geography and politics in Israel since 1967. Elisha Efrat. London: Cass, 1988: 225 p. (ill) *ISBN: 0714633038. Bibliography — p.219-222.*

12 Intense preferences, strong beliefs and democratic decision-making. Peter Jones. *Politic. Stud.* **XXXVI:1** 3:1988 pp. 7 – 29

13 Leadership and social cleavages — political processes among the Indians in Fiji. I.S. Chauhan. Jaipur: Rawat, 1988: 173 p. *ISBN: 81 7033 047 5.*

14 Modernization in the People's Republic of China — the politicization of the elderly. Philip Olson. *Sociol. Q.* **29:2** Summer:1988 pp. 241 – 262

J.6: Political behaviour. Elections. Politics [Comportement politique. Élections. Politique]

15 Movilidad electoral y modernización en México — 1961-1985 *[In Spanish]*; [Electoral mobility and modernization in Mexico — 1961-1985]. Consuelo Lima Moreno; Monique Robert Godbout. *Rev. Mexicana Soc.* **L:2** 4-6:1988 pp. 125 – 160

16 The myth of the corporate political jungle — politicization as a political strategy. Jonathan I. Klein. *J. Manag. Stu.* **25:1** 1:1988 pp. 1 – 12

17 Out of hate — a sociology of defection from neo-Nazism. James A. Aho. *Cur. Res. P.* **XI:4** 1988 pp. 159 – 68

18 Peace & revolution — the moral crisis of American pacifism. Guenter Lewy. Grands Rapid,Mi.: William B. Eerdmans Publishing, 1988: 283 p. *ISBN: 0802836402; LofC: 88-1374.*

19 Political elite — a sociological study of legislators of Rajasthan. R.C. Swarankar. Jaipur: Rawat, 1988: vii, 236 p. *ISBN: 81 7033 046 7.*

20 Political reasoning and cognition — a Piagetian view. Shawn W. Rosenberg; Dana Ward *[Ed.]*; Stephen Chilton *[Ed.]*. Durham: Duke University Press, 1988: 204 p. *ISBN: 0822308568. Includes index; Bibliography — p.189-200.*

21 Politische Persönlichkeit und politische Repräsentation — zur demokratietheoretischen Bedeutung subjektiver Faktoren und ihrer Sozialisationsgeschichte *[In German]*; [Political personality and political representation — on the relevance of subjective factors and their socialization for democratic theory]. Bernhard Claussen. Frankfurt am Main: Haag u. Herchen, 1988: 112 p. *ISBN: 3892282951.* [Materialien zur sozialwissenschaftlichen Forschung. : No. 6]

22 Popular culture and political power. Fred Inglis. Brighton: Wheatsheaf Books, 1988: 256 p. *ISBN: 0745003346. Includes index.*

23 Popular cultures and political practice. Richard S. Gruneau *[Ed.]*. Toronto: Garamond Press, 1988: 100 p. *ISBN: 0920059562.*

24 Populist politics, communications media and large scale societal integration. Craig Calhoun. *Sociol. Theory* **6:2** Fall:1988 pp. 219 – 241

25 The power dynamics of the Nigerian society — people, politics and power. Arthur Agwuncha Nwankwo. Enugu: Fourth Dimension, 1988: 235 p. *ISBN: 9781563087.*

26 Reagan, Thatcher, and social welfare — typical and nontypical behaviour for presidents and prime ministers. Dorothy H. Clayton; Robert J. Thompson. *Pres. Stud. Q.* **XVIII:3** Summer:1988 pp. 565 – 581

27 Rechtsextremistische Orientierungen bei Jugendlichen — empirische Ergebnisse und Erklärungsmuster einer Untersuchung zur politischen Sozialisation *[In German]*; [Right-wing extremist orientations amongst youths — empirical results and explanatory models of a study in political socialization]. Wilhelm Heitmeyer. Weinheim: Juventa, 1988: 244 p. *ISBN: 3779904071.* [Jugendforschung.]

28 Regards sur l'Iran *[In French]*; [Views on Iran] *[Summary]*. Firouzeh Nahavandi *[Contrib.]*; Poopak Ta'Ati *[Contrib.]*; Francine Timothy-Mahak *[Contrib.]*; Homa Firouzbakhch *[Contrib.]*; Haïdeh Salehi-Esfahani; Theresa Battesti *[Contrib.]*; Farrokh Gaffary *[Contrib.]*; Mohammad Réza Djalili *[Contrib.]*; Vida Nassehi-Behnam *[Contrib.]*. **Civilisations** , *XXXVIII:2*, 1988 pp. 7 – 252

J.6: Political behaviour. Elections. Politics *[Comportement politique. Élections. Politique]*

29 Der Rheinhausen-Effekt — wahl- und parteipolitische Folgen eines kollektiven Widerstandes. Methodische und empirische Ergebnisse einer Längsschnitt-Untersuchung *[In German]*; The "Rheinhausen effect" — analyzing the implications of local protest for party identification and electoral behavior *[Summary]*. Dieter Urban. *Soz. Welt.* **39:4** 1988 pp. 435 – 458

30 Sins of the children. Social change, democratic politics, and the successor generation in Western Europe. Harvey Waterman. *Comp. Polit.* **20: 4** 7:1988 pp. 401 – 422

31 Social identity and mass politics in Spain. Peter McDonough; Samuel H. Barnes; Antonio López Pina. *Comp. Poli. S.* **21:2** 7:1988 pp. 200 – 230

32 Social status, urbanisation and the ethnic dimension of voting behaviour in Australia. James Forrest. *Ethn. Racial* **11:4** 11:1988 pp. 489 – 505

33 Sociedad civil, cultura política y democracia. Los obstáculos de la transición política *[In Spanish]*; [Society, political culture and democracy. Obstacles for political transition]. José Alvaro Moisés. *Rev. Mexicana Soc.* **L:3** 7-9:1988 pp. 37 – 60

34 Sociologie des militants et sociologie du parti. Le cas de la SFIO sous Guy Mollet *[In French]*; Sociology of the militants and of the party. The case of the SFIO under Guy Mollet *[Summary]*. Marc Sadoun. *R. Fr. Sci. Pol.* **38:3** 6:1988 pp. 348 – 369

35 Soviet grassroots — citizen participation in local Soviet government. Jeffrey W. Hahn. Princeton: Princeton University Press, 1988: 320 p. *ISBN: 0691077673; LofC: 87-28966. Bibliography — p.291-308.*

36 Strong leadership — Thatcher, Reagan and an eminent person. Graham Little. Oxford: Oxford Univversity Press, 1988: 289 p. *ISBN: 0195547594.*

37 Testing Ajzen and Fishbein's attitudes model — the prediction of voting. A. Echebarria Echabe; D. Paez Rovira; J.F. Valencia Garate. *Eur. J. Soc. Psychol.* **18:2** 4-6:1988 pp. 181 – 189

J.7: Army. Military sociology — *Armée. Sociologie militaire*

1 La enseñanza superior militar en España *[In Spanish]*; [Higher military training in Spain]. Diego López Garrido. *Sistema* **84** 5:1988 pp. 43 – 70

2 Les militaires égyptiens. Esprit de corps et révolution *[In French]*; Egyptian soldiers and power — Esprit de Corps and revolution *[Summary]*. Tewfik Aclimandos. *Peup. Médit.* **41-42** 10:1987-3:1988 pp. 87 – 104

3 The psychology of conflict and combat. Ben Shalit. New York: Praeger, 1988: x, 205 p. *ISBN: 0275927539; LofC: 87-23729. Bibliography — p.187-196.*

4 Reforging the Iron Cross — the search for tradition in the West German armed forces. Donald Abenheim; G. Craig *[Foreword]*. Princeton, N.J.: Princeton U.P., 1988: 316 p. *ISBN: 0691055343. Bibliography.*

5 Women and the military system — proceedings of a symposium arranged by the International Peace Bureau and Peace Union of Finland. Eva Isaksson *[Ed.]*. Brighton: Wheartsheaf, 1988: 320 p. *ISBN: 074500475x. Includes bibliography and index.*

J.8: International relations — Relations internationales

1 Accidental nuclear war. Paul Smoker [Ed.]; Morris Bradley [Ed.]; Michael Intriligator [Contrib.]; Dagobert Brito [Contrib.]; Michel Haag [Contrib.]; Patricia Axelrod [Contrib.]; Dean Babst [Contrib.]; Robert Aldridge [Contrib.]; Pertti Järvinen [Contrib.]; Ian Welsh [Contrib.] and others. Collection of 9 articles. **Cur. Res. P.** , *XI:1-2*, 1988 pp. 2 – 79

2 Balkan i medunarodno pravo susedstva [In Serbo-Croatian]; The Balkans and the international law of the neighbourhood [Summary]. Čedomir Vučković. *Med. Prob.* **XL:1:2** 1988 pp. 50 – 60

3 Crises and the unexpected. George H. Quester. *J. Interd. Hist.* **XVIII:4** Spring:1988 pp. 701 – 719

4 Dialectics of war — an essay in the social theory of total war and peace. Martin Shaw. London: Pluto Press, 1988: 154 p. *ISBN: 0745302580.* Includes index.

5 Disarmament, arms control, and peace in the nuclear age — political objectives and relevant research. S. Plous. *J. Soc. Issues* **44:2** 1988 pp. 133 – 154

6 Leadership and negotiation in the Middle East. Barbara Kellerman [Ed.]; Jeffrey Z. Rubin [Ed.]; Seymour Feshbach [Foreword]. New York: Praeger in cooperation with the Society for the Psychological Study of Social Issues, 1988: x, 299 p. *ISBN: 0275924890; LofC: 88-10337.* Bibliography — p.281-283. Includes index.

7 Nuclear fear — a history of images. Spencer R. Weart. Cambridge, Mass.: Harvard University Press, 1988: 535 p. (1ill) *ISBN: 0674628357; LofC: 87-25995.* Includes index.

8 Nuclear war as a source of adolescent worry — relationships with age, gender, trait emotionality and drug use. Scott B. Hamilton; Susan van Mouwerik; Eugene R. Oetting; Frederick Beauvais; William G. Keilin. *J. Soc. Psychol.* **128:6** 12:1988 pp. 745 – 763

9 Odpowiedzialność międzynarodowa państwa za szkodę jądrową [In Polish]; (International liability for nuclear damage by a state. General issues). Anna Wyrozumska. *Pań. Prawo* **XLIII:8** 8:1988 pp. 56 – 66

10 Peace fair or warfare — educating the community. Joseph de Rivera; James Laird. *J. Soc. Issues* **44:2** 1988 pp. 59 – 80

11 Preventing famine — policies and prospects for Africa. Donald Curtis; Michael Hubbard [Ed.]; A. W. Shepherd [Ed.]. London: Routledge, 1988: xi, 250 p. *ISBN: 0415007119; LofC: 87-28267.* Bibliography — p.237-241. Includes index.

12 Psychology and the promotion of peace. Richard V. Wagner [Ed.]; Joseph de Rivera [Ed.]; Mary Watkins [Ed.]; Elise Boulding [Contrib.]; James Laird [Contrib.]; Ervin Staub [Contrib.]; Philip E. Tetlock [Contrib.]; S. Plous [Contrib.]; Paul Wehr [Contrib.]; Stephen P. Cohen [Contrib.] and others. Collection of 10 articles. **J. Soc. Issues** , *44:2*, 1988 pp. 1 – 202

13 The social dynamics of peace and conflict — culture in international security. Robert A. Rubinstein [Ed.]; Mary LeCron Foster [Ed.]. Boulder: Westview Press, 1988: 206 p. *ISBN: 0813376149; LofC: 88- 017594.*

14 Stellar-inertial guidance — a study in the sociology of military technology. Donald Mackenzie. *Sociol. Sci.* **XXII** 1988 pp. 187 – 242

J.8: International relations *[Relations internationales]*

15 The theory of hegemonic war. Robert Gilpin. *J. Interd. Hist.* **XVIII:4** Spring:1988 pp. 591 – 613
16 Transnational networks in global development — Canada and the Third World. Dan A. Chekki. *Int. Soc. Sci. J.* **117** 8:1988 pp. 383 – 397
17 L'U.R.S.S. et son autre *[In French]*; [The USSR and its other]. Marie Mendras. *Eur. J. Soc.* **XXIX:2** 1988 pp. 229 – 257
18 War and misperception. Robert Jervis. *J. Interd. Hist.* **XVIII:4** Spring:1988 pp. 675 – 700
19 War memorials as political memory. James M. Mayo. *Geogr. Rev.* **78:1** 1:1988 pp. 62 – 75
20 Why doesn't everyone work to prevent nuclear war? A decision theory analysis. Kenneth Fuld; John A. Nevin. *J. Appl. Soc. Psychol.* **18:1** 1:1988 pp. 59 – 65

K: Social problems. Social services. Social work — *Problèmes sociaux. Services sociaux. Travail social*

K.1: Social problems — *Problèmes sociaux*

Sub-divisions: Child neglect and abuse *[Enfants martyrs et abandon d'enfant]*; Crime *[Délits]*; Criminal justice *[Justice criminelle]*; Drugs *[Drogue]*; Poverty *[Pauvreté]*

1 Abuse and victimization across the life span. Martha B. Straus *[Ed.]*. Baltimore: Johns Hopkins University Press, 1988: x, 270 p. (ill) *ISBN: 0801836360; LofC: 87-46306. Includes index.* [The Johns Hopkins series in contemporary medicine and public health.]
2 Assessing the validity of a sequential drug use pattern using the 1985 National Household Survey on Drug Abuse. C. Lazaro; L. LoSciuto; L. Porcellini; R. Santos. *Proc. Am. Stat. Ass.* pp. 329 – 333
3 Battered women — implications for social control. Nanette J. Davis. *Cr. Law Soc. Chan.* **12:4** 1988 pp. 345 – 372
4 Central and East European social research — parts 1 & 2. Arien Mack *[Ed.]*; Timothy Garton Ash *[Contrib.]*; Elemér Hankiss *[Contrib.]*; Laszlo Bruszt *[Contrib.]*; Robert Manchin *[Contrib.]*; Mira Marody *[Contrib.]*; Lena Kolarska-Bobinska *[Contrib.]*; Marek Ziołkowski *[Contrib.]*; Krzysztof Kowak *[Contrib.]*; H. Gordon Skilling *[Contrib.] and others. Collection of 14 articles.* **Soc. Res.**, *55:1-2*, Spring-Summer:1988 pp. 3 – 318
5 Changing trends in drug use — an initial follow-up of a local heroin using community. Andrew Fraser; Michael George. *Br. J. Addict.* **83:6** 6:1988 pp. 655 – 663
6 Childhood loss in alcoholics and narcotic addicts. Chris Tennant; Elsa Bernardi. *Br. J. Addict.* **83:6** 6:1988 pp. 695 – 703
7 Conflict in natural disasters — a codification of consensus and conflict theories. Robert A. Stallings. *Soc. Sci. Q.* **69:3** 9:1988 pp. 569 – 586
8 Determinants of benefit-program participation among the urban homeless — results from a 16 - city study. James D. Wright; Eleanor Weber. *Eval. Rev.* **12:4** 8:1988 pp. 376 – 395

K.1: Social problems [Problèmes sociaux]

9 Ending lives. Robert Campbell; Diané Collinson *[Ed.]*. Oxford: Basil Blackwell in association with the Open University, 1988: xviii, 203 p. *ISBN: 0631153292; LofC: 87-29366. Includes index.*

10 The evaluation of a "cooperative counselling" alcohol service which uses family and affected others to reach and influence problem drinkers. F.E. Yates. *Br. J. Addict.* **83:11** 11:1988 pp. 1309 – 1319

11 Expectations about appropriate drinking contexts — comparisons of parents, adolescents and best friends. Jeffrey Wilks; Victor J. Callan. *Br. J. Addict.* **83:9** 9:1988 pp. 1055 – 1062

12 Family abuse and its consequences — new directions in research. Gerald T. Hotaling *[Ed.]*. Newbury Park, CA: Sage Publications, 1988: 318 p. *ISBN: 0803927207.*

13 The generality of deviance in late adolescence and early adulthood. Wayne D. Osgood; Lloyd D. Johnston; Patrick M. O'Malley; Jerald G. Bachman. *Am. Sociol. R.* **53:1** 2:1988 pp. 81 – 93

14 "Iatrogenic crisis" admission for benzodiazepine dependence. Neil Joughin; Gillian Russell. *Inter. J. Therap. Comm.* **9:1** 1988 pp. 41 – 48

15 Language, interaction, and social problems. Douglas W. Maynard *[Contrib.]*; Jack Whalen *[Contrib.]*; Don H. Zimmermann *[Contrib.]*; Marilyn R. Whalen *[Contrib.]*; Hugh Mehan *[Contrib.]*; John Wills *[Contrib.]*; Carol Brooks Gardner *[Contrib.]*; Paul Drew *[Contrib.]*; Elizabeth Holt *[Contrib.]*; Gail Jefferson *[Contrib.] and others*. *Soc. Prob.* , *35:4*, 10:1988 pp. 311 – 492

16 Methodology for obtaining a representative sample of homeless persons — the Los Angeles Skid Row Study. M. Audrey Burnham; Paul Koegel. *Eval. Rev.* **12:2** 4:1988 pp. 117 – 152

17 A multivariate model of job stress and alcohol consumption. Michael M. Harris; Mary L. Fennell. *Sociol. Q.* **29:3** Fall:1988 pp. 391 – 406

18 The nature of alcoholism — opinions of Canadian alcohol intervention workers. S. Israelstam; K. Sykora. *Br. J. Addict.* **83:10** 10:1988 pp. 1215 – 1219

19 Опыт социологического исследования негативных явлений в молодежной среде *[In Russian]*; A sociological study in some negative phenomena among the young people *[Summary]*. V.S. Ajanasyee; N.V. Kofyrin. *Vest. Lenin. Univ. 6* **20:3** 1988 pp. 53 – 66

20 Peer influence and adolescent substance abuse — a promising side? Harith Swadi; Harry Zeitlin. *Br. J. Addict.* **83:2** 2:1988 pp. 153 – 157

21 Personal violence and public order — the prosecution of "domestic" violence in England and Wales. Andrew Sanders. *Int. J. S. Law* **16:3** 8:1988 pp. 359 – 382

22 Police response to runaway and missing children — a conceptual framework for research and policy. Cheryl Maxson; Margaret A. Little; Malcolm W. Klein. *Crime Delin.* **34:1** 1:1988 pp. 84 – 102

23 Policing and punishing the drinking driver — a study of general and specific deterrence. Ross Homel. New York: Springer-Verlag, 1988: 318 p. *ISBN: 038796715x. Bibliography — p.273-293*. [Research in criminology.]

24 Poverty, policy and food security in Southern Africa. Coralie Bryant *[Ed.]*. Boulder, Colo.: Lynne Rienner, 1988: xii, 291 p. *ISBN: 0720119723.*

K.1: Social problems [Problèmes sociaux]

25 The rise and fall of social problems — a public arenas model. Stephen Hilgartner; Charles L. Bosk. *A.J.S.* **94:1** 7:1988 pp. 53 – 78

26 "Rogues and vagabonds" — vagrant underlife in Britain 1815-1985. Lionel Rose. London: Routledge & Kegan Paul, 1988: ix, 254 p. (ill) *ISBN: 0710208111. Includes bibliography and index.*

27 La santé des adolescents — approche longitudinale des consommations de drogues et des troubles somatiques et psychosomatiques *[In French]*; [Adolescents' health — longitudinal analysis of drug-taking and somatic and psychosomatic disorders]. Marie Choquet; Sylvie Ledoux *[Ed.]*; Hede Menke *[Ed.]*. Paris: La Documentation française, 1988: 141 p. *ISBN: 2110019883. Bibliography — p.137-141.* [Analyses et prospectives.]

28 The social impact of the Chernobyl disaster. David R. Marples. Basingstoke: Macmillan, 1988: xviii, 313 p. *ISBN: 0333464214. Includes index.*

29 Socio-economic and psychological causes of suicide in Jheneidah District. H. Rahman. New Delhi: Northern Book Store, 1988: x, 74 p.

30 The sociology of suicide. Steve Taylor. London: Longman, 1988: 96 p. (ill) *ISBN: 0582355656; LofC: 88-535. Bibliography — p.93-94. Includes ndex.* [Sociology in focus series.]

31 Street children of Cali. Lewis Aptekar. Durham: Duke University Press, 1988: 235 p. *ISBN: 0822308347; LofC: 87-034324. Bibliography.*

32 Structure of drug use behaviors and consequences among young adults — multitrait-multimethod assessment of frequency, quantity, work site, and problem substance use. Judith A. Stein; Michael D. Newcomb; P. M. Bentler. *J. Appl. Psychol.* **73:4** 11:1988 pp. 595 – 605

33 Substance abuse and public policy. Mark Fraser; Nance Kohlert. *Soc. Ser. R.* **62:1** 3:1988 pp. 103 – 126

34 Suicide in gaol — the construction and measurement of a phenomenon. Suzanne E. Hatty. *Aust. J. Soc. Iss.* **23:3** 8:1988 pp. 184 – 195

35 A survival time analysis of criminal sanctions for misdemeanor offenders — a case for alternatives to incarceration. Gerald R. Wheeler; Rodney V. Hissong. *Eval. Rev.* **12:5** 10:1988 pp. 510 – 527

36 Teenage paternity, child support, and crime. Maureen A. Pirog-Good. *Soc. Sci. Q.* **69:3** 9:1988 pp. 527 – 546

37 Television advertisements for alcoholic drinks do reinforce under-age drinking. P.P. Aitken; D.R. Eadie; D.S. Leathar; R.E.J. McNeill; A.C. Scott. *Br. J. Addict.* **83:12** 12:1988 pp. 1399 – 1419

38 Tempête de "neige" en Amazonie colombienne *[In French]*; Tempestà de "nieve" en Amazonia colombiana *[Spanish summary]*; "Snow" storm in Colombian Amazonia *[Summary]*; Tempestade de "neve" na Amazõnia colombiana *[Portuguese summary]*. Alain Delpirou. *Cah. Amer. Lat.* **7** 1988 pp. 89 – 96

39 Tranquilisers as a social problem. Jonathan Gabe; Michael Bury. *Sociol. Rev.* **36:2** 5:1988 pp. 320 – 352

40 Trends in drinking problems and attitudes in the United States — 1979-1984. Michael E. Hilton. *Br. J. Addict.* **83:12** 12:1988 pp. 1421 – 1427

41 Trends in the use and misuse of alcohol and other psychoactive drugs in the United Kingdom — some perplexing connections. Martin A. Plant; David F. Peck; John C. Duffy. *Br. J. Addict.* **83:8** 8:1988 pp. 943 – 947

K.1: Social problems [Problèmes sociaux]

42 Vice. Philip J. Cook [Ed.]; Donald E. Petersen [Ed.]; Michael P. Scarf [Ed.]; Jerome H. Skolnick [Contrib.]; John McConahay [Contrib.]; Katharine T. Bartlett [Contrib.]; Carl E. Schneider [Contrib.]; David A.J. Richards [Contrib.]; John Kaplan [Contrib.]; D.J. West [Contrib.] and others. Collection of 13 articles. **Law Cont. Pr.**, *51:1*, Winter:1988 pp. 1 – 374

43 Where the beer truck stopped — drinking in a northern Australian town — a research report. Maggie Brady. Casuarina, Australia: Australian National University, North Australia Research Unit, 1988: xvii, 95 p. (ill) ISBN: 0731502736. Bibliography — p.93-95.

Child neglect and abuse [Enfants martyrs et abandon d'enfant]

44 Accusations of child sexual abuse. Hollida Wakefield; Ralph Underwager [Ed.]. Springfield,Ill.: Charles C. Thomas, 1988: 499p. ISBN: 0398054231; LofC: 87-030346. Bibliography.

45 The battle and the backlash — the child sexual abuse war. David Hechler. Lexington, Mass.: D. C. Heath, 1988: xiv, 375 p. ISBN: 066914097x.

46 Child abuse. Angela Park. London: Gloucester Press, 1988: 62 p. (col.ill) ISBN: 0863137784. Includes index. [Understanding social issues.]

47 Child abuse — violences and sexualities towards young people. Jeff Hearn. **Sociology 22:4** 11:1988 pp. 531 – 544

48 Children enslaved. Roger Sawyer. London: Routledge, 1988: xviii, 238 p. ISBN: 0415002737. Bibliography — p.219-230.

49 The disclosure of child abuse. Helen Kiel [Contrib.]; Judith Cashmore [Contrib.]; Kay Bussey [Contrib.]; Helen Winefield [Contrib.]; Sally N. Castell-McGregor [Contrib.]. Collection of 3 articles. **Aust. J. Soc. Iss.**, *23:1*, 2:1988 pp. 3 – 27

50 La droga y los establecimientos penitenciarios [In Spanish]; [Drugs and prison]. Francisco Bueno Arus. **Rev. Fom. Soc. 43:170** 4-6:1988 pp. 139 – 148

51 Early prediction and prevention of child abuse. Kevin Browne [Ed.]; Cliff Davies [Ed.]; Peter Stratton [Ed.]. Chichester: Wiley, 1988: 315 p. (ill) ISBN: 0471916358. Includes index and bibliographies.

52 Les enfants victimes d'abus sexuels et la réponse judiciaire à la sanction de leurs droits [In French]; [Child victims of sexual abuse and the judicial response to the sanctioning of their rights]. Lyne Bachand [Ed.]. Cowansville: Yvon Blais, 1988: 249 p. ISBN: 2890736474. [essays for the] 1987 Prix Charles-Coderre.

53 Family secrets — child sexual abuse. Mary McIntosh [Contrib.]; Mary MacLeod [Contrib.]; Esther Saraga [Contrib.]; Linda Gordon [Contrib.]; Liz Kelly [Contrib.]; Jenny Kitzinger [Contrib.]; Ann Scott [Contrib.]; Mica Nava [Contrib.]; Elizabeth Woodcraft [Contrib.]; Gina Betcher [Contrib.] and others. Collection of 15 articles. **Feminist R.**, 28, Spring:1988 pp. 6 – 17

54 Fertility patterns — their relationship to child physical abuse and child neglect. Susan J. Zuravin. **J. Marriage Fam. 50:4** 11:1988 pp. 983 – 993

55 Innocent victims — the question of child abuse. Alan Gilmour. London: Joseph, 1988: ix, 198 p. ISBN: 071812958x.

56 Natal and non-natal fathers as sexual abusers in the United Kingdom — a comparative analysis. Michael Gordon; Susan J. Creighton. **J. Marriage Fam. 50:1** 2:1988 pp. 99 – 105

INTERNATIONAL BIBLIOGRAPHY OF SOCIOLOGY — 1988

K.1: Social problems *[Problèmes sociaux]* — Child neglect and abuse *[Enfants martyrs et abandon d'enfant]*

57 Whose neglect? The role of poverty-related factors in child neglect cases and court decisions in the United States. Leroy H. Pelton; Marguerite G. Rosenthal. *Int. J. Law Fam.* **2:2** 1988 pp. 167 – 182

58 Women and children at risk — a feminist perspective on child abuse. Evan Stark; Anne H. Flitcraft. *Int. J. Health. Ser.* **18:1** 1988 pp. 97 – 118

Crime *[Délits]*

59 Aboriginal and nonaboriginal recidivism in Western Australia — a failure rate analysis. Roderick G. Broadhurst; Ross A. Maller; Maxwell G. Maller; Jennifer Duffecy. *J. Res. Crim. Delin.* **25:1** 2:1988 pp. 83 – 108

60 Against criminology. Stanley Cohen. New Brunswick; Oxford: Transaction Books, 1988: 310 p. *ISBN: 0887381537; LofC: 87-16237.*

61 Age, crime and the early life course. Yossi Shavit; Arye Rattner. *A.J.S.* **93:6** 5:1988 pp. 1457 – 1470

62 An assessment of the design, implementation and effectiveness of Neighbourhood Watch in London. Trevor Bennett. *Howard J. Crim. Just.* **27:4** 11:1988 pp. 241 – 255

63 Bouryokudanhanzai nohenka to Bouryokudanhanzai taisakujou no shomondai *[In Japanese]*; [Changes in organized crime and policy implications]. Kanehiro Hoshino. ***Hanzai to Hikou*** *Vol.73. 1988.* pp. 129 – 152

64 Chugakusei Hikoh *[In Japanese]*; [Delinquency of junior school students]. Kazunori Kikuchi *[Ed.]*; Mamoru Horiuchi *[Ed.]*. Japan: Gakuji Shuppan, 1988

65 Community organizations and crime. Wesley G. Skogan. *Crime Just.* **10** 1988 pp. 39 – 78

66 Community types, crime, and police services on Canadian Indian reserves. Carol Pitcher LaPrairie. *J. Res. Crim. Delin.* **25:4** 11:1988 pp. 375 – 391

67 Competing perspectives on cross-national crime — an evaluation of theory and evidence. W. Lawrence Neuman; Ronald J. Berger. *Sociol. Q.* **29:2** Summer:1988 pp. 281 – 313

68 Considering sex offenders — a model of addiction. Judith Lewis Herman. *Signs* **13:4** Summer:1988 pp. 695 – 724

69 Convicted rapists' perceptions of self and victim — role taking and emotions. Diana Scully. *Gender Soc.* **2:2** 6:1988 pp. 200 – 213

70 Co-offending and criminal careers. Albert J. Reiss. *Crime Just.* **10** 1988 pp. 117 – 170

71 The creation of dangerous violent criminals. Lonnie H. Athens. London: Routledge, 1988: 109 p. *ISBN: 041502837x. Bibliography — p.104-105.*

72 Crime and justice. Lily E. Christ *[Contrib.]*; Alfred M. Fuerst *[Contrib.]*; A.H. Reed *[Contrib.]*; A. Bukoff; J.B. Waller *[Contrib.]*; K.S. Murty *[Contrib.]*; Abdullah M. Al-Lanqawi *[Contrib.]*; Chaiho C. Wang *[Contrib.]*; Herbert F. Spirer *[Contrib.]*. Collection of 5 articles. **Proc. Am. Stat. Ass.** , pp. 386 – 411

73 Crime and moral luck. Steven Sverdlik. *Am. Phil. Q.* **25:1** 1:1988 pp. 79 – 86

74 Crime and the elderly — an annotated bibliography. Ron H. Aday. New York: Greenwood, 1988: xiii, 118 p. *ISBN: 0313254702; LofC: 88-30051.* Includes index. [Bibliographies and indexes in gerontology.]

K.1: Social problems *[Problèmes sociaux]* — *Crime [Délits]*

75 Crime in the Caribbean — robbers, hustlers and warriors. Cynthia Mahabir. *Int. J. S. Law* **16:3** 8:1988 pp. 315 – 338

76 Crime severity and criminal career progression. Kimberly L. Kempf. *J. Crim. Law* **79:2** Summer:1988 pp. 524 – 540

77 Crime victim and offender mediation as a social work strategy. Burt Galaway. *Soc. Ser. R.* **62:4** 12:1988 pp. 668 – 683

78 Crime, community and police. V. K. Mohanan. Delhi: Gian, 1987: 172 p. *ISBN: 81 212 0107 1.*

79 Crime, corruption and reform — the Australian experience in a comparative context. Robert Williams. *Aust. Stud.* **1** 1988 pp. 72 – 83

80 Crime, localities and the multi-agency approach. Alice Sampson; Paul Stubbs; David Smith; Geoffrey Pearson; Harry Blagg. *Br. J. Crimin.* **28:4** Autumn:1988 pp. 478 – 493

81 Crime-victim stories — New York City's urban folklore. Eleanor F. Wachs. Bloomington: Indiana University Press, 1988: 138 p. *ISBN: 0253204917; LofC: 87-046243.*

82 La criminalidad como problema social (en la crisis del Estado benefactor) *[In Spanish]*; [Criminality as a social problem (in the crisis of the welfare state)]. Roberto Bergalli. *Sistema* **83** 3:1988 pp. 123 – 137

83 Critical criminology no shiten to mondaiten *[In Japanese]*; [Valuation of critical criminology]. Motonori Hirana. ***Fukuoka U. Review of Literature & Humanities*** *Vol.20-1; No.76 - 1988.* 1-33

84 Cross-national determinants of child homicide. Robert Fiala; Gary LaFree. *Am. Sociol. R.* **53:3** 6:1988 pp. 432 – 445

85 Cultural and economic sources of homicide in the United States. Larry Baron; Murray A. Straus. *Sociol. Q.* **29:3** Fall:1988 pp. 371 – 390

86 A day in the life of 195 drug addicts and abusers — crimes committed and how the money was spent. Bruce Johnson; Kevin Anderson; Eric D. Wish. *Social Soc. Res.* **72:3** April:1988 pp. 185 – 191

87 Delinquency and drug abuse — implications for social services. J. David Hawkins; Jeffrey M. Jenson; Richard F. Catalano; Denise M. Lishner. *Soc. Ser. R.* **62:2** 6:1988 pp. 258 – 284

88 Delinquency and regular solvent abuse — an unfavourable combination? Allan M. Jacobs; A. Hamide Ghodse. *Br. J. Addict.* **83:8** 8:1988 pp. 965 – 968

89 Donald Cressey's contributions to the study of organized crime — an evaluation. Joseph L. Albini. *Crime Delin.* **34:3** 7:1988 pp. 338 – 354

90 The economics of crime deterrence — a survey of theory and evidence. Samuel Cameron. *Kyklos* **41: 2** 1988 pp. 301 – 323

91 Die Eigendynamik der Rückfallkriminalität *[In German]*; The dynamics of recidivism *[Summary]*. Dieter Hermann; Hans-Jürgen Kerner. *Kölner Z. Soz. Soz. psy.* **40:3** 1988 pp. 485 – 504

92 The equity-control model as a predictor of vandalism among college students. Sylvia Warzecha DeMore; Jeffrey D. Fisher; Reuben M. Baron. *J. Appl. Soc. Psychol.* **18:1** 1:1988 pp. 80 – 91

93 Examining three-wave deterrence models — a question of temporal order and specification. Raymond Paternoster. *J. Crim. Law* **79:1** Spring:1988 pp. 135 – 179

94 Explaining criminal behaviour — interdisciplinary approaches. Wouter Buikhuisen *[Ed.]*; Sarnoff A. Mednick *[Ed.]*. Leiden: E.J. Brill, 1988: vi, 260 p. (ill.) *ISBN: 9004085149. Includes bibliographies and indexes.*

K.1: Social problems *[Problèmes sociaux]* — Crime *[Délits]*

95 Explaining fear of crime. Steven Box; Chris Hale; Glen Andrews. *Br. J. Crimin.* **28**:3 Summer:1988 pp. 340 – 356

96 Fear of crime in public housing. William M. Rohe; Raymond J. Burby. *Envir. Behav.* **20**:5 11:1988 pp. 700 – 720

97 Feminism and criminology in Britain. Loraine Gelsthorpe; Allison Morris. *Br. J. Crimin.* **28**:2 Spring:1988 pp. 93 – 110

98 Les fluctuations de la criminalité en Belgique *[In French]*; [Fluctuations in Belgian criminality]. Nicole Lempereur; Pierre Guilmot *[Ed.]*; Raymond Screvens *[Ed.]*. Bruxelles: Centre National de Criminologie, -: 346 p. *ISBN: 2802704222. Bibliography — p.303-304.*

99 Fragments of an economic theory of the Mafia. Diego Gambetta. *Eur. J. Soc.* **XXIX**:1 1988 pp. 127 – 45

100 A general theory of expropriative crime — an evolutionary ecological approach. Lawrence E. Cohen; Richard Machalek. *A.J.S.* **94**:3 11:1988 pp. 465 – 501

101 Geographic mobility and criminal behavior. Charles R. Tittle; Raymond Paternoster. *J. Res. Crim. Delin.* **25**:3 8:1988 pp. 301 – 343

102 The geography of crime. David J. Evans *[Ed.]*; David Herbert *[Ed.]*. London: Routledge Kegan Paul, 1988: xv, 360 p. *ISBN: 0415004535.*

103 Governments, victims and policies in two countries. Paul Rock. *Br. J. Crimin.* **28**:1 Winter:1988 pp. 44 – 66

104 Hikou to Chiikishakai *[In Japanese]*; [Juvenile delinquency and community]. Kanehiro Hoshino. ***Kokoro no Kagaku*** Vol.22. 1988. pp. 40 – 46

105 A history of British criminology. Paul Rock *[Ed.]*; David Garland *[Contrib.]*; Leon Radzinowicz *[Contrib.]*; Morris Terence *[Contrib.]*; J.P. Martin *[Contrib.]*; David Downes *[Contrib.]*; Paul Rock *[Contrib.]*; Ken Pease *[Contrib.]*; D.J. West *[Contrib.]*; Loraine Gelsthorpe *[Contrib.]* and others. Collection of 13 articles. **Br. J. Crimin.**, 28:2, Spring:1988 pp. 131 – 183

106 How young house burglars choose targets. Richard Wright; Robert H. Logie. *Howard J. Crim. Just.* **27**:2 5:1988 pp. 92 – 104

107 The informal regulation of illegal economic activities — comparisons between the squatter property market and organized crime. Alan Smart. *Int. J. S. Law* **16**:1 2:1988 pp. 91 – 101

108 Juvenile delinquency. Arnold Binder. *Ann. R. Psych.* **39**: 1988 pp. 253 – 282

109 К вопросу о связи правонарушающего поведения несовершеннолетних с некоторыми социально-демографическими процессами *[In Russian]*; To the question of relations between juvenile delinquency and some socio-demographic processes *[Summary]*. I.V. Volgareva. *Vest. Lenin. Univ.* **6 1:6** 3:1988 pp. 65 – 69

110 Kriminalität als Modernisierungsrisiko? Das „Hermes-Syndrom" der entwickelten Industriegesellschaften *[In German]*; Criminality as a risk of modernity *[Summary]*. Baldo Blinkert. *Soz. Welt.* **39**:4 1988 pp. 397 – 412

111 Macroeconomic and social-control policy influences on crime rate changes, 1948-1985. Joel A. Devine; Joseph F. Sheley; M. Dwayne Smith. *Am. Sociol. R.* **53**:3 6:1988 pp. 407 – 420

112 Mediation in South Yorkshire. David Smith; Henry Blagg; Nick Derricourt. *Br. J. Crimin.* **28**:3 Summer:1988 pp. 378 – 395

K.1: Social problems *[Problèmes sociaux]* — *Crime [Délits]*

113 A new look at an old problem — finding temporal patterns in homicide series — the Canadian case; *[French summary]*. Estela Bee Dagum; Guy Huot; Marietta Morry. *Can. R. Stat.* **16:2** 6:1988 pp. 117 – 131

114 The perceived seriousness of white collar crime and conventional crime. Albert R. Hauber; Leo G. Toornvliet; Hans M. Willemse. *Corr. Reform* **3:1** 1988 pp. 41 – 64

115 Perspectives in criminology. S. Venugopal Rao *[Ed.]*. New Delhi: Vikas, 1988: xiii, 351 p.

116 The politics of juvenile crime. John Pitts. London: Sage, 1988: 192 p. (ill) *ISBN: 0803981325. Includes bibliography and index.* [Sage contemporary criminology.]

117 Psychological contributions to criminology. D.J. West. *Br. J. Crimin.* **28:2** Spring:1988 pp. 77 – 92

118 Public care or distorted family relationships — the antecedents of violent crime. Brian Minty. *Howard J. Crim. Just.* **27:3** 8:1988 pp. 172 – 187

119 The purpose of knowledge — pragmatism and the praxis of Marxist criminology. Pat O'Malley. *Cr. Law Soc. Chan.* **12:1** 1988 pp. 65 – 79

120 Radical criminology in Britain — the emergence of a competing paradigm. Jock Young. *Br. J. Crimin.* **28:2** Spring:1988 pp. 159 – 183

121 Regional variations in homicide, capital punishment, and perceived crime severity in the United States. K.D. Harries. *Geog.ann. B.* **70B:3** 1988 pp. 325 – 334

122 Revisiting Thurstone's and Coomb's scales on the seriousness of crimes and offences. I. Borg. *Eur. J. Soc. Psychol.* **18:1** 1-3:1988 pp. 53 – 62

123 Romantic fictions — the re-emergence of the crime as politics debate. John Tierney. *Sociol. Rev.* **36:1** 2:1988 pp. 133 – 145

124 The roots of football hooliganism — an historical and sociological study. Eric Dunning; Patrick Murphy *[Ed.]*; John Williams *[Ed.]*. London: Routledge & Kegan Paul, 1988: x, 273 p. *ISBN: 0710213360. Includes index.*

125 Seductions of crime — moral and sensual attractions in doing evil. Jack Katz. New York: Basic Books, 1988: 367 p. *ISBN: 0465076157; LofC: 88-047691.*

126 Selected juvenile delinquency correlates in Kuwait. K.S. Murty; Abdullah M. Al-Lanqawi. *Proc. Am. Stat. Ass.* pp. 395 – 400

127 Sitting in judgment — the sentencing of white collar criminals. Stanton Wheeler; Kenneth Mann *[Ed.]*; Austin Sarat *[Ed.]*. New Haven, Conn.: Yale University Press, 1988: 199 p. *ISBN: 0300039832.* [Yale studies on white-collar crime.]

128 Social organization and differential association — a research note from a longitudinal study of violent juvenile offenders. Craig Reinarman; Jeffrey Fagan. *Crime Delin.* **34:3** 7:1988 pp. 307 – 327

129 The social production of criminal homicide — a comparative study of disaggregated rates in American cities. Kirk R. Williams; Robert L. Flewelling. *Am. Sociol. R.* **53:3** 6:1988 pp. 421 – 431

130 Social structure and criminal victimization. Douglas A. Smith; G. Roger Jarjoura. *J. Res. Crim. Delin.* **25:1** 2:1988 pp. 27 – 52

131 State punishment — political principles and community values. Nicola Lacey. London: Routledge, 1988: xiii, 222 p. *ISBN: 0415001714; LofC: 87-27018. Includes index.* [International library of philosophy.]

K.1: Social problems *[Problèmes sociaux]* — *Crime [Délits]*

132 Structural criminology. John Hagan; et al. Cambridge: Polity, 1988: viii, 294 p. (ill) *ISBN: 0745605168. Bibliography — p.263-285. Includes index.*

133 Surviving sexual violence. Liz Kelly. Cambridge: Polity, 1988: 273 p. (ill) *ISBN: 0745604625. Includes bibliography and index.* [Feminist perspectives.]

134 Time and punishment — an intertemporal model of crime. Michael L. Davis. *J. Polit. Ec.* **96:2** 4:1988 pp. 383 – 390

135 Unemployed, crime and offenders. Iain Crow. London: Routledge, 1988: 162 p. *ISBN: 041501834x. Bibliography.*

136 Urban unemployment drives urban crime. Carol W. Kohfeld; John Sprague. *Urban Aff. Q.* **24:2** 12:1988 pp. 215 – 241

137 Victim and observer characteristics as determinants of responsibility attributions to victims of rape. Barbara Krahe. *J. Appl. Soc. Psychol.* **18:1** 1:1988 pp. 50 – 58

138 Were Cloward and Ohlin strain theorists? Delinquency and opportunity revisited. Francis T. Cullen. *J. Res. Crim. Delin.* **25:3** 8:1988 pp. 214 – 241

139 White collar crime — re-examination of a concept. Joseph Bensman. *Int. J. Pol. C. S.* **2:1** Fall:1988 pp. 4 – 14

Criminal justice *[Justice criminelle]*

140 The abandonment of delinquent behaviour — promoting the turnaround. Richard L. Jenkins *[Ed.]*; Waln K. Brown *[Ed.]*. New York: Praeger, 1988: 229 p. *ISBN: 0275929280; LofC: 87-1135. Includes bibliography and index.*

141 An analysis of juvenile correctional treatment. Steven P. Lab; John T. Whitehead. *Crime Delin.* **34:1** 1:1988 pp. 60 – 83

142 Architecturally mediated effects of social density in prison. Marc A. Schaeffer; Andrew Baum; Paul B. Paulus; Gerald G. Gaes. *Envir. Behav.* **20:1** 1:1988 pp. 3 – 19

143 Children in jails. Ira M. Schwartz *[Ed.]*; Linda Harris *[Contrib.]*; Laurie Levi *[Contrib.]*; Meda Chesney-Lind *[Contrib.]*; David Steinhart *[Contrib.]*; Mark Soler *[Contrib.]*; Harry F. Swanger *[Contrib.]*. Collection of 6 articles. **Crime Delin.** , *34:2*, 4:1988 pp. 131 – 227

144 Children in justice. Ian O'Connor; Pamela Sweetapple *[Ed.]*. Melbourne: Longman Cheshire, 1988: 135 p. *ISBN: 0582712408.*

145 Chivalry, justice or paternalism? The female offender in the juvenile justice system. Joy Wundersitz; Ngaire Naffine; Fay Gale. *Aust. N.Z. J. Soc.* **24:3** 11:1988 pp. 359 – 376

146 A comparative analysis of juvenile court responses to drug and alcohol offenses. Anne L. Schneider. *Crime Delin.* **34:1** 1:1988 pp. 103 – 124

147 A comparison of prison use in England, Canada, West Germany, and the United States — a limited test of punitive hypothesis. James P. Lynch. *J. Crim. Law* **79:1** Spring:1988 pp. 180 – 217

148 Corrective services in New South Wales. Bill Cullen *[Ed.]*; Michael Dowding *[Ed.]*; John Griffin *[Ed.]*. North Ryde, N.S.W.: Law Book Company, 1988: 347 p. *ISBN: 045520781x. Includes bibliographies.*

149 Crime and justice. Lily E. Christ *[Contrib.]*; Alfred M. Fuerst *[Contrib.]*; A.H. Reed *[Contrib.]*; A. Bukoff; J.B. Waller *[Contrib.]*; K.S. Murty *[Contrib.]*; Abdullah M. Al-Lanqawi *[Contrib.]*; Chaiho C. Wang *[Contrib.]*; Herbert F. Spirer *[Contrib.]*. Collection of 5 articles. **Proc. Am. Stat. Ass.** , pp. 386 – 411

K.1: Social problems *[Problèmes sociaux]* — *Criminal justice [Justice criminelle]*

150 Destructuring, privatization, and the promise of juvenile diversion — compromising community-based corrections. Daniel J. Curran. *Crime Delin.* **34:4** 10:1988 pp. 363 – 378

151 Differentiating the effects of juvenile court sentences on eliminating recidivism. John D. Wooldredge. *J. Res. Crim. Delin.* **25:3** 8:1988 pp. 264 – 300

152 Donald Cressey and the sociology of the prison. John Irwin. *Crime Delin.* **34:3** 7:1988 pp. 328 – 337

153 Driving under the influence — the impact of legislative reform on court sentencing practices. Rodney Kingsnorth; Michael Jungsten. *Crime Delin.* **34:1** 1:1988 pp. 3 – 28

154 Effects of criminal sanctions on drunk drivers — beyond incarceration. Gerald R. Wheeler; Rodney V. Hissong. *Crime Delin.* **34:1** 1:1988 pp. 29 – 42

155 Evaluation of New Jersey's intensive supervision program. Frank S. Pearson. *Crime Delin.* **34:4** 10:1988 pp. 437 – 448

156 Female offenders and the probation service. George Mair; Nicola Brockington. *Howard J. Crim. Just.* **27:2** 5:1988 pp. 117 – 126

157 Free South Africa's children — a symposium on children in detention. Gay McDougall *[Contrib.]*; Edward M. Kennedy *[Contrib.]*; Barbara A. Mikulski *[Contrib.]*; Jerry Coovadia *[Contrib.]*; Patrick Makhoba *[Contrib.]*; Pule Nape *[Contrib.]*; Sylvia Jele *[Contrib.]*; Audrey Coleman *[Contrib.]*; Michael Rice *[Contrib.]*; Marumo Moerane *[Contrib.] and others*. Collection of 9 articles. **Hum. Rights Q.** , *10:1*, 2:1988 pp. 10 – 108

158 Gender, justice and welfare in South Australia — a study of the female status offender. Rebecca Bailey-Harris; Ngaire Naffine. *Int. J. Law Fam.* **2:2** 1988 pp. 214 – 233

159 Girls in jail. Meda Chesney-Lind. *Crime Delin.* **34:2** 4:1988 pp. 150 – 168

160 House arrest and correctional policy — doing time at home. Richard A. Ball; C.Ronald Huff *[Ed.]*; J.Robert Lilly *[Ed.]*. Newbury Park, Ca.: Sage Publications, 1988: 180 p. *ISBN: 0803929692. Bibliographical references — p.169-177.* [Studies in crime,law and justice. : Vol. 3]

161 The influence of race in juvenile justice processing. Donna M. Bishop; Charles E. Frazier. *J. Res. Crim. Delin.* **25:3** 8:1988 pp. 242 – 263

162 Informal justice? Roger Matthews *[Ed.]*. London: Sage, 1988: 214 p. (ill) *ISBN: 0803981481. Includes bibliography and index.* [Sage contemporary criminology.]

163 Insiders — women's experience of prison. Una Padel *[Ed.]*; Prue Stevenson *[Ed.]*. London: Virago, 1988: 202 p. *ISBN: 0860688674.*

164 Junge Frauen und Männer vor Gericht — geschlechtsspezifische Kriminalität und Kriminalisierung *[In German]*; Young men and women in court — sex differences in criminality and criminalization *[Summary]*. Rainer Geißler; Norbert Marißen. *Kölner Z. Soz. Soz. psy.* **40:3** 1988 pp. 505 – 526

165 Juvenile sentence reform and its evaluation — a demonstration of the need for more precise measures of offense seriousness in juvenile justice research. Patricia M. Harris. *Eval. Rev.* **12:6** 12:1988 pp. 655 – 666

166 The law and criminology of drunk driving. James B. Jacobs. *Crime Just.* **10** 1988 pp. 171 – 229

167 Leave of absence for West German prisoners. Legal principle and administrative practice. Dirk Zyl van Smit. *Br. J. Crimin.* **28:1** Winter:1988 pp. 1 – 18

INTERNATIONAL BIBLIOGRAPHY OF SOCIOLOGY — 1988

K.1: Social problems *[Problèmes sociaux]* — Criminal justice *[Justice criminelle]*

168 Mental disorder and criminal law in Australia and New Zealand. I.G. Campbell. Sydney: Butterworths, 1988: 237 p. *ISBN: 0409494828*.

169 Mind games. Where the action is in prisons. Kathleen McDermott; Roy D. King. *Br. J. Crimin.* **28:3** Summer:1988 pp. 357 – 377

170 The national punishment survey and public policy consequences. Sherwood E. Zimmerman; David J. van Alstyne; Christopher S. Dunn. *J. Res. Crim. Delin.* **25:2** 5:1988 pp. 120 – 149

171 Non-custodial alternatives in Europe. Norman Bishop. Helsinki: Helsinki Institute for Crime Prevention and Control, 1988: 364 p. *ISBN: 951471444x. eng; English, French or Russian; Includes bibliographical references (p. 149-153)*.

172 Old and new — Japan's mechanisms for crime control and social justice. Carl B. Becker. *Howard J. Crim. Just.* **27:4** 11:1988 pp. 283 – 296

173 Older offenders — perspectives in criminology and criminal justice. Belinda McCarthy *[Ed.]*; Robert H. Langworthy *[Ed.]*. New York: Praeger, 1988: xxviii, 222 p. *ISBN: 0275927342; LofC: 87-7147. Bibliography — p.197-214. Includes index.*

174 Physical environment and jail social climate. James G. Houston; Don C. Gibbons; Joseph F. Jones. *Crime Delin.* **34:4** 10:1988 pp. 449 – 466

175 Prison crowding. Paul B. Paulus. New York: Spreinger-Verlag, 1988: x, 115 p. *ISBN: 0387966501. Bibliography — p.101-107*. [Research in criminology.]

176 Prison crowding — public attitudes toward strategies of population control. Sandra Evans Skovron; Joseph E. Scott; Francis T. Cullen. *J. Res. Crim. Delin.* **25:2** 5:1988 pp. 150 – 169

177 Prison officers and their world. Kelsey Kauffman. Cambridge, Mass.: Harvard U. P., 1988: 290 p. *ISBN: 0674707168. Bibliography — p.279-283.*

178 Prison populations — a system out of control? Alfred Blumstein. *Crime Just.* **10** 1988 pp. 231 – 266

179 Punishment and social structure revisited — unemployment and imprisonment in the United States, 1948-1984. James Inverarity; Daniel McCarthy. *Sociol. Q.* **29:2** Summer:1988 pp. 263 – 279

180 Race and the criminal justice process. Two empirical studies on social inquiry reports and ethnic minority defendants. Robert Waters. *Br. J. Crimin.* **28:1** Winter:1988 pp. 82 – 96

181 Reparation in the service of diversion — the subordination of a good idea. Gwynn Davis; Jacky Boucherat; David Watson. *Howard J. Crim. Just.* **27:2** 5:1988 pp. 127 – 134

182 Sentencing and the penal system — text and materials. Christopher Harding; Laurence Koffman *[Ed.]*. London: Sweet & Maxwell, 1988: xxvii, 401 p. *ISBN: 0421357703. Bibliography — p.385-396.Includes index.*

183 Sitting in judgment — the sentencing of white collar criminals. Stanton Wheeler; Kenneth Mann *[Ed.]*; Austin Sarat *[Ed.]*. New Haven, Conn.: Yale University Press, 1988: 199 p. *ISBN: 0300039832.* [Yale studies on white-collar crime.]

184 State punishment — political principles and community values. Nicola Lacey. London: Routledge, 1988: xiii, 222 p. *ISBN: 0415001714; LofC: 87-27018. Includes index.* [International library of philosophy.]

185 Structured discretion, racial bias, and the death penalty — the first decade after Furman in Texas. Sheldon Ekland-Olson. *Soc. Sci. Q.* **69:4** 12:1988 pp. 853 – 873

K.1: Social problems [Problèmes sociaux] — Criminal justice [Justice criminelle]

186 La toxicomanie en milieu carcéral — approche statistique *[In French]*; [Drug addiction in the prison environment — a statistical approach]. G. Badet; B. Fustier; M. Verpeaux. *Econ. Cen.E.* :1 1988 pp. 41 – 54

187 Treatment of sex offenders in social work and mental health settings. John S. Wodarski *[Ed.]*; Daniel Whitaker *[Ed.]*. New York: Haworth, 1988: 161 p. *ISBN: 0866567917.*

188 The uses of criminology, the rehabilitative ideal, and justice. Kenneth Polk; Don C. Gibbons. *Crime Delin.* **34:3** 7:1988 pp. 263 – 276

189 Youthful offender designations and sentencing in the New York criminal courts. Ruth D. Peterson. *Soc. Prob.* **35:2** 4:1988 pp. 111 – 130

Drugs [Drogue]

190 Adolescent smoking — research and health policy. Paul D. Cleary; Jan L. Hitchcock; Norbert Semmer; Laura J. Flinchbaugh; John M. Pinney. *Milbank Q.* **66:1** 1988 pp. 137 – 171

191 Alcohol abuse and culturally marginal American Indians. Michael P. Nofz. *Fam. Soc.* **69:2** 2:1988 pp. 67 – 73

192 Alcohol and suicide in Scandinavia. Thor Norström. *Br. J. Addict.* **83:5** 5:1988 pp. 553 – 559

193 The alcoholic family — drinking problems in a family context. Peter Steinglass; Linda A. Bennett *[Ed.]*. London: Hutchinson, 1988: xvi, 381 p. *ISBN: 0091729491. Bibliography — p365-371.*

194 Alcoholism, anxiety and depression. Marc A. Schuckit; Maristela G. Monteiro. *Br. J. Addict.* **83:12** 12:1988 pp. 1373 – 1380

195 Alcohol-shousha ni taisuru ippan jumin no shakaiteki taido kenkyu *[In Japanese]*; [An empirical study on social attitudes of the general population toward alcoholics]. Shinji Shimazu. *Japanese Journal of Social Psychiatry Vol.11; No.1 - 1988.* pp. 55 – 62

196 Changing patterns of smoking — are there economic causes? Vanessa Fry; Panos Pashardes *[Ed.]*. London: Institute for Fiscal Studies, 1988: 58 p. *ISBN: 0902992694. Bibliography — p.58.* [IFS report series. : No. 30]

197 Consequences of adolescent drug use — impact on the lives of young adults. Michael D. Newcomb; Peter M. Bentler *[Ed.]*. : Sage Publications, 1988: 285 p. *ISBN: 0803928475.*

198 Dancing on a volcano — the Latin American drug trade. Scott B. MacDonald. Westport, Conn.: Praeger, 1988: 176 p. *ISBN: 0275927520; LofC: 88-9950.* Includes bibliography and index.

199 A day in the life of 195 drug addicts and abusers — crimes committed and how the money was spent. Bruce Johnson; Kevin Anderson; Eric D. Wish. *Social Soc. Res.* **72:3** April:1988 pp. 185 – 191

200 Dealing with drugs — consequences of government control. Ronald Hamowy *[Ed.]*. : Pacific Research Institute for Public Policy, 1988: 385 p. *ISBN: 0669156787. Bibliography — p.353-360.*

201 Drinkers at risk in Western Australia. Debra G. Blaze-Temple; Colin W. Binns; Tony Radalj; Michael Phillips. *Br. J. Addict.* **83:11** 11:1988 pp. 1281 – 1287

202 Drinking, driving, and the legal profession. Roy Light. *Howard J. Crim. Just.* **27:3** 8:1988 pp. 188 – 197

K.1: Social problems [Problèmes sociaux] — Drugs [Drogue]

203 Droga y sociedad en Columbia — el poder y el estigma *[In Spanish]*; [Drugs and society in Colombia — power and stigma]. Alvaro Camacho Guizado. Bogotá: Cerec, 1988: 174 p. *ISBN: 9589061273.*

204 Drug abuse and treatment — a study of social conditions and contextual strategies. Anders Bergmark; Lars Oscarsson *[Ed.]*. Stockholm: Almqvist & Wiksell, 1988: 318 p. *ISBN: 9122012427. Bibliography.* [Stockholmer studies in social work. : Vol. 4]

205 Drug consumption among university students in Spain. D. Queipo; F.J. Alvarez; A. Velasco. *Br. J. Addict.* **83:1** 1:1988 pp. 91 – 98

206 Drug taking, crime and the illicit supply system. Philip T. Bean; Christine K. Wilkinson. *Br. J. Addict.* **83:5** 5:1988 pp. 533 – 539

207 Effects of alcoholic beverage prices and legal drinking ages on youth alcohol use. Douglas Coate; Michael Grossman. *J. Law Econ.* **XXXI:1** 4:1988 pp. 145 – 171

208 Epidemic cocaine abuse — America's present, Britain's future? Herbert D. Kleber. *Br. J. Addict.* **83:12** 12:1988 pp. 1359 – 1371

209 The epidemiology of alcohol consumption in Spain. Maria-Elena Rodriguez; M. Douglas Anglin. *Int. J. Soc. Psyc.* **34:2** Summer:1988 pp. 102 – 111

210 Historia de la drogadicción en Colombia *[In Spanish]*; [History of drug addiction in Colombia]. Augusto Pérez Gómez *[Ed.]*. Bogotá: Tercer Mundo, 1988: 190 p. *ISBN: 9586012026.* [Colección cuarenta años uniandes.]

211 Longitudinally foretelling drug usage in adolescence — early childhood personality and environmental precursors. Jack Block; Jeanne H. Block; Susan Keyes. *Child. Devel.* **59:2** 4:1988 pp. 336 – 355

212 Mémoire et socialisation — femmes alcooliques et associations d'anciens buveurs *[In French]*; [Memory and socialization — alcoholic women and associations of former drinkers]. Marcel Drulhe. *Cah. Int. Soc.* **35:LXXXV** 7-12:1988 pp. 313 – 324

Poverty [Pauvreté]

213 Affordable housing and the homeless. Jürgen Friedrichs *[Ed.]*. Berlin: Walter de Gruyter, 1988: 191 p. *ISBN: 0899254519. A selection of papers initially presented at a symposium on affordable housing, organized by the Ad Hoc Group of Housing and the Built Environment of the International Sociological Association at the University of Hamburg, 1987.*

214 Asuntos humanitarios, la pobreza y el medio ambiente *[In Spanish]*; [Humanitarian topics — poverty and the environment] *[Summary]*. Vicente Sánchez. *Eure* **XIV:43** 10:1988 pp. 91 – 98

215 Confronting poverty in developing countries — definitions, information and policies. Paul Glewwe; J. van der Gaag *[Ed.]*. Washington, D. C.: The World Bank, 1988: vii, 48 p. *ISBN: 0821310836. Bibliography — p..45-48.* [LSMS working paper. : No. 48]

216 Dynamics of hunger in underdeveloped countries. Selim Jahan. *J. Soc. Stud. Dhaka* **:41** 7:1988 pp. 78 – 97

217 Estratégias para a diminuição da pobreza no Brasil *[In Portuguese]*; [Strategies to reduce poverty in Brazil]. Nei Roberto da Silva Oliveira. *Rev. Ciê. Pol.* **31** 4-6:1988 pp. 21 – 40

K.1: Social problems *[Problèmes sociaux]* — *Poverty [Pauvreté]*

218 Extent and measurement of poverty in India — a case study of Rajasthan. Keshav Dev Gaur. Delhi: Mittal, 1988: xix, 240 p. *ISBN: 81 7099 054 8.*

219 Face à la pauvreté — politique sociale, assistance publique et travail social *[In French]*; [Faced with poverty — social policy, public assistance and social work]. Charles Beer *[Ed.]*. Genève: Éditions Institut d'études sociales, 1988: 226 p. *ISBN: 2882240112. Includes bibliographical references.* [Annales du centre de recherche sociale. : No. 26]

220 Famine. G.A. Harrison *[Ed.]*. Oxford: Oxford University Press, 1988: xvi, 166 p. *Includes bibliography and index.*

221 Famine — social crisis and historical change. David Arnold. Oxford: Basil Blackwell, 1988: x, 154 p. *ISBN: 0631151184; LofC: 88-22133. Includes index.*

222 Food and poverty — India's half won battle. Gilbert Etienne. New Delhi: Sage, 1988: 272 p. *ISBN: 81 7036 076 5.*

223 Homeless families. George Thorman. Springfield: Charles C. Thomas, 1988: 142 p. *ISBN: 0398055246; LofC: 88-020069. Bibliography.*

224 Homelessness and the homeless — responses and innovations. H. Peter Oberlander; Arthur L. Fallick *[Ed.]*. Vancouver: University of British Columbia.Center for Human Settlements, 1988: 147 p. *ISBN: 088865345x.*

225 Homelessness and the London housing market. Glen Bramley *[Ed.]*. Bristol: University of Bristol, School for Advanced Urban Studies, 1988: 163 p. *ISBN: 0862923093.* [Occasional paper.]

226 Homelessness in the U.S.A. Ian Loveland. *Urban Law P.* **9:4** 1988 pp. 231 – 276

227 Individual and structural explanations of poverty. Leonard Beeghley. *Pop. Res. Pol. R.* **7:3** 1988 pp. 201 – 222

228 Land, poverty and politics in the Philippines. Mamerto Canlas; Mariano Miranda *[Ed.]*; James Putzel *[Ed.]*. London: CIIR, 1988: 80 p. *ISBN: 1852870028. Includes index.*

229 Longitudinal aspects of childhood poverty. Greg J. Duncan; Willard L. Rodgers. *J. Marriage Fam.* **50:4** 11:1988 pp. 1007 – 1021

230 The mentally ill homeless — what is myth and what is fact? James D. Wright. *Soc. Prob.* **35:2** 4:1988 pp. 182 – 191

231 Nowhere to go — the tragic odyssey of the homeless mentally ill. Edwin Fuller Torrey. New York: Harper and Row, 1988: xvi, 256 p. *ISBN: 0060159936.*

232 Pobreza en Chile *[In Spanish]*; [Poverty in Chile]. Eugenio Ortega R.; Ernesto Tironi *[Ed.]*. Santiago, Chile: Centro de Estudios del Desarrollo, 1988: 208 p., 3 p. of plates (ill.) *Includes bibliographical references.*

233 The poor and the poorest — some interim findings. Michael Lipton. Washington, D. C.: The World Bank, 1988: v, 68 p. *ISBN: 0821310348. Includes bibliographical references.* [World Bank discussion papers. : No. 25]

234 Poverty and disease — need for structural change. S. Akbar Zaidi. *Soc. Sci. Med.* **27:2** 1988 pp. 119 – 127

235 Poverty measurement — some issues. Sushma Sagar. Jaipur: RBSA Pub, 1988: viii, 171 p. *ISBN: 81 85176 18 3.*

236 The poverty of nations — a global perspective of mass poverty in the Third World. Jayan Tanuja Bandyopadhyaya. Ahmedabad: Allied, 1988: vii, 320 p.

K.1: Social problems *[Problèmes sociaux]* — *Poverty [Pauvreté]*

237 Processes of impoverishment in Bangladesh — reconceptualizing poverty and resources. Florence E. McCarthy; Shelley Feldman. *J. Soc. Stud. Dhaka* :**39** 1:1988 pp. 1 – 21
238 Rural poverty in India — problems in planning and strategy for poverty alleviation. Anand Prasad Mishra. New Delhi: Deep
239 Ubóstwo jako kwestia społeczna *[In Polish]*; (Poverty as a social problem). Lucyna Frackiewicz. *Pra. Zab. Społ.* **9**:*1988* pp. 1 – 12
240 Whose neglect? The role of poverty-related factors in child neglect cases and court decisions in the United States. Leroy H. Pelton; Marguerite G. Rosenthal. *Int. J. Law Fam.* **2:2** 1988 pp. 167 – 182

K.2: Social policy — *Politique sociale*

1 21 seiki heno kadai — kourei-shakai to shakai hoshou *[In Japanese]*; [Problems toward the 21st century — aged society and social welfare]. Tadashi Fukutake. Tokyo: University of Tokyo Press, 1988: 214 p.
2 Accommodation for elderly persons in newly industrializing countries — the Hong Kong experience. David R. Phillips. *Int. J. Health. Ser.* **18:2** 1988 pp. 255 – 280
3 AIDS — ethics and public policy. Christine Pierce *[Ed.]*; Donald Vandeveer *[Ed.]*. Belmont: Wadsworth, 1988: 241 p. *ISBN: 0534082866; LofC: 87-10695.*
4 America no roujin fukushi — sono hatten to tokusei ni tsuite *[In Japanese]*; [Social welfare for the aged in the United States]. Yoshiko Someya. ***Toshimondai Kenkyu** Vol.40; No.3 - 1988.* pp. 129 – 144
5 Argentina — social sectors in crisis. World Bank. Washington, DC.: World Bank, 1988: xiii, 104 p. Argentina [A World Bank country study.]
6 Between social networks and formal social services. Howard Litwin; Gail Auslander. *Age. Soc.* **8:3** 9:1988 pp. 269 – 285
7 Care of the elderly — policy and practice. David J. Hunter; Neil P. McKeganey *[Ed.]*; Isobel A. MacPherson *[Ed.]*. Abderdeen: Aberdeen University Press, 1988: 183 p. *ISBN: 0080364160. Includes index.*
8 Career patterns in child care — implications for service. David Thorpe. *Br. J. Soc. W.* **18:2** 4:1988 pp. 137 – 154
9 Child care and convenience — the effects of labor market entry costs on economic self- sufficiency among public housing residents. Philip K. Robins. *Soc. Sci. Q.* **69:1** 3:1988 pp. 122 – 136
10 Child care — monitoring practice. Isobel Freeman *[Ed.]*; Stuart Montgomery *[Ed.]*. London: Jessica Kingsley Publishers, 1988: 133 p. *Bibliographies.* [Research highlights in social work.]
11 Childcare in New Zealand — people, programmes, politics. Anne B. Smith; David A. Swain *[Ed.]*. Wellington: Allen & Unwin, 1988: xi, 218 p *ISBN: 0868614599. Includes indexes; Bibliography — p.. 198-209.*
12 Class and gender in Australian income security. Sheila Shaver. *Aust. N.Z. J. Soc.* **24:3** 11:1988 pp. 377 – 397
13 Desarrollo social de América Latina — políticas y restricciones institucionales *[In Spanish]*; [Social development in Latin America — policies and institutional restrictions]. Roberto Guimarães. *Soc. Part.* **44** 12:1988 pp. 33 – 59

K.2: Social policy [Politique sociale]

14 Dimensions of substitute child care — a comparative study of foster and residential care practice. M. J. Colton. Aldershot: Avebury, 1988: xi,301 p. *ISBN: 0566056127. Bibliography — p272-301.*

15 Equity in Australia. M. Sant *[Ed.]*; I. Burnley *[Contrib.]*; J. Forrest *[Contrib.]*; E. Young *[Contrib.]*; J.H. Holmes *[Contrib.]*; J.H. Humphreys *[Contrib.]*; A. Conacher *[Contrib.]*; F.C. Bell *[Contrib.]*; D. Rumley *[Contrib.]*. Collection of 8 articles. **Geoforum**, *19:3*, 1988 pp. 263 – 379

16 Factors predicting admission of elderly people to local authority residential care. Ian Sinclair; Lorraine Stanforth; Pat O'Connor. *Br. J. Soc. W.* **18:3** 6:1988 pp. 251 – 268

17 La faillite de l'Etat dans l'approvisionnement alimentaire des citadins — mythe ou réalité? *[In French]*; The bankruptcy of the Egyptian state in supplying food to cities — myth or reality? *[Summary]*. Nadia Khouri-Dagher. *Peup. Médit.* **41-42** 10:1987-3:1988 pp. 193 – 209

18 Families and economic distress — coping strategies and social policy. Linda C. Majka *[Ed.]*; Patricia Voydanoff *[Ed.]*. Newbury Park: Sage Publications, 1988: 306 p. *LofC: 87-034674; ISBN: 0-8039-2999-4. Bibliography.*

19 Federal categorical grants and social policies — an empirical study. Daniel J. Finnegan. *Soc. Ser. R.* **62:4** 12:1988 pp. 614 – 631

20 The future of the British welfare state — public attitudes, citizenship and social policy under the conservative governments of the 1980s. Peter Taylor-Gooby. *Eur. Sociol. R.* **4:1** 5:1988 pp. 1 – 19

21 Gendai nihon no shakai-hoshou seisaku no kousei to doutai *[In Japanese]*; [The constitution and dynamics of social welfare policy in contemporary Japan]. Masayuki Fujimura. ***Jimbun Gakuho*** *Vol.202. 1988.* pp. 1 – 45

22 Handlungstheorie und Sozialethik. Reflexionsstufen einer Ethik sozialen Handelns *[In German]*; [The theory of action and social ethics — stages in an ethic of social action]. Hans-Joachim Höhn. *Jahr. Christ. Sozialwiss.* **29** 1988 pp. 29 – 60

23 Health and social policy responses to unemployment in Europe. Thomas Kieselbach; Per-Gunnar Svensson. *J. Soc. Issues* **44:4** 1988 pp. 173 – 191

24 De hervorming van de sociale zekerheid en het sociaal-economisch beleid in België *[In Dutch]*; [The reform of social security and social-economic policy in Belgium]. F. Spinnewyn. *Maan. Econ.* **52:5** 1988 pp. 340 – 348

25 Home from home? — private residential care for elderly people. David R. Phillips; John A. Vincent *[Ed.]*; Sarah Blacksell *[Ed.]*. Sheffield: Joint Unit for Social Services Research, 1988: vi, 129 p. *ISBN: 0907484107. Bibliography — p.121-129.* [Social services monographs.]

26 Inter-agency collaboration in the all-Wales strategy — initial comments on a vanguard area. Morag McGrath. *Soc. Pol. Admin.* **22:1** 5:1988 pp. 53 – 67

27 Is there a crisis of the welfare state? Cross-national evidence from Europe, North America, and Japan. Jens Alber. *Eur. Sociol. R.* **4:3** 12:1988 pp. 181 – 208

28 Issues in the analysis of welfare recipiency. John Coder *[Contrib.]*; Patricia Ruggles *[Contrib.]*; Thomas S. Flory *[Contrib.]*; Alberto P. Martini *[Contrib.]*; Alice Robbin *[Contrib.]*; Enrique Lamas *[Contrib.]*; John McNeil *[Contrib.]*; Cynthia Harpine *[Contrib.]*; Harlene C. Gogan *[Contrib.]*; Michele Adler *[Contrib.]* and others. Collection of 6 articles. **Proc. Am. Stat. Ass.**, pp. 261 – 295

K.2: Social policy [Politique sociale]

29 Lineamientos para una política social orientada a superar la crisis [In Spanish]; [Lineaments for a social policy designed to beat the crisis]. Rolando Franco. *Rev. Parag. Sociol.* **25:**73 9-12:1988 pp. 107 – 125

30 Long-term care and AIDS — perspectives from experience with the elderly. A.E. Benjamin. *Milbank Q.* **66:**3 1988 pp. 415 – 443

31 The moral dilemmas of positive discrimination. John Edwards. *Soc. Pol. Admin.* **22:**3 12:1988 pp. 210 – 221

32 Ontwikkelingen in het Nederlandse stelsel van sociale zekerheid gekarakteriseerd en bekritiseerd [In Dutch]; [Developments in the Netherlands' system of social security characterised and criticised]. F.G. van den Heuvel. *Maan. Econ.* **52:**5 1988 pp. 349 – 362

33 The past and future of home- and community-based long-term care. William G. Weissert; Cynthia Matthews Cready; James E. Pawelak. *Milbank Q.* **66:**2 1988 pp. 309 – 388

34 Policy entrepreneurs and policy divergence — John R. Commons and William Beveridge. David Brian Robertson. *Soc. Ser. R.* **62:**3 9:1988 pp. 504 – 531

35 Poor support — poverty in the American family. David T. Ellwood. New York: Basic Books, 1988: xii, 271 p. (ill.) *ISBN: 0465059961. Bibliography — p.245-262.*

36 Postmaterialism at work in social welfare policy — the Swedish case. Richard Hoefer. *Soc. Ser. R.* **62:**3 9:1988 pp. 383 – 395

37 Program participation issues — food stamps and social security. Roberta Barnes [Contrib.]; Kevin Treesh [Contrib.]; Christine Ross [Contrib.]; Sharon K. Long [Contrib.]; Pat Doyle [Contrib.]; Denton R. Vaughan [Contrib.]; Susan Grad [Contrib.]. Collection of 6 articles. **Proc. Am. Stat. Ass.** , pp. 200 – 234

38 Public opinion about a child support assurance system. Tom Corbett; Irwin Garfinkel; Nora Cate Schaeffer. *Soc. Ser. R.* **62:**4 12:1988 pp. 632 – 648

39 Public welfare expenditure in OECD countries — towards a reconciliation of inconsistent findings. Julia S. O'Connor; Robert J. Brym. *Br. J. Soc.* **XXXIX:**1 3:1988 pp. 47 – 68

40 Rented housing and market rents — a social policy critique. John Ivatts. *Soc. Pol. Admin.* **22:**3 12:1988 pp. 197 – 209

41 Residential group care for children considered emotionally disturbed, 1966-1981. Thomas M. Young; Martha M. Dore; Donnell M. Pappenfort. *Soc. Ser. R.* **62:**1 3:1988 pp. 158 – 170

42 Rodinná a společenská péče o staré lidi [In Polish]; Family and social care of old people [Summary]. Eliška Rendlová. *Demografie* 3:1988 pp. 220 – 227

43 Roujin Fukushi Gairon [In Japanese]; [Welfare for the aged in Japan]. Kazuko Enomoto. Kyoto: Genbun-sha, 1988: 165 p.

44 Roujin no tameno day care service [In Japanese]; [Day care services for the elderly]. Akemi Soeda. ***Sougou Toshi Kenkyū*** *Vol.32. 1988.* pp. 125 – 144

45 Shakai keikaku-ron no mondai kousei — shakai keikaku ni okeru "keikaku"-teki na mono to "shakai-teki" naru mono [In Japanese]; [Some issues in social planning theory]. Shogo Takegawa. ***Journal of the Faculty of Literature*** *Vol.35. 1988.* pp. 127 – 164

46 Social engineering in Singapore. Barry Wilkinson. *J. Cont. Asia* **18: 2** 1988 pp. 165 – 188

K.2: Social policy [Politique sociale]

47 Social marketing in the alcohol policy arena. Glen G. Murray; Ronald R. Douglas. *Br. J. Addict.* **83:5** 5:1988 pp. 505 – 511
48 Social security after 1988. Peter Barclay. *Soc. Pol. Admin.* **22:1** 5:1988 pp. 3 – 9
49 Social security and the transition to adulthood. Neville Harris. *J. Soc. Pol.* **17:4** 10:1988 pp. 501 – 524
50 Social services law. John Williams. London: Fourmat, 1988: xxii, 338 p. *ISBN: 185190039x. Includes index.*
51 Sociale zekerheidsstelsels nader beschouwd *[In Dutch]*; [Social security systems under closer scrutiny]. N.H. Douben. *Maan. Econ.* **52:5** 1988 pp. 327 – 339
52 Stato sociale e società civile — alcune considerazioni in prospettiva sturziana *[In Italian]*; [Welfare state and human society — some considerations from a Sturzian perspective]. Gianfranco Morra. *Sociologia [Rome]* **XXII:1** 1988 pp. 3 – 14
53 Struggle for justice. Richard Korn *[Contrib.]*; Adjoa A. Aiyetoro *[Contrib.]*; Gilda Zwerman *[Contrib.]*; Harry Mika *[Contrib.]*; Jim Thomas *[Contrib.]*; M. Kamm Laurence *[Contrib.]*; Jenny Hocking *[Contrib.]*; Deborah Baskin *[Contrib.]*; Margaret A. Burnham *[Contrib.]*. Collection of 10 articles. **Soc. Just.**, *15:1,* Spring:1988 pp. 1 – 185
54 Toward a typology of benefit-granting in Islam. Kazuo Ohtsuka. *Orient* **XXIV:** 1988 pp. 141 – 151
55 The use and effects of welfare — a survey of recent evidence. Greg J. Duncan; Saul D. Hoffman. *Soc. Ser. R.* **62:2** 6:1988 pp. 238 – 257
56 Welfare dependence and welfare policy — a statistical study. Vicky N. Albert. New York: Greenwood Press, 1988: xvi, 195 p. (ill) *ISBN: 031326175x; LofC: 88-15495. Bibliography — p.183-187. Includes index.* [Studies in social welfare policies and programs.]
57 Welfare state and welfare society. Alex Robertson. *Soc. Pol. Admin.* **22:3** 12:1988 pp. 222 – 234
58 Women's access to pensions and the structure of eligibility rules — systems of production and reproduction. Jill Quadango. *Sociol. Q.* **29:4** Winter:1988 pp. 541 – 558
59 Yūryou roujin home no jittai — keiken jisyou no bunseki shikaku ni yoru mondai-ten *[In Japanese]*; [About the actual state of commercial nursing — homes for the aged]. Kiyo Tamura. ***The Doho Daigaku Ronso*** *Vol.58. 1988.* pp. 1 – 30

K.3: Social work

1 Action sociale et décentralisation — tendances et prospectives *[In French]*; [Social action and decentralization — trends and perspectives]. Jacques Tymen *[Ed.]*. Paris: l'Harmattan, 1988: 367 p. *ISBN: 2738401503*. [Logiques sociales.]

2 Alternative criteria for theory evaluation. Stanley L. Witkin; Shimon Gottschalk. *Soc. Ser. R.* **62:2** 6:1988 pp. 211 – 224

3 An analysis of the implementation of single-case evaluation by practitioners. Elizabeth A.R. Robinson; Denise E. Bronson; Betty J. Blythe. *Soc. Ser. R.* **62:2** 6:1988 pp. 285 – 301

4 Can the ecological model guide social work practice? Aaron M. Brower. *Soc. Ser. R.* **62:3** 9:1988 pp. 411 – 429

5 Crime victim and offender mediation as a social work strategy. Burt Galaway. *Soc. Ser. R.* **62:4** 12:1988 pp. 668 – 683

6 Dangerous clients — further observations on the limitation of mayhem. Herschel Prins. *Br. J. Soc. W.* **18:6** 12:1988 pp. 593 – 610

7 Dependency and its relationship to the assessment of care needs of elderly people. Ian Gibbs; Jonathan Bradshaw. *Br. J. Soc. W.* **18:6** 12:1988 pp. 577 – 592

8 Employment and economic problems. Catherine S. Chilman *[Ed.]*; Fred M. Cox *[Ed.]*; Elam W. Nunnally *[Ed.]*. Newbury Park: Sage, 1988: 269 p. *ISBN: 080392707x; LofC: 88-6539. Bibliography — p.237-254. Includes index.* [Families in trouble series. : Vol. 1]

9 Foster and residential care practices compared. Matthew Colton. *Br. J. Soc. W.* **18:1** 1988 pp. 25 – 42

10 Foster families for adolescents — the healing potential of time-limited placements. Celia Downes. *Br. J. Soc. W.* **18:5** 10:1988 pp. 473 – 488

11 Guidelines for social workers in coping with violent clients. Sally Johnson. *Br. J. Soc. W.* **18:4** 8:1988 pp. 377 – 390

12 HIV-AIDS — a social work perspective. M. Bamford *[Ed.]*; Roger Gaitley *[Ed.]*; Riva Miller *[Ed.]*. Birmingham: British Association of Social Workers, 1988: v,125 p. *ISBN: 0900102659. Bibliography — p.119-120.*

13 Infant mortality and social work — legacy of success. Terri Combs-Orme. *Soc. Ser. R.* **62:1** 3:1988 pp. 83 – 102

14 The influence of class and race on clinical assessments by MSW students. Robert Paviour. *Soc. Ser. R.* **62:4** 12:1988 pp. 684 – 693

15 Interview med børn *[In Danish]*; [Interviews with children]. Mogens Kjær Jensen. København: Socialforskningsinstituttet, 1988: 235 p. (ill.) *ISBN: 8774873423; LofC: 89-104212. Danish, Norwegian, and Swedish; Includes bibliographies.* [Rapport.]

16 Let's get political — political participation among social workers. Margarita Frederico; T.C. Puckett. *Aust. J. Soc. Iss.* **23:3** 8:1988 pp. 219 – 230

17 Levels of social work provisions in relation to needs in a developing society. M.S. Gore. *Indian J. Soc. W.* **XLIX:1** 1:1988 pp. 1 – 10

18 Local authority plans on client access to social work case records. Suzy Braye; Brian Corby; Chris Mills. *Envir. Plan.A.* **14:2** 3-4:1988 pp. 49 – 67

19 Marshaling social support — formats, processes and effects. Benjamin H. Gottlieb *[Ed.]*. Newbury Park: Sage, 1988: 337 p. *ISBN: 0803927150; LofC: 87-26305. Includes bibliographies.*

K.3: Social work

20 The metamodel and clinical social work. Eleanor Reardon Tolson. New York: Columbia University Press, 1988: 247 p. *ISBN: 0231055587. Bibliography — p211-233.*

21 Private and agency practitioners — some data and observations. Srinika Jayaratne; Kristine Siefert; Wayne A. Chess. *Soc. Ser. R.* **62:2** 6:1988 pp. 324 – 336

22 Problems of police-social work interaction — some American lessons. Mike Stephens. *Howard J. Crim. Just.* **27:2** 5:1988 pp. 81 – 91

23 Psychotherapy, distributive justice, and social work. Jerome Carl Wakefield. *Soc. Ser. R.* **62:2** 6:1988 pp. 187 – 210

24 Psychotherapy, distributive justice, and social work — part 2 — psychotherapy and the pursuit of justice. Jerome Carl Wakefield. *Soc. Ser. R.* **62:3** 9:1988 pp. 353 – 382

25 Public issues, private pain — poverty, social work and social policy. Saul Becker *[Ed.]*; Stewart MacPherson *[Ed.]*. London: Social Services Insight, 1988: xiii, 380 p. *ISBN: 1871018005. Bibliography — p.357-374.*

26 Relationships among task complexity, structure, job performance and satisfaction in social service organisations. Sumati N. Dubey; Yassef Meller. *Indian J. Soc. W.* **XLIX:4** 10:1988 pp. 321 – 336

27 Religion and social work practice in contemporary American society. Frank M. Loewenberg. New York: Columbia University Press, 1988: xii, 176 p. (ill.) *ISBN: 0231064527. Bibliography, p. [153]-165.*

28 Research paradigms in social work — from stalemate to creative synthesis. Colin Peile. *Soc. Ser. R.* **62:1** 3:1988 pp. 1 – 19

29 Setting objectives and measuring achievement in social care. Tony Bovaird; Ian Mallinson. *Br. J. Soc. W.* **18:3** 6:1988 pp. 309 – 324

30 Social programme evaluation in the USA — trends and issues. Edward Allan Brawley; Emilia E. Martinez-Brawley. *Br. J. Soc. W.* **18:4** 8:1988 pp. 391 – 414

31 Social support — theory, research and intervention. Alan Vaux. Westport, Conn.: Praeger, 1988: 368 p. (ill) *ISBN: 027592811x; LofC: 88-5888. Includes bibliography and index.*

32 Social work and received ideas. Chris Rojek; Geraldine Peacock *[Ed.]*; Stewart Collins *[Ed.]*. London: Routledge, 1988: viii, 198 p. *ISBN: 0415012740. Bibliography — p.183-191.*

33 Social work and the unemployed. Katherine Hooper Briar. Silver Spring,Md.: National Association of Social Workers, 1988: 222 p. *ISBN: 0871011530; LofC: 87-034846.*

34 South African social work and the norm of injustice. Gary R. Lowe. *Soc. Ser. R.* **62:1** 3:1988 pp. 20 – 39

35 Super problem solvers — a systematic case study. William J. Reid; Pamela Strother. *Soc. Ser. R.* **62:3** 9:1988 pp. 430 – 445

36 Supervision, role strain and social services departments. Michael Clare. *Br. J. Soc. W.* **18:5** 10:1988 pp. 489 – 508

37 Working with children and their families. Martin Herbert. London: British Psychological Society, 1988: 226 p. *ISBN: 0901715794.* [Psychology in action.]

K.4: Social services — Services sociaux

1 The arguments against a national health program — science or ideology? Vicente Navarro. *Int. J. Health. Ser.* **18:2** 1988 pp. 179 – 190
2 Bureaucracy and the Pacific health services. Sitaleki A. Finau. *J. Pac. Stud.* **14:** 1988 pp. 131 – 144
3 The challenge of double jeopardy — toward a mental health agenda for aging women. Dean Rodeheaver; Nancy Datan. *Am. Psychol.* **43:8** 8:1988 pp. 648 – 654
4 The changing character of the medical profession. John B. McKinlay *[Contrib.]*; Donald Light *[Contrib.]*; Sol Levine *[Contrib.]*; Fredric D. Wolinsky *[Contrib.]*; Marie R. Haug *[Contrib.]*; Vicente Navarro *[Contrib.]*; John D. Stoeckle *[Contrib.]*; David Coburn *[Contrib.]*; G.V. Larkin *[Contrib.]*; Elianne Riska *[Contrib.] and others. Collection of 12 articles.* **Milbank Q.** , *66:2 Suppl.,* 1988 pp. 1 – 204
5 Children's mental health — the gap between what we know and what we do. Leonard Saxe; Theodore Cross; Nancy Silverman. *Am. Psychol.* **43:10** 10:1988 pp. 800 – 807
6 Choosing alternative medicine — a comparison of the beliefs of patients visiting a general practitioner and a homoeopath. Adrian Furnham; Chris Smith. *Soc. Sci. Med.* **26:7** 1988 pp. 685 – 689
7 Chronic illness and disability. Catherine S. Chilman *[Ed.]*; Elam W. Nunnally *[Ed.]*; Fred M. Cox *[Ed.]*. Newbury Park: Sage, 1988: 288 p. (ill) *ISBN: 0803927037; LofC: 88-6539. Bibliography — p.248-276. Includes index.* [Families in trouble series. : Vol. 2]
8 A comparison of the resource intensity of inpatients in urban and rural nonteaching hospitals. Michael J. Long; James C. Fisher; Janice L. Dreachslin. *Int. J. Health. Ser.* **18:2** 1988 pp. 323 – 334
9 Consent and the incompetent patient — ethics, law and medicine. S. R. Hirsch *[Ed.]*; John Harris *[Ed.]*. London: Gaskell, 1988: x, 101 p. *ISBN: 0902241222.* [Gaskell psychiatry series.]
10 Continuing care of old people — a medical viewpoint. Richard Lewis; John Wattis. *Age. Soc.* **8:2** 6:1988 pp. 189 – 209
11 Contributions of patients to general practitioner consultations in relation to their understanding of doctor's instructions and advice. E.J. Robinson; M.J. Whitfield. *Soc. Sci. Med.* **27:9** 1988 pp. 895 – 900
12 Cooperation in mental health — an Italian project in Nicaragua. Benedetto Saraceno; Fabrizio Asioli; Alessandro Liberati; Gianni Tognoni. *Carib. Stud.* **21:3-4** 7-12:1988 pp. 91 – 100
13 Corporatization and the social transformation of doctoring. John B. McKinlay; John D. Stoeckle. *Int. J. Health. Ser.* **18:2** 1988 pp. 191 – 206
14 Deliberate misdiagnosis in mental health practice. Stuart A. Kirk; Herb Kutchins. *Soc. Ser. R.* **62:2** 6:1988 pp. 225 – 237
15 The development of Canadian nursing — professionalization and proletarianization. David Coburn. *Int. J. Health. Ser.* **18:3** 1988 pp. 437 – 456
16 The development of medical sociology in Finland. Eero Lahelma; Elianne Riska. *Soc. Sci. Med.* **27:3** 1988 pp. 223 – 229

K.4: Social services *[Services sociaux]*

17 Doctors and rules — a sociology of professional values. Joseph M. Jacob; D. MacRae *[Foreword]*. London: Routledge, 1988: xv, 250 p. *ISBN: 0415006880; LofC: 88-1950. Includes bibliography and index.*

18 Elderly people, their medicines, and their doctors. Ann Cartwright; Christopher Smith *[Ed.]*. London: Routledge, 1988: ix, 195 p. *ISBN: 0415006848.*

19 Ethics — the heart of health care. David Seedhouse. Chichester: Wiley, 1988: xvi, 157 p. (ill) *ISBN: 0471918741; LofC: 87-037253. Bibliography — p.155-156.Includes index.* [A Wiley medical publication.]

20 Ethnicity, gender, and utilization of mental health services in a Medicaid population. Helena Temkin-Greener; Kathryn T. Clark. *Soc. Sci. Med.* **26:10** 1988 pp. 989 – 996

21 Experience in mental health — community care and social policy. Kathleen Jones. London: Sage, 1988: 165 p. *ISBN: 0803980655. Bibliographies.*

22 Field applications of operations research in primary health care within developing countries - part II. Robert Maxwell *[Foreword]*; Sumner L. Levine *[Ed.]*; Barnett R. Parker *[Contrib.]*; Sally K. Stansfield; Antoine Augustin *[Contrib.]*; Reginald Boulos *[Contrib.]*; Jeanne S. Newman *[Contrib.]*; Sherilynn F. Spear *[Contrib.]*; Ellen vor der Bruegge *[Contrib.]*; Charles B. Hamilton *[Contrib.] and others. Collection of 6 articles.* **Socio. Econ.** , *:1,* :1988 pp. 1 – 50

23 For the patient's good — the restoration of benificence in health care. Edmund D. Pellegrino; David C. Thomasma *[Ed.]*. Oxford: Oxford University Press, 1988: xii, 240 p. *ISBN: 0195043197.*

24 Forgotten millions. David Cohen. London: Paladin, 1988: 236 p. *ISBN: 0586086676. Bibliography — p.227-230. Includes index.*

25 Free care — a quantitative analysis of health and cost effects of a national health program for the United States. Steffie Woolhandler; David U. Himmelstein. *Int. J. Health. Ser.* **18:3** 1988 pp. 393 – 400

26 Governo local, processo político e equipamentos socials — um balanço bibliográfico *[In Portuguese]*; [Local government, political process and social services — a bibliographical checklist]. Maria Helena Guimarães de Castro. *Bol. Inf. Bibl. Soc.* **:25** :1988 pp. 56 – 82

27 Health and health care among travellers. Jan Pahl; Michael Vaile. *J. Soc. Pol.* **17:2** 4:1988 pp. 195 – 213

28 Health and the social power of women. Carol P. MacCormack. *Soc. Sci. Med.* **26:7** 1988 pp. 677 – 683

29 Health care and the older citizen — economic, demographic, and financial aspects. C. Carl Pegels. Rockville, Maryland: Aspen, 1988: x, 278 p. *ISBN: 0871897717.*

30 The health of the republic — epidemics, medicine, and moralism as challenges to democracy. Dan E. Beauchamp. Philadelphia: Temple University Press, 1988: 298 p. *ISBN: 0877225583. Bibliography.* [Health, society, and policy.]

31 Health services utilisation in urban India — a study. C.A.K. Yesudian. Delhi: Mittal, 1988: xii, 322 p. *ISBN: 81 7099 024 6.*

32 Health, apartheid and frontline states. Anthony Zwi *[Contrib.]*; Shula Marks *[Contrib.]*; Neil Andersson *[Contrib.]*; Derek Yach *[Contrib.]*; Sharon Fonn *[Contrib.]*; Malcolm Steinberg *[Contrib.]*; Max Price *[Contrib.]*; Julie Cliff

K.4: Social services *[Services sociaux]*

[Contrib.]; Abdul Razak Noormahomed *[Contrib.]*; David Sanders *[Contrib.] and others. Collection of 9 articles.* **Soc. Sci. Med.** , *27:8*, 1988 pp. 661 – 745

33 Hidden menace in the universal child immunization program. Debabar Banerji. *Int. J. Health. Ser.* **18:2** 1988 pp. 293 – 300

34 Hospital utilization, performance measures and health status — econometric analyses of Dutch micro-data. Reinier Corstiaan Johannes Antonius van Vliet. Alblasserdam: Offsetdrukkerij Kanters B.V., 1988: 351 p. *ISBN: 9090022686. eng: dut; Bibliography — p.319-331.*

35 Hospitalised schizophrenics — their socio-sexual life and rehabilitation. R. K. Upadhyay. Delhi: Mittal, 1987: xi, 215 p. *ISBN: 81 7099 018 1.*

36 Human relations and primary health care delivery in rural Nepal — the case of Deurali. Nanda R. Shrestha. *Prof. Geogr.* **40:2** 5:1988 pp. 202 – 214

37 Ideology and reality — representation and participation in local service management. Uri Yanay. *Br. J. Soc. W.* **18:1** 1988 pp. 43 – 56

38 Images of general practice — the perceptions of the doctor. Michael Calnan. *Soc. Sci. Med.* **27:6** 1988 pp. 579 – 586

39 In the shadow of the city — community health and the urban poor. Trudy Harpham *[Ed.]*; Tim Lusty *[Ed.]*; Patrick Vaughan *[Ed.].* Oxford: Oxford University Press, 1988: xviii, 237 p. (ill) *ISBN: 0192615912. Bibliography — p213-227. Includes index.*

40 Innovations in reproductive health care — menstrual regulation policies and programs in Bangladesh. Ruth Mueller-Dixon. *Stud. Fam. Pl.* **19:3** 5-6:1988 pp. 129 – 140

41 Is there a religious factor in health care utilization? A review. Preston L. Schiller; Jeffery S. Levin. *Soc. Sci. Med.* **27:12** 1988 pp. 1369 – 1379

42 IVF technology and the argument from potential. Peter Singer; Karen Dawson. *Philos. Pub.* **17:2** Spring:1988 pp. 87 – 104

43 Lay evaluation of medicine and medical practice — report of a pilot study. Michael Calnan. *Int. J. Health. Ser.* **18:2** 1988 pp. 311 – 322

44 Life and death decision making. Baruch A. Brody. New York: Oxford University Press, 1988: xii, 250 p. *ISBN: 019505007x.*

45 The management of clinicians in the National Health Service. Ellie Scrivens. *Soc. Pol. Admin.* **22:1** 5:1988 pp. 22 – 34

46 Management problems in health care. Günter Fandel *[Ed.].* Berlin: Springer-Verlag, 1988: 296 p. *ISBN: 3540192433.*

47 The Mandwa project — an experiment in community participation. Noshir H. Antia. *Int. J. Health. Ser.* **18:1** 1988 pp. 153 – 164

48 Measuring health — a practical approach. George Teeling Smith *[Ed.].* Chichester: Wiley, 1988: 268 p. *ISBN: 0471918490. Contains bibliographies.*

49 Measuring small area variation in hospital use — site-of-care versus patient origin data. Catherine G. McLaughlin. *Socio. Econ.* **:4** 1988 pp. 177 – 184

50 Medical geography — selected papers from the 1986 Rutgers symposium. Robert Earickson *[Contrib.]*; Michael Greenberg *[Contrib.]*; Marian Craig *[Contrib.]*; Surinder M. Bhardwaj *[Contrib.]*; Madhusudana N. Rao *[Contrib.]*; Maggie Pearson *[Contrib.]*; D.R. Phillips *[Contrib.]*; J. Vincent *[Contrib.]*; Graham Betham *[Contrib.]*; G. Brent Hall *[Contrib.] and others. Collection of 21 articles.* **Soc. Sci. Med.** , *26:1*, 1988 pp. 1 – 199

K.4: Social services [Services sociaux]

51 The medical profession and the pharmaceutical industry — an unhealthy alliance. Joel Lexchin. *Int. J. Health. Ser.* **18:4** 1988 pp. 603 – 616

52 Medicine and culture — varieties of treatment in the United States, England, West Germany, and France. Lynn Payer. New York: Holt, 1988: 204 p. *ISBN: 0805004432.*

53 Methadone and public policy. Edward Senay. *Br. J. Addict.* **83:3** 3:1988 pp. 257 – 263

54 Modernization and medical care. Eugene B. Gallagher. *Sociol. Pers.* **31:1** 1:1988 pp. 59 – 87

55 One foot in Eden — a sociological study of the range of therapeutic community practice. M. Bloor; Neil P. McKeganey *[Ed.]*; Dick Fonkert *[Ed.]*. London: Routledge, 1988: - *ISBN: 0415008220.*

56 Optimization of task allocation for community health workers in Haiti. Barnett R. Parker; Sally K. Stansfield; Antoine Augustin; Reginald Boulos; Jeanne S. Newman. *Socio. Econ.* **:1** :1988 pp. 3 – 14

57 Organ substitution technology — ethical, legal, and public policy issues. Deborah Mathieu *[Ed.]*. Boulder: Westview, 1988: 340 p. *ISBN: 0813305446.*

58 Overlooked, overworked — women's unpaid and paid work in the health services' "cost crisis". Nona Y. Glazer. *Int. J. Health. Ser.* **18:1** 1988 pp. 119 – 138

59 Patients first — reality or rhetoric? Valerie Williamson. *Soc. Pol. Admin.* **22:3** 12:1988 pp. 245 – 258

60 Permanence and change in Asian health care traditions. Beatrix Pfleiderer *[Contrib.]*; Paul Michael Taylor *[Contrib.]*; Louis Golomb *[Contrib.]*; Laurel Kendall *[Contrib.]*; Unni Wikan *[Contrib.]*; Nadja Reissland *[Contrib.]*; Richard Burghart *[Contrib.]*; Mitchell G. Weiss *[Contrib.]*; Amit Desai *[Contrib.]*; Sushrut Jadhav *[Contrib.] and others. Collection of 18 articles.* **Soc. Sci. Med.** , *27:5*, 1988 pp. 411 – 567

61 Perspectives on utility-based decision models in primary health care within developing countries. Stewart N. Blumenfeld; Jeanne S. Newman; Barnett R. Parker. *Socio. Econ.* **:1** :1988 pp. 45 – 50

62 Pharmacies as alternative sources of medical care — the case of Cincinnati. Roger Mark Selya. *Soc. Sci. Med.* **26:4** 1988 pp. 409 – 416

63 Polypharmacy — its cost burden and barrier to medical care in a drug-oriented health care system. Anthony E. Isenalumhe; Osawaru Oviawe. *Int. J. Health. Ser.* **18:2** 1988 pp. 335 – 342

64 Poverty, health services, and health status in rural America. Donald L. Patrick; Jane Stein; Miquel Porta; Carol Q. Porter; Thomas C. Ricketts. *Milbank Q.* **66:1** 1988 pp. 105 – 136

65 The present problems and future needs of primary health care in Malaysia. Ho Tak Ming. *Int. J. Health. Ser.* **18:2** 1988 pp. 281 – 292

66 Private sector care for chronically mentally ill individuals — the more things change, the more they stay the same. William R. Shadish. *Am. Psychol.* **44:8** 8:1988 pp. 1142 – 1147

67 The profitization of health promotion. Nancy Milio. *Int. J. Health. Ser.* **18:4** 1988 pp. 573 – 586

68 Psychology and public policy in the "health care revolution". Charles A. Kiesler; Teru L. Morton. *Am. Psychol.* **43:12** 12:1988 pp. 993 – 1003

K.4: Social services *[Services sociaux]*

69 Quality/ capacity substitution in the delivery of mental health care. John G. Cross. *Socio. Econ.* :**3** 1988 pp. 145 – 151

70 The quantification of health. P. Kind; R. Rosser. *Eur. J. Soc. Psychol.* **18:1** 1-3:1988 pp. 63 – 78

71 Questioni e metodi delle neuroscienze *[In Italian]*; Questions and methods of neurosciences *[Summary]*. Antonio Di Meo *[Contrib.]*; Giovanni Berlinguer *[Contrib.]*; Alberto Oliverio *[Contrib.]*; Gian Luigi Gessa *[Contrib.]*; Gaetano Di Chiara *[Contrib.]*. **Crit. Marx.** , *26:1*, 1-2:1988 pp. 13 – 51

72 Racial inequalities in health — a challenge to the British National Health Service. Carol Baxter; David Baxter. *Int. J. Health. Ser.* **18:4** 1988 pp. 563 – 572

73 Racism, the National Health Service, and the health of black people. Louis Kushnick. *Int. J. Health. Ser.* **18:3** 1988 pp. 457 – 470

74 Rationing medicine. Robert H. Blank. New York: Columbia University Press, 1988: x, 290 p. *ISBN: 0231065361. Bibliography — p[253]-273.*

75 Reducing attrition among village health workers in rural Nigeria. Herman H. Gray; James Ciroma. *Socio. Econ.* :**1** :1988 pp. 39 – 44

76 Regelmatigheden bij de invloedsverdeling — een empirische toetsing aan de gezondheidszorg- sector *[In Dutch]*; Regularities in the distribution of influence — the public health care as an empirical test *[Summary]*. J.M. Bos. *Sociol. Gids* **XXXV:6** 11-12:1988 pp. 380 – 396

77 Rights & reponsibilities of doctors. British Medical Association. London: British Medical Association, 1988: xxiv, 135 p. *ISBN: 0727902369.*

78 Rigor in health-related research — toward an expanded conceptualization. John W. Ratcliffe; Amalia Gonzalez-del-Valle. *Int. J. Health. Ser.* **18:3** 1988 pp. 361 – 392

79 The role of social support and life stress events in use of mental health services. Cathy Donald Sherbourne. *Soc. Sci. Med.* **27:12** 1988 pp. 1393 – 1400

80 Selective or comprehensive primary health care? Daniel Grodos *[Contrib.]*; de Xavier Béthune *[Contrib.]*; Kenneth S. Warren *[Contrib.]*; Julia A. Walsh *[Contrib.]*; Kenneth W. Newell *[Contrib.]*; W. Henry Mosley *[Contrib.]*; Duane L. Smith *[Contrib.]*; John H. Bryant *[Contrib.]*; Andrew Green *[Contrib.]*; Carol Barker *[Contrib.]* and others. Collection of 14 articles. **Soc. Sci. Med.** , *26:9*, 1988 pp. 877 – 977

81 Sex differences in health complaints estimated from self- and proxy survey responses. Michael P. Massagli; Brian R. Clarridge. *Proc. Am. Stat. Ass.* pp. 317 – 322

82 The significance of interprofessional stereotyping in the health and social services. Michael Broussine; Philip Cox; Fred Davies. *Envir. Plan.A.* **14:3** 5-6:1988 pp. 57 – 67

83 El sistema unico de salud y seguridad social — una respuesta a la crisis *[In Spanish]*; [The single system of health and social security — a response to the crisis]. Carlos Godoy Arteaga. Tegucigalpa: Litografía Lopez, 1988: 119 p.

84 Social provision and service delivery — problems of equity, health, and health care in rural Australia. John S. Humphreys. *Geoforum* **19:3** 1988 pp. 323 – 338

K.4: Social services *[Services sociaux]*

85 Social work and psychotropic drug treatments. David Cohen. *Soc. Ser. R.* **62:4** 12:1988 pp. 576 – 599

86 Storia e sviluppi delle neuroscienze *[In Italian]*; (Neurosciences history and developments). Alberto Oliverio. *Crit. Marx.* **26:2** 3-4:1988 pp. 99 – 110

87 Strategies to plan and assess alternative programs to train rural-based health workers in Papua New Guinea. F. Sherilynn Spear; Ellen von der Bruegge; Charles B. Hamilton; N. Stewart Blumenfeld. *Socio. Econ.* **:1** :1988 pp. 23 – 28

88 Stress and coping in relation to health and disease. A.J.J.M. Vingerhoets *[Contrib.]*; F.H.G. Marcelissen *[Contrib.]*; James P. Henry *[Contrib.]*; L.J.P. van Doornen *[Contrib.]*; E.J.C. de Geus *[Contrib.]*; J.F. Orlebeke *[Contrib.]*; Susan Folkman *[Contrib.]*; Richard S. Lazarus; Zahava Solomon *[Contrib.]*; Hanoch Flum *[Contrib.]* and others. Collection of 14 articles. *Soc. Sci. Med.*, *26:3*, 1988 pp. 277 – 392

89 Tracking cancer prevention activities. Robert Parke. *Proc. Am. Stat. Ass.* pp. 311 – 316

90 The well baby lottery — motivational procedures for increasing attendance at maternal and child health clinics. John P. Elder; Rene Salgado. *Int. J. Health. Ser.* **18:1** 1988 pp. 165 – 172

91 "We'll take care of it for you?" Health care in the Canadian community. Robert G. Evans. *Dædalus* **117:4** Fall:1988 pp. 155 – 190

92 Will cost effectiveness analysis worsen the cost effectiveness of health care? David U. Himmelstein; Steffie Woolhandler; David H. Bor. *Int. J. Health. Ser.* **18:1** 1988 pp. 1 – 10

93 Women's health and social change — the case of lay midwives. Bonnie J. Kay; Irene H. Butter; Deborah Chang; Kathleen Houlihan. *Int. J. Health. Ser.* **18:2** 1988 pp. 223 – 236

94 Youth unemployment and health effects. Thomas Kieselbach. *Int. J. Soc. Psyc.* **34:2** Summer:1988 pp. 83 – 96

AUTHOR INDEX
INDEX DES AUTEURS

Abarca, S: **F.5**: 95.
Abaza, M: **F.5**: 21, 70.
Abbott, A: **B.1.3**: 30.
Abdelmaki, L: **G.1**: 10.
Abe, M: **B.1.3**: 28.
Abel, E: **F.7**: 4.
Abenheim, D: **J.7**: 4.
Abercrombie, N: **A.1**: 8.
Abidi, N: **I.2**: 66.
Aborn, M: **A.5**: 7.
Aboud, F: **F.7**: 100.
Abouhani, A: **G.1**: 10.
Abraham, G: **B.1.1**: 18.
Abrams, D: **C.3**: 45.
Abrams, P: **J.3**: 14.
Abrous, D: **F.5**: 70.
Abu-Laban, B: **A.1**: 17.
Abuzar, M: **F.1**: 29.
Achilli, E: **D.9.1**: 1.
Achío, M: **F.5**: 95.
Acker, J: **F.5**: 30.
Aclimandos, T: **J.7**: 2.
Acock, A: **F.4.2**: 33, 79. **F.6**: 20.
Acosta-Belén, E: **F.7**: 31.
Adachi, K: **G.3.2**: 26.
Adams, B: **F.4.2**: 143.
Adams, J: **F.7**: 111.
Adams, R: **F.3**: 42.
Adamson, N: **F.5**: 11.
Aday, R: **K.1**: 74.
Adebayo, A: **F.3**: 37. **F.4.2**: 35.
Adelmann, P: **I.4**: 20.
Adjali, S: **G.1**: 10.
Adler, M: **K.2**: 28.
Adler, P: **H.4**: 2–3.

Agbola, T: **G.3.2**: 89.
Aggleton, P: **F.3**: 101, 127.
Agnew, R: **D.9**: 2.
Agostinelli, J: **F.4.2**: 25.
Agrawal, B: **G.3.1**: 85.
Ahern, F: **B.2**: 6.
Ahlburg, D: **I.4**: 5.
Ahmat, S: **D.9.5**: 18.
Ahmed, A: **D.5**: 83.
Ahn, T: **D.9.5**: 23.
Aho, J: **J.6**: 17.
Ahrne, G: **E.2**: 7.
Aida, K: **F.8**: 13.
Aikawa, Y: **G.3.1**: 42.
Aina, T: **F.3**: 103.
Ainlay, S: **F.3**: 11.
Aisenberg, N: **D.9.5**: 26.
Aitken, P: **K.1**: 37.
Aiyetoro, A: **K.2**: 53.
Ajanasyee, V: **K.1**: 19.
Akbar, J: **G.3.2**: 11.
Akin, J: **F.3**: 29.
Akiwowo, A: **A.1**: 39.
Akubue, A: **D.9.3**: 6.
Al Hammad, M: **G.3.2**: 143.
Al-Haj, M: **F.7**: 6.
Al-Lanqawi, A: **K.1**: 72, 126.
Alaiz, F: **J.2**: 2.
Alanen, L: **F.2**: 83.
Alatriste, C: **G.2**: 2.
Alawiye, C: **C.2**: 101.
Alawiye, O: **C.2**: 101.
Albanese, P: **H.1**: 5.
Alber, J: **K.2**: 27.

INTERNATIONAL BIBLIOGRAPHY OF SOCIOLOGY — 1988

Alberigo, G: **D.5**: 72.
Albert, A: **F.4.2**: 42.
Albert, H: **B.1.1**: 11.
Albert, V: **K.2**: 56.
Albertoni, E: **E.2**: 73.
Albertsen, N: **B.1.1**: 21.
Albini, J: **A.2**: 1. **K.1**: 89.
Albuquerque, de, K: **F.8**: 28.
Alcoff, L: **F.5**: 4.
Alden, J: **G.3.2**: 113.
Aldridge, R: **J.8**: 1.
Alexander, J: **D.1.1**: 11.
Ali, A: **D.9.3**: 6. **I.3**: 41.
Ali, I: **G.3.1**: 31.
Ali, K: **G.3.1**: 45.
Allamani, A: **I.3**: 4.
Allan, G: **F.2**: 48.
Aloisi, M: **D.5**: 81.
Alonso, A: **D.1.1**: 13.
Alpert, G: **G.2**: 12.
Alstyne, van, D: **K.1**: 170.
Altergott, K: **F.2**: 38.
Altheide, D: **C.5**: 18.
Altshuler, M: **F.7**: 56.
Alvarado, M: **D.7**: 92.
Alvarez, F: **K.1**: 205.
Alvarez de la Torre, G: **G.3.2**: 146.
Alvim, M: **F.2**: 78.
Aly, J: **D.8**: 17.
Amadieu, J: **I.6**: 13.
Amano, M: **D.9**: 16.
Amato, P: **F.4.1**: 51.
Ambert, A: **F.4.2**: 113.
Ameur, M: **G.1**: 10.
Amir, S: **D.9.8**: 2. **H.3**: 24.
Ancian, J: **J.3**: 15.
Andersen, M: **D.5**: 77.
Anderson, B: **E.1**: 2.
Anderson, C: **F.6**: 26.
Anderson, D: **D.9.3**: 2. **G.3.1**: 10.
Anderson, J: **C.1**: 26.

Anderson, K: **F.4.2**: 132. **K.1**: 86.
Anderson, R: **F.3**: 118.
Andersson, N: **K.4**: 32.
Anderton, T: **D.5**: 66.
Andics, H: **F.7**: 83.
Andors, P: **I.2**: 62.
Andreff, W: **E.3**: 17.
Andrew, C: **F.5**: 76.
Andrews, G: **K.1**: 95.
Andzenge, D: **F.7**: 42.
Anglin, M: **K.1**: 209.
Anker, R: **I.2**: 65.
Annerstedt, J: **H.4**: 13.
Anselme, M: **G.3.2**: 20, 82.
Anson, J: **G.3.2**: 36.
Anson, O: **F.3**: 117.
Antia, N: **K.4**: 47.
Antonides, G: **H.5**: 6.
Antonovsky, A: **F.4.2**: 19.
Antrobus, J: **C.3**: 46.
Aoi, K: **F.5**: 74.
Appelgryn, A: **F.7**: 91.
Appleyard, R: **F.8**: 74.
Apps, J: **D.9.5**: 12.
Aptekar, L: **F.2**: 86. **K.1**: 31.
Araji, S: **G.3.1**: 32.
Arayici, A: **D.9.6**: 2. **F.8**: 86.
Arbena, J: **I.7**: 19.
Arber, S: **B.3**: 6.
Archer, A: **I.6**: 3.
Archer, J: **C.7**: 2.
Archer, M: **D.1.1**: 7.
Ardoino, J: **A.1**: 30.
Arefeen, H: **F.6**: 24.
Arias, P: **I.2**: 15.
Arlacchi, P: **H.5**: 5.
Arnold, D: **K.1**: 221.
Arnone, H: **C.3**: 5.
Aron, R: **F.7**: 23.
Aronowitz, S: **D.6**: 22.
Aronson, B: **G.1**: 15.

Arshanapalli, G: **I.6**: 16.
Arthur, R: **C.6**: 14.
Asch, A: **F.3**: 11, 106. **F.5**: 107.
Ascolani, A: **G.3.2**: 139.
Ash, T: **A.3**: 3.
Ashforth, B: **C.5**: 19.
Ashton, D: **I.2**: 47.
Ashton, T: **I.3**: 14.
Ashworth, G: **F.5**: 101. **G.3.2**: 48. **H.7**: 5.
Asioli, F: **K.4**: 12.
Askew, I: **F.3**: 39.
Asplund, G: **I.5**: 26.
Assaad, R: **G.3.2**: 27.
Association internationale des sociologues de langue française: **A.3**: 12.
Association professionnelle des sociologues: **A.3**: 12.
Astington, J: **C.2**: 9.
Athappily, K: **F.4.1**: 39.
Athens, L: **K.1**: 71.
Atkinson, C: **C.3**: 17.
Atkinson, P: **B.1.3**: 9.
Attwood, D: **G.3.1**: 84.
Audinarayana, N: **F.4.1**: 31.
Auerbach, J: **I.3**: 20.
Augustin, A: **K.4**: 22, 56.
Auslander, G: **K.2**: 6.
Austin, R: **E.2**: 52.
Averill, J: **C.2**: 68. **F.4.1**: 2.
Avery, R: **C.2**: 96.
Avis, M: **C.7**: 20.
Avison, W: **F.3**: 130.
Avrunin, G: **C.3**: 52.
Awaji, T: **G.1**: 15.
Awalt, S: **F.4.1**: 41.
Axelrod, P: **J.8**: 1.
Ayalon, H: **F.7**: 34.
Ayoub, J: **D.1.2**: 10.
Azmitia, M: **C.3**: 32.
Azmon, Y: **J.4**: 11.
Azumi, K: **I.6**: 46.

Baacke, D: **D.7**: 130.
Baba, Y: **B.1.1**: 17.
Babcock, M: **C.2**: 63.
Babst, D: **J.8**: 1.
Babüroğlu, O: **C.5**: 47.
Bachand, L: **K.1**: 52.
Bachman, J: **C.7**: 42. **K.1**: 13.
Back, L: **D.8**: 3.
Backer, T: **C.1**: 27.
Badet, G: **K.1**: 186.
Baduel, P: **G.1**: 10.
Baer, W: **H.7**: 2.
Baglioni, A: **I.4**: 21.
Baglioni, G: **I.6**: 29.
Bahr, S: **F.2**: 31.
Baier, K: **B.1.1**: 23.
Bailey, F: **C.6**: 8.
Bailey-Harris, R: **K.1**: 158.
Bain, G: **I.6**: 44.
Bainham, A: **F.4.2**: 3.
Baird, R: **D.4**: 12.
Baker, D: **F.7**: 71.
Baker, L: **F.3**: 93.
Baker, M: **F.2**: 33.
Baker, T: **B.1.3**: 7.
Balakrishnan, T: **F.3**: 50.
Baldi, S: **F.7**: 8.
Baldwin, J: **C.2**: 69.
Bale, J: **I.7**: 14.
Ball, M: **D.7**: 81.
Ball, R: **K.1**: 160.
Baltagi, A: **G.3.2**: 82, 100.
Balza, S: **G.3.2**: 3.
Bamford, C: **I.2**: 36.
Bamford, M: **K.3**: 12.
Bandarage, A: **F.5**: 99.
Bandyopadhyaya, J: **K.1**: 236.
Banerjee, B: **D.1.3**: 1.
Banerjee, P: **D.1.1**: 31.
Banerji, D: **K.4**: 33.
Banks, B: **G.3.1**: 31.

Banks, M: **I.2**: 53.
Bannerman, P: **D.5**: 23.
Banton, M: **F.7**: 66, 85.
Banyikwa, W: **G.3.2**: 135.
Baoill, D: **D.7**: 8.
Baqee, L: **F.3**: 21.
Bar-Haïm, G: **I.4**: 1.
Bar-Tal, D: **D.6**: 31.
Barak, B: **C.7**: 31.
Barber, P: **C.4**: 18.
Barcan, A: **D.9**: 5.
Barcelo, R: **H.4**: 50.
Barclay, P: **K.2**: 48.
Barham, S: **F.5**: 62.
Barik, B: **E.2**: 8.
Barker, C: **K.4**: 80.
Barlösius, E: **H.5**: 8.
Barnes, B: **C.3**: 30.
Barnes, M: **C.2**: 78.
Barnes, R: **K.2**: 37.
Barnes, S: **J.6**: 31.
Barnett, P: **C.2**: 45.
Baron, J: **I.1**: 4.
Baron, L: **K.1**: 85.
Baron, R: **C.5**: 3. **K.1**: 92.
Barouch, G: **J.5**: 6.
Barrera, M: **F.7**: 59.
Barrett, F: **C.4**: 34.
Barrett, J: **F.3**: 84.
Barrett, M: **F.7**: 40.
Barrett, R: **G.3.2**: 136.
Barro, R: **F.3**: 79.
Barsh, R: **F.7**: 24.
Barsky, O: **G.3.1**: 4.
Barthel, D: **D.7**: 36.
Bartlema, J: **B.3**: 14.
Bartlett, K: **K.1**: 42.
Barton, M: **I.2**: 57.
Bartra, R: **H.4**: 9.
Baruch, S: **F.3**: 7.
Barwise, P: **D.7**: 135.

Baskin, D: **K.2**: 53.
Basu, A: **F.3**: 5, 28. **G.3.2**: 101.
Batchelor, W: **C.1**: 27.
Bator, C: **C.2**: 71.
Battesti, T: **J.6**: 28.
Baubérot, J: **D.5**: 75.
Baudouin, J: **G.3.2**: 82, 110.
Bauer, M: **I.5**: 13.
Bauer, T: **E.3**: 17.
Baughman, A: **F.3**: 35.
Baum, A: **K.1**: 142.
Bauman, Z: **C.3**: 51. **F.7**: 51.
Baumeister, R: **C.2**: 34, 51.
Baumgartner, F: **C.5**: 43.
Baumgartner, M: **G.2**: 10.
Baviskar, B: **G.3.1**: 84.
Baxter, C: **K.4**: 72.
Baxter, D: **C.2**: 27. **K.4**: 72.
Baxter, J: **E.2**: 28. **H.1**: 6. **I.3**: 13.
Bay, K: **F.2**: 46.
Baydar, N: **F.4.2**: 78.
Bayer, G: **I.3**: 2.
Bayer, R: **I.3**: 18.
Bayley, D: **G.2**: 17.
Bazac, D: **F.2**: 10.
Bazzani, F: **D.3**: 16.
Beagles-Roos, J: **D.7**: 125.
Bean, P: **K.1**: 206.
Beardsworth, A: **C.6**: 17.
Beauchamp, D: **K.4**: 30.
Beaumont, P: **I.6**: 36.
Beauvais, F: **J.8**: 8.
Beccalli, B: **I.2**: 29.
Beck, E: **I.3**: 30.
Becker, C: **K.1**: 172.
Becker, G: **F.3**: 79.
Becker, H: **F.2**: 62.
Becker, M: **B.3**: 15.
Becker, S: **K.3**: 25.
Beckett, J: **F.7**: 1.
Beeghley, L: **E.2**: 9. **K.1**: 227.

Beek, W: **D.5**: 35.
Beer, C: **K.1**: 219.
Beer, W: **F.4.2**: 119.
Beer, de, J: **F.1**: 23.
Begag, A: **F.1**: 16.
Behuniak, P: **D.9.2**: 1.
Beit-Hallahmi, B: **D.5**: 50.
Bekele, A: **I.2**: 11.
Beli, Z: **I.3**: 5.
Bell, F: **K.2**: 15.
Bell, N: **F.4.2**: 110.
Bellingham, B: **F.2**: 76.
Bellone, E: **D.6**: 29.
Bellucci, S: **F.8**: 92.
Belokon', I: **G.3.1**: 48.
Belsher, G: **C.2**: 47.
Belsky, J: **F.4.2**: 107.
Ben-Rafael, E: **F.7**: 34.
Benabdellah, A: **G.1**: 10.
Bender, B: **J.3**: 25.
Bengtson, V: **F.2**: 9.
Beniger, J: **A.5**: 7.
Benin, M: **F.4.2**: 25.
Benington, J: **I.7**: 7.
Benjamin, A: **K.2**: 30.
Bennett, L: **K.1**: 193.
Bennett, N: **F.4.1**: 7.
Bennett, T: **K.1**: 62.
Bennett-Alexander, D: **I.3**: 7.
Bennis, W: **C.6**: 5.
Bensman, J: **B.1.3**: 20. **K.1**: 139.
Benson, J: **I.6**: 15.
Benson, L: **F.7**: 37.
Bentler, P: **B.3**: 8. **K.1**: 32, 197.
Benton, P: **C.2**: 61.
Bercken, W: **D.5**: 21.
Bercusson, B: **B.1.1**: 16.
Berding, H: **F.7**: 109.
Bergalli, R: **K.1**: 82.
Berger, J: **E.3**: 18.
Berger, R: **D.4**: 5. **K.1**: 67.

Bergmark, A: **K.1**: 204.
Berkane, M: **B.3**: 8.
Berkman, L: **F.2**: 63.
Berkowitz, M: **I.2**: 35. **I.4**: 15.
Berkowitz, S: **E.1**: 7.
Berlinguer, G: **K.4**: 71.
Bernard, R: **F.7**: 47.
Bernardi, E: **K.1**: 6.
Bernardini, C: **D.6**: 29. **D.9.9**: 2.
Bernhardt, E: **I.2**: 10.
Bernheim, B: **C.7**: 3.
Bernoussi, El, N: **F.5**: 70.
Berti, A: **C.2**: 20.
Bertino, S: **F.4.2**: 146.
Best, H: **A.1**: 15.
Betcher, G: **K.1**: 53.
Betham, G: **G.1**: 13.
Béthune, D: **K.4**: 80.
Bettoni, C: **F.7**: 29.
Betts, K: **F.8**: 66.
Bhachu, P: **F.7**: 22, 61.
Bharat, S: **F.4.2**: 52.
Bhardwaj, S: **G.1**: 13.
Bhargava, G: **F.4.2**: 17. **F.8**: 41, 93.
Bhowmik, K: **B.1.3**: 27.
Bhrolcháin, M: **F.3**: 25.
Bianca, D: **D.9.3**: 1.
Bianchi, S: **F.4.2**: 91.
Biber, D: **D.7**: 48.
Bielli, C: **F.3**: 18.
Bifani, P: **F.5**: 89.
Bigelow, J: **D.3**: 15.
Billig, M: **C.7**: 21.
Billings, R: **C.2**: 24.
Bills, D: **I.5**: 3.
Bilmes, J: **D.7**: 22.
Binder, A: **K.1**: 108.
Bini, P: **I.2**: 31.
Binns, C: **K.1**: 201.
Birnbaum, R: **D.9.5**: 14.
Bishop, D: **K.1**: 161.

Bishop, N: **K.1**: 171.
Bisson, J: **G.1**: 10.
Biswas, P: **F.4.2**: 46.
Biswas, S: **F.1**: 30.
Blacker, F: **H.4**: 21.
Blackley, P: **H.3**: 9.
Blacksell, S: **K.2**: 25.
Blagg, H: **K.1**: 80, 112.
Blaha, J: **E.3**: 17.
Blair, S: **I.3**: 61.
Blair, T: **G.3.2**: 104.
Blanc, A: **F.4.1**: 7.
Blanchet, D: **F.1**: 10. **F.2**: 4.
Blangiardo, G: **F.3**: 45.
Blank, R: **K.4**: 74.
Blankstein, K: **C.2**: 71.
Blau, J: **D.8**: 18.
Blau, P: **F.4.1**: 24.
Blaze-Temple, D: **K.1**: 201.
Blea, I: **F.7**: 52.
Bledsoe, T: **G.3.2**: 79.
Blinkert, B: **K.1**: 110.
Blinn, L: **F.4.2**: 133.
Bloch, M: **F.2**: 73.
Block, E: **G.3.2**: 21.
Block, J: **K.1**: 211.
Bloom, D: **F.4.1**: 7.
Bloor, M: **K.4**: 55.
Blore, I: **G.3.2**: 88.
Blossfeld, H: **I.2**: 8.
Blossfield, H: **I.2**: 27.
Blum, T: **F.4.1**: 24. **I.3**: 61.
Blumberg, H: **C.3**: 12.
Blumenfeld, S: **K.4**: 61.
Blumenfeld, Stewart, N: **K.4**: 87.
Blumstein, A: **K.1**: 178.
Blumstein, P: **C.3**: 34.
Bly, P: **G.3.2**: 134.
Blythe, B: **K.3**: 3.
Bobbitt, S: **D.9.9**: 5.
Bobo, L: **F.7**: 92.

Boden, L: **G.1**: 15.
Boden, M: **C.1**: 5.
Bogard, W: **G.1**: 2.
Bograd, M: **F.4.1**: 19.
Boismenu, G: **J.3**: 12.
Boland, R: **C.5**: 15.
Bolaños, B: **F.5**: 95.
Bolger, N: **C.1**: 23.
Bolin, A: **F.6**: 19.
Bologh, R: **C.5**: 17.
Bonacich, P: **H.4**: 22.
Bond, S: **F.3**: 123.
Bondi, L: **D.9.1**: 2.
Bonfil, R: **E.3**: 10.
Bonitatibus, G: **C.2**: 14.
Bonney, N: **E.2**: 30. **H.3**: 5.
Bookman, A: **F.5**: 104.
Booth, D: **B.1.1**: 35.
Bor, D: **K.4**: 92.
Borg, I: **K.1**: 122.
Borg, M: **D.5**: 33.
Borgatta, E: **A.1**: 13.
Borman, K: **I.4**: 29.
Bornstein, G: **C.3**: 25.
Boruch, R: **B.2**: 2. **F.4.2**: 32.
Borys, B: **H.4**: 3.
Borzeix, A: **I.6**: 25.
Bos, J: **K.4**: 76.
Bose, A: **F.2**: 34.
Bosk, C: **K.1**: 25.
Bosker, R: **E.2**: 62.
Boston, T: **F.7**: 88.
Boswell, T: **I.6**: 5.
Bottomley, G: **F.7**: 63.
Boubekeur, S: **G.1**: 10.
Bouchard, M: **C.2**: 85.
Boucherat, J: **K.1**: 181.
Boudon, R: **D.6**: 5.
Bouhaba, M: **G.1**: 10.
Bouhamama, D: **D.3**: 29.
Boulding, E: **J.8**: 12.

Boulos, R: **K.4**: 22, 56.
Bourdillon, M: **D.5**: 25.
Bovaird, T: **K.3**: 29.
Bowden, R: **B.3**: 22.
Bowers, T: **C.7**: 35.
Bowles, M: **H.4**: 47.
Box, S: **K.1**: 95.
Boyce, A: **F.6**: 17.
Boyce, W: **C.4**: 32.
Boyd, J: **F.2**: 3, 28.
Boyden, J: **I.2**: 11.
Boys, C: **I.4**: 4.
Bozett, F: **F.4.2**: 102.
Bozon, M: **F.4.1**: 10.
Braaten, J: **C.1**: 10.
Brack, La, B: **F.4.2**: 17.
Bradley, M: **J.8**: 1.
Bradshaw, J: **K.3**: 7.
Brady, A: **F.5**: 105.
Brady, M: **K.1**: 43.
Brakel, van, J: **B.1.1**: 22.
Bramley, G: **K.1**: 225.
Brandt, A: **F.3**: 7.
Brannen, J: **B.2**: 7. **F.4.2**: 39.
Brant, L: **F.2**: 46.
Brante, T: **I.5**: 21.
Brasioli, D: **F.8**: 55.
Braun, F: **D.7**: 46.
Brawley, E: **K.3**: 30.
Bray, D: **I.5**: 11.
Braye, S: **K.3**: 18.
Brazzell, J: **F.6**: 20.
Brea, J: **F.8**: 38.
Breakwell, G: **C.2**: 49. **F.2**: 26, 28. **I.4**: 24.
Brechin, S: **C.5**: 4.
Brečka, S: **D.7**: 105.
Brennan, J: **G.1**: 15. **I.2**: 22.
Bresnen, M: **C.6**: 17.
Breton, R: **D.5**: 40. **F.1**: 27. **J.2**: 5.
Breum, M: **F.3**: 89.
Briar, K: **K.3**: 33.

Brierton, T: **I.3**: 37.
Briger, R: **F.4.1**: 48.
Brinkerhoff, M: **F.4.1**: 27.
Brinkman, P: **D.9.5**: 7.
Brinton, M: **F.5**: 41.
Briskin, L: **F.5**: 11.
British Medical Association: **K.4**: 77.
Brito, D: **J.8**: 1.
Broadhurst, R: **K.1**: 59.
Brock, C: **D.9**: 4.
Brock, D: **F.2**: 46.
Brockington, N: **K.1**: 156.
Brockner, J: **I.3**: 42. **I.6**: 37.
Broda, J: **I.3**: 48.
Brodie, R: **D.7**: 99.
Brody, B: **K.4**: 44.
Brody, C: **B.3**: 5.
Brody, G: **F.4.1**: 58.
Bromley, D: **D.5**: 41. **F.2**: 28.
Bronfman, M: **F.3**: 146.
Bronson, D: **K.3**: 3.
Bronstein, P: **F.4.2**: 101.
Brooks, A: **I.3**: 38.
Brooks Gardner, C: **K.1**: 15.
Broomhill, R: **F.5**: 90.
Brotchie, J: **G.3.2**: 134.
Brothun, M: **F.5**: 43.
Broussine, M: **K.4**: 82.
Brower, A: **K.3**: 4.
Brown, C: **I.2**: 52.
Brown, D: **F.4.1**: 16.
Brown, J: **C.2**: 28. **D.6**: 7. **I.6**: 37.
Brown, K: **F.7**: 90.
Brown, L: **F.5**: 1. **F.8**: 38.
Brown, M: **C.3**: 13.
Brown, R: **C.4**: 9. **I.2**: 30.
Brown, S: **C.6**: 9. **F.5**: 101.
Brown, W: **E.2**: 43. **F.4.1**: 45. **K.1**: 140.
Browne, K: **K.1**: 51.
Bruce, J: **G.3.1**: 25. **H.3**: 12.
Bruce, R: **D.7**: 45.

Bruch, C: **D.4**: 1.
Bruegge, von der, E: **K.4**: 87.
Bruegge, vor der, E: **K.4**: 22.
Brumfiel, E: **C.4**: 6.
Brunal, E: **E.3**: 17.
Brunet, F: **E.2**: 44.
Bruszt, L: **A.3**: 3.
Brutsaert, H: **C.2**: 104.
Bryant, C: **K.1**: 24.
Bryant, J: **K.4**: 80.
Brym, R: **F.8**: 97. **K.2**: 39.
Bryman, A: **B.1.3**: 6, 22. **C.6**: 17.
Bryson, L: **G.2**: 6.
Buchbinder, H: **D.9.5**: 25.
Bucher, H: **F.2**: 36.
Buchheit, R: **D.7**: 71.
Buchowski, M: **D.5**: 36.
Buckingham, S: **F.3**: 97.
Buckner, K: **C.2**: 102.
Bude, H: **A.1**: 5.
Budinich, P: **D.6**: 29.
Bühl, W: **E.3**: 8.
Bueno Arus, F: **K.1**: 50.
Buikhuisen, W: **K.1**: 94.
Bukoff, A: **K.1**: 72.
Bulcroft, K: **F.4.2**: 42.
Bullivant, B: **F.7**: 25.
Bumpass, L: **F.4.2**: 81.
Bunčák, J: **D.1.3**: 14.
Bunting, T: **G.3.2**: 106.
Burby, R: **K.1**: 96.
Burger, E: **G.1**: 15.
Burger, J: **C.2**: 88.
Burgess, Y: **I.4**: 23.
Burghart, R: **K.4**: 60.
Burish, T: **C.1**: 11.
Burlingame, V: **F.2**: 53.
Burm, R: **F.8**: 16.
Burnham, M: **K.1**: 16. **K.2**: 53.
Burnkrant, R: **C.7**: 41.
Burnley, I: **K.2**: 15.

Burns, J: **J.4**: 4.
Burns, L: **G.3.2**: 86.
Burt, S: **F.5**: 61.
Burton, J: **E.3**: 32. **F.1**: 20.
Burton, R: **D.5**: 41.
Bury, M: **F.3**: 118. **K.1**: 39.
Busching, B: **D.5**: 41.
Buss, T: **F.7**: 48.
Bussey, K: **K.1**: 49.
Butler, R: **C.5**: 42.
Buttel, F: **E.3**: 16.
Butter, I: **K.4**: 93.
Buttiglione, R: **J.5**: 37.
Buxton, W: **D.6**: 32.
Bynner, J: **B.1.3**: 10.
Bynum, W: **C.1**: 1.
Cain, B: **F.2**: 53.
Caine, B: **F.5**: 3.
Caldwell, J: **F.1**: 13. **F.3**: 2.
Caldwell, P: **F.3**: 2.
Calhoun, C: **H.3**: 2. **J.6**: 24.
Callahan, J: **D.3**: 2.
Callan, E: **D.3**: 14.
Callan, V: **K.1**: 11.
Calnan, M: **K.4**: 38, 43.
Calvanese, F: **F.8**: 54.
Calvet, L: **D.7**: 66.
Calvora, R: **D.6**: 20, 23.
Camacho Guizado, A: **K.1**: 203.
Camara, E: **D.5**: 1.
Cameron, S: **K.1**: 90.
Cammen, H: **G.3.2**: 112.
Campagna, D: **F.6**: 28.
Campbell, D: **D.7**: 31.
Campbell, I: **K.1**: 168.
Campbell, J: **H.4**: 31.
Campbell, L: **F.4.1**: 72.
Campbell, R: **H.4**: 31. **K.1**: 9.
Campbell, T: **D.7**: 31.
Campinos-Dubernet, M: **I.4**: 8.
Canavagh, G: **D.5**: 76.

Cancian, F: **F.4.1**: 4.
Canclini, N: **C.6**: 6. **D.1.1**: 29.
Canel, P: **G.3.2**: 92, 94.
Canlas, M: **K.1**: 228.
Cannings, K: **H.4**: 25.
Cannon, L: **F.5**: 86.
Cansot, M: **F.8**: 70.
Cant, B: **F.6**: 25.
Cantelon, H: **I.7**: 11–12.
Card, C: **C.3**: 23.
Cardenas, G: **F.8**: 68.
Cardozier, V: **D.9.5**: 1.
Carey, M: **C.1**: 11.
Carley, K: **B.3**: 9.
Carlopio, J: **H.4**: 16.
Carlson, C: **F.4.2**: 131.
Carlson, L: **C.1**: 26.
Carlson, R: **C.1**: 26.
Carmeli, Y: **D.8**: 19.
Carmichael, G: **F.4.1**: 63.
Carmichael, L: **D.9.5**: 15.
Carnes, A: **H.4**: 35.
Caron, A: **C.2**: 73.
Caron, R: **C.2**: 73.
Carriere, J: **G.3.2**: 15.
Carroll, B: **D.1.1**: 44.
Carroll, L: **F.6**: 8.
Carroll, S: **B.3**: 13.
Carron, J: **F.3**: 54.
Carter, A: **F.5**: 83.
Carter, I: **G.3.1**: 13.
Carter-Greer, K: **F.4.2**: 32.
Cartwright, A: **K.4**: 18.
Carvalho, J: **E.2**: 20.
Casetti, E: **G.3.2**: 140.
Cashmore, J: **K.1**: 49.
Cassidy, J: **F.4.2**: 89.
Cassim, M: **G.3.2**: 113.
Casswell, S: **I.3**: 14.
Castagnino, D: **F.3**: 54.
Castaño, H: **G.3.2**: 37.

Castell-McGregor, S: **K.1**: 49.
Castilhos Brito, M: **F.5**: 89.
Castles, F: **F.4.1**: 61.
Castor, S: **F.8**: 80.
Castro, G: **A.1**: 31.
Castro-Almeida, C: **F.8**: 70.
Castro, de, M: **K.4**: 26.
Catalano, R: **K.1**: 87.
Catanese, A: **G.3.2**: 121.
Cate, M: **C.3**: 40.
Catherwood, M: **C.4**: 2.
Catton, W: **F.4.1**: 69.
Celentano, D: **I.2**: 54.
Centre National de la Recherche Scientifique: **A.3**: 12.
Cernescu, T: **F.2**: 16.
Chachage, C: **H.2**: 1.
Chaffee, L: **D.7**: 40.
Chakrabarty, D: **I.2**: 52.
Chakraborty J.: **F.3**: 56.
Chalas, Y: **D.1.1**: 39.
Chaliand, G: **F.7**: 40.
Chamberlain, K: **D.5**: 44.
Chan, F: **C.7**: 14.
Chan, T: **C.7**: 14.
Chanana, K: **F.5**: 52.
Chance, M: **C.1**: 36.
Chandani, A: **F.3**: 8.
Chandler, J: **I.7**: 22.
Chandrasekhar, S: **F.8**: 60.
Chang, D: **K.4**: 93.
Chang, K: **F.8**: 85.
Chaplin, W: **C.2**: 102.
Chapman, G: **C.4**: 33.
Charfi, F: **G.3.2**: 15.
Charlton, M: **D.7**: 130.
Charnes, A: **D.9.5**: 23.
Charny, I: **F.7**: 105.
Charvoz, A: **D.9.2**: 5.
Chaudhuri, A: **B.3**: 26.
Chauhan, I: **J.6**: 13.

Chazan, R: **E.3**: 10.
Cheatwood, D: **D.4**: 9.
Checkland, P: **C.3**: 17.
Cheepen, C: **C.3**: 36.
Chekki, D: **F.4.1**: 18. **F.4.2**: 17, 142. **J.8**: 16.
Chelte, A: **I.6**: 46.
Cherkaoui, M: **E.2**: 46.
Cherunilam, F: **F.8**: 30.
Chesney-Lind, M: **K.1**: 143, 159.
Chess, W: **K.3**: 21.
Chester, G: **D.7**: 3.
Chetwynd, J: **D.7**: 99.
Cheung, P: **F.4.1**: 55.
Chevalier, Y: **F.7**: 95.
Chevallier, P: **F.2**: 81.
Chiara, M: **D.6**: 29.
Chiara, Di, G: **K.4**: 71.
Chiarante, G: **D.6**: 29, 34.
Chiba, M: **D.4**: 7.
Chiesa, B: **E.3**: 10.
Chilman, C: **F.4.2**: 62. **K.3**: 8. **K.4**: 7.
Chilton, P: **D.7**: 116.
Chilton, S: **E.3**: 1. **J.6**: 20.
Chiswick, B: **F.8**: 67.
Choinière, R: **F.3**: 61.
Cholvy, G: **D.5**: 79.
Choquet, M: **K.1**: 27.
Chottopadhyay, S: **D.5**: 60.
Chowdhry, D: **F.2**: 21.
Christ, L: **K.1**: 72.
Christensen, K: **I.2**: 60.
Christenson, J: **G.3.1**: 41.
Christian-Smith, L: **F.5**: 2.
Christman, J: **C.2**: 86.
Chung, R: **F.7**: 27.
Chunsuvimol, B: **G.3.1**: 47.
Chusmir, L: **F.5**: 45.
Ciattini, A: **D.3**: 30.
Ciechocinska, M: **G.1**: 17.
Cierpka, M: **F.4.2**: 148.
Cintra, A: **G.3.2**: 131.
Ciotea, F: **C.3**: 4.
Cipriani, F: **I.3**: 4.
Ciroma, J: **K.4**: 75.
Clapp, R: **G.3.1**: 24.
Clare, M: **K.3**: 36.
Clark, C: **D.5**: 58.
Clark, J: **C.5**: 23. **H.4**: 30.
Clark, K: **K.4**: 20.
Clark, M: **C.3**: 27. **C.7**: 28. **F.2**: 55.
Clark, P: **C.5**: 21.
Clark, W: **F.2**: 55. **G.3.2**: 74.
Clarke, C: **F.7**: 9.
Clarridge, B: **K.4**: 81.
Claussen, B: **J.3**: 21. **J.6**: 21.
Clawson, D: **I.6**: 46. **J.5**: 3.
Clayton, D: **J.6**: 26.
Cleary, P: **K.1**: 190.
Clement, W: **E.2**: 6.
Clichevsky, N: **G.3.2**: 133.
Cliff, J: **K.4**: 32.
Clogg, C: **B.3**: 15.
Cloke, P: **G.3.1**: 33.
Close, P: **F.4.2**: 97.
Clum, G: **C.7**: 35.
Clyne, M: **F.7**: 29.
Coalter, F: **I.7**: 5.
Coate, D: **K.1**: 207.
Coates, T: **C.1**: 27.
Cobalti, A: **I.4**: 16.
Coburn, D: **K.4**: 4, 15.
Cochran, J: **E.2**: 9.
Cochrane, R: **F.4.1**: 44.
Code, L: **F.5**: 61.
Coder, J: **K.2**: 28.
Coenen-Huther, J: **F.4.2**: 136.
Cohen, D: **K.4**: 24, 85.
Cohen, E: **I.5**: 13.
Cohen, L: **K.1**: 100.
Cohen, S: **C.3**: 5. **E.3**: 10. **J.8**: 12. **K.1**: 60.
Colbjørnsen, T: **E.2**: 50. **H.3**: 21.

Colclough, G: **G.3.1**: 49.
Coleman, A: **F.2**: 75.
Coleman, J: **C.4**: 7.
Coleman, M: **F.4.2**: 94.
Collins, C: **J.4**: 8.
Collins, J: **C.2**: 6. **F.8**: 79.
Collins, R: **B.1.3**: 15.
Collins, S: **K.3**: 32.
Collinson, D: **K.1**: 9.
Collmann, J: **F.7**: 33.
Colombo, R: **D.9.5**: 2.
Colomy, P: **A.2**: 1.
Colosi, M: **I.3**: 3.
Colton, M: **K.2**: 14. **K.3**: 9.
Coltrane, S: **F.4.2**: 100.
Combs-Orme, T: **K.3**: 13.
Comer, J: **D.9**: 7.
Commins, P: **D.7**: 8.
Conacher, A: **K.2**: 15.
Condor, S: **F.2**: 28–29.
Condran, G: **F.4.1**: 75.
Congdon, P: **E.3**: 3.
Conger, J: **C.6**: 5. **D.1.2**: 6.
Conklin, G: **F.4.1**: 25. **F.4.2**: 17.
Connell, J: **F.8**: 46.
Connidis, I: **F.4.2**: 99.
Conrad, P: **I.3**: 61.
Contreras, A: **D.9.2**: 3.
Conway, J: **I.2**: 34.
Conway, P: **F.2**: 53.
Cook, C: **G.2**: 4.
Cook, K: **A.1**: 13. **E.1**: 4.
Cook, P: **K.1**: 42.
Coole, D: **F.5**: 106.
Coombs, C: **C.3**: 52.
Coombs, R: **F.4.2**: 41.
Cooney, T: **F.4.1**: 65.
Coope, P: **D.7**: 99.
Cooper, C: **I.3**: 12. **I.4**: 21.
Cooper, J: **J.2**: 6.
Cooper, T: **D.7**: 134.

Cooper, W: **D.9.5**: 23.
Coovadia, J: **F.2**: 75.
Copans, J: **D.5**: 87.
Coppens, Y: **D.6**: 24.
Coquery-Vidrovitch, C: **G.3.2**: 150.
Coram, B: **B.3**: 11.
Corbett, G: **D.7**: 53.
Corbett, T: **K.2**: 38.
Corbí, J: **D.6**: 7.
Corby, B: **K.3**: 18.
Corfman, K: **C.7**: 17.
Corkhill, A: **F.7**: 30.
Corless, I: **F.3**: 100.
Cornehls, J: **G.2**: 2.
Corns, C: **J.3**: 17.
Corsaro, W: **C.3**: 11.
Cortés, F: **G.3.1**: 57.
Costa, M: **F.5**: 6.
Costa, P: **C.2**: 99.
Costello, C: **C.2**: 47.
Cotlear, D: **G.3.1**: 54.
Cotterrell, R: **B.1.1**: 16.
Coulloudon, V: **J.6**: 10.
Coulmas, F: **D.7**: 7, 76.
Coulon, C: **D.5**: 82.
Coupland, J: **D.7**: 33.
Coupland, N: **D.7**: 33.
Courcy, R: **D.5**: 79.
Courgeau, D: **F.8**: 18.
Cousens, P: **F.3**: 121.
Cowan, C: **F.4.2**: 101.
Cowan, J: **D.6**: 1.
Cowan, N: **C.2**: 25.
Coward, R: **F.2**: 35.
Cox, F: **F.4.2**: 62. **K.3**: 8. **K.4**: 7.
Cox, P: **K.4**: 82.
Craen, van de, P: **D.7**: 76.
Craig, D: **D.7**: 75.
Craig, G: **J.7**: 4.
Craig, M: **G.1**: 13.
Cramer, D: **C.3**: 42.

Cramer, P: **C.2**: 89.
Crane, D: **I.6**: 19.
Crane, J: **B.2**: 3.
Crawford, J: **C.2**: 61. **F.3**: 121.
Cray, D: **C.5**: 42.
Cready, C: **K.2**: 33.
Creedy, J: **I.4**: 10.
Creighton, S: **K.1**: 56.
Crester, G: **E.2**: 43.
Crimmins, E: **F.2**: 12.
Crimp, D: **F.3**: 98.
Cromie, S: **F.5**: 96.
Crompton, R: **I.4**: 22.
Crooks, P: **F.4.2**: 98.
Cross, J: **K.4**: 69.
Cross, M: **F.7**: 38.
Cross, T: **K.4**: 5.
Crouch, A: **C.5**: 14.
Crouch, C: **I.6**: 28.
Crow, I: **K.1**: 135.
Crow, M: **C.5**: 32.
Cruise O'Brien, D: **D.5**: 82.
Cuéllar, O: **G.3.1**: 57.
Cullen, B: **K.1**: 148.
Cullen, F: **I.3**: 35. **K.1**: 138, 176.
Cummings, S: **G.2**: 2. **G.3.2**: 105.
Cummins, J: **D.9**: 21.
Cunard, J: **D.7**: 45.
Cunha, M: **F.7**: 86.
Curran, D: **K.1**: 150.
Curran, M: **I.2**: 20.
Curtis, D: **J.8**: 11.
Curtis, J: **C.6**: 9. **E.2**: 57.
Cushman, J: **D.1.1**: 4.
Cushman, T: **D.1.3**: 16.
Cushner, K: **F.2**: 19.
Czawartosz, Z: **D.1.3**: 12.
D'Agostino, F: **B.1.3**: 26.
d'Argemir, D: **F.4.2**: 24.
D'Sa, E: **F.1**: 20.
D'Souza, S: **F.3**: 144.

Dagum, E: **K.1**: 113.
Dahlgren, P: **D.7**: 149.
Dahlström, E: **A.3**: 7.
Dahme, H: **B.1.1**: 20.
Dahya, B: **F.8**: 96.
Dalal, A: **D.5**: 47.
Dalal, F: **F.7**: 114.
Dale, A: **B.3**: 6. **I.2**: 36.
Dale Wright, N: **D.3**: 21.
Dalto, G: **I.3**: 16.
Daly, M: **G.3.2**: 2.
Damachi, U: **I.5**: 6.
Dance, K: **C.1**: 2.
Daniels, R: **F.7**: 7.
Dann, G: **F.8**: 87.
Danser, D: **D.5**: 58.
Dant, T: **F.2**: 39.
Daoyi, Z: **D.6**: 8, 24.
Darmaputera, E: **D.1.1**: 35.
Darnell, A: **D.5**: 42.
Daro, D: **F.4.2**: 67.
Dasgupta, A: **H.3**: 11.
Dasgupta, B: **G.3.1**: 50.
Datan, N: **K.4**: 3.
David, M: **H.3**: 1.
Davidson, N: **F.5**: 7.
Davies, C: **K.1**: 51.
Davies, F: **K.4**: 82.
Davies, H: **H.7**: 3.
Davies, P: **F.3**: 101.
Davis, A: **D.7**: 97.
Davis, D: **F.3**: 140.
Davis, G: **F.4.1**: 23. **K.1**: 181.
Davis, J: **F.7**: 15.
Davis, K: **F.7**: 116. **I.3**: 61.
Davis, M: **K.1**: 134.
Davis, N: **E.2**: 11. **E.3**: 10. **K.1**: 3.
Davis, P: **E.2**: 12, 16.
Davis, R: **D.3**: 13.
Davis, W: **C.2**: 60, 66.
Dawes, R: **C.7**: 4.

Dawson, K: **K.4**: 42.
Day, R: **C.1**: 28.
Debert, G: **J.2**: 10.
DeFreitas, G: **F.8**: 65.
Dekker, P: **G.3.2**: 84. **J.6**: 2.
Delaney, J: **I.6**: 37, 39, 41.
DeLey, W: **F.4.2**: 73.
Delpirou, A: **K.1**: 38.
Demirović, A: **A.1**: 37.
Demo, D: **F.4.2**: 79.
DeMore, S: **K.1**: 92.
Demos, V: **D.7**: 71.
Dempsey, K: **F.4.2**: 11.
Denhardt, K: **J.4**: 3.
Denis, M: **D.7**: 7.
Denis, W: **I.3**: 8.
Dennis, C: **I.2**: 52.
Dennis, M: **F.4.2**: 32.
Denton, N: **G.3.2**: 51, 68.
DePaul, M: **D.3**: 24.
Derricourt, N: **K.1**: 112.
Desai, A: **K.4**: 60.
Desplanques, G: **F.3**: 53.
Dessens, J: **I.2**: 58.
Detlefsen, M: **D.6**: 7.
Deutsch, S: **I.3**: 60.
Devereux, J: **C.2**: 49. **I.4**: 24.
Devine, J: **K.1**: 111.
DeViney, S: **I.3**: 17.
Dewe, P: **I.6**: 45.
Dex, S: **I.3**: 53.
Dhanagare, D: **G.3.1**: 14.
Dhaouadi, M: **E.3**: 22.
Dhombres, J: **D.6**: 20.
Dhruvarajan, V: **D.5**: 46. **F.4.2**: 17, 114.
Diallo, A: **F.3**: 119.
Diamant, L: **F.6**: 22.
Diamond, M: **C.5**: 25.
Diawara I.: **D.1.2**: 3.
Díaz-Salazar, R: **D.5**: 4.
Dickens, L: **I.5**: 4.

Dickens, P: **E.2**: 65.
Dickey, J: **D.7**: 3.
Diedrick, P: **F.4.2**: 20.
Diehl, M: **C.7**: 37.
Diekmann, A: **I.3**: 50.
DiGaetano, A: **G.3.2**: 53.
Diggory, P: **F.3**: 72.
Dighe, A: **D.7**: 29. **G.3.1**: 19.
Dijk, T: **D.7**: 114–115.
Dijk, van, J: **B.2**: 1.
Дилигенский, : **C.1**: 22.
Dimakopoulos, K: **F.8**: 104.
Dinesh, B: **F.2**: 72.
Dingwall, R: **F.4.2**: 77.
DiPrete, T: **I.4**: 9.
Director, M: **D.7**: 45.
Disla, C: **D.7**: 78.
Dittmar, N: **D.7**: 77.
Djalili, M: **J.6**: 28.
Dodge, K: **C.3**: 13.
Doherty, P: **G.3.2**: 63.
Doig, J: **D.9.4**: 1.
Doise, W: **C.3**: 24.
Dolinski, D: **C.2**: 40.
Domanski, H: **I.2**: 28.
Dometrius, N: **D.9.9**: 1.
Dominelli, L: **F.5**: 12.
Donaldson, P: **D.5**: 62.
Donnan, H: **F.4.1**: 43.
Donohew, L: **C.3**: 3.
Doornen, van, L: **K.4**: 88.
Döpke, S: **F.7**: 29.
Dorais, L: **F.7**: 17.
Doray, B: **H.4**: 14.
Dore, M: **B.1.3**: 31. **K.2**: 41.
Dornbuch, S: **F.4.2**: 134.
Dorney, L: **F.5**: 61.
Douben, N: **K.2**: 51.
Douglas, R: **K.2**: 47.
Douglas, W: **J.2**: 1.
Douglass, M: **G.3.2**: 73.

Dow, J: **D.7**: 71.
Dowd, J: **F.2**: 3, 28.
Dowding, M: **K.1**: 148.
Downes, C: **K.3**: 10.
Downes, D: **K.1**: 105.
Downing, J: **D.7**: 83, 140.
Doyle, M: **F.3**: 132.
Doyle, P: **K.2**: 37.
Dragadze, T: **G.3.1**: 30.
Dragomirescu, D: **I.4**: 17.
Dreachslin, J: **K.4**: 8.
Dressler, W: **F.7**: 111.
Drew, P: **D.1.3**: 6. **D.7**: 54. **K.1**: 15.
Drewes-Nielsen, L: **I.2**: 50.
Dreyer, L: **E.2**: 47.
Dreyfus, H: **D.6**: 1.
Dreyfus, S: **D.6**: 1.
Driel, van, B: **D.7**: 120.
Driver, A: **F.4.2**: 17.
Driver, E: **F.4.2**: 17.
Driver, F: **G.1**: 12.
Drobizheva, L: **D.1.1**: 9.
Drulhe, M: **K.1**: 212.
Drummond, P: **D.7**: 136.
Dubey, K: **G.3.2**: 77.
Dubey, S: **K.3**: 26.
Dubinskas, F: **H.4**: 23.
DuBois, B: **I.2**: 34.
Dubresson, A: **G.3.2**: 18, 92.
Dubuisson, W: **F.8**: 72.
Ducastelle, C: **F.8**: 88.
Duclos, L: **A.3**: 11.
Dülen, van, R: **D.3**: 35.
Duffecy, J: **K.1**: 59.
Duffy, J: **K.1**: 41.
Dufourcq, E: **D.5**: 63.
Dugger, K: **F.5**: 51.
Duncan, G: **K.1**: 229. **K.2**: 55.
Duncan, I: **J.5**: 19.
Duncan, O: **B.3**: 5.
Duncan, W: **F.4.1**: 68.

Dunham, R: **G.2**: 12.
Dunkel, W: **C.2**: 82.
Dunkle, R: **F.2**: 53.
Dunn, C: **K.1**: 170.
Dunning, E: **K.1**: 124.
Dunstan, G: **D.3**: 33.
Durham, D: **H.5**: 3.
Duru, M: **D.9.5**: 6.
Dutta, R: **D.1.3**: 10.
Dworkin, J: **I.6**: 37.
Dwyer, D: **H.3**: 12. **I.3**: 36.
Dyring, A: **D.6**: 19, 24.
Eadie, D: **K.1**: 37.
Eagle, E: **D.9.8**: 1.
Eagles, M: **J.6**: 4.
Earickson, R: **G.1**: 13.
Earl, P: **H.1**: 4.
Easterlin, R: **F.2**: 12. **F.3**: 51.
Echabe, A: **J.6**: 37.
Eckert, P: **E.2**: 1.
Edelman, G: **D.6**: 1.
Edelstein, M: **G.1**: 3.
Edmonston, B: **F.4.2**: 123.
Edwards, A: **D.1.2**: 9. **G.2**: 6.
Edwards, C: **D.1.3**: 2.
Edwards, D: **H.7**: 3.
Edwards, J: **K.2**: 31.
Edwards, L: **I.2**: 17.
Edwards P.K.: **I.6**: 44.
Eekelaar, J: **F.4.2**: 77.
Eells, L: **F.4.1**: 8.
Efrat, E: **J.6**: 11.
Egerton, M: **C.2**: 76.
Eggebeen, D: **I.2**: 13.
Ehara, T: **D.9.9**: 3.
Ehara, Y: **D.7**: 143. **F.5**: 9.
Ehizulen, A: **I.3**: 29.
Ehrenberg, A: **D.7**: 135.
Einsiedel, E: **D.7**: 87.
Eisenberg, N: **C.3**: 38.
Eisenstein, Z: **F.5**: 66.

Eiser, C: **D.9.3**: 9.
Eiser, J: **C.7**: 27. **D.9.3**: 9.
Ekehammar, B: **E.2**: 59.
Ekland-Olson, S: **K.1**: 185.
El-Attar, S: **F.1**: 21.
El-Din, H: **G.3.2**: 95.
Elchardus, M: **B.1.3**: 23.
Elder, J: **K.4**: 90.
Elford, J: **F.3**: 151.
Ellickson, P: **D.9.3**: 1.
Elliot, B: **F.7**: 36.
Ellis, F: **G.3.1**: 63.
Ellsworth, E: **F.5**: 2.
Ellwood, D: **K.2**: 35.
Elms, A: **C.1**: 26.
Elshtain, J: **F.5**: 101.
Elson, D: **F.5**: 37. **I.2**: 64.
Ember, C: **D.1.3**: 2.
Emery, R: **C.2**: 32.
Emler, N: **C.3**: 37.
Emmert, M: **C.5**: 32.
Endo, K: **G.3.1**: 20.
Engel, U: **E.2**: 68.
Engelhardt, R: **F.1**: 4. **F.3**: 15.
Engineer, A: **F.5**: 92.
Ennaji, M: **D.7**: 7, 62.
Enninger, W: **D.7**: 71.
Enomoto, K: **K.2**: 43.
Ensminger, M: **I.2**: 54.
Entzinger, H: **F.7**: 38.
Ephross, P: **C.4**: 10.
Eplan, L: **G.3.2**: 121.
Erbslöh, B: **E.2**: 39.
Erfle, S: **J.6**: 4.
Espenshade, T: **H.3**: 2.
Esquivel Vilchis, G: **F.5**: 89.
Estabrooks, M: **H.4**: 33.
Ester, P: **G.3.2**: 84. **J.6**: 2.
Estes, R: **E.3**: 29. **H.6**: 2.
Etienne, B: **F.8**: 69.
Etienne, G: **K.1**: 222.

Ettema, J: **D.7**: 113.
Evangelista, I: **D.7**: 78.
Evans, D: **K.1**: 102.
Evans, G: **G.3.1**: 2.
Evans, R: **F.7**: 12. **K.4**: 91.
Evans, T: **D.9.3**: 3.
Everitt, J: **F.5**: 46.
Evers, G: **I.2**: 48.
Everson, S: **C.2**: 21.
Evetts, J: **F.4.2**: 34.
Ewen, S: **D.1.1**: 1.
Eysenck, S: **F.2**: 77.
Factor, R: **A.5**: 2.
Fagan, J: **A.2**: 1. **K.1**: 128.
Faison, R: **F.5**: 50.
Fallick, A: **K.1**: 224.
Fandel, G: **K.4**: 46.
Fandrem, J: **H.5**: 3.
Fantasia, R: **I.6**: 46.
Farber, B: **A.5**: 3. **D.9**: 25.
Fargues, P: **F.3**: 52.
Farkus, G: **I.2**: 57.
Farley, R: **F.7**: 3.
Farr, M: **F.3**: 23.
Farrell, D: **B.1.1**: 30.
Fassio, F: **A.1**: 2.
Faucher, A: **A.1**: 7.
Feagin, J: **G.3.2**: 41.
Feagin, S: **C.2**: 70.
Feather, N: **D.3**: 12.
Fee, E: **F.3**: 102.
Feingold, A: **C.3**: 29.
Feldman, S: **C.5**: 37. **I.6**: 37. **K.1**: 237.
Feng, L: **I.2**: 71.
Fennell, M: **K.1**: 17.
Fenner, F: **F.3**: 119.
Fenton, S: **F.7**: 104.
Ferber, von, C: **I.3**: 45.
Fernandes, R: **D.5**: 74.
Fernandez, R: **D.9.2**: 3. **I.2**: 67.
Fernando, S: **C.1**: 30.

Ferrand, M: **F.3**: 38.
Ferrarotti, F: **D.7**: 93.
Feshbach, N: **C.2**: 62.
Feshbach, S: **J.8**: 6.
Festy, P: **F.4.1**: 66.
Feyerabend, P: **D.6**: 15.
Feyisetan, B: **F.3**: 62.
Fiala, R: **K.1**: 84.
Field, M: **F.4.2**: 57. **I.5**: 14.
Fielding, N: **B.1.3**: 1. **I.4**: 12.
Fielding, T: **E.2**: 65.
Fife-Schaw, C: **C.2**: 49. **F.2**: 26, 28. **I.4**: 24.
Figueroa, O: **G.3.2**: 133.
Filion, P: **G.3.2**: 106.
Filoramo, G: **D.5**: 49.
Filsinger, E: **F.4.1**: 1.
Finau, S: **K.4**: 2.
Finch, W: **F.4.1**: 21.
Fincham, F: **C.2**: 32.
Findlay, A: **F.8**: 61, 94.
Fine, B: **H.6**: 1.
Fine, G: **F.2**: 79.
Fine, M: **F.3**: 11, 106. **F.5**: 107.
Finestein, I: **F.7**: 28.
Finholt, T: **F.3**: 122.
Finlay, B: **F.4.1**: 71.
Finlay, W: **I.6**: 2.
Finnäs, F: **F.4.1**: 11.
Finnegan, D: **K.2**: 19.
Finnegan, R: **D.7**: 26.
Finocchiaro, E: **G.3.2**: 5.
Finquelievich, S: **G.3.2**: 69.
Fiorito, J: **I.6**: 32.
Firebaugh, G: **F.7**: 116.
Firouzbakhch, H: **J.6**: 28.
Fischer, A: **F.7**: 82.
Fischer, S: **D.5**: 19.
Fisher, B: **F.5**: 53.
Fisher, D: **C.2**: 90.
Fisher, J: **K.1**: 92. **K.4**: 8.
Fisher, S: **F.3**: 133.

Fishman, J: **D.7**: 7–8, 71, 75–76. **F.7**: 29.
Fiske, D: **C.2**: 91.
Flaitz, J: **D.7**: 58.
Flap, H: **I.2**: 45.
Fletcher, R: **F.4.2**: 1, 50.
Flett, G: **C.2**: 71.
Flewelling, R: **K.1**: 129.
Fligstein, N: **I.2**: 67.
Flinchbaugh, L: **K.1**: 190.
Flitcraft, A: **K.1**: 58.
Florey, F: **F.3**: 26.
Florian, A: **G.3.1**: 68.
Flory, T: **H.3**: 1. **K.2**: 28.
Flowers, R: **F.7**: 39.
Floyd, F: **C.3**: 7.
Flum, H: **K.4**: 88.
Flynn, A: **F.3**: 39.
Foddy, M: **C.2**: 52.
Foege, W: **F.3**: 7.
Foley, D: **F.2**: 46.
Folger, R: **B.1.3**: 5.
Folkman, S: **C.2**: 84. **K.4**: 88.
Fonkert, D: **K.4**: 55.
Fonn, S: **K.4**: 32.
Fonseca, C: **G.3.1**: 7.
Foot, D: **F.2**: 57.
Forbes, J: **F.7**: 72.
Ford, R: **E.2**: 3.
Forehand, R: **F.4.1**: 58.
Foreman, M: **F.3**: 103.
Forgas, J: **C.1**: 32.
Forjaz, M: **I.7**: 10.
Forlani, F: **C.5**: 31.
Forrest, J: **E.2**: 56. **J.6**: 32. **K.2**: 15.
Foschi, M: **E.2**: 67.
Fossen, von, A: **J.5**: 12.
Fossett, M: **F.7**: 18.
Foster, L: **F.7**: 50.
Foster, M: **J.8**: 13.
Fournier, G: **F.8**: 9–10.
Fox, D: **F.3**: 102.

Fox, J: **F.3**: 110.
Fox, K: **F.3**: 46.
Frackiewicz, L: **K.1**: 239.
Francia, di, G: **D.6**: 9, 29.
Franco, R: **K.2**: 29.
Franco, V: **D.3**: 34.
Frank, G: **F.3**: 11.
Frank, R: **C.2**: 77.
Frankena, W: **D.3**: 7.
Franklin, M: **G.3.1**: 26.
Franklin, R: **E.2**: 35.
Frantzioch, M: **F.8**: 77.
Franz, C: **C.1**: 26.
Fraser, A: **K.1**: 5.
Fraser, M: **K.1**: 33.
Frazier, C: **K.1**: 161.
Frederico, M: **K.3**: 16.
Freedman, S: **C.5**: 45.
Freeman, I: **K.2**: 10.
Freeman, J: **I.6**: 10.
Freeman, R: **F.6**: 31.
Freiberger, W: **F.2**: 46.
Freidenberg, J: **F.8**: 21.
Frémont, A: **G.1**: 8.
Frey, W: **G.3.2**: 151.
Fried, A: **F.3**: 16.
Fried, Y: **C.5**: 19.
Friedberg, A: **F.8**: 76.
Friedman, A: **I.3**: 55.
Friedman, D: **B.1.3**: 4.
Friedrichs, J: **G.3.2**: 66. **K.1**: 213.
Frisch, D: **B.3**: 27.
Frith, S: **D.8**: 12.
Frost, R: **D.7**: 97.
Fry, V: **K.1**: 196.
Fryer, D: **F.4.2**: 61.
Fuchs, M: **D.1.1**: 18.
Fuchs, R: **G.3.2**: 35.
Fuchs, S: **D.1.2**: 11.
Fuchs, V: **F.5**: 108.
Fuente Alcantara, F: **D.5**: 61.

Fuentes, P: **G.3.2**: 35.
Fuenzalida, V: **D.7**: 139.
Fuerst, A: **K.1**: 72.
Fujimura, M: **K.2**: 21.
Fukami, C: **I.6**: 32.
Fukutake, T: **K.2**: 1.
Fulcher, J: **I.6**: 24.
Fuld, K: **J.8**: 20.
Fuller, S: **D.6**: 30.
Funnell, D: **G.3**: 6.
Furger, F: **A.1**: 6.
Furnham, A: **C.1**: 18. **F.7**: 112. **K.4**: 6.
Furtună, C: **D.1.3**: 11.
Furuta, T: **H.4**: 37.
Fustier, B: **K.1**: 186.
Fyfe, G: **D.8**: 14.
Fyfe, J: **I.3**: 27.
Gaag, J: **K.1**: 215.
Gabe, J: **K.1**: 39.
Gabriel, Y: **I.5**: 28.
Gadant, M: **F.5**: 70, 78. **I.6**: 14.
Gaes, G: **K.1**: 142.
Gaffary, F: **D.7**: 146. **J.6**: 28.
Gagnon, M: **C.2**: 85.
Gagnon, R: **D.9.5**: 9.
Gair, W: **D.7**: 122.
Gaitley, R: **K.3**: 12.
Galaway, B: **K.1**: 77.
Gale, D: **G.3.2**: 83.
Gale, F: **K.1**: 145.
Galea, R: **F.3**: 93.
Galen, van, J: **D.9.2**: 5.
Galilea, S: **G.3.2**: 133.
Gallagher, A: **C.7**: 36.
Gallagher, D: **I.6**: 32.
Gallagher, E: **K.4**: 54.
Galland, O: **D.9.3**: 10.
Gallego, V: **F.3**: 114.
Gallhofer, I: **C.1**: 38.
Gallie, D: **I.1**: 2.
Galloway, J: **D.6**: 18.

Galster, G: **F.7**: 113. **G.3.2**: 50.
Galván Díaz, F: **F.3**: 126.
Gama, De, K: **J.3**: 16.
Gambetta, D: **K.1**: 99.
Gambles, D: **C.7**: 7.
Gane, M: **B.1.3**: 19.
Gangrade, K: **F.2**: 34.
Ganguli, H: **F.6**: 5.
Ganguly, I: **G.2**: 16.
Gânju, M: **F.2**: 16.
Ganong, L: **F.4.2**: 94.
Garand, J: **C.6**: 21.
Garate, J: **J.6**: 37.
Garber, S: **I.3**: 1.
Garcia, D: **A.5**: 7.
Garcia, E: **D.9.2**: 3.
García, O: **D.7**: 78.
García Ferrer, A: **F.1**: 2.
García y Griego, M: **F.8**: 78.
Gareau, F: **A.1**: 3, 20.
Garelli, F: **D.5**: 15, 49.
Garen, J: **H.3**: 27.
Garfinkel, I: **K.2**: 38.
Garibaldo, F: **C.5**: 31.
Garland, D: **K.1**: 105.
Garner, M: **F.7**: 29.
Garrido, D: **J.7**: 1.
Garrier, G: **G.3.1**: 58.
Garza Toledo, de la, E: **E.2**: 25.
Gaspersz, J: **I.2**: 48.
Gaul, R: **C.2**: 89.
Gault, U: **C.2**: 61.
Gaur, K: **K.1**: 218.
Gawryszewski, A: **G.3.1**: 27.
Gay, G: **D.9.2**: 3.
Gaye, M: **G.3.2**: 147.
Gazzola, A: **G.3.2**: 82.
Gecas, V: **F.4.2**: 147.
Geißler, R: **K.1**: 164.
Gelles, R: **F.4.2**: 74.
Gellner, E: **J.1**: 3.

Gelsthorpe, L: **F.5**: 8. **K.1**: 105.
George, M: **K.1**: 5.
Gerbner, G: **D.7**: 147–148.
Gerhards, J: **C.2**: 65.
Gerholm, T: **D.5**: 89.
Gerosa, E: **F.2**: 58.
Gerstein, D: **C.1**: 4.
Gerstein, L: **I.3**: 2.
Gerstel, N: **F.4.1**: 67.
Gersten, J: **C.5**: 17.
Gessa, G: **K.4**: 71.
Geuns, van, R: **I.2**: 48.
Geurts, J: **B.1.1**: 22.
Geus, de, E: **K.4**: 88.
Gey, S: **D.7**: 84.
Geyer, H: **G.3.2**: 148.
Ghetău, V: **F.3**: 60.
Ghodse, A: **K.1**: 88.
Gibbons, D: **A.2**: 1. **K.1**: 174, 188.
Gibbons, J: **F.7**: 29.
Gibbs, I: **K.3**: 7.
Gibson, J: **F.5**: 44.
Gibson, M: **F.7**: 61.
Giesbers, H: **D.7**: 76.
Gijsels, H: **F.7**: 96.
Gilbert, R: **C.1**: 9.
Gildemeister, R: **D.1.3**: 9.
Giles, H: **F.2**: 28–29.
Gillis, A: **F.5**: 16.
Gillis-Knox, J: **F.4.1**: 41.
Gillmor, D: **G.3.1**: 16.
Gillmore, M: **E.1**: 4.
Gilman, S: **D.8**: 5. **F.3**: 7.
Gilmore, L: **I.3**: 14.
Gilmour, A: **K.1**: 55.
Gilpin, R: **J.8**: 15.
Gingold, L: **F.5**: 89.
Gingras, Y: **D.9.5**: 9.
Ginsberg, R: **D.9.4**: 1.
Girard, C: **G.3.2**: 92, 94.
Giriappa, S: **G.3.1**: 73.

Gismondi, M: **D.5**: 6.
Gittelsohn, A: **F.3**: 140.
Glass, R: **G.3.2**: 8.
Glasser, T: **D.7**: 113.
Glazer, N: **K.4**: 58.
Gledhill, J: **J.3**: 25.
Gleizal, J: **J.3**: 12.
Glenn, C: **C.5**: 6.
Glenn, N: **F.4.1**: 5.
Glewwe, P: **K.1**: 215.
Glezer, H: **I.3**: 28.
Gliasáin, M: **D.7**: 8.
Glick, P: **I.2**: 56.
Glytsos, N: **F.8**: 91.
Gnaneshwar, V: **G.3.2**: 75.
Godara, R: **G.3.1**: 28.
Godbey, G: **I.7**: 4.
Godbout, M: **J.6**: 15.
Godoy Arteaga, C: **K.4**: 83.
Godwin, D: **F.4.2**: 124.
Goetz, A: **F.5**: 101. **F.8**: 38.
Gogan, H: **K.2**: 28.
Gohn, M: **G.3.2**: 93.
Gokturk, S: **C.5**: 38.
Golata, E: **F.3**: 73.
Gold, S: **F.8**: 89.
Goldberg, W: **F.4.2**: 145.
Golding, G: **D.3**: 32.
Golding, P: **G.3.2**: 42.
Goldman, A: **D.3**: 5.
Goldstein, M: **C.1**: 12.
Golomb, L: **K.4**: 60.
Gómez de León C., J: **F.3**: 146.
Gómez Sánchez, L: **B.1.1**: 7.
González, H: **D.7**: 109.
González, M: **F.5**: 95.
González, O: **G.3.2**: 133.
González Arévalo, A: **F.5**: 89.
Gonzalez-del-Valle, A: **K.4**: 78.
Goodale, T: **I.7**: 4.
Goodfellow, M: **B.2**: 6.
Goodfriend, A: **D.7**: 123.
Goodin, R: **B.3**: 21.
Goodman, M: **D.3**: 39. **G.3.2**: 10.
Goodman, P: **I.3**: 1.
Goodnow, J: **F.2**: 70.
Goodsell, C: **G.3.2**: 62.
Gopnik, A: **C.2**: 9.
Gordon, L: **K.1**: 53.
Gordon, M: **A.1**: 27. **K.1**: 56.
Gordon, P: **F.7**: 11.
Gordon, R: **I.3**: 13.
Gordon, S: **F.4.1**: 4.
Gore, M: **K.3**: 17.
Gorlach, K: **J.5**: 30.
Gorsuch, R: **D.5**: 34.
Gosetti, G: **H.4**: 46.
Gotlib, I: **C.2**: 45.
Gotō, N: **G.3.2**: 71.
Gottdiener, M: **G.3.2**: 41.
Gottlieb, B: **K.3**: 19.
Gottschalk, S: **K.3**: 2.
Götz, H: **I.5**: 10.
Gould, H: **E.2**: 4.
Gould, S: **C.7**: 31.
Gould, W: **F.8**: 62, 94.
Graad, de, N: **F.2**: 14.
Graaf, De, N: **F.4.2**: 16.
Graaf, de, P: **D.9.3**: 7. **F.2**: 14. **F.4.2**: 16.
Grad, S: **K.2**: 37.
Grady, W: **F.3**: 26.
Graen, G: **I.5**: 7.
Graen, M: **I.5**: 7.
Graetz, B: **I.5**: 25.
Grafton-Wasserman, D: **F.3**: 34.
Graham, G: **B.1.1**: 6. **F.5**: 24. **I.6**: 46.
Grainger, K: **D.7**: 33.
Grămadă, C: **D.1.3**: 11.
Grando, J: **I.4**: 8.
Grannemann, B: **C.2**: 100.
Graumann, C: **C.1**: 24.
Gravelin, B: **G.3.2**: 138.

Graversen, G: **I.6**: 23.
Graves, L: **I.2**: 26.
Gray, H: **K.4**: 75.
Greatbatch, D: **D.7**: 141.
Greely, A: **D.5**: 26.
Green, A: **K.4**: 80.
Green, E: **F.3**: 24.
Green, F: **I.6**: 42.
Green, R: **F.4.2**: 98.
Green, S: **E.2**: 36.
Greenbaum, A: **D.5**: 59.
Greenberg, B: **D.7**: 88.
Greenberg, J: **B.1.3**: 5. **C.3**: 9.
Greenberg, M: **G.1**: 13.
Greene, J: **J.3**: 4.
Greene, M: **F.2**: 46.
Greene, R: **H.3**: 15.
Greenfeld, L: **A.1**: 36.
Greenfield, P: **D.7**: 125.
Greenhalgh, S: **F.3**: 63.
Greenwood, J: **C.1**: 21.
Gregory, P: **F.6**: 11.
Greif, G: **F.4.2**: 38.
Greil, A: **F.3**: 69.
Grevengoed, N: **D.5**: 38.
Griffeth, R: **F.5**: 47.
Griffin, G: **I.6**: 15.
Griffin, J: **K.1**: 148.
Grimmer, P: **E.1**: 9.
Groce, N: **F.3**: 11.
Grodos, D: **K.4**: 80.
Grofman, B: **J.6**: 9.
Gromski, W: **C.2**: 40.
Gronau, R: **H.3**: 20.
Gronow, J: **D.1.1**: 14.
Groot, L: **F.3**: 85.
Gros, C: **G.3.1**: 23.
Grossman, M: **K.1**: 207.
Grosz, E: **F.5**: 3.
Grotevant, H: **F.4.2**: 131.

Group for the Advancement of Psychiatry: **J.2**: 13.
Gruen, R: **C.2**: 84.
Grünbaum, A: **C.1**: 34.
Grünewald, W: **F.3**: 67.
Gruneau, R: **J.6**: 23.
Grusky, D: **I.4**: 3.
Gubrium, J: **F.3**: 108. **F.4.2**: 130.
Gudykunst, W: **D.7**: 59.
Guest, D: **I.6**: 45.
Gueullette, A: **E.3**: 17.
Gugler, J: **G.3.2**: 156.
Guillauma, Y: **D.7**: 119.
Guillaume, S: **D.1.1**: 36.
Guillon, M: **F.8**: 103.
Guilmot, P: **K.1**: 98.
Guimarães, R: **K.2**: 13.
Gullestad, M: **F.2**: 67.
Gunner, E: **D.1.1**: 8.
Gunsteren, van, H: **G.1**: 1.
Gupta, A: **F.8**: 42.
Gupta, D: **F.3**: 109.
Gupta, R: **I.2**: 65.
Gupta, S: **D.1.1**: 31.
Guralnik, J: **F.1**: 25.
Gurevitch, Z: **C.3**: 31.
Guseinov, O: **D.3**: 18.
Gustafson, S: **C.2**: 17.
Gustavsen, B: **I.3**: 11.
Gustman, A: **I.2**: 32.
Gutiérrez, G: **D.5**: 56.
Gutkind, P: **I.2**: 52. **I.5**: 24.
Gutman, H: **D.1.3**: 20.
Gutton, J: **F.2**: 54.
Guy, J: **D.1.1**: 8.
Gwartney-Gibbs, P: **I.2**: 44.
Haag, G: **F.2**: 36.
Haag, M: **J.8**: 1.
Haaken, J: **C.1**: 13.
Haas, M: **D.9.3**: 11.
Habaieb, El, A: **G.3.2**: 15.
Haberfeld, Y: **I.2**: 43.

Habermas, J: **D.1.1**: 25.
Hachen, D: **B.3**: 2. **I.2**: 24.
Hackett, D: **D.5**: 54.
Hada, S: **F.8**: 13.
Hadden, J: **D.5**: 32.
Haeberle, S: **G.2**: 13.
Haffner, S: **F.7**: 2.
Hagan, J: **F.5**: 16. **K.1**: 132.
Hage, J: **B.1.1**: 27.
Hagelstange, T: **E.2**: 39.
Hagen, A: **D.7**: 76.
Hagen, E: **I.2**: 19.
Hagenaars, J: **B.3**: 10.
Hagestad, G: **F.4.2**: 20.
Hahn, H: **F.3**: 11.
Hahn, J: **J.6**: 35.
Haile, A: **F.4.1**: 12.
Haimes, E: **F.4.2**: 49.
Haindl, E: **F.2**: 36, 52.
Haines, T: **I.3**: 59.
Halaby, C: **I.2**: 3.
Halamska, M: **J.5**: 22.
Hale, C: **K.1**: 95.
Hall, A: **H.3**: 4.
Hall, E: **I.2**: 12.
Hall, G: **G.1**: 13.
Hall, J: **C.4**: 30. **D.5**: 41.
Hall, P: **G.3.2**: 108. **I.2**: 21.
Hallebone, E: **C.3**: 53.
Halliday, F: **F.5**: 101.
Hallinan, M: **D.9**: 13.
Hallpike, C: **E.3**: 23.
Halperin, R: **H.1**: 2.
Halverson, C: **C.2**: 50.
Hamaguchi, H: **A.1**: 29.
Hamel, R: **D.7**: 74.
Hamilton, C: **K.4**: 22, 87.
Hamilton, S: **J.8**: 8.
Hamilton, V: **D.4**: 13.
Hammarström, A: **I.2**: 70.
Hammer, M: **C.3**: 46.

Hammond, E: **I.6**: 8.
Hammond, P: **D.5**: 37.
Hamnett, C: **G.3.2**: 85.
Hamowy, R: **K.1**: 200.
Hamzaoui, S: **I.6**: 34.
Hankiss, E: **A.3**: 3.
Hannan, M: **C.5**: 27. **I.6**: 10.
Hansel, B: **F.2**: 19.
Hansen, C: **B.1.1**: 3.
Hansen, N: **F.8**: 68.
Hanson, S: **E.2**: 29. **G.3.2**: 47.
Hansot, E: **D.9.3**: 4.
Hansson, R: **F.4.1**: 2.
Hara, J: **B.3**: 23.
Harada, T: **J.4**: 6.
Harcum, E: **C.1**: 7.
Hardert, R: **D.9**: 25.
Hardesty, S: **H.3**: 7.
Harding, C: **K.1**: 182.
Hare, P: **C.3**: 12.
Harel, Z: **F.2**: 53.
Hareven, T: **F.2**: 18.
Hargrove, B: **D.5**: 41.
Harper, D: **H.4**: 40.
Harper, M: **G.3.1**: 29.
Harpham, T: **K.4**: 39.
Harpine, C: **K.2**: 28.
Harrell-Bond, B: **F.8**: 43.
Harries, K: **K.1**: 121.
Harrington, M: **D.9.5**: 26.
Harris, F: **F.7**: 87.
Harris, J: **D.7**: 8. **K.4**: 9.
Harris, L: **K.1**: 143.
Harris, M: **K.1**: 17.
Harris, N: **K.2**: 49.
Harris, P: **C.3**: 15. **K.1**: 165.
Harris, R: **I.6**: 36.
Harris, S: **D.6**: 24.
Harris, Z: **A.5**: 7.
Harrison, F: **H.2**: 4.
Harrison, G: **K.1**: 220.

Harrison, M: **F.4.2**: 76.
Harrison, R: **I.2**: 38. **I.4**: 6.
Hart, G: **F.3**: 101.
Hart, J: **C.2**: 100. **H.3**: 28.
Hart, P: **I.2**: 72.
Hartman, S: **F.5**: 47.
Hartmann, M: **E.2**: 40.
Hartmann, P: **D.7**: 29. **G.3.1**: 19.
Harvey, J: **I.7**: 12.
Hassibi, M: **C.2**: 74.
Hathaway, W: **D.5**: 38.
Hatty, S: **K.1**: 34.
Hauber, A: **K.1**: 114.
Haug, M: **K.4**: 4.
Haug, W: **F.3**: 1.
Hauser, R: **I.4**: 3.
Hawkesworth, M: **F.5**: 15.
Hawkins, J: **K.1**: 87.
Hayashi, S: **H.4**: 10.
Hayes, D: **I.3**: 6.
Hayes, J: **F.5**: 96.
Hayward, M: **F.3**: 26.
Hazlehurst, K: **C.3**: 39. **F.7**: 89.
Hazuda, H: **F.7**: 2.
Healey, P: **G.3.2**: 31.
Healy, D: **C.2**: 22.
Hearn, J: **K.1**: 47.
Heaven, P: **F.7**: 112.
Heaven, R: **F.2**: 28.
Hebbert, M: **G.3.2**: 113.
Hechler, D: **K.1**: 45.
Hechter, M: **B.1.3**: 4.
Hecker, S: **D.7**: 32.
Hedges, R: **F.4.1**: 35.
Hedl, J: **C.7**: 14.
Hedström, P: **E.2**: 71.
Heery, E: **I.6**: 9.
Heeter, C: **D.7**: 88.
Heilman, M: **I.3**: 52.
Hein, J: **F.8**: 98.
Heine, H: **I.5**: 5.
Heiner, R: **C.5**: 8.
Heitmeyer, W: **J.6**: 27.
Helkama, K: **D.3**: 37.
Heller, M: **D.7**: 52.
Helman, S: **D.5**: 24.
Helmes-Hayes, R: **A.1**: 26.
Hemans, L: **C.2**: 88.
Hemmings, S: **F.6**: 25.
Henderson, J: **G.3.2**: 129.
Henderson, V: **F.2**: 85.
Hendrick, S: **C.3**: 22.
Hendriks, A: **F.3**: 89.
Hendrix, L: **F.5**: 110.
Hennis, W: **B.1.1**: 19.
Henry, E: **G.3.2**: 133.
Henry, J: **K.4**: 88.
Henwood, K: **F.2**: 28.
Hepworth, M: **D.7**: 15.
Héran, F: **C.3**: 43. **F.4.1**: 10.
Herbert, D: **I.7**: 26. **K.1**: 102.
Herbert, M: **K.3**: 37.
Herman, J: **K.1**: 68.
Hermann, D: **K.1**: 91.
Hermans, H: **C.2**: 97.
Hernández, T: **F.5**: 89.
Hernández Sánchez, A: **H.4**: 11.
Hernes, H: **J.3**: 24.
Herron, J: **D.9.5**: 24.
Hershatter, G: **F.5**: 82.
Hertzog, C: **C.2**: 74.
Herva, S: **B.1.1**: 10.
Hervieu-Léger, D: **D.5**: 79.
Herwegen, S: **I.5**: 6.
Herzlich, C: **D.7**: 108.
Hess, P: **F.3**: 78.
Hesselink, A: **C.1**: 14.
Heuvel, A: **F.4.2**: 121.
Heuvel, van den, F: **K.2**: 32.
Hickson, D: **C.5**: 42.
Higginbotham, E: **F.5**: 86.
Higgins, E: **C.2**: 79. **C.3**: 3.

Higgins, I: **F.3**: 34.
Higgins, R: **C.3**: 16.
Hijab, N: **I.2**: 59.
Hilgartner, S: **K.1**: 25.
Hill, A: **F.1**: 13.
Hill, L: **I.6**: 3.
Hill, M: **F.4.1**: 6.
Hill, R: **J.2**: 6.
Hilton, D: **C.2**: 31.
Hilton, M: **K.1**: 40.
Himmelstein, D: **K.4**: 25, 92.
Hindess, B: **C.7**: 10.
Hiramatsu, H: **B.3**: 20.
Hirana, M: **K.1**: 83.
Hiraoka, K: **B.1.3**: 28.
Hirata, H: **I.3**: 34.
Hiro, D: **D.5**: 85.
Hirohara, M: **G.3.2**: 113.
Hirsch, B: **F.4.2**: 106.
Hirsch, J: **J.5**: 4.
Hirsch, S: **K.4**: 9.
Hirschhorn, M: **A.1**: 22.
Hirschon, R: **F.8**: 64.
Hirst, P: **B.1.1**: 16.
Hissong, R: **K.1**: 35, 154.
Hitchcock, J: **K.1**: 190.
Hobart, C: **F.4.1**: 16. **F.4.2**: 21, 112.
Hobbs, R: **D.7**: 97.
Hobson, C: **I.6**: 37.
Hochet, A: **F.8**: 69.
Hocking, J: **K.2**: 53.
Hodge, R: **D.7**: 42.
Hodgson, D: **F.1**: 19.
Hodson, R: **I.3**: 33.
Hoefer, R: **K.2**: 36.
Hoffman, S: **K.2**: 55.
Hoffman, T: **F.7**: 82.
Hofstetter, R: **F.7**: 48.
Hofstetter, C, R: **I.2**: 34.
Hogan, D: **F.3**: 3.
Hoge, D: **D.5**: 78.

Hogg, M: **C.3**: 45.
Höhn, H: **K.2**: 22.
Holban, I: **D.9**: 6.
Hollander, R: **I.3**: 61.
Hollands, B: **I.7**: 11.
Hollinger, R: **C.5**: 23.
Holloh, D: **I.5**: 6.
Holman, T: **F.4.1**: 32.
Holmes, J: **K.2**: 15.
Holmes, M: **H.3**: 7.
Holt, E: **D.7**: 54. **K.1**: 15.
Holtmann, D: **E.2**: 39.
Homans, H: **F.3**: 127.
Home, R: **D.6**: 3.
Homel, R: **K.1**: 23.
Honeyford, R: **F.7**: 107.
Honig, E: **F.5**: 82.
Honneth, A: **D.1.1**: 40.
Hood, B: **F.3**: 133.
Hooker, K: **C.2**: 74.
Hooper, A: **H.7**: 3.
Hoover, G: **E.3**: 6.
Hoover, S: **D.5**: 71.
Hope, S: **C.7**: 20.
Hopkinson, P: **D.5**: 70.
Horch, H: **C.5**: 36.
Horio, T: **D.9**: 12.
Horiuchi, M: **K.1**: 64.
Horley, J: **D.1.1**: 44.
Horowitz, M: **C.6**: 14.
Horton, C: **J.3**: 7.
Horvath, P: **C.1**: 25.
Hoshino, K: **K.1**: 63, 104.
Hoskins, C: **D.1.1**: 29.
Hossain, Z: **F.5**: 110.
Hosseini, J: **H.6**: 2.
Hotaling, G: **F.4.2**: 68. **K.1**: 12.
Hotta, I: **A.2**: 6.
Hottovy, T: **G.3.2**: 21.
Houlihan, B: **I.7**: 16.
Houlihan, K: **K.4**: 93.

INTERNATIONAL BIBLIOGRAPHY OF SOCIOLOGY — 1988

House, J: **C.4**: 31.
Houston, J: **K.1**: 174.
Hout, M: **D.5**: 26. **I.4**: 18.
Hout, van, R: **D.7**: 7.
Hovell, M: **I.2**: 34.
Howard, A: **I.5**: 11.
Howard, G: **I.2**: 6.
Howard, J: **F.6**: 30.
Howard-Pitney, B: **D.7**: 25.
Howe, A: **F.2**: 64.
Hoyle, B: **G.3.2**: 122.
Hoyo Bernat, J: **F.1**: 2.
Hsia, H: **D.7**: 28.
Hubbard, M: **J.8**: 11.
Hubert, J: **D.9.2**: 1.
Hubscher, R: **G.3.1**: 58.
Hudson, J: **G.1**: 14.
Huff, C: **K.1**: 160.
Hughes, P: **F.1**: 20.
Huh, K: **D.9.8**: 8.
Huiban, L: **F.3**: 115.
Hull, F: **A.3**: 9. **I.6**: 46.
Hull, H: **C.4**: 5.
Hull, V: **F.1**: 13.
Hummon, D: **I.7**: 24.
Humphrey, C: **F.3**: 151.
Humphrey, H: **F.4.2**: 14.
Humphrey, M: **F.4.2**: 14.
Humphreys, J: **K.2**: 15. **K.4**: 84.
Hundley, G: **I.6**: 11, 43.
Hunnicutt, B: **I.3**: 57.
Hunt, A: **I.2**: 61.
Hunt, C: **F.2**: 8. **F.3**: 88.
Hunter, A: **D.9**: 14.
Hunter, D: **K.2**: 7.
Hunter, J: **C.4**: 12.
Hunter, W: **D.3**: 32. **I.6**: 4.
Huot, G: **K.1**: 113.
Hurd, A: **D.5**: 53.
Hurh, W: **F.7**: 14.
Hurrelmann, K: **D.1.3**: 18.

Hurstel, F: **F.4.2**: 87.
Hurtado, J: **G.3.2**: 133.
Husain, M: **G.3.2**: 122.
Hutchens, R: **F.2**: 40.
Hutchings, N: **F.4.2**: 75.
Huttman, J: **G.3.2**: 87.
Hwang, S: **G.3.2**: 49.
Hyde, J: **C.3**: 21.
Hyman, R: **I.6**: 27.
Iakovlev, I: **D.9.5**: 16.
Ibrahim, A: **D.1.2**: 2. **F.3**: 119.
Ibrahim, F: **F.8**: 39.
Ichikawa, T: **D.1.1**: 33.
Ideris, A: **F.3**: 119.
Igbineweka, A: **I.3**: 29.
Iglesias de Ussel, J: **F.4.2**: 13.
Ihinger-Tallman, M: **F.4.2**: 48.
Iida, T: **D.5**: 14.
Iijima, N: **F.5**: 28.
Ikoshi, K: **B.1.3**: 17.
Illich, I: **D.7**: 1.
Imada, T: **E.2**: 49.
Imanyi, G: **I.5**: 23.
Imazu, K: **D.9.9**: 4.
Imperiale, G: **F.8**: 21.
Inaba, A: **F.4.2**: 120.
Inglis, F: **J.6**: 22.
Ingoldsby, B: **F.3**: 36.
Innes, C: **C.1**: 33.
Innes, J: **C.1**: 32.
Innocenti, S: **I.3**: 4.
Inō, K: **B.1.3**: 28.
Inoue, T: **D.7**: 129.
Intriligator, M: **J.8**: 1.
Inverarity, J: **K.1**: 179.
Irwin, J: **A.2**: 1. **K.1**: 152.
Isaacs, H: **I.2**: 34.
Isaksson, E: **J.7**: 5.
Isenalumhe, A: **K.4**: 63.
Ishigami, F: **H.6**: 3.
Ishihara, T: **I.4**: 19.

INTERNATIONAL BIBLIOGRAPHY OF SOCIOLOGY — 1988

Ishii-Kuntz, M: **F.6**: 1.
Ishikawa, A: **I.1**: 7.
Ishikawa, H: **C.2**: 30.
Ishikawa, M: **F.8**: 13.
Isono, F: **F.4.2**: 10.
Israel, J: **C.7**: 39.
Israelstam, S: **K.1**: 18.
Ito, K: **D.1.1**: 3.
Ivanov, S: **F.3**: 59.
Иванов, : **A.1**: 23.
Ivatts, J: **K.2**: 40.
Ives, J: **G.3.1**: 8.
Iwao, K: **F.2**: 49.
Izraeli, D: **F.5**: 22.
Jabber, P: **E.3**: 11.
Jackson, H: **C.7**: 20.
Jackson, J: **C.1**: 37.
Jackson, K: **I.3**: 61.
Jackson, M: **I.6**: 35.
Jackson, P: **D.2**: 3. **I.2**: 53.
Jacob, J: **K.4**: 17.
Jacobs, A: **K.1**: 88.
Jacobs, D: **H.4**: 7.
Jacobs, J: **K.1**: 166.
Jacobs, L: **E.3**: 10.
Jacquart, M: **F.4.1**: 32.
Jadhav, S: **K.4**: 60.
Jahan, S: **K.1**: 216.
Jahangir, B: **G.3.1**: 56.
Jahoda, G: **C.2**: 39. **F.2**: 66.
Jain, A: **F.3**: 142.
Jain, R: **F.7**: 44.
James, D: **F.4.2**: 66. **F.7**: 53.
Jamison, A: **H.4**: 13.
Jansen, S: **J.3**: 2.
Jansen, W: **I.2**: 58.
Jarjoura, G: **K.1**: 130.
Jarratt, K: **F.2**: 84.
Jarvie, I: **D.5**: 39.
Järvinen, P: **J.8**: 1.
Jasis, M: **I.2**: 34.
Jasso, G: **B.1.3**: 21.
Jayaratne, S: **K.3**: 21.
Jayasinghe, K: **F.3**: 23.
Jefferson, G: **K.1**: 15.
Jele, S: **F.2**: 75.
Jencks, C: **D.9**: 26. **I.2**: 55.
Jenkins, R: **K.1**: 140.
Jenkins, S: **F.8**: 58.
Jennings, R: **D.7**: 13.
Jensen, J: **F.8**: 84.
Jensen, L: **C.7**: 7.
Jenson, J: **I.2**: 19. **K.1**: 87.
Jenswold, J: **H.4**: 6.
Jervis, R: **J.8**: 18.
Jex, S: **I.3**: 36.
Jiménez Alvarez, A: **F.5**: 89.
Jiobu, R: **F.7**: 60, 77.
Joas, H: **B.1.1**: 2. **D.1.1**: 40.
Joerges, B: **H.4**: 5, 45.
Joesoef, M: **F.3**: 35.
Johansson, I: **B.1.2**: 4.
Johnson, A: **D.3**: 26.
Johnson, B: **K.1**: 86.
Johnson, C: **F.4.2**: 111.
Johnson, D: **D.5**: 3. **F.4.2**: 141. **G.3.1**: 10.
Johnson, J: **F.3**: 48. **I.2**: 12.
Johnson, L: **D.7**: 145.
Johnson, N: **F.3**: 77, 149.
Johnson, P: **D.3**: 22.
Johnson, R: **C.6**: 1.
Johnson, S: **D.5**: 41. **K.3**: 11.
Johnson, V: **F.6**: 9.
Johnson, W: **I.2**: 1.
Johnston, D: **H.3**: 23.
Johnston, J: **F.4.1**: 72.
Johnston, L: **K.1**: 13.
Jolley, J: **B.1.3**: 25.
Jones, B: **H.4**: 32, 51.
Jones, D: **D.9**: 2.
Jones, F: **E.2**: 12, 16, 70.
Jones, G: **F.2**: 5.

Jones, J: **C.1**: 27. **K.1**: 174.
Jones, K: **K.4**: 21.
Jones, P: **G.3.1**: 35. **J.6**: 12.
Jones, S: **D.8**: 1.
Jones, W: **D.5**: 38.
Jong, de, P: **C.2**: 2.
Jonsdottir, G: **F.5**: 12.
Joravsky, D: **C.1**: 35.
Jordan, J: **D.9.8**: 9.
Jørgensen, J: **D.7**: 51.
Jorgensen, S: **F.3**: 42.
Joshi, P: **J.2**: 7.
Jouët, J: **I.3**: 51.
Joughin, N: **K.1**: 14.
Joyce, W: **J.2**: 6.
Jozefonvicz, J: **D.6**: 18.
Jozefowicz, M: **D.6**: 18.
Juillard, J: **D.6**: 18.
Jules, D: **D.9**: 20.
Jungsten, M: **K.1**: 153.
Jurgensen, M: **F.7**: 30.
Kabanoff, B: **C.5**: 1.
Kadi, El, G: **G.3.2**: 144.
Kagehiro, D: **C.3**: 33.
Kajita, T: **F.7**: 62.
Kakhk, I: **A.1**: 35.
Kalleberg, A: **H.3**: 21. **I.3**: 9.
Kallen, J: **D.7**: 8.
Kallus, K: **A.1**: 35.
Kalra, S: **C.6**: 18.
Kamalkhani, Z: **F.8**: 75.
Kamann, D: **H.4**: 42.
Kanaya, H: **A.1**: 14.
Kanbargi, R: **I.2**: 9.
Kanchanabucha, K: **G.3.1**: 72.
Kane, P: **D.9.9**: 6.
Kaneko, I: **F.2**: 65.
Kannisto, V: **F.2**: 56.
Kanungo, R: **C.6**: 5.
Kapferer, B: **F.7**: 84.
Kapitza, S: **D.6**: 12, 24.

Kaplan, H: **C.6**: 1.
Kaplan, J: **K.1**: 42.
Kaplan, M: **G.3.2**: 121.
Karger, H: **I.6**: 33.
Karpf, A: **D.7**: 91.
Kasari, C: **F.2**: 80.
Kashyap, A: **J.3**: 3.
Kasten, E: **F.7**: 13.
Kasun, J: **F.3**: 49.
Katano, T: **A.3**: 8.
Katase, K: **F.6**: 27.
Kato, K: **F.4.2**: 140.
Katra, W: **D.1.1**: 30.
Katz, J: **K.1**: 125.
Katz, M: **I.6**: 20.
Katz, R: **D.7**: 5. **F.4.1**: 48.
Kauffman, K: **K.1**: 177.
Kaur, M: **F.5**: 87.
Kavadlo, C: **D.5**: 52.
Kavolis, V: **D.5**: 7.
Kawai, T: **A.2**: 3.
Kawakoshi, J: **B.1.1**: 15.
Kawanishi, H: **D.1.1**: 22.
Kawatei, M: **B.1.3**: 28.
Kay, B: **C.6**: 9. **K.4**: 93.
Kay, D: **F.5**: 38.
Kay, M: **C.4**: 32.
Keane, J: **J.5**: 17.
Keating, M: **G.3.2**: 109.
Kędelski, M: **F.3**: 73.
Kedourie, E: **F.7**: 5.
Keeney, W: **F.7**: 113.
Keeping, J: **D.5**: 77.
Keil, T: **C.6**: 17.
Keilin, W: **J.8**: 8.
Keilman, N: **F.3**: 85.
Keith, V: **F.4.1**: 71.
Kellerhals, J: **F.4.2**: 136.
Kellerman, B: **J.8**: 6.
Kelley, P: **D.5**: 70.
Kellner, D: **D.7**: 89.

Kelly, C: **C.4**: 15.
Kelly, J: **I.6**: 9. **J.5**: 9.
Kelly, L: **K.1**: 53, 133.
Kelly, M: **I.4**: 21.
Kelly, R: **C.2**: 92.
Kempf, K: **K.1**: 76.
Kempson, R: **D.7**: 68.
Kendall, L: **K.4**: 60.
Kendon, A: **D.7**: 39.
Kennedy, E: **F.2**: 75.
Kennedy, I: **D.3**: 36.
Kennedy, K: **F.3**: 39.
Kennell, J: **D.5**: 38.
Keown, J: **F.3**: 17.
Kepel, G: **D.5**: 88.
Kepplinger, H: **D.7**: 104.
Kerblay, B: **F.4.2**: 129.
Keren, G: **I.7**: 1.
Kern, B: **I.1**: 5.
Kern, H: **I.1**: 5.
Kerner, H: **K.1**: 91.
Kernis, M: **C.2**: 100.
Kerr, J: **F.2**: 46.
Keshavarz, M: **D.7**: 57.
Kestenbaum, B: **F.2**: 46.
Kesteren, Van, J: **I.2**: 18.
Kets de Vries, M: **C.6**: 16.
Kettler, D: **B.1.1**: 24.
Keyes, S: **K.1**: 211.
Kfir, A: **F.8**: 76.
Khadda, N: **F.5**: 70.
Khalifa, M: **F.3**: 20.
Khan, J: **I.5**: 9.
Khan, M: **I.2**: 65.
Khan, R: **D.6**: 20, 25.
Khan, Z: **F.6**: 24.
Kharitonov, V: **F.3**: 14.
Khatri, A: **F.4.2**: 17.
Khoo, S: **F.4.2**: 90.
Khouri-Dagher, N: **K.2**: 17.
Khramov, N: **D.7**: 103.

Kida, K: **C.2**: 67.
Kida, T: **C.2**: 23.
Kidane, A: **F.4.1**: 12.
Kiecolt, K: **C.7**: 33. **F.4.2**: 33.
Kiefer, M: **D.7**: 130.
Kiel, H: **K.1**: 49.
Kiernan, K: **F.6**: 33.
Kiernan, N: **B.2**: 6.
Kieselbach, T: **K.2**: 23. **K.4**: 94.
Kiesler, C: **K.4**: 68.
Kiesler, S: **F.3**: 122.
Kikuchi, K: **K.1**: 64.
Kilburg, R: **I.5**: 16.
Kilduff, M: **C.5**: 49.
Killian, C: **E.3**: 6.
Kim, K: **F.7**: 14.
Kim, Q: **E.3**: 15.
Kim, Y: **D.7**: 18.
Kimenyi, M: **F.3**: 9.
Kimura, K: **C.6**: 11.
Kimura, M: **E.1**: 10.
Kind, P: **K.4**: 70.
Kindahl, J: **F.8**: 19.
King, C: **C.2**: 16.
King, D: **F.1**: 20. **F.5**: 19. **J.4**: 1.
King, J: **G.3.2**: 54.
King, R: **G.3.2**: 127. **K.1**: 169.
Kingdom, E: **B.1.1**: 16.
Kingsnorth, R: **K.1**: 153.
Kinicki, A: **F.5**: 47.
Kipnis, B: **F.8**: 23.
Kippax, S: **C.2**: 61.
Kirk, S: **K.4**: 14.
Kirkland, J: **I.4**: 4.
Kitahara, A: **G.3.1**: 46.
Kitcher, P: **B.1.1**: 1.
Kito, T: **E.2**: 74.
Kitzinger, J: **K.1**: 53.
Kivett, V: **F.2**: 32, 35.
Kivnick, H: **F.2**: 23.
Kjær Jensen, M: **K.3**: 15.

Klandermans, B: **I.6**: 40.
Klatell, D: **I.7**: 21.
Kleber, H: **K.1**: 208.
Kleeman, W: **C.5**: 29.
Kleemeier, L: **G.3.1**: 69.
Klein, J: **J.6**: 16.
Klein, M: **K.1**: 22.
Klennert, K: **G.3.1**: 70.
Kliemke, C: **F.2**: 36.
Klijzing, E: **F.3**: 85.
Kline, S: **D.7**: 47.
Kluegel, J: **F.4.1**: 62. **H.1**: 1.
Knaap, van der, G: **I.2**: 48.
Knibbs, C: **C.2**: 31.
Knoke, D: **C.5**: 9.
Knottnerus, J: **D.1.3**: 3.
Knowles, J: **D.9.2**: 5.
Knudsen, K: **E.2**: 10.
Kobak, R: **C.2**: 5.
Kobayashi, K: **A.3**: 1.
Koberg, C: **F.5**: 45.
Kobielski, J: **C.7**: 1.
Koch, J: **I.7**: 9.
Kocks, M: **F.2**: 36.
Koctürk, T: **F.4.2**: 2.
Koegel, P: **K.1**: 16.
Koenig, M: **F.3**: 21, 56.
Koffman, L: **K.1**: 182.
Kofyrin, N: **K.1**: 19.
Kohfeld, C: **K.1**: 136.
Kohlert, N: **K.1**: 33.
Kohli, M: **F.2**: 27.
Kohout, J: **I.5**: 22.
Kojima, K: **D.8**: 13.
Kola, L: **F.2**: 53.
Kolarska-Bobinska, L: **A.3**: 3.
Kolenda, K: **D.3**: 20.
Kollock, P: **C.3**: 34.
Kolodny, R: **F.6**: 9.
Kolody, B: **F.4.1**: 42.
Komarovsky, M: **F.5**: 20.

Komenaka, A: **D.7**: 71.
Kominski, R: **H.3**: 8.
Koning, R: **C.1**: 14, 16–17, 29.
Konno, T: **J.3**: 10.
Kontuly, T: **G.3**: 2.
Koocher, G: **G.2**: 1.
Koomen, W: **C.4**: 24.
Korcelli, P: **F.8**: 29. **G.3**: 4.
Korman, A: **F.7**: 110.
Korn, R: **K.2**: 53.
Korovkin, M: **C.6**: 7.
Kosmitzki, C: **C.2**: 64.
Koster, A: **C.1**: 15.
Kotler, T: **C.3**: 1.
Koumoto, M: **D.5**: 51.
Koushki, P: **I.7**: 3.
Koutmoto, M: **D.5**: 17.
Kouzmin, L: **F.7**: 29.
Kovalchenko, I: **A.1**: 16.
Kovel, J: **C.1**: 31.
Kowak, K: **A.3**: 3.
Kraemer, K: **G.3.2**: 54.
Kragt, van de, A: **C.7**: 4.
Krahe, B: **K.1**: 137.
Krakover, S: **G.3.2**: 140.
Kranzberg, M: **A.5**: 7.
Krauze, T: **B.3**: 17.
Kravdal, O: **F.4.1**: 70.
Krefft, A: **I.2**: 34.
Kremer, J: **C.7**: 36.
Kress, G: **D.7**: 42.
Krieger, N: **F.3**: 94.
Kriesberg, L: **J.5**: 21.
Kriger, N: **D.1.1**: 8.
Krishna Iyer, V: **G.3.2**: 32.
Krishnan, V: **F.3**: 74.
Kristeva, J: **D.1.3**: 7.
Kröber, G: **D.6**: 20.
Kronenfeld, J: **I.3**: 61.
Krosnick, J: **C.7**: 6.
Krout, J: **F.2**: 35, 41.

Krout, P: **F.2**: 35.
Krueger, J: **C.2**: 103.
Kruglanski, A: **D.6**: 31.
Kruijt, B: **I.2**: 48.
Krulic, J: **F.8**: 69.
Krulis-Randa, J: **C.6**: 15.
Kuan, H: **F.7**: 26.
Kuchiba, M: **B.1.2**: 1.
Kuczynski, P: **J.5**: 28.
Küenzlen, G: **D.5**: 27.
Künzler, J: **F.2**: 36.
Kultgen, J: **I.4**: 7.
Kumada, T: **B.1.1**: 26.
Kumagai, F: **F.4.2**: 29.
Kumar, N: **G.3.2**: 75.
Kumon, M: **F.4.2**: 27.
Kunkel, D: **D.7**: 94.
Kupiszewski, M: **F.8**: 4.
Kurabayashi, Y: **D.8**: 7.
Kurup, K: **A.3**: 10.
Kurzman, C: **D.6**: 21.
Kusayaangi, C: **D.7**: 43.
Kushner, K: **I.2**: 57.
Kushnick, L: **K.4**: 73.
Kutchins, H: **K.4**: 14.
Kuvacic, I: **D.3**: 8.
Kuz'min, S: **I.2**: 33.
Kuzina, I: **F.3**: 14.
Kwilecki, S: **D.5**: 48.
LaGory, M: **F.2**: 43.
Laan, van der, L: **I.2**: 48.
Lab, S: **K.1**: 141.
Laborie, J: **G.3.2**: 153.
Labouze, E: **D.6**: 18.
Lacey, L: **G.3.2**: 99.
Lacey, N: **K.1**: 131.
Lachmann, R: **D.8**: 10.
Lacombe, D: **F.6**: 18.
Ładyka, J: **C.7**: 23.
LaFontaine, H: **D.9.2**: 1.
LaFree, G: **K.1**: 84.

Lahelma, E: **K.4**: 16.
Lahmann, H: **F.1**: 9.
Laino, G: **G.3.2**: 38, 82.
Laird, J: **J.8**: 10, 12.
Laki, M: **E.3**: 17.
Lakshmanna, M: **F.3**: 40.
Lal, H: **G.3.2**: 6.
Lal, S: **F.3**: 8.
Lalonde, F: **C.2**: 85.
Lam, C: **C.7**: 14.
Lam, J: **F.3**: 129.
Lamas, E: **K.2**: 28.
Lambert, R: **C.6**: 9.
Lambert, Y: **D.5**: 79.
Lamont, M: **D.1.3**: 4.
Lampert, N: **J.2**: 6.
Lancaster, S: **C.2**: 52.
Landis, K: **C.4**: 31.
Landry, P: **F.2**: 9.
Landry, S: **F.4.2**: 106.
Landsverk, J: **F.4.2**: 41.
Lang, J: **C.5**: 29.
Langumier, J: **G.3.2**: 153.
Langworthy, R: **K.1**: 173.
Lansbury, R: **I.6**: 23.
Lapeyronnie, D: **E.3**: 20.
LaPrairie, C: **K.1**: 66.
Larbalestier, J: **F.7**: 1.
Lareau, A: **D.1.3**: 4.
Larionescu, M: **B.1.1**: 37.
Larkin, G: **K.4**: 4.
Larrea Maldonado, C: **G.3.2**: 58.
Larsen, M: **J.3**: 25.
Lassalle, J: **I.7**: 20.
Lassman, P: **A.2**: 4.
Lasswell, T: **E.2**: 43.
Lastra de Suarez, Y: **D.7**: 74.
Latessa, E: **I.3**: 35.
Latham, G: **I.3**: 19.
Laudenslager, M: **C.2**: 43. **F.4.1**: 2.
Laurence, M: **K.2**: 53.

Lavee, Y: **F.4.2**: 139.
Lavigne, M: **E.3**: 17.
Law, J: **D.8**: 14.
Lawless, P: **G.3.2**: 128.
Lawrence, K: **H.4**: 1.
Lawry, R: **D.3**: 23.
Lawson, A: **F.6**: 2.
Lawuyi, O: **D.5**: 28.
Laxmi Devi, A: **G.3.1**: 36.
Layder, D: **B.1.2**: 5.
Layton, L: **C.1**: 26.
Lazaro, C: **K.1**: 2.
Lazarus, R: **C.2**: 84. **K.4**: 88.
Lazerson, M: **H.4**: 28.
Lealand, G: **D.1.1**: 17.
Learmonth, A: **G.1**: 5.
Leathar, D: **K.1**: 37.
Lebon, A: **F.8**: 70.
Lebowitz, M: **B.1.1**: 34.
Leclerc, J: **D.7**: 56.
Leclerc, M: **D.7**: 67.
Leclercq, J: **D.5**: 65.
Lederberg, J: **F.3**: 7.
Ledoux, S: **K.1**: 27.
Lee, C: **F.3**: 12.
Lee, D: **G.3.2**: 121.
Lee, G: **F.4.1**: 40.
Lee, R: **D.5**: 31.
Lee, S: **C.3**: 2. **F.4.1**: 26.
Leggett, D: **D.7**: 95.
Lehmann, D: **C.7**: 17.
Lehrer, E: **F.4.1**: 14.
Leicht, K: **I.5**: 17.
Leifer, E: **C.6**: 10.
Leighton, A: **F.3**: 120.
Leinbach, T: **F.3**: 135.
Leite, M: **D.8**: 9.
Leitko, T: **F.3**: 69.
Leiulfsrud, H: **E.2**: 17.
Lele, J: **D.7**: 20, 60.
Lempereur, N: **K.1**: 98.

Lempert, W: **I.6**: 17.
Lempert-Lenderink, J: **A.5**: 6.
Lenbardt, G: **F.7**: 71.
Lengermann, J: **I.3**: 61.
Lennerlöf, L: **I.3**: 26.
Lenz, R: **F.3**: 116.
Leon, F: **F.3**: 39.
León, De, B: **D.5**: 11.
Leopold, J: **I.6**: 21.
Lepervanche, M: **F.5**: 3.
Lequin, Y: **F.8**: 82.
Leridon, H: **F.4.1**: 50.
Lerner, J: **C.2**: 74.
Lesbet, D: **G.3.2**: 4, 82.
Leslie, L: **D.9.5**: 7.
Lesnoff-Caravaglia, G: **F.2**: 53.
Lesthaeghe, R: **F.3**: 55.
Leung, M: **F.5**: 86.
Leung, S: **F.1**: 18.
Leveau, R: **D.5**: 88. **F.8**: 69.
Lever-Tracy, C: **E.2**: 21.
Levi, G: **D.6**: 29.
Levi, L: **K.1**: 143.
Levin, J: **D.5**: 22.
Levine, M: **F.2**: 24.
Levine, R: **G.2**: 1.
Levine, S: **K.4**: 4, 22.
Levitt, B: **C.5**: 26.
Levy, J: **F.2**: 47.
Levy, S: **F.3**: 34.
Lewin, D: **I.6**: 37.
Lewis, B: **F.3**: 93.
Lewis, D: **C.2**: 19.
Lewis, I: **F.2**: 66.
Lewis, J: **F.4.2**: 92.
Lewis, M: **H.4**: 47.
Lewis, N: **F.3**: 107.
Lewis, R: **F.7**: 70. **K.4**: 10.
Lewy, G: **J.6**: 18.
Lexchin, J: **K.4**: 51.
Leyens, J: **C.4**: 3.

Li, P: **F.7**: 74, 103.
Lian, K: **F.7**: 68.
Liberati, A: **K.4**: 12.
Lichter, D: **F.8**: 11. **I.2**: 41.
Lieberson, S: **A.1**: 4.
Liem, J: **I.2**: 40.
Liem, R: **I.2**: 40.
Liff, S: **I.2**: 39.
Light, D: **K.4**: 4.
Light, R: **K.1**: 202.
Lilienfeld, A: **F.3**: 140.
Lilly, J: **K.1**: 160.
Limousin, A: **F.8**: 69.
Limra, A: **F.4.2**: 123.
Linck, T: **G.3.1**: 62.
Linde, C: **D.7**: 37.
Lindemann, A: **F.7**: 94.
Linden, van der, P: **C.4**: 11.
Lindley, R: **I.2**: 61.
Lindsay, J: **C.4**: 16.
Lindstrom, F: **D.9**: 25.
Lines, J: **G.3.2**: 121.
Linhart, D: **I.6**: 25.
Linn, M: **C.3**: 21.
Liotine, M: **H.4**: 1.
Lipton, M: **K.1**: 233.
Lishner, D: **K.1**: 87.
Liston, A: **F.4.1**: 46.
Lithman, Y: **D.5**: 89.
Litrento, O: **D.4**: 15.
Little, B: **D.1.1**: 44.
Little, G: **J.6**: 36.
Little, M: **K.1**: 22.
Litwin, H: **K.2**: 6.
Liu, C: **F.7**: 26.
Liu, R: **D.7**: 7.
Lloyd, C: **F.3**: 59.
Lloyd, S: **C.3**: 40. **F.4.2**: 45.
Lloyd-Bostock, S: **D.4**: 8.
Locher, U: **F.8**: 3.
Locke Anderson, W: **B.1.1**: 36.

Locksley, G: **D.7**: 142.
Loewenberg, F: **K.3**: 27.
Loewy, E: **F.3**: 90.
Logie, R: **K.1**: 106.
Loken, B: **D.7**: 25.
Lomsky-Feder, E: **F.2**: 11.
Lomuto, C: **I.3**: 4.
London, C: **D.9**: 11.
Long, E: **C.3**: 40.
Long, M: **K.4**: 8.
Long, S: **K.2**: 37.
Longhurst, B: **D.6**: 13.
Longino, C: **F.2**: 59.
López, T: **J.6**: 8.
Lopez Castro, G: **F.8**: 20.
LoSciuto, L: **K.1**: 2.
Losito, M: **A.1**: 1.
Louw-Potgieter, J: **C.2**: 83. **F.7**: 57.
Loveland, I: **K.1**: 226.
Lovera Sánchez, M: **G.3.2**: 96.
Lovrich, N: **D.7**: 100.
Lowe, G: **K.3**: 34.
Lucas, R: **F.8**: 32.
Ludwick-Rosenthal, R: **C.1**: 39.
Luger, K: **D.7**: 130.
Luhmann, N: **D.1.2**: 11.
Lull, J: **D.7**: 150.
Lunt, P: **D.9.8**: 7.
Lupfer, M: **D.5**: 70.
Lupri, E: **F.4.1**: 27.
Lustgarten, L: **B.1.1**: 16.
Lusty, T: **K.4**: 39.
Luthardt, W: **J.3**: 21.
Lye, D: **F.4.1**: 75.
Lynch, J: **K.1**: 147.
Lynn, R: **D.9.8**: 3.
Lynne, G: **C.7**: 25.
Lyon, D: **H.4**: 20.
Lyth, I: **C.2**: 15.
MacCormack, C: **F.5**: 72.
MacDonald, G: **F.7**: 1.

Macdonald, K: **I.4**: 28.
MacDonald, S: **K.1**: 198.
MacGaffey, W: **D.1.1**: 8.
Machado, D: **G.3.2**: 133.
Machalek, R: **K.1**: 100.
Mack, A: **A.3**: 3. **F.3**: 7.
Mackenzie, D: **J.8**: 14.
Mackey, W: **F.4.2**: 109.
Mackie, V: **F.5**: 13.
MacLean, D: **C.2**: 73.
Maclean, M: **F.4.2**: 80.
MacLeod, M: **K.1**: 53.
MacPherson, I: **K.2**: 7.
MacPherson, S: **K.3**: 25.
MacRae, A: **B.3**: 12.
MacRae, D: **K.4**: 17.
Macunovich, D: **F.3**: 51.
Madami, P: **F.5**: 70. **I.6**: 14.
Madrid, J: **D.1.1**: 29.
Maeno, H: **F.4.2**: 135.
Maffenini, W: **F.8**: 35.
Magala, S: **J.6**: 3.
Maggiore, D: **F.6**: 21.
Maguire, M: **I.3**: 58.
Mahabir, C: **K.1**: 75.
Maher, C: **G.3.2**: 120.
Mahfoudh, D: **F.5**: 70. **I.6**: 38.
Mahler, J: **C.5**: 33.
Mahon, E: **F.5**: 109.
Maillu, D: **F.6**: 23.
Maio, Di, G: **D.6**: 29.
Mair, G: **K.1**: 156.
Mair, L: **F.5**: 34.
Maitre, J: **D.5**: 79.
Majewski, J: **F.7**: 102.
Majka, L: **K.2**: 18.
Major, I: **E.3**: 17.
Makannah, T: **G.3.2**: 137.
Makas, E: **F.3**: 11.
Makhoba, P: **F.2**: 75.
Makinde, M: **D.6**: 2.

Malaysia. Jabatan Perangkaan: **G.3.2**: 142.
Mallat, C: **D.5**: 90.
Maller, M: **K.1**: 59.
Maller, R: **K.1**: 59.
Mallinckrodt, A: **J.5**: 8.
Mallinson, I: **K.3**: 29.
Mallory, G: **C.5**: 42.
Malmberg, G: **G.3.2**: 145.
Mamberg, M: **C.2**: 10.
Manchin, R: **A.3**: 3. **E.2**: 63.
Manciaux, M: **F.3**: 87.
Maney, M: **F.7**: 115.
Mangelsdorf, K: **I.4**: 27.
Mangen, D: **F.2**: 9.
Mangiafico, L: **F.8**: 51.
Mangoni, F: **G.3.2**: 24.
Manicas, P: **D.6**: 33.
Manis, M: **C.3**: 50.
Mann, J: **F.3**: 119.
Mann, K: **K.1**: 127.
Mann, M: **J.1**: 4.
Mannan, M: **F.3**: 43.
Mannari, H: **C.5**: 22. **I.3**: 31.
Manning, C: **H.4**: 15.
Manona, C: **G.3.2**: 152.
Manor, O: **C.2**: 58.
Mansueto, A: **D.5**: 43.
Mantell, J: **F.3**: 92.
Manz, W: **H.5**: 8.
Manzanal, M: **G.3.2**: 1.
Mar, J: **D.1.1**: 2.
Maranto, C: **I.6**: 6.
Marceau, J: **H.4**: 12.
Marcelissen, F: **K.4**: 88.
March, J: **C.5**: 26.
Marchi, M: **I.3**: 4.
Marchuk, G: **D.6**: 18.
Marcus, N: **I.7**: 21.
Mardones, J: **J.1**: 1.
Marie, A: **G.3.2**: 92.

Marie, C: **F.8**: 69.
Marin, B: **I.5**: 13, 18.
Marinov, M: **D.6**: 7.
Marißen, N: **K.1**: 164.
Markovsky, B: **E.1**: 5.
Marks, S: **K.4**: 32.
Markus, M: **C.5**: 10.
Marmot, M: **I.3**: 43.
Marody, M: **A.3**: 3.
Marotel, G: **F.8**: 48.
Marples, D: **K.1**: 28.
Marquand, D: **J.2**: 11.
Marques, J: **C.4**: 3–4.
Marsh, R: **C.5**: 22. **H.1**: 7. **I.3**: 31.
Marshall, C: **D.9.4**: 1.
Marshall, G: **E.2**: 14, 51, 54.
Marsiglio, W: **F.4.2**: 8, 126.
Marsland, D: **A.1**: 28.
Martell, R: **I.3**: 52.
Martin, C: **C.3**: 19.
Martin, J: **K.1**: 105.
Martin, L: **D.1.3**: 20.
Martin, M: **E.3**: 7.
Martin, P: **F.4.2**: 20. **F.8**: 63.
Martin, R: **C.4**: 13.
Martin, S: **C.6**: 1.
Martin, W: **H.4**: 19.
Martín-Barbero, J: **D.1.1**: 29.
Martínez, M: **D.7**: 78.
Martinez-Brawley, E: **K.3**: 30.
Martini, A: **K.2**: 28.
Martins, H: **A.2**: 4.
Martohardjono, G: **D.7**: 20.
Marullo, S: **J.5**: 15.
Marwell, G: **C.4**: 23, 29.
Maryanski, A: **A.1**: 34. **B.1.1**: 13.
Masaoka, K: **F.2**: 18.
Masarani, F: **C.5**: 38.
Maschino, M: **D.1.1**: 16.
Mascie-Taylor, C: **F.6**: 17.
Masina, L: **C.5**: 31.

Mason, K: **F.4.2**: 88.
Massagli, M: **K.4**: 81.
Massengill, D: **I.3**: 24.
Masser, I: **G.3.2**: 113.
Massey, D: **G.3.2**: 51, 68. **I.2**: 48.
Massot, J: **F.8**: 70.
Masters, M: **I.6**: 41.
Masters, W: **F.6**: 9.
Mastrobuoni, O: **C.1**: 8.
Mastrofski, S: **J.3**: 4.
Matabane, P: **D.7**: 137.
Mathien, T: **B.1.3**: 18.
Mathieu, D: **K.4**: 57.
Matilal, B: **D.7**: 2.
Matsuda, Y: **D.8**: 7.
Matsudaira, M: **G.3.2**: 22.
Matsueda, R: **A.2**: 1. **C.2**: 18.
Matsui, K: **C.5**: 48.
Matsuoka, M: **E.3**: 14.
Matsuyama, H: **F.2**: 45.
Matta, B: **F.8**: 71.
Matthews, A: **F.2**: 35.
Matthews, M: **D.9.1**: 2.
Matthews, R: **K.1**: 162.
Matthews, S: **F.4.2**: 116.
Mattick, , P: **A.5**: 7.
Mattingly, M: **G.3.2**: 123.
Mattinson, J: **F.4.1**: 64.
Mauksch, H: **I.2**: 68.
Mauldin, W: **F.3**: 44.
Mautz, R: **I.5**: 5.
Maw, C: **D.9.8**: 1.
Mawlawi, R: **D.7**: 85.
Maxfield, M: **J.3**: 11.
Maxson, C: **K.1**: 22.
Maxwell, E: **D.9**: 9.
Maxwell, N: **F.8**: 8.
Maxwell, R: **D.9**: 9. **K.4**: 22.
May, M: **F.4.2**: 83.
Mayberry, M: **D.9.2**: 5.
Mayer, E: **G.3.1**: 7.

Mayer, J: **C.2**: 10. **D.5**: 79. **F.3**: 107.
Mayer, K: **I.2**: 8, 27.
Mayer, L: **B.3**: 13.
Mayes, T: **C.2**: 39.
Maynard, D: **D.7**: 64. **K.1**: 15.
Mayo, J: **C.5**: 29. **G.3.2**: 126. **J.8**: 19.
Mays, V: **C.1**: 27.
Mazey, S: **F.5**: 65.
Mazuera, M: **F.5**: 89.
Mazur, A: **F.3**: 152.
McAdams, D: **C.1**: 26.
McAllister, I: **D.5**: 45. **I.5**: 25. **J.2**: 9.
McAllister, J: **D.6**: 7.
McAuley, P: **C.4**: 2.
McBarnet, D: **B.1.1**: 16.
McCallum, J: **I.3**: 22.
McCarthy, B: **K.1**: 173.
McCarthy, D: **K.1**: 179.
McCarthy, F: **K.1**: 237.
McClellan, B: **D.9**: 23.
McClintock, C: **D.1.2**: 4.
McConahay, J: **K.1**: 42.
McConnell, T: **C.3**: 26.
McCorduck, P: **D.6**: 1.
McCormack, G: **E.3**: 13.
McCormick, J: **J.3**: 6.
McCracken, J: **D.1.1**: 8.
McCrae, R: **C.2**: 99.
McCrate, E: **F.3**: 30.
McDermott, J: **H.4**: 8.
McDermott, K: **K.1**: 169.
McDonald, M: **D.1.1**: 33.
McDonald, S: **D.1.1**: 33.
McDonough, P: **J.6**: 31.
McDougall, G: **F.2**: 75.
McElroy, J: **F.8**: 28.
McFarlane, B: **D.8**: 2.
McGarty, C: **C.7**: 9.
McGee, T: **G.3.2**: 141.
McGeevor, P: **I.2**: 22.
McGhee, J: **F.4.2**: 61.

McGoldrick, A: **I.3**: 12.
McGrath, M: **K.2**: 26.
McGrath, P: **I.6**: 16.
McGregor, J: **J.4**: 2.
Мчедлов, : **D.3**: 25.
McHoul, A: **D.8**: 16.
McIntosh, M: **K.1**: 53.
McIntyre, A: **C.6**: 3.
McKay, S: **D.7**: 61.
McKeganey, N: **K.2**: 7. **K.4**: 55.
McKerlie, D: **E.2**: 24.
McKinlay, J: **K.4**: 4, 13.
McKinney, K: **F.6**: 26.
McLanahan, S: **F.4.2**: 81.
McLaughlin, B: **C.2**: 42.
McLaughlin, C: **K.4**: 49.
McLaughlin, J: **A.5**: 1.
McLaughlin, S: **F.5**: 60.
McLuhan, M: **D.7**: 106.
McMahan, J: **F.3**: 23.
McMahon, R: **F.4.2**: 144.
McMurry, J: **F.4.1**: 35.
McNair, B: **D.7**: 98.
McNeil, J: **K.2**: 28.
McNeill, R: **K.1**: 37.
McPhail, M: **F.5**: 11.
McPherson, A: **D.9.2**: 4.
McRae, S: **I.2**: 69.
McTavish, D: **F.2**: 35.
Medeiros, F: **G.3.1**: 12.
Mednick, M: **C.1**: 20.
Mednick, S: **K.1**: 94.
Meek, M: **D.7**: 72.
Meeker, B: **B.1.1**: 27.
Meguru, Y: **F.4.2**: 137.
Mehan, H: **K.1**: 15.
Mehendale, S: **D.6**: 18.
Meier, A: **J.5**: 20.
Meijnen, W: **E.2**: 62.
Meja, V: **B.1.1**: 24.
Melian, M: **F.3**: 54.

Meller, Y: **K.3**: 26.
Melo, de, J: **D.1.1**: 29.
Melton, G: **G.2**: 1.
Melucci, A: **J.5**: 17.
Memon, P: **H.7**: 6.
Menahem, G: **F.4.2**: 60.
Méndez, Z: **F.5**: 95.
Mendras, M: **J.8**: 17.
Menke, H: **K.1**: 27.
Menta, B: **G.3.1**: 3.
Meo, Di, A: **D.6**: 27, 29. **K.4**: 71.
Merchiers, J: **I.1**: 1.
Mercure, D: **I.3**: 49.
Meredith, B: **F.4.2**: 92.
Merelman, R: **C.5**: 29.
Merten, K: **D.7**: 17.
Merten, P: **E.3**: 27.
Mertz, E: **D.7**: 14.
Meslé, F: **F.3**: 139.
Messerschmidt, D: **G.3.1**: 44.
Mest, G: **F.3**: 11.
Mestrovic, S: **B.1.1**: 28.
Metz, R: **B.3**: 7.
Meulen, van der, T: **I.2**: 48.
Meyer, M: **E.3**: 10.
Meyer, S: **F.4.1**: 49.
Mhlanga, C: **G.3.2**: 98.
Michael, C: **F.7**: 65.
Michaels, G: **F.4.2**: 145.
Mickiewicz, E: **D.7**: 131. **J.2**: 6.
Midgley, J: **H.3**: 4.
Mier, P: **J.5**: 17.
Migalski, M: **J.6**: 9.
Miguel, de, A: **F.7**: 35.
Mika, H: **K.2**: 53.
Mikulincer, M: **C.2**: 48.
Mikulski, B: **F.2**: 75.
Milberg, S: **C.7**: 28.
Miles, A: **F.5**: 102.
Milio, N: **K.4**: 67.
Millar, K: **C.7**: 13.

Miller, E: **I.2**: 68.
Miller, H: **F.8**: 26.
Miller, L: **F.5**: 47.
Miller, M: **F.3**: 138. **F.8**: 70.
Miller, N: **F.3**: 95.
Miller, P: **C.3**: 38.
Miller, R: **K.3**: 12.
Miller, W: **B.1.1**: 8.
Mills, C: **G.3.2**: 116. **K.3**: 18.
Mills, J: **C.7**: 5.
Milroy, B: **F.5**: 76.
Milza, O: **F.8**: 59.
Milza, P: **F.8**: 69.
Minami, T: **F.4.2**: 120.
Minault, G: **F.5**: 75.
Miner, J: **I.6**: 19.
Ming, H: **K.4**: 65.
Mingat, A: **D.9.5**: 6.
Minkowski, A: **F.1**: 24.
Minty, B: **K.1**: 118.
Miossec, J: **G.3.2**: 15.
Miranda, M: **K.1**: 228.
Mirus, R: **D.1.1**: 29.
Mishra, A: **K.1**: 238.
Misra, B: **G.3.1**: 51.
Misra, H: **G.3.2**: 43, 81.
Misztal, B: **J.5**: 5, 26.
Mitchell, M: **B.1.3**: 25.
Mitchell, N: **J.3**: 6.
Mittar, V: **G.3.2**: 25.
Miyares, J: **G.1**: 15.
Miyauchi, T: **D.1.3**: 17.
Miyazawa, S: **J.5**: 24.
Mlay, W: **F.8**: 1.
Moberg, D: **G.3.1**: 39.
Mochizuki, T: **F.3**: 3.
Modak, M: **F.4.2**: 136.
Model, S: **H.3**: 6.
Moen, M: **J.5**: 29.
Moen, P: **F.5**: 54, 80.
Moerane, M: **F.2**: 75.

Mohammed, P: **F.5**: 34.
Mohanan, V: **K.1**: 78.
Mohanty, C: **F.5**: 25.
Mohanty, R: **E.2**: 22.
Mohr, R: **F.6**: 14.
Moigne, Le, G: **F.8**: 70.
Moilanen, I: **F.4.2**: 53.
Moisés, J: **J.6**: 33.
Molina, A: **H.4**: 38.
Molotch, H: **G.3.2**: 125.
Monahan, L: **F.8**: 43.
Mongardini, C: **E.3**: 5.
Monteiro, M: **K.1**: 194.
Monteith, R: **F.3**: 48, 54.
Monteón González, H: **F.7**: 75.
Montgomery, M: **F.4.1**: 55.
Montgomery, S: **K.2**: 10.
Moodie, T: **D.1.1**: 8.
Moody, H: **F.2**: 22.
Mookherjee, H: **F.3**: 64.
Moore, J: **F.7**: 41.
Moore, W: **I.6**: 7.
Mora, P: **F.5**: 95.
Moreales, S: **G.3.2**: 133.
Morel, B: **G.3.2**: 15.
Moreno, C: **J.6**: 15.
Morettini, A: **I.3**: 4.
Morgan, G: **D.7**: 53.
Morgan, L: **F.4.1**: 73.
Morgan, S: **F.4.1**: 75.
Morgen, S: **F.5**: 104.
Morgia, C: **G.3.2**: 40.
Mori, S: **B.1.3**: 28.
Morin, S: **C.1**: 27.
Morioka, K: **F.5**: 73.
Morra, G: **K.2**: 52.
Morrill, R: **G.3.2**: 28.
Morris, A: **F.5**: 8.
Morris, C: **D.3**: 28.
Morris, H: **D.3**: 1.
Morris, L: **F.3**: 54.

Morris, M: **F.4.2**: 30.
Morris-Suzuki, T: **H.4**: 4.
Morrison, D: **D.9.5**: 2. **F.8**: 11.
Morrison, J: **D.5**: 77.
Morry, M: **K.1**: 113.
Morss, J: **F.2**: 82.
Mortimer, J: **I.4**: 29.
Mortimer-Szymcak, H: **F.5**: 84.
Morton, T: **K.4**: 68.
Mosco, V: **D.7**: 34.
Mosley, M: **D.6**: 24. **D.7**: 102.
Mosley, W: **K.4**: 80.
Moss, P: **F.4.2**: 39.
Mott, F: **F.4.2**: 8.
Mougenot, C: **G.3.2**: 97.
Moulin, H: **C.4**: 1.
Mountjoy, A: **G.3**: 3.
Moutardier, M: **H.5**: 2.
Mouwerik, van, S: **J.8**: 8.
Mouzelis, N: **A.1**: 33.
Mühlhäusler, P: **D.7**: 75.
Mueller, C: **F.5**: 39.
Mueller-Dixon, R: **K.4**: 40.
Münch, R: **E.3**: 31.
Münstermann, H: **D.7**: 7.
Mufune, P: **E.2**: 27.
Muir, K: **F.5**: 93.
Mukherjee, R: **H.3**: 22.
Mulkay, M: **C.2**: 36.
Mullen, B: **C.2**: 53.
Muller, E: **H.3**: 3.
Mullins, M: **D.5**: 29.
Mulroy, E: **F.4.2**: 64.
Mumby, D: **C.5**: 5.
Mumford, M: **C.2**: 17.
Mundy, P: **F.2**: 80.
Muñoz Cruz, H: **D.7**: 74.
Murai, K: **F.4.2**: 55.
Murai, M: **G.3.2**: 26.
Murakami, M: **B.1.3**: 28.
Murch, M: **F.4.1**: 23.

Murcott, A: **F.3**: 76.
Murdock, S: **G.3.2**: 49.
Murphy, A: **D.7**: 73.
Murphy, C: **J.3**: 5.
Murphy, J: **A.1**: 21.
Murphy, P: **K.1**: 124.
Murphy, R: **C.3**: 44.
Murray, D: **D.7**: 24.
Murray, G: **K.2**: 47.
Murray, M: **I.2**: 52.
Murty, K: **F.4.2**: 44. **K.1**: 72, 126.
Musa, A: **D.9.6**: 1.
Muta, K: **F.4.2**: 28.
Myerscough, J: **D.8**: 8.
Myles, J: **E.2**: 26.
Naegeler, G: **C.1**: 40.
Naerssen, T: **G.3.2**: 80.
Naffine, N: **K.1**: 145, 158.
Nagatsu, M: **F.4.2**: 93.
Nagel, S: **G.3.2**: 19.
Nahavandi, F: **C.6**: 19. **J.6**: 28.
Naidoo, J: **F.4.2**: 17. **F.7**: 15.
Najimi, A: **G.3.2**: 114.
Najman, J: **D.5**: 77.
Nakagawa, N: **D.8**: 6.
Nakagiri, S: **E.1**: 3.
Nakai, N: **G.3.2**: 113.
Nakajima, M: **B.1.1**: 9.
Nakosteen, R: **F.8**: 19.
Naoi, A: **I.4**: 26.
Nape, P: **F.2**: 75.
Narayan, R: **F.5**: 100.
Nasri Messara, A: **J.3**: 1.
Nassehi, A: **D.1.2**: 13.
Nassehi-Behnam, V: **J.6**: 28.
Nathan, P: **I.5**: 16.
Natsoulas, T: **C.2**: 56.
Nauck, B: **F.4.2**: 26.
Nava, M: **K.1**: 53.
Navarro, R: **G.3.2**: 30, 92.
Navarro, V: **K.4**: 1, 4.

Ndatshe, V: **D.1.1**: 8.
Nearine, R: **D.9.2**: 1.
Nebe, J: **G.3.2**: 52.
Nebraska Sociological Feminist Collective: **B.1.3**: 11.
Nedelmann, B: **D.1.1**: 15.
Nederman, C: **J.2**: 3.
Needell, J: **H.5**: 1.
Neelsen, J: **E.2**: 69.
Negrine, R: **D.7**: 123.
Negrón, L: **F.8**: 56.
Neidert, L: **F.7**: 3.
Neilson, I: **C.2**: 39.
Neira Alva, E: **G.3.2**: 13.
Neiss, R: **C.2**: 46.
Nelkin, D: **F.3**: 7.
Nell, V: **C.2**: 33.
Nelson, A: **G.3.2**: 121.
Nelson, C: **I.2**: 56.
Nelson, K: **G.3.2**: 23.
Nelson, L: **D.5**: 41.
Nelson, R: **D.5**: 73.
Nelson, T: **C.3**: 50.
Nerlove, M: **F.3**: 41.
Ness, G: **C.5**: 4.
Neubaum, E: **F.4.1**: 58.
Neufeld, R: **C.1**: 2, 39.
Neuman, W: **D.4**: 5. **K.1**: 67.
Neumann, K: **D.7**: 130.
Neusner, J: **D.6**: 35. **E.3**: 10.
Neustadtl, A: **J.5**: 3.
Nevin, J: **C.7**: 8. **J.8**: 20.
Newcomb, M: **K.1**: 32, 197.
Newell, C: **F.1**: 12.
Newell, K: **K.4**: 80.
Newland, K: **F.5**: 101.
Newman, J: **D.5**: 38. **K.4**: 22, 56, 61.
Newman, R: **I.6**: 7.
Newson, J: **D.9.5**: 25.
Newton, K: **G.3.2**: 121.
Ng, C: **H.4**: 44.
Nicolae, I: **F.1**: 14.

Nicolaï, R: **C.7**: 40. **D.7**: 7.
Nicolas, P: **G.3.2**: 147.
Nieuwoudt, J: **F.7**: 91.
Nijnatten, van, C: **F.4.2**: 7.
Nilsson, I: **E.2**: 59.
Nishihara, K: **D.6**: 16.
Nishishita, A: **F.2**: 51.
Nishiyama, Y: **G.3.2**: 117.
Nkomo, M: **D.9**: 8.
Noble, I: **I.2**: 5.
Nock, S: **F.4.2**: 15.
Noël, L: **C.7**: 26.
Noesjirwan, J: **C.2**: 61.
Nofz, M: **K.1**: 191.
Noh, S: **F.3**: 130.
Noormahomed, A: **K.4**: 32.
Nordmann, E: **F.4.2**: 148.
Norström, T: **F.8**: 100. **K.1**: 192.
Novak, M: **F.2**: 30.
Nowak, K: **J.5**: 28.
Nowak, M: **I.2**: 25.
Nozawa, S: **G.3.2**: 70.
Numata, K: **D.5**: 18.
Nunley, E: **C.2**: 68. **F.4.1**: 2.
Nunnally, E: **F.4.2**: 62. **K.3**: 8. **K.4**: 7.
Nurse, L: **C.5**: 46.
Nwankwo, A: **J.6**: 25.
O'Brien, S: **E.2**: 3.
O'Bryant, S: **F.4.2**: 117.
O'Callaghan, E: **F.5**: 10.
O'Connor, I: **K.1**: 144.
O'Connor, J: **K.2**: 39.
O'Connor, P: **K.2**: 16.
O'Donnell, C: **I.2**: 21.
O'Donovan, K: **F.4.2**: 115. **F.5**: 33.
O'Flaherty, K: **F.4.1**: 8.
O'Malley, P: **K.1**: 13, 119.
O'Neill, O: **F.2**: 71.
O'Rand, A: **I.3**: 17.
O'Reilly, P: **C.4**: 20.
Oakes, G: **B.1.1**: 25. **D.3**: 35.

Oberg, J: **D.7**: 144.
Oberlander, H: **K.1**: 224.
Oberle, M: **F.3**: 48.
Obudho, R: **G.3.2**: 98.
Ochberg, R: **C.1**: 26.
Ochiai, H: **D.2**: 1.
Ochs, E: **D.7**: 55.
Ocon, S: **G.3.2**: 35.
Oda, T: **E.3**: 19.
Oetting, E: **J.8**: 8.
Offen, K: **F.5**: 5.
Ogan, C: **D.7**: 111.
Ogawa, K: **C.3**: 20.
Ogawa, T: **I.4**: 13.
Ogiso, M: **C.5**: 39.
Ohashi, T: **F.2**: 15.
Ohlin, L: **A.2**: 1. **F.4.2**: 71.
Ohm, R: **D.9**: 25.
Ohno, M: **D.1.1**: 23.
Ohtsuka, K: **K.2**: 54.
Oishi, Y: **H.7**: 4.
Ojeda, G: **F.3**: 27.
Ojima, F: **D.9.8**: 5.
Ojo, M: **D.5**: 8.
Okada, N: **D.1.2**: 5.
Okafor, F: **G.3.2**: 55.
Okahara, M: **C.2**: 67.
Okamura, K: **I.3**: 32.
Oksa, J: **H.4**: 39.
Okumura, T: **D.1.1**: 24.
Olesen, D: **D.6**: 24.
Oliveira, N: **K.1**: 217.
Oliver, M: **G.3.2**: 76.
Oliver, P: **C.4**: 23, 29.
Oliverio, A: **D.6**: 29. **K.4**: 71, 86.
Olofsson, G: **J.5**: 1.
Olsen, J: **C.7**: 7.
Olshansky, S: **F.3**: 75.
Olson, D: **D.7**: 69.
Olson, P: **J.6**: 14.
Omark, D: **C.1**: 36.

INTERNATIONAL BIBLIOGRAPHY OF SOCIOLOGY — 1988

Omodei, M: **C.3**: 1.
Omuta, G: **G.3.2**: 44.
Omvedt, G: **G.3.1**: 59.
Onda, M: **H.1**: 3.
Oni, G: **F.3**: 134.
Ono, M: **D.1.1**: 28.
Ono, Y: **F.4.1**: 22.
Onunwa, U: **F.5**: 94.
Oommen, T: **A.2**: 5.
Opp, K: **J.5**: 11.
Oppen, M: **I.3**: 46.
Oppenheimer, V: **F.4.1**: 60.
Orbell, J: **C.7**: 4.
Orcutt, J: **F.5**: 50.
Orense, V: **F.3**: 39.
Orlebeke, J: **K.4**: 88.
Ornelas, R: **F.3**: 143.
Ortega R., E: **K.1**: 232.
Orthner, D: **F.4.1**: 53.
Oscarsson, L: **K.1**: 204.
Osgood, W: **K.1**: 13.
Oshagbemi, T: **D.9.5**: 17.
Osipov, G: **A.1**: 32.
Oskamp, S: **D.7**: 138.
Ostow, R: **F.7**: 81.
Otani, S: **C.4**: 19.
Otani, T: **D.4**: 2.
Otero, G: **H.4**: 9.
Otnes, P: **H.5**: 7.
Overton, J: **G.3.1**: 31.
Oviawe, O: **K.4**: 63.
Owen, B: **I.5**: 19.
Owen, M: **F.2**: 85.
Owiro, A: **G.3.2**: 130.
Ozolins, U: **F.7**: 29.
Ozonoff, D: **G.1**: 15.
Pabst, M: **F.4.2**: 38.
Padel, U: **K.1**: 163.
Padovani, L: **G.3.2**: 46, 82.
Padua, N: **D.9.5**: 21.
Page, T: **C.7**: 41.

Page, Le, R: **D.7**: 75.
Pahl, J: **K.4**: 27.
Pahl, R: **F.4.2**: 125. **I.1**: 6. **I.2**: 46.
Paicheler, G: **C.3**: 37.
Pakulski, J: **J.5**: 25.
Palard, J: **D.5**: 79.
Paletz, D: **D.7**: 118.
Palloni, A: **F.3**: 144.
Palmer, G: **F.4.2**: 43.
Palmieri, A: **F.8**: 34.
Palmore, J: **F.3**: 31.
Palomino, H: **I.7**: 6.
Pandey, A: **F.3**: 10.
Pandey, J: **D.1.1**: 41.
Pang, G: **F.4.1**: 28.
Pankhurst, J: **D.1.1**: 45.
Pantham, T: **J.1**: 2.
Papageorgiou, M: **D.9.9**: 5.
Papert, S: **D.6**: 1.
Pappenfort, D: **K.2**: 41.
Paquette, L: **C.2**: 23.
Paquin, L: **E.2**: 31.
Paradeise, C: **I.2**: 2.
Paradis, L: **G.2**: 2.
Parcel, T: **I.2**: 37.
Pardo Galvan, S: **F.8**: 20.
Pargament, K: **D.5**: 38.
Pargetter, R: **D.3**: 15.
Paridon, van, W: **I.2**: 48.
Parikh, S: **D.5**: 42.
Parilla, P: **C.5**: 23.
Parish, T: **C.2**: 93.
Park, A: **K.1**: 46.
Park, K: **F.4.2**: 103.
Park, P: **A.1**: 38.
Parke, R: **K.4**: 89.
Parker, B: **K.4**: 22, 56, 61.
Parker, H: **C.7**: 14.
Parkes, C: **F.4.1**: 2.
Parks, A: **F.2**: 37.
Parpart, J: **F.5**: 81.

Parr, J: **F.5**: 31.
Pashardes, P: **K.1**: 196.
Passevant, C: **E.2**: 15.
Paternoster, R: **K.1**: 93, 101.
Paterson, R: **D.7**: 136.
Patil, B: **D.7**: 29. **G.3.1**: 19.
Patil, M: **D.1.1**: 46.
Patnoe, S: **C.1**: 19.
Paton, G: **C.2**: 26.
Patrick, D: **K.4**: 64.
Patterson, D: **D.5**: 12.
Patterson, J: **F.3**: 13.
Patton, C: **F.3**: 99.
Patton, T: **E.1**: 5.
Paulhus, D: **C.3**: 19.
Paulino, B: **D.7**: 78.
Paulley, N: **G.3.2**: 134.
Paulus, P: **K.1**: 142, 175.
Paunonen, S: **C.2**: 34.
Pausewang, S: **G.3.1**: 22.
Pauwels, A: **F.7**: 29.
Paviour, R: **K.3**: 14.
Pawelak, J: **K.2**: 33.
Payeng, H: **E.3**: 9.
Payer, L: **K.4**: 52.
Peacock, G: **K.3**: 32.
Peacock, J: **D.5**: 12.
Peacock, W: **E.3**: 6.
Pearce, P: **I.7**: 25.
Pearson, D: **F.7**: 64.
Pearson, F: **K.1**: 155.
Pearson, G: **K.1**: 80.
Pearson, M: **G.1**: 13.
Pearson, N: **C.7**: 2.
Pearson, R: **B.2**: 2. **I.2**: 64.
Pease, K: **K.1**: 105.
Peck, D: **K.1**: 41.
Peek, C: **F.4.2**: 110.
Pegels, C: **K.4**: 29.
Peile, C: **K.3**: 28.
Peinado López, M: **F.5**: 32.

Pelham, A: **F.2**: 55.
Pellegrino, E: **K.4**: 23.
Pelosi, N: **C.1**: 27.
Pelton, L: **K.1**: 57.
Penman, R: **D.7**: 21.
Penn, R: **I.4**: 2. **I.6**: 1.
Penny, R: **C.7**: 9.
Peraldi, M: **F.8**: 48. **G.3.2**: 39, 82.
Perera, H: **F.3**: 39.
Pérez Gómez, A: **K.1**: 210.
Pérez Moreda, V: **F.1**: 5.
Perin, C: **D.1.2**: 1.
Perlo, V: **F.7**: 20.
Perloff, J: **C.2**: 7.
Perman, L: **I.2**: 55.
Perrineau, P: **J.5**: 10.
Perrucci, C: **F.4.2**: 96.
Persons, J: **C.2**: 7.
Peschard, J: **J.6**: 7–8.
Pessar, P: **F.8**: 105.
Petch, A: **F.2**: 68.
Peters, A: **D.7**: 82.
Peters, G: **C.5**: 20.
Peters, R: **F.4.2**: 144.
Peters, V: **B.3**: 3.
Petersen, A: **F.2**: 1.
Petersen, D: **I.3**: 24. **I.6**: 20. **K.1**: 42.
Petersen, J: **G.3.2**: 121.
Petersen, L: **D.5**: 30.
Peterson, B: **D.7**: 112.
Peterson, E: **F.2**: 31.
Peterson, K: **D.9.4**: 1.
Peterson, M: **C.6**: 13.
Peterson, R: **K.1**: 189.
Peterson, S: **C.5**: 41.
Petre, I: **D.9.5**: 5.
Petschen, S: **D.7**: 11.
Pettigrew, T: **F.7**: 108.
Pettit, G: **C.3**: 13.
Peyrot, M: **F.4.1**: 35.
Pfennig, W: **F.8**: 99.

Pflaumer, P: **F.1**: 1.
Pfleiderer, B: **K.4**: 60.
Phillips, D: **G.1**: 13. **K.2**: 2, 25.
Phillips, J: **C.5**: 45. **F.3**: 21, 56.
Phillips, M: **K.1**: 201.
Phillips, R: **F.3**: 39. **F.4.2**: 84.
Philo, G: **D.1.1**: 29.
Picard, R: **D.7**: 126.
Piccione, F: **F.8**: 50.
Picciotto, S: **B.1.1**: 16.
Piccone, P: **D.3**: 35.
Pichňa, J: **B.1.3**: 29.
Pickard-Cambridge, C: **G.3.2**: 61.
Pickvance, C: **I.2**: 16.
Pierce, C: **K.2**: 3.
Pierce, J: **D.7**: 100.
Pierret, J: **D.7**: 108.
Pilkington, E: **F.7**: 97.
Pillai, V: **F.3**: 86.
Pillemer, K: **F.4.2**: 95.
Pilon-Lê, L: **F.7**: 17.
Pina, A: **J.6**: 31.
Pinder, D: **G.3.2**: 122.
Pineda Bravo, G: **G.3.1**: 71.
Pinnelli, A: **F.4.2**: 146.
Pinney, J: **K.1**: 190.
Pinto, D: **F.8**: 69.
Pirie, M: **F.5**: 26.
Pirog-Good, M: **K.1**: 36.
Pitt, D: **G.3.1**: 8.
Pittman, J: **F.4.1**: 53. **F.4.2**: 45.
Pittman-Lindeman, M: **F.3**: 100.
Pitts, J: **K.1**: 116.
Placencia, M: **G.3.2**: 59.
Plank, van der, P: **D.7**: 76.
Plant, M: **K.1**: 41.
Platts, M: **D.3**: 9.
Platzer, S: **D.9**: 12.
Pligt, van der, J: **C.7**: 27.
Pliner, P: **C.2**: 71.
Plous, S: **J.8**: 5, 12.

Plowman, D: **I.6**: 12.
Pockley, P: **D.6**: 20.
Poffenberger, D: **F.6**: 28.
Poggi, G: **H.2**: 3.
Poggie, J: **I.3**: 47.
Pokrovskaya, M: **H.3**: 16.
Polk, K: **A.2**: 1. **K.1**: 188.
Pollak, M: **F.3**: 113.
Pollnac, R: **I.3**: 47.
Pollock, L: **D.3**: 4.
Pondy, L: **C.5**: 15.
Pongratz, H: **F.2**: 61.
Popescu, S: **A.1**: 9.
Popp, A: **F.8**: 71.
Porcellini, L: **K.1**: 2.
Porket, J: **D.9.8**: 10.
Porta, M: **K.4**: 64.
Porter, C: **K.4**: 64.
Porter, K: **F.3**: 69.
Porter, R: **C.1**: 1. **H.5**: 4.
Portis, L: **E.2**: 15.
Post, K: **I.2**: 52.
Potel, J: **D.5**: 79.
Potepan, M: **I.6**: 42.
Potrykowska, A: **F.8**: 2. **G.3**: 4. **G.3.1**: 27.
Potter, R: **G.3**: 3.
Potts, M: **F.3**: 72.
Poulat, E: **D.5**: 79.
Poulton, G: **C.5**: 16.
Poverny, L: **F.4.1**: 21.
Powell, C: **C.2**: 26.
Powell, G: **I.2**: 26.
Powell, J: **D.7**: 122. **G.1**: 11.
Powell, W: **F.2**: 53.
Powell-Griner, E: **F.3**: 137.
Powers, D: **D.9.5**: 13.
Prahl, R: **C.4**: 29.
Prakasa, R: **G.3.2**: 155.
Pramod, S: **G.3.1**: 9.
Prasad, A: **G.3.1**: 3.
Pratt, G: **E.2**: 29. **G.3.2**: 47.

Pratt, M: **D.3**: 32.
Pravda, A: **J.2**: 6.
Preisendörfer, P: **I.2**: 7. **I.3**: 50. **I.4**: 23.
Premack, S: **C.4**: 12.
Prentice, A: **F.5**: 58.
Presser, H: **F.4.2**: 51.
Price, M: **K.4**: 32.
Price, N: **E.2**: 2.
Pride, J: **D.7**: 7.
Prins, H: **K.3**: 6.
Prioux, F: **F.3**: 71.
Pritchard, M: **D.9.3**: 9.
Probert, B: **H.4**: 43.
Procter, M: **B.3**: 6.
Prokopenko, V: **C.7**: 22.
Pronovost, G: **I.7**: 17.
Prosser, T: **B.1.1**: 16.
Prout, A: **F.4.2**: 40.
Psacharopoulos, G: **D.9.5**: 8.
Puchol, L: **F.2**: 7.
Puckett, T: **K.3**: 16.
Pugliese, E: **F.8**: 54.
Pullen, G: **C.4**: 5.
Punter, J: **H.7**: 3.
Putte, Van Den, B: **B.3**: 25.
Putzel, J: **K.1**: 228.
Pycroft, C: **I.2**: 52.
Pytel-Tafel, E: **F.8**: 25.
Quadango, J: **K.2**: 58.
Quah, S: **F.4.1**: 3.
Quang Ba, T: **F.7**: 55.
Quayle, E: **C.4**: 2.
Queipo, D: **K.1**: 205.
Quéniart, A: **F.4.2**: 4.
Quesnel, A: **F.1**: 8.
Quester, G: **J.8**: 3.
Quijano, A: **A.3**: 4.
Quinlan, M: **E.2**: 21. **I.4**: 25.
Raab, C: **D.9.2**: 4.
Racioppi, F: **F.3**: 18.
Radalj, T: **K.1**: 201.

Radlett, M: **F.3**: 103.
Radley, A: **C.2**: 54.
Radu, N: **D.1.3**: 11.
Radzinowicz, L: **K.1**: 105.
Raffalovice, L: **H.3**: 17.
Rafoth, B: **D.7**: 41.
Raha, M: **F.4.1**: 52.
Rahman, H: **K.1**: 29.
Rahman, M: **D.9.5**: 20.
Rai, K: **G.3.1**: 85.
Raigoza, J: **F.7**: 54.
Rainwater, L: **I.2**: 55.
Rajaiah, B: **F.5**: 68.
Rajendra, S: **G.3.1**: 18.
Rakodi, C: **J.4**: 10.
Rallis, T: **G.3.2**: 132.
Ramírez Solero, A: **G.1**: 4.
Ramu, G: **E.2**: 5. **F.4.1**: 37–38. **F.4.2**: 17.
Rancaño, M: **G.3.1**: 21.
Randolph, B: **G.3.2**: 85.
Ranfla González, A: **G.3.2**: 146.
Ranger, T: **D.1.1**: 8.
Rani, J: **F.5**: 68.
Rankin, C: **I.6**: 4.
Rannikko, P: **H.4**: 39.
Ransel, D: **F.4.2**: 37.
Rantakallio, P: **F.4.2**: 53.
Rao, K: **F.3**: 50. **F.4.2**: 44.
Rao, M: **G.1**: 13.
Rao, V: **F.3**: 136.
Raphael, R: **F.5**: 55.
Rapoport, A: **C.3**: 25.
Rapoport, D: **J.5**: 14.
Rapoport, T: **F.2**: 11.
Rapoport-Albert, A: **E.3**: 10.
Rash, J: **F.2**: 19.
Rasinski, K: **C.2**: 12.
Raskin, R: **C.2**: 95.
Rasmussen, D: **F.8**: 9–10.
Rasnake, R: **D.1.1**: 10.
Ratcliff, R: **E.2**: 41.

Ratcliffe, J: **K.4**: 78.
Rathgeber, E: **I.2**: 14.
Rattner, A: **F.2**: 2.
Ratzsch, D: **D.6**: 7.
Raulin, A: **G.3.2**: 17.
Ravuvu, A: **G.3.1**: 67.
Ray, B: **D.9.2**: 5.
Reason, P: **B.1.3**: 13.
Reddy, C: **I.2**: 19.
Reddy, P: **F.3**: 2.
Reddy, T: **F.4.1**: 29.
Redekop, P: **I.7**: 18.
Reed, A: **K.1**: 72.
Reeke, G: **D.6**: 1.
Reese, W: **D.9**: 23.
Reeves, M: **D.9.5**: 4.
Regan, D: **C.5**: 49.
Regis, H: **D.7**: 19.
Regnault, H: **G.3.2**: 15.
Rehorick, D: **D.6**: 32.
Reich, M: **G.1**: 15.
Reid, W: **K.3**: 35.
Reinarman, C: **A.2**: 1. **K.1**: 128.
Reinhardt, N: **G.3.1**: 60.
Reis, H: **C.3**: 27.
Reiss, A: **K.1**: 70.
Reissland, N: **K.4**: 60.
Reitz, J: **F.8**: 73.
Rellini, G: **F.8**: 70.
Renard, D: **G.3.2**: 12.
Renaud, M: **I.3**: 39.
Rendlová, E: **K.2**: 42.
Reskin, B: **F.5**: 29.
Reskina, S: **D.9.3**: 8.
Resnick, M: **D.7**: 71.
Reygadas, L: **J.6**: 5, 8.
Reynaud, J: **I.6**: 22.
Rhodes, A: **C.6**: 4.
Riagáin, P: **D.7**: 8.
Riandey, B: **F.1**: 26.
Rice, M: **F.2**: 75.

Rice, R: **D.7**: 128.
Richard, L: **F.6**: 16.
Richards, D: **K.1**: 42.
Richardson, A: **D.9.9**: 8.
Richardson, J: **D.5**: 41. **D.7**: 120.
Richardson, L: **C.3**: 41.
Richie, T: **C.2**: 100.
Richter, K: **F.4.2**: 23.
Ricketts, E: **E.2**: 19.
Ricketts, T: **K.4**: 64.
Rickford, J: **D.7**: 75.
Ricolfi, L: **D.5**: 49.
Rigby, K: **C.7**: 34.
Rigg, J: **F.8**: 37.
Rijsman, J: **C.4**: 4.
Rimani, S: **F.8**: 103.
Rimmer, D: **G.3.1**: 79.
Río García, L: **F.5**: 77.
Riordan, C: **C.2**: 53.
Riordan, J: **D.9**: 24. **F.2**: 17.
Rioseco, F: **G.3.2**: 3.
Riska, E: **I.5**: 15. **K.4**: 4, 16.
Risman, B: **F.4.2**: 103. **F.6**: 29.
Risseeuw, C: **F.5**: 71.
Ritzer, G: **B.1.1**: 29. **I.4**: 28.
Rivera, de, J: **J.8**: 10, 12.
Rizzo, T: **C.3**: 11.
Robb, M: **F.4.2**: 118.
Robbin, A: **K.2**: 28.
Robbins, T: **D.5**: 10, 57.
Robertson, A: **K.2**: 57.
Robertson, D: **K.2**: 34.
Robertson, J: **D.1.1**: 19.
Robey, D: **C.5**: 10.
Robins, K: **D.7**: 15.
Robins, L: **D.7**: 23.
Robins, P: **K.2**: 9.
Robinson, B: **D.8**: 11. **F.4.2**: 58.
Robinson, D: **F.3**: 119.
Robinson, E: **K.3**: 3. **K.4**: 11.
Robinson, J: **I.6**: 48.

Robinson, M: **J.4**: 9.
Robinson, R: **E.2**: 11.
Robinson, V: **E.2**: 48.
Robitaille, N: **F.3**: 61.
Rochefort, M: **G.3.2**: 92.
Rochowiak, D: **C.1**: 6.
Rock, P: **K.1**: 103, 105.
Rockwell, R: **F.3**: 95.
Rodeheaver, D: **F.3**: 58. **K.4**: 3.
Rodgers, W: **C.7**: 42. **K.1**: 229.
Rodrigo, J: **J.4**: 5.
Rodríguez, H: **F.5**: 95.
Rodríguez, J: **D.5**: 13.
Rodriguez, M: **K.1**: 209.
Rodriguez, N: **F.5**: 23.
Rodríguez A, N: **F.8**: 22.
Rofé, Y: **F.4.1**: 36.
Rogers, B: **F.5**: 56.
Rogers, E: **D.7**: 128.
Rogge, J: **D.7**: 130. **F.8**: 47.
Rohe, W: **K.1**: 96.
Rohlinger, H: **F.4.2**: 63.
Rojek, C: **K.3**: 32.
Rola, L: **C.7**: 25.
Roland, A: **C.2**: 94.
Rolandi Ricci, M: **F.8**: 70.
Romaine, S: **D.7**: 75.
Roman, L: **F.5**: 2.
Román, M: **J.5**: 16.
Roman, P: **I.3**: 61.
Romer, C: **F.3**: 87.
Romney, A: **B.2**: 9.
Roniger, L: **C.3**: 18.
Roos, J: **C.2**: 59.
Roosens, E: **F.8**: 24.
Ropers, R: **G.3.2**: 90.
Rorty, A: **C.2**: 42.
Rose, D: **E.2**: 51, 60.
Rose, L: **K.1**: 26.
Rose, R: **C.5**: 28.
Rose, S: **H.4**: 34.

Röseberg, U: **D.6**: 7.
Rosecrance, J: **I.7**: 8.
Rosen, P: **D.7**: 101.
Rosen, S: **F.7**: 21.
Rosenbaum, S: **D.4**: 12.
Rosenberg, A: **A.1**: 24. **D.6**: 33.
Rosenberg, C: **F.3**: 7.
Rosenberg, S: **J.6**: 20.
Rosenblatt, A: **C.3**: 9.
Rosenblatt, P: **F.4.1**: 2.
Rosenkrantz, B: **F.3**: 7.
Rosenmayr, L: **F.2**: 36.
Rosenstein, R: **F.2**: 46.
Rosenthal, M: **K.1**: 57.
Rosenthal, R: **G.2**: 1.
Rosenwaike, I: **F.3**: 153.
Rosenwald, G: **C.1**: 41.
Rosenzweig, M: **F.3**: 111.
Rosner, T: **F.4.2**: 116.
Rosnow, R: **D.7**: 38.
Ross, C: **G.3.2**: 121. **K.2**: 37.
Ross, J: **F.3**: 32.
Ross, M: **F.3**: 91.
Rosser, R: **K.4**: 70.
Rossi, P: **F.3**: 129.
Rothbart, M: **C.2**: 103.
Rothenberg, L: **C.4**: 22.
Rothenbuhler, E: **D.7**: 107.
Rothman, S: **C.2**: 29.
Roussel, M: **G.3.2**: 92.
Roussillon, A: **A.1**: 10.
Roux, B: **G.3.2**: 15.
Rovine, M: **F.4.2**: 107.
Rovira, D: **J.6**: 37.
Rowland, R: **F.5**: 98.
Rowles, G: **F.2**: 35. **G.3.1**: 52.
Rowse, T: **F.7**: 1.
Roy, W: **H.4**: 22.
Rozelle, R: **I.3**: 13.
Ruback, R: **C.1**: 33.
Rubin, D: **D.7**: 41.

Rubin, J: **J.8**: 6.
Rubinstein, R: **J.8**: 13.
Rüland, J: **J.4**: 7.
Ruff, A: **G.3.2**: 34.
Ruggiero, K: **G.3.1**: 5.
Ruggles, P: **K.2**: 28.
Rugina, A: **J.2**: 12.
Rule, B: **A.1**: 17.
Rule, J: **D.9**: 3.
Rumley, D: **K.2**: 15.
Runciman, W: **B.1.1**: 31.
Ruppert, H: **F.8**: 39.
Russell, G: **F.4.2**: 66. **K.1**: 14.
Russell, R: **I.6**: 46.
Rustagi, K: **D.6**: 18.
Руткевич, : **E.2**: 66.
Rwezaura, B: **F.4.2**: 18, 31.
Ryan, E: **F.2**: 28.
Ryan, M: **D.7**: 89.
Ryan, R: **C.2**: 96.
Rychtaříková, J: **F.3**: 139.
Rydin, Y: **G.3.2**: 91.
Rykiel, Z: **F.8**: 17, 33, 44. **G.1**: 9.
Rytina, S: **F.4.1**: 24.
Saarinen, A: **F.5**: 14.
Sabatelli, R: **F.4.1**: 47.
Sabatier, R: **F.3**: 103. **F.7**: 99.
Sackett, L: **F.7**: 1.
Sacks, M: **D.1.1**: 45.
Sadler, P: **H.4**: 24.
Sadoun, M: **J.6**: 34.
Sadri, A: **D.1.1**: 27.
Sadri, M: **D.1.1**: 27.
Saeed, K: **H.3**: 25.
Sáez Buanaventura, C: **F.5**: 77.
Safford, J: **A.1**: 25.
Sagar, S: **K.1**: 235.
Sagaza, H: **A.1**: 29.
Sah, U: **D.5**: 47.
Sahai, I: **G.3.1**: 47.
Sahayam, M: **F.2**: 25.

Said, E: **J.5**: 13.
Saint-Gérard, Y: **J.3**: 9.
Saito, S: **B.1.1**: 14.
Sajo, T: **J.4**: 7.
Saka, Y: **A.3**: 6.
Saklofske, D: **F.2**: 77.
Sala-Diakanda, M: **F.1**: 7.
Salaff, J: **F.4.2**: 56.
Salehi-Esfahani, H: **J.6**: 28.
Salgado, R: **K.4**: 90.
Salt, J: **F.8**: 94.
Salts, C: **F.4.1**: 46.
Salzinger, S: **C.3**: 46.
Samha, M: **F.3**: 6.
Sampson, A: **K.1**: 80.
Sampson, R: **C.3**: 28. **D.3**: 32.
Samson, C: **F.6**: 2.
Samson, I: **E.3**: 17.
Sanbonmatsu, M: **G.3.2**: 26.
Sánchez, V: **G.1**: 7. **K.1**: 214.
Sánchez Carrero, P: **F.5**: 77.
Sánchez Molinero, J: **C.4**: 14.
Sanda, A: **A.1**: 18.
Sandelands, L: **I.3**: 10.
Sander, U: **D.7**: 130.
Sanders, A: **K.1**: 21.
Sanders, B: **D.7**: 1.
Sanders, C: **F.4.1**: 2.
Sanders, D: **K.4**: 32.
Sanders, G: **C.7**: 18.
Sanders, J: **D.4**: 13.
Sandstrom, K: **F.2**: 79.
Sandu, D: **B.3**: 1, 4.
Sanger, W: **F.6**: 15.
Sant, M: **K.2**: 15.
Santana, R: **G.3.1**: 62.
Santillán, M: **F.5**: 89.
Santos, R: **K.1**: 2.
Saraceno, B: **K.4**: 12.
Saraga, E: **K.1**: 53.
Saraswathi, S: **F.2**: 20.

Saraswathi, T: **D.1.3**: 10.
Sarat, A: **K.1**: 127.
Sardar, Z: **H.4**: 36.
Saris, W: **B.3**: 25. **C.1**: 38.
Sarkar, J: **E.2**: 58.
Sashkin, M: **D.9.4**: 1.
Sassen, S: **F.8**: 81.
Sati, P: **F.2**: 60.
Sato, H: **F.4.2**: 104.
Sato, T: **C.4**: 21. **D.7**: 96.
Sato, Y: **G.3.1**: 37.
Saunier, D: **D.6**: 24.
Sauvage, P: **D.5**: 65.
Savage, M: **E.2**: 45, 65.
Savells, J: **D.1.1**: 12.
Savitch, H: **G.3.2**: 119.
Sawai, A: **A.5**: 4.
Sawhill, I: **E.2**: 19.
Sawyer, R: **K.1**: 48.
Saxe, L: **K.4**: 5.
Saxena, H: **G.3.1**: 6.
Saxer, U: **D.7**: 130.
Sayigh, R: **F.5**: 79. **F.8**: 83.
Scaff, L: **D.1.1**: 47.
Scarduelli, P: **E.3**: 24.
Scarf, M: **K.1**: 42.
Scarr, D: **F.7**: 78.
Scarr, S: **F.7**: 49.
Scattergood, H: **I.4**: 2.
Sceery, A: **C.2**: 5.
Schaeffer, M: **K.1**: 142.
Schaeffer, N: **K.2**: 38.
Schaeffer, P: **F.8**: 12.
Schall, J: **D.3**: 10.
Scheckenbach, M: **F.3**: 140.
Scheer, J: **F.3**: 11.
Scheff, T: **C.2**: 80.
Scheffel, D: **F.3**: 57.
Scheidt, R: **F.2**: 35. **G.3.1**: 34.
Scheingold, S: **B.1.1**: 16.
Schelp, L: **G.2**: 15.

Scher, A: **I.7**: 6.
Scher, S: **C.2**: 51.
Scherer, L: **C.2**: 24.
Scheuch, E: **B.3**: 19. **E.1**: 1.
Schiller, P: **D.5**: 22.
Schillinger, E: **H.4**: 6.
Schlesinger, P: **D.1.1**: 29.
Schlobinski, P: **D.7**: 77.
Schmid, M: **B.1.1**: 12.
Schmidt, G: **H.4**: 27.
Schneider, A: **K.1**: 146.
Schneider, C: **K.1**: 42.
Schneider, E: **F.1**: 25.
Schneider, J: **F.3**: 11.
Schoeff, D: **D.9.3**: 1.
Schoen, R: **F.1**: 15, 22. **F.4.1**: 33, 62.
Schoenberger, E: **I.5**: 1.
Schoenherr, R: **D.5**: 67.
Schooler, C: **I.4**: 26.
Schott, T: **F.4.1**: 41.
Schröer, A: **I.3**: 45.
Schubert, J: **C.6**: 2.
Schuckit, M: **K.1**: 194.
Schuller, T: **D.1.1**: 38.
Schulze, E: **F.4.1**: 49.
Schulze, H: **F.2**: 36.
Schuman, H: **F.7**: 92.
Schumann, M: **I.1**: 5.
Schuppe, M: **D.1.2**: 7.
Schur, E: **F.6**: 3.
Schuster, C: **C.1**: 27.
Schuurman, F: **G.3.2**: 80.
Schwager, K: **B.3**: 24.
Schwalbe, M: **C.6**: 20.
Schwartz, B: **F.3**: 29.
Schwartz, I: **K.1**: 143.
Schwartz, J: **D.6**: 1. **F.4.1**: 24.
Schwartz, M: **G.2**: 8.
Schwartz, P: **F.6**: 29.
Schwartz, R: **I.2**: 63.
Schwenk, C: **C.2**: 11. **C.3**: 14.

Schwochau, S: **I.6**: 37, 41.
Sciolla, L: **D.5**: 49.
Scott, A: **D.6**: 11. **K.1**: 37, 53.
Scott, I: **J.4**: 4.
Scott, J: **C.4**: 27–28. **K.1**: 176.
Screvens, R: **K.1**: 98.
Scrivens, E: **K.4**: 45.
Scully, D: **K.1**: 69.
Searles, P: **D.4**: 5.
Secombe, M: **D.7**: 6.
Seddon, E: **F.4.1**: 61.
Seedhouse, D: **K.4**: 19.
Seeman, T: **F.2**: 63.
Segal, S: **F.3**: 44.
Segal, Z: **C.2**: 3.
Segre, S: **A.1**: 1.
Seguin, M: **F.6**: 16.
Segura, A: **G.3.2**: 82.
Sehgal, V: **F.1**: 30.
Seibel, H: **I.5**: 6.
Seidel, A: **C.5**: 29.
Seidner, L: **C.2**: 62.
Seitz, P: **I.3**: 33.
Selden, M: **G.3**: 1.
Selengant, C: **D.5**: 2.
Selier, F: **F.8**: 40.
Sell, R: **F.8**: 53.
Seller, M: **D.3**: 33.
Seltzer, J: **F.4.2**: 91.
Selya, R: **K.4**: 62.
Semmer, N: **K.1**: 190.
Semmoud, B: **G.3.2**: 15.
Semyonov, M: **F.7**: 10.
Sen, A: **F.3**: 125.
Sen, P: **D.7**: 2.
Senay, E: **K.4**: 53.
Sergevnin, S: **D.4**: 11.
Serow, W: **F.1**: 3. **F.8**: 9–10.
Serr, B: **F.7**: 115.
Setti, L: **G.3.1**: 72.
Severy, L: **F.3**: 39.

Sgritta, G: **D.6**: 6.
Shadish, W: **K.4**: 66.
Shai, D: **F.3**: 153.
Shalin, D: **A.2**: 2.
Shalit, B: **J.7**: 3.
Shamir, B: **I.7**: 2.
Shankar, P: **G.3.1**: 15.
Shanon, B: **D.7**: 12.
Shanta, K: **F.3**: 33.
Shapiro, M: **D.7**: 35.
Shapiro, R: **F.4.1**: 17. **F.5**: 70.
Sharabi, H: **E.3**: 21.
Sharma, P: **F.5**: 88.
Sharma, R: **G.3.2**: 65.
Sharot, S: **F.7**: 34.
Sharp, D: **D.6**: 1.
Sharp, R: **F.5**: 90.
Shaver, S: **K.2**: 12.
Shavit, Y: **F.2**: 2.
Shaw, A: **F.7**: 45.
Shaw, D: **G.3**: 5.
Shaw, G: **I.7**: 23.
Shaw, M: **J.8**: 4.
Shaw, R: **C.2**: 95.
Shedler, J: **C.3**: 50.
Shehayeb, D: **G.3.2**: 95.
Sheley, J: **K.1**: 111.
Shenhav, Y: **I.2**: 43.
Shenk, D: **F.2**: 35.
Shepherd, A: **J.8**: 11.
Shepherd, C: **F.5**: 34.
Shepherd, J: **E.3**: 3.
Shepherd, M: **C.1**: 1.
Sherbourne, C: **K.4**: 79.
Sherman, S: **F.2**: 43.
Shetreet, S: **J.3**: 23.
Shibano, S: **D.9.3**: 5.
Shields, J: **D.5**: 78.
Shimazu, S: **K.1**: 195.
Shin, E: **F.8**: 85.
Shin, H: **G.3.1**: 43.

Shin, K: **E.2**: 72.
Shinagawa, L: **F.4.1**: 28.
Shingals, Y: **E.2**: 42.
Shinohara, T: **G.2**: 9.
Shiobara, T: **D.1.1**: 21.
Shlapentokh, V: **I.6**: 46.
Shokeid, M: **F.8**: 6.
Shortland, M: **D.6**: 24.
Shouji, Y: **G.3.2**: 26.
Shrauger, J: **C.2**: 92.
Shreir, S: **J.5**: 36.
Shrestha, N: **F.3**: 13. **F.8**: 45. **K.4**: 36.
Shrum, W: **C.5**: 35.
Shu, G: **D.9.2**: 3.
Shughart, W: **F.3**: 9.
Shulman, L: **F.3**: 92.
Shupe, A: **D.5**: 32.
Sibuye, B: **D.1.1**: 8.
Sickmeier, M: **I.2**: 37.
Sidanius, J: **E.2**: 59.
Siddique, S: **D.9.5**: 18.
Sieber, J: **A.3**: 5.
Sieber, K: **E.1**: 9.
Siefert, K: **K.3**: 21.
Siegers, J: **F.3**: 85.
Sigelman, L: **D.9.9**: 1.
Sigman, M: **F.2**: 80.
Signorielli, N: **D.7**: 147–148.
Silber, J: **F.1**: 17.
Silj, A: **D.7**: 92.
Silk, M: **D.5**: 55.
Siller, S: **I.2**: 42.
Sills, A: **G.3.2**: 42.
Silva, de, V: **F.3**: 23.
Silvéréano, F: **D.9**: 15.
Silverman, N: **K.4**: 5.
Simard, P: **F.8**: 70.
Siméon, J: **D.1.1**: 37.
Simmons, C: **C.2**: 16.
Simmons, R: **F.3**: 21, 56.
Simon, M: **I.3**: 52.
Simon-Nahum, P: **F.7**: 23.
Simonton, D: **C.2**: 1. **D.1.1**: 20.
Simpson, J: **F.5**: 16.
Sinclair, I: **K.2**: 16.
Singelmann, J: **E.2**: 39.
Singer, P: **K.4**: 42.
Singh, A: **C.2**: 4. **D.5**: 47. **G.3.2**: 77. **H.4**: 18.
Singh, D: **F.2**: 13.
Singh, I: **G.3.1**: 17.
Singh, R: **D.7**: 20, 60. **G.3.1**: 82.
Singh, S: **D.1.1**: 6. **G.3.1**: 75.
Singleton, R: **B.1.3**: 2.
Sinha, A: **D.5**: 47.
Sipan, C: **I.2**: 34.
Sixel, F: **H.2**: 2.
Sjostrom, B: **F.7**: 31.
Skeels, J: **I.6**: 16.
Skilling, H: **A.3**: 3.
Skinner, J: **I.2**: 1.
Sklair, L: **E.3**: 28.
Skogan, W: **K.1**: 65.
Skolnick, J: **G.2**: 17. **K.1**: 42.
Skovron, M: **F.8**: 21.
Skovron, S: **K.1**: 176.
Skutnabb-Kangas, T: **D.9**: 21.
Slack, A: **F.5**: 67. **F.6**: 13.
Sladkowski, W: **D.1.1**: 32.
Slater, M: **A.5**: 5.
Slater, R: **D.9.4**: 1.
Slesina, W: **I.3**: 45.
Slomczynski, K: **B.3**: 17.
Sly, D: **F.1**: 3.
Small, R: **C.7**: 19.
Small, S: **F.4.2**: 108.
Smart, A: **K.1**: 107.
Smetana, J: **F.4.2**: 86.
Smith, A: **K.2**: 11.
Smith, B: **H.7**: 1.
Smith, C: **K.4**: 6, 18.
Smith, D: **C.7**: 38. **J.3**: 7. **K.1**: 80, 112, 130. **K.4**: 80.

Smith, E: **C.2**: 44.
Smith, G: **B.1.2**: 6.
Smith, K: **F.5**: 80. **H.3**: 18.
Smith, M: **G.3.2**: 45. **K.1**: 111.
Smith, N: **H.3**: 26.
Smith, P: **C.6**: 13. **I.3**: 56.
Smith, R: **E.2**: 38. **G.3.2**: 56.
Smith, S: **C.7**: 30.
Smith, T: **D.6**: 18.
Smith-Hefner, N: **D.7**: 49.
Smit, van, D: **K.1**: 167.
Smoker, P: **J.8**: 1.
Smolicz, J: **D.1.1**: 43. **D.7**: 6.
Smyer, M: **B.2**: 6.
Snippenburg, van, L: **F.5**: 18.
Snowden, L: **F.4.1**: 41.
Snowden, R: **F.3**: 39.
Snyder, C: **C.3**: 16.
Snyderman, M: **C.2**: 29.
Soble, S: **G.1**: 15.
Société française de sociologie: **A.3**: 12.
Sockell, D: **I.6**: 37.
Soeda, A: **K.2**: 44.
Sokolowski, R: **D.6**: 1.
Soler, M: **K.1**: 143.
Solomon, R: **A.5**: 7. **C.2**: 75.
Solomon, Z: **K.4**: 88.
Solomos, J: **F.7**: 98.
Somerville, P: **C.7**: 36.
Someya, Y: **K.2**: 4.
Sommer, R: **C.2**: 98. **C.5**: 29.
Sommers, S: **C.2**: 64.
Sonigo, P: **F.3**: 119.
Sonnert, G: **J.2**: 8.
Soos, K: **E.3**: 17.
Soothill, K: **A.1**: 8.
Sorell, G: **F.4.2**: 110.
Sorin, M: **D.9.5**: 5.
Sormano, A: **B.2**: 4.
Soule, W: **I.4**: 9.
Sourani, T: **F.4.2**: 19.

South, N: **J.3**: 18.
South, S: **F.5**: 48–49.
Southall, A: **G.3.1**: 80.
Southam, C: **I.2**: 6.
Spain, D: **G.2**: 5.
Spain. Instituto de la Mujer: **F.5**: 85.
Spanou, C: **J.5**: 7.
Sparks, C: **D.7**: 117.
Spear, S: **K.4**: 22.
Speare, A: **G.3.2**: 151, 154.
Spears, R: **C.7**: 27.
Spear, Sherilynn, F: **K.4**: 87.
Spector, P: **I.3**: 36.
Spector, W: **F.2**: 46.
Speier, H: **D.6**: 17.
Spencer, L: **J.2**: 4.
Spenner, K: **E.2**: 61.
Spilman, M: **I.3**: 61.
Spinnewyn, F: **K.2**: 24.
Spirer, H: **K.1**: 72.
Spitze, G: **F.4.2**: 122.
Sprague, J: **K.1**: 136.
Sprecher, S: **F.6**: 26.
Sprengers, M: **I.2**: 45.
Sprey, J: **F.4.2**: 128.
Sprigge, T: **C.2**: 41.
Sproull, N: **B.1.3**: 12.
Sridhar, K: **D.7**: 71.
Srivastva, S: **C.4**: 34.
St-Jacques, C: **I.3**: 39.
St. James-Emler, A: **C.3**: 37.
Stack, S: **E.2**: 52.
Stahl, C: **F.8**: 74.
Stahl, H: **A.1**: 12.
Stahura, J: **F.7**: 16.
Stall, R: **C.1**: 27.
Stallings, R: **K.1**: 7.
Stalpers, J: **D.7**: 76.
Станев, : **B.3**: 18.
Stanforth, L: **K.2**: 16.
Stanley, B: **A.3**: 5.

Stansfield, S: **K.4**: 22, 56.
Stanton, M: **F.3**: 36.
Stapleton, D: **D.9.8**: 4.
Stark, E: **K.1**: 58.
Stark, O: **C.7**: 3. **F.1**: 11. **F.8**: 32, 36.
Starkey, K: **C.5**: 21.
Stasser, G: **B.1.3**: 3.
Statham, A: **I.2**: 68.
Stathopoulos, M: **D.4**: 14.
Staub, E: **J.8**: 12.
Stauffer, J: **D.7**: 97.
Steckel, J: **C.7**: 17.
Steel, B: **D.7**: 100.
Steele, V: **D.2**: 2.
Steger, M: **D.7**: 100.
Stehr, N: **B.1.1**: 24.
Stein, J: **G.3.2**: 121. **K.1**: 32. **K.4**: 64.
Steinberg, B: **D.9.2**: 2.
Steinberg, M: **K.4**: 32.
Steiner, K: **C.5**: 29.
Steinglass, P: **K.1**: 193.
Steinhart, D: **K.1**: 143.
Steinmeier, T: **I.2**: 32.
Stenbeck, M: **B.3**: 5.
Stephens, M: **D.9**: 17. **J.3**: 20. **K.3**: 22.
Sterling, T: **A.5**: 7.
Stern, M: **F.7**: 2.
Stern, R: **I.6**: 46.
Sternberg, R: **C.2**: 44, 78.
Stets, J: **F.4.1**: 15.
Stevens, E: **D.4**: 10.
Stevens, G: **F.4.1**: 33.
Stevens, J: **F.4.2**: 54.
Stevenson, P: **K.1**: 163.
Stewart, A: **C.1**: 26.
Stewart, D: **D.7**: 32.
Stewman, S: **C.5**: 24.
Stichter, S: **F.5**: 81.
Stipek, D: **C.2**: 62.
Stockley, D: **F.7**: 50.
Stockmann, R: **I.2**: 49.

Stoeckle, J: **K.4**: 4, 13.
Stojanov, C: **I.6**: 47.
Stokes, C: **F.3**: 138.
Stolzenberg, R: **I.3**: 23.
Stone, D: **D.9.5**: 22.
Stopes-Roe, M: **F.4.1**: 44.
Strassberg, B: **D.5**: 5.
Strasser, H: **E.2**: 39.
Stratton, P: **K.1**: 51.
Strauman, T: **C.2**: 79.
Straus, M: **F.5**: 36. **K.1**: 1, 85.
Strauss, A: **A.3**: 2.
Strauss, G: **I.6**: 37.
Streiff-Fenart, J: **F.4.1**: 30. **F.5**: 70.
Strober, M: **F.4.2**: 134.
Stroebe, M: **F.4.1**: 2.
Stroebe, W: **C.3**: 47. **F.4.1**: 2.
Stromback, T: **I.4**: 11.
Stromgaard, P: **G.1**: 16.
Strother, P: **K.3**: 35.
Strube, M: **C.3**: 8.
Strubelt, W: **F.2**: 36.
Struck, E: **F.8**: 27.
Stubbs, P: **K.1**: 80.
Studlar, D: **J.2**: 9.
Stycos, J: **F.3**: 22.
Subbamma, M: **D.5**: 84.
Suchindran, C: **F.3**: 10.
Suedfeld, P: **C.6**: 12.
Sugarman, D: **F.5**: 36.
Sugaya, Y: **G.3.1**: 38.
Sugimoto, Y: **E.3**: 13.
Sugita, K: **I.3**: 34.
Suitor, J: **F.4.2**: 95.
Sulak, D: **F.4.1**: 55.
Sullivan, M: **F.1**: 20.
Suls, J: **C.7**: 18.
Sundar, R: **F.3**: 28.
Sundaram, J: **I.2**: 52.
Sundeen, R: **C.5**: 7.
Surkyn, J: **F.3**: 55.

Sutcliffe, A: **G.3.2**: 103.
Sutton, G: **F.8**: 19.
Suzuki, I: **D.5**: 20.
Suzuki, M: **B.1.1**: 33.
Suzuki, T: **F.4.1**: 57.
Svanberg, I: **F.7**: 37.
Sven Reher, D: **F.1**: 5.
Svensson, P: **K.2**: 23.
Sverdlik, S: **K.1**: 73.
Swadi, H: **K.1**: 20.
Swain, D: **K.2**: 11.
Swanger, H: **K.1**: 143.
Swanson, G: **C.7**: 16.
Swarankar, R: **J.6**: 19.
Swarnkar, G: **G.3.1**: 53.
Sweetapple, P: **K.1**: 144.
Switzer, L: **D.7**: 86.
Sykora, K: **K.1**: 18.
Syme, S: **I.3**: 44.
Sypher, H: **C.3**: 3.
Szelenyi, I: **E.2**: 63.
Széll, G: **I.6**: 26.
Szirman, A: **H.3**: 14.
Szivos, S: **C.3**: 6.
Szmajke, A: **C.2**: 40.
Sztompka, P: **B.1.1**: 5. **J.5**: 23.
Szyszczak, E: **F.5**: 33.
Ta'Ati, P: **J.6**: 28.
Tabboni, S: **C.7**: 11.
Tabory, E: **F.5**: 22.
Taft, R: **C.1**: 28.
Tagle, S: **J.6**: 6, 8.
Tagliagambe, S: **D.6**: 28.
Taguchi, H: **F.3**: 150.
Tahir, G: **D.9.6**: 1.
Taitz, J: **D.4**: 16.
Takahashi, Y: **E.2**: 18.
Takajashi, Y: **G.3.2**: 70.
Takase, T: **C.5**: 40.
Takegawa, S: **K.2**: 45.
Takenaka, H: **E.2**: 18.

Takeuchi, K: **D.9.5**: 11.
Tamney, J: **D.5**: 41.
Tamura, E: **D.9**: 22.
Tamura, K: **F.4.1**: 74. **K.2**: 59.
Tamura, M: **F.4.1**: 74.
Tanabe, S: **A.1**: 11.
Tanaka, H: **D.7**: 30. **E.3**: 4.
Taniguchi, Y: **J.5**: 32.
Tank, H: **G.3.2**: 124.
Tansey, B: **F.4.2**: 12.
Tapari, B: **F.1**: 20.
Tar, I: **G.3.1**: 61.
Tarrius, A: **F.8**: 48. **G.3.2**: 82.
Tarrow, S: **C.7**: 29.
Tarver, J: **F.8**: 26.
Tashakkori, A: **F.4.1**: 9.
Tausky, C: **I.6**: 46.
Taylor, G: **G.3.2**: 42.
Taylor, M: **J.5**: 33.
Taylor, P: **D.9.5**: 19. **K.4**: 60.
Taylor, R: **F.3**: 34. **F.7**: 73, 80. **I.6**: 31.
Taylor, S: **C.2**: 28. **K.1**: 30.
Taylor-Gooby, P: **K.2**: 20.
Tazelaar, F: **I.2**: 45.
Tedin, K: **F.5**: 44.
Teeling Smith, G: **K.4**: 48.
Teklu, T: **F.3**: 80.
Tellegen, A: **C.2**: 34.
Temkin-Greener, H: **K.4**: 20.
Tennant, C: **K.1**: 6.
Tent, J: **D.9.5**: 10.
Teper, S: **F.3**: 72.
Terada, A: **F.2**: 50.
Terence, M: **K.1**: 105.
Tesser, A: **C.7**: 13.
Tetlock, P: **J.8**: 12.
Teulings, A: **I.6**: 30.
Tewari, R: **G.3.1**: 76.
Thabane, M: **D.1.1**: 8.
Thakur, B: **G.3.1**: 81.
Thaman, R: **D.7**: 90.

Thanh-Dam, T: **F.6**: 32.
Thapa, S: **F.3**: 23.
Thé, de, H: **F.3**: 119.
Theorell, T: **I.2**: 70. **I.3**: 43.
Thiessen, V: **F.4.2**: 63.
Thoma, S: **F.4.1**: 1.
Thomas, A: **C.2**: 74.
Thomas, H: **C.5**: 15.
Thomas, J: **K.2**: 53.
Thomas, L: **D.3**: 27. **F.3**: 7.
Thomas, R: **D.9**: 18.
Thomas-Hope, E: **F.8**: 49, 94.
Thomasma, D: **K.4**: 23.
Thompson, F: **B.1.1**: 36.
Thompson, J: **D.7**: 27.
Thompson, K: **D.3**: 13.
Thompson, P: **F.5**: 17.
Thompson, R: **J.6**: 26.
Thompson, V: **F.4.1**: 9.
Thompson, W: **G.2**: 1.
Thorbek, S: **G.3.2**: 158.
Thoreson, R: **I.5**: 16.
Thorman, G: **K.1**: 223.
Thornton, J: **D.3**: 3.
Thornton, M: **F.7**: 73, 80.
Thorpe, D: **K.2**: 8.
Thurman, Q: **F.3**: 129.
Tice, D: **C.2**: 34.
Tickamyer, A: **H.3**: 10.
Tickamyer, C: **H.3**: 10.
Tickner, J: **F.5**: 101.
Ticktin, H: **J.2**: 6.
Tien, H: **F.3**: 12.
Tierney, J: **K.1**: 123.
Tietze, G: **H.4**: 41.
Tight, M: **D.9**: 1.
Tilly, C: **J.5**: 27.
Timothy-Mahak, F: **J.6**: 28.
Tinler, J: **F.3**: 103.
Tips, W: **G.3.1**: 66.
Tironi, E: **D.1.3**: 13. **K.1**: 232.

Titarenko, A: **D.3**: 18.
Tittle, C: **K.1**: 101.
Tixier, P: **C.5**: 13. **I.5**: 13.
Tobin, S: **F.2**: 53.
Tocatlian, J: **A.5**: 7.
Todd, P: **I.2**: 52.
Tognoni, G: **K.4**: 12.
Togunde, O: **F.3**: 62.
Tokii, S: **I.5**: 20.
Tollison, R: **F.3**: 9.
Tolnay, S: **F.3**: 58.
Tolson, E: **K.3**: 20.
Tomlinson, R: **G.3.2**: 64.
Tomori, O: **F.3**: 119.
Tongsawate, M: **G.3.1**: 66.
Tonry, M: **F.4.2**: 71.
Toornvliet, L: **K.1**: 114.
Torpey, J: **D.3**: 17.
Torres, D: **C.5**: 30.
Torrey, E: **K.1**: 231.
Tourangeau, R: **C.2**: 12.
Touré, S: **D.6**: 24.
Toussaint, M: **J.6**: 5, 8.
Tovey, H: **D.7**: 8.
Townsend, M: **F.3**: 27.
Trachen, A: **G.3.2**: 15.
Trager, L: **F.8**: 7. **G.3.2**: 57.
Travers, E: **C.3**: 6.
Travis, L: **I.3**: 35.
Traylen, G: **C.7**: 36.
Trebici, V: **F.1**: 6.
Treesh, K: **K.2**: 37.
Treibel, A: **F.7**: 76.
Tremonti, G: **C.1**: 14, 29.
Trent, K: **F.5**: 48.
Tribalat, M: **F.4.1**: 54.
Tribe, K: **B.1.1**: 19.
Tribillon, J: **G.3.2**: 92.
Trost, J: **F.4.2**: 127.
Trouillas, P: **D.1.1**: 5.
Troussier, J: **I.1**: 1.

Trovato, F: **F.4.1**: 34.
Trueba, H: **D.9.2**: 3.
Trueba Lara, J: **F.7**: 75.
Tsay, C: **G.3.2**: 154.
Tsitsipis, L: **D.7**: 63.
Tsukatani, T: **G.1**: 15.
Tsuya, N: **F.3**: 83.
Tuan, Y: **G.3.2**: 7.
Tucker, S: **C.2**: 16.
Tulasciewicz, W: **D.9**: 4.
Turnbull, P: **I.3**: 25.
Turner, B: **D.1.1**: 26.
Turner, J: **A.1**: 34. **B.1.1**: 4, 13. **D.1.3**: 21. **D.9**: 25.
Turner, R: **D.9**: 25.
Twine, N: **D.7**: 79.
Tyack, D: **D.9.3**: 4.
Tymen, J: **K.3**: 1.
Tyson, R: **D.5**: 12.
Tyson, S: **C.5**: 2.
Uchida, C: **C.7**: 38.
Udry, J: **F.6**: 6.
Ueda, T: **I.3**: 40.
Uga, H: **C.1**: 3.
Uglow, S: **J.3**: 19.
Uitti, C: **C.4**: 32.
Ukadike, N: **D.7**: 127.
Ukai, K: **J.5**: 35.
Ulbrich, P: **F.4.1**: 13.
Ulloa, T: **G.1**: 4.
Ultee, W: **I.2**: 58.
Umberson, D: **C.4**: 31.
Umezawa, T: **I.5**: 8.
Umino, M: **B.3**: 23.
Underwager, R: **K.1**: 44.
Université du Québec: **D.9.5**: 3.
Unwin, P: **G.3**: 3.
Upadhyay, R: **K.4**: 35.
Ura, M: **F.4.2**: 120.
Urban, D: **J.6**: 29.
Urban, J: **I.2**: 70.

Urevbu, A: **D.6**: 20, 26.
Urriola, R: **G.3.2**: 58.
Urry, J: **A.1**: 8.
Useem, M: **G.3.1**: 72.
Ushijama, C: **E.2**: 37.
Utomo, B: **F.3**: 35.
Vaile, M: **K.4**: 27.
Vaillancourt, F: **D.7**: 65.
Valdman, A: **D.7**: 75.
Valentei, D: **F.4.2**: 22.
Valerie A.: **E.3**: 12.
Valladares, L: **F.2**: 78.
Valle, R: **F.4.1**: 42.
Vallin, J: **F.3**: 139, 144.
Valsiner, J: **C.2**: 37.
Valverde, L: **D.9.2**: 3.
Van Hasselt, V: **F.4.2**: 72.
Vandell, D: **F.2**: 85.
Vander Hill, C: **I.7**: 9.
Vandergeest, P: **E.3**: 2, 16.
Vandeveer, D: **K.2**: 3.
Varikas, E: **E.3**: 30.
Varma, V: **C.2**: 87.
Vásquez, I: **F.5**: 89.
Vassil, T: **C.4**: 10.
Vasudeva Rao, D: **G.3.1**: 78.
Vaughan, D: **K.2**: 37.
Vaughan, P: **K.4**: 39.
Vaughn, B: **F.4.2**: 118.
Vaux, A: **K.3**: 31.
Veenhoven, R: **C.2**: 81.
Veer, van der, P: **E.2**: 23.
Veer, van der, R: **C.2**: 37.
Veevers, J: **F.4.1**: 56.
Vega, J: **F.6**: 7.
Vega, W: **F.4.1**: 42.
Veglery, A: **F.8**: 52.
Velasco, A: **K.1**: 205.
Velasquez, M: **D.5**: 76.
Velden, van der, R: **E.2**: 62.
Vélis, J: **D.9**: 15.

Velody, I: **A.2**: 4.
Velpen, J: **J.5**: 2.
Veltman, C: **D.7**: 7, 70.
Venkata Reddy, K: **G.3.1**: 77.
Venkatacharya, K: **F.3**: 80.
Venu Gopal, C: **C.7**: 24.
Venugopal Rao, S: **K.1**: 115.
Verdieck, M: **D.5**: 78.
Verdugo, N: **D.9.8**: 6.
Verdugo, R: **D.9.8**: 6.
Verdun-Jones, S: **F.6**: 31.
Verea Campos, M: **F.8**: 78.
Vergara, R: **G.3.2**: 149.
Verma, G: **B.1.3**: 14.
Verma, R: **B.1.3**: 14.
Vernon, R: **F.3**: 27.
Véron, J: **I.2**: 4.
Verpeaux, M: **K.1**: 186.
Vialle, A: **F.8**: 70.
Vicari, S: **G.3.2**: 125.
Vichi, M: **F.4.2**: 146.
Vichnevskij, A: **F.3**: 81.
Vichnievski, A: **F.3**: 4.
Vidal, D: **D.5**: 9.
Vidich, A: **D.3**: 38.
Vigil, J: **F.7**: 58.
Vilarino, J: **D.5**: 67.
Villar Gaviria, A: **E.2**: 64.
Villaverde Castro, J: **G.3.2**: 15.
Villeneuve-Gokalp, C: **F.4.1**: 50.
Vimard, P: **F.1**: 8.
Vincent, J: **G.1**: 13. **K.2**: 25.
Vingerhoets, A: **K.4**: 88.
Виноградов, : **A.1**: 19.
Visano, L: **D.1.3**: 8.
Visaria, P: **F.3**: 142.
Visker, R: **D.3**: 11.
Vita, V: **D.7**: 121.
Vitouch, P: **D.7**: 130.
Vliet, R: **K.4**: 34.
Vogel, J: **E.2**: 33.

Vogelsang, R: **G.3**: 2.
Voges, W: **F.2**: 61.
Voisard, J: **F.8**: 88.
Volait, M: **G.3.2**: 9.
Volanth, A: **C.2**: 10.
Volgareva, I: **K.1**: 109.
Volkema, R: **H.4**: 29.
Vollbrecht, R: **D.7**: 130.
Volst, A: **I.3**: 21.
Voogd, H: **H.7**: 5.
Voorden, van, W: **I.2**: 48.
Vos, D: **F.4.2**: 23.
Vos, J: **B.3**: 26.
Voss, T: **I.2**: 7.
Voydanoff, P: **F.4.2**: 65. **K.2**: 18.
Voyé, L: **D.5**: 79.
Vučković, C: **J.8**: 2.
Vwakyanakazi, M: **E.3**: 26.
Vyakarnam, S: **G.3.1**: 29.
Vyas, M: **E.2**: 42.
Wachs, E: **K.1**: 81.
Wada, S: **B.3**: 23.
Wade, R: **G.3.1**: 83.
Wadsworth, M: **F.4.2**: 80.
Wagenaar, W: **I.7**: 1.
Wagenborg, J: **C.1**: 14–16. **C.4**: 8.
Wagner, A: **G.3.2**: 29, 92.
Wagner, I: **I.3**: 21.
Wagner, R: **J.8**: 12.
Wajcman, J: **H.4**: 43.
Wakabayashi, M: **I.5**: 7.
Wakefield, H: **K.1**: 44.
Wakefield, J: **K.3**: 23–24.
Walb, S: **A.1**: 8.
Walby, S: **F.5**: 35.
Waldren, T: **F.4.2**: 110.
Walker, A: **I.2**: 5.
Walker, F: **F.7**: 27.
Walker, J: **C.5**: 43. **F.2**: 8.
Walker, L: **F.7**: 42.
Walker, M: **D.4**: 4.

INTERNATIONAL BIBLIOGRAPHY OF SOCIOLOGY — 1988

Walkup, J: **C.2**: 38.
Wallace, M: **C.6**: 12. **I.5**: 17.
Wallace, R: **F.5**: 59.
Wallbott, H: **C.2**: 72.
Wallemacq, A: **I.3**: 49.
Waller, J: **K.1**: 72.
Wallimann, I: **I.6**: 47.
Wallin, E: **E.2**: 71.
Walmsley, D: **G.3.2**: 78.
Walsh, J: **K.4**: 80.
Walsh, R: **F.6**: 26.
Walters, V: **I.3**: 59.
Walton, C: **I.5**: 12.
Wan, C: **C.7**: 18.
Wan, H: **G.3.1**: 64.
Wang, C: **K.1**: 72.
Wang, F: **F.3**: 82.
Wang, G: **D.1.1**: 4.
Wangel, A: **I.3**: 54.
Wanitzek, U: **F.4.2**: 18, 31.
Wanta, W: **D.7**: 95.
Ward, D: **J.6**: 20.
Ward, K: **C.7**: 15.
Ward, M: **F.4.2**: 118.
Ward, R: **F.2**: 43.
Warde, A: **A.1**: 8.
Warland, R: **F.3**: 138.
Warman, A: **G.3.1**: 55.
Warr, P: **I.2**: 53.
Warren, C: **F.3**: 48, 54.
Warren, K: **K.4**: 80.
Wartes, J: **D.9.2**: 5.
Waschkuhn, A: **J.3**: 21.
Wasko, J: **D.7**: 34.
Watababe, S: **F.8**: 13.
Watanabe, H: **F.4.1**: 20.
Watanabe, S: **C.4**: 26.
Watari, A: **A.1**: 11.
Waterman, A: **D.3**: 19.
Waterman, H: **J.6**: 30.
Waters, R: **K.1**: 180.

Watkins, J: **C.1**: 27.
Watkins, M: **J.8**: 12.
Watson, D: **K.1**: 181.
Watson, J: **F.4.2**: 66.
Watson, L: **I.3**: 30.
Watson, S: **F.5**: 27.
Watt, W: **D.5**: 86.
Wattis, J: **K.4**: 10.
Watts, J: **I.4**: 21.
Weart, S: **C.2**: 35.
Weaver, C: **F.4.1**: 5.
Webb, J: **I.2**: 39.
Weber, E: **K.1**: 8.
Weber, G: **D.1.2**: 13.
Weber, H: **I.5**: 13.
Webley, P: **C.7**: 27.
Webster, F: **G.3.2**: 134.
Webster, M: **E.2**: 67.
Weclawowicz, G: **G.3.2**: 16.
Weeks, D: **C.7**: 15.
Wehner, E: **C.2**: 16.
Wehr, P: **J.8**: 12.
Weidlich, W: **E.1**: 8.
Weil, P: **F.8**: 69.
Weingarten, F: **A.5**: 7.
Weinstein, M: **F.3**: 70.
Weiskrantz, L: **C.2**: 57.
Weiss, J: **C.5**: 34.
Weiss, M: **K.4**: 60.
Weiss, R: **F.4.1**: 2.
Weissert, W: **K.2**: 33.
Wejnert, B: **J.5**: 31.
Wekwete, K: **G.3.2**: 111.
Welch, P: **D.9**: 10.
Welch, S: **G.3.2**: 79.
Welfeld, I: **G.3.2**: 102.
Welldon, E: **F.4.2**: 36.
Weller, L: **F.4.1**: 36.
Weller, S: **B.2**: 9.
Wellman, B: **E.1**: 7.
Welis, E: **D.7**: 99.

Welsh, I: **J.8**: 1.
Weltz, F: **I.1**: 3.
Wendel Abramo, L: **H.4**: 49.
Wenden, de, C: **F.8**: 69.
Wenger, M: **B.1.2**: 3.
Wensierski, P: **J.5**: 18.
Wenston, S: **F.2**: 84.
West, D: **K.1**: 42, 105, 117.
West, P: **E.2**: 32.
Westeman, K: **C.7**: 2.
Wester, F: **B.3**: 3.
Westergaard, J: **I.2**: 5.
Westergård-Nielsen, N: **H.3**: 26.
Westwood, S: **F.7**: 22.
Wettstein, H: **C.2**: 13.
Wetzel, P: **D.7**: 16.
Weyr, T: **F.7**: 32.
Whalen, J: **K.1**: 15.
Whalen, M: **K.1**: 15.
Wheeler, G: **K.1**: 35, 154.
Wheeler, S: **K.1**: 127.
Whitaker, B: **F.7**: 40.
Whitaker, D: **K.1**: 187.
Whitbeck, L: **F.4.2**: 147.
White, J: **I.7**: 7.
White, M: **I.2**: 69.
White, P: **C.2**: 8. **F.8**: 94–95. **G.3.2**: 33, 48.
White, S: **J.2**: 6.
Whitehand, J: **G.3.2**: 107.
Whitehead, G: **C.7**: 30.
Whitehead, J: **K.1**: 141.
Whitfield, K: **I.4**: 10.
Whitfield, M: **K.4**: 11.
Whiting, B: **D.1.3**: 2.
Whittaker, W: **F.8**: 31.
Widerszpil, S: **E.2**: 55.
Widlak, P: **F.4.2**: 96.
Wiener-Hughes, G: **F.2**: 19.
Wigdor, B: **F.2**: 57.
Wigle, S: **C.2**: 93.
Wihtol de Wenden, C: **F.8**: 102.

Wikan, U: **K.4**: 60.
Wild, M: **G.3.1**: 35.
Wildavsky, A: **J.4**: 12.
Wiley, N: **B.1.3**: 16.
Wilkens, L: **F.3**: 23.
Wilkes, J: **I.4**: 1.
Wilkins, R: **F.7**: 87.
Wilkinson, B: **K.2**: 46.
Wilkinson, C: **K.1**: 206.
Wilkinson, S: **F.3**: 104.
Wilks, J: **K.1**: 11.
Willaume, M: **D.1.1**: 32.
Willemse, H: **K.1**: 114.
Willemyns, R: **D.7**: 76.
Willer, D: **E.1**: 5.
Williams, A: **I.7**: 23.
Williams, C: **I.3**: 15. **I.5**: 2.
Williams, F: **D.7**: 128.
Williams, G: **D.5**: 77.
Williams, J: **C.2**: 22. **D.7**: 75. **D.8**: 4. **H.3**: 7. **K.1**: 124. **K.2**: 50.
Williams, K: **I.6**: 18. **K.1**: 129.
Williams, P: **D.5**: 64.
Williams, R: **F.8**: 90. **K.1**: 79.
Williamson, V: **K.4**: 59.
Willis, E: **I.2**: 51.
Wills, J: **K.1**: 15.
Wilpert, C: **F.8**: 57.
Wilshire, P: **C.3**: 15.
Wilson, A: **F.2**: 19.
Wilson, B: **D.5**: 16. **D.7**: 82.
Wilson, D: **C.5**: 42.
Wilson, F: **F.8**: 5.
Wilson, J: **I.7**: 15.
Wilson, K: **D.7**: 44. **F.2**: 85.
Wilson, P: **F.4.2**: 125.
Wimpelberg, R: **D.9.4**: 1.
Winchester, H: **G.3.2**: 33, 48.
Windley, P: **F.2**: 35. **G.3.1**: 34.
Windsor, P: **F.5**: 101.
Wineberg, H: **F.3**: 47, 65.

Winefield, H: **K.1**: 49.
Winford, D: **D.7**: 75.
Winkler, E: **D.3**: 3.
Winkler, G: **H.4**: 41.
Winn, S: **F.3**: 105.
Winson, A: **J.6**: 1.
Winter, D: **C.1**: 26.
Wischer, R: **F.2**: 36.
Wish, E: **K.1**: 86.
Witkin, S: **K.3**: 2.
Witte, J: **F.1**: 9.
Witten, M: **D.1.1**: 34.
Wodarski, J: **K.1**: 187.
Wolf, D: **F.4.2**: 105.
Wolf, F: **D.7**: 23.
Wolf, R: **D.6**: 10.
Wolinsky, F: **K.4**: 4.
Wolpin, K: **F.3**: 111.
Wong, B: **F.7**: 46.
Wong, S: **D.7**: 61.
Wood, C: **E.2**: 20.
Wood, G: **G.3.1**: 40.
Wood, J: **D.6**: 18. **F.3**: 70.
Wood, W: **F.3**: 96.
Woodcraft, E: **K.1**: 53.
Wooden, M: **I.2**: 23.
Woodward, A: **E.2**: 17.
Wooldredge, J: **K.1**: 151.
Woolgar, S: **D.6**: 14.
Woolhandler, S: **K.4**: 25, 92.
Wootton, A: **D.1.3**: 6.
World Bank: **F.8**: 14. **G.3.1**: 17. **K.2**: 5.
Worthington, E: **D.5**: 58.
Wright, A: **F.3**: 145.
Wright, C: **D.9.2**: 5.
Wright, E: **E.2**: 72.
Wright, J: **B.2**: 8. **K.1**: 8, 230.
Wright, R: **F.3**: 68. **K.1**: 106.
Wright, von, G: **D.6**: 4.
Wulff, H: **F.7**: 69.
Wundersitz, J: **K.1**: 145.

Wuthnow, R: **C.5**: 35. **D.1.1**: 34.
Wyatt, R: **C.5**: 11.
Wyrozumska, A: **J.8**: 9.
Yach, D: **K.4**: 32.
Yadav, C: **G.3.2**: 118.
Yagasaki, S: **A.3**: 8.
Yagi, H: **F.4.2**: 138.
Yakunin, V: **D.9.3**: 8.
Yamagishi, T: **E.1**: 4.
Yamamoto, H: **A.3**: 8.
Yamamoto, K: **G.3.2**: 60.
Yamamoto, T: **G.3.2**: 72.
Yan, X: **B.3**: 16.
Yanagawa, Y: **C.5**: 44.
Yanagishita, M: **F.1**: 25.
Yanay, U: **K.4**: 37.
Yapi-Diahou, A: **G.3.2**: 18, 92.
Yasukochi, K: **G.2**: 11.
Yates, F: **K.1**: 10.
Yazaki, T: **G.3.2**: 115.
Yearley, S: **E.3**: 25.
Yeboah, S: **F.7**: 106.
Yelsma, P: **F.4.1**: 39.
Yesudian, C: **K.4**: 31.
Yetton, P: **C.5**: 14.
Yirmiya, N: **F.2**: 80.
Yitzhaki, S: **F.1**: 11.
Yllö, K: **F.4.1**: 19.
Yokoi, T: **B.1.3**: 24.
Yokoyama, Y: **E.1**: 6.
Yonakuni, N: **B.1.1**: 32.
Yoneyama, T: **D.1.1**: 3.
Yorisaki, T: **G.3.2**: 113.
Yoshino, H: **H.3**: 19.
Yoshizawa, N: **B.1.2**: 2.
Yoshizumi, K: **F.6**: 10.
Young, C: **F.8**: 101.
Young, D: **D.9.8**: 4.
Young, E: **G.2**: 14. **K.2**: 15.
Young, F: **G.3.2**: 67.
Young, J: **K.1**: 120.

Young, L: **D.5**: 67.
Young, M: **D.1.1**: 38.
Young, R: **C.5**: 12.
Young, T: **K.2**: 41.
Yu, B: **C.7**: 14.
Yun, H: **I.2**: 52.
Yúnez N., A: **G.3.1**: 65.
Yuzawa, Y: **F.4.2**: 82.
Yzerbyt, V: **C.4**: 3–4.
Zaidi, S: **K.1**: 234.
Zaki, K: **F.3**: 149.
Zald, M: **J.5**: 34.
Zalokar, N: **I.4**: 14.
Zaman, G: **I.3**: 5.
Zameck, von, W: **H.4**: 17.
Zanardo, A: **D.3**: 6.
Zapata, F: **I.5**: 27.
Zaragoza, A: **I.7**: 13.
Zarling, C: **F.4.2**: 106.
Zeidner, M: **D.5**: 50.
Zeigler, L: **C.3**: 35.
Zeitlin, H: **K.1**: 20.
Zeitlin, M: **E.2**: 41.
Zerbi de, G: **F.5**: 70.
Zerzan, J: **H.4**: 35.
Zhang, W: **G.3.2**: 157.
Zhu, J: **F.3**: 119.
Zick, C: **H.3**: 18.
Zika, S: **D.5**: 44.
Zimmerman, S: **K.1**: 170.
Zimmermann, D: **K.1**: 15.
Ziołkowski, M: **A.3**: 3.
Zion, C: **I.2**: 56.
Zouwen, V: **B.2**: 10.
Зуев, : **H.4**: 26.
Zuravin, S: **F.3**: 66.
Zwerman, G: **K.2**: 53.
Zwi, A: **K.4**: 32.

PLACENAME INDEX
INDEX DES ENDROITS

Afghanistan
  D.7: 140. **G.3.2**: 114.

Africa
  Entries also appear under:
  ALGERIA; BOTSWANA; EAST AFRICA; EGYPT; ETHIOPIA; GHANA; IVORY COAST; KENYA; LIBERIA; MALAWI; MAURITIUS; NIGERIA; SENEGAL; SIERRA LEONE; SOUTH AFRICA; SOUTHERN AFRICA; SUB-SAHARAN AFRICA; SUDAN; TANZANIA; TOGO; TUNISIA; UGANDA; WEST AFRICA; ZAIRE; ZAMBIA; ZIMBABWE
  D.5: 82. **F.1**: 7. **F.3**: 95. **F.6**: 23. **F.7**: 73. **F.8**: 1, 47. **G.3.1**: 10, 79. **G.3.2**: 150. **I.2**: 14. **J.8**: 11.

Algeria
  F.4.1: 30.

Americas
  Entries also appear under:
  CENTRAL AMERICA; NORTH AMERICA

Andes
  D.1.1: 10. **G.3.1**: 7. **G.3.2**: 149.

Argentina
  G.3.1: 4–5. **G.3.2**: 1. **I.7**: 6.

Asia
  Entries also appear under:
  AFGHANISTAN; BANGLADESH; CHINA; HONG KONG; INDIA; INDONESIA; JAPAN; MALAYSIA; NEPAL; PAKISTAN; PHILIPPINES; SINGAPORE; SOUTH KOREA; SOUTHEAST ASIA; SRI LANKA; TAIWAN; THAILAND
  F.6: 32. **F.8**: 37. **G.3.1**: 17. **G.3.2**: 65. **H.4**: 44. **I.2**: 62.

Australia
  C.1: 28. **D.6**: 3. **D.7**: 6, 39, 124, 145. **D.8**: 2. **D.9.3**: 2–3. **D.9.5**: 22. **E.2**: 12, 21, 56. **F.2**: 8. **F.4.1**: 51, 63. **F.5**: 27, 62, 90. **F.7**: 30, 33, 50, 63, 84, 90. **F.8**: 66, 79. **G.1**: 11. **G.3.2**: 2, 120. **I.2**: 21, 51. **I.3**: 28. **I.4**: 2. **I.5**: 2, 25. **I.6**: 12. **J.6**: 32. **K.1**: 23, 43, 59, 79, 144, 148, 158, 168, 201. **K.2**: 12. **K.4**: 84.

Austria
  F.7: 83.

Bangladesh
  D.9.5: 20. **F.3**: 21, 43, 56. **F.6**: 24. **G.3.1**: 40. **K.1**: 237. **K.4**: 40.

Barbados
  D.9: 10.

Belgium
  D.5: 65. **D.7**: 73. **F.7**: 96. **F.8**: 24. **G.3.2**: 97. **J.5**: 2. **K.1**: 98. **K.2**: 24.

Bolivia
  D.1.1: 10.

Botswana
  F.8: 26. **G.3.1**: 25.

Brazil
  D.5: 1, 11, 73. **E.2**: 20. **F.1**: 4. **F.2**: 78. **F.3**: 15. **F.8**: 55. **G.3.2**: 93, 131. **H.5**: 1. **I.7**: 10. **J.2**: 10. **K.4**: 26.

Bulgaria
  I.6: 47.

California
  F.4.1: 28. **F.7**: 58, 60, 77. **G.3.2**: 90. **I.5**: 19. **K.1**: 153.

Canada
  Entries also appear under:
  ONTARIO; QUEBEC
  A.1: 7, 17. **C.6**: 9. **D.1.1**: 36. **D.5**: 29. **D.7**: 56, 100. **D.9.5**: 25. **E.2**: 6, 26, 57. **F.2**: 30, 33, 57. **F.3**: 50, 68. **F.4.1**: 16, 34. **F.4.2**: 99, 132. **F.5**: 61, 76. **F.6**: 16, 18, 31. **F.7**: 8, 15, 55, 74, 103. **G.3.2**: 34, 106. **I.2**: 47, 58. **I.3**: 59. **J.2**: 5. **J.3**: 12. **K.1**: 18, 52, 66, 103, 113, 147, 224. **K.4**: 91.

Caribbean
  Entries also appear under:
  BARBADOS; DOMINICAN REPUBLIC; HAITI; JAMAICA; PUERTO RICO
  D.7: 19. **D.8**: 17. **D.9**: 11, 20. **D.9.9**: 8. **F.5**: 34. **F.7**: 44. **F.8**: 49, 87. **G.3.2**: 35. **K.1**: 75.

Central Africa
  Entries also appear under:
  BOTSWANA; MALAWI; TANZANIA; UGANDA; ZAIRE; ZAMBIA; ZIMBABWE

Central America
  Entries also appear under:

Central America continued

COSTA RICA; MEXICO
D.5: 6.

Central Europe
Entries also appear under:
AUSTRIA; CZECHOSLOVAKIA; HUNGARY; POLAND; ROMANIA; SWITZERLAND

Chile
D.7: 139. **E.2**: 41. **G.3.2**: 3. **K.1**: 232.

China
C.7: 14. **D.1.1**: 20. **F.3**: 82. **F.5**: 82. **F.7**: 21, 37. **G.3**: 1. **J.6**: 14.

Colombia
F.2: 86. **F.3**: 27. **G.3.1**: 60. **K.1**: 31, 38, 203, 210.

Costa Rica
D.5: 64. **G.1**: 4. **J.6**: 1.

Czechoslovakia
F.3: 139. **I.5**: 22. **J.2**: 4.

Denmark
I.3: 55.

Dominican Republic
F.3: 24. **F.8**: 80.

East Africa
Entries also appear under:
ETHIOPIA; KENYA; MALAWI; MAURITIUS; SUDAN; TANZANIA; UGANDA; ZAMBIA
G.1: 16.

Eastern Europe
Entries also appear under:
BULGARIA; CZECHOSLOVAKIA; HUNGARY; POLAND; YUGOSLAVIA
F.4.2: 129. **G.3.2**: 87.

Ecuador
F.8: 22, 38. **G.3.2**: 59.

Egypt
A.1: 10. **F.3**: 22, 46. **F.8**: 53. **G.3.2**: 9, 27.

England
D.8: 3. **F.3**: 123, 132. **F.7**: 69, 97. **G.3.2**: 85, 107, 119. **I.1**: 2. **J.3**: 11, 20. **K.1**: 21, 62, 118, 147, 163, 169, 225.

Estonia
A.1: 35.

Ethiopia
F.4.1: 12. **G.3.1**: 22. **I.2**: 18.

Europe
Entries also appear under:

Europe continued

EASTERN EUROPE; SCANDINAVIA; SOUTHEAST EUROPE; SOUTHERN EUROPE; WESTERN EUROPE
C.3: 35. **D.7**: 92, 142. **F.8**: 57. **H.4**: 12. **I.2**: 64. **I.4**: 8. **I.6**: 42. **K.1**: 171. **K.2**: 27. **K.4**: 52.

Fiji
F.7: 78. **G.3.1**: 31, 67. **J.6**: 13.

Finland
E.2: 7. **H.4**: 39.

France
A.1: 22, 30. **A.3**: 12. **D.1.1**: 5, 16, 32. **D.2**: 2. **D.5**: 75, 88. **D.7**: 58, 108, 119. **D.9**: 15. **D.9.3**: 10. **E.2**: 15. **E.3**: 7. **F.2**: 54. **F.3**: 87, 139. **F.4.1**: 30. **F.7**: 86. **F.8**: 48, 59, 82, 86, 88, 103. **G.1**: 8. **G.3.1**: 58. **G.3.2**: 17, 20, 110, 119. **H.5**: 2. **I.6**: 13. **J.3**: 12, 15. **J.5**: 10. **K.3**: 1.

Francophone Africa
Entries also appear under:
ALGERIA; IVORY COAST; SENEGAL; TUNISIA; ZAIRE

Germany East
E.1: 1. **F.7**: 81. **I.5**: 10. **J.5**: 8, 18.

Germany West
C.2: 64. **D.1.1**: 25. **D.1.2**: 7. **D.7**: 83. **D.9.3**: 7. **D.9.5**: 10. **E.1**: 1. **E.2**: 39. **F.1**: 9. **F.7**: 71, 76, 109. **F.8**: 77, 91. **G.3.2**: 52. **I.2**: 8. **I.3**: 50. **I.6**: 18. **J.6**: 27, 29. **J.7**: 4. **K.1**: 147, 167.

Ghana
C.2: 101. **G.3.2**: 137.

Greece
D.9.5: 8. **E.3**: 30. **F.4.1**: 17. **F.8**: 64, 91.

Gujarat
D.1.3: 10.

Guyana
E.2: 38.

Haiti
E.2: 31. **F.7**: 79. **F.8**: 80. **K.4**: 56.

Hawaii
D.9.3: 11.

Holland
Entries also appear under:
NETHERLANDS

Hong Kong
F.7: 26. **J.4**: 4.

Hungary
E.2: 63. **F.4.2**: 105. **G.3.1**: 61. **I.2**: 16.

Iceland
F.5: 12.

India
Entries also appear under:

GUJARAT; PUNJAB; RAJASTHAN; UTTAR PRADESH; WEST BENGAL

A.2: 5. **C.2**: 94. **C.7**: 24. **D.1.1**: 6, 18. **D.5**: 9. **D.7**: 29. **D.8**: 4. **E.2**: 4, 22. **E.3**: 9. **F.1**: 27. **F.2**: 20, 34. **F.3**: 2, 28, 135, 142. **F.4.1**: 18, 25, 31, 39. **F.4.2**: 142. **F.5**: 52. **F.7**: 4. **F.8**: 60, 90. **G.3.1**: 9, 14–15, 19, 51, 59, 76, 82–83. **G.3.2**: 32, 77, 88, 155. **H.3**: 22. **I.2**: 65–66. **J.1**: 2. **J.3**: 3. **K.1**: 222, 238. **K.4**: 31.

Indochina
Entries also appear under:

LAOS; VIETNAM

Indonesia
Entries also appear under:

JAVA

D.1.1: 35. **D.9**: 18. **E.3**: 24. **F.3**: 35, 116. **F.8**: 14. **J.4**: 1.

Iran
C.6: 19. **C.7**: 12. **D.7**: 57, 146. **F.4.1**: 9. **F.4.2**: 6.

Iraq
G.3.1: 32.

Ireland
F.5: 105, 109. **H.4**: 42.

Israel
D.5: 50. **D.9.2**: 2. **D.9.8**: 2. **F.2**: 11. **F.4.1**: 36, 48. **F.5**: 22. **F.7**: 6. **F.8**: 23, 76. **J.4**: 11. **J.6**: 11.

Italy
C.3: 11. **D.1.3**: 5. **D.5**: 15. **D.7**: 121. **F.3**: 45. **F.5**: 6. **F.8**: 50, 54–55, 92. **G.3.2**: 24, 38, 40, 125, 139. **I.2**: 31. **I.3**: 4. **I.4**: 16. **I.6**: 14, 28–29.

Ivory Coast
K.1: 215.

Jamaica
E.2: 38. **F.3**: 29. **F.5**: 10. **H.2**: 4.

Japan
A.2: 3. **A.3**: 8. **C.2**: 94. **C.4**: 21. **C.5**: 22. **D.1.1**: 19, 21, 28, 33. **D.1.2**: 8. **D.4**: 13. **D.5**: 17, 51. **D.7**: 16, 47. **D.8**: 7. **D.9**: 12, 19, 22. **D.9.5**: 11. **D.9.8**: 3. **D.9.9**: 3. **E.3**: 13. **F.2**: 18. **F.3**: 3. **F.4.1**: 57. **F.4.2**: 10, 28–29, 104. **F.5**:

Japan continued
41. **F.8**: 13. **G.3.1**: 37, 56. **G.3.2**: 22, 26, 62, 71–72, 125. **H.4**: 4. **I.2**: 17. **I.3**: 22, 31, 34. **I.4**: 26. **I.5**: 7. **K.1**: 172. **K.2**: 21, 27, 43, 59.

Java
D.7: 49. **H.4**: 15.

Jordan
F.3: 6.

Kentucky
H.3: 10.

Kenya
G.3.2: 130.

Laos
G.3.1: 2.

Latin America
Entries also appear under:

CENTRAL AMERICA

A.3: 4. **D.7**: 74. **F.3**: 29. **G.3.1**: 24. **G.3.2**: 35. **I.5**: 27. **I.7**: 19. **K.1**: 198. **K.2**: 13.

Lebanon
D.5: 90. **F.8**: 83. **J.3**: 1.

Liberia
G.3.2: 99.

Malawi
G.3: 5.

Malaysia
D.5: 31. **F.4.1**: 46. **F.7**: 44. **G.3.1**: 64. **G.3.2**: 141–142.

Marshall Islands
F.3: 34.

Massachusetts
K.1: 177.

Mauretania
G.3.2: 153.

Mauritius
F.8: 60.

Mexico
B.1.3: 8. **D.9.5**: 21. **E.2**: 25. **F.3**: 126, 146. **F.7**: 75. **F.8**: 20, 78. **G.3.1**: 21, 62, 71. **G.3.2**: 96, 146. **H.3**: 7. **H.4**: 9. **I.2**: 42. **J.6**: 5–7.

Michigan
K.4: 49.

Middle East
Entries also appear under:

IRAN; IRAQ; ISRAEL; JORDAN; LEBANON; SAUDI ARABIA; TURKEY

E.3: 21–22. **G.3.2**: 143. **J.8**: 6.

Morocco
D.7: 62.
Nepal
G.3.1: 44. **K.4**: 36.
Netherlands
A.5: 6. **F.1**: 3, 28. **F.2**: 62. **F.4.2**: 7. **F.7**: 38. **I.2**: 58. **I.3**: 55. **J.6**: 2. **K.4**: 34.
New Jersey
K.1: 155.
New York
D.7: 78. **F.7**: 46. **F.8**: 6, 52. **G.3.2**: 119. **K.1**: 81, 170, 189.
New Zealand
D.1.1: 17. **E.2**: 12. **F.7**: 27, 68, 89. **G.3.1**: 13. **I.2**: 44, 51. **I.3**: 14. **K.1**: 168. **K.2**: 11.
Nigeria
D.1.2: 3. **D.5**: 28. **D.9.5**: 17. **F.3**: 62, 134. **F.5**: 42. **G.3.2**: 44, 55, 57, 89, 123. **I.3**: 29. **I.5**: 6, 23. **J.6**: 25. **K.4**: 75.
North Africa
Entries also appear under:
ALGERIA; EGYPT; MOROCCO; TUNISIA
North America
Entries also appear under:
CANADA; U.S.A.
D.9.9: 8. **F.4.1**: 18. **F.4.2**: 142. **F.7**: 13. **F.8**: 84. **K.2**: 27.
North Carolina
D.5: 12. **H.3**: 10.
Northern Ireland
C.7: 36.
Norway
E.2: 7, 10. **F.4.1**: 70. **F.8**: 75. **H.3**: 21.
Ohio
F.5: 93. **K.4**: 62.
Oklahoma
F.7: 41.
Ontario
A.1: 26. **F.7**: 47. **J.3**: 5.
Pacific Region
Entries also appear under:
MARSHALL ISLANDS
D.7: 55. **K.4**: 2.
Pakistan
F.4.1: 43. **F.8**: 40, 90. **G.3.1**: 45, 70.

Papua New Guinea
F.1: 20. **K.4**: 87.
Paraguay
F.3: 54.
Peru
G.3.2: 145.
Philippines
D.5: 66. **D.7**: 109. **F.8**: 7. **J.4**: 7. **K.1**: 228.
Poland
D.5: 5. **F.5**: 84. **G.1**: 9, 17. **I.2**: 28.
Puerto Rico
F.8: 56. **J.5**: 16.
Punjab
F.3: 5. **F.8**: 42.
Quebec
D.9.5: 9. **F.3**: 61. **F.7**: 17. **F.8**: 3, 72. **K.1**: 66.
Rajasthan
J.6: 19. **K.1**: 218.
Romania
F.1: 14.
Russia
D.6: 28.
Sahel
Entries also appear under:
SENEGAL
Saudi Arabia
I.7: 3.
Scandinavia
Entries also appear under:
DENMARK; FINLAND; ICELAND; NORWAY; SWEDEN
D.7: 126. **I.5**: 15. **I.6**: 23. **J.3**: 24. **K.1**: 192. **K.3**: 15.
Scotland
D.9.2: 4. **G.3.2**: 109. **J.2**: 9. **K.2**: 7.
Senegal
D.5: 87. **F.2**: 73. **G.3.2**: 30, 147.
Sierra Leone
G.3.2: 137.
Singapore
F.4.1: 3, 26. **F.4.2**: 56. **G.3.2**: 56. **K.2**: 46.
South Africa
C.2: 83. **D.7**: 14, 86. **D.9**: 8. **D.9.5**: 19. **E.2**: 47. **F.7**: 12, 57, 82, 91. **G.3.2**: 148, 152.

INTERNATIONAL BIBLIOGRAPHY OF SOCIOLOGY — 1988

South America
Entries also appear under:
ARGENTINA; BOLIVIA; BRAZIL; CHILE; COLOMBIA; ECUADOR; GUYANA; PARAGUAY; PERU; VENEZUELA

South Korea
F.3: 31. **G.3.1**: 43. **G.3.2**: 14.

Southeast Asia
D.1.1: 4. **D.9.5**: 18. **F.8**: 99.

Southeast Europe
J.8: 2.

Southern Africa
Entries also appear under:
BOTSWANA; MALAWI; SOUTH AFRICA; ZAMBIA; ZIMBABWE
G.3.2: 61. **K.1**: 24.

Southern Europe
Entries also appear under:
GREECE; ITALY; SPAIN
G.3.1: 12.

Spain
D.5: 4. **D.7**: 40. **F.1**: 2, 5. **F.4.2**: 13. **F.5**: 32, 77, 85. **F.7**: 35. **J.6**: 31. **K.1**: 205, 209.

Sri Lanka
F.5: 99. **F.7**: 84. **G.3.2**: 158.

St Vincent and the Grenadines
E.2: 2.

Sub-Saharan Africa
Entries also appear under:
BOTSWANA; ETHIOPIA; GHANA; IVORY COAST; KENYA; LIBERIA; MALAWI; MAURITIUS; NIGERIA; SENEGAL; SIERRA LEONE; SOUTH AFRICA; SUDAN; TANZANIA; TOGO; UGANDA; ZAIRE; ZAMBIA; ZIMBABWE
F.5: 81. **F.8**: 62. **G.3.2**: 98.

Sudan
E.3: 32. **F.8**: 39.

Sweden
C.5: 50. **D.7**: 112. **E.2**: 7, 33. **F.3**: 20. **F.4.2**: 2, 73. **F.5**: 54. **F.8**: 100. **G.2**: 15. **I.2**: 10, 12. **I.5**: 26. **I.6**: 24.

Switzerland
F.2: 58. **K.1**: 219.

Taiwan
C.3: 35. **G.3.2**: 154.

Tanzania
F.4.2: 31. **G.3.1**: 69. **G.3.2**: 135.

Tennessee
H.3: 10.

Texas
F.7: 67. **G.3.2**: 49.

Thailand
E.2: 74. **F.3**: 29. **G.3.1**: 46, 66, 72. **G.3.2**: 158.

Togo
F.1: 8.

Tunisia
F.8: 48. **G.3.2**: 100. **I.6**: 38.

Turkey
D.7: 111. **D.9.6**: 2. **F.4.2**: 2. **F.8**: 27, 104.

U.S.A.
Entries also appear under:
CALIFORNIA; HAWAII; KENTUCKY; MASSACHUSETTS; MICHIGAN; NEW JERSEY; NEW YORK; NORTH CAROLINA; OHIO; OKLAHOMA; TENNESSEE; TEXAS; VIRGINIA; WASHINGTON; WEST VIRGINIA; WISCONSIN
A.1: 25. **C.2**: 64. **C.3**: 35. **C.7**: 42. **D.1.1**: 1. **D.1.2**: 1. **D.4**: 1, 13. **D.5**: 1, 55, 71, 76. **D.7**: 14, 36, 47, 61, 88–89, 99–100, 118, 122, 138. **D.9**: 1, 23. **D.9.3**: 4. **D.9.5**: 1, 7, 12–14, 24, 26. **E.3**: 14. **F.1**: 9, 19, 25. **F.2**: 12, 18, 22, 31, 37, 43, 55, 59, 87. **F.3**: 3, 14, 26, 36, 92, 149, 153. **F.4.1**: 4, 15, 33, 39, 42, 46. **F.4.2**: 38, 51, 62, 64, 68, 71–73, 88. **F.5**: 7, 36, 39, 55, 60, 104. **F.6**: 3, 14, 21, 28. **F.7**: 7, 14, 28, 31–32, 39, 52, 59, 61, 72–73, 80, 87–88, 110. **F.8**: 51, 63, 68, 78, 85, 90, 100. **G.2**: 8. **G.3.1**: 49, 52. **G.3.2**: 23, 42, 45, 50–51, 68, 74, 79, 83, 86, 102, 105, 125, 151. **H.3**: 6–7, 21. **H.4**: 22. **I.2**: 41, 58, 60, 68. **I.3**: 18, 20, 30, 47, 57. **I.4**: 2, 12, 15, 18. **I.6**: 7, 10, 42. **I.7**: 8, 21–22, 24. **J.3**: 4, 22. **J.6**: 18. **K.1**: 40, 45, 57, 85, 120–121, 127, 129, 140, 159–160, 175, 178, 197, 200, 208, 223, 226–227. **K.2**: 3–4, 18–19, 34–35, 55–56. **K.3**: 22, 27–28, 30, 33. **K.4**: 7, 30, 52, 64, 74.

U.S.S.R.
Entries also appear under:
ESTONIA; RUSSIA
A.1: 19, 35. **C.1**: 35. **D.1.1**: 45. **D.5**: 21, 59. **D.6**: 28. **D.7**: 98, 131, 144. **D.9**: 24. **D.9.3**: 8. **E.2**: 66. **F.2**: 17, 64. **F.3**: 81. **F.4.2**: 37, 55, 129. **F.7**: 56. **F.8**: 89, 97. **G.3.1**: 30. **H.4**: 6. **I.5**: 14. **J.6**: 10, 35. **J.8**: 17. **K.1**: 19, 28.

Uganda
F.4.1: 45.

United Kingdom
Entries also appear under:
ENGLAND; NORTHERN IRELAND; SCOTLAND; WALES
A.1: 28. **C.5**: 16. **D.4**: 8. **D.7**: 83, 98, 123. **D.8**: 1, 8. **D.9.5**: 4, 17. **E.2**: 14, 32, 48, 51, 54. **F.3**: 17. **F.4.1**: 64. **F.5**: 8, 56, 83. **F.6**: 25. **F.7**: 38,

United Kingdom continued
   45, 70, 98, 107. **F.8**: 61, 96. **G.3.2**: 42. **H.3**: 5, 28. **I.2**: 5, 22, 61, 69, 72. **I.3**: 12, 25, 53, 55. **I.4**: 2, 12, 22. **I.6**: 8, 24, 27–28, 36, 45. **I.7**: 7, 22. **J.3**: 7, 18–20. **K.1**: 26, 41, 56, 97, 103, 116, 124, 135, 196, 208. **K.2**: 10, 20, 25. **K.3**: 25, 37. **K.4**: 77.

Uttar Pradesh
   F.1: 29. **G.3.2**: 43, 81. **J.5**: 19.

Venezuela
   A.1: 31.

Vietnam
   A.3: 7.

Virginia
   H.3: 10.

Wales
   K.1: 21, 169.

Washington
   G.3.2: 28.

West Africa
   Entries also appear under:
   GHANA; IVORY COAST; LIBERIA; NIGERIA; SENEGAL; SIERRA LEONE; TOGO
   G.3.2: 67, 136.

West Bengal
   G.2: 16. **G.3.1**: 50.

West Virginia
   H.3: 10.

Western Europe
   Entries also appear under:
   BELGIUM; FRANCE; IRELAND; ITALY; SPAIN; SWITZERLAND; UNITED KINGDOM
   D.5: 72, 89. **F.3**: 71, 110. **F.8**: 95. **G.3.2**: 112. **J.6**: 30.

Wisconsin
   K.2: 38.

Yugoslavia
   J.2: 4.

Zaire
   E.3: 26.

Zambia
   E.2: 27. **J.4**: 10.

Zimbabwe
   D.5: 25. **D.9.8**: 9. **G.3.2**: 111.

SUBJECT INDEX

Abandoned children **F.4.2**: 37.
Aborigines **C.3**: 39. **D.7**: 39, 124. **F.7**: 1, 33, 90. **K.1**: 59.
Abortion **D.3**: 15, 39. **F.3**: 17–18, 38, 138.
Absenteeism **I.3**: 1, 14.
Academic achievement **D.9.3**: 7. **D.9.5**: 6. **D.9.8**: 4–5, 8. **F.4.1**: 71. **F.7**: 61.
Academic freedom **D.9**: 1, 12.
Academic profession **F.5**: 43, 74, 84.
Accident
Entries also appear under:
NUCLEAR ACCIDENTS; WORK ACCIDENTS
Accidents **D.7**: 37. **F.3**: 87.
Achievement **F.8**: 77.
Achievement motivation
Entries also appear under:
ACADEMIC ACHIEVEMENT
Acid rain **D.7**: 100.
Action research **A.3**: 1.
Actors **B.2**: 4.
Addiction
Entries also appear under:
DRUG ADDICTION
K.1: 68.
Administration
Entries also appear under:
EDUCATION ADMINISTRATION; PUBLIC ADMINISTRATION
Adolescence **C.2**: 5, 74. **C.4**: 32. **E.2**: 68. **F.3**: 86–87. **F.4.2**: 41, 46, 58, 86, 108, 126. **F.6**: 6, 20, 30. **K.1**: 11, 13, 20, 211.
Adolescents **C.3**: 46. **C.7**: 34. **D.5**: 50, 58. **D.7**: 50. **E.2**: 1. **F.2**: 77. **F.4.2**: 59. **F.6**: 27. **J.8**: 8. **K.1**: 190, 197.
Adopted children **F.4.2**: 115.
Adult education **D.9**: 17. **D.9.5**: 12. **D.9.6**: 1.
Adulthood **F.2**: 11, 23. **K.2**: 49.
Adults **D.3**: 32.

Advertising **D.7**: 25, 32, 36, 47, 99, 133. **F.8**: 93. **I.7**: 24. **K.1**: 37.
Aesthetics **B.1.3**: 20. **D.1.1**: 15.
Affectivity **C.2**: 5. **C.3**: 3, 7.
Affiliation
Entries also appear under:
POLITICAL AFFILIATION; RELIGIOUS AFFILIATION
Age
Entries also appear under:
OLD AGE
Age at marriage **F.4.1**: 31, 57, 63, 71.
Age discrimination **F.2**: 24.
Age groups **C.6**: 2. **F.1**: 10. **F.2**: 2–4. **F.3**: 70. **F.6**: 2. **J.8**: 8. **K.1**: 61.
Aged
Entries also appear under:
CARE OF THE AGED
F.1: 3, 25. **F.2**: 7, 25, 37–38, 41–43, 45, 50–52, 54–56, 58–61, 63, 65. **F.4.2**: 95, 99, 105. **F.8**: 10. **G.3.1**: 11. **G.3.2**: 117. **I.3**: 17. **J.6**: 14. **K.1**: 74, 173. **K.2**: 1, 4, 30, 43. **K.4**: 18, 29.
Ageing **F.1**: 28. **F.2**: 26–35, 40, 43, 45, 47, 49, 57, 62. **F.4.1**: 40. **G.3.1**: 1, 34, 52. **I.2**: 35. **I.5**: 11. **K.4**: 3.
Aggregate demand **D.7**: 99.
Agrarian policy **G.3.1**: 2.
Agrarian reform **G.3.1**: 23.
Agrarian relations **G.3.1**: 3.
Agrarian society **G.3.1**: 21.
Agricultural development
Entries also appear under:
GREEN REVOLUTION
Agricultural enterprises
Entries also appear under:
FAMILY FARMS
I.4: 19.
Agricultural labour **F.8**: 63. **G.3.1**: 17. **H.4**: 15.
Agriculture **G.3.1**: 7, 26. **H.4**: 39.

AIDS **C.1**: 27. **D.7**: 108. **D.8**: 5. **F.3**: 88–92, 95–101, 103, 112–115, 123–124, 126–127. **F.6**: 1, 8–9, 14. **F.7**: 99. **G.2**: 1. **I.3**: 3. **K.2**: 3, 30. **K.3**: 12.
Air pollution **G.1**: 3.
Air traffic **D.7**: 37.
Alcohol **D.7**: 133. **I.3**: 4, 14, 35. **K.1**: 10–11, 17, 23, 37, 40–41, 146, 153–154, 166, 192, 202, 207, 209. **K.2**: 47.
Alcoholism **K.1**: 18, 43, 191, 193–195, 212.
Alexander, Jeffrey. **B.1.1**: 2.
Alienation **D.1.3**: 7. **D.5**: 30. **F.7**: 48. **J.5**: 10.
Altruism **C.2**: 77. **C.7**: 3–4, 20.
Alzheimer's disease **F.3**: 108.
Amerindians **F.7**: 13, 72. **K.1**: 66.
Amish **D.1.1**: 12. **D.5**: 69.
Anarchism **F.5**: 1.
Ancestor cults **D.5**: 28, 51.
Animal
  Entries also appear under:
  DOMESTIC ANIMALS
Anomie **G.3.2**: 72. **J.4**: 12.
Anthropological methodology
  Entries also appear under:
  PARTICIPANT OBSERVATION
Anthropology
  Entries also appear under:
  CULTURAL ANTHROPOLOGY; MEDICAL ANTHROPOLOGY; POLITICAL ANTHROPOLOGY; SOCIAL ANTHROPOLOGY; URBAN ANTHROPOLOGY
D.1.1: 2.
Anthropology of education **D.9.5**: 24.
Anti-nuclear movements **D.7**: 83. **J.5**: 15.
Anti-semitism **F.7**: 94–95, 109.
Anxiety **C.2**: 15, 49. **K.1**: 194.
Apartheid **F.2**: 23. **F.7**: 12. **K.3**: 34. **K.4**: 32.
Arabs **E.3**: 21. **F.3**: 52. **F.7**: 6. **I.2**: 59.
Arbitration **I.6**: 19–20.
Architecture **G.3.2**: 11, 62. **K.1**: 142.
Armed forces **J.7**: 4.
Arms limitation **C.1**: 9. **J.8**: 5.

Artificial intelligence **D.6**: 1.
Artificial reproduction **F.4.2**: 49.
Arts
  Entries also appear under:
  PERFORMING ARTS; VISUAL ARTS
  D.7: 40. **D.8**: 5, 8, 18.
ASEAN **F.8**: 99.
Asians **F.4.1**: 28. **F.7**: 15, 61, 80. **F.8**: 84, 96.
Aspirations **F.2**: 12. **F.6**: 20.
Assistance **I.3**: 2.
Associations **C.2**: 18.
Atheism **D.5**: 21.
Attitude change **C.7**: 6, 12. **F.4.1**: 9. **F.4.2**: 6. **F.5**: 50.
Attitudes
  Entries also appear under:
  POLITICAL ATTITUDES; RACIAL ATTITUDES
  C.7: 7, 14, 25, 27, 33, 37. **D.6**: 25. **F.3**: 20. **F.4.1**: 51. **F.4.2**: 88. **F.5**: 51. **F.6**: 4, 10, 20, 30. **F.8**: 3. **G.2**: 12. **G.3.2**: 26. **I.6**: 15. **J.3**: 11, 13. **J.6**: 37. **K.1**: 40, 176, 195.
Attitudes to work **I.3**: 10, 53.
Attribution **C.1**: 18. **C.2**: 31, 40, 48–49, 53, 72, 88.
Audiences **D.7**: 135, 143, 149. **D.8**: 13.
Authoritarian leadership **C.6**: 18.
Authoritarianism **C.2**: 83. **C.7**: 34. **D.5**: 70.
Authority **F.4.2**: 86–87.
Automation
  Entries also appear under:
  OFFICE AUTOMATION
  H.4: 2–4, 49, 51.
Bank
  Entries also appear under:
  WORLD BANK
Banking **H.4**: 47.
Bargaining
  Entries also appear under:
  COLLECTIVE BARGAINING
  I.6: 12, 22.
Basques **D.7**: 40.
Behavioural sciences **C.1**: 4.
Behaviourism **B.1.1**: 4.
Belief
  Entries also appear under:
  FOLK BELIEFS; RELIGIOUS BELIEFS

C.2: 9. C.4: 14. J.6: 12.
Bibliographies A.5: 1. D.5: 53. D.7: 134, 148. F.5: 105. F.6: 21. F.7: 65, 105. I.7: 18. K.1: 74. K.4: 26.
Bilingualism D.7: 51.
Biology
Entries also appear under:
HUMAN BIOLOGY; SOCIAL BIOLOGY
B.1.1: 1. F.1: 24.
Biotechnology D.9: 3. K.4: 42.
Birth F.3: 50. F.4.1: 70. F.4.2: 8.
Birth intervals F.3: 84.
Birth place F.8: 23.
Birth rate F.3: 52, 61, 71, 80.
Birth spacing F.3: 47.
Black market H.5: 5.
Blacks D.4: 3. D.7: 136. F.2: 37. F.4.2: 54. F.5: 19, 51. F.7: 11–12, 20, 65, 72–73, 80, 88, 91, 98, 111. G.3.2: 76. I.2: 57.
Blindness D.7: 82.
Botany C.2: 98.
Boys F.2: 8.
Breast-feeding F.4.2: 2, 43.
Broadcasting
Entries also appear under:
RELIGIOUS BROADCASTING
D.7: 96, 98, 101, 131.
Buddhism D.5: 29.
Budget
Entries also appear under:
HOUSEHOLD BUDGETS
Bureaucracy C.5: 48. D.3: 26. F.5: 23. F.7: 33. I.6: 4. K.4: 2.
Business community A.1: 28. H.4: 12.
Business management C.4: 28.
Business organization C.6: 5. H.4: 28.
Cambodians F.7: 17.
Capital
Entries also appear under:
INDUSTRIAL CAPITAL
H.6: 1.
Capital punishment K.1: 121.
Capitalism D.1.1: 26. G.3.2: 127. H.4: 2, 33–34. J.1: 1, 4. J.2: 12.
Capitalist development F.5: 99.
Capitalist economy F.8: 22.

Care of the aged F.2: 48. F.4.2: 92. K.2: 7, 16, 25, 42, 59. K.3: 7. K.4: 10.
Caring F.3: 108. F.4.2: 116. K.2: 30, 33. K.3: 29.
Carnivals D.2: 3.
Case studies C.1: 34.
Casework K.3: 3, 15.
Castes E.2: 4–5, 22–23. F.7: 72. F.8: 24.
Catholic Church D.5: 64, 61, 67–68, 81. F.4.1: 68.
Catholicism D.5: 62, 66, 74, 76, 79. F.3: 19. F.5: 109.
Catholics D.5: 65, 78. F.5: 59.
Causality B.1.1: 27. C.5: 10. C.7: 20. F.3: 51.
Cause C.2: 31.
Causes of death F.3: 153.
Censorship D.7: 3.
Character
Entries also appear under:
NATIONAL CHARACTER
H.3: 19. K.4: 4.
Charisma C.6: 4, 19. D.5: 10, 82.
Charismatic leaders C.6: 5.
Child abuse F.3: 66. F.4.2: 67, 73. F.6: 28. K.1: 45–48, 52, 54–56.
Child adoption F.3: 31. F.4.2: 12, 14, 31, 49.
Child care D.4: 1. F.2: 67. F.4.2: 38–39, 51, 107. I.3: 20. K.2: 8, 10–11, 38.
Child development C.1: 23. C.2: 20, 62, 74, 96, 101. C.3: 13, 46. D.1.3: 1–2. D.7: 125. F.2: 66. F.5: 100.
Child fostering F.4.2: 14, 37. K.2: 14. K.3: 9–10.
Child labour I.2: 9, 11.
Child mortality F.3: 134–135.
Child neglect F.2: 87. F.3: 66. K.1: 54, 57.
Child psychology A.5: 1. C.2: 9, 73, 89. D.1.3: 2. F.2: 77, 81. F.3: 104. F.4.2: 89.
Child rearing F.4.2: 41, 54, 108.
Childhood F.2: 76, 78, 82–83. F.3: 87. K.1: 6, 229.
Children
Entries also appear under:

ABANDONED CHILDREN; ADOPTED CHILDREN; DISABLED CHILDREN; GIFTED CHILDREN
C.3: 11. **C.7**: 2. **D.1.2**: 12. **D.1.3**: 5. **D.9**: 7. **F.2**: 69, 72–73, 75, 79, 86. **F.3**: 43, 111. **F.4.1**: 16. **F.4.2**: 3, 7, 53, 78–80, 90–91, 94, 134, 147. **F.7**: 100. **I.2**: 13. **J.3**: 8. **K.1**: 22, 31, 84, 143–144, 157. **K.3**: 15, 37. **K.4**: 5.

Children in care **K.1**: 118. **K.2**: 14, 41. **K.3**: 9.

Children's rights **F.2**: 68, 71. **K.1**: 52.

Chinese **D.1.1**: 4. **F.7**: 7, 26–27, 46, 68, 74–75. **F.8**: 51.

Choice **C.7**: 10. **F.3**: 41.

Christian churches
Entries also appear under:
HUTTERITES

Christian orders
Entries also appear under:
DOMINICANS

Christianity
Entries also appear under:
CATHOLICISM
D.5: 62–68, 70, 72–75, 77–78, 81. **D.9**: 4. **F.3**: 19. **F.4.1**: 68. **F.5**: 59.

Christians **A.1**: 6. **D.5**: 70. **J.5**: 29.

Church and state **D.5**: 64.

Cinema **D.7**: 89, 146. **D.8**: 2.

Circumcision **F.5**: 67. **F.6**: 13.

Circus **D.8**: 19.

Cities **F.2**: 65. **G.3**: 1. **G.3.2**: 6–7, 11, 21, 33, 40, 50, 71, 74, 81, 96, 115, 118, 124, 143. **J.4**: 7. **K.1**: 129.

Citizenship **G.1**: 1. **J.3**: 24. **K.2**: 20.

Civil liberties **J.3**: 2.

Civil servants **J.4**: 6.

Civil service **I.3**: 29. **J.4**: 1, 4.

Civil-military relations **J.7**: 4.

Civilization **D.1.1**: 18, 20. **H.2**: 1.

Class
Entries also appear under:
MIDDLE CLASS; SOCIAL CLASSES; UNDERCLASS; WORKING CLASS
E.2: 13–14, 29, 34, 38, 52, 65, 70, 75. **F.4.1**: 6. **F.5**: 30, 86. **F.7**: 53. **J.3**: 27. **J.6**: 4. **K.2**: 12. **K.3**: 14.

Class consciousness **E.2**: 39.

Class formation **E.2**: 8, 69.

Class identification **E.2**: 9–11.

Class structure **E.2**: 12, 16, 28, 39, 51.

Class struggle **D.5**: 43. **E.2**: 40.

Clientelism **C.6**: 7.

Cliques **B.3**: 16.

Co-operatives
Entries also appear under:
COOPERATIVE SECTOR
G.3.1: 84.

Coal mines **I.3**: 1.

Coffee **J.6**: 1.

Cognition
Entries also appear under:
SOCIAL COGNITION
A.1: 15. **C.2**: 9–11, 20, 37, 44, 57. **C.3**: 7. **J.6**: 20.

Cognitive development **D.7**: 125.

Cohabitation **F.4.1**: 7, 21, 49. **F.4.2**: 90.

Cold War **D.7**: 98.

Collective action **C.4**: 23, 29. **C.5**: 9. **C.7**: 1, 29.

Collective bargaining **D.9.9**: 7. **I.6**: 39.

Collective security **F.7**: 24. **J.8**: 13.

Colonialism **D.7**: 66.

Colour names **D.7**: 53.

Communal violence **E.2**: 22.

Communalism **F.7**: 64. **J.3**: 3.

Communication
Entries also appear under:
INTERCULTURAL COMMUNICATION; INTERPERSONAL COMMUNICATION; MASS COMMUNICATION; NONVERBAL COMMUNICATION; ORAL COMMUNICATION
C.3: 3–4, 7, 25, 49. **C.5**: 5. **D.7**: 16–28, 30–45, 47–49. **D.9.5**: 22. **F.4.1**: 39.

Community
Entries also appear under:
BUSINESS COMMUNITY; ETHNIC COMMUNITIES; RURAL COMMUNITIES; URBAN COMMUNITIES
C.3: 28. **D.1.1**: 13. **G.2**: 7, 9, 11, 17. **J.3**: 26. **J.6**: 4. **J.8**: 10. **K.1**: 5, 66, 78, 104.

Community development **F.3**: 22. **G.2**: 2.

Community organizations **G.2**: 3. **G.3.2**: 10. **K.1**: 65.

Community participation **G.2**: 1, 15. **J.3**: 4.

Commuting **F.8**: 18.

Company management
Entries also appear under:
BUSINESS MANAGEMENT

INTERNATIONAL BIBLIOGRAPHY OF SOCIOLOGY — 1988

Comparative analysis **A.3**: 8. **B.1.1**: 5.
Compensation **I.6**: 4.
Competition **C.3**: 25. **C.4**: 6. **I.2**: 39.
Competitiveness **C.2**: 16.
Complex societies **C.4**: 6.
Computerization **H.4**: 26.
Computers **B.1.3**: 3. **B.3**: 3. **C.1**: 5. **H.4**: 5, 33, 40. **I.3**: 21.
Concepts **B.1.1**: 5. **C.5**: 20.
Conflict
Entries also appear under:
GENERATION CONFLICTS; INTERPERSONAL CONFLICTS; MARITAL CONFLICT; RACIAL CONFLICT; RELIGIOUS CONFLICTS
C.2: 83. **C.5**: 1. **E.2**: 35. **J.7**: 3.
Conflict resolution **C.3**: 5, 35, 39. **F.7**: 89. **G.2**: 10.
Conflict theory **C.3**: 20.
Confucianism **C.3**: 35.
Consensus **C.7**: 18, 30.
Conservation
Entries also appear under:
SOIL CONSERVATION
Conservatism **F.7**: 88. **K.2**: 20.
Conservatives **J.1**: 1.
Constitution **J.3**: 3.
Consumer behaviour **H.5**: 1, 6.
Consumption **C.7**: 31. **H.5**: 7. **J.5**: 7.
Contextual analysis **C.2**: 72.
Contraception **F.3**: 24–27, 34–35, 43–44, 46, 54.
Contract
Entries also appear under:
LABOUR CONTRACT
Cooking **H.5**: 8.
Co-operative sector **H.4**: 6.
Corporate crime **K.1**: 114.
Corporate culture **C.5**: 50. **I.5**: 26.
Corporate power **H.4**: 7.
Corporatism **C.3**: 35.
Correlation **B.3**: 15.
Corruption **K.1**: 79.
Cosmetics **F.5**: 28.
Cost
Entries also appear under:
TRANSPORT COSTS

Cost of living **H.5**: 2.
Cost-benefit analysis **I.4**: 15.
Counselling **C.2**: 82. **K.1**: 10.
Coup d'etat **J.5**: 9.
Courts
Entries also appear under:
JUVENILE COURTS
D.4: 4. **F.2**: 87. **F.7**: 19. **J.3**: 23. **K.1**: 57, 164.
Courtship **F.4.1**: 8, 55.
Creativity **F.8**: 77.
Credit **J.4**: 2.
Cressey, Donald. **K.1**: 89, 152.
Crime
Entries also appear under:
CORPORATE CRIME
D.3: 31. **F.2**: 2. **F.5**: 8. **G.2**: 3, 7, 17. **J.3**: 26. **K.1**: 59–68, 70–71, 73–86, 89–91, 93–104, 106–113, 115–118, 120–125, 127–139, 206. **K.3**: 5.
Crime prevention **K.1**: 23, 62, 80, 90, 172.
Criminal justice **D.4**: 3, 13. **F.7**: 11, 39. **J.3**: 12. **K.1**: 127, 131, 142, 144–148, 150–156, 158–164, 166–170, 172–182, 187–189.
Criminal law **K.1**: 162, 202.
Criminal sentencing **D.4**: 9. **K.1**: 127, 151, 154, 171, 182, 189.
Criminality **K.1**: 82, 110, 164.
Criminology **F.5**: 8. **K.1**: 60, 83, 97, 105, 115, 117, 119–120, 132, 166, 173, 188.
Criticism **B.1.1**: 11.
Cross-cultural analysis **C.2**: 94. **F.4.2**: 109, 133.
Cross-national analysis **F.5**: 48.
Cults
Entries also appear under:
ANCESTOR CULTS
D.5: 10.
Cultural anthropology **D.1.1**: 3.
Cultural change **C.7**: 12. **F.4.1**: 9. **F.4.2**: 6. **F.8**: 77.
Cultural dependence **A.1**: 3.
Cultural dynamics **F.3**: 55.
Cultural history **D.1.1**: 6. **D.2**: 2.
Cultural identity **D.1.1**: 4, 10, 35–36.

Cultural interaction **D.8**: 1.
Cultural relations **J.8**: 13.
Cultural values **D.1.2**: 8. **I.3**: 22.
Culture
Entries also appear under:
CORPORATE CULTURE; POLITICAL CULTURE; SUBCULTURE; WORKING CLASS CULTURE
A.3: 8. **B.1.2**: 1. **C.1**: 30. **C.2**: 87. **C.5**: 34. **C.6**: 6, 13. **C.7**: 23. **D.1.1**: 7–9, 11, 14, 18–19, 24, 26, 28, 30, 32–34, 37, 47. **D.1.2**: 3. **D.6**: 27. **D.8**: 3. **D.9.5**: 24. **F.3**: 5. **G.3.2**: 40. **I.7**: 24. **K.1**: 85.
Cybernetics **D.9.5**: 14.
Damage **J.8**: 9.
Darwin, Charles. **C.1**: 6.
Data collection **B.2**: 9.
Data processing **I.3**: 55.
Daughters **F.4.1**: 75. **F.4.2**: 92.
Death **D.1.2**: 13. **F.1**: 17. **F.3**: 150.
Decentralization **J.4**: 1.
Decision **C.5**: 8.
Decision making
Entries also appear under:
GROUP DECISION MAKING
C.4: 1, 21. **C.5**: 37, 42. **F.8**: 1. **H.6**: 2. **J.6**: 12.
Decision models **K.4**: 61.
Decision theory **C.4**: 30. **J.8**: 20.
Deforestation **G.3.1**: 8.
Delinquency
Entries also appear under:
JUVENILE DELINQUENCY
F.5: 16. **I.7**: 20. **K.1**: 64, 87–88, 138.
Delinquent rehabilitation **K.1**: 140, 188.
Demand
Entries also appear under:
AGGREGATE DEMAND
Democracy **B.1.1**: 16. **D.7**: 117. **G.3.2**: 13. **H.3**: 3. **I.6**: 8, 47. **J.2**: 11. **J.6**: 12, 33.
Democratization **D.9.1**: 1.
Demographic change **D.5**: 40, 67. **F.1**: 27. **F.3**: 2–5.
Demographic research **F.1**: 13, 26.
Demography **C.5**: 24. **E.2**: 20. **F.1**: 5–7, 12, 19, 24, 30. **F.3**: 53, 81. **F.4.1**: 11, 52. **F.8**: 50, 101.
Dentistry **I.4**: 21.

Dependence relationships **C.1**: 13. **C.3**: 53. **F.2**: 39. **K.3**: 7.
Deprivation **D.9**: 2.
Desegregation **G.3.2**: 61.
Deterrence **K.1**: 23, 90, 93, 202.
Developed countries **G.3.1**: 33.
Developing countries **A.1**: 3. **E.3**: 22. **F.3**: 13, 32, 78, 86. **F.5**: 37. **F.8**: 37, 45. **G.3.1**: 29, 63, 84. **G.3.2**: 25, 80–81, 86, 156. **H.3**: 12. **H.4**: 36. **I.2**: 52. **I.3**: 54. **I.5**: 24. **J.8**: 16. **K.1**: 215–216, 233, 236. **K.4**: 39, 61.
Development planning **F.7**: 24.
Development policy **F.8**: 14. **G.3**: 1. **G.3.1**: 66, 69, 72. **J.4**: 7.
Development studies **F.2**: 21. **F.3**: 88. **F.5**: 34.
Deviance **K.1**: 13.
Diabeves **F.4.1**: 35.
Dialects **D.7**: 77.
Diet **F.3**: 136.
Directories **A.3**: 12.
Disability **C.7**: 14. **F.3**: 11, 106. **K.4**: 7.
Disabled children **D.7**: 82. **D.9**: 24. **F.2**: 80.
Disabled persons **D.1.3**: 15. **F.3**: 125.
Disarmament **J.8**: 5.
Disasters **D.7**: 144. **K.1**: 28.
Discourse analysis **D.7**: 115.
Discrimination
Entries also appear under:
AGE DISCRIMINATION; POSITIVE DISCRIMINATION; RACIAL DISCRIMINATION; RELIGIOUS DISCRIMINATION; SEX DISCRIMINATION
C.4: 4. **C.7**: 37. **F.3**: 91, 106. **F.7**: 102.
Diseases
Entries also appear under:
OCCUPATIONAL DISEASES
C.2: 55. **F.3**: 107, 109, 118, 131. **G.1**: 5. **K.1**: 234. **K.4**: 88.
Dissent **F.7**: 21.
Dissidents **F.7**: 57.
Distribution **E.2**: 13. **F.5**: 30. **I.2**: 33.
Distributive justice **K.3**: 23–24.
Division of labour **F.4.2**: 11, 25, 63. **F.5**: 31, 37. **H.4**: 14. **I.3**: 21, 34.

Divorce **C.2**: 93. **D.5**: 68. **F.4.1**: 23, 45, 51, 65, 67–74. **F.4.2**: 77, 79–80, 82, 84, 111, 113.
Divorced persons **I.2**: 1.
Dollar **F.3**: 29.
Domestic animals **F.4.2**: 42.
Domestic violence **F.4.1**: 15, 19, 27. **F.4.2**: 67–69, 71–75. **F.5**: 23. **K.1**: 1, 3, 12, 21.
Domestic workers **F.3**: 28. **F.5**: 6. **I.3**: 15.
Domination **C.5**: 5, 13. **D.6**: 10. **G.3.1**: 24.
Dominicans **F.8**: 56.
Drinkers **K.1**: 201.
Drug abuse **K.1**: 20, 32, 87, 186, 197, 204–206, 208, 210–211.
Drug addiction **K.1**: 6, 86. **K.4**: 53.
Drug trafficking **K.1**: 198, 203, 206.
Drugs **D.9.3**: 9. **F.4.2**: 41. **I.3**: 35. **J.8**: 8. **K.1**: 10, 17–18, 27, 41, 43, 50, 86, 146, 190–198, 200–212. **K.4**: 85.
Durkheim, Emile. **B.1.1**: 8–9, 28. **B.1.3**: 19. **C.1**: 8. **D.1.1**: 11. **D.5**: 43. **E.3**: 31.
Dysfunction
Entries also appear under:
ORGANIZATIONAL DYSFUNCTIONS
Early motherhood **C.4**: 32.
Early retirement **I.3**: 12.
Earnings **D.9.8**: 6. **F.3**: 74. **F.7**: 43. **F.8**: 71. **H.3**: 2, 5, 7, 13, 21. **I.4**: 10.
Eastern bloc **A.1**: 19.
Ecological movements **J.5**: 6.
Ecology
Entries also appear under:
HUMAN ECOLOGY
G.1: 14. **G.3.1**: 9–10. **J.5**: 6.
Economic analysis **H.1**: 6.
Economic behaviour **F.2**: 72. **H.1**: 5.
Economic change **E.2**: 60. **E.3**: 9.
Economic conditions **D.5**: 76. **F.1**: 29. **F.7**: 20.
Economic development **D.9.5**: 25. **F.3**: 5. **F.4.1**: 25. **H.3**: 3, 11. **J.2**: 10.
Economic elites **G.3.2**: 105.
Economic growth **E.2**: 74. **F.3**: 4. **H.1**: 7.
Economic hardship **K.2**: 18.

Economic inequality **F.7**: 10, 113.
Economic policy **F.5**: 90.
Economic power **F.5**: 49. **H.4**: 7.
Economic psychology **H.1**: 4–6.
Economic sociology **H.1**: 3, 7.
Economic theory **F.3**: 55. **K.1**: 99.
Economics of education **D.9.5**: 7, 20.
Education
Entries also appear under:
ADULT EDUCATION; ANTHROPOLOGY OF EDUCATION; ECONOMICS OF EDUCATION; HIGHER EDUCATION; MINORITY EDUCATION; TECHNICAL EDUCATION; THEORY OF EDUCATION
D.1.2: 3. **D.3**: 25, 29. **D.9**: 2, 4, 8–9, 12, 14, 16, 18–19, 22–24. **D.9.2**: 2–3. **D.9.3**: 9. **D.9.5**: 9. **D.9.8**: 10. **F.4.2**: 29. **F.7**: 71. **I.2**: 14. **I.6**: 11.
Education administration **D.9.5**: 17.
Educational expenditure **D.9**: 3. **D.9.5**: 20.
Educational opportunities **D.9**: 13, 26.
Educational output **D.9.5**: 3, 23.
Educational planning **D.9.5**: 13, 25.
Educational policy **D.9**: 7, 10–13, 18, 21, 24, 26. **D.9.1**: 1. **D.9.2**: 4.
Effect
Entries also appear under:
PSYCHOLOGICAL EFFECTS
Ego **C.2**: 96. **C.7**: 16.
Electoral behaviour **J.6**: 9, 29.
Electronics industry **I.3**: 6. **I.6**: 45.
Eligibility **K.2**: 58.
Elites
Entries also appear under:
ECONOMIC ELITES; POLITICAL ELITES
D.3: 26. **E.2**: 41, 47, 73. **G.3.1**: 18. **J.2**: 4.
Emigrants **F.8**: 6.
Emigration **F.8**: 3, 50, 54, 87, 97, 100.
Emotions **C.2**: 59–82. **C.3**: 1. **F.4.1**: 4. **J.8**: 8.
Empathy **C.2**: 56.
Employees **I.3**: 2.
Employers **I.5**: 18.
Employers' organizations **I.6**: 12.
Employment
Entries also appear under:
YOUTH EMPLOYMENT

D.9: 14. **F.2**: 7. **F.4.1**: 53, 64. **F.4.2**: 39, 66. **F.5**: 54, 68. **F.7**: 48, 110. **F.8**: 67. **H.4**: 43. **I.2**: 7, 14, 17, 35, 45. **I.6**: 13.

Employment discrimination **F.5**: 29. **F.7**: 10. **I.2**: 43, 56. **I.3**: 46.

Employment opportunities **F.2**: 40.

Employment stability **I.3**: 50.

Endogamy **F.4.1**: 28, 36.

Energy
Entries also appear under:
NUCLEAR ENERGY

English language **D.7**: 58.

Enterprises
Entries also appear under:
AGRICULTURAL ENTERPRISES; MULTINATIONAL ENTERPRISES; PRIVATE ENTERPRISES; SMALL AND MEDIUM SIZED ENTERPRISES
H.4: 41. **I.1**: 3. **I.6**: 6.

Entrepreneurs **F.5**: 96. **H.4**: 48.

Entrepreneurship **C.5**: 34. **F.7**: 46.

Environment
Entries also appear under:
PHYSICAL ENVIRONMENT; RURAL ENVIRONMENT; URBAN ENVIRONMENT; WORK ENVIRONMENT
C.5: 47. **G.1**: 2–3, 10. **G.3.2**: 133. **I.5**: 5. **J.5**: 7. **K.1**: 174, 214.

Environmental impact studies **G.1**: 7.

Environmental policy **G.3.1**: 8. **G.3.2**: 62. **J.5**: 8, 18.

Environmental psychology **K.1**: 102.

Environmental quality **G.3.2**: 5.

Epidemiology **F.3**: 96. **G.1**: 5. **I.3**: 4. **K.1**: 43. **K.4**: 30.

Epistemology **D.6**: 30.

Equal opportunity **D.9**: 13, 26. **E.2**: 36, 52. **I.2**: 17, 21, 39, 61.

Equity **D.9.2**: 3. **D.9.5**: 8. **K.2**: 15. **K.4**: 84.

Eroticism **F.6**: 11.

Ethics
Entries also appear under:
MEDICAL ETHICS; PROFESSIONAL ETHICS; PROTESTANT ETHICS
C.6: 8. **D.3**: 17, 21, 24, 28, 34–35, 39. **D.5**: 80. **D.7**: 113, 134. **F.6**: 14, 31. **J.4**: 3. **K.1**: 9. **K.2**: 22. **K.4**: 30.

Ethnic assimilation **F.7**: 60, 71.

Ethnic communities **F.7**: 4, 17, 45–46, 68.

Ethnic consciousness **F.7**: 66.

Ethnic factors **F.7**: 24.

Ethnic groups **C.2**: 39. **D.7**: 125. **F.7**: 78, 84. **G.2**: 12. **G.3.2**: 52. **H.3**: 24. **J.3**: 13.

Ethnic minorities **D.5**: 29. **F.7**: 6–7, 25, 27–28, 30, 37–38, 77, 103. **G.3.2**: 17. **K.1**: 180.

Ethnic pluralism **F.7**: 10.

Ethnic policy **F.7**: 71, 98.

Ethnicity **D.5**: 42. **D.7**: 59. **F.7**: 57–69. **G.3.2**: 49. **J.6**: 32. **K.4**: 20.

Ethnocentrism **B.1.1**: 3.

Ethnography **C.4**: 32.

Ethnolinguistics **D.8**: 17.

Ethnomethodology **B.1.3**: 9.

Ethology **C.2**: 43. **C.7**: 5.

Eugenics **F.3**: 72.

European Community **F.5**: 65. **F.8**: 104. **J.4**: 5.

Euthanasia **K.1**: 9.

Evaluation
Entries also appear under:
PROGRAMME EVALUATION
A.3: 10. **B.2**: 10. **C.1**: 21. **I.2**: 26. **K.3**: 3.

Evangelism **D.5**: 71.

Everyday life **C.2**: 84. **D.1.1**: 39. **D.3**: 18. **D.8**: 11. **F.2**: 38. **H.4**: 45.

Evolution **D.1.2**: 4. **E.3**: 12, 14.

Exchange **H.6**: 1.

Exile **F.5**: 38.

Existentialism **F.5**: 1.

Expectation **D.1.3**: 3. **D.9**: 2. **F.3**: 30. **K.1**: 11.

Expenditure
Entries also appear under:
PUBLIC EXPENDITURE

Experimental groups **C.4**: 4.

Experimental methods **C.1**: 24.

Experimental psychology **C.1**: 19.

Experts **B.3**: 9.

Explanation **B.1.2**: 1.

Extended family **F.4.1**: 25. **F.4.2**: 104, 140.

Extreme right **J.5**: 10. **J.6**: 27.

Facial expressions **C.2**: 72.

Factor analysis **B.1.3**: 10.
Factories **C.5**: 22. **I.3**: 31.
Failure
Entries also appear under:
SCHOOL FAILURE
C.2: 89.
Family
Entries also appear under:
NUCLEAR FAMILY; SOCIOLOGY OF THE FAMILY
C.1: 12. **C.3**: 13. **C.4**: 17. **C.7**: 3, 12. **D.5**: 17, 46. **D.9**: 19. **E.1**: 10. **E.2**: 17. **F.2**: 31, 45, 49, 74. **F.3**: 82, 111, 118. **F.4.1**: 9, 18, 21, 51, 69. **F.4.2**: 1, 5–6, 15–17, 19–22, 24, 29, 42, 47–48, 50, 55–56, 60–61, 70, 102, 110, 116, 124, 129–137, 140–142, 148. **F.5**: 80. **F.6**: 12. **F.8**: 7, 32. **G.3.1**: 30. **I.2**: 40. **I.4**: 19. **K.1**: 1, 10, 53. **K.4**: 7.
Family disintegration **F.4.2**: 76–84.
Family farms **G.3.1**: 39, 60. **H.4**: 50.
Family history **F.4.2**: 28.
Family law **D.4**: 6, 14. **F.4.2**: 3, 10, 18, 31, 38, 77.
Family life **F.4.2**: 12, 45, 146.
Family planning **D.5**: 62. **F.3**: 19–22, 28, 31–33, 36–37, 39–40, 42, 49, 58–59, 82.
Family policy **F.4.2**: 56, 62, 66. **K.2**: 18, 35, 55.
Family relations **C.3**: 10. **F.4.1**: 72. **F.4.2**: 86–89, 91–96, 98–100, 102–104, 106–107, 109–122. **K.1**: 118, 193.
Family size **F.4.1**: 3.
Family structure **F.4.2**: 11, 25, 27, 33, 46, 60, 63, 65, 85, 97, 105, 146. **I.2**: 4.
Family therapy **F.4.2**: 144. **K.3**: 35, 37.
Famine **J.8**: 11. **K.1**: 216, 220–221.
Farmers **G.3.1**: 44, 54, 70.
Farming **G.3.1**: 24.
Fascism **J.6**: 17.
Fashion **D.2**: 2.
Fatalism **C.7**: 19.
Fatherhood **F.4.2**: 66, 87, 100–101, 126.
Fathers **F.4.2**: 58. **K.1**: 56.
Fear **C.2**: 35, 60. **J.8**: 7. **K.1**: 95–96.
Feelings **C.2**: 10, 54, 65. **C.3**: 15. **C.7**: 28. **I.3**: 10.

Feminism **B.1.3**: 11. **D.3**: 17. **D.7**: 3. **F.4.1**: 19. **F.4.2**: 134. **F.5**: 1–12, 14–26, 66, 106. **I.6**: 14. **K.1**: 97.
Fertility **F.3**: 2, 34, 36, 51, 53–55, 58–59, 61–63, 65–68, 70, 72–74, 78, 81–83, 85–86. **K.1**: 54.
Feudalism **H.2**: 3.
Field work
Entries also appear under:
PARTICIPANT OBSERVATION
Filipinos **F.8**: 51.
Films **D.7**: 89, 97, 103, 124. **F.7**: 90.
Finance **I.6**: 21.
Fishermen **I.3**: 47.
Fishery management **I.3**: 47.
Folk beliefs **C.1**: 18.
Folklore **K.1**: 81.
Food **F.3**: 76. **K.1**: 222.
Food industry **I.2**: 37.
Food preparation
Entries also appear under:
COOKING
Food security **K.1**: 24.
Food supply **K.2**: 17.
Forced migration **F.8**: 43.
Forecasts
Entries also appear under:
POPULATION FORECASTS
C.7: 25. **J.6**: 37.
Foreigners **F.7**: 76. **I.3**: 46.
Forestry **H.4**: 39.
Foucault, Michel. **D.1.3**: 20.
Fraser, Malcolm. **J.6**: 36.
Freedom
Entries also appear under:
ACADEMIC FREEDOM; CIVIL LIBERTIES
A.1: 28.
French language **D.7**: 67.
Friendship **C.3**: 11, 28. **D.1.3**: 5.
Fringe benefits **I.3**: 16.
Frustration **F.4.2**: 46.
Functional analysis **G.3.2**: 53.
Functionalism **B.1.1**: 2.
Fundamentalism **D.5**: 70.
Gambling **I.7**: 1, 8.
Game theory **B.3**: 21–22. **C.4**: 1.

Games **C.6**: 11.
Gangs **F.7**: 58.
Geertz, Clifford. **B.1.2**: 1.
Gender **B.1.1**: 20. **C.7**: 2. **D.1.3**: 9. **D.4**: 16. **D.9**: 16. **D.9.3**: 3–4. **E.2**: 13, 28–30. **F.2**: 47. **F.4.1**: 67. **F.4.2**: 137. **F.5**: 16, 30, 34–35, 37–39, 41, 45, 76. **F.6**: 2. **F.7**: 33, 49. **H.3**: 26. **H.4**: 25, 44. **H.5**: 4. **H.6**: 2. **I.2**: 20, 36, 44. **I.3**: 7, 16–17, 34. **I.4**: 1, 9, 20. **I.6**: 15, 20. **J.8**: 8. **K.1**: 95, 158. **K.2**: 12. **K.4**: 20.
Gender differentiation **D.3**: 32. **F.3**: 43. **F.5**: 28–29, 31, 36, 40, 42. **H.3**: 20. **I.4**: 14. **I.5**: 23.
Gender relations **F.4.1**: 49.
Gender roles **D.7**: 36. **E.2**: 9, 67. **F.4.1**: 20. **F.4.2**: 33. **F.5**: 50–51, 54.
Generation conflicts **F.4.2**: 95. **F.5**: 73.
Generation differences **F.2**: 15.
Genetics **F.1**: 24.
Genocide **F.7**: 51, 105.
Geographic mobility **F.8**: 18. **K.1**: 101.
Geography
Entries also appear under:
HUMAN GEOGRAPHY; URBAN GEOGRAPHY
F.3: 96. **G.1**: 13. **I.7**: 14. **K.4**: 50.
German language **D.7**: 77.
Germans **F.7**: 30.
Gerontology **F.2**: 64.
Gifted children **D.9**: 24.
Girls **F.7**: 69. **K.1**: 145, 159.
Gods **D.5**: 9, 20.
Goffman, Erving. **D.1.3**: 6, 17.
Government
Entries also appear under:
LOCAL GOVERNMENT
Graduates **F.5**: 74. **I.2**: 22. **I.4**: 4.
Gramsci, Antonio. **D.3**: 6. **D.5**: 43.
Greeks **D.7**: 6.
Green Revolution **G.3.1**: 14. **H.4**: 15.
Group behaviour **C.3**: 45. **C.4**: 10. **C.6**: 14.
Group decision making **B.1.3**: 3. **C.4**: 1, 22.

Group dynamics **C.4**: 9, 17. **C.5**: 31. **F.4.2**: 136.
Group identity **C.3**: 45. **C.4**: 3, 15.
Group membership **F.7**: 86.
Group participation **C.4**: 24.
Group protest **F.2**: 6. **F.5**: 18.
Group psychotherapy **C.4**: 2.
Group size **C.4**: 23.
Group theory **C.4**: 14, 30, 34. **E.2**: 69.
Guilt **D.3**: 1.
Habit
Entries also appear under:
READING HABITS
Habits **C.2**: 69.
Haitians **F.8**: 72.
Happiness **C.2**: 59, 81. **F.4.1**: 5, 36.
Hare, Richard M. **D.3**: 7.
Hasidism **D.5**: 19.
Hate **J.6**: 17.
Hausa **D.1.2**: 3.
Health
Entries also appear under:
MENTAL HEALTH; PUBLIC HEALTH
C.2: 55. **C.3**: 1. **C.7**: 18. **E.2**: 32. **F.3**: 11, 104, 106, 110–111, 117, 131. **F.4.2**: 40. **F.5**: 26, 72. **I.2**: 70. **I.3**: 18, 36, 38, 61. **K.2**: 23. **K.4**: 7, 27–28, 32, 34, 45, 60, 70, 88, 94.
Health care
Entries also appear under:
MEDICAL CARE; PRIMARY HEALTH CARE; PRIVATE HEALTH CARE
D.5: 22. **F.3**: 92. **K.4**: 27, 29, 41, 48, 68–69, 76, 84, 91.
Health economics **K.4**: 29.
Health policy **K.1**: 190. **K.2**: 3. **K.4**: 40.
Health services **K.4**: 2, 20, 24, 31, 39, 46, 56, 64, 75, 79, 82, 87.
Hermeneutics **B.1.1**: 11.
Heuristics **B.1.2**: 6.
Hierarchy **F.4.2**: 15. **H.4**: 28.
High technology **H.4**: 23.
Higher education **D.9**: 1, 3. **D.9.5**: 2–8, 10–26. **D.9.9**: 3.
Hill, Reuben. **F.4.2**: 143.
Hirshman, A. **C.5**: 44.
Hispanics **D.7**: 70. **F.3**: 153. **F.7**: 31–32, 52, 58–59, 67. **F.8**: 65. **G.3.2**: 49. **I.2**:

57.
Historical analysis **A.1**: 15. **B.3**: 19. **C.1**: 13.
Historicism **B.1.3**: 24.
Historiography **E.3**: 10.
History
Entries also appear under:
CULTURAL HISTORY; FAMILY HISTORY; MILITARY HISTORY; POLITICAL HISTORY; RELIGIOUS HISTORY; SOCIAL HISTORY; URBAN HISTORY
A.1: 16. **B.3**: 19. **D.1.1**: 25. **D.7**: 14, 112, 129. **F.5**: 106. **I.7**: 4, 11. **K.1**: 105. **K.4**: 86.
History of medicine **C.1**: 1.
History of social research **A.2**: 3.
History of sociology **B.1.3**: 24. **D.1.1**: 47.
HIV **F.3**: 112, 123. **K.3**: 12.
Hobbes, Thomas. **B.1.1**: 30.
Holidays **I.6**: 42.
Home economics **F.5**: 17.
Homelessness **G.3.2**: 90. **K.1**: 22, 213, 223–226, 230–231.
Homicide **K.1**: 84–85, 113, 121, 129.
Homogamy **I.2**: 58.
Homosexuality **C.7**: 7. **F.3**: 99, 113. **F.4.1**: 21. **F.4.2**: 102. **F.6**: 4, 14, 16, 21–22, 25, 29. **K.2**: 3.
Honour **D.3**: 8.
Hospitals **K.4**: 34, 49.
Hours of work **I.3**: 49, 57.
Household budgets **H.5**: 2.
Household income **H.3**: 5.
Households **E.2**: 30. **F.1**: 9. **F.4.2**: 11, 23–24, 63, 105. **F.8**: 27. **G.2**: 5. **H.4**: 34.
Housework **H.4**: 17. **I.3**: 15.
Housing
Entries also appear under:
SOCIAL HOUSING; URBAN HOUSING
F.5: 27. **G.3.1**: 25, 68. **G.3.2**: 88, 93, 96–97, 100, 102. **K.1**: 213.
Housing market **G.3.2**: 85. **K.1**: 225.
Housing policy **D.1.3**: 14. **G.3.2**: 14, 86–87, 89, 91. **I.2**: 16. **K.1**: 224.
Human biology **F.6**: 6.
Human ecology **C.5**: 6.
Human geography **G.1**: 8–9, 11–12.

Human relations **A.1**: 34. **C.3**: 48. **K.4**: 36.
Human resources **I.2**: 45. **I.3**: 19. **I.4**: 14.
Human rights **F.3**: 89. **J.3**: 6, 10.
Humanity **J.3**: 10.
Humour **C.2**: 26, 36.
Husbands **F.3**: 35. **F.4.1**: 53. **I.3**: 32.
Hutterites **F.3**: 36.
Identification
Entries also appear under:
CLASS IDENTIFICATION
Identity
Entries also appear under:
CULTURAL IDENTITY; NATIONAL IDENTITY
C.3: 24. **C.5**: 25. **C.7**: 37. **D.1.1**: 25. **D.4**: 16. **D.5**: 37. **F.5**: 45, 98. **J.6**: 31.
Ideology **C.5**: 5. **C.7**: 21–23. **D.1.2**: 10. **D.4**: 1. **D.5**: 21, 46. **D.6**: 22. **D.7**: 14, 27, 89, 99. **D.8**: 10. **F.3**: 49. **F.4.2**: 47. **G.3.1**: 24. **J.5**: 3.
Illegal immigration **F.8**: 67, 78.
Illiteracy **D.9.6**: 2.
Images **C.2**: 35. **C.6**: 9. **F.3**: 114. **H.4**: 5. **H.6**: 3. **J.8**: 7. **K.4**: 38.
Imagination **C.2**: 70.
Immigrant adaptation **D.7**: 18.
Immigrants **D.7**: 70. **F.4.1**: 30. **F.7**: 96. **F.8**: 51–52, 58, 75, 84–86, 90, 103. **H.3**: 6.
Immigration
Entries also appear under:
ILLEGAL IMMIGRATION
F.1: 10. **F.8**: 41, 54, 59–60, 65–66, 69–73, 79, 82, 88, 93, 101–102. **G.3.1**: 50. **H.3**: 13.
Income
Entries also appear under:
HOUSEHOLD INCOME; LOW INCOME
F.4.2: 61. **G.3.2**: 44. **H.3**: 12. **K.2**: 12.
Income determination **I.2**: 28.
Income distribution **H.3**: 25.
Income inequality **H.3**: 3, 14, 17, 27.
Income redistribution **F.3**: 68.
Indians **E.2**: 48. **F.7**: 78.
Indicator **B.1.3**: 10. **B.3**: 10. **H.3**: 19.
Indigenism **A.1**: 18, 38–39.
Indigenous population
Entries also appear under:
ABORIGINES

Individual behaviour **C.2**: 76. **C.7**: 1, 15–16, 18, 25, 28. **F.3**: 104. **F.4.1**: 1, 66.
Individualism **B.1.1**: 8. **D.1.1**: 26. **D.3**: 20. **J.5**: 17.
Individuals **I.6**: 43.
Induction **C.2**: 31.
Industrial capital **G.3.2**: 141.
Industrial management **D.3**: 21.
Industrial productivity **H.4**: 18.
Industrial psychology **H.4**: 18, 31. **I.3**: 42.
Industrial society **D.1.1**: 12. **D.5**: 69. **F.8**: 5. **J.5**: 18. **K.1**: 110.
Industrial sociology **I.1**: 2–3, 5, 7.
Industrial workers **E.2**: 5. **I.5**: 5–6.
Industry
Entries also appear under:
FOOD INDUSTRY
H.4: 34. **I.3**: 34. **I.6**: 17.
Infant mortality **E.2**: 53. **F.3**: 32, 59, 138, 141–143, 145, 151. **K.3**: 13.
Infertility **F.3**: 69.
Inflation **H.6**: 3.
Informal sector **G.3.2**: 25, 58–59. **H.2**: 4. **I.2**: 14, 46.
Information **A.1**: 19. **A.5**: 5. **C.2**: 92, 103. **C.5**: 37. **D.7**: 100. **F.3**: 97. **H.7**: 4. **I.2**: 3, 25.
Information services **A.5**: 6.
Information society **D.7**: 5, 15. **H.4**: 19–20.
Information technology **C.5**: 10. **G.3.2**: 21, 54. **H.4**: 4, 21.
In-group **C.4**: 3–4, 13.
Inheritance **F.4.1**: 45. **H.4**: 50.
Injustice **F.7**: 111. **K.3**: 34.
Innovation **C.5**: 21, 40. **G.3.2**: 123.
Institutions
Entries also appear under:
POLITICAL INSTITUTIONS; RELIGIOUS INSTITUTIONS
C.2: 15. **K.1**: 174.
Intellectual development **F.4.2**: 96.
Intellectuals **E.2**: 35.
Intelligence **C.2**: 4. **D.3**: 10.
Intelligence tests **C.2**: 29.

Intelligentsia **E.2**: 55.
Interactionism **D.1.3**: 8.
Intercultural communication **D.7**: 18.
Interdependence **D.1.2**: 4.
Interest groups **J.5**: 3.
Interethnic relations **F.4.1**: 26.
Intergenerational relations **D.7**: 33. **F.4.1**: 69. **F.4.2**: 20, 81, 104, 121. **F.5**: 73.
Intergroup relations **C.2**: 83. **C.3**: 24–25, 45, 47. **C.4**: 15. **C.7**: 37. **F.7**: 80.
Intermarriage **F.4.1**: 11, 24, 26, 28, 30, 36, 43.
Internal migration **F.8**: 14, 18, 20, 42.
International migration **F.8**: 48–54, 56–61, 63, 65–68, 71–75, 77–91, 93, 95–97, 99–101, 103–105. **H.3**: 13.
International organizations **C.5**: 4. **D.9**: 17.
International system **E.3**: 6.
Interpersonal attraction **C.3**: 9.
Interpersonal communication **C.3**: 36, 49. **D.7**: 43, 93.
Interpersonal conflicts **C.3**: 26, 47, 52.
Interpersonal relations **C.3**: 1, 7, 10, 14, 19, 22, 27, 34, 40–42, 46. **F.2**: 43. **F.4.2**: 93.
Interviewers **B.2**: 4.
Interviews **B.2**: 1, 9–10. **K.3**: 15.
Intimacy **F.6**: 30.
Inuit **F.3**: 61.
Inventions **A.3**: 9.
Investment decision **H.6**: 2.
Iranians **F.8**: 75.
Islam
Entries also appear under:
SHIISM; SUFISM
D.5: 82–90. **D.9**: 18. **F.5**: 92. **F.8**: 102. **I.3**: 41. **K.2**: 54.
Islamic law **D.5**: 23.
Israelis **F.8**: 6.
Japanese **D.5**: 29. **F.7**: 7, 77.
Japanese language **D.7**: 79.
Jews **B.1.1**: 18. **D.5**: 2. **D.9.8**: 2. **F.7**: 23, 28, 51, 56, 81–83, 95, 110. **F.8**: 89, 97. **H.3**: 24.

INTERNATIONAL BIBLIOGRAPHY OF SOCIOLOGY — 1988

Job change **I.5**: 4.
Job requirements **I.3**: 24.
Job satisfaction **I.3**: 47. **K.3**: 26.
Job search **I.2**: 3.
Journalism **D.7**: 85, 105, 113, 140.
Judaism **D.5**: 59.
Judgement
  Entries also appear under:
    SOCIAL JUDGEMENT
  C.2: 75. **C.4**: 3. **D.1.1**: 37. **D.3**: 12, 29.
Judiciary power **J.3**: 23.
Jung, Carl. **F.7**: 114.
Juries **F.7**: 115.
Jurisprudence **F.7**: 115.
Justice
  Entries also appear under:
    CRIMINAL JUSTICE; DISTRIBUTIVE JUSTICE; SOCIAL JUSTICE
  C.4: 17. **F.4.2**: 136. **K.1**: 158, 188. **K.2**: 53.
Juvenile courts **K.1**: 146, 151.
Juvenile delinquency **G.2**: 7. **K.1**: 104, 106, 109, 116, 128, 140–141, 144–145, 150.
Kazakh **F.7**: 37.
Kinship **E.2**: 38. **F.2**: 48. **F.4.1**: 6, 67. **F.4.2**: 105.
Kinship system
  Entries also appear under:
    ENDOGAMY
Knowledge
  Entries also appear under:
    SOCIOLOGY OF KNOWLEDGE
  B.1.3: 29. **B.3**: 9. **C.2**: 31. **D.6**: 6, 10. **D.7**: 100. **K.1**: 119.
Koreans **F.7**: 14. **F.8**: 51, 85.
Labour
  Entries also appear under:
    AGRICULTURAL LABOUR; CHILD LABOUR; DIVISION OF LABOUR
  A.3: 6. **F.4.2**: 24. **F.8**: 94. **H.4**: 47. **I.2**: 33, 48, 52. **I.5**: 24, 27.
Labour contract **I.3**: 33.
Labour disputes **E.2**: 21.
Labour force **D.9.8**: 2. **G.3.2**: 141. **H.4**: 32. **I.2**: 19, 49, 65. **I.3**: 27, 32. **I.5**: 25.
Labour market **F.3**: 30, 85. **F.5**: 32. **F.7**: 10. **I.2**: 2, 7, 16, 19–23, 30–32, 37, 43, 50, 55, 57, 67. **I.3**: 16. **I.4**: 10.
Labour market segmentation **F.8**: 65. **H.3**: 17. **I.2**: 8, 27–28, 47.
Labour migration **F.8**: 13, 16, 45, 49, 53, 62, 81, 104–105.
Labour movements **I.6**: 24.
Labour redundancy **I.2**: 5, 23. **I.3**: 25.
Labour relations **I.3**: 55. **I.6**: 18, 23–24, 27–29, 36, 47.
Labour supply **I.2**: 1, 51.
Labour turnover **I.3**: 50.
Land market **G.3.2**: 91.
Land property **G.3.2**: 37.
Land settlement **J.6**: 11.
Land tenure **G.3.1**: 17, 25, 71.
Land use **G.1**: 14. **G.3.1**: 33. **G.3.2**: 96.
Language
  Entries also appear under:
    SIGN LANGUAGE; WRITTEN LANGUAGES
  C.2: 57, 95. **D.7**: 9, 14, 53, 56, 59, 63–64, 66, 68, 70, 116. **K.1**: 15.
Language acquisition **D.7**: 55.
Language change **D.7**: 50. **E.2**: 1.
Language planning **D.7**: 61–62.
Language policy **D.7**: 6, 11, 73.
Laotians **F.7**: 17.
Latent structure analysis **B.3**: 10.
Latvians **D.7**: 6.
Law
  Entries also appear under:
    CRIMINAL LAW; FAMILY LAW; ISLAMIC LAW; MARITAL LAW; NATURAL LAW; SOCIOLOGY OF LAW
  D.3: 36. **D.4**: 1, 8, 10, 16. **F.3**: 17. **F.6**: 14. **G.3.2**: 32, 130. **I.6**: 43. **J.3**: 16. **J.8**: 2. **K.1**: 166, 200, 207. **K.2**: 50. **K.4**: 57, 77.
Lawyers **D.4**: 2.
Leaders
  Entries also appear under:
    CHARISMATIC LEADERS
  C.6: 9, 19. **I.5**: 25.
Leadership
  Entries also appear under:
    AUTHORITARIAN LEADERSHIP; POLITICAL LEADERSHIP
  C.6: 2, 11–17, 21. **D.9.4**: 1. **J.5**: 15. **J.6**: 13, 36.
Learning **C.2**: 48. **C.5**: 26. **G.3.2**: 123.
Legal aspects **F.6**: 31.
Legal profession **K.1**: 202.

Legal reform **D.4**: 5-6. **F.4.2**: 18. **K.1**: 153.
Legislation **F.4.1**: 31. **F.5**: 65. **I.3**: 38.
Legislative power **J.6**: 19.
Legitimacy **C.5**: 13. **J.2**: 4.
Legitimation **C.7**: 16.
Leisure **D.9.5**: 11. **F.4.1**: 32. **I.3**: 57. **I.7**: 2, 4, 7, 10-11, 13, 15, 17, 26.
Leisure policy **I.7**: 16.
Level of education **D.9.8**: 2, 6. **F.7**: 43.
Lewin, Kurt. **C.1**: 19.
Liability **J.8**: 9.
Liberalism **F.6**: 7.
Life expectancy **F.2**: 56. **F.3**: 136.
Life styles **D.1.1**: 1, 15, 44. **D.1.2**: 5. **F.4.2**: 16. **G.3.2**: 60.
Life tables **F.1**: 17. **F.3**: 67.
Linguistic minorities **D.7**: 61.
Linguistics
Entries also appear under:
SOCIOLINGUISTICS
D.7: 46, 50-55, 57-59, 61-70, 72-74, 77-78, 81-82. **E.2**: 1. **F.4.1**: 33.
Literacy **D.4**: 10. **D.7**: 1, 26, 69, 72. **D.9**: 15, 20. **F.5**: 68.
Literature **C.2**: 70. **D.1.1**: 30. **D.3**: 22. **D.8**: 11, 16.
Living conditions **F.2**: 10, 52. **F.3**: 117, 147. **G.1**: 17. **G.3.2**: 36.
Local government **G.3.2**: 107. **J.4**: 7-8, 10. **J.6**: 35. **K.3**: 18. **K.4**: 26.
Local politics **J.4**: 9.
Logic **D.9.8**: 8.
Lorenz curves **F.1**: 11.
Love **C.2**: 78. **F.4.1**: 64. **F.6**: 11.
Low income **F.2**: 55. **F.4.2**: 54.
Luhmann, Niklas. **B.1.1**: 17.
Macroeconomics **K.1**: 111.
Mafia **K.1**: 99.
Magic **D.5**: 25.
Male sterilization **F.3**: 23.
Malnutrition **D.7**: 90.
Management
Entries also appear under:
BUSINESS MANAGEMENT; FISHERY MANAGEMENT; INDUSTRIAL MANAGEMENT; MIDDLE MANAGEMENT; PERSONNEL MANAGEMENT; URBAN MANAGEMENT
C.5: 11, 15-16, 18, 34. **C.6**: 5. **H.4**: 10, 24-25, 29. **I.3**: 47. **I.5**: 7, 10. **I.6**: 19. **K.4**: 45-46.
Management techniques **I.5**: 9.
Managers **C.5**: 50. **F.5**: 42. **I.5**: 8, 11-12, 22-23, 26.
Mannheim, Karl. **A.5**: 4. **B.1.1**: 24. **D.6**: 13, 17.
Manufacturing **D.9.5**: 16. **I.3**: 30. **I.4**: 2. **I.5**: 1.
Maori **F.7**: 64, 89.
Marginality **E.2**: 2. **F.3**: 143. **F.7**: 12.
Marital conflict **F.4.1**: 15, 42.
Marital interaction **F.3**: 130. **F.4.1**: 35, 59.
Marital law **F.4.1**: 23, 45. **F.4.2**: 77.
Marital roles **F.4.1**: 6, 25, 37-38.
Marital satisfaction **F.4.1**: 5, 32, 35, 39-41, 48. **F.4.2**: 25.
Marital separation **F.4.1**: 66, 69, 72-73, 75. **F.4.2**: 76.
Marital stability **F.4.1**: 1, 7, 12, 14, 41, 61.
Marital status **F.4.1**: 5.
Marketing
Entries also appear under:
ADVERTISING
F.2: 15. **F.3**: 27, 46. **G.3.2**: 84. **K.2**: 47.
Markets
Entries also appear under:
BLACK MARKET; HOUSING MARKET; LABOUR MARKET; LAND MARKET
G.3.2: 144. **H.4**: 28. **H.5**: 4. **I.3**: 56.
Marriage
Entries also appear under:
AGE AT MARRIAGE; INTERMARRIAGE; REMARRIAGE
C.7: 12. **F.3**: 65. **F.4.1**: 4, 9, 13, 17, 44, 47, 51, 63-64. **F.4.2**: 1, 6, 144. **F.6**: 2. **F.8**: 36, 41, 93.
Marshall, Alfred. **D.3**: 11.
Marx, Karl. **D.5**: 43. **E.3**: 16.
Marxism **B.1.1**: 35. **D.7**: 105. **E.2**: 14. **J.2**: 7. **K.1**: 119.
Mass communication **D.7**: 27, 30.
Mate selection **F.4.1**: 10, 20, 46, 56.
Maternity leave **I.3**: 28.

INTERNATIONAL BIBLIOGRAPHY OF SOCIOLOGY — 1988

Mathematical models **B.3**: 20. **C.4**: 25. **C.5**: 17. **G.3.2**: 129.

Mead, G.H. **A.2**: 2.

Meaning **C.2**: 11, 61, 84, 97. **C.5**: 25.

Measurement **E.2**: 3, 43, 70. **F.2**: 9. **F.4.1**: 47.

Media
Entries also appear under:
PRESS
D.1.2: 7. **D.1.3**: 19. **D.7**: 28–29, 44, 69, 83, 85–88, 90–101, 103–107, 109, 111–121, 123–126, 128–131, 133–136, 138–141, 143–149. **F.7**: 90. **G.3.1**: 19. **K.1**: 37.

Mediation **F.4.2**: 77. **K.1**: 77, 112. **K.3**: 5.

Medical anthropology **F.3**: 109.

Medical care **F.4.2**: 27. **K.4**: 54, 62, 74.

Medical ethics **D.3**: 33, 36. **K.4**: 9, 14, 17, 19, 23, 44, 57, 77.

Medical personnel **D.7**: 23. **I.2**: 66.

Medical research **G.2**: 1.

Medical sociology **F.3**: 39, 109, 118. **K.4**: 16–18.

Medicine
Entries also appear under:
HISTORY OF MEDICINE; SURGERY
D.7: 91. **K.4**: 6, 52.

Memory **C.2**: 50, 61, 99. **J.8**: 19. **K.1**: 212.

Men **F.3**: 20, 37. **F.4.2**: 35. **F.5**: 45, 55–56. **I.4**: 20. **K.1**: 164.

Menstruation **K.4**: 40.

Mental deficiencies **C.2**: 32.

Mental health **C.3**: 9. **F.3**: 133. **F.4.1**: 13, 42. **F.4.2**: 53. **F.5**: 77, 102. **I.2**: 12, 53. **I.5**: 16. **K.1**: 168, 187, 194, 230. **K.4**: 3, 5, 12, 14, 20–21, 69, 79.

Mental illness **F.3**: 121, 129–130. **F.4.1**: 59. **K.1**: 231. **K.4**: 24, 66, 85.

Mental stress **F.2**: 51. **F.4.2**: 45. **I.4**: 21. **K.1**: 17.

Mentally disabled **C.3**: 6. **F.3**: 120.

Methodology **A.1**: 2, 27. **B.1.3**: 19, 22, 24–25. **B.3**: 24. **C.5**: 46. **D.7**: 28.

Metropolis **G.3.2**: 88.

Metropolitan areas **G.3.2**: 112, 140, 151.

Mexicans **F.4.1**: 42. **F.8**: 68.

Microcomputers **I.3**: 51.

Microelectronics **H.4**: 38.

Middle class **E.2**: 26, 48.

Middle management **H.4**: 47.

Migrant workers **E.2**: 21. **F.8**: 21, 37, 57, 63, 68, 95.

Migrants **F.3**: 153. **F.4.1**: 54. **F.4.2**: 26. **F.8**: 15, 23, 48, 96, 98.

Migration
Entries also appear under:
FORCED MIGRATION; INTERNAL MIGRATION; INTERNATIONAL MIGRATION; LABOUR MIGRATION; RURALURBAN MIGRATION; SEASONAL MIGRATION; URBANRURAL MIGRATION
F.2: 4, 42. **F.3**: 6. **F.8**: 1, 5, 10–11, 24, 27–28, 32, 35–36, 91, 94. **G.3.2**: 117, 138, 146.

Migration policy **F.8**: 30, 62, 66.

Militancy **I.6**: 14.

Militants **J.6**: 34.

Militarism **J.7**: 5.

Military **J.7**: 1, 3.

Military and politics **J.7**: 2.

Military history **J.7**: 4.

Millenarianism **D.5**: 11, 24.

Mills, C. Wright. **A.2**: 6.

Mine
Entries also appear under:
COAL MINES

Minorities
Entries also appear under:
ETHNIC MINORITIES; LINGUISTIC MINORITIES
F.7: 39–40. **F.8**: 98.

Minority education **D.9**: 7, 21.

Minority groups **C.4**: 13. **F.8**: 99.

Mode of production **B.1.3**: 32. **F.5**: 110.

Modelling **B.3**: 14. **F.1**: 15. **F.4.2**: 124. **F.7**: 108.

Models
Entries also appear under:
DECISION MODELS; MATHEMATICAL MODELS
B.1.3: 3. **B.3**: 2, 10. **D.9.2**: 3. **F.1**: 22. **F.3**: 42, 50, 73–74, 84. **F.4.2**: 146. **F.8**: 91. **H.4**: 27. **I.2**: 32. **I.3**: 2. **I.4**: 17. **K.1**: 92. **K.3**: 4, 20.

Modernity **D.1.1**: 14, 35. **D.5**: 86. **E.3**: 18, 31. **K.1**: 110.

Modernization **B.1.1**: 3. **D.7**: 79. **E.3**: 13, 17, 19, 24. **G.3.2**: 115. **I.2**: 49. **J.2**: 8. **J.6**: 14–15. **K.4**: 54.

Morality
Entries also appear under:
POLITICAL MORALITY
C.3: 26. **D.3**: 4, 7, 12, 14–16, 18, 29, 38. **D.5**: 7. **I.6**: 17.

Morals **D.3**: 6, 25, 30–32, 37. **K.1**: 125.

Morbidity **F.3**: 116.

Mortality
Entries also appear under:
CHILD MORTALITY; INFANT MORTALITY
F.3: 136, 139, 144, 146–147, 149, 152. **F.4.1**: 56. **G.3.2**: 36.

Motherhood
Entries also appear under:
EARLY MOTHERHOOD; SURROGATE MOTHERHOOD
F.4.2: 4, 8, 36, 106. **H.3**: 2.

Mothers **F.4.2**: 23, 40, 92.

Motivation **C.2**: 2, 16. **D.1.3**: 14. **I.3**: 29. **I.4**: 24.

Mountains **G.3.1**: 54.

Multiculturalism **D.7**: 6. **F.7**: 50. **F.8**: 66.

Multilingualism **D.7**: 61.

Multinational enterprises **H.4**: 12. **I.2**: 64.

Music **D.8**: 6.

Muslims **D.5**: 88. **F.4.1**: 43.

Myth **K.1**: 230.

Name
Entries also appear under:
COLOUR NAMES

Narcissism **C.2**: 95. **C.6**: 14.

Narratives **C.1**: 26. **D.7**: 63.

National character **D.1.1**: 16.

National identity **D.7**: 67.

Nationalism **D.7**: 40. **D.9**: 22. **F.5**: 78. **F.7**: 63, 84. **J.2**: 4–5, 8–9, 13.

Natural law **D.4**: 15.

Nature **A.2**: 5. **D.3**: 16.

Neighbourhood associations **G.3.2**: 10.

Neighbourhoods **D.1.2**: 1. **G.2**: 4–5, 10, 13. **K.1**: 62, 95.

Network analysis **B.1.1**: 26. **B.3**: 16. **C.4**: 28. **E.1**: 7.

New technology **D.7**: 44, 142. **F.2**: 26. **H.4**: 16, 27, 47. **I.6**: 8, 22–23.

News **D.7**: 115, 141, 149.

Nihilism **D.5**: 33.

Non-verbal communication **D.7**: 32, 42. **F.2**: 80.

Nostalgia **D.1.1**: 19.

Nuclear accidents **F.3**: 45. **J.8**: 9. **K.1**: 28.

Nuclear energy **C.2**: 35. **C.7**: 27. **D.7**: 104. **J.8**: 7.

Nuclear family **F.4.2**: 109.

Nuclear war **J.8**: 1, 8, 20.

Nuclear weapons **C.2**: 35. **J.8**: 5, 7.

Nuptiality **F.4.1**: 34, 54–56, 60.

Nursery schools **C.3**: 11. **D.1.3**: 5.

Nutrition **H.5**: 8.

Objectivity **C.6**: 4.

Obligation **C.3**: 23.

Observation
Entries also appear under:
PARTICIPANT OBSERVATION

Occupation
Entries also appear under:
ACADEMIC PROFESSION

Occupational choice **I.4**: 4, 14.

Occupational diseases **I.3**: 46.

Occupational groups **I.4**: 21.

Occupational mobility **F.4.2**: 120. **I.2**: 3. **I.4**: 3, 10–11, 16–18. **I.5**: 7.

Occupational promotion **H.4**: 25. **I.3**: 7. **I.4**: 9.

Occupational psychology **I.4**: 13.

Occupational qualification **I.5**: 22.

Occupational roles **F.4.2**: 65.

Occupational safety **I.3**: 3, 18, 38, 46, 54, 59. **I.6**: 48.

Occupational segregation **I.2**: 44.

Occupational sociology **I.3**: 36. **I.4**: 26.

Occupational status **F.3**: 74. **I.4**: 6. **I.5**: 15.

Occupational strategy **I.4**: 1, 5, 23. **K.2**: 8.

Occupational stratification **I.4**: 3.

Occupational structure **G.3.1**: 46. **I.4**: 18, 22.

Occupations **E.2**: 61. **F.5**: 47. **I.2**: 30–31. **I.4**: 19–20, 28. **I.5**: 20.

Offenders **K.1**: 70, 77, 112, 145, 156, 158, 173, 187, 189. **K.3**: 5.

Office automation **I.3**: 21.

Oil **C.7**: 27.
Old age **F.2**: 23, 39.
Old age policy **F.2**: 22.
Older workers **I.2**: 36.
Oligarchy **C.5**: 36. **G.3.1**: 21.
Oligopoly **I.3**: 30.
One-parent families **F.4.2**: 13, 52–53, 64, 103. **G.2**: 4.
Operations research **A.3**: 10.
Opinion
Entries also appear under:
PUBLIC OPINION
Oral communication **D.7**: 22, 24.
Organization
Entries also appear under:
BUSINESS ORGANIZATION; SOCIOLOGY OF ORGANIZATIONS; WORK ORGANIZATION
C.4: 22, 30. **C.5**: 24–27. **H.4**: 27. **I.3**: 27.
Organization of research **A.3**: 2.
Organization of space **F.5**: 76.
Organization of work **I.3**: 30.
Organization theory **C.5**: 20, 28.
Organizational analysis **C.5**: 2, 44, 46.
Organizational behaviour **C.5**: 1, 5, 19, 34, 39–40. **H.4**: 31. **I.4**: 23.
Organizational change **C.5**: 10, 15, 21–22. **I.3**: 31.
Organizational dysfunctions **I.6**: 10.
Organizational structure **C.5**: 17, 36, 47.
Organizations
Entries also appear under:
COMMUNITY ORGANIZATIONS; INTERNATIONAL ORGANIZATIONS; VOLUNTARY ORGANIZATIONS
C.5: 6, 8–9, 12–13, 28, 30–33, 35, 37, 42, 44. **C.6**: 13. **F.5**: 42, 56. **H.4**: 21. **I.5**: 23.
Out-groups **C.4**: 13.
Pacifism **J.6**: 18. **J.8**: 4.
Pakistanis **F.7**: 45.
Paradigms **B.1.3**: 13. **D.6**: 35.
Parent-child relations **C.2**: 50, 93, 99. **C.3**: 10. **F.2**: 85. **F.4.2**: 3, 30, 46, 78, 86–87, 89, 91, 93, 95, 100, 103, 106–109, 111, 118. **I.4**: 24.
Parenthood **F.4.2**: 35, 66, 76, 121, 145. **F.5**: 54.
Parents **D.1.2**: 12. **D.5**: 58. **D.9.3**: 7. **F.2**: 68. **F.4.1**: 71. **F.4.2**: 59, 147.

Parliament **J.3**: 1.
Parsons, Talcott. **E.1**: 10.
Participant observation **F.2**: 79.
Partisanship **J.6**: 29.
Paternalism **I.3**: 34.
Patients **D.7**: 23. **F.3**: 118, 145. **K.4**: 6, 11, 59.
Patriarchy **E.3**: 21.
Peace **G.3.1**: 23. **J.8**: 5, 10, 12.
Peace movements **J.5**: 20.
Peasant movements **G.3.1**: 59.
Peasant societies **F.5**: 21.
Peasantry **E.2**: 8. **G.3.1**: 54–55, 57–58, 60–65. **J.5**: 19.
Peer groups **K.1**: 20.
Penal policy **K.1**: 160, 170.
Penal sanctions **K.1**: 167.
Pensions **K.2**: 58.
Perception
Entries also appear under:
ROLE PERCEPTIONS; SOCIAL PERCEPTION; VISUAL PERCEPTION
C.2: 32. **C.3**: 9. **D.6**: 20. **D.7**: 68. **F.3**: 145. **F.4.1**: 38. **F.7**: 73. **I.6**: 20.
Perception of others **C.3**: 31.
Perestroika **A.1**: 23. **C.1**: 22. **E.2**: 66.
Performing arts **D.8**: 7.
Periodicals **A.5**: 2. **D.7**: 129. **F.4.1**: 4.
Persian language **D.7**: 57.
Personal aggression **C.7**: 2.
Personal power **C.3**: 30. **C.6**: 6.
Personality **C.2**: 83–104. **C.3**: 4. **E.2**: 61. **K.1**: 211.
Personality development **D.1.3**: 18.
Personnel management **I.3**: 19, 29.
Phenomenology **C.1**: 24.
Philosophy
Entries also appear under:
SOCIAL PHILOSOPHY
A.1: 24. **D.4**: 12.
Photography **D.7**: 35.
Physical environment **D.7**: 31. **K.1**: 174.
Physically disabled **F.3**: 132. **F.5**: 107.
Physicians **F.3**: 39, 145. **F.8**: 85. **I.5**: 14–15. **K.4**: 11, 38.

Piaget, Jean. **A.5**: 1. **D.3**: 37. **J.6**: 20.
Pilgrimages **D.5**: 74.
Planning methods **C.5**: 11.
Plantations **F.1**: 8.
Pluralism
Entries also appear under:
ETHNIC PLURALISM; SOCIAL PLURALISM
C.3: 35.
Poles **D.7**: 6.
Police **C.3**: 33. **I.4**: 12. **J.3**: 7, 11–12, 15–16, 22. **K.1**: 22, 78, 95. **K.3**: 22.
Policing **G.2**: 12, 17. **I.4**: 12. **J.3**: 4–5, 13, 15, 17–20, 26. **K.1**: 66.
Policy analysis **D.7**: 35. **H.4**: 1.
Policy making **K.2**: 34.
Political action **E.3**: 20. **J.5**: 6.
Political affiliation **C.4**: 15. **J.6**: 4.
Political anthropology **J.3**: 25.
Political attitudes **J.6**: 17, 27, 29.
Political behaviour **J.5**: 3. **J.6**: 26.
Political consciousness **C.2**: 20.
Political control **A.3**: 7.
Political culture **F.7**: 84. **J.6**: 23, 33.
Political economy **I.6**: 27.
Political elite **J.6**: 2, 19.
Political history **D.9.5**: 10.
Political institutions **J.3**: 21.
Political leadership **C.6**: 3, 8.
Political morality **D.3**: 13.
Political participation **J.6**: 35. **K.3**: 16.
Political parties
Entries also appear under:
WORKING CLASS PARTIES
J.5: 19.
Political psychology **D.3**: 22. **J.2**: 11, 13. **J.6**: 20, 36.
Political representation **J.3**: 21. **J.6**: 21.
Political socialization **J.6**: 20, 27.
Political sociology **J.1**: 4.
Political theory **F.5**: 106.
Politicization **J.5**: 16. **J.6**: 14, 16.
Politics
Entries also appear under:
URBAN POLITICS
D.2: 3. **F.4.2**: 43. **F.5**: 22, 107. **I.7**: 15.

Pollution
Entries also appear under:
ACID RAIN; AIR POLLUTION
Polyandry **F.4.1**: 52.
Polygamy **F.4.1**: 52. **F.6**: 23.
Poor **C.2**: 4. **D.9**: 7. **J.4**: 2.
Popper, Karl. **B.1.1**: 12.
Popular culture **D.1.1**: 1, 17. **D.8**: 1. **F.5**: 2. **I.7**: 19. **J.6**: 23.
Popular music **D.8**: 12.
Popular religion **D.5**: 11, 14, 20.
Population
Entries also appear under:
RURAL POPULATION; URBAN POPULATION
F.1: 10–11, 15, 22, 29. **F.3**: 1, 15, 49. **K.1**: 195.
Population dynamics **C.5**: 27. **F.1**: 4, 8. **F.3**: 6, 14.
Population forecasts **F.1**: 2, 23, 25. **F.3**: 75.
Population growth **F.1**: 3. **F.3**: 9, 13, 78.
Population movements **F.1**: 14, 16.
Population policy **F.3**: 8, 31, 40–41, 82. **F.8**: 38, 101.
Population theory **C.5**: 12.
Populism **J.2**: 10.
Pornography **D.7**: 87, 118. **F.6**: 18.
Portuguese **F.7**: 86.
Positive discrimination **K.2**: 31.
Positivism **E.3**: 4.
Post-Fordism **H.4**: 32.
Post-industrial society **G.3.2**: 117.
Postmodernism **A.1**: 21. **G.3.2**: 116.
Poverty
Entries also appear under:
RURAL POVERTY; URBAN POVERTY
D.1.1: 24. **D.1.3**: 10. **F.2**: 87. **F.7**: 87. **K.1**: 57, 213–239. **K.2**: 35. **K.3**: 25. **K.4**: 64.
Power **D.6**: 28. **E.1**: 4. **F.4.1**: 37–38. **F.4.2**: 137. **G.3.1**: 43.
Pragmatism **K.1**: 119.
Pregnancy **D.5**: 77. **F.3**: 30, 76. **F.4.1**: 41. **F.4.2**: 74. **F.6**: 20.
Prejudice
Entries also appear under:
RACIAL PREJUDICE
F.3: 103. **F.7**: 99.
Presidency **J.6**: 26.

Press **D.7**: 83, 86, 104, 108, 114, 117–121, 126, 144. **F.8**: 41. **I.3**: 56.
Prices **K.1**: 207.
Pride **C.2**: 62.
Priests **D.5**: 67, 78.
Primary health care **K.4**: 36, 61, 80.
Primary schools **D.9.3**: 3.
Primatology **C.2**: 43.
Prisons **C.1**: 33. **I.5**: 19. **K.1**: 34, 50, 142, 147–148, 152, 159, 163, 169, 174–179, 186.
Privacy
Entries also appear under:
RIGHT OF PRIVACY
Private enterprises **H.4**: 6.
Private health care **K.4**: 66.
Private sector **K.3**: 21.
Privatization **K.1**: 150.
Probability **B.3**: 27.
Problem solving **C.3**: 13, 32. **H.4**: 29.
Production **E.3**: 17. **F.8**: 27. **G.3.1**: 48. **H.6**: 1.
Production systems **H.4**: 14, 32, 50. **K.2**: 58.
Productivity
Entries also appear under:
INDUSTRIAL PRODUCTIVITY
H.4: 31. **I.2**: 33.
Profession
Entries also appear under:
LEGAL PROFESSION
Professional ethics **D.3**: 2, 20, 23. **I.4**: 7. **I.5**: 12.
Professional workers **G.3.2**: 84. **I.5**: 1.
Professionalism **C.5**: 30. **I.4**: 12.
Professionalization **I.5**: 20. **I.7**: 16.
Programme evaluation **K.3**: 30.
Proletarianization **E.2**: 51.
Property
Entries also appear under:
LAND PROPERTY
H.4: 8.
Prostitution **F.5**: 85. **F.6**: 15, 24, 28, 32. **G.3.2**: 48.
Protestant ethic **D.3**: 26.
Protestantism **D.5**: 73, 75.

Protestants **D.3**: 35. **D.5**: 80.
Prototypes **C.2**: 2.
Psychiatry **C.1**: 1, 30. **C.4**: 2. **K.4**: 55.
Psychoanalysis **C.1**: 31, 34, 40. **C.5**: 25.
Psycholinguistics **D.7**: 68.
Psychological effects **F.4.1**: 52. **I.2**: 40. **I.4**: 26.
Psychological factors **C.1**: 9.
Psychologists **I.5**: 16.
Psychology
Entries also appear under:
CHILD PSYCHOLOGY; ECONOMIC PSYCHOLOGY; ENVIRONMENTAL PSYCHOLOGY; EXPERIMENTAL PSYCHOLOGY; INDUSTRIAL PSYCHOLOGY; POLITICAL PSYCHOLOGY; SOCIAL PSYCHOLOGY
C.1: 5, 7, 10, 13, 20, 24, 27–28, 33, 35, 41. **C.2**: 33. **C.3**: 37, 52. **D.4**: 8. **F.3**: 124, 133. **F.4.2**: 119. **F.5**: 98, 107. **F.6**: 22. **F.7**: 49, 76. **I.4**: 29. **I.5**: 16. **I.7**: 25. **J.7**: 3. **J.8**: 12. **K.1**: 71, 117. **K.4**: 68.
Psychometrics **F.4.2**: 131.
Psychopathology **C.1**: 12.
Psychotherapy
Entries also appear under:
GROUP PSYCHOTHERAPY
C.2: 87. **K.3**: 23–24.
Public administration **J.4**: 3, 11–12.
Public choice **C.7**: 10.
Public expenditure **K.2**: 39.
Public goods **C.3**: 25.
Public health **K.4**: 30, 76.
Public interest **D.1.2**: 6. **D.7**: 122.
Public opinion **D.7**: 58. **F.3**: 129. **F.6**: 18. **I.6**: 44. **K.2**: 20, 38.
Public policy **F.5**: 54. **F.6**: 18. **G.3.2**: 69. **J.5**: 7. **K.1**: 33. **K.4**: 53, 57, 68.
Public sector **I.5**: 9. **I.6**: 4, 43. **I.7**: 16. **J.4**: 5.
Public services **F.5**: 42. **I.5**: 23.
Punishment
Entries also appear under:
CAPITAL PUNISHMENT
D.4: 13. **F.4.2**: 73. **K.1**: 134, 170.
Pupils **F.4.2**: 40. **F.7**: 61.
Puritanism **D.5**: 35.
Qualitative analysis **F.3**: 108.
Quality of life **C.7**: 42. **F.8**: 87. **H.3**: 22–23.

Quantitative analysis **B.3**: 19, 24.
Quantitative methods **B.3**: 26.
Quechua **D.1.1**: 10.
Race **C.1**: 30. **D.4**: 4. **E.2**: 34, 52, 75. **F.3**: 103. **F.5**: 86. **F.7**: 19, 48–49, 53, 63, 66, 99, 102. **F.8**: 73. **J.3**: 27. **K.1**: 95, 161, 180. **K.3**: 14.
Race relations **D.7**: 124, 136. **E.2**: 31. **F.4.1**: 26. **F.7**: 70–92. **G.3.1**: 49. **J.6**: 9.
Racial attitudes **F.7**: 73, 91–92.
Racial conflict **F.7**: 89.
Racial differentiation **F.3**: 149. **F.4.1**: 62. **H.3**: 27. **I.2**: 41.
Racial discrimination **F.2**: 69. **F.7**: 70, 75, 94–100, 104–110, 112–116.
Racial prejudice **F.7**: 108, 112, 116.
Racial segregation **G.3.2**: 61.
Racism **F.3**: 88. **F.7**: 70, 96, 104, 106–107, 115.
Radio **D.7**: 121, 125, 145.
Railway networks **H.4**: 22.
Rape **D.4**: 5. **F.5**: 50. **F.6**: 7. **K.1**: 137.
Rationalism **B.1.1**: 18.
Rationality **B.1.1**: 12, 24. **C.5**: 39–40. **C.7**: 10, 32.
Rationalization **H.5**: 8.
Reading habits **C.2**: 33.
Reagan, Ronald. **J.6**: 36.
Reason **D.6**: 4.
Recidivism **K.1**: 59, 91, 151.
Reciprocity **G.3.1**: 24.
Recruitment **I.2**: 20, 25, 56.
Reference works **J.5**: 36.
Referendums **D.5**: 68. **F.4.1**: 68.
Reform
Entries also appear under:
AGRARIAN REFORM; LEGAL REFORM
D.7: 139. **K.1**: 79. **K.2**: 24.
Refugees **F.5**: 93. **F.7**: 6. **F.8**: 64, 75, 83, 89, 92, 98–99, 105.
Reggae **D.8**: 1, 3.
Regional development **H.7**: 4.
Regional integration **F.8**: 53.
Regression analysis **F.4.1**: 14.

Regulation **K.1**: 107.
Relative deprivation **F.7**: 91.
Relativism **D.3**: 30.
Religion
Entries also appear under:
POPULAR RELIGION; SOCIOLOGY OF RELIGION
D.3: 10. **D.5**: 6, 9, 16, 18, 22, 37–43, 52, 57, 60, 76. **F.1**: 27. **F.4.1**: 52. **F.4.2**: 114. **F.8**: 90. **K.3**: 27. **K.4**: 41.
Religion and politics **D.5**: 4, 32, 55.
Religiosity **D.5**: 27, 44.
Religious affiliation **D.5**: 77.
Religious beliefs **D.5**: 58. **F.4.2**: 59.
Religious broadcasting **D.5**: 71.
Religious change **D.5**: 5, 17, 45.
Religious conflicts **D.5**: 31.
Religious conversion **D.5**: 2, 10, 26.
Religious discrimination **I.3**: 37.
Religious fundamentalism **D.5**: 85–86.
Religious history **D.5**: 54.
Religious institutions **F.8**: 52.
Religious life **D.5**: 12. **G.3.1**: 47.
Religious movements **D.5**: 2, 10, 51. **D.7**: 120.
Religious orders **D.5**: 63.
Religious practice **I.3**: 24.
Religious revival **D.9**: 18.
Religious syncretism **D.5**: 1.
Remarriage **C.2**: 93. **F.4.1**: 8, 16. **F.4.2**: 21, 78, 110, 112. **H.3**: 18.
Remittances **F.8**: 32, 91.
Repression **D.1.2**: 9.
Research
Entries also appear under:
ACTION RESEARCH; DEMOGRAPHIC RESEARCH; MEDICAL RESEARCH; OPERATIONS RESEARCH; ORGANIZATION OF RESEARCH; SOCIAL RESEARCH; SOCIOLOGICAL RESEARCH
A.1: 17. **A.3**: 11. **B.1.3**: 25. **B.2**: 5. **B.3**: 3, 7. **C.1**: 33, 38. **C.2**: 34. **C.4**: 20. **C.5**: 43. **D.4**: 9. **D.7**: 28, 30, 87. **D.9.2**: 5. **D.9.5**: 9. **D.9.9**: 4. **F.4.1**: 47. **F.4.2**: 48, 139. **F.5**: 14, 86. **G.2**: 1. **G.3**: 6. **I.6**: 16, 37. **K.1**: 190. **K.3**: 2, 28.
Research and development **A.3**: 9.
Research methods **B.1.3**: 1–2, 5, 12, 27. **C.2**: 97. **D.7**: 128. **F.4.2**: 124.

Research policy **H.4**: 13.
Research techniques **B.1.3**: 3, 8. **E.2**: 25.
Research trends **D.9**: 16. **F.4.2**: 142.
Residence **F.3**: 149. **F.7**: 113. **G.3.2**: 12. **J.6**: 4.
Residential mobility **F.3**: 133. **F.7**: 51.
Residential segregation **F.7**: 67, 92. **G.3.2**: 49–50, 52, 68, 74, 100.
Responsibility **C.2**: 32, 40. **F.2**: 48. **F.3**: 108.
Retail trade **G.3.2**: 17.
Retirement
Entries also appear under:
EARLY RETIREMENT
D.1.2: 8. **F.2**: 24, 60–61. **I.3**: 17, 22, 32.
Revisionism **F.1**: 19.
Revolution **J.2**: 7.
Right **J.5**: 29.
Right of privacy **D.7**: 44.
Rights
Entries also appear under:
HUMAN RIGHTS
D.3: 10. **F.2**: 71. **J.5**: 24.
Riots **F.7**: 97.
Risk **B.3**: 2. **I.3**: 16.
Rites of passage **F.5**: 55. **F.6**: 19.
Ritual **D.1.3**: 16. **I.7**: 24.
Role **C.6**: 10. **D.7**: 31. **E.2**: 35.
Role perceptions **K.1**: 69.
Role taking **C.6**: 20.
Role theory **C.5**: 1.
Rural areas **F.2**: 32, 37, 52. **F.3**: 14. **G.3.1**: 10, 12, 14, 31, 34, 68. **I.2**: 15. **K.4**: 64, 84.
Rural communities **G.2**: 15. **G.3.1**: 43.
Rural development **D.9.6**: 1. **G.3.1**: 63, 66–71, 74, 76, 79–80, 82–85. **G.3.2**: 154.
Rural economics **H.5**: 4.
Rural environment **F.2**: 41. **G.3.1**: 9, 11.
Rural life **D.7**: 29. **G.3.1**: 19.
Rural planning **G.3.1**: 33.
Rural policy **G.3.1**: 23. **J.4**: 2.
Rural population **F.3**: 14. **G.3.1**: 30.
Rural poverty **G.3.1**: 17. **J.4**: 9. **K.1**: 238.
Rural society **G.3.1**: 15, 18, 20.
Rural sociology **F.4.2**: 22, 104. **F.8**: 42. **G.3.1**: 13, 41.
Rural women **F.5**: 87–88. **G.3.1**: 36.
Rural youth **F.2**: 13.
Rural-urban relations **G.3**: 3, 5–6. **G.3.2**: 57.
Rural-urban migration **F.8**: 7, 39–40. **G.3.2**: 145.
Russian language **D.7**: 53.
Safety
Entries also appear under:
OCCUPATIONAL SAFETY; WORK SAFETY
Salisbury, John of. **J.2**: 3.
Sanction
Entries also appear under:
PENAL SANCTIONS
Sati **D.5**: 47.
Satisfaction
Entries also appear under:
JOB SATISFACTION; MARITAL SATISFACTION
C.3: 22.
School
Entries also appear under:
NURSERY SCHOOLS; PRIMARY SCHOOLS
School attendance **F.4.2**: 40.
School failure **D.9.8**: 7.
Schooling **D.9**: 14. **F.3**: 30.
Schools **D.9.3**: 5. **D.9.4**: 1.
Schopenhauer, Arthur. **B.1.1**: 28.
Science
Entries also appear under:
BEHAVIOURAL SCIENCES
D.6: 4, 9, 12, 19–29, 33–34. **D.7**: 102. **D.9.5**: 16. **H.4**: 36. **I.4**: 1.
Scientific personnel **I.2**: 43.
Scientific publications **A.5**: 3.
Scientist
Entries also appear under:
SOCIAL SCIENTISTS
Scientists **D.3**: 38. **D.6**: 8.
Seasonal fluctuations **F.3**: 71.
Seasonal migration **F.8**: 13.
Seasonality **K.1**: 113.
Secondary analysis **B.3**: 25.
Secondary schools **D.9.3**: 4, 7–8.
Secrecy **C.3**: 41. **C.5**: 37.

Sects **D.5**: 77.
Secularization **D.4**: 14. **D.5**: 15, 45, 49, 72.
Segregation
Entries also appear under:
OCCUPATIONAL SEGREGATION; RACIAL SEGREGATION; RESIDENTIAL SEGREGATION
J.4: 11.
Self **C.2**: 5, 63, 86, 90, 94. **D.1.3**: 17, 20. **K.1**: 69.
Self-employed workers **I.2**: 60.
Self-concept **C.2**: 101.
Self-consciousness **C.2**: 69, 100. **C.7**: 31.
Self-esteem **C.2**: 49, 104. **C.3**: 42. **F.4.2**: 108. **I.3**: 42.
Self-evaluation **C.2**: 92.
Self-help **C.7**: 38. **G.3.2**: 123.
Self-management **I.6**: 26.
Semiotics **D.7**: 42, 106.
Sensation **C.2**: 38.
Sex **D.5**: 50. **F.1**: 18. **F.5**: 48–49. **K.1**: 164.
Sex differentiation **C.2**: 39, 76. **C.7**: 20. **F.3**: 133.
Sex discrimination **D.9.3**: 3. **D.9.5**: 26. **F.5**: 33, 56, 66, 107. **I.2**: 26, 56.
Sex education **F.6**: 27.
Sex roles **F.5**: 7, 45, 47.
Sex therapy **F.6**: 31.
Sexism **F.3**: 88.
Sexual assault **F.6**: 31. **K.1**: 68, 133, 187.
Sexual behaviour **F.6**: 1–2, 5–6, 8–10.
Sexual mutilation **F.6**: 13.
Sexual permissiveness **F.6**: 26.
Sexual reproduction **F.3**: 45, 56. **F.6**: 17. **K.4**: 40.
Sexuality **F.6**: 3, 5, 30.
Shift work **F.4.2**: 51.
Shifting cultivation **G.1**: 16.
Shiism **D.5**: 90.
Siblings **F.4.2**: 117–119.
Sign language **D.7**: 39.
Simmel, Georg. **B.1.1**: 20. **D.1.1**: 47.
Simulation **B.1.3**: 3. **E.3**: 27.

Simulation techniques **C.1**: 5.
Skilled workers **I.4**: 2.
Skills **D.9**: 14. **H.4**: 2.
Slavery **K.1**: 48.
Slums **D.1.3**: 10. **G.3.2**: 80, 98. **H.2**: 4.
Small and medium sized enterprises **F.8**: 89. **H.4**: 28.
Small groups **C.5**: 31. **I.3**: 40.
Small towns **G.3.2**: 152.
Smoking **K.1**: 190, 196.
Sociability **C.3**: 43.
Social action **D.1.1**: 18. **D.5**: 61. **E.1**: 2. **K.2**: 22.
Social anthropology **D.1.1**: 40. **F.7**: 69.
Social behaviour **C.2**: 37. **C.7**: 13, 16, 39. **I.3**: 2.
Social biology **C.2**: 43.
Social change **C.5**: 27. **C.6**: 15. **D.5**: 32. **E.2**: 74. **E.3**: 1, 3–4, 8–9, 12, 14–15, 21, 23, 26–27, 32. **F.3**: 83. **F.4.1**: 17. **F.7**: 62. **H.4**: 27. **J.2**: 12. **J.3**: 17. **J.6**: 30.
Social classes **D.5**: 50. **E.2**: 3, 5–7, 15, 17, 30–32, 53–54. **F.3**: 151. **F.4.2**: 5. **F.7**: 79, 88. **F.8**: 22. **H.4**: 8.
Social cognition **C.3**: 3. **D.1.3**: 3.
Social conditions **C.2**: 64. **C.6**: 15.
Social conflicts **B.3**: 21. **D.7**: 40.
Social conformity **C.2**: 80. **D.1.3**: 16.
Social consciousness **E.2**: 55.
Social control **D.1.2**: 9–10. **F.5**: 72. **F.6**: 6. **G.3.2**: 69. **I.3**: 58. **I.5**: 19. **K.1**: 3, 111. **K.4**: 28.
Social co-operation **C.2**: 16. **C.6**: 7.
Social development **D.1.3**: 14. **E.3**: 6–7, 29. **F.2**: 85. **K.2**: 13.
Social differentiation **E.2**: 56, 66. **H.4**: 9.
Social doctrines **E.3**: 7.
Social exchange **E.1**: 4–5.
Social forces **H.4**: 6.
Social group work **C.4**: 10.
Social history **D.7**: 93. **D.9**: 23. **E.3**: 7. **F.4.2**: 84. **F.6**: 15, 25. **G.2**: 16.
Social housing **K.1**: 96.

INTERNATIONAL BIBLIOGRAPHY OF SOCIOLOGY — 1988

Social inequality **E.2**: 20, 32–33, 57. **E.3**: 6. **F.4.1**: 24. **G.3.1**: 14.

Social influence **C.3**: 37.

Social integration **D.1.3**: 13, 15. **D.9.2**: 2. **E.2**: 66. **F.2**: 52. **F.3**: 121, 125. **F.7**: 107. **F.8**: 52, 72.

Social interaction **C.3**: 12, 32, 44, 49. **C.6**: 10. **D.1.3**: 6, 17, 21. **D.7**: 43. **F.3**: 106.

Social judgement **C.3**: 50. **C.7**: 9.

Social justice **B.1.1**: 16. **K.1**: 172.

Social life **D.1.1**: 21.

Social mobility **D.9.5**: 5. **E.2**: 18, 37, 45–46, 58, 63. **I.4**: 17.

Social mobilization **J.5**: 15.

Social movements **E.3**: 20. **F.5**: 11. **G.3.2**: 80. **J.5**: 1, 6–7, 11, 17, 24, 26, 32, 35, 37.

Social networks **B.3**: 20. **C.3**: 46. **C.4**: 20, 25–29, 31–32. **F.2**: 63. **F.4.2**: 45, 54, 106. **G.3.2**: 76. **I.2**: 7. **K.2**: 6. **K.3**: 31. **K.4**: 79.

Social norms **C.4**: 14.

Social order **D.4**: 10.

Social perception **E.2**: 67.

Social philosophy **B.1.1**: 6.

Social planning **K.2**: 45.

Social pluralism **D.1.1**: 43. **J.3**: 1.

Social policy
Entries also appear under:
OLD AGE POLICY
F.3: 128. **G.1**: 15. **H.4**: 41. **K.2**: 19–21, 23–24, 29, 47, 54, 56. **K.3**: 25. **K.4**: 21.

Social problems **D.7**: 9, 64. **H.4**: 26. **K.1**: 15, 25, 39, 82, 239.

Social psychology **B.1.3**: 5. **C.1**: 4, 18–19, 21–23, 32, 36–37. **C.3**: 33, 45, 47. **C.7**: 21. **D.6**: 31. **F.3**: 42. **F.7**: 57, 108. **H.4**: 16. **I.4**: 13.

Social relations **C.3**: 51. **C.5**: 20. **F.2**: 51.

Social reproduction **E.1**: 9.

Social research **A.1**: 15. **A.2**: 3. **A.3**: 3–6. **B.1.3**: 2, 5, 7, 11–12, 22, 28–29. **B.2**: 7. **G.3.1**: 22. **K.1**: 4.

Social sciences **A.1**: 3, 6–7, 10, 16–17, 19–20, 24–25, 37. **A.2**: 4. **A.3**: 7, 11. **A.5**: 6. **B.1.1**: 1, 11–12. **B.1.3**: 22. **C.1**: 4, 18. **D.9.5**: 2.

Social scientists **A.5**: 5.

Social security **K.2**: 24, 38, 49, 51.

Social services **K.2**: 6, 50. **K.3**: 26, 36. **K.4**: 26, 37, 82.

Social status **E.2**: 43, 59, 67–68. **J.6**: 32.

Social stratification **E.2**: 49, 60–62, 70. **F.4.2**: 24.

Social structure **B.1.1**: 4, 26. **C.3**: 30. **C.6**: 20. **C.7**: 33. **D.1.1**: 24. **D.1.3**: 18. **D.7**: 50. **E.1**: 1–3, 7, 9–10. **E.2**: 1, 74. **F.2**: 50. **F.5**: 51. **G.3.1**: 42. **I.2**: 46. **K.1**: 130.

Social systems **E.1**: 6, 8. **E.3**: 27.

Social theory **A.1**: 6. **B.1.1**: 14, 31. **B.1.3**: 1. **C.5**: 38. **C.7**: 10. **F.5**: 35. **G.1**: 2. **K.3**: 2, 32.

Social values **D.1.2**: 1, 4, 7. **K.1**: 131.

Social welfare **F.3**: 4. **J.6**: 26. **K.1**: 219. **K.2**: 1, 4, 21, 36.

Social work **F.3**: 112. **F.4.2**: 62. **F.8**: 58. **K.1**: 77, 187, 219. **K.3**: 2, 4–5, 12–13, 17–18, 20, 23–25, 27–29, 31–34, 37. **K.4**: 7, 85.

Social workers **E.2**: 34. **I.6**: 33. **J.3**: 22. **K.3**: 11, 14, 16, 22.

Socialism **A.2**: 2. **D.3**: 18. **D.9.8**: 10. **I.2**: 16. **J.2**: 12.

Socialist countries **E.2**: 63.

Socialist states **D.3**: 8. **E.3**: 17.

Socialists **E.3**: 17.

Socialization
Entries also appear under:
POLITICAL SOCIALIZATION
C.3: 11. **D.1.3**: 2, 5, 9–10, 18–19. **D.7**: 130. **F.2**: 14. **H.4**: 25. **K.1**: 212.

Society
Entries also appear under:
INDUSTRIAL SOCIETY

Socio-economic development **A.1**: 33. **D.9**: 8. **F.3**: 78. **G.1**: 4. **G.3.1**: 73–74, 78. **G.3.2**: 154. **I.7**: 3.

Sociolinguistics **D.7**: 46, 52, 55, 57, 59–60, 63, 72, 74–77, 81.

Sociological analysis **F.3**: 85. **I.2**: 29. **I.5**: 27.

Sociological research **A.2**: 5. **F.6**: 29. **F.7**: 76.

Sociological theory **A.1**: 18, 39. **E.3**: 1, 4, 12, 18, 20. **F.2**: 27, 84. **H.5**: 8.

Sociologists **A.1**: 31, 37. **A.3**: 12.

Sociology
Entries also appear under:
ECONOMIC SOCIOLOGY; HISTORY OF SOCIOLOGY; MEDICAL SOCIOLOGY; OCCUPATIONAL SOCIOLOGY; POLITICAL SOCIOLOGY; RURAL SOCIOLOGY; URBAN SOCIOLOGY
A.1: 2, 5, 11, 13–15, 21–23, 26–36, 38. **A.3**: 12. **A.5**: 3. **B.1.1**: 26, 33. **B.3**: 19, 23. **C.1**: 40. **C.3**: 48. **D.5**: 79. **E.3**: 8. **F.7**: 51, 104. **H.5**: 8. **I.3**: 45. **J.6**: 34.

Sociology of development **B.1.1**: 35. **E.3**: 16, 28.

Sociology of knowledge **D.1.2**: 13. **D.6**: 2, 11, 13, 16, 30–33. **E.3**: 25. **F.5**: 3.

Sociology of law **D.4**: 7, 11.

Sociology of organizations **C.5**: 38.

Sociology of religion **D.5**: 54, 57.

Sociology of the family **F.4.2**: 125, 127–128, 132, 138, 143.

Sociology of work **I.1**: 1–2. **I.3**: 58.

Sociometry **C.1**: 38.

Soil conservation **C.7**: 25.

Soils **G.1**: 16.

Solidarity **D.5**: 43.

Solvent abuse **K.1**: 88.

Songs **D.8**: 17.

Sons **F.4.1**: 75.

Spanish language **D.7**: 78.

Spatial dimension **C.2**: 39. **E.2**: 29. **G.1**: 17. **H.4**: 42. **I.6**: 36.

Speech **D.7**: 48, 82.

Spencer, Herbert. **E.3**: 12.

Sport **C.2**: 53. **D.7**: 95. **I.7**: 6, 11, 14, 16, 18–22. **K.1**: 124.

Squatters **F.1**: 4. **F.3**: 15. **G.2**: 2. **G.3.2**: 98–99, 101. **K.1**: 107.

Standard of living **F.2**: 55. **F.5**: 80. **H.3**: 11, 18.

State
Entries also appear under:
CHURCH AND STATE
D.5: 42. **H.4**: 7. **J.1**: 4.

State formation **J.3**: 25.

State structure **E.2**: 75. **F.7**: 53. **J.3**: 27.

Statistical analysis **B.3**: 6, 24, 26.

Statistical methods **B.3**: 22. **F.1**: 30.

Statistics **F.8**: 103.

Stereotypes **C.3**: 50. **C.7**: 40. **F.5**: 47. **K.4**: 82.

Sterilization
Entries also appear under:
MALE STERILIZATION
F.3: 48.

Stochastic processes **F.1**: 30.

Stratification **F.5**: 41.

Strauss, Leo. **D.1.1**: 27.

Strikes **I.6**: 16, 35.

Structural change **K.1**: 234.

Students **C.2**: 2. **C.3**: 10. **C.7**: 14. **D.9.3**: 10. **D.9.5**: 11. **F.4.1**: 20, 46. **F.4.2**: 93. **F.6**: 1, 8, 10. **I.4**: 1. **K.1**: 64, 205.

Subculture **F.2**: 8.

Suburban areas **D.1.2**: 1. **G.2**: 10. **G.3.1**: 35. **G.3.2**: 68.

Sufism **D.5**: 82.

Suicide **K.1**: 9, 29–30, 34, 192.

Supervisors **I.3**: 2.

Supply
Entries also appear under:
FOOD SUPPLY; LABOUR SUPPLY
K.1: 206.

Surgery **K.4**: 57.

Surrogate motherhood **F.4.2**: 14, 57.

Surveys **B.2**: 1. **C.5**: 43. **F.1**: 26. **F.4.1**: 47. **K.4**: 48.

Symbolism **C.5**: 33. **F.3**: 114.

Sympathy **C.2**: 56.

Systems theory **C.3**: 17, 28. **E.2**: 40. **E.3**: 19.

Tagore, Rabindranath, **D.5**: 60.

Teacher training **D.9.9**: 3.

Teachers **D.9.3**: 3. **D.9.8**: 8. **D.9.9**: 4, 7. **I.6**: 39.

Teaching **D.9.9**: 2.

Technical education **I.4**: 24.

Technicians **I.5**: 1–2.

Technological change **F.5**: 87. **G.3.1**: 45. **H.4**: 43. **I.6**: 1.

Technology

INTERNATIONAL BIBLIOGRAPHY OF SOCIOLOGY — 1988

Entries also appear under:
BIOTECHNOLOGY; HIGH TECHNOLOGY; INFORMATION TECHNOLOGY; NEW TECHNOLOGY
D.6: 25-26. **D.7**: 5, 44. **E.3**: 25. **F.2**: 28-29. **G.3.2**: 69. **H.4**: 5, 8, 13, 19-20, 35-36, 38, 40, 42, 44-46. **I.2**: 50-51.

Telecommunications **D.7**: 45.

Television **D.7**: 88, 92, 98, 102, 107, 121-122, 125, 131, 133-136, 138-139, 142, 149-150. **G.3.1**: 85. **I.7**: 21-22. **K.1**: 37.

Terrorism **C.3**: 5. **D.7**: 147-148. **J.5**: 2, 14, 33.

Thatcher, Margaret. **J.6**: 36.

Theology **D.5**: 72.

Theory of education **D.9**: 11.

Therapy
Entries also appear under:
FAMILY THERAPY
C.1: 21. **C.3**: 53. **F.3**: 46. **K.4**: 55.

Thurstone scale **K.1**: 122.

Time **B.1.3**: 23. **D.1.1**: 38. **G.1**: 17.

Time series **B.3**: 7.

Tobacco **D.7**: 25. **K.1**: 196.

Tolerance **C.7**: 26. **F.6**: 16. **F.7**: 21.

Tourism **G.3.2**: 56. **I.7**: 24-25.

Town
Entries also appear under:
SMALL TOWNS

Towns **G.2**: 16. **G.3.2**: 5, 55.

Trade
Entries also appear under:
RETAIL TRADE
H.5: 4.

Trade union membership **I.6**: 7, 11, 38, 45.

Trade unionism **I.3**: 56. **I.6**: 41-42.

Trade unions **F.8**: 102. **I.6**: 1, 4, 6, 8-10, 13-15, 19, 21-22, 32-34, 44, 48.

Tradition **D.1.1**: 43. **D.2**: 1.

Traditional society **F.3**: 56.

Traffic
Entries also appear under:
AIR TRAFFIC

Training
Entries also appear under:
TEACHER TRAINING; VOCATIONAL TRAINING
G.3.2: 123. **I.3**: 19. **J.7**: 1.

Transport
Entries also appear under:
URBAN TRANSPORT

Transport costs **H.5**: 2.

Transport planning **G.3.2**: 134.

Transport policy **H.4**: 1.

Travel **F.3**: 132. **I.7**: 3.

Tribal society **E.2**: 58.

Tropical zones **G.3.1**: 79.

Trusts **C.3**: 18.

Tunisians **F.8**: 103.

Turks **F.4.2**: 2.

Twins **F.2**: 85.

Typology **D.1.1**: 44. **F.5**: 96. **H.4**: 48.

Tyranny **J.2**: 3.

Underclass **E.2**: 19.

Underdevelopment **E.3**: 22, 28.

Underemployment **F.8**: 11. **I.2**: 41.

Unemployed **I.2**: 12. **K.1**: 135. **K.3**: 33.

Unemployment
Entries also appear under:
URBAN UNEMPLOYMENT
F.4.2: 61. **I.2**: 5, 23, 40, 53-54, 58, 69-71. **K.1**: 179. **K.2**: 23. **K.4**: 94.

Uneven development **G.3.1**: 49. **G.3.2**: 126.

United Nations **F.7**: 24.

Universities **D.9**: 3. **D.9.5**: 2, 6, 10-11, 17, 19, 25. **F.3**: 133. **F.5**: 43.

Urban anthropology **G.3.2**: 156.

Urban areas **F.3**: 14. **G.3.2**: 63, 100.

Urban communities **G.3.2**: 26, 76.

Urban design **G.3.2**: 126-127.

Urban development **G.3**: 1. **G.3.2**: 123-125, 129. **J.4**: 7.

Urban economics **G.3.2**: 25, 59.

Urban environment **G.3.2**: 69, 77.

Urban geography **G.3.2**: 47, 118.

Urban growth **G.3.2**: 138-140, 145, 151.

Urban history **G.3.2**: 146.

Urban housing **D.1.3**: 14. **G.3.2**: 85-91, 93, 95-97, 99, 101-102.

Urban life **G.3.2**: 22, 48.

Urban management **G.3.2**: 24, 34.

Urban planning **F.8**: 48. **G.3.2**: 108, 112, 114–115, 130.

Urban policy **G.3.2**: 1–2, 23, 42, 45, 56, 61, 64, 79, 104–105, 108–109, 111, 119–120, 122–123, 128, 134, 142, 149–150.

Urban politics **G.3.2**: 53.

Urban population **F.1**: 16. **F.3**: 147. **G.3.2**: 28, 36, 137.

Urban poverty **G.3.2**: 32, 35, 44, 75. **K.4**: 39.

Urban renewal **G.3.2**: 83, 106, 116.

Urban services **G.3.2**: 27, 75.

Urban sociology **D.7**: 77. **E.2**: 18, 56. **E.3**: 3, 26. **F.3**: 152. **F.4.1**: 37–38. **F.4.2**: 22. **F.7**: 113. **G.3.2**: 8, 41, 84.

Urban structure **F.8**: 95.

Urban transport **G.3.2**: 133–136.

Urban unemployment **K.1**: 136.

Urbanism **G.3.2**: 60, 82.

Urbanization **G.3.1**: 50. **G.3.2**: 137–156, 158. **J.6**: 32.

Urban-rural migration **G.3**: 2.

Utopias **D.5**: 19.

Vagrancy **K.1**: 26, 31.

Values **D.1.1**: 43. **D.1.2**: 6, 8, 12. **D.3**: 12, 38. **D.4**: 15. **D.5**: 45, 77. **D.6**: 26. **E.2**: 62. **F.2**: 14. **F.4.1**: 46. **F.4.2**: 147. **I.3**: 22. **I.5**: 25.

Vandalism **K.1**: 92.

Veblen, Thorstein. **E.3**: 14.

Victims **F.4.2**: 75. **J.3**: 11. **K.1**: 1.

Victims of crime **K.1**: 77, 81, 103, 112, 130, 137, 181. **K.3**: 5.

Victims of rape **K.1**: 69.

Videos **D.9.3**: 9.

Vietnamese **F.8**: 89.

Villages **F.4.2**: 24. **F.8**: 37. **G.3.1**: 15–16, 35, 37–38, 42, 47–48, 51, 72, 83. **H.4**: 39.

Violence
Entries also appear under:
COMMUNAL VIOLENCE; DOMESTIC VIOLENCE
D.7: 148. **D.9.3**: 11. **I.7**: 20. **K.1**: 71. **K.3**: 11.

Visual arts **D.8**: 4, 14.

Visual perception **C.2**: 39.

Vocational rehabilitation **I.4**: 15.

Vocational training **I.4**: 8, 24.

Voluntary organizations **C.5**: 16, 36, 43. **G.2**: 8. **G.3.1**: 66.

Voting **J.6**: 9, 37.

Voting behaviour **J.6**: 32.

Voting turnout **I.6**: 41.

Wage determination **H.3**: 25.

Wage differentials **F.5**: 40. **H.3**: 20, 24, 26–27.

Wages **I.3**: 30.

Waldenses **G.3.1**: 5.

Walloons **D.5**: 65.

War
Entries also appear under:
COLD WAR; NUCLEAR WAR
J.1: 4. **J.8**: 4, 15, 18–19.

Wealth **H.3**: 28.

Weapons
Entries also appear under:
NUCLEAR WEAPONS
C.7: 38.

Weber, Max. **A.1**: 22. **A.2**: 4. **B.1.1**: 18–19, 32–33. **C.5**: 48. **D.1.1**: 14, 18, 27, 47. **E.3**: 16, 31. **H.2**: 3. **H.5**: 8.

Welfare
Entries also appear under:
SOCIAL WELFARE
F.4.2: 7. **G.3.2**: 26. **H.3**: 11. **K.1**: 158. **K.2**: 43, 55–56.

Welfare economics **K.2**: 39.

Welfare state **F.8**: 58. **K.1**: 82. **K.2**: 20, 27, 52, 57.

Well-being **C.7**: 42. **D.5**: 44. **F.2**: 32. **F.4.2**: 78, 117. **H.3**: 28.

Welsh language **D.7**: 81.

West Indians **F.7**: 38, 97.

Westernization **E.3**: 30.

Whites **D.9.8**: 6. **E.2**: 47. **F.4.2**: 54. **F.5**: 51. **F.7**: 43, 91–92. **I.2**: 13, 57.

Widowhood **F.4.1**: 2. **H.3**: 18.

Widows **F.4.2**: 117.

Wives + **F.3**: 26. **F.4.1**: 3, 53. **F.7**: 14.

Women
Entries also appear under:
RURAL WOMEN

B.1.3: 11. **C.3**: 53. **D.1.3**: 9. **D.5**: 44. **D.7**: 25, 36, 49, 129. **D.9.5**: 26. **E.2**: 9, 28. **E.3**: 30. **F.2**: 25, 61. **F.3**: 18, 117. **F.4.1**: 4, 42. **F.4.2**: 64, 88, 105. **F.5**: 26, 33, 43, 52, 59–62, 65–66, 68, 70–77, 79–82, 86, 90, 93, 96, 98–102, 105, 107. **F.6**: 13. **F.7**: 15. **G.2**: 4. **G.3.1**: 32, 53, 85. **G.3.2**: 158. **H.2**: 4. **H.3**: 12. **H.4**: 48. **I.2**: 1, 12, 19. **I.3**: 53. **I.6**: 9, 38. **J.5**: 7. **J.7**: 5. **K.1**: 3, 156, 158, 163–164, 212. **K.2**: 58. **K.4**: 3, 28.

Women and politics **F.5**: 12, 39, 104, 106.

Women workers **F.3**: 85. **F.5**: 45. **I.2**: 18, 29, 61. **I.3**: 48. **I.4**: 5.

Women's education **F.5**: 88.

Women's employment **F.4.2**: 85, 122. **F.5**: 40, 76. **F.8**: 11, 21. **H.3**: 20. **I.2**: 4, 49, 64–66.

Women's liberation movements **F.5**: 11. **J.5**: 16, 36.

Women's rights **F.5**: 78, 83, 109.

Women's role † **F.5**: 21, 48–49, 53, 80.

Women's status **D.5**: 84. **F.3**: 62. **F.4.2**: 100. **F.5**: 71, 84, 92.

Women's work **C.5**: 50. **F.5**: 29, 74. **H.4**: 32, 34, 44. **I.2**: 21, 50, 59, 62–63, 68. **I.4**: 22. **I.5**: 26.

Work accidents **I.3**: 1.

Work at home **I.2**: 15, 42, 60.

Work environment **I.3**: 4.

Work ethic **F.7**: 25. **I.3**: 41.

Work experience **I.4**: 29.

Work organization **I.3**: 9, 55–56.

Work place **I.3**: 37.

Work safety **I.3**: 46.

Workers
Entries also appear under:
DOMESTIC WORKERS; INDUSTRIAL WORKERS; MIGRANT WORKERS; OLDER WORKERS; PROFESSIONAL WORKERS; SKILLED WORKERS; SOCIAL WORKERS; WOMEN WORKERS
F.8: 16. **H.4**: 47, 49. **I.2**: 40, 67. **I.3**: 59. **I.5**: 2, 24. **I.6**: 46.

Workers' participation **I.5**: 4. **I.6**: 25–26, 32.

Workers' representation **I.6**: 30.

Working class **B.1.3**: 8. **E.2**: 21, 25. **G.3.2**: 88.

Working class culture **I.7**: 11.

Working class parties **J.6**: 4.

Working conditions **I.3**: 6, 35, 45, 48. **K.1**: 17.

Working groups **I.3**: 40.

Working mothers **F.2**: 73. **F.4.2**: 39. **I.2**: 10, 13. **I.3**: 20.

World Bank **G.3.1**: 71.

World religion
Entries also appear under:
CHRISTIANITY; ISLAM; JUDAISM

Writing **D.7**: 35, 41, 48, 79.

Written languages **D.7**: 24.

Youth
Entries also appear under:
RURAL YOUTH
C.2: 49. **C.7**: 42. **D.1.2**: 6. **E.2**: 32. **F.2**: 5–7, 10–12, 17, 19–21. **F.4.1**: 65. **F.5**: 18. **F.7**: 58. **F.8**: 71. **H.3**: 13. **I.2**: 32, 47, 57, 69–71. **J.6**: 10. **K.1**: 19, 207. **K.4**: 94.

Youth culture **D.1.1**: 23.

Youth employment **I.2**: 72.

Zinoviev, Aleksander. **A.1**: 2.

Zoning **G.3.2**: 131.

INDEX DES MATIÈRES

Abandon d'enfant **F.2**: 87. **F.3**: 66. **K.1**: 54, 57.

Aborigènes **C.3**: 39. **D.7**: 39, 124. **F.7**: 1, 33, 90. **K.1**: 59.

Absentéisme **I.3**: 1, 14.

Accidents **D.7**: 37. **F.3**: 87.

Accidents du travail **I.3**: 1.

Accidents nucléaires **F.3**: 45. **J.8**: 9. **K.1**: 28.

Accomplissement **F.8**: 77.

Accomplissement scolaire **D.9.3**: 7. **D.9.5**: 6. **D.9.8**: 4–5, 8. **F.4.1**: 71. **F.7**: 61.

Acquisition de connaissances **C.2**: 48. **C.5**: 26. **G.3.2**: 123.

Acquisition du langage **D.7**: 55.

Acteurs **B.2**: 4.

Action collective **C.4**: 23, 29. **C.5**: 9. **C.7**: 1, 29.

Action politique **E.3**: 20. **J.5**: 6.

Action sociale **D.1.1**: 18. **D.5**: 61. **E.1**: 2. **K.2**: 22.

Activité bancaire **H.4**: 47.

Activité militante **I.6**: 14.

Adaptation des immigrants **D.7**: 18.

Adhésion syndicale **I.6**: 7, 11, 38, 45.

Administration de l'enseignement **D.9.5**: 17.

Administration locale **G.3.2**: 107. **J.4**: 7–8, 10. **J.6**: 35. **K.3**: 18. **K.4**: 26.

Administration publique **J.4**: 3, 11–12.

Adolescence **C.2**: 5, 74. **C.4**: 32. **E.2**: 68. **F.3**: 86–87. **F.4.2**: 41, 46, 58, 86, 108, 126. **F.6**: 6, 20, 30. **K.1**: 11, 13, 20, 211.

Adolescents **C.3**: 46. **C.7**: 34. **D.5**: 50, 58. **D.7**: 50. **E.2**: 1. **F.2**: 77. **F.4.2**: 59. **F.6**: 27. **J.8**: 8. **K.1**: 190, 197.

Adoption d'enfant **F.3**: 31. **F.4.2**: 12, 14, 31, 49.

Adultes **D.3**: 32.

Affectivité **C.2**: 5. **C.3**: 3, 7.

Affiliation politique **C.4**: 15. **J.6**: 4.

Affiliation religieuse **D.5**: 77.

Âge **F.1**: 3, 25. **F.2**: 7, 25, 37–38, 41–43, 45, 50–52, 54–56, 58–61, 63, 65. **F.4.2**: 95, 99, 105. **F.8**: 10. **G.3.1**: 11. **G.3.2**: 117. **I.3**: 17. **J.6**: 14. **K.1**: 74, 173. **K.2**: 4, 30, 43. **K.4**: 18, 29.

Âge adulte **F.2**: 11, 23. **K.2**: 49.

Âge au mariage **F.4.1**: 31, 57, 63, 71.

Âgisme **F.2**: 24.

Agression personnelle **C.7**: 2.

Agression sexuelle **F.6**: 31. **K.1**: 68, 133, 187.

Agriculteurs **G.3.1**: 44, 54, 70.

Agriculture **G.3.1**: 7, 26. **H.4**: 39.

Agriculture itinérante **G.1**: 16.

Agriexploitation **G.3.1**: 24.

Aide à l'enfance **D.4**: 1. **F.2**: 67. **F.4.2**: 38–39, 51, 107. **I.3**: 20. **K.2**: 8, 10–11, 38.

Aide aux gens âgés **F.2**: 48. **F.4.2**: 92. **K.2**: 7, 16, 25, 42, 59. **K.3**: 7. **K.4**: 10.

Aires métropolitaines **G.3.2**: 112, 140, 151.

Alcool **D.7**: 133. **I.3**: 4, 14, 35. **K.1**: 10–11, 17, 23, 37, 40–41, 146, 153–154, 166, 192, 202, 207, 209. **K.2**: 47.

Alcoolisme **K.1**: 18, 43, 191, 193–195, 212.

Alexander, Jeffrey **B.1.1**: 2.

Aliénation **D.1.3**: 7. **D.5**: 30. **F.7**: 48. **J.5**: 10.

Aliments **F.3**: 76. **K.1**: 222.

Allaitement naturel **F.4.2**: 2, 43.

Alphabétisation **D.4**: 10. **D.7**: 1, 26, 69, 72. **D.9**: 15, 20. **F.5**: 68.

Altruisme **C.2**: 77. **C.7**: 3–4, 20.

Aménagement de l'espace **F.5**: 76.

Aménagement urbain **F.8**: 48. **G.3.2**: 108, 112, 114–115, 130.

Amerindiens **F.7**: 13, 72. **K.1**: 66.

Amish **D.1.1**: 12. **D.5**: 69.

Amitié **C.3**: 11, 28. **D.1.3**: 5.

Analphabétisme **D.9.6**: 2.

Analyse comparative **A.3**: 8. **B.1.1**: 5.

Analyse contextuelle **C.2**: 72.

Analyse coût-avantage **I.4**: 15.

Analyse de discours **D.7**: 115.

Analyse de régression **F.4.1**: 14.

Analyse de réseau **B.1.1**: 26. **B.3**: 16. **C.4**: 28. **E.1**: 7.

Analyse de structure latente **B.3**: 10.

Analyse des politiques gouvernementales **D.7**: 35. **H.4**: 1.

Analyse économique **H.1**: 6.

Analyse factorielle **B.1.3**: 10.

Analyse fonctionnelle **G.3.2**: 53.

Analyse historique **A.1**: 15. **B.3**: 19. **C.1**: 13.

Analyse organisationnelle **C.5**: 2, 44, 46.

Analyse qualitative **F.3**: 108.

Analyse quantitative **B.3**: 19, 24.

Analyse secondaire **B.3**: 25.

Analyse sociologique **F.3**: 85. **I.2**: 29. **I.5**: 27.

Analyse statistique **B.3**: 6, 24, 26.

Analyse transculturelle **C.2**: 94. **F.4.2**: 109, 133.

Analyse transnationale **F.5**: 48.

Anarchisme **F.5**: 1.

Angoisse **C.2**: 15, 49. **K.1**: 194.

Animaux domestiques **F.4.2**: 42.

Anomie **G.3.2**: 72. **J.4**: 12.

Anthropogéographie **G.1**: 8–9, 11–12.

Anthropologie **D.1.1**: 2.

Anthropologie culturelle **D.1.1**: 3.

Anthropologie de l'éducation continued

Anthropologie de l'éducation **D.9.5**: 24.

Anthropologie médicale **F.3**: 109.

Anthropologie politique **J.3**: 25.

Anthropologie sociale **D.1.1**: 40. **F.7**: 69.

Anthropologie urbaine **G.3.2**: 156.

Antillais **F.7**: 38, 97.

Antisémitisme **F.7**: 94–95, 109.

Apartheid **F.2**: 23. **F.7**: 12. **K.3**: 34. **K.4**: 32.

Appartenance au groupe **F.7**: 86.

Arabes **E.3**: 21. **F.3**: 52. **F.7**: 6. **I.2**: 59.

Arbitrage **I.6**: 19–20.

Architecture **G.3.2**: 11, 62. **K.1**: 142.

Armes **C.7**: 38.

Armes nucléaires **C.2**: 35. **J.8**: 5, 7.

Art culinaire **H.5**: 8.

Arts **D.7**: 40. **D.8**: 5, 8, 18.

Arts du spectacle **D.8**: 7.

Arts visuels **D.8**: 4, 14.

ASEAN **F.8**: 99.

Asiatiques **F.4.1**: 28. **F.7**: 15, 61, 80. **F.8**: 84, 96.

Aspects juridiques **F.6**: 31.

Aspirations **F.2**: 12. **F.6**: 20.

Assimilation ethnique **F.7**: 60, 71.

Assistance **I.3**: 2.

Assistance socio-psychologique **C.2**: 82. **K.1**: 10.

Association **C.2**: 18.

Associations de quartier **G.3.2**: 10.

Athéisme **D.5**: 21.

Attitude envers le travail **I.3**: 53.

Attitude moraliste envers le travail **F.7**: 25. **I.3**: 41.

Attitudes **C.7**: 7, 14, 25, 27, 33, 37. **D.6**: 25. **F.3**: 20. **F.4.1**: 51. **F.4.2**: 88. **F.5**: 51. **F.6**: 4, 10, 20, 30. **F.8**: 3. **G.2**: 12. **G.3.2**: 26. **I.6**: 15. **J.3**: 11, 13. **J.6**: 37. **K.1**: 40, 176, 195.

Attitudes politiques **J.6**: 17, 27, 29.

Attitudes raciales **F.7**: 73, 91–92.

Attraction interpersonnelle **C.3**: 9.

Hausa **D.1.2**: 3.

Autoassistance **C.7**: 38. **G.3.2**: 123.
Autogestion **I.6**: 26.
Automation **H.4**: 2–4, 49, 51.
Autoritarisme **C.2**: 83. **C.7**: 34. **D.5**: 70.
Autorité **F.4.2**: 86–87.
Avantages accessoires **I.3**: 16.
Avortement **D.3**: 15, 39. **F.3**: 17–18, 38, 138.
Banque mondiale **G.3.1**: 71.
Basques **D.7**: 40.
Behaviorisme **B.1.1**: 4.
Bibliographies **A.5**: 1. **D.5**: 53. **D.7**: 134, 148. **F.5**: 105. **F.6**: 21. **F.7**: 65, 105. **I.7**: 18. **K.1**: 74. **K.4**: 26.
Bien-être **C.7**: 42. **D.5**: 44. **F.2**: 32. **F.4.2**: 7, 78, 117. **G.3.2**: 26. **H.3**: 11, 28. **K.1**: 158. **K.2**: 43, 55–56.
Bien-être social **F.3**: 4. **J.6**: 26. **K.1**: 219. **K.2**: 1, 4, 21, 36.
Biens publics **C.3**: 25.
Bilinguisme **D.7**: 51.
Biologie **B.1.1**: 1. **F.1**: 24.
Biologie humaine **F.6**: 6.
Biologie sociale **C.2**: 43.
Biotechnologie **D.9**: 3. **K.4**: 42.
Blancs **D.9.8**: 6. **E.2**: 47. **F.4.2**: 54. **F.5**: 51. **F.7**: 43, 91–92. **I.2**: 13, 57.
Bloc oriental **A.1**: 19.
Bonheur **C.2**: 59, 81. **F.4.1**: 5, 36.
Botanique **C.2**: 98.
Bouddhisme **D.5**: 29.
Budgets des ménages **H.5**: 2.
Bureaucratie **C.5**: 48. **D.3**: 26. **F.5**: 23. **F.7**: 33. **I.6**: 4. **K.4**: 2.
Bureautique **I.3**: 21.
Buveurs **K.1**: 201.
Cadres **C.5**: 50. **F.5**: 42. **I.5**: 8, 11–12, 22–23, 26.
Cadres moyens **H.4**: 47.
Café **J.6**: 1.
Capital **H.6**: 1.
Capital industriel **G.3.2**: 141.
Capitalisme **D.1.1**: 26. **G.3.2**: 127. **H.4**: 2, 33–34. **J.1**: 1, 4. **J.2**: 12.

Caractère **H.3**: 19.
Caractère national **D.1.1**: 16.
Carnavals **D.2**: 3.

Castes **E.2**: 4–5, 22–23. **F.7**: 72. **F.8**: 24.
Catholic Church **D.5**: 64.
Catholicisme **D.5**: 62, 66, 74, 76, 79. **F.3**: 19. **F.5**: 109.
Catholiques **D.5**: 65, 78. **F.5**: 59.
Causalité **B.1.1**: 27. **C.5**: 10. **C.7**: 20. **F.3**: 51.
Cause **C.2**: 31.
Cécité **D.7**: 82.
Censure **D.7**: 3.
Chances d'éducation **D.9**: 13, 26.
Chances d'obtenir un emploi **F.2**: 40.
Changement culturel **C.7**: 12. **F.4.1**: 9. **F.4.2**: 6. **F.8**: 77.
Changement d'attitude **C.7**: 6, 12. **F.4.1**: 9. **F.4.2**: 6. **F.5**: 50.
Changement d'organisation **C.5**: 10, 15, 21–22. **I.3**: 31.
Changement démographique **D.5**: 40, 67. **F.1**: 27. **F.3**: 2–5.
Changement économique **E.2**: 60. **E.3**: 9.
Changement linguistique **D.7**: 50. **E.2**: 1.
Changement religieux **D.5**: 5, 17, 45.
Changement social **C.5**: 27. **C.6**: 15. **D.5**: 32. **E.2**: 74. **E.3**: 1, 3–4, 8–9, 12, 14–15, 21, 23, 26–27, 32. **F.3**: 83. **F.4.1**: 17. **F.7**: 62. **H.4**: 27. **J.2**: 12. **J.3**: 17. **J.6**: 30.
Changement structurel **K.1**: 234.
Changement technologique **F.5**: 87. **G.3.1**: 45. **H.4**: 43. **I.6**: 1.
Charisme **C.6**: 4, 19. **D.5**: 10, 82.
Châtiment **D.4**: 13. **F.4.2**: 73. **K.1**: 134, 170.
Chefs d'entreprise **F.5**: 96. **H.4**: 48.
Chiisme **D.5**: 90.
Chinois **D.1.1**: 4. **F.7**: 7, 26–27, 46, 68, 74–75. **F.8**: 51.
Chirurgie **K.4**: 57.
Choix collectif **C.7**: 10.
Choix d'une profession **I.4**: 4, 14.

Choix du conjoint **F.4.1**: 10, 20, 46, 56.
Chômage **F.4.2**: 61. **I.2**: 5, 23, 40, 53–54, 58, 69–71. **K.1**: 179. **K.2**: 23. **K.4**: 94.
Chômage partiel **F.8**: 11. **I.2**: 41.
Chômage urbain **K.1**: 136.
Chômeurs **I.2**: 12. **K.1**: 135. **K.3**: 33.
Chrétiens **A.1**: 6. **D.5**: 70. **J.5**: 29.
Christianisme **D.5**: 62–68, 70, 72–75, 77–78, 81. **D.9**: 4. **F.3**: 19. **F.4.1**: 68. **F.5**: 59.
Cinéma **D.7**: 89, 146. **D.8**: 2.
Circoncision **F.5**: 67. **F.6**: 13.
Circulation aérienne **D.7**: 37.
Cirque **D.8**: 19.
Citoyenneté **G.1**: 1. **J.3**: 24. **K.2**: 20.
Civilisation **D.1.1**: 18, 20. **H.2**: 1.
Classe **E.2**: 13–14, 29, 34, 38, 52, 65, 70, 75. **F.4.1**: 6. **F.5**: 30, 86. **F.7**: 53. **J.3**: 27. **J.6**: 4. **K.2**: 12. **K.3**: 14.
Classe moyenne **E.2**: 26, 48.
Classe ouvrière **B.1.3**: 8. **E.2**: 21, 25. **G.3.2**: 88.
Classes sociales **D.5**: 50. **E.2**: 3, 5–7, 15, 17, 30–32, 53–54. **F.3**: 151. **F.4.2**: 5. **F.7**: 79, 88. **F.8**: 22. **H.4**: 8.
Clientélisme **C.6**: 7.
Cliques **B.3**: 16.
Code déontologique médical **D.3**: 33, 36. **K.4**: 9, 14, 17, 19, 23, 44, 57, 77.
Cognition **A.1**: 15. **C.2**: 9–11, 20, 37, 44, 57. **C.3**: 7. **J.6**: 20.
Cognition sociale **C.3**: 3. **D.1.3**: 3.
Cohabitation **F.4.1**: 7, 21, 49. **F.4.2**: 90.
Collectivité **C.3**: 28. **D.1.1**: 13. **G.2**: 7, 9, 11, 17. **J.3**: 26. **J.6**: 4. **J.8**: 10. **K.1**: 5, 66, 78, 104.
Collectivités rurales **G.2**: 15. **G.3.1**: 43.
Collectivités urbaines **G.3.2**: 26, 76.
Colonialisme **D.7**: 66.
Colonisation rurale **J.6**: 11.
Commandement autoritaire **C.6**: 18.
Commerce **H.5**: 4.
Commerce de détail **G.3.2**: 17.
Commercialisation **F.2**: 15. **F.3**: 27, 46. **G.3.2**: 84. **K.2**: 47.

Communalisme **F.7**: 64. **J.3**: 3.
Communautés ethniques **F.7**: 4, 17, 45–46, 68.
Communautés européennes **F.5**: 65. **F.8**: 104. **J.4**: 5.
Communication **C.3**: 3–4, 7, 25, 49. **C.5**: 5. **D.7**: 16–28, 30–45, 47–49. **D.9.5**: 22. **F.4.1**: 39.
Communication de masse **D.7**: 27, 30.
Communication interculturelle **D.7**: 18.
Communication interpersonnelle **C.3**: 36, 49. **D.7**: 43, 93.
Communication non-verbale **D.7**: 32, 42. **F.2**: 80.
Communication orale **D.7**: 22, 24.
Compensation **I.6**: 4.
Compétences **D.9**: 14. **H.4**: 2.
Compétitivité **C.2**: 16.
Comportement de l'organisation **C.5**: 1, 5, 19, 34, 39–40. **H.4**: 31. **I.4**: 23.
Comportement du consommateur **H.5**: 1, 6.
Comportement du groupe **C.3**: 45. **C.4**: 10. **C.6**: 14.
Comportement économique **F.2**: 72. **H.1**: 5.
Comportement électoral **J.6**: 9, 29, 32.
Comportement individuel **C.2**: 76. **C.7**: 1, 15–16, 18, 25, 28. **F.3**: 104. **F.4.1**: 1, 66.
Comportement politique **J.5**: 3. **J.6**: 26.
Comportement sexuel **F.6**: 1–2, 5–6, 8–10.
Comportement social **C.2**: 37. **C.7**: 13, 16, 39. **I.3**: 2.
Conception de soi **C.2**: 101.
Concurrence **C.3**: 25. **C.4**: 6. **I.2**: 39.
Condamnation pénale **D.4**: 9. **K.1**: 127, 151, 154, 171, 182, 189.
Conditions de travail **I.3**: 6, 35, 45, 48. **K.1**: 17.
Conditions de vie **F.2**: 10, 52. **F.3**: 117, 147. **G.1**: 17. **G.3.2**: 36.
Conditions économiques **D.5**: 76. **F.1**: 29. **F.7**: 20.
Conditions sociales **C.2**: 64. **C.6**: 15.

Conflit **C.2**: 83. **C.5**: 1. **E.2**: 35. **J.7**: 3.
Conflit conjugal **F.4.1**: 15, 42.
Conflits de générations **F.4.2**: 95. **F.5**: 73.
Conflits du travail **E.2**: 21.
Conflits interpersonnels **C.3**: 26, 47, 52.
Conflits raciaux **F.7**: 89.
Conflits religieux **D.5**: 31.
Conflits sociaux **B.3**: 21. **D.7**: 40.
Conformité sociale **C.2**: 80. **D.1.3**: 16.
Confucianisme **C.3**: 35.
Conjoncture démographique **F.1**: 14, 16.
Connaissance **B.1.3**: 29. **B.3**: 9. **C.2**: 31. **D.6**: 6, 10. **D.7**: 100. **K.1**: 119.
Conscience de classe **E.2**: 39.
Conscience de soi **C.2**: 69, 100. **C.7**: 31.
Conscience ethnique **F.7**: 66.
Conscience politique **C.2**: 20.
Conscience sociale **E.2**: 55.
Consensus **C.7**: 18, 30.
Conservateurs **J.1**: 1.
Conservation des sols **C.7**: 25.
Conservatisme **F.7**: 88. **K.2**: 20.
Consommation **C.7**: 31. **H.5**: 7. **J.5**: 7.
Constitution **J.3**: 3.
Construction de l'état **J.3**: 25.
Contestation de groupe **F.2**: 6. **F.5**: 18.
Contraception **F.3**: 24–27, 34–35, 43–44, 46, 54.
Contrat de travail **I.3**: 33.
Contremaîtres **I.3**: 2.
Contrôle politique **A.3**: 7.
Conversion religieuse **D.5**: 2, 10, 26.
Coopération sociale **C.2**: 16. **C.6**: 7.
Corporatisme **C.3**: 35.
Corrélation **B.3**: 15.
Corruption **K.1**: 79.
Cosmétique **F.5**: 28.
Courbes de Lorenz **F.1**: 11.
Courtisement **F.4.1**: 8, 55.
Coût de la vie **H.5**: 2.
Coût du transport **H.5**: 2.
Créativité **F.8**: 77.

Crédit continued
Crédit **J.4**: 2.
Cressey, Donald **K.1**: 89, 152.
Crime commerciale **K.1**: 114.
Criminalité **K.1**: 82, 110, 164.
Criminologie **F.5**: 8. **K.1**: 60, 83, 97, 105, 115, 117, 119–120, 132, 166, 173, 188.
Critique **B.1.1**: 11.
Croissance démographique **F.1**: 3. **F.3**: 9, 13, 78.
Croissance économique **E.2**: 74. **F.3**: 4. **H.1**: 7.
Croissance urbaine **G.3.2**: 138–140, 145, 151.
Croyance **C.2**: 9. **C.4**: 14. **J.6**: 12.
Croyances populaires **C.1**: 18.
Croyances religieuses **D.5**: 58. **F.4.2**: 59.
Culpabilité **D.3**: 1.
Culte des ancêtres **D.5**: 28, 51.
Cultes **D.5**: 10.
Culture **A.3**: 8. **B.1.2**: 1. **C.1**: 30. **C.2**: 87. **C.5**: 34. **C.6**: 6, 13. **C.7**: 23. **D.1.1**: 7–9, 11, 14, 19, 24, 26, 28, 30, 32–34, 37, 47. **D.1.2**: 3. **D.6**: 27. **D.8**: 3. **D.9.5**: 24. **F.3**: 5. **G.3.2**: 40. **I.7**: 24. **K.1**: 85.
Culture d'entreprise **C.5**: 50. **I.5**: 26.
Culture ouvrière **I.7**: 11.
Culture politique **F.7**: 84. **J.6**: 23, 33.
Culture populaire **D.1.1**: 1, 17. **D.8**: 1. **F.5**: 2. **I.7**: 19. **J.6**: 23.
Cybernétique **D.9.5**: 14.
Darwin, Charles **C.1**: 6.
Débilité mentale **C.2**: 32.
Déboisement **G.3.1**: 8.
Décentralisation **J.4**: 1.
Décision **C.5**: 8.
Décision d'investissement **H.6**: 2.
Dégats **J.8**: 9.
Délinquance **F.5**: 16. **I.7**: 20. **K.1**: 87–88, 138.
Délinquance juvénile **G.2**: 7. **K.1**: 104, 106, 109, 116, 128, 140–141, 144–145, 150.

Délinquants **K.1**: 70, 77, 112, 145, 156, 158, 173, 187, 189. **K.3**: 5.

Délits **D.3**: 31. **F.2**: 2. **F.5**: 8. **G.2**: 3, 7, 17. **J.3**: 26. **K.1**: 59–68, 70–71, 73–86, 89–91, 93–104, 106–113, 115–118, 120–125, 127–139, 206. **K.3**: 5.

Demande globale **D.7**: 99.

Démocratie **B.1.1**: 16. **D.7**: 117. **G.3.2**: 13. **H.3**: 3. **I.6**: 8, 47. **J.2**: 11. **J.6**: 12, 33.

Démocratisation **D.9.1**: 1.

Démographie **C.5**: 24. **E.2**: 20. **F.1**: 5–7, 12, 19, 24, 30. **F.3**: 53, 81. **F.4.1**: 11, 52. **F.8**: 50, 101.

Dentisterie **I.4**: 21.

Déontologie **D.3**: 2, 20, 23. **I.4**: 7. **I.5**: 12.

Dépendance culturelle **A.1**: 3.

Dépenses publiques **K.2**: 39.

Désarmement **J.8**: 5.

Désastres **D.7**: 144. **K.1**: 28.

Déségrégation **G.3.2**: 61.

Désintégration de la famille **F.4.2**: 76–84.

Détermination du revenu **I.2**: 28.

Développement capitaliste **F.5**: 99.

Développement cognitif **D.7**: 125.

Développement de l'enfant **C.1**: 23. **C.2**: 20, 62, 74, 96, 101. **C.3**: 13, 46. **D.1.3**: 1–2. **D.7**: 125. **F.2**: 66. **F.5**: 100.

Développement de la personnalité **D.1.3**: 18.

Développement des collectivités **F.3**: 22. **G.2**: 2.

Développement économique **D.9.5**: 25. **F.3**: 5. **F.4.1**: 25. **H.3**: 3, 11. **J.2**: 10.

Développement inégal **G.3.1**: 49. **G.3.2**: 126.

Développement intellectuel **F.4.2**: 96.

Développement régional **H.7**: 4.

Développement rural **D.9.6**: 1. **G.3.1**: 63, 66–71, 74, 76, 79–80, 82–85. **G.3.2**: 154.

Développement social **D.1.3**: 14. **E.3**: 6–7, 29. **F.2**: 85. **K.2**: 13.

Développement socio-économique continued

Développement socio-économique **A.1**: 33. **D.9**: 8. **F.3**: 78. **G.1**: 4. **G.3.1**: 73–74, 78. **G.3.2**: 154. **I.7**: 3.

Développement urbain **G.3**: 1. **G.3.2**: 123–125, 129. **J.4**: 7.

Déviance **K.1**: 13.

Diabète **F.4.1**: 35.

Dialectes **D.7**: 77.

Différences de generations **F.2**: 15.

Différenciation raciale **F.3**: 149. **F.4.1**: 62. **H.3**: 27. **I.2**: 41.

Différenciation sexuelle **C.2**: 39, 76. **C.7**: 20. **D.3**: 32. **F.3**: 43, 133. **F.5**: 28–29, 31, 36, 40, 42. **H.3**: 20. **I.4**: 14. **I.5**: 23.

Différenciation sociale **E.2**: 56, 66. **H.4**: 9.

Difficultés économiques **K.2**: 18.

Diffusion religieuse **D.5**: 71.

Dimension de la famille **F.4.1**: 3.

Dimension du groupe **C.4**: 23.

Dimension spatiale **C.2**: 39. **E.2**: 29. **G.1**: 17. **H.4**: 42. **I.6**: 36.

Diplômés d'université **F.5**: 74. **I.2**: 22. **I.4**: 4.

Direction de l'entreprise **C.5**: 34. **F.7**: 46.

Discrimination **C.4**: 4. **C.7**: 37. **F.3**: 91, 106. **F.7**: 102.

Discrimination dans l'emploi **F.5**: 29. **F.7**: 10. **I.2**: 43, 56. **I.3**: 46.

Discrimination positive **K.2**: 31.

Discrimination raciale **F.2**: 69. **F.7**: 70, 75, 94–100, 104–110, 112–116.

Discrimination religieuse **I.3**: 37.

Discrimination sexuelle **D.9.3**: 3. **D.9.5**: 26. **F.5**: 33, 56, 66, 107. **I.2**: 26, 56.

Disponibilités alimentaires **K.2**: 17.

Dissensus **F.7**: 21.

Dissidents **F.7**: 57.

Dissuasion **K.1**: 23, 90, 93, 202.

Distribution **E.2**: 13. **F.5**: 30. **I.2**: 33.

Division du travail **F.4.2**: 11, 25, 63. **F.5**: 31, 37. **H.4**: 14. **I.3**: 21, 34.

Divorce continued

Divorce **C.2**: 93. **D.5**: 68. **F.4.1**: 23, 45, 51, 65, 67–74. **F.4.2**: 77, 79–80, 82, 84, 111, 113.
Divorcés **I.2**: 1.
Doctrines sociales **E.3**: 7.
Dollar **F.3**: 29.
Domination **C.5**: 5, 13. **D.6**: 10. **G.3.1**: 24.
Dominicains **F.8**: 56.
Drogue **D.9.3**: 9. **F.4.2**: 41. **I.3**: 35. **J.8**: 8. **K.1**: 10, 17–18, 27, 41, 43, 50, 146, 200. **K.4**: 85.
Droit **D.3**: 10, 36. **D.4**: 1, 8, 10, 16. **F.2**: 71. **F.3**: 17. **F.6**: 14. **G.3.2**: 32, 130. **I.6**: 43. **J.3**: 16. **J.5**: 24. **J.8**: 2. **K.1**: 166, 200, 207. **K.2**: 50. **K.4**: 57, 77.
Droit à la vie privée **D.7**: 44.
Droit criminel **K.1**: 162, 202.
Droit de la famille **D.4**: 6, 14. **F.4.2**: 3, 10, 18, 31, 38, 77.
Droit matrimonial **F.4.1**: 23, 45. **F.4.2**: 77.
Droit naturel **D.4**: 15.
Droits de l'homme **F.3**: 89. **J.3**: 6, 10.
Durkheim, Emile **B.1.1**: 8–9, 28. **B.1.3**: 19. **C.1**: 8. **D.1.1**: 11. **D.5**: 43. **E.3**: 31.
Dynamique culturelle **F.3**: 55.
Dynamique de groupe **C.4**: 9, 17. **C.5**: 31. **F.4.2**: 136.
Dynamique de la population **C.5**: 27. **F.1**: 4, 8. **F.3**: 6, 14.
Dysfonctions de l'organisation **I.6**: 10.
Échange social **E.1**: 4–5.
Échec **C.2**: 89.
Échec scolaire **D.9.8**: 7.
Échelle de Thurstone **K.1**: 122.
Écoles **D.9.3**: 5. **D.9.4**: 1.
Écoles maternelles **C.3**: 11. **D.1.3**: 5.
Écoles primaires **D.9.3**: 3.
Écoles secondaires **D.9.3**: 4, 7–8.
Écologie **G.1**: 14. **G.3.1**: 9–10. **J.5**: 6.
Écologie humaine **C.5**: 6.
Économie capitaliste **F.8**: 22.
Économie de bien-être **K.2**: 39.

Économie de l'éducation continued

Économie de l'éducation **D.9.5**: 7, 20.
Économie de la santé **K.4**: 29.
Économie domestique **F.5**: 17.
Économie politique **I.6**: 27.
Économie rurale **H.5**: 4.
Économie urbaine **G.3.2**: 25, 59.
Écriture **D.7**: 35, 41, 48, 79.
Éducation **D.1.2**: 3. **D.3**: 25, 29. **D.9**: 2, 4, 8–9, 12, 14, 16, 18–19, 22–24. **D.9.2**: 2–3. **D.9.3**: 9. **D.9.5**: 9. **D.9.8**: 10. **F.4.2**: 29. **F.7**: 71. **I.2**: 14. **I.6**: 11.
Éducation des adultes **D.9**: 17. **D.9.5**: 12. **D.9.6**: 1.
Éducation des minorités **D.9**: 7, 21.
Éducation sexuelle **F.6**: 27.
Effectifs en ouvriers **D.9.8**: 2. **G.3.2**: 141. **H.4**: 32. **I.2**: 19, 49, 65. **I.3**: 27, 32. **I.5**: 25.
Effets psychologiques **F.4.1**: 52. **I.2**: 40. **I.4**: 26.
Égalité de chances **D.9**: 13, 26. **E.2**: 36, 52. **I.2**: 17, 21, 39, 61.
Église catholique **D.5**: 61, 67–68, 81. **F.4.1**: 68.
Église et État **D.5**: 64.
Ego **C.2**: 96. **C.7**: 16.
Élaboration d'une politique **K.2**: 34.
Élèves **F.4.2**: 40. **F.7**: 61.
Éligibilité **K.2**: 58.
Élite **D.3**: 26. **E.2**: 41, 47, 73. **G.3.1**: 18. **J.2**: 4.
Élite économique **G.3.2**: 105.
Élite politique **J.6**: 2, 19.
Émigrants **F.8**: 6.
Émigration **F.8**: 3, 50, 54, 87, 97, 100.
Émotion **C.2**: 59–82. **C.3**: 1. **F.4.1**: 4. **J.8**: 8.
Empathie **C.2**: 56.
Emploi **D.9**: 14. **F.2**: 7. **F.4.1**: 53, 64. **F.4.2**: 39, 66. **F.5**: 54, 68. **F.7**: 48, 110. **F.8**: 67. **H.4**: 43. **I.2**: 7, 14, 17, 35, 45. **I.6**: 13.
Emploi des jeunes **I.2**: 72.
Employés **I.3**: 2.

Employeurs **I.5**: 18.
En-groupe **C.4**: 3–4, 13.
Endogamie **F.4.1**: 28, 36.
Énergie nucléaire **C.2**: 35. **C.7**: 27. **D.7**: 104. **J.8**: 7.
Enfance **F.2**: 76, 78, 82–83. **F.3**: 87. **K.1**: 6, 229.
Enfants **C.3**: 11. **C.7**: 2. **D.1.2**: 12. **D.1.3**: 5. **D.9**: 7. **F.2**: 69, 72–73, 79, 86. **F.3**: 43, 111. **F.4.1**: 16. **F.4.2**: 3, 7, 53, 78–80, 90–91, 94, 134, 147. **F.7**: 100. **I.2**: 13. **J.3**: 8. **K.1**: 22, 31, 84, 144, 157. **K.3**: 15, 37. **K.4**: 5.
Enfants à la garde de l'État **K.1**: 118. **K.2**: 14, 41. **K.3**: 9.
Enfants abandonnés **F.4.2**: 37.
Enfants adoptés **F.4.2**: 115.
Enfants doués **D.9**: 24.
Enfants handicapés **D.7**: 82. **D.9**: 24. **F.2**: 80.
Enfants martyrs **F.3**: 66. **F.4.2**: 67, 73. **F.6**: 28. **K.1**: 45–48, 52, 54–56.
Enquêtes **B.2**: 1. **C.5**: 43. **F.1**: 26. **F.4.1**: 47. **K.4**: 48.
Enquêteurs **B.2**: 4.
Enseignants **D.9.3**: 3. **D.9.8**: 8. **D.9.9**: 4, 7. **I.6**: 39.
Enseignement **D.9.9**: 2.
Enseignement supérieur **D.9**: 1, 3. **D.9.5**: 2–8, 10–26. **D.9.9**: 3.
Enseignement technique **I.4**: 24.
Entreprise agricole **I.4**: 19.
Entreprises **H.4**: 41. **I.1**: 3. **I.6**: 6.
Entreprises multinationales **H.4**: 12. **I.2**: 64.
Entreprises privées **H.4**: 6.
Entretiens **B.2**: 1, 9–10. **K.3**: 15.
Environnement **C.5**: 47. **G.1**: 2–3, 10. **G.3.2**: 133. **I.5**: 5. **J.5**: 7. **K.1**: 174, 214.
Environnement physique **D.7**: 31. **K.1**: 174.
Envois de fonds **F.8**: 32, 91.
Epidémiologie **F.3**: 96. **G.1**: 5. **I.3**: 4. **K.1**: 43. **K.4**: 30.
Épistémologie **D.6**: 30.

Équité **D.9.5**: 8. **K.2**: 15. **K.4**: 84.
Erotisme **F.6**: 11.
Esclavage **K.1**: 48.
Espacement des naissances **F.3**: 47.
Espérance de vie **F.2**: 56. **F.3**: 136.
Esprit de parti **J.6**: 29.
Esthétique **B.1.3**: 20. **D.1.1**: 15.
Esthétique urbaine **G.3.2**: 126–127.
Estime de soi **C.2**: 49, 104. **C.3**: 42. **F.4.2**: 108. **I.3**: 42.
État providence **F.8**: 58. **K.1**: 82. **K.2**: 20, 27, 52, 57.
État socialiste **D.3**: 8. **E.3**: 17.
Éthique **C.6**: 8. **D.3**: 17, 21, 24, 28, 34–35, 39. **D.5**: 80. **D.7**: 113, 134. **F.6**: 14, 31. **J.4**: 3. **K.1**: 9. **K.2**: 22. **K.4**: 30.
Éthique protestante **D.3**: 26.
Ethnicité **D.5**: 42. **D.7**: 59. **F.7**: 57–61, 63–69. **G.3.2**: 49. **J.6**: 32. **K.4**: 20.
Ethnocentrisme **B.1.1**: 3.
Ethnographie **C.4**: 32.
Ethnolinguistiques **D.8**: 17.
Ethnométhodologie **B.1.3**: 9.
Ethologie **C.2**: 43. **C.7**: 5.
Étrangers **F.7**: 76. **I.3**: 46.
Études littéraires **J.3**: 10.
Études sur le développement **F.2**: 21. **F.3**: 88. **F.5**: 34.
Études sur les effets mésologiques **G.1**: 7.
Étudiants **C.2**: 2. **C.3**: 10. **C.7**: 14. **D.9.3**: 10. **D.9.5**: 11. **F.4.1**: 20, 46. **F.4.2**: 93. **F.6**: 1, 8, 10. **I.4**: 1. **K.1**: 64, 205.
Eugénisme **F.3**: 72.
Euthanasie **K.1**: 9.
Évaluation **A.3**: 10. **B.2**: 10. **C.1**: 21. **I.2**: 26. **K.3**: 3.
Évaluation de programme **K.3**: 30.
Évaluation de soi **C.2**: 92.
Evangélisme **D.5**: 71.
Éventail des salaires **F.5**: 40. **H.3**: 20, 24, 26–27.
Évolution **D.1.2**: 4. **E.3**: 12, 14.
Évolution des emplois **I.5**: 4.

Exilé **F.5**: 38.
Existentialisme **F.5**: 1.
Expectation **D.1.3**: 3. **D.9**: 2. **F.3**: 30. **K.1**: 11.
Expérience du travail **I.4**: 29.
Experts **B.3**: 9.
Explication **B.1.2**: 1.
Expression faciale **C.2**: 72.
Extrême droite **J.5**: 10. **J.6**: 27.
Fabrication industrielle **D.9.5**: 16. **I.3**: 30. **I.4**: 2. **I.5**: 1.
Facteurs ethniques **F.7**: 24.
Facteurs psychologiques **C.1**: 9.
Faible revenu **F.2**: 55. **F.4.2**: 54.
Famille **C.1**: 12. **C.3**: 13. **C.4**: 17. **C.7**: 3, 12. **D.5**: 17, 46. **D.9**: 19. **E.1**: 10. **E.2**: 17. **F.2**: 31, 45, 49, 74. **F.3**: 82, 111, 118. **F.4.1**: 9, 18, 21, 51, 69. **F.4.2**: 1, 5–6, 15–17, 19–22, 24, 29, 42, 47–48, 50, 55–56, 60–61, 70, 102, 110, 116, 124, 129–137, 140–142, 148. **F.5**: 80. **F.6**: 12. **F.8**: 7, 32. **G.3.1**: 30. **I.2**: 40. **I.4**: 19. **K.1**: 1, 10. **K.4**: 7.
Famille conjugale **F.4.2**: 109.
Famille étendue **F.4.1**: 25. **F.4.2**: 104, 140.
Famine **J.8**: 11. **K.1**: 216, 220–221.
Fascisme **J.6**: 17.
Fatalisme **C.7**: 19.
Fécondité **F.3**: 2, 34, 36, 51, 53–55, 58–59, 61–63, 65–68, 70, 72–74, 78, 81–83, 85–86. **K.1**: 54.
Féminisme **B.1.3**: 11. **D.3**: 17. **D.7**: 3. **F.4.1**: 19. **F.4.2**: 134. **F.5**: 1–12, 14–26, 66, 106. **I.6**: 14. **K.1**: 97.
Femmes **B.1.3**: 11. **C.3**: 53. **D.1.3**: 9. **D.5**: 44. **D.7**: 25, 36, 49, 129. **D.9.5**: 26. **E.2**: 9, 28. **E.3**: 30. **F.2**: 25, 61. **F.3**: 18, 117. **F.4.1**: 4, 42. **F.4.2**: 64, 88, 105. **F.5**: 26, 33, 43, 52, 59–62, 65–66, 68, 70–77, 79–82, 86, 90, 93, 96, 98–102, 105, 107. **F.6**: 13. **F.7**: 15. **G.2**: 4. **G.3.1**: 32, 53, 85. **G.3.2**: 158. **H.2**: 4. **H.3**: 12. **H.4**: 48. **I.2**: 1, 12, 19. **I.3**: 53. **I.6**: 9, 38. **J.5**: 7. **J.7**: 5. **K.1**: 3, 156, 158, 163–164, 212. **K.2**: 58. **K.4**: 3, 28.

Femmes et politique **F.5**: 12, 39, 104, 106.
Femmes rurales **F.5**: 87–88. **G.3.1**: 36.
Féodalisme **H.2**: 3.
Fermes familiales **G.3.1**: 39, 60. **H.4**: 50.
Fierté **C.2**: 62.
Fille **F.4.1**: 75. **F.4.2**: 92.
Finance **I.6**: 21.
Fixation du salaire **H.3**: 25.
Folklore **K.1**: 81.
Fonction publique **I.3**: 29. **J.4**: 1, 4.
Fonctionnaires **J.4**: 6.
Fonctionnalisme **B.1.1**: 2.
Fondamentalisme religieux **D.5**: 85–86.
Force armée **J.7**: 4.
Forces sociales **H.4**: 6.
Foresterie **H.4**: 39.
Formation **G.3.2**: 123. **I.3**: 19. **J.7**: 1.
Formation de classe **E.2**: 8, 69.
Formation des enseignants **D.9.9**: 3.
Formation professionnelle **I.4**: 8, 24.
Foucault, Michel **D.1.3**: 20.
Fraser, Malcolm **J.6**: 36.
Fratrie **F.4.2**: 117–119.
Fréquentation scolaire **F.4.2**: 40.
Frustration **F.4.2**: 46.
Gains **D.9.8**: 6. **F.3**: 74. **F.7**: 43. **F.8**: 71. **H.3**: 2, 5, 7, 13, 21. **I.4**: 10.
Geertz, Clifford **B.1.2**: 1.
Génétique **F.1**: 24.
Génocide **F.7**: 51, 105.
Genre **B.1.1**: 20. **C.7**: 2. **D.1.3**: 9. **D.4**: 16. **D.9**: 16. **D.9.3**: 3–4. **E.2**: 13, 28–30. **F.2**: 47. **F.4.1**: 67. **F.4.2**: 137. **F.5**: 16, 30, 34–35, 37–39, 41, 45, 76. **F.6**: 2. **F.7**: 33, 49. **H.3**: 26. **H.4**: 25, 44. **H.5**: 4. **H.6**: 2. **I.2**: 20, 36, 44. **I.3**: 7, 16–17, 34. **I.4**: 1, 9, 20. **I.6**: 15, 20. **J.8**: 8. **K.1**: 95, 158. **K.2**: 12. **K.4**: 20.
Gens de maison **F.3**: 28. **F.5**: 6. **I.3**: 15.
Géographie **F.3**: 96. **I.7**: 14. **K.4**: 50.
Géographie urbaine **G.3.2**: 47, 118.
Gérontologie **F.2**: 64.

Gestion **C.5**: 11, 15–16, 18, 34. **C.6**: 5. **H.4**: 10, 24–25, 29. **I.3**: 47. **I.5**: 7, 10. **I.6**: 19. **K.4**: 45–46.

Gestion d'entreprises **C.4**: 28.

Gestion des pêches **I.3**: 47.

Gestion du personnel **I.3**: 19, 29.

Gestion industrielle **D.3**: 21.

Gestion urbaine **G.3.2**: 24, 34.

Goffman, Erving **D.1.3**: 6, 17.

Gramsci, Antonio **D.3**: 6. **D.5**: 43.

Grecs **D.7**: 6.

Grèves **I.6**: 16, 35.

Grossesse **D.5**: 77. **F.3**: 30, 76. **F.4.1**: 41. **F.4.2**: 74. **F.6**: 20.

Group d'âge **C.6**: 2. **F.1**: 10. **F.2**: 2–4. **F.3**: 70. **F.6**: 2. **J.8**: 8. **K.1**: 61.

Groupements professionnels **I.4**: 21.

Groupes d'égaux **K.1**: 20.

Groupes d'intérêt **J.5**: 3.

Groupes de travail **I.3**: 40.

Groupes ethniques **C.2**: 39. **D.7**: 125. **F.7**: 78, 84. **G.2**: 12. **G.3.2**: 52. **H.3**: 24. **J.3**: 13.

Groupes expérimentaux **C.4**: 4.

Groupes minoritaires **C.4**: 13. **F.8**: 99.

Groupes restreints **C.5**: 31. **I.3**: 40.

Guerre **J.1**: 4. **J.8**: 4, 15, 18–19.

Guerre froide **D.7**: 98.

Guerre nucléaire **J.8**: 1, 8, 20.

Habitudes **C.2**: 69.

Habitudes de lecture **C.2**: 33.

Handicapés **D.1.3**: 15. **F.3**: 125.

Handicapés mentaux **C.3**: 6. **F.3**: 120.

Handicapés physiques **F.3**: 132. **F.5**: 107.

Hare, Richard M. **D.3**: 7.

Herméneutique **B.1.1**: 11.

Heures de travail **I.3**: 49, 57.

Heuristique **B.1.2**: 6.

Hierarchie **F.4.2**: 15. **H.4**: 28.

Hill, Reuben **F.4.2**: 143.

Hirshman, A. **C.5**: 44.

Hispanique **D.7**: 70. **F.3**: 153. **F.7**: 31–32, 52, 58–59, 67. **F.8**: 65. **G.3.2**: 49. **I.2**:

Hispanique continued
57.

Histoire **A.1**: 16. **B.3**: 19. **D.1.1**: 25. **D.7**: 14, 112, 129. **F.5**: 106. **I.7**: 4, 11. **K.4**: 86.

Histoire culturelle **D.1.1**: 6. **D.2**: 2.

Histoire de la famille **F.4.2**: 28.

Histoire de la médicine **C.1**: 1.

Histoire de la sociologie **B.1.3**: 24. **D.1.1**: 47.

Histoire militaire **J.7**: 4.

Histoire politique **D.9.5**: 10.

Histoire religieuse **D.5**: 54.

Histoire sociale **D.7**: 93. **D.9**: 23. **E.3**: 7. **F.4.2**: 84. **F.6**: 15, 25. **G.2**: 16.

Histoire urbaine **G.3.2**: 146.

Historicisme **B.1.3**: 24.

HIV **F.3**: 112, 123. **K.3**: 12.

Hobbes, Thomas **B.1.1**: 30.

Homicide **K.1**: 84–85, 113, 121, 129.

Hommes **F.3**: 20, 37. **F.4.2**: 35. **F.5**: 45, 55–56. **I.4**: 20. **K.1**: 164.

Hommes de loi **D.4**: 2.

Homogamie **I.2**: 58.

Homosexualité **C.7**: 7. **F.3**: 99, 113. **F.4.1**: 21. **F.4.2**: 102. **F.6**: 4, 14, 16, 21–22, 25, 29. **K.2**: 3.

Hôpitaux **K.4**: 34, 49.

Huile **C.7**: 27.

Humour **C.2**: 26, 36.

Hutterite **F.3**: 36.

Identification à une classe sociale **E.2**: 9–11.

Identité **C.3**: 24. **C.5**: 25. **C.7**: 37. **D.1.1**: 25. **D.4**: 16. **D.5**: 37. **F.5**: 45, 98. **J.6**: 31.

Identité culturelle **D.1.1**: 4, 10, 35–36.

Identité de groupe **C.3**: 45. **C.4**: 3, 15.

Identité nationale **D.7**: 67.

Idéologie **C.5**: 5. **C.7**: 21–23. **D.1.2**: 10. **D.4**: 1. **D.5**: 21, 46. **D.6**: 22. **D.7**: 14, 27, 89, 99. **D.8**: 10. **F.3**: 49. **F.4.2**: 47. **G.3.1**: 24. **J.5**: 3.

Images **C.2**: 35. **C.6**: 9. **F.3**: 114. **H.4**: 5. **H.6**: 3. **J.8**: 7. **K.4**: 38.

Imagination **C.2**: 70.
Immigrants D.7: 70. **F.4.1**: 30. **F.7**: 96. **F.8**: 51–52, 58, 75, 84–86, 90, 103. **H.3**: 6.
Immigration F.1: 10. **F.8**: 41, 54, 59–60, 65–66, 69–73, 79, 82, 88, 93, 101–102. **G.3.1**: 50. **H.3**: 13.
Immigration clandestine **F.8**: 67, 78.
Indicateur **B.1.3**: 10. **B.3**: 10. **H.3**: 19.
Indiens **E.2**: 48. **F.7**: 78.
Indigénisme **A.1**: 18, 38–39.
Individualisme **B.1.1**: 8. **D.1.1**: 26. **D.3**: 20. **J.5**: 17.
Individus **I.6**: 43.
Induction **C.2**: 31.
Industrie **H.4**: 34. **I.3**: 34. **I.6**: 17.
Industrie alimentaire **I.2**: 37.
Inégalité de revenu **H.3**: 3, 14, 17, 27.
Inégalité économique **F.7**: 10, 113.
Inégalité sociale **E.2**: 20, 32–33, 57. **E.3**: 6. **F.4.1**: 24. **G.3.1**: 14.
Inflation **H.6**: 3.
Influence sociale **C.3**: 37.
Information A.1: 19. **A.5**: 5. **C.2**: 92, 103. **C.5**: 37. **D.7**: 100. **F.3**: 97. **H.7**: 4. **I.2**: 3, 25.
Informatisation **H.4**: 26.
Injustice **F.7**: 111. **K.3**: 34.
Innovations **C.5**: 21, 40. **G.3.2**: 123.
Institutions **C.2**: 15. **K.1**: 174.
Institutions politiques **J.3**: 21.
Institutions religieuses **F.8**: 52.
Intégration régionale **F.8**: 53.
Intégration sociale **D.1.3**: 13, 15. **D.9.2**: 2. **E.2**: 66. **F.2**: 52. **F.3**: 121, 125. **F.7**: 107. **F.8**: 52, 72.
Intellectuels **E.2**: 35.
Intelligence **C.2**: 4. **D.3**: 10.
Intelligentsia **E.2**: 55.
Interaction conjugale **F.3**: 130. **F.4.1**: 35, 59.
Interaction culturelle **D.8**: 1.
Interaction sociale C.3: 12, 32, 44, 49. **C.6**: 10. **D.1.3**: 6, 17, 21. **D.7**: 43. **F.3**: 106.

Interactionnisme **D.1.3**: 8.
Interdépendance **D.1.2**: 4.
Intérêt public **D.1.2**: 6. **D.7**: 122.
Intermariage **F.4.1**: 11, 24, 26, 28, 30, 36, 43.
Intervalles génésiques **F.3**: 84.
Intimité **F.6**: 30.
Inuit **F.3**: 61.
Invalidité **C.7**: 14. **F.3**: 106. **K.4**: 7.
Inventions **A.3**: 9.
Iraniens **F.8**: 75.
Islam **D.5**: 82–90. **D.9**: 18. **F.5**: 92. **F.8**: 102. **I.3**: 41. **K.2**: 54.
Japonais **D.5**: 29. **F.7**: 7, 77.
Jeunesse C.2: 49. **C.7**: 42. **D.1.2**: 6. **E.2**: 32. **F.2**: 5–7, 10–12, 17, 19–21. **F.4.1**: 65. **F.5**: 18. **F.7**: 58. **F.8**: 71. **H.3**: 13. **I.2**: 32, 47, 57, 69–71. **J.6**: 10. **K.1**: 19, 207. **K.4**: 94.
Jeunesse rurale **F.2**: 13.
Jeux d'argent **I.7**: 1, 8.
Journalisme **D.7**: 85, 105, 113, 140.
Judaïsme **D.5**: 59.
Jugement **C.2**: 75. **C.4**: 3. **D.1.1**: 37. **D.3**: 12, 29.
Jugement social **C.3**: 50. **C.7**: 9.
Juifs B.1.1: 18. **D.5**: 2. **D.9.8**: 2. **F.7**: 23, 28, 51, 56, 81–83, 95, 110. **F.8**: 89, 97. **H.3**: 24.
Jung, Carl **F.7**: 114.
Jurisprudence **F.7**: 115.
Jury **F.7**: 115.
Justice **C.4**: 17. **F.4.2**: 136. **K.1**: 158, 188.
Justice criminelle D.4: 3, 13. **F.7**: 11, 39. **J.3**: 12. **K.1**: 127, 131, 142, 144–148, 150–156, 158–164, 166–170, 172–182, 187–189.
Justice distributive **K.3**: 23–24.
Justice sociale **B.1.1**: 16. **K.1**: 172.
Kazakh **F.7**: 37.
Langage **C.2**: 57, 95. **D.7**: 9, 14, 53, 56, 59, 63–64, 66, 68, 70, 116. **K.1**: 15.
Langage par signes **D.7**: 39.
Langue allemande **D.7**: 77.

Langue anglaise **D.7**: 58.
Langue espagnole **D.7**: 78.
Langue française **D.7**: 67.
Langue gallois **D.7**: 81.
Langue japonaise **D.7**: 79.
Langue russe **D.7**: 53.
Langues écrites **D.7**: 24.
Leaders **C.6**: 9, 19. **I.5**: 25.
Leaders charismatiques **C.6**: 5.
Leadership **C.6**: 2, 11–17, 21. **D.9.4**: 1. **J.5**: 15. **J.6**: 13, 36.
Leadership politique **C.6**: 3, 8.
Législation **F.4.1**: 31. **F.5**: 65. **I.3**: 38.
Légitimation **C.7**: 16.
Légitimité **C.5**: 13. **J.2**: 4.
Lewin, Kurt **C.1**: 19.
Libéralisme **F.6**: 7.
Liberté **A.1**: 28.
Liberté de l'enseignement **D.9**: 1, 12.
Libertés civiles **J.3**: 2.
Lieu de naissance **F.8**: 23.
Lieu de travail **I.3**: 37.
Limitation des armements **C.1**: 9. **J.8**: 5.
Linguistique **D.7**: 46, 50–55, 57–59, 61–70, 72–74, 77–78, 81–82. **E.2**: 1. **F.4.1**: 33.
Littérature **C.2**: 70. **D.1.1**: 30. **D.3**: 22. **D.8**: 11, 16.
Logement **F.5**: 27. **G.3.1**: 25, 68. **G.3.2**: 88, 93, 96–97, 100, 102. **K.1**: 213.
Logement urbain **D.1.3**: 14. **G.3.2**: 85–91, 93, 95–97, 99, 101–102.
Logements sociaux **K.1**: 96.
Logique **D.9.8**: 8.
Loi islamique **D.5**: 23.
Loisir **D.9.5**: 11. **F.4.1**: 32. **I.3**: 57. **I.7**: 2, 4, 7, 10–11, 13, 15, 17, 26.
Luhmann, Niklas **B.1.1**: 17.
Lutte de classes **D.5**: 43. **E.2**: 40.
Macroéconomie **K.1**: 111.
Mafia **K.1**: 99.
Magie **D.5**: 25.
Maintien de l'ordre **G.2**: 12, 17. **I.4**: 12. **J.3**: 4–5, 13, 15, 17–20, 26. **K.1**: 66.

Malades **D.7**: 23. **F.3**: 118, 145. **K.4**: 6, 11, 59.
Maladie mentale **F.3**: 121, 129–130. **F.4.1**: 59. **K.1**: 231. **K.4**: 24, 66, 85.
Maladies **C.2**: 55. **F.3**: 107, 109, 118, 131. **G.1**: 5. **K.1**: 234. **K.4**: 88.
Maladies professionnelles **I.3**: 46.
Malnutrition **D.7**: 90.
Mannheim, Karl **A.5**: 4. **B.1.1**: 24. **D.6**: 13, 17.
Maori **F.7**: 64, 89.
Marché **G.3.2**: 144. **H.4**: 28. **H.5**: 4. **I.3**: 56.
Marché du logement **G.3.2**: 85. **K.1**: 225.
Marché du travail **F.3**: 30, 85. **F.5**: 32. **F.7**: 10. **I.2**: 2, 7, 16, 19–23, 30–32, 37, 43, 50, 55, 57, 67. **I.3**: 16. **I.4**: 10.
Marché foncier **G.3.2**: 91.
Marché noir **H.5**: 5.
Marginalité **E.2**: 2. **F.3**: 143. **F.7**: 12.
Mari **F.3**: 35. **F.4.1**: 53. **I.3**: 32.
Mariage **C.7**: 12. **F.3**: 65. **F.4.1**: 4, 9, 13, 17, 44, 47, 51, 63–64. **F.4.2**: 1, 6, 144. **F.6**: 2. **F.8**: 36, 41, 93.
Marshall, Alfred **D.3**: 11.
Marx, Karl **D.5**: 43. **E.3**: 16.
Marxisme **B.1.1**: 35. **D.7**: 105. **E.2**: 14. **J.2**: 7. **K.1**: 119.
Maternité **F.4.2**: 4, 8, 36, 106. **H.3**: 2.
Maternité de substitution **F.4.2**: 14, 57.
Maternité précoce **C.4**: 32.
Mead, G.H. **A.2**: 2.
Médecine **D.7**: 91. **K.4**: 6, 52.
Médecins **F.3**: 39, 145. **F.8**: 85. **I.5**: 14–15. **K.4**: 11, 38.
Médiation **F.4.2**: 77. **K.1**: 77, 112. **K.3**: 5.
Médicaments **K.1**: 86, 190–198, 200–212.
Mémoire **C.2**: 50, 61, 99. **J.8**: 19. **K.1**: 212.
Ménages **E.2**: 30. **F.1**: 9. **F.4.2**: 11, 23–24, 63, 105. **F.8**: 27. **G.2**: 5. **H.4**: 34.
Menstruation **K.4**: 40.
Mère **F.4.2**: 23, 40, 92.

Mères travailleuses **F.2**: 73. **F.4.2**: 39. **I.2**: 10, 13. **I.3**: 20.
Mesure **E.2**: 3, 43, 70. **F.2**: 9. **F.4.1**: 47.
Méthode de production **B.1.3**: 32. **F.5**: 110.
Méthode expérimentale **C.1**: 24.
Méthodes de planification **C.5**: 11.
Méthodes de recherche **B.1.3**: 1–2, 5, 12, 27. **C.2**: 97. **D.7**: 128. **F.4.2**: 124.
Méthodes statistiques **B.3**: 22. **F.1**: 30.
Méthodologie **A.1**: 2, 27. **B.1.3**: 19, 22, 24–25. **B.3**: 24. **C.5**: 46. **D.7**: 28.
Métropole **G.3.2**: 88.
Mexicains **F.4.1**: 42. **F.8**: 68.
Microélectronique **H.4**: 38.
Microordinateurs **I.3**: 51.
Migranteurs **F.3**: 153. **F.4.1**: 54. **F.4.2**: 26. **F.8**: 15, 23, 48, 96, 98.
Migration **F.2**: 4, 42. **F.3**: 6. **F.8**: 1, 5, 10–11, 24, 27–28, 32, 35–36, 91, 94. **G.3.2**: 117, 138, 146.
Migration de travail **F.8**: 13, 16, 45, 49, 53, 62, 81, 104–105.
Migration forcée **F.8**: 43.
Migration internationale **F.8**: 48–54, 56–61, 63, 65–68, 71–75, 77–91, 93, 95–97, 99–101, 103–105. **H.3**: 13.
Migration interne **F.8**: 14, 18, 20, 42.
Migration rurale-urbaine **F.8**: 7, 39–40. **G.3.2**: 145.
Migration saisonnière **F.8**: 13.
Migration urbaine-rurale **G.3**: 2.
Migrations alternantes **F.8**: 18.
Milieu de travail **I.3**: 4.
Milieu rural **F.2**: 41. **G.3.1**: 9, 11.
Milieu urbain **G.3.2**: 69, 77.
Milieux d'affaires **A.1**: 28. **H.4**: 12.
Militaires **J.7**: 1, 3.
Militaires et politique **J.7**: 2.
Militants **J.6**: 34.
Militarisme **J.7**: 5.
Millénarisme **D.5**: 11, 24.
Mills, C. Wright **A.2**: 6.
Mines de houille **I.3**: 1.

Minorités continued
Minorités **F.7**: 39–40. **F.8**: 98.
Minorités ethniques **D.5**: 29. **F.7**: 6–7, 25, 27–28, 30, 37–38, 77, 103. **G.3.2**: 17. **K.1**: 180.
Minorités linguistiques **D.7**: 61.
Mobilisation sociale **J.5**: 15.
Mobilité géographique **F.8**: 18. **K.1**: 101.
Mobilité professionnelle **F.4.2**: 120. **I.2**: 3. **I.4**: 3, 10–11, 16–18. **I.5**: 7.
Mobilité résidentielle **F.3**: 133. **F.7**: 51.
Mobilité sociale **D.9.5**: 5. **E.2**: 18, 37, 45–46, 58, 63. **I.4**: 17.
Mode **D.2**: 2.
Modèles **B.3**: 2.
Modèles de décision **K.4**: 61.
Modèles mathématiques **B.3**: 20. **C.4**: 25. **C.5**: 17. **G.3.2**: 129.
Modelisation **B.3**: 14. **F.1**: 15. **F.4.2**: 124. **F.7**: 108.
Modernisation **B.1.1**: 3. **D.7**: 79. **E.3**: 13, 17, 19, 24. **G.3.2**: 115. **I.2**: 49. **J.2**: 8. **J.6**: 14–15. **K.4**: 54.
Modernité **D.1.1**: 14, 35. **D.5**: 86. **E.3**: 18, 31. **K.1**: 110.
Modes de vie **D.1.1**: 1, 15, 44. **D.1.2**: 5. **F.4.2**: 16. **G.3.2**: 60.
Moi **C.2**: 5, 63, 86, 90, 94. **D.1.3**: 17, 20. **K.1**: 69.
Montagnes **G.3.1**: 54.
Moralité **C.3**: 26. **D.3**: 4, 7, 12, 14–16, 18, 29, 38. **D.5**: 7. **I.6**: 17.
Moralité politique **D.3**: 13.
Morbidité **F.3**: 116.
Mort **D.1.2**: 13. **F.1**: 17. **F.3**: 150.
Mortalité **F.3**: 136, 139, 144, 146–147, 149, 152. **F.4.1**: 56. **G.3.2**: 36.
Mortalité des enfants **F.3**: 134–135.
Mortalité infantile **E.2**: 53. **F.3**: 32, 59, 138, 141–143, 145, 151. **K.3**: 13.
Motivation **C.2**: 2, 16. **D.1.3**: 14. **I.3**: 29. **I.4**: 24.
Mouvements écologiques **J.5**: 6.
Mouvements ouvriers **I.6**: 24.
Mouvements pacifistes **J.5**: 20.

Mouvements paysans **G.3.1**: 59.
Mouvements religieux **D.5**: 2, 10, 51. **D.7**: 120.
Mouvements sociaux **E.3**: 20. **F.5**: 11. **G.3.2**: 80. **J.5**: 1, 6–7, 11, 17, 24, 26, 32, 35, 37.
Moyens de communication **D.1.2**: 7. **D.1.3**: 19. **D.7**: 28–29, 44, 69, 83, 85–88, 90–101, 103–107, 109, 111–121, 123–126, 128–131, 133–136, 138–141, 143–149. **F.7**: 90. **G.3.1**: 19. **K.1**: 37.
Multilinguisme **D.7**: 61.
Musique **D.8**: 6.
Musique populaire **D.8**: 12.
Musulman **D.5**: 88. **F.4.1**: 43.
Mutilations sexuelles **F.6**: 13.
Mythes **K.1**: 230.
Naissance **F.3**: 50. **F.4.1**: 70. **F.4.2**: 8.
Narcissisme **C.2**: 95. **C.6**: 14.
Nationalisme **D.7**: 40. **D.9**: 22. **F.5**: 78. **F.7**: 63, 84. **J.2**: 4–5, 8–9, 13.
Nations unies **F.7**: 24.
Nature **A.2**: 5. **D.3**: 16.
Négociation **I.6**: 12, 22.
Négociation collective **D.9.9**: 7. **I.6**: 39.
Nihilisme **D.5**: 33.
Niveau d'enseignement **D.9.8**: 2, 6. **F.7**: 43.
Niveau de vie **F.2**: 55. **F.5**: 80. **H.3**: 11, 18.
Noirs **D.4**: 3. **D.7**: 136. **F.2**: 37. **F.4.2**: 54. **F.5**: 19, 51. **F.7**: 11–12, 20, 65, 72–73, 80, 88, 91, 98, 111. **G.3.2**: 76. **I.2**: 57.
Noms de couleur **D.7**: 53.
Normes sociales **C.4**: 14.
Nostalgie **D.1.1**: 19.
Nouvelles **D.7**: 115, 141, 149.
Nuptialité **F.4.1**: 34, 54–56, 60.
Nutrition **H.5**: 8.
Objectivité **C.6**: 4.
Obligation **C.3**: 23.
Observation participante **F.2**: 79.
Occidentalisation **E.3**: 30.

Offre **K.1**: 206.
Offre de main d'oeuvre **I.2**: 1, 51.
Oligarchie **C.5**: 36. **G.3.1**: 21.
Oligopole **I.3**: 30.
Opinion publique **D.7**: 58. **F.3**: 129. **F.6**: 18. **I.6**: 44. **K.2**: 20, 38.
Ordinateurs **B.1.3**: 3. **B.3**: 3. **C.1**: 5. **H.4**: 5, 33, 40. **I.3**: 21.
Ordre social **D.4**: 10.
Ordres religieux **D.5**: 63.
Organisation communautaire **G.2**: 3. **G.3.2**: 10. **K.1**: 65.
Organisation de l'entreprise **C.6**: 5. **H.4**: 28.
Organisation de la recherche **A.3**: 2.
Organisation du travail **I.3**: 9, 55–56.
Organisations **C.4**: 22, 30. **C.5**: 6, 8–9, 12–13, 24–28, 30–33, 35, 37, 42, 44. **C.6**: 13. **F.5**: 42, 56. **H.4**: 21, 27. **I.3**: 27. **I.5**: 23.
Organisations bénévoles **C.5**: 16, 36, 43. **G.2**: 8. **G.3.1**: 66.
Organisations internationales **C.5**: 4. **D.9**: 17.
Ouvrages de référence **J.5**: 36.
Ouvriers industriels **E.2**: 5. **I.5**: 5–6.
Ouvriers qualifiés **I.4**: 2.
Pacifisme **J.6**: 18. **J.8**: 4.
Paix **G.3.1**: 23. **J.8**: 5, 10, 12.
Paradigmes **B.1.3**: 13. **D.6**: 35.
Parenté **E.2**: 38. **F.2**: 48. **F.4.1**: 6, 67. **F.4.2**: 105.
Parents **D.1.2**: 12. **D.5**: 58. **D.9.3**: 7. **F.2**: 68. **F.4.1**: 71. **F.4.2**: 59, 147.
Parlement **J.3**: 1.
Parole **D.7**: 48, 82.
Parsons, Talcott **E.1**: 10.
Participation au groupe **C.4**: 24.
Participation de la collectivité **G.2**: 1, 15. **J.3**: 4.
Participation électorale **I.6**: 41.
Participation politique **J.6**: 35. **K.3**: 16.
Partis ouvriers **J.6**: 4.
Partis politiques **J.5**: 19.
Paternalisme **I.3**: 34.

Paternité **F.4.2**: 66, 87, 100–101, 126.
Paternité-maternité **F.4.2**: 35, 66, 76, 121, 145. **F.5**: 54.
Patriarcat **E.3**: 21.
Pauvres **C.2**: 4. **D.9**: 7. **J.4**: 2.
Pauvreté **D.1.1**: 24. **D.1.3**: 10. **F.2**: 87. **F.7**: 87. **K.1**: 57, 213–239. **K.2**: 35. **K.3**: 25. **K.4**: 64.
Pauvreté rurale **G.3.1**: 17. **J.4**: 9. **K.1**: 238.
Pauvreté urbaine **G.3.2**: 32, 35, 44, 75. **K.4**: 39.
Pays développés **G.3.1**: 33.
Pays en développement **A.1**: 3. **E.3**: 22. **F.3**: 13, 32, 78, 86. **F.5**: 37. **F.8**: 37, 45. **G.3.1**: 29, 63, 84. **G.3.2**: 25, 80–81, 86, 156. **H.3**: 12. **H.4**: 36. **I.2**: 52. **I.3**: 54. **I.5**: 24. **J.8**: 16. **K.1**: 215–216, 233, 236. **K.4**: 39, 61.
Pays socialistes **E.2**: 63.
Paysannerie **E.2**: 8. **G.3.1**: 54–55, 57–58, 60–65. **J.5**: 19.
Peine de mort **K.1**: 121.
Pélerinages **D.5**: 74.
Penchant **K.1**: 68.
Pension **K.2**: 58.
Perception **C.2**: 32. **C.3**: 9. **D.7**: 68. **F.3**: 145. **F.4.1**: 38. **F.7**: 73. **I.6**: 20.
Perception d'autrui **C.3**: 31.
Perception de rôle **K.1**: 69.
Perception sociale **E.2**: 67.
Perception visuelle **C.2**: 39.
Père **F.4.2**: 58. **K.1**: 56.
Perestroika **A.1**: 23. **C.1**: 22. **E.2**: 66.
Périodiques **A.5**: 2. **D.7**: 129. **F.4.1**: 4.
Permissivité sexuelle **F.6**: 26.
Personnalité **C.2**: 83–104. **C.3**: 4. **E.2**: 61. **K.1**: 211.
Personnel médical **D.7**: 23. **I.2**: 66.
Personnel scientifique **I.2**: 43.
Petites et moyennes entreprises **F.8**: 89. **H.4**: 28.
Petites villes **G.3.2**: 152.
Peur **C.2**: 35, 60. **J.8**: 7. **K.1**: 95–96.
Phénoménologie **C.1**: 24.

Philippins **F.8**: 51.
Philosophie **A.1**: 24. **D.4**: 12.
Philosophie sociale **B.1.1**: 6.
Photographie **D.7**: 35.
Piaget, Jean **A.5**: 1. **D.3**: 37. **J.6**: 20.
Placement familial **F.4.2**: 14, 37. **K.2**: 14. **K.3**: 9–10.
Planification de l'éducation **D.9.5**: 13, 25.
Planification de la famille **D.5**: 62. **F.3**: 19–22, 28, 31–33, 36–37, 39–40, 42, 49, 58–59, 82.
Planification des transports **G.3.2**: 134.
Planification du développement **F.7**: 24.
Planification linguistique **D.7**: 61–62.
Planification rurale **G.3.1**: 33.
Planification sociale **K.2**: 45.
Plantation **F.1**: 8.
Pluie d'acide **D.7**: 100.
Pluralisme **C.3**: 35.
Pluralisme ethnique **F.7**: 10.
Pluralisme social **D.1.1**: 43. **J.3**: 1.
Police **C.3**: 33. **I.4**: 12. **J.3**: 7, 11–12, 15–16, 22. **K.1**: 22, 78, 95. **K.3**: 22.
Politique agraire **G.3.1**: 2.
Politique de développement **F.8**: 14. **G.3**: 1. **G.3.1**: 66, 69, 72. **J.4**: 7.
Politique de l'environnement **G.3.1**: 8. **G.3.2**: 62. **J.5**: 8, 18.
Politique de la recherche **H.4**: 13.
Politique de la vieillesse **F.2**: 22.
Politique démographique **F.3**: 8, 31, 40–41, 82. **F.8**: 38, 101.
Politique des loisirs **I.7**: 16.
Politique des transports **H.4**: 1.
Politique du logement **D.1.3**: 14. **G.3.2**: 14, 86–87, 89, 91. **I.2**: 16. **K.1**: 224.
Politique économique **F.5**: 90.
Politique ethnique **F.7**: 71, 98.
Politique familiale **F.4.2**: 56, 62, 66. **K.2**: 18, 35, 55.
Politique linguistique **D.7**: 6, 11, 73.
Politique migratoire **F.8**: 30, 62, 66.
Politique pénale **K.1**: 160, 170.

Politique publique continued

Politique publique **F.5**: 54. **F.6**: 18. **G.3.2**: 69. **J.5**: 7. **K.1**: 33. **K.4**: 53, 57, 68.

Politique rurale **G.3.1**: 23. **J.4**: 2.

Politique sanitaire **K.1**: 190. **K.2**: 3. **K.4**: 40.

Politique sociale **F.3**: 128. **H.4**: 41. **K.2**: 19–21, 23–24, 29, 47, 54, 56. **K.3**: 25. **K.4**: 21.

Politique urbaine **G.3.2**: 1–2, 23, 42, 45, 53, 56, 61, 64, 79, 104–105, 108–109, 111, 119–120, 122–123, 128, 134, 142, 149–150.

Politisation **J.5**: 16. **J.6**: 14, 16.

Pollution de l'air **G.1**: 3.

Polyandrie **F.4.1**: 52.

Polygamie **F.4.1**: 52. **F.6**: 23.

Popper, Karl **B.1.1**: 12.

Population **F.1**: 10–11, 15, 22, 29. **F.3**: 1, 15, 49. **K.1**: 195.

Population rurale **F.3**: 14. **G.3.1**: 30.

Population urbaine **F.1**: 16. **F.3**: 147. **G.3.2**: 28, 36, 137.

Populisme **J.2**: 10.

Pornographie **D.7**: 87, 118. **F.6**: 18.

Positivisme **E.3**: 4.

Post-fordisme **H.4**: 32.

Postmoderisme **A.1**: 21. **G.3.2**: 116.

Pouvoir de l'entreprise **H.4**: 7.

Pouvoir économique **F.5**: 49. **H.4**: 7.

Pouvoir judiciaire **J.3**: 23.

Pouvoir législatif **J.6**: 19.

Pouvoir personnel **C.3**: 30. **C.6**: 6.

Pragmatisme **K.1**: 119.

Pratique religieuse **I.3**: 24.

Préjugé **F.3**: 103. **F.7**: 99.

Préjugé racial **F.7**: 108, 112, 116.

Présidence **J.6**: 26.

Presse **D.7**: 83, 86, 104, 108, 114, 117–121, 126, 144. **F.8**: 41. **I.3**: 56.

Prêtres **D.5**: 67, 78.

Prévention de la délinquance **K.1**: 23, 62, 80, 90, 172.

Prévisions **C.7**: 25. **J.6**: 37.

Prévisions démographiques **F.1**: 2, 23, 25. **F.3**: 75.

Primatologie **C.2**: 43.

Prise de décision **C.4**: 1, 21. **C.5**: 37, 42. **F.8**: 1. **H.6**: 2. **J.6**: 12.

Prise de décision en groupe **B.1.3**: 3. **C.4**: 1, 22.

Prise de rôle **C.6**: 20.

Prison **K.1**: 50, 163.

Prisons **C.1**: 33. **I.5**: 19. **K.1**: 34, 142, 147–148, 152, 159, 169, 174–179, 186.

Privation **D.9**: 2.

Privation relative **F.7**: 91.

Privatisation **K.1**: 150.

Prix **K.1**: 207.

Probabilité **B.3**: 27.

Problèmes sociaux **D.7**: 9, 64. **H.4**: 26. **K.1**: 15, 25, 39, 82, 239.

Processus stochastiques **F.1**: 30.

Production **E.3**: 17. **F.8**: 27. **G.3.1**: 48. **H.6**: 1.

Productivité **H.4**: 31. **I.2**: 33.

Productivité industrielle **H.4**: 18.

Profession legale **K.1**: 202.

Professionnalisation **I.5**: 20. **I.7**: 16.

Professionnalisme **C.5**: 30. **I.4**: 12.

Professions **E.2**: 61. **F.5**: 47. **I.2**: 30–31. **I.4**: 19–20, 28. **I.5**: 20.

Professorat **F.5**: 43, 74, 84.

Prolétarisation **E.2**: 51.

Promotion professionnelle **H.4**: 25. **I.3**: 7. **I.4**: 9.

Propriété **H.4**: 8.

Propriété foncière **G.3.2**: 37.

Prostitution **F.5**: 85. **F.6**: 15, 24, 28, 32. **G.3.2**: 48.

Protestantisme **D.5**: 73, 75.

Protestants **D.3**: 35. **D.5**: 80.

Prototypes **C.2**: 2.

Psychanalyse **C.1**: 31, 34, 40. **C.5**: 25.

Psychiâtrie **C.1**: 1, 30. **C.4**: 2. **K.4**: 55.

Psycholinguistique **D.7**: 68.

Psychologie continued

Psychologie **C.1**: 5, 7, 10, 13, 20, 24, 28, 33, 35, 41. **C.2**: 33. **C.3**: 37, 52. **D.4**: 8. **F.3**: 124, 133. **F.4.2**: 119. **F.5**: 98, 107. **F.6**: 22. **F.7**: 49, 76. **I.4**: 29. **I.5**: 16. **I.7**: 25. **J.7**: 3. **K.1**: 71, 117. **K.4**: 68.

Psychologie de l'enfant **A.5**: 1. **C.2**: 9, 73, 89. **D.1.3**: 2. **F.2**: 77, 81. **F.3**: 104. **F.4.2**: 89.

Psychologie de l'environnement **K.1**: 102.

Psychologie économique **H.1**: 4–6.

Psychologie expérimentale **C.1**: 19.

Psychologie industrielle **H.4**: 18, 31. **I.3**: 42.

Psychologie politique **D.3**: 22. **J.2**: 11, 13. **J.6**: 20, 36.

Psychologie sociale **B.1.3**: 5. **C.1**: 4, 18–19, 21–23, 32, 36–37. **C.3**: 33, 45, 47. **C.7**: 21. **D.6**: 31. **F.3**: 42. **F.7**: 57, 108. **H.4**: 16. **I.4**: 13.

Psychologues **I.5**: 16.

Psychométrie **F.4.2**: 131.

Psychopathologie **C.1**: 12.

Psychothérapie **C.2**: 87. **K.3**: 23–24.

Psychothérapie de groupe **C.4**: 2.

Public **D.7**: 135, 143, 149. **D.8**: 13.

Publications scientifiques **A.5**: 3.

Publicité **D.7**: 25, 32, 36, 47, 99, 133. **F.8**: 93. **I.7**: 24. **K.1**: 37.

Puériculture **F.4.2**: 41, 54, 108.

Puritanisme **D.5**: 35.

Qualification professionnelle **I.5**: 22.

Qualification requise pour l'emploi **I.3**: 24.

Qualité de l'environnement **G.3.2**: 5.

Qualité de la vie **C.7**: 42. **F.8**: 87. **H.3**: 22–23.

Quartier **D.1.2**: 1. **G.2**: 4–5, 10, 13. **K.1**: 62, 95.

Quechua **D.1.1**: 10.

Race **C.1**: 30. **D.4**: 4. **E.2**: 34, 52, 75. **F.3**: 103. **F.5**: 86. **F.7**: 19, 48–49, 53, 63, 66, 99, 102. **F.8**: 73. **J.3**: 27. **K.1**: 95, 161, 180. **K.3**: 14.

Racisme **F.3**: 88. **F.7**: 70, 96, 104, 106–107, 115.

Radio **D.7**: 121, 125, 145.

Radiodiffusion **D.7**: 96, 98, 101, 131.

Rationalisation **H.5**: 8.

Rationalisme **B.1.1**: 18.

Rationalité **B.1.1**: 12, 24. **C.5**: 39–40. **C.7**: 10, 32.

Réadaptation des délinquants **K.1**: 140, 188.

Réadaptation professionnelle **I.4**: 15.

Reagan, Ronald **J.6**: 36.

Recherche **A.1**: 17. **A.3**: 11. **B.1.3**: 25. **B.2**: 5. **B.3**: 3, 7. **C.1**: 33, 38. **C.4**: 20. **C.5**: 43. **D.4**: 9. **D.7**: 28, 30, 87. **D.9.5**: 9. **D.9.9**: 4. **F.4.1**: 47. **F.4.2**: 48, 139. **F.5**: 14, 86. **G.2**: 1. **G.3**: 6. **I.6**: 16. **K.1**: 190. **K.3**: 2, 28.

Recherche action **A.3**: 1.

Recherche d'emploi **I.2**: 3.

Recherche démographique **F.1**: 13, 26.

Recherche et développement **A.3**: 9.

Recherche médicale **G.2**: 1.

Recherche sociale **A.1**: 15. **A.2**: 3. **A.3**: 3–6. **B.1.3**: 2, 5, 7, 11–12, 22, 28–29. **B.2**: 7. **G.3.1**: 22. **K.1**: 4.

Recherche sociologique **A.2**: 5. **F.6**: 29. **F.7**: 76.

Récidivisme **K.1**: 59, 91, 151.

Réciprocité **G.3.1**: 24.

Récits **C.1**: 26. **D.7**: 63.

Recrutement **I.2**: 20, 25, 56.

Redistribution du revenu **F.3**: 68.

Référendum **D.5**: 68. **F.4.1**: 68.

Réforme **D.7**: 139. **K.1**: 79. **K.2**: 24.

Réforme agraire **G.3.1**: 23.

Réforme légale **D.4**: 5–6. **F.4.2**: 18. **K.1**: 153.

Réfugiés **F.5**: 93. **F.7**: 6. **F.8**: 64, 75, 83, 89, 92, 98–99, 105.

Reggae **D.8**: 1, 3.

Régimes fonciers **G.3.1**: 17, 25, 71.

Règlement de conflits **C.3**: 5, 35, 39. **F.7**: 89. **G.2**: 10.

Réglementation **K.1**: 107.

Régulation sociale continued

Régulation sociale **D.1.2**: 9–10. **F.5**: 72. **F.6**: 6. **G.3.2**: 69. **I.3**: 58. **I.5**: 19. **K.1**: 3, 111. **K.4**: 28.
Relation agraire **G.3.1**: 3.
Relations culturelles **J.8**: 13.
Relations de dépendance **C.1**: 13. **C.3**: 53. **F.2**: 39. **K.3**: 7.
Rélations des sexes **F.4.1**: 49.
Relations du travail **I.3**: 55. **I.6**: 18, 23–24, 27–29, 36, 47.
Relations entre générations **D.7**: 33. **F.4.1**: 69. **F.4.2**: 20, 81, 104, 121. **F.5**: 73.
Relations familiales **C.3**: 10. **F.4.1**: 72. **F.4.2**: 86–89, 91–96, 98–100, 102–104, 106–107, 109–122. **K.1**: 118, 193.
Relations humaines **A.1**: 34. **C.3**: 48. **K.4**: 36.
Relations interethniques **F.4.1**: 26.
Relations intergroupes **C.2**: 83. **C.3**: 24–25, 45, 47. **C.4**: 15. **C.7**: 37. **F.7**: 80.
Relations interpersonnelles **C.3**: 1, 7, 10, 14, 19, 22, 27, 34, 40–42, 46. **F.2**: 43. **F.4.2**: 93.
Relations raciales **D.7**: 124, 136. **E.2**: 31. **F.4.1**: 26. **F.7**: 70–92. **G.3.1**: 49. **J.6**: 9.
Relations sociales **C.3**: 51. **C.5**: 20. **F.2**: 51.
Relativisme **D.3**: 30.
Religion **D.3**: 10. **D.5**: 6, 9, 16, 22, 37–40, 42–43, 52, 57, 60, 76. **F.1**: 27. **F.4.1**: 52. **F.4.2**: 114. **F.8**: 90. **K.3**: 27. **K.4**: 41.
Religion et politique **D.5**: 4, 32, 55.
Religion populaire **D.5**: 11, 14, 20.
Religiosité **D.5**: 27, 44.
Remariage **C.2**: 93. **F.4.1**: 8, 16. **F.4.2**: 21, 78, 110, 112. **H.3**: 18.
Rendement de l'éducation **D.9.5**: 3, 23.
Rénovation urbaine **G.3.2**: 83, 106, 116.
Répartition du revenu **H.3**: 25.
Répertition en zones **G.3.2**: 131.

Répertoires continued

Répertoires **A.3**: 12.
Représentation politique **J.3**: 21. **J.6**: 21.
Répression **D.1.2**: 9.
Reproduction sexuelle **F.3**: 45, 56. **F.6**: 17. **K.4**: 40.
Reproduction sociale **E.1**: 9.
Réseau ferroviaire **H.4**: 22.
Réseaux sociaux **B.3**: 20. **C.3**: 46. **C.4**: 20, 25–29, 31–32. **F.2**: 63. **F.4.2**: 45, 54, 106. **G.3.2**: 76. **I.2**: 7. **K.2**: 6. **K.3**: 31. **K.4**: 79.
Reserche opérationnelle **A.3**: 10.
Résidence **F.3**: 149. **F.7**: 113. **G.3.2**: 12. **J.6**: 4.
Résolution de problème **C.3**: 13, 32. **H.4**: 29.
Responsabilité **C.2**: 32, 40. **F.2**: 48. **F.3**: 108.
Responsabilité civile **J.8**: 9.
Ressources humaines **I.2**: 45. **I.3**: 19. **I.4**: 14.
Retraite **D.1.2**: 8. **F.2**: 24, 60–61. **I.3**: 17, 22, 32.
Retraite anticipée **I.3**: 12.
Réveil religieux **D.9**: 18.
Revenu **F.4.2**: 61. **G.3.2**: 44. **H.3**: 12. **K.2**: 12.
Revenu des ménages **H.3**: 5.
Révisionnisme **F.1**: 19.
Révolution **J.2**: 7.
Révolution verte **G.3.1**: 14. **H.4**: 15.
Richesse **H.3**: 28.
Risque **B.3**: 2. **I.3**: 16.
Rites de passage **F.5**: 55. **F.6**: 19.
Rituelle **D.1.3**: 16. **I.7**: 24.
Rôle **C.6**: 10. **D.7**: 31. **E.2**: 35.
Rôle de sexes **D.7**: 36. **E.2**: 9, 67. **F.4.1**: 20. **F.4.2**: 33. **F.5**: 50–51, 54.
Rôles conjugaux **F.4.1**: 6, 25, 37–38.
Rôles professionnels **F.4.2**: 65.
Rôles sexuels **F.5**: 7, 45, 47.
Rotation de la main-d'oeuvre **I.3**: 50.
Saisonnalité **K.1**: 113.

Salisbury, John of **J.2**: 3.
Sanctions pénales **K.1**: 167.
Sans-abri **G.3.2**: 90. **K.1**: 22, 213, 223–226, 230–231.
Santé **C.2**: 55. **C.3**: 1. **C.7**: 18. **E.2**: 32. **F.3**: 11, 104, 106, 110–111, 117, 131. **F.4.2**: 40. **F.5**: 26, 72. **I.2**: 70. **I.3**: 18, 36, 38. **K.2**: 23. **K.4**: 7, 27–28, 32, 34, 45, 60, 70, 94.
Santé mentale **C.3**: 9. **F.3**: 133. **F.4.1**: 13, 42. **F.4.2**: 53. **F.5**: 77, 102. **I.2**: 12, 53. **I.5**: 16. **K.1**: 168, 187, 194, 230. **K.4**: 3, 5, 12, 14, 20–21, 69, 79.
Santé publique **K.4**: 30, 76.
Sati **D.5**: 47.
Satisfaction **C.3**: 22.
Satisfaction au travail **I.3**: 47. **K.3**: 26.
Satisfaction conjugale **F.4.1**: 5, 32, 35, 39–41, 48. **F.4.2**: 25.
Schopenhauer, Arthur **B.1.1**: 28.
Science **D.6**: 4, 9, 12, 19–23, 25–28, 33–34. **D.7**: 102. **D.9.5**: 16. **H.4**: 36. **I.4**: 1.
Sciences du comportement **C.1**: 4.
Sciences sociales **A.1**: 3, 6–7, 10, 16–17, 19–20, 24–25, 37. **A.2**: 4. **A.3**: 7, 11. **A.5**: 6. **B.1.1**: 1, 11–12. **B.1.3**: 22. **C.1**: 4, 18. **D.9.5**: 2.
Scientifiques **D.3**: 38. **D.6**: 8.
Scolarité **D.9**: 14. **F.3**: 30.
Secret **C.3**: 41. **C.5**: 37.
Secteur coopératif **H.4**: 6.
Secteur informel **G.3.2**: 25, 58–59. **H.2**: 4. **I.2**: 14, 46.
Secteur privé **K.3**: 21.
Secteur public **I.5**: 9. **I.6**: 4, 43. **I.7**: 16. **J.4**: 5.
Sécularisation **D.4**: 14. **D.5**: 15, 45, 72.
Sécurité alimentaire **K.1**: 24.
Sécurité collective **F.7**: 24. **J.8**: 13.
Sécurité du travail **I.3**: 3, 18, 38, 46, 54, 59. **I.6**: 48.
Sécurité sociale **K.2**: 24, 38, 49, 51.
Segmentation du marché du travail **F.8**: 65. **H.3**: 17. **I.2**: 8, 27–28, 47.
Ségrégation **J.4**: 11.

Ségrégation professionnelle **I.2**: 44.
Ségrégation raciale **G.3.2**: 61.
Ségrégation résidentielle **F.7**: 67, 92. **G.3.2**: 49–50, 52, 68, 74, 100.
Sémiotique **D.7**: 42, 106.
Sensation **C.2**: 38.
Sentiments **C.2**: 10, 54, 65. **C.3**: 15. **C.7**: 28. **I.3**: 10.
Séparation maritale **F.4.1**: 66, 69, 72–73, 75. **F.4.2**: 76.
Séries temporelles **B.3**: 7.
Services d'information **A.5**: 6.
Services de santé **K.4**: 2, 20, 24, 31, 39, 46, 56, 64, 75, 79, 82, 87.
Services publics **F.5**: 42. **I.5**: 23.
Services sociaux **K.2**: 6, 50. **K.3**: 26, 36. **K.4**: 26, 37, 82.
Services urbains **G.3.2**: 27, 75.
Sexe **D.5**: 50. **F.1**: 18. **F.5**: 48–49. **K.1**: 164.
Sexisme **F.3**: 88.
Sexualité **F.6**: 3, 5, 30.
SIDA **C.1**: 27. **D.7**: 108. **D.8**: 5. **F.3**: 88–92, 95–101, 103, 112–115, 123–124, 126–127. **F.6**: 1, 8–9, 14. **F.7**: 99. **G.2**: 1. **I.3**: 3. **K.2**: 3, 30. **K.3**: 12.
Simmel, Georg **B.1.1**: 20. **D.1.1**: 47.
Simulation **B.1.3**: 3. **E.3**: 27.
Situation de famille **F.4.1**: 5.
Sociabilité **C.3**: 43.
Socialisation **C.3**: 11. **D.1.3**: 2, 5, 9–10, 18–19. **F.2**: 14. **H.4**: 25. **K.1**: 212.
Socialisation politique **J.6**: 20, 27.
Socialisme **A.2**: 2. **D.3**: 18. **D.9.8**: 10. **I.2**: 16. **J.2**: 12.
Socialistes **E.3**: 17.
Société agraire **G.3.1**: 21.
Société de l'information **D.7**: 5, 15. **H.4**: 19–20.
Société industrielle **D.1.1**: 12. **D.5**: 69. **F.8**: 5. **J.5**: 18. **K.1**: 110.
Société paysanne **F.5**: 21.
Société post-industrielle **G.3.2**: 117.
Société rurale **G.3.1**: 15, 18, 20.

Société traditionnelle **F.3**: 56.
Société tribale **E.2**: 58.
Sociétés complexes **C.4**: 6.
Sociolinguistique **D.7**: 46, 52, 55, 57, 59–60, 63, 72, 74–77, 81.
Sociologie **A.1**: 2, 5, 13, 15, 21–23, 26–28, 30–36, 38. **A.3**: 12. **A.5**: 3. **B.1.1**: 26. **B.3**: 19, 23. **C.1**: 40. **C.3**: 48. **E.3**: 8. **F.7**: 51, 104. **H.5**: 8. **I.3**: 45. **J.6**: 34.
Sociologie de la connaissance **D.1.2**: 13. **D.6**: 2, 11, 13, 16, 30–33. **E.3**: 25. **F.5**: 3.
Sociologie de la famille **F.4.2**: 125, 127–128, 132, 138, 143.
Sociologie de la profession **I.3**: 36. **I.4**: 26.
Sociologie de la religion **D.5**: 54, 57.
Sociologie des organisations **C.5**: 38.
Sociologie du développement **B.1.1**: 35. **E.3**: 16, 28.
Sociologie du droit **D.4**: 11.
Sociologie du travail **I.1**: 1–2. **I.3**: 58.
Sociologie économique **H.1**: 3, 7.
Sociologie industrielle **I.1**: 2–3, 5.
Sociologie médicale **F.3**: 39, 109, 118. **K.4**: 16–18.
Sociologie politique **J.1**: 4.
Sociologie rurale **F.4.2**: 22, 104. **F.8**: 42. **G.3.1**: 13, 41.
Sociologie urbaine **D.7**: 77. **E.2**: 18, 56. **E.3**: 3, 26. **F.3**: 152. **F.4.1**: 37–38. **F.4.2**: 22. **F.7**: 113. **G.3.2**: 8, 41, 84.
Sociologues **A.1**: 31, 37. **A.3**: 12.
Sociométrie **C.1**: 38.
Soins **F.3**: 108. **F.4.2**: 116. **K.2**: 30, 33. **K.3**: 29.
Soins mécíaux privée **K.4**: 66.
Soins médicaux **D.5**: 22. **F.3**: 92. **F.4.2**: 27. **K.4**: 27, 29, 36, 41, 48, 54, 61–62, 68–69, 74, 76, 80, 84, 91.
Solidarité **D.5**: 43.
Soufisme **D.5**: 82.
Sous-classe **E.2**: 19.
Sous-développement **E.3**: 22, 28.
Spécialistes en sciences sociales **A.5**: 5.

Spencer, Herbert **E.3**: 12.
Sport **C.2**: 53. **D.7**: 95. **I.7**: 6, 11, 14, 16, 18–22. **K.1**: 124.
Squatters **F.1**: 4. **F.3**: 15. **G.2**: 2. **G.3.2**: 98–99, 101. **K.1**: 107.
Stabilité conjugale **F.4.1**: 1, 7, 12, 14, 41, 61.
Stabilité d'emploi **I.3**: 50.
Statistique **F.8**: 103.
Statut professionnel **F.3**: 74. **I.4**: 6. **I.5**: 15.
Statut social **E.2**: 43, 59, 67–68. **J.6**: 32.
Stéréotypes **C.3**: 50. **C.7**: 40. **F.5**: 47. **K.4**: 82.
Stérilisation **F.3**: 48.
Stérilisation masculine **F.3**: 23.
Stérilité **F.3**: 69.
Stratification professionnelle **I.4**: 3.
Stratification sociale **E.2**: 49, 60–62, 70. **F.4.2**: 24.
Strauss, Leo **D.1.1**: 27.
Structure de classe **E.2**: 12, 16, 28, 39, 51.
Structure de l'État **E.2**: 75. **F.7**: 53. **J.3**: 27.
Structure de l'organisation **C.5**: 17, 36, 47.
Structure de la famille **F.4.2**: 11, 25, 27, 33, 46, 60, 63, 65, 85, 97, 105, 146. **I.2**: 4.
Structure professionnelle **G.3.1**: 46. **I.4**: 18, 22.
Structure sociale **B.1.1**: 4, 26. **C.3**: 30. **C.6**: 20. **C.7**: 33. **D.1.1**: 24. **D.1.3**: 18. **D.7**: 50. **E.1**: 1–2, 7, 9–10. **E.2**: 1, 74. **F.2**: 50. **F.5**: 51. **G.3.1**: 42. **I.2**: 46. **K.1**: 130.
Structure urbaine **F.8**: 95.
Subculture **F.2**: 8.
Suicide **K.1**: 9, 29–30, 34, 192.
Surabondance de main d'oeuvre **I.2**: 5, 23. **I.3**: 25.
Symbolisme **C.5**: 33. **F.3**: 114.
Sympathie **C.2**: 56.
Syncrétisme religieux **D.5**: 1.
Syndicalisme **I.3**: 56. **I.6**: 41–42.

Syndicats **F.8**: 102. **I.6**: 1, 4, 6, 8–10, 13–15, 19, 21–22, 32–34, 44, 48.
Système international **E.3**: 6.
Système social **E.1**: 6, 8. **E.3**: 27.
Systèmes de production **H.4**: 14, 32, 50. **K.2**: 58.
Tabac **D.7**: 25. **K.1**: 196.
Tables de mortalité **F.1**: 17. **F.3**: 67.
Tagore, Rabindranath **D.5**: 60.
Taux de natalité **F.3**: 52, 61, 71, 80.
Techniciens **I.5**: 1–2.
Techniques de gestion **I.5**: 9.
Techniques de recherche **B.1.3**: 3, 8. **E.2**: 25.
Techniques de simulation **C.1**: 5.
Technologie **D.6**: 25–26. **D.7**: 5, 44. **E.3**: 25. **F.2**: 28–29. **G.3.2**: 69. **H.4**: 5, 8, 13, 19–20, 35–36, 38, 40, 42, 44–46. **I.2**: 50–51.
Technologie de l'information **C.5**: 10. **G.3.2**: 21, 54. **H.4**: 4, 21.
Technologie de pointe **H.4**: 23.
Technologies nouvelles **D.7**: 44, 142. **F.2**: 26. **H.4**: 16, 27, 47. **I.6**: 8, 22–23.
Télécommunications **D.7**: 45.
Télévision **D.7**: 88, 92, 98, 102, 107, 121–122, 125, 131, 133–136, 138–139, 142, 149–150. **G.3.1**: 85. **I.7**: 21–22. **K.1**: 37.
Tendances de recherche **D.9**: 16. **F.4.2**: 142.
Tension mentale **F.2**: 51. **F.4.2**: 45. **I.4**: 21. **K.1**: 17.
Terrorisme **C.3**: 5. **D.7**: 147–148. **J.5**: 2, 14, 33.
Tests d'aptitude **C.2**: 29.
Thatcher, Margaret **J.6**: 36.
Théologie **D.5**: 72.
Théorie de l'éducation **D.9**: 11.
Théorie de l'organisation **C.5**: 20, 28.
Théorie de la décision **C.4**: 30. **J.8**: 20.
Théorie de la population **C.5**: 12.
Théorie de systèmes **C.3**: 17, 28. **E.2**: 40. **E.3**: 19.
Théorie des jeux **B.3**: 21–22. **C.4**: 1.
Théorie du conflit **C.3**: 20.
Théorie du groupe **C.4**: 14, 30, 34. **E.2**: 69.
Théorie du rôle **C.5**: 1.
Théorie économique **F.3**: 55. **K.1**: 99.
Théorie politique **F.5**: 106.
Théorie sociale **A.1**: 6. **B.1.1**: 31. **B.1.3**: 1. **C.5**: 38. **C.7**: 10. **F.5**: 35. **G.1**: 2. **K.3**: 2, 32.
Théorie sociologique **A.1**: 18, 39. **E.3**: 1, 4, 12, 18, 20. **F.2**: 27, 84. **H.5**: 8.
Thérapie **C.1**: 21. **C.3**: 53. **F.3**: 46. **K.4**: 55.
Thérapie familiale **F.4.2**: 144. **K.3**: 35, 37.
Tolérance **C.7**: 26. **F.6**: 16. **F.7**: 21.
Tourisme **G.3.2**: 56. **I.7**: 24–25.
Toxicomanie **K.1**: 6, 20, 32, 86–87, 186, 197, 204–206, 208, 210–211. **K.4**: 53.
Tradition **D.1.1**: 43. **D.2**: 1.
Traffic de la drogue **K.1**: 198, 203, 206.
Traitement des données **I.3**: 55.
Transport urbain **G.3.2**: 134–136.
Travail **A.3**: 6. **F.4.2**: 24. **F.8**: 94. **H.4**: 47. **I.2**: 33, 48, 52. **I.5**: 24, 27.
Travail à domicile **I.2**: 15, 42, 60.
Travail agricole **F.8**: 63. **G.3.1**: 17. **H.4**: 15.
Travail des cas individuels **K.3**: 3, 15.
Travail des enfants **I.2**: 9, 11.
Travail ménager **H.4**: 17. **I.3**: 15.
Travail par roulement **F.4.2**: 51.
Travail social **F.3**: 112. **F.4.2**: 62. **F.8**: 58. **K.1**: 77, 187, 219. **K.3**: 2, 4–5, 12–13, 17–18, 20, 23–25, 27–29, 31–34, 37. **K.4**: 7, 85.
Travail social des groupes **C.4**: 10.
Travailleurs **F.8**: 16. **H.4**: 47, 49. **I.2**: 40, 67. **I.3**: 59. **I.5**: 2, 24. **I.6**: 46.
Travailleurs âgés **I.2**: 36.
Travailleurs migrants **E.2**: 21. **F.8**: 21, 37, 57, 63, 68, 95.
Travailleurs professionnels **G.3.2**: 84. **I.5**: 1.

Travailleurs sociaux continued

Travailleurs sociaux **E.2**: 34. **I.6**: 33. **J.3**: 22. **K.3**: 11, 14, 16, 22.

Travailleuses **F.3**: 85. **F.5**: 45. **I.2**: 18, 29, 61. **I.3**: 48. **I.4**: 5.

Tribunal **D.4**: 4. **F.2**: 87. **F.7**: 19. **J.3**: 23. **K.1**: 57.

Tribunaux **K.1**: 164.

Tribunaux pour enfants **K.1**: 146, 151.

Trusts **C.3**: 18.

Typologie **D.1.1**: 44. **F.5**: 96. **H.4**: 48.

Tyrannie **J.2**: 3.

Universités **D.9**: 3. **D.9.5**: 2, 6, 10–11, 17, 19, 25. **F.3**: 133. **F.5**: 43.

Urbanisation **G.3.1**: 50. **G.3.2**: 137–156, 158. **J.6**: 32.

Urbanisme **G.3.2**: 60, 82.

Usage de solvants **K.1**: 88.

Usage du tabac **K.1**: 190, 196.

Usines **C.5**: 22. **I.3**: 31.

Utilisation des terres **G.1**: 14. **G.3.1**: 33. **G.3.2**: 96.

Utopie **D.5**: 19.

Vacances **I.6**: 42.

Vagabondage **K.1**: 26, 31.

Valeurs **D.1.1**: 43. **D.1.2**: 6, 8, 12. **D.3**: 12, 38. **D.4**: 15. **D.5**: 45, 77. **D.6**: 26. **E.2**: 62. **F.2**: 14. **F.4.1**: 46. **F.4.2**: 147. **I.3**: 22. **I.5**: 25.

Valeurs culturelles **D.1.2**: 8. **I.3**: 22.

Valeurs sociales **D.1.2**: 1, 4, 7. **K.1**: 131.

Vandalisme **K.1**: 92.

Variations saisonnières **F.3**: 71.

Veblen, Thorstein **E.3**: 14.

Veuvage **F.4.1**: 2. **H.3**: 18.

Veuve **F.4.2**: 117.

Victimes **F.4.2**: 75. **J.3**: 11. **K.1**: 1.

Vidéo **D.9.3**: 9.

Vie familiale **F.4.2**: 12, 45, 146.

Vie quotidienne **C.2**: 84. **D.1.1**: 39. **D.3**: 18. **D.8**: 11. **F.2**: 38. **H.4**: 45.

Vie religieuse **D.5**: 12. **G.3.1**: 47.

Vie rurale **D.7**: 29. **G.3.1**: 19.

Vie sociale **D.1.1**: 21.

Vie urbaine **G.3.2**: 22, 48.

Vieillesse **F.2**: 23, 39.

Vieillissement **F.1**: 28. **F.2**: 26–35, 40, 43, 45, 47, 49, 57, 62. **F.4.1**: 40. **G.3.1**: 1, 34, 52. **I.2**: 35. **I.5**: 11. **K.4**: 3.

Vietnamiens **F.8**: 89.

Villages **F.4.2**: 24. **F.8**: 37. **G.3.1**: 15–16, 35, 37–38, 42, 47–48, 51, 72, 83. **H.4**: 39.

Ville **F.2**: 65. **G.3**: 1. **G.3.2**: 6–7, 11, 21, 33, 40, 50, 71, 74, 81, 96, 115, 118, 124, 143. **J.4**: 7. **K.1**: 129.

Viol **D.4**: 5. **F.5**: 50. **F.6**: 7. **K.1**: 137.

Violence **D.7**: 148. **D.9.3**: 11. **I.7**: 20. **K.1**: 71. **K.3**: 11.

Violence communale **E.2**: 22.

Violence domestique **F.4.1**: 15, 19, 27. **F.4.2**: 67–69, 71–75. **F.5**: 23. **K.1**: 1, 3, 12, 21.

Vote **J.6**: 9, 37.

Voyages **F.3**: 132. **I.7**: 3.

Weber, Max **A.1**: 22. **A.2**: 4. **B.1.1**: 18–19, 32–33. **C.5**: 48. **D.1.1**: 14, 18, 27, 47. **E.3**: 16, 31. **H.2**: 3. **H.5**: 8.

Zinoviev, Aleksander **A.1**: 2.

Zone tropicale **G.3.1**: 79.

Zones rurales **F.2**: 32, 37, 52. **F.3**: 14. **G.3.1**: 10, 12, 14, 31, 34, 68. **I.2**: 15. **K.4**: 64, 84.

Zones suburbaines **D.1.2**: 1. **G.2**: 10. **G.3.1**: 35. **G.3.2**: 68.

Zones urbaines **F.3**: 14. **G.3.2**: 63, 100.